THE GEORGIA FRONTIER

Volume III:
Descendants of Virginia, North Carolina, and South Carolina Families

By Jeannette Holland Austin

CLEARFIELD

Printed for
Clearfield Company by
Genealogical Publishing Co.
Baltimore, Maryland
2005

Reprinted for
Clearfield Company by
Genealogical Publishing Co.
Baltimore, Maryland
2006, 2007

Volume III ISBN-13: 978-0-8063-5275-6
Volume III ISBN-10: 0-8063-5275-2
Set ISBN-13: 978-0-8063-5272-5
Set ISBN-10: 0-8063-5272-8

Made in the United States of America

Table of Contents

Preface

After General James Oglethorpe's initial settling of Europeans from England, Scotland, and the Palatine to the Georgia colony and the dissolution of the trustee's charter, in order to settle and prosper the land, King George of England offered substantial land grants as enticements to other colonials.

As early as 1752, colonists from New England, Virginia and the Carolinas poured into Georgia, bringing with them their families, servants and whole religious congregations. By the time of the American Revolution, these settlements had produced expensive coastal cotton and rice plantations. After the war, veterans established homesteads by taking up land grants for their services. Thereafter, a series of land lotteries were used during the early 1800's to draw new settlers. Then, the final largest conquest and distribution of land occurred when numerous tribes of Cherokees and Creeks were evacuated. In 1832, the tribal lands in the mid and western regions were put into a State lottery.

These volumes trace family histories from Oglethorpe's first settlers through all of the pioneering periods and include some descendants in the modern times.

This collection comprises a forty-year period of extensive research and study of the pioneers from other countries and states into Georgia. This volume includes 125 families.

Jeannette Holland Austin

Ables of Paulding County

Anson A. Ables was born 1 March 1829, and died on 17 September 1862 in Paulding County. He was married on 9 October 1853 in Paulding County to Celia A. Bone, a daughter of Bailey Bone and his wife, Nancy (Evans) Bone. SEE Bone. Issue:[1]

I.   John M. Ables, born 24 July 1854 in Paulding County, died 15 May 1912 in Paulding County, buried in the Dallas City Cemetery. Wife, S. Louisa, born 1854 in Georgia. Issue:[2]
    A.   William Snoden Ables, born 1879 in Dallas, Paulding County.

II.   Nancy Ables, born 1856 in Paulding County.

III.   Loretta C. Ables, born 1858 in Paulding County, married George O. Wilkins on 6 November 1881 in Paulding County.

IV.   Jefferson D. Ables, born 26 February 1861 in Paulding County, died 2 February 1919 in Paulding County, buried in the Dallas City Cemetery. Wife, F. L. He worked on the farm of Paton Peacock, in Cobb County, 1880.

Adair of Ireland, Pennsylvania, South Carolina; Madison, Morgan & Paulding Counties

Thomas Adair, son of Alexander Adair (born 1660) was born 1679 in Genoch, County of Antrim, Ireland, emigrated to Chester County, Pennsylvania, where he died. The name of his wife is unknown. Issue:[3]

I.   James Robert Adair, born 1709 in County of Antrim, Ireland, married Ester McBride on 11 January 1734. He was known as an Indian Trader and received a land grant on Duncan's Creek in Laurens County, South Carolina.

II.   Joseph Adair, born 1711 in County of Antrim, Ireland, died 1801 in Laurens County, South Carolina, buried on Duncan's Creek. He married (1) Susannah Long (2) Sarah Laferty in 1732). He was a member of the Duncan's Creek Presbyterian Church. Colonel Levi Casey certified that he served as a Revolutionary War Soldier. Issue by 1st wife:
    A.   Joseph Adair, Jr., Revolutionary War Soldier of South Carolina, married Sarah Dillard. Issue:
        1. John Adair, a Revolutionary War Soldier of South Carolina, was born in 1759 on Duncan's Creek in South Carolina, and died in 1812 in Morgan County, Georgia. He entered military service in 1779, and was captured near

---

[1] 1870 Paulding County Census.

[2] 1880 Paulding County Census, Dallas.

[3] Page 93, Minutes of the Court of Ordinary, Jackson County, Georgia (1796-1809), Estate of William Adair, deceased (Bozeman Adair, administrator); Jackson County Estates and Marriages; 1850 Jackson County Census; Madison County Marriages; 1850-1870 Paulding County Census; 1850-1860 Stewart County Census; Paulding County Marriages.

Charlotte, North Carolina[4], and became a prisoner in Camden, South Carolina. He married Jane Jones. She married 2nd, Green Jackson (died 1852). Issue:[5]

> a. Joseph Alexander Adair, married 1811, Elizabeth McCord.
> b. John Fisher Adair, born 1785, died 1856, married (1) Tylitha Brantley and (2) Mary Radcliff Slaven. Known child:

> > 1. George Washington Adair, born 1 March 1823 in Morgan County, died 1899 in Atlanta. He married Mary J., born 1831 in Georgia. He was a real estate entrepreneur in Atlanta, and amassed a great deal of property in the Atlanta area. Issue:[6]

L-R: John J. Thrasher, George Washington Collier, and Col. George W. Adair, Sr.

> > > i. Robin Adair, born 1859 Georgia, clothier's clerk.
> > > ii. Kacl Adair, born 1852 Georgia, dry goods clerk.
> > > iii. Forest Adair, born 1854 Georgia, real estate clerk.
> > > iv. Sallie Adair, born 1857 Georgia.
> > > v. Anne Adair, born 1859 Georgia.
> > > vi. George Adair, born 1874 Georgia.
> c. Mary Radcliff Adair married Mr. Slaven.
> d. Hiram Adair of Upson County, a soldier during the War of 1812.
> e. Jones Adair married (1) Woods and (2) Polly Ann Shields.
> f. Elizabeth Adair married Miles Garrett of Alabama.
> g. William Adair, lived in Morgan County.
> h. Mary Adair married John Apperson of Alabama.
> i. Farmar Adair.
> j. Susan Adair.
> k. Sarah Adair, died young.
> l. James M. Adair, married Sarah Dean.

III. William Adair, born 1719 in County Antrim, Ireland, died in Mercer County, Kentucky, buried in the Whitehall Cemetery. He married Mary Moore in 1749. Mary was born 5 June 1717 in Carnmoney, County of Antrim, Ireland, a daughter of James Moore and his wife, Elizabeth Newfville Moore. Issue:

> A. James Adair, son of William Adair of Kentucky, was born 1747 in Chester County, South Carolina, married Rebecca Montgomery.

---

[4] Letter from General Smallwood to Lord Cornwallis, Commander of the British forces, Southern Department, dated 24 October 1780....."Sir, the prisoners taken in the neighborhood of Charlotte, North Carolina, viz...John Adair, etc....I understand are very desirous of obtaining an exchange..." The Henry Laurens Chapter of the DAR of Laurens County, South Carolina, placed a tablet at the Duncan Creek Presbyterian Church, listing 16 Revolutionary War Soldiers, including Joseph Adair, Sr. and Joseph Adair, Jr.

[5] Roster of Revolutionary War Soldiers in Georgia, Volume III, by McCall.

[6] 1880 Fulton County Census, Atlanta, District 92.

B. William Adair, son of William Adair of Kentucky, was born 1749 in Virginia, died 1804 in Jackson County, Georgia. Wife, Sarah. (died 5 August 1842) Issue:

1. Bozeman Adair, Sr., son of William Adair of Jackson County, was born 1771 in Virginia, died April 1857 in Dallas, Paulding County, Georgia. Paulding County Misc. Estates, Book A (1852-1877), page 294: J. L. Adair, J. B. Adair, Absalom Jones and William Adair, securities on the Administrator's Bond for the Estate of Bozeman Adair, Sr. Madison. His LWT was presented for probate in the Paulding Superior Court and the following heirs filed a Caveat by John B. Adair, William Adair, Permelia Tolbert, Jone Bone, in right of his wife, Sarah, and James C. Lane, in right of his wife; John Bone, Jr. in right of his wife vs. James L. Adair. The original case was tried before Judge Hammond in March of 1859, however, the case went to the Supreme Court of Georgia (Volume 30, Supreme Court Reports), and was decided at the March Term of 1860. "That said will was procured, and deceased induced to execute the same, by the undue and unlawful influence of James L. Adair and Mitchell S. Adair, principal legatees in said will, and sons of deceased; said influence exercised at a time when deceased was extremely weak and imbecile from old age and sickness....That deceased was induced to sign said paper by the false and fraudulent representation made bo him by said James L. and Mitchell S. Adair, in relation to the conduct of the other children of deceased...The case came on for trial in the Superior Court, the appeal from the judgment of the Ordinary, rejecting the paper prounded as the last will and testament of Bozeman Adair, deceased. On the trial, it was procen that at the time the alleged will was executed, deceased was very weak and feeble, and about eighty-six years of age; he spoke very low." The Judgment was reversed and sent back to the trial judge. Issue:

   a. Judith Adair, daughter of Bozeman Adair, was born September 1790 in South Carolina, died 7 September 1823 in Madison County. She married Elijah Williams on 7 August 1806 in Madison County. SEE Williams.

   b. William Andrew Adair, son of Bozeman Adair, was born 1792 South Carolina, died May 1867 in Dallas, Paulding County. He married Mary Meroney (born 1798) on 18 October 1815. He was a Captain in the Militia in 1816-1829; also served in the War of 1812 as a Captain in Ware County. Later, he was a Justice of the Peace in Madison and Paulding Counties. Issue:

      i. John L. Adair, son of William Andrew Adair, was born 1819 Madison County, married Mary A. Hesleps on 15 December 1841. Issue:

         a. James Adair, born 1844.

         b. John G. Adair, born 1846, married on 16 January 1881, Martha Duncan.

         c. Martha Ann Adair, born 1848.

         d. Mary Jane Adair, born 1850.

      ii. Milla E. Adair, daughter of William Andrew Adair, was born 1822 Madison County, married Wilbourne Tolbert on 10 December 1841.

      iii. Nathan M. Adair, son of William Andrew Adair, was born 1822 Madison County, married Tilathia Raper on 24 March 1844. Issue:

3

a. Francis D. Adair, born 1846.

b. Jasper Newton Adair, born December 1848, died 10 September 1914, married in 1867, Mary J. Millican.

iv. Sarah Ann E. Adair, daughter of William Andrew Adair, was born 1826 Madison County, married George Silvester Parris on 26 June 1852. SEE Parris.

v. Emily C. Adair, daughter of William Andrew Adair, was born 1829 Madison County, died 24 December 1891, married John D. Sanford Foote (born 1820, died 3 October 1888) on 22 September 1852.

vi. James B. Adair, son of William Andrew Adair, was born 1831 Madison County, married Martha J. Cornett (born 1837) on 21 September 1857. They were residents of Lamar County, Alabama, in 1880. Issue:[7]

a. John W. Adair, born December 1858, married Malinda.

b. Mary Adair, born 1861.

c. James D. Adair, born July 1862 in Madison County.

d. Joseph H. Adair, born 1865 in Madison County.

e. Vina A. Adair, born 25 August 1878 in Lamar County, Alabama, died 9 June 1941.

vii. Mary A. Adair, daughter of William Andrew Adair, was born 1833 Madison County.

viii. Francis Adair, son of William Andrew Adair, was born 1835 Madison County.

c. Whitmell Harrington Adair, son of Bozeman Adair, was born 1794 South Carolina, died after 1874 in Paulding County. He married (1) Sarah Sorrells on 18 January 1816 in Madison County (2) Rachael Colbert in 1865 Madison County. He was a Justice of the Peace in Madison County between 1819 and 1830; member of the House of Representatives from Madison County in 1829, 1831, 1833, 1834 and 1835; also served in the Senate. Issue:

i. Dorcas Adair, daughter of Whitmell Harrington Adair, was born 1817 Madison County, died 1842, married Thomas C. Walker on 27 January 1838.

ii. William S. Adair, son of Whitmell Harrington Adair, was born 18 March 1819 Madison County, died 23 September 1889 Cobb County, buried in Mars Hill Cemetery, Acworth. He married Elmira Jane Walker, born 19 March 1819, died 7 January 1903, buried Mars Hill Cemetery. They were residents of Oregon and Red Rock, Cobb County, in 1880.[8] Issue:

a. Talitha Ann Adair, born 1839.

b. Sarah C. Adair, born 1840.

c. Mary E. Adair, born 1843.

d. Martha Delany Adair, born 1845.

---

[7] 1880 Lamar County, Alabama Census, Township 16, Beat 10.

[8] 1880 Cobb County Census, Oregon and Red Rock.

  e. Elisha W. Adair, born 1847, married Elizabeth
    Bone. SEE Bone.
  f. James E. Adair, born 23 April 1849, died 5
    November 1929, married Rena Waldrop.
  g. William J. Adair, born 22 November 1852, died 4
    April 1826.
  h. Adolphus Adair, born 1859.

iii. James Bozeman Adair, son of Whitmell Harrington
Adair, was born 1823 Madison County, died 10 April
1897 Paulding County. He married Margaret Elizabeth
Buford, born 1837 in Georgia. They were residents of
Dallas, Georgia, in 1880. Issue:[9]

  a. Sally Amanda Adair, born 1859 Paulding County,
    married on 5 January 1881, Rufus W. Ray..
  b. James Leonard Adair, born 30 September 1860 in
    Paulding County, died 6 August 1913.
  c. Whitmill H. Adair, born 25 May 1865 in Paulding
    County, died 18 February 1923..
  d. Louise E. Adair, born 26 May 1869 in Paulding
    County, died 19 December 1934..
  e. Cicero Clark Adair, born 18 Auyust 1871 in
    Paulding County, died 6 October 1927.
  f. Joseph Warren Adair, born 9 September 1880 in
    Paulding County, died 26 October 1973.
  g. Elmira Cordelia Adair, born 23 November 1873
    Paulding County. (mulatto)
  h. Margaret Elizabeth Adair, born 20 July 1876 in
    Paulding County, died 3 May 1968, married Zollie
    Wade..

iv. Sara Ann Adair, daughter of Whitmell Harrington Adair,
was born 19 May 1825 Madison County, died 26
December 1886 Paulding County. She married Jesse
Hitchcock, Jr. on 17 February 1847. SEE Hitchcock.

v. Jane Adair, daughter of Whitmell Harrington Adair, was
born 4 July 1827 in Madison County, died 8 July 1887,
married John Brooks on 26 December 1841.

vi. Permelia Ann Adair, daughter of Whitmell Harrington
Adair, was born 1829 Madison County, married Green B.
Harris on 2 March 1848.

vii. L. Adair, son of Whitmell Harrington Adair, was born
between 1830-1840, died between 1840-1850.

viii. Mitchell Andrew Adair, son of Whitmell Harrington
Adair, was born November 1831 in Madison County. He
married (1) Amanda Matthews on 25 September 1853) (2)
Sydney A. (1869), and (3) Fannie (in 1890). He was a
resident of Jonesboro, Craighead County, Arkansas, in
1880. Issue:[10]

---

[9] 1880 Paulding County Census, Dallas.

[10] 1880 Census of Craighead County, Arkansas Census, Jonesboro.

a. Mary A. Adair, born 1856 Georgia.
b. Martha J. Adair, born 1858 Georgia.
c. Mitchell A. Adair, born 1871 Georgia.
d. William W. Adair, born 1873 Georgia.
ix. Whitmell H. Adair, Jr., son of Whitmell Harrington Adair, was born 1834 Madison County, married Sarah Elizabeth Carter (born 1843) on 27 January 1859. Issue:
a. James Glenn Adair, born 29 February 1860, died 15 May 1949.
x. John Gibson Adair, son of Whitmell Harrington Adair, was born 4 February 1839 Madison County, died 15 August 1891, married Elizabeth Sailors on 17 November 1859. Issue:
a. William J. Adair, born 11 October 1860, died 27 July 1878.
b. John Alexander Whitmill Adair, born 2 March 1864, died 2 February 1939.
c. James Mitchell Adair, born 5 April 1866, died 9 April 1951, marrid Mennie Albertie.
d. Patrick Adair, born 4 February 1871, died 11 February 1938.
e. Dock Adair, born 21 November 1873, died 28 February 1957, married Maggie Ward.
f. Thomas L. Adair, born 1876, died 1958.
g. George L. Adair, born December 1878, died 1956, married Sammie Ward.
h. Memie C. Adair, born 10 September 1882, died 4 January 1884.
i. Mattie Elizabeth Adair, born 27 June 1885, died 27 September 1963.
xi. Louisa H. Adair, daughter of Whitmell Harrington Adair, was born 1842 Paulding County, died 1891 Paulding County. She married Tilmon Powell Brown on 21 November 1871.
xii. Lucy J. Adair, daughter of Whitmell Harrington Adair, was born 1845 Paulding County. She married John Sailors on 17 December 1863.
d. John Bluett Adair, son of Bozeman Adair, was born 1802 Jackson County, died 1868 Paulding County. He married Pheriby C. Anderson (born 1809 in Georgia) on 16 October 1822 in Madison County. The LWT of John Bluett Adair dated 3 September 1868 in Paulding County, Book D (1867-1872), page 31-32. He served in the Militia as (2) Lieutenant 1821-1823, as Captain 1824-1830, and as Colonel 1833 - . Issue:
i. Emily C. Adair, daughter of John Bluett Adair, was born 1824 Madison County, married Pleasant W. Bone on 28 July 1840.
ii. Bozeman H. Adair, son of John Bluett Adair, was born 27 August 1826 Madison County, died 26 April 1880 in Lamar County, Alabama, married Elizabeth Adeline Deloach (born 1830) on 13 July 1850. They had a farm in Dallas. Issue:

6

(1) James L. Adair, born 1847 in Paulding County, died 17 August 1881, lawyer, resident of Dallas, Georgia, in 1880. He married Mary E. Thompson on 12 November 1872 (born 1856 Georgia). Issue:[11]

    i. Gary F. Adair (daughter), born 1874 in Paulding County.

    ii. Hiram W. Adair, born 1878 in Paulding County.

(2) Asbury H. Adair, born 1849 in Paulding County, married 18 October 1868, Mary F. Baxter in Paulding County.

(3) Adeliine Adair, born 2 February 1851 in Paulding County, died 11 December 1910.

(4) John Henry Adair, born 1853 in Paulding County, married on 30 October 1873, Georgia Ann Baxter.

(5) Zachariah Adair, born April 1855 in Paulding County, died 1900, married Betty Aimee Robertson in 1873.

(6) George W. Adair, born 1857 Paulding County.

(7) Fereby Adair, born 1859 Paulding County.

(8) Jefferson D. Adair, born 1862 in Paulding County.

(9) Thomas Jackson Adair, born 20 October 1865, died 29 January 1960.

(10) Charles Lafayette Adair, born 1869.

(11) Condes Adair, born 1873.

(12) Robert Lee Adair, born 10 November 1874, died 25 December 1912, married Nora Cook.

iii. John W. Adair, son of John Bluett Adair, was born 1833 Madison County, married on 6 September 1855, P. M. Hollis.

iii. Harriett Adair, daughter of John Bluett Adair, was born 23 November 1835 in Madison County, died 14 February 1920, married John Baxter on 23 November 1854. SEE Baxter.

iv. James Sanders Adair, son of John Bluett Adair, was born January 1837 in Madison County, died 13 September 1911, married Rosanna Martin (born 1834) on 9 September 1860. They were residents of Dallas, Georgia, in 1880. Issue:[12]

    a. James Bozeman Adair, born 3 August 1864 in Paulding County, died 26 October 1943.

    b. Henry Lee Adair, born 17 November 1867 in Paulding County, died 11 November 1949.

---

[11] 1880 Paulding County Census, Dallas.

[12] 1880 Paulding County, Census, Dallas.

c. Alice A. Adair, born 23 January 1870 in Paulding County, died 31 October 1916, married on 8 July 1889, M. T. Petty.

d. Louanna Moselle Adair, born 13 March 1873 in Paulding County, died 5 October 1960.

e. Sarah A. Malinda Adair, born 8 July 1874 in Paulding County, died 22 June 1933.

f. Georgiann Adair, born 29 July 1876 in Paulding County, died 10 March 1965, married John Lemon Barnett.

g. Martha A. Adair, born 1879 in Paulding County.

h. Robert Emmitt Adair, born April 1882 in Paulding County.

v. Martha Jane Adair, daughter of John Bluett Adair, was born 1839 Madison County.

vi. William Harrison S. Adair, son of John Bluett Adair, was born 3 January 1841 Madison County, died 1 July 1910, married Nancy Jane Craton (born 1847) on 12 July 1867. They were residents of Dallas, Georgia, in 1880. Issue:[13]

a. Memory Amanda Adair, born July 1868 in Paulding County, died 1946.

b. John E. Adair, born 23 December 1869, died 31 August 1933 in Paulding County.

c. Thomas Franklin Adair, born 15 November 1871 in Paulding County, died June 1952, married Ida Jane Lyle.

e. Lula Jane Adair, born 15 March 1873 in Paulding County, died 1959, married 18 December 1892, Thomas Lane.

e. Martha B. Adair, born 1874 in Paulding County, married on 20 August 1895, John Garner.

f. Amy Florence Adair, born 10 July 1881 in Paulding County, died August 1973.

g. Mary Josephine Adair, born May 1883 in Paulding County, married on 8 January 1905, Albert W. Carroll.

h. Joseph Henry Adair, born 2 February 1884, died 1 November 1903.

i. William H. Adair, born February 1887, died 1954, married 6 January 1907, Leila Murdock.

j. Frances N. Adair, born January 1890, died 1922, married 14 April 1908, Benjamin F. Wright.

vii. Henry Clay Adair, son of John Bluett Adair, was born 1843 Madison County, died 1965.

viii.Sarah E. Adair, daughter of John Bluett Adair, was born 1845 Madison County.

ix. Mary F. Adair, daughter of John Bluett Adair, was born 22 March 1847 Dallas, Paulding County, died 14 June 1901, married Charles C. Gamel. SEE Gamel.

---

[13] Ibid.

          x.   Pheriby Emmaline Adair, daughter of John Bluett Adair, was born 23 September 1852 in Dallas, Paulding County, died 15 September 1911, married William I. Craton on 30 November 1869. SEE Craton.

e. James Lee Adair, son of Bozeman Adair, was born 1805 Jackson County, died 1864 Dallas, Paulding County. He married Caroline Evans on 4 September 1822 in Madison County. LWT of James L. Adair dated 25 February 1864, probated 21 March 1864 Paulding County, Book C (1861-1867), page 350. He was the first postmaster at Villa Rica in 1831; also a Justice o f the Inferior Court. Issue:

      i.   William Levi Adair, son of James Lee Adair, was born 1829 Carroll County, died 22 July 1864, married Adaline Gann Issue:

          a.   Mary Adair, born 1850.
          b.   Sarah Adair, born 1853.
          c.   Salina Laura Adair, born 3 January 1855, died 30 March 1939.
          d.   Milton R. Adair, born 4 February 1857, died 22 January 1936.
          e.   Thomas F. Adair, born 7 June 1860, died 1 December 1883.
          f.   William Bozeman Adair, born 1863, died 1856, married on 26 February 1885, Lucy J. Pace.

      ii.   Sarah Frances Adair, daughter of James Lee Adair, was born 1830, died ca 1857 in Paulding County, married John W. Hollis on 30 April 1850.

      iii.   Martha Adair, daughter of James Lee Adair, was born 1832, married William J. Matthews.

      iv.   Emiline Adair, daughter of James Lee Adair, was born 2 February 1836 Carroll County, died 26 August 1894 in Cobb County, married Ezekiel W. Moody on 25 December 1857.

      v.   Judith Adair, daughter of James Lee Adair, was born 1838 Madison County. She married (1) Richard J. Carter on 8 January 1858; (2) Nickalus Hawkins Bullock in 1866; (3) Jesse Hitchcock on 13 October 1892. Issue by Hawkins Bullock: William Bullock, born 1867 and John Pickney Bullock, born 1871 in Paulding County.

      vi.   Thomas B. Adair, son of James Lee Adair, was born 1840 Madison County.

      vii.   Bozeman Adair, son of James Lee Adair, was born 1843 Paulding County, died 1889, married Georgia Ella Alexander in 1875. Issue:

          a.   Henry B. Adair.
          b.   Mattie J. Adair.

      viii. James Kermit Adair, son of James Lee Adair, was born 20 February 1847, died 31 July 1938 in Fisher County, Texas. He married (1) Nancy Baxter in 1864 and (2) Theodocia Wells on 18 October 1885.

        Issue by (2) wife:

          a.   Sarah C. Adair, born 1866.

  b. William H. Adair, born 1 November 1866, died 8 March 1940, married India Virginia Rasberry.

  c. John Thomas Adair, born 4 April 1871, died 1950. Issue:

    i. Marjorie Adair, born 17 March 1889, died 20 May 1962.

    ii. Dill Adair, born 1891.

 ix. John W. Adair, son of James Lee Adair, was born 13 February 1849 Paulding County, died 30 April 1918, married Salina M. Bullock on 10 November 1872. Issue:

  a. Albert Lonzo Adair, born 12 August 1873, died 3 September 1960.

  b. Sherman L. Adair, born 7 March 1881, died 14 March 1975.

  c. Alexander J. Adair, born November 1886.

  d. George P. Adair, born July 1896.

f. Mitchell S. Adair, son of Bozeman Adair, was born 1810 Jackson County, died 1857 Dallas, Paulding County. He married (1) Rebecca Walker (born 1813 in Georgia) on 29 December 1831 in Madison County (2) Amanda Matthews on 25 September 1853. They were residents of Paulding County, in 1850. Issue:

  i. Bozeman Adair, son of Mitchell S. Adair, was born 1833 Paulding County, married Salina Gann (born 1838 Georgia) on 19 June 1863. SEE Gann. He was a waggoner by occupation, and a resident of Caseys, in Fulton County, 1880. Issue:[14]

   a. Mary Ella Adair, born 1864 Georgia.

   b. Joseph A. Adair, born 1872 Georgia.

   c. George Dawson Adair, born 13 May 1875 Georgia, died 1 January 1923, married Ernestine Waggoner..

   d. Ida A. Adair, born 1877 Georgia.

  ii. Jonathan W. Adair, son of Mitchell S. Adair, was born 28 November 1834 Madison County, died 12 August 1913, married Temple Walker (born 1840) on 18 August 1859. He was a dairy farmer and a resident of Caseys, Fulton County, in 1880. Issue:[15]

   a. Rufus L. Adair, born 1860 Alabama.

   b. Julia R. Adair, born 1864 Alabama.

   c. Mary L. Adair, born 1869 Alabama.

   d. Sarah R. Adair, born 1871 Georgia.

   e. Emma Adair, born 1874 Georgia.

   f. Ella Adair, born 1876 Georgia.

   g. Lizzie Adair, born 1878 Georgia.

   h. Joseph Adair, born 1879 Georgia.

   i. Emer Adair, born January 1884 Georgia.

---

[14] 1880 Fulton County Census, Caseys District.

[15] Ibid.

iii. William Adair, son of Mitchell S. Adair, was born 1837
Madison County, died 1907, married Margaret Hollis
(born 1827) on 9 August 1855. They resided in Pumpkin
Vine Creek, in Paulding County. Issue:[16]
   a. Robert Adair, born 28 July 1859, died 5 March 1933.
   b. Margaret Eugenia Adair, born 1862 Georgia,
   married on 9 August 1886, H. H. McPherson..
   c. Mary Rebecca Adair, born 8 February 1865, died
   23 October 1892.
iv. Joseph Adair, son of Mitchell S. Adair, was born 1839
Madison County.
v. Sarah Ann Adair, daughter of Mitchell S. Adair, was
born 10 April 1843 Paulding County, died 24 March 1895,
married John W. Hollis on 25 December 1859.
vi. George B. Adair, son of Mitchell S. Adair, was born 1842
Paulding County.
vii. James Adair, son of Mitchell S. Adair, was born 1845,
married Mary A. Clark. Issue:
   a. Willie Adair.
   b. Eva B. Adair.
   c. Ophelia Adair.
   d. Mary Adair.
   e. James E. Adair.
   f. Frank Adair.
viii. Mary Adair, daughter of Mitchell S. Adair, was born 1849
Paulding County.
ix. Thomas Adair, son of Mitchell S. Adair, was born 1852
Paulding County.
g. Sally Adair, daughter of Bozeman Adair, was born 1798
Jackson County, died between 1870-1880 in Dallas, Paulding
County. She married John Bone on 8 May 1814 in Madison
County. SEE Bone.
h. Lucy Adair, daughter of Bozeman Adair, was born 1800
Jackson County, married Jonathan Sanders on 8 May 1817 in
Madison County.
i. Permelia Adair, daughter of Bozeman Adair, was born 1805 in
Jackson County, married Allen Tolbert on 24 July 1824.
Removed to Stewart County, Georgia.
2. Robert Adair, son of William Adair of Jackson County, died 1804 in
Jackson County, Georgia, married Betsy Reed on 28 July 1800 in Jackson
County. Page 93, Minutes of the Court of Ordinary of Jackson County
(1796-1809) dated 12 May 1804, Bozeman Adair, administrator of the
Estate of Robert Adair. Robert's widow objected to Bozeman Adair's
administration of the estate.
3. John Adair, son of William Adair of Jackson County, died 1804 in Jackson
County, married Jane Jones in 1786. 3 December 1804, Robert Williamson
and Robey William were appointed administrators of the Estate of John
Adair. In 1813, Jane, widow of John Adair, applied for the Letters of
Administration of her husband's estate.

---

[16] 1880 Paulding County Census, Pumpkin Vine District.

4. Joseph Adair, son of William Adair of Jackson County, was born ca 1775 in Virginia, died before 1850 in Jackson County. He married Elizabeth McCord on 7 April 1808 in Jackson County.

C. Betsy Adair, daughter of William Adair of Kentucky, was born ca 1756 in Chester County, South Carolina, married John Moore.

D. John Adair, son of William Adair of Kentucky, Governor of Kentucky, was born 9 January 1757 in Chester County, South Carolina, died 18 May 1840 in Mercer County, Kentucky. He married Catherine Palmer on 9 September 1784.

E. Alexander Adair, son of William Adair of Kentucky, was born in Chester County, South Carolina.

Austin of North Carolina & Atlanta

William M. Austin, born 1823 in North Carolina, farmer, died before 1860, married Sarah (born 1825 in North Carolina); listed on the 1850 Union County, North Carolina Census and the 1880 Cabarrus, North Carolina Census, Bethel Church District. Issue:

I. Milton A. Austin, born 1843 in Union County, North Carolina, died 1863.

II. Hampton D. Austin was born January 1845 in North Carolina, married Caroline (born September 1845 in North Carolina, listed on the 1850 Union County, North Carolina Census, 1880 Cabarrus County, North Carolina Census, and the 1900 Mecklenburg County Census. Issue:[17]

A. M. V. Austin (daughter), born 1866 in North Carolina.

B. J. L. Austin (daughter), born 1868 in North Carolina.

C. R. A. Austin (son), born 1869 in North Carolina.

D. Sanford C. Austin, born 1870 in North Carolina, died 1929 in Cobb County, married on 13 July 1893 in Mecklenburg County, North Carolina, Blandina Hargett (born 17 October 1877 in North Carolina, died 23 September 1934 in Smyrna, Cobb County, the daughter of W. B. Hargett and his wife, Mary (Nicholson) Hargett of North Carolina.[18] Issue:

1. Charles Louis Austin was born 27 September 1901, died 1 December 1977 in Atlanta, buried in the Westview Cemetery.[19] He married Ruby Louise Richardson (born 1900 in Atlanta, died 1995, buried in the Georgia Memorial Cemetery, Smyrna, Cobb County, on 19 March 1924 in Birmingham, Alabama, a daughter of Rufus Richardson and his wife, Josephine (Gallaway) Richardson. Issue:

---

[17] 1880 Cabarrus, North Carolina Census, Bethel Church District.

[18] State of Georgia Amendment to Death Certificate, Blandia Austin.

[19] State of Georgia, Certificate of Death No. 7434 of Charles L. Austin.

a. Frances Louise Austin, born 25 July 1929 in Birmingham, Alabama, married Harry M. Tice of Atlanta.

b. Kenneth Edward Austin, born 22 April 1934 in Atlanta, died December 1973 in Atlanta. Wife, Edith (married 1952 in Atlanta).

c. Clarence Louis "Buddy" Austin, born 31 July 1936 in Atlanta, died 25 January 1988[20] in Orange County, New Jersey, buried in the Georgia Memorial Cemetery, Smyrna, Cobb County. He married (1) Mary Ann Scott (2) Joy.

d. Jerry Franklin Austin, born 10 December 1942 in Atlanta, died on 3 March 1993 in Fayetteville, Georgia. SEE Holland.

E. Alice Austin, born 1871 in North Carolina.

F. Z. V. Austin (son), born 1872 in North Carolina.

G. Walter Austin, born 1873 in North Carolina.

H. Peter Austin, born 1875 in North Carolina.

I. Harrison D. Austin, born December of 1881 in Mecklenburg County, North Carolina.[21]

III. William C. Austin, born 1847 in Union County, North Carolina.

IV. Jonathan C. Austin, born 1849 in Union County, North Carolina.

V. J. T. Austin (son), born 1856 in Union County, North Carolina.

Baxter of Madison County

Nathaniel Baxter was born 3 November 1803 in North Carolina, and died 5 September 1894. He married on 23 July 1829 in Madison County, Elizabeth Bone (born 15 April 1815 Madison County, died 23 April 1889), a daughter of John Bone and his wife, Sally (Adair) Bone. SEE Bone. Issue:[22]

I. Mitchell M. Baxter, born 1831 in Madison County, farmer. He married (1) Muscogee C. Robertson (born 1834 in South Carolina) on 17 March 1849 in Paulding County, who died before 1860. In 1880, his wife was Mary A. F., born 1840 Georgia. In 1850-1860, Mitchell's family were residents of Dallas, Paulding County, and in 1880, they were residents of Spring Hill, Hampstead County, Arkansas.

Issue by (1) wife:
A. Wesley H. Baxter, born 1850 in Dallas, Paulding County, died before 1860.

Issue by (2) wife:

---

[20] State of New Jersey Death Certificate of Clarence Louis Austin.

[21] 1900 Census of Mecklenburg County, North Carolina, Charlotte, Township #1.

[22] 1830-1860 Madison County Census; Madison County Marriages; 1880 Hampstead County, Arkansas Census.; 1880 Paulding County Census.

B. Eliza Jane Baxter, born 1858 in Dallas, Paulding County.

C. Martha E. Baxter, born 1860 in Dallas, Paulding County.

D. Mary M. Baxter, born 1863 in Dallas, Paulding County, Georgia.

E. Margaret A. J. Baxter, born 1867 in Indiana.

F. Robert E. L. Baxter, born 1870 Hampstead County, Arkansas.

G. Delaney A. Baxter (daughter), born 1873 Hampstead County, Arkansas.

H. Emma A. Baxter, born 1875 Hampstead County, Arkansas.

I. Richard S. Baxter, born 1877 Hampstead County, Arkansas.

J. Thomas J. Baxter, born 1879 Hampstead County, Arkansas.

II. John A. Baxter, born 4 April 1834 in Madison County, died 31 August 1925, buried in the Dallas City Cemetery.. He married Harriett N. Adair (born 23 November 1834, died 15 February 1920, buried in the Dallas City Cemetery) on 23 November 1854 in Paulding County.

III. Nathaniel Baxter, born 1840 Madison County.

IV. Sarah A. Baxter, born 1844 Madison County.

V. James J. Baxter, born 1 November 1845, died 8 December 1934, married Nancy E. Moody Brock.

VI. Mary F. Baxter, born 1848 Madison County, married 18 October 1868, Asberry H. Adair (born 1849). SEE Adair.

VII. Eli Barney Baxter, born 1851 Madison County. He married (1) Caroline J. Moody on 1 December 1870 in Paulding County, and (2) Adaline Adair (born 1851 in Georgia) on 6 October 1872 in Paulding County. They were residents of Dallas, Georgia in 1880. Issue by (1) wife:
   A. Stockley S. Baxter, born 1871 Dallas, Paulding County.
Issue by (2) wife:
   B. Almedia Baxter, born 1874 Dallas, Paulding County.
   C. Arminda C. Baxter, born 1875 Dallas, Paulding County.
   D. Cicero H. Baxter, born 1877 Dallas, Paulding County.

VIII. Lucy Baxter, born 15 September 1852, died 30 March 1943, married on 25 April 1872, Arch Holland. SEE Holland.

IX. Daniel Columbus Baxter, born 1856 Madison County.

X. Columbus Baxter, born 1857 in Paulding County.

Another family, William Baxter, was born 1802 in North Carolina, farmer, married Rebecca B. McKleroy (born 1801 in Georgia) on 9 July 1822 in Madison County. Issue:

I. Julia Baxter, born 1832 Madison County.

II. Caroline Baxter, born 1834 Madison County.

III. Eliza Baxter, born 1837 Madison County.

IV. Mary A. Baxter, born 1839 Madison County.

V. John D. Baxter, born 1844 Madison County.

VI.   Almeda Baxter, born 1846 Madison County.

Beckham of Virginia and Columbia County

Simon Beckham was born ca 1660, died September 1716 in Essex County, Virginia. Wife, Lydia. Essex County, Virginia, Order Book No. 3, 1703-1708, page 89: "10 July 1704. Certificate according to Act of the Assembly, granted to Simon Beckham for 50 acres of land, due by his, the said Beckham's own transportation into this Colony, who, in Court assigned the same to Larkin Chew. Larkin Chew is believed to have speculated in land, as he received land patents for some 2,700 acres. The 1704 Quit Rent Rolls of the Colony of Virginia show that Simon Beckham of Essex County was the owner of 100 acres.

Wills & Deeds, Essex County, Vol. 11, 1702-1704, page 218. 10 April 1704, an inventory of the Estate of Robert Halsey, deceased, was taken by Court Order on 10 November 1703. Simon Beckham's name appeared as being obligated for 700 pounds of tobacCounty Also, in Essex County Wills and Deeds, Vol. 12, 1704-1707, page 211 – June 1706, the name of Simon Beckham and his wife, Lydia Beckham appear as witnesses to a power of attorney from Daniel and Marh Maburt. Proved 60 June 1706. Essex County, Virginia Deed and Will Book 14, 1711-1716, page 665 (not dated), probated on 19 September 1716, the LWT of Simon Beckham, deceased. Issue:[23]

I.   James Beckham, died 1759 in Essex County, Virginia.

II.   William Beckham, emigrated from England to America in 1701, settling in Orange County, Virginia. Some o f his children settled in Orange and nearby counties, while others removed to the Carolinas and to Georgia. Wife, Tabitha. Issue:

A.   William Beckham, born 1709 in Essex County, Virginia, died November 1777 in Granville County, North Carolina, his LWT dated 4 June 1776 and probated November of 1777. Wife: Phillis Randolph. Orange County, Virginia Deed Book I, 14 June 1735, Alexander Spotswood to William Beckham for the natural life of his son, Simon Beckham. Issue:

   1.   Simon Beckham, son of William Beckham, was born ca 1729 in Orange County, Virginia, died 29 December 1785. He married Susanna McMillican on 2 June 1749.

   2.   William Beckham, Captain, son of William Beckham, was born 1734 in Buckingham County, Virginia, died 9 September 1812 in Columbia County, Georgia. Wife, Catherine. His first known deed in Columbia County was dated 9 September 1794, Moses Marshall and his wife, Mary, Benjamin Garrison and John Doss, for 80 pounds, deed to William Beckham, 160 acres located on Greenbriar Creek, which had been granted to William Chandler on 1 August 1769 and sold by him to Benjamin Bevans, then by him, in deed of gift, to his four children, the "begotten of the body of Rebecca Garrison", Mary, Benjamin, Sarah and Dorcas. Another deed dated 30 August 1799, Anderson Crawford, Sheriff of Columbia County, deeded to William Beckham, the guardian for Thomas

---

[23] Essex County, Virginia Wills & Deeds; Orange County, Virginia Wills & Deeds; Columbia County Wills & Deeds; Richmond County Marriages.

Cobbs, a minor, for $65, a tract of 119 acres of land seized as the property of John L. Dixon on a suit of Thomas Cobbs, Esquire, on Greenbrier Creek in Columbia County. The LWT of William Beckham dated 5 November 1812, in Columbia County, in which he named his wife, Catherine, and grandsons: Thomas and Lewis Cobbs (sons of John Cobbs, deceased); Alfred, Simpson and G. Beckham Ellis (children of Charles Ellis); Catherine Cobbs. Great grandchildren were: William Beckham and Adeline Cobbs (daughter of grandson, Thomas Cobbs). Issue:

- i. Elizabeth Beckham married (1) John Cobbs ca 1782 and (2) Charles Ellis on 7 February 1798. SEE Cobbs.
- ii. Sherwood Beckham married on 9 April 1794, Mary Stephens in Richmond County
- iii. Solomon Beckham married Susannah Weathers on 18 September 1787 in Richmond County. A Georgia newspaper recorded dated 14 September 1812 provided the death date and year of birth.

3. John Beckham, son of William Beckham, married Elizabeth Henderson on 13 August 1761.
4. Thomas Beckham, son of William Beckham, died 1796 in Edgefield County, South Carolina. Wife, Mary.
5. Phillis Beckham, daughter of William Beckham, died 1791 in Granville County, North Carolina. She married (1) William Williams before 1758 and (2) John Mitchell on 22 December 1777.
6. Mary Beckham, daughter of William Beckham.

B. Henry Beckham.

C. Thomas Beckham.

D. Simon Beckham.

E. Stephen Beckham.

Bell of Paulding County

Ernest Coleman Bell, born on 5 February 1897 in Braswell, died in Paulding County, married on 7 November 1920, Donnie Viola Holland (born 5 May 1904, died 2 April 1980). SEE Holland. Both were buried in the New Hope Cemetery in Dallas, Georgia.

I. Wilma Ione Bell, born on 28 November 1921 Paulding County, married on 27 April 1940 in Paulding County, Lawrence Vester Bivens, born 25 December 1914 in Cobb County. SEE Bivins.

II. Kenneth Ernest Bell, born 17 January 1924 in Paulding County, married 7 November 1946 Norina Roundtree, born 12 April 1926 in Floyd County. Issue:

A. Kenneth James Bell, born 23 May 1956 Fulton County, married 28 January 1979, Beverly Bailey (born 18 July 1952). Issue: Marie Kenneth Bell and Joshua Ernest Bell.

B. Ernest Blake Bell, born 23 August 1958, married on 27 August 1977, Sylvia Brown (born 1 October 1958). Issue: Narcissa Nicole Bell.

III. Wyatt Coleman Bell, born 14 October 1927 in Demopolis, Alabama, married on 25 November 1848, Margaret Elizabeth Crowe (born 3 October 1927). Issue:

A. Ronald Coleman Bell, born 11 October 1954 Paulding County, died 3 March 1956, buried New Hope Cemetery, Paulding County.

B. Lydia Margaret Bell, born 21 May 1949 Paulding County, married 14 August 1967 Daniel James Williams (born 11 September 1948). Issue:
   1. James Wyatt Williams.
   2. Matthew Daniel Williams, born 27 Feruary 1974.

C. Myra Susan Bell, born 24 May 1950 Paulding County, married 21 September 1968 William Robert Moody (born 29 March 1949). Daughter:
   1 Donna Lyn Moody.

D. Donnie Lynn Bell, born 26 May 1951 in Paulding County, married 10 July 1971 Wyatt Blair Elliot II (born 20 April 1950). Issue:
   1. Michael Joshua Elliot.
   2. Caleb Steven Elliot.

IV. Rachel Wynette Bell, daughter of Ernest Coleman Bell, born 22 November 1936, died 1 September 1974, married Daryl Robertson Brockington (born 23 February 1954). Issue:

A. Sera Elizabeth Brockington.
B. David Oliver Brockington.

V. Doris Jeanette Bell, daughter of Ernest Coleman Bell, born 6 February 1933, and married (1) on 29 July 1949, John Wendall Crocker (born 8 April 1930), (divorced), and (2) on 8 November 1963, David Johnson (born on 18 April 1937), divorced, and (3) on 24 June 1972, Donald Franklin Royals (born on 7 March 1936). Issue:

A. John Wendall Johnson, born 18 August 1954, married Jonella Marie Payne (born 29 August 1956) on 17 September 1978. Their Issue:

   1. April Marie Johnson.
   2. Erin Jeannette Johnson.

VI. James Calvin Bell, son of Ernest Coleman Bell, born 28 August 1935, died 30 July 1956, buried New Hope Cemetery, Paulding County.

VII. Patricia June Bell, daughter of Ernest Coleman Bell, born 6 January 1938 in Paulding County, married 6 April 1958, Thurmon Eugene Atkinson (born 27 May 1933). Issue:

A. Holly Jeanette Atkinson.
B. Daryl Eugene Atkinson.

VIII. Infant san of Ernest Coleman Bell was born 24 March 1942, and was buried in the High Shoals Cemetery, Paulding County.

Edward Bird was born ca 1640 and died 1697 in Accomack County, Virginia, his LWT dated 12 April 1697, probated 3 August 1697. Edward Bird was transported into Virginia on 10 May 1664 along with 17 other persons by Richard Kellum, who received 900 acres in Accomack County, headed by Mathepungo Creek. [24] Wife, Jane. [25] They had two known children, viz: a daughter who married William Rodgers or Rogers (his estate inventoried in Accomack County in 1738) and John Bird (below). Locating other children of this couple would, no doubt, be helpful in clearing up the connections of the Bird family with the families of Scarbrough, Eborne and Bull.

John Bird was born ca 1670, and died in 1728 in Accomack County, Virginia. His LWT dated 26 January 1727/8, was probated on 5 March 1727/8. He named his children as Nathaniel, Solomon, Major, Eborn and Daniel. John Bird probably married Miss Scarbrough, a member of the famous Colonel Edmund Scarbrough family who owned thousands of acres in Accomack and Northampton Counties and who controlled the politics of that region for many years, as the name is well-remembered for generations in the naming of the Bird females, as was the Ebourne (Eborne) name. In Colonial times, Virginia's southeastern shore along Accomack and Northampton Counties was settled by notable wealthy persons such as Colonel Edmund Scarbrough, who transported many persons into the colony and obtained large land grants for it. The land was subjugated by the unpopular Governor Berkeley who did favors for his friends. The Birds, Scarbroughs and Bulls all seemed to belong to the tightly strung existence of the colonial heirachy. When traveling from the eastern shore, one one crosses the river on a ferry to the distant shore, and at once begins to notice the isolated circumstances of old-ruling churchyards with their graveyards planted with cedars and surrounded by black iron fences. One can imagine Nathaniel Bacon and his rebels trying to change local politics, galloping across old corn fields, going against Governor Berkeley.

Issue:

I.   Nathaniel Bird, his LWT dated 30 December 1778, probated 29 February 1780 in Accomack County, Virginia, named his wife, Margaret, and his brother, Solomon.

II.   Solomon Bird, his LWT dated 28 September 1784, probated on 30 November 1784 in Accomack County, Virginia. Wife, Frances. [26] Witnesses were: Nathaniel Bird and Major Bird. Issue:

---

[24] Cavaliers and Pioneers, Vol. I, by Nell Marion Nugent.

[25] The wife of Edward Bird could be Jane Spiers, a relative of John Spiers, his LWT dated 19 November 1693, probated 18 December 1693 in Accomack County which named wife, Sarah; son, John. The LWT was proved by Jane Bird and Bridget Bird. .Another plausible theory is that his wife was Jane Ebourne, a daughter of William Ebourne, who died intestate in 1677 in Accomack County (inventory of estate). William Ebourne was transported into Virginia by John Browne on 27 November 1652, for which Brown received 1000 acres in Northampton County near Matchepongo. (ibid).

[26] The wife of Solomon Bird is believed to be Frances Bull, the granddaughter of Tobias Bull II, whose LWT was dated 4 May 1751, probated 25 November 1760 in Accomack County, Virginia, naming a granddaughter, Frances Bird.

A. John W. Bird, born 1746, died 1829 (not named in the LWT of his father). He married (1) in 1768, Mary and (2) Ester Ross, in 1790.

B. Esther Bird.

C. Rebecca Bird.

D. Esther Bird.

E. Scarbrough Bird.

F. Solomon Bird, Jr., born ca 1755, was listed on the 1787, 1790 and 1800 Edgefield County, South Carolina Census. His LWT dated 2 October 1810, probated 7 December 1810 in Edgefield County named his wife, Nancy, and children. His daughter, Rachel Jourdan, was listed. Apparently two of his children came to Georgia, viz....Rachel with her husband, Jesse Jordan to DeKalb County; and Billions (or Billings) Bird who went to Elbert County. Issue:
    1. Rachel Bird, born 1790 in Edgefield County, South Carolina, died in DeKalb County, Georgia. She married ca 1810 in Edgefield County, Jesse Jordan. SEE Jordan.
    2. Esther Bird, married Mr. Smith.
    3. Mary Bird.
    4. Eborn Bird, born ca 1795 in Edgefield County.
    5. Billions (or Billings) Bird, born 1797 in Edgefield County, died before 1850 in DeKalb County Georgia. He married on 15 February 1815 in Elbert County, Charity Tyner.
    6. Elijah Bird. There is an Account of Elijah Bird on the Estate of J. L. Williams (1854) in DeKalb County.[27]

G. Elijah Bird. Edgefield County deed dated 5 April 1793 of Francis Bremar to Elijah Bird of Edgefield County.

H. Daniel Bird, Sr., born ca 1750, died 1806. Daniel Bird, a Revolutionary War Soldier, served in the South Carolina Militia in 1782, sometimes furnishing supplies to the army. [28] A deed dated 16 February 1787, of James Murehead of Edgefield County, South Carolina, to Daniel Bird of the same place, for 50 pounds, 125 acres, being part of 250 acres granted to Anne Millar on 6 February 1773 in Granville County on Logg Creek, bounded on the Northeast by Timothy Rairden and by land surveyed on a Dutch Bounty Warrant. Edgefield County Deed Book 3, pp. 241-245.
There is a Bill of Sale dated 5 October 1790 of Daniel Bird, Planter, to Jean Nobles, spinister, for a Negro woman, in Edgefield County.

I. Frances Bird.

J. Hezekiah Bird. Wife, Peggy. His LWT dated 14 July 1808, probated 7 October 1808 in Edgefield County, named daughter, Kitty.

III. Major Bird, born ca 1710.

---

[27] DeKalb County, Georgia Probate Records by Jeannette Holland Austin, page 244.

[28] South Carolina Patriots in the American Revolution by Moss.

IV. Eborn Bird.

V. Daniel Bird, born ca 1720, of Accomack County, Virginia appears to be the progenitor of the family in Edgefield County, South Carolina and in Elbert and DeKalb Counties, Georgia. Wife, Margaret.[29]

Daniel Bird died 1758 in Accomack County, Virginia, his (nuncupative) LWT dated 1751, but probated on 29 March 1758, naming his daughter, Susannah, to whom he left the land "where I now live containing 125 acres". Daughters, Mary and Scarburgh Bird, Rachel Mason, and Elizabeth Parks. To: Solomon Bird. Wife, Margaret was to have use of the land during her widowhood. This will was proven by the testimony of Henry Fletcher and William Melson. Later, Henry Fletcher and William Melson filed depositions in the suit of Susannah Bird, Complainant, versus Margaret Bird, Middleton Mason and Rachel, his wife; Benjamin Parks and Elizabeth, his wife; Mary Bird and Scarburgh Bird, Defendants. The depositions were ordered recorded to be established as the LWT of Daniel Bird, deceased, and it was also ordered that the former administration which had been granted to said estate be revoked, and that the defendant, the widow of the said testator, be summoned to take upon her the administration of said estate.[30]

Issue:

A. Mary Bird.
B. Scarburgh Bird.
C. Rachel Bird married in 1736, Accomack County, Middleton Mason who died 1772 in Accomack County.
D. Elizabeth Bird married Benjamin Parks.
E. Susannah Bird

---

[29] Hitchen's Lessee vs. Ejectment Proceedings, Hall:

> "That Catherine Moore being seized in fee of the premises in question by
> deed dated 7 September 1726 conveyed the same to her son-in-law, Thomas Stockly,
> of Sussex County, Delaware, being 200 acres in *Jolly's Neck* adjoining the land of
> *Hancock Curtis*, and being a tract of land formerly belonging to John Bayley;
> That soon afterwards the said Catherine died possessed of the premises after
> whose death George Philby, the eldest son and heir at law, entered into the
> oremises and was thereof seized and possessed; the said Thomas Stockly being
> then and always afterwards until his death resident in the Province of Maryland
> or Pennsylvania; That the said George Philby being so in possession by deed dated
> 7 March 1737, conveyed the premises to *Daniel Byrd*, and that *Daniel Bird*, by virtue
> of said deed entered into the premises and was thereof possessed; and by his deed
> dated 6 March 1739, conveyed the same to George Philby, the younger; ...."
> Accomack Land Causes.

[30] Accomack County, Virginia Wills (1752-1757), page 39.

Bittick of Tennessee & Monroe County

Samuel F. Bittick was born 16 April 1790 in Pulaski, Giles County, Tennessee, and married on 16 August 1824, Elizabeth Frasier Goodrum. Known issue:

I.   Cyrus Samuel Bittick, born 1 December 1826 in Franklin, William County, Tennessee, died 27 August 1871 in Tennessee. He was married on 30 October 1856 in Monroe County, Georgia to Emmaline E. Goodrum (born 16 November 1838, died 30 October 1856 in Monroe County), a daughter of John Goodrum. Issue:

A. John Goodrum Bittick, born 3 February 1858 in Tennessee, died on 6 October 1917 in Georgia. He was married on 19 December 1882 in Monroe County to Jennie Bob Simmons (born 21 February 1863, died 26 June 1936 in Monroe County), the daughter of Robert Simmons and his wife, Elizabeth (Chambliss) Simmons. SEE Chambliss. Issue:

1. Robert Cyrus Bittick, born 28 February 1884 in Monroe County, died 5 April 1923, married Mattie Nixon.
2. Eula Grace Bittick, born 3 December 1885 in Monroe County, married Arthur Sasser
3. Rollie Joe Bittick, born 25 June 1888 in Monroe County, married Sarah Haygood.
4. John Goodrum Bittick, Jr., born 16 July 1891 in Monroe County.
5. Lawson Cary Bittick, born 10 August 1894 in Monroe County, died 29 November 1953 in Monroe County, married on 25 February 1926, Ruth Thompson.

B. Mary Elizabeth Bittick, born 30 March 1860 in Tennessee, died 1928, Mount Olivet, Nashville County, Tennessee.

C. James F. Bittick, born 12 April 1862 in Tennessee.

D. Cyrus Samuel Bittick, born 26 November 1864 in Tennessee.

Bivins of Paulding County

Lawrence Vester Bivins was born 25 December 1914 in Cobb County and married on 27 April 1940 in Paulding County, Wilma Ione Bell, born 28 November 1921 in Paulding County. Issue:

I.   Donnie Joan Bivins, born 10 April 1941 in DeKalb County, married on 14 June 1964, James Donald Champion. Child: Gretchen Sloan Champion, born 17 August 1971.

II.   Cora Rosemary Bivins, born 18 May 1949 in Paulding County, married Alfred Keith Butler, born 10 May 1949 in Paulding County, on 6 February 1969. Issue: Bradly Keith Butler, born 28 May 1970, Marietta, Patrick Christian Butler, born 24 September 1974 in Marietta, Alice Elizabeth Butler, born 12 April 1977 in Marietta.

III.   Cherry Bell Bivins, born 23 January 1951 in Paulding County, married Fred Christian Waddell, Jr., born 18 September 1948 in Nassau, New York, on 26 July 1969; divorced 30 June 1980. Issue: Jeffery Jason Waddell, born 13 August 1974 and Wendy Lynn Waddell, born 16 December 1975.

John Bone was born ca 1740, probably in Pennsylvania, and died 1796 in Jackson County, Georgia, where his estate is mentioned, but no details are provided. He married Elizabeth Jordan on 19 January of 1762 in Prince George Parish, South Carolina. He appears to be linked with those Bones who migrated from Pennsylvania to Rowan County, North Carolina. According to the Revolutionary War Pension of his son, George Bone, the family resided in Marlboro County, South Carolina during the 1760's, but removed before 1778 to Richmond County, North Carolina (from where George was drafted in 1779) . [31]

Aaron Knight, Revolutionary War Soldier, served in the war with both George and Lewis Bone, and made affidavits certifying to their service. George Bone mentioned that his "brother" had predeceased him". Issue:[32]

I.   George Bone, Revolutionary War Soldier, born 1763 in Marlboro County, South Carolina. He died August 1845 in Chesterfield County, South Carolina. Wife, Penelope. According to his pension, he enlisted from Richmond County, North Carolina where he father had gone to live in 1777. Voucher #2443. "State of South Carolina, Auditor's Office, Salisbury District, Lower Board. 19 July 1784. This may certify that George Bone exhibited his claim and was allowed the sum of Eleven Pounds, Five Shillings. William Love, John Auld, M. L. Chiles." In 1831, he moved back to Chesterfield County, where he died. [33]

---

[31] NOTE____ Richmond county was taken from Anson County in 1779, and borders the State of South Carolina.

[32] Revolutionary War Pensions of George, John and Lewis Bone; Madison County deed dated 1806, John Bone "of Clarke County"; 1820 Clarke County Census; Madison County Estates; 1820-1860 Madison County Census; Madison County Marriages; 1850-1900 Paulding County Census; Personal records of Mrs. Alfred V. Thomson, 2325 Barbe St., Lake Charles LA 70601; Dallas City Cemetery, Paulding County; Paulding County Marriages; 1870 Paulding County Census; 1850 Chesterfield County, South Carolina Census.

[33] Pension of George Bone

"Chesterfield Court House
May 3, 1837

F.L. Edwards, Esquire:

Sir, early in the year of 1834, George Bone applied to me to prepare his
Declaration in order to obtain a Pension under the Act of June 7th, 1832.
I then prepared his declaration and instructed him to attend at March
Court (1834) with a clergyman and one or two respectable citizens who
Would give the certificate required in the instructions from the Department
And with such other proof of service as he could get.

He did not attend. He afterward applied to me to prepare his declaration
Again, stating as his reason for not attending that he could not get the
individuals upon whose certificate he depended to attend at the time
appointed, but thought that he could procure the certificate by the next court
after this second application to me, this was in 1836. He failed to attend again.

But meeting with him afterward he mentioned the subject of his declaration and I absolutely refused to have anything further to do with the matter, as I had been at considerable trouble and he had wholly neglected the matter.

He stated that he had failed to attend because he could not provide the attendance of any clergyman who could give the requisite certificate, and that he understood from what I had said that the certificate of a clergyman was absolutely necessary. This was in the early part of this year and I prepared the declaration which was sent to you believing that his failures had provided from the facts stated by him, and knowing that I had instructed him to procure the certificate of a clergyman. As the certificate of Aaron Knight – I am informed it was taken at the instance of the *brother of this applicant* who has been some time dead. Aaron Knight lived in Georgia at the time of giving the certificate forwarded to you. I know nothing of him myself but I know he has the character in this community of a man of truth and of having been a Revolutionary soldier. I am informed that Aaron Knight and Moses Knight are both now dead.

The facts he stated with regards the times of preparing the several declarations for the said George Bone, I am able to say are correct having prepared the two first and having three now before me. Hoping the above may be satisfactory, I am your Obedient Servant.

M. J. Harred."

Declaration of George Bone, in order to obtain the benefit of the Act of Congress, passed June 7, 1832

"....that he was born in what is now the District of Marlboro, in the State aforesaid, in January in the year of our Lord one thousand seven hundred and sixty three, that his age was set down in a Bible given to this deponent by his father, when a boy at school, that many leaves of the Bible have since been destroyed and amongst them on wich his age was written.

That this deponent went into the revolutionary service in December in the year one thousand seven hundred and seventy eight, at which time he volunteered for one month under Captain Tristan Thomas, Stephens, orderly sergeant, that he does not recollect the names of the other officers of Captain Thomas' Company, nor does he know that it was attached to any battalion or regiment, but appears to act alone against the Tories of Marlboro District. That he served the whole month under Captain Thomas but was not in any engagement during the time. At the expiration of one month he returned to his father's, who shortly afterwards removed to Richmond County, North Carolina, taking this deponent with him. That in March of 1779, he was drafted in Richmond County, North Caroina for three months under Captain John Speed, Major John Jones and Colonel Thomas Crawford; he does not recollect that the regiment was called. Before marching, they were joined by Colonel Wade who took command of the regiment; he then marched under the said officers from the house of Colonel Crawford in Richmond County, by way of Green's Swamp to Betting Bridge or Downing Creek where a number of Tories were there lying under the command of Colonel Hester McNeill; the night before we attacked them Colonel Fanning, with a

Known issue of George Bone:

A. Martha Bone married Mr. Stogner, applied for her father's pension in 1856 from Chesterfield County.

B. John W. Bone, alive in 1856 according to his sister, Martha's application for pension.

II. Lewis Bone, Revolutionary War Soldier, was born ca 1765 in Marlboro County, South Carolina, died ca 1819 in Chesterfield County, South Carolina. He married ca 1789, Mary Killingsworth who died in the Spring of 1845 in Chesterfield District.[34]

---

number of Tories, joined Colonel McNeill though the force of Colonel Wade was greatly inferior to that of McNeill and Fanning, he made the attack and was completely defeated. In this engagement, the deponent received five bullet holes through his coat and had his horse shot out from under him – at the moment of surrender, deponent's gun was loaded and he shot the captain and made his escape upon his horse – that he was out in this tour the whole three months for which he was drafted.

That some times afterwards he volunteered under the same officers (except Colonel Wade), Colonel Thomas Crawford having the command and marched from Pee Dee River in Richmond County, to near Wilmington, North Carolina in order to join General Rutherford's army, intending to assist him in driving the British, who had possession of Wilmington. Rutherford's army was on the opposite side of the river and that he (Colonel Crawford) could not cross. The next day, after Colonel Crawford arrived near the town, the British marched out and crossed the river toward Colonel Crawford's camp, who immediately retreated a few miles. The next day General Rutherford took possession of the town and this deponent returned home with Colonel Crawford's Regiment, having served four months in this tour – making in this whole a service of eight months in the Militia.

That he never received any discharge – that he lived in Richmond County, North Carolina from the time his father settled there as above stated until 1831. In January of 1831, he removed to Marlboro District in South Carolina where he resided until February 1832, when he removed to Chesterfield District where he now resides. This deponent does not know or recollect any of his companions in arms who are now alive having lately learned that Aaron Knight who lived in the State of Georgia and Moses Knight who lived in Richmond County, North Carolina, are both dead."

[34] Pension of Lewis Bone

"State of South Carolina
Chesterfield District

Personally appeared Aggy Molton before me, Turner Bryan, Judge of the Court of Ordinary for said District, who, after being duly sworn, saith that she is about eighty years of age; and that she was well acquainted with Lewis Bone and Mary Killingsworth; who was married to said Lewis Bone as was said, by them and the neighbors generally by one Reverend Lewis, a Baptist minister of the Gospel and that the said Lewis Bone and his said wife, Mary, resided together as man and wife during their joint lives and that Henry Bone, their son, was born in wedlock about one year after marriage and that the said Lewis Bone paid the marriage expenses.

Aggy Morton (her mark)

24

Henry Bone, son, gave his declaration on 2 February 1850 in Chesterfield District as to the service of his father, and named his siblings.

Issue of Lewis Bone:

A. Henry Bone, born 1790, one year after parent's marriage, died after 1850 in Chesterfield County. He married Elizabeth, born 1800. Issue:

1. Jacob Bone, born 1828 Chesterfield County.
2. Andrew Bone, born 1831 Chesterfield County.
3. Mary Bone, born 1833 Chesterfield County.
4. Martha Bone, born 1836 Chesterfield County.

Sworn before me this first January 1849
Turner Bryan, Judge of the Court of Ordinary"

"State of South Carolina
Chesterfield District

Aaron Knight of the District and State aforesaid, personally came before me, Turner Bryan, Judge of the Court of Ordinary of the District aforesaid in the State aforesaid and being duly sworn, saith: That he knew Lewis Bone in his lifetime; Deponent knows he was old enough to have served in the War of the Revolution. Deponent's father, Aaron Knight, served in the War of the Revolution and deponent has often heard his father (who is now dead) say that Lewis Bone served with him in the said war and that said Lewis Bone was a good whig and a good soldier. Deponent believes that his father and the said Lewis Bone served together under General Wade. Deponent always understood and believes that Lewis Bone served sometimes in the neighborhood of Charleston, South Carolina, particularly on Sullivan's Island. Deponent has been informed and believes that said Lewis Bone was in the Battle of Bettis Bridge or Downing Creek in North Carolina and that he was there wounded and taken prisoner by Colonel Fanning who commanded the British and Tories in that battle. Deponent has heard his father say that he served six months in the neighborhood of Charleston and that Lewis Bone was with him the whole time. Deponent is now upwards of fifty nine years of age. Deponent knows Lewis Bone and Mary Bone were regarded and proper as husband and wife. Lewis Bone died upwards of thirty years ago, leaving Mary surviving. Mary, the widow, never married again but continued a widow until she died. Said Mary Bone died as deponent believes in the Spring of 1845. Henry Bone is a son of the said Lewis and Mary Bone. There are now living of the children of the said Lewis and Mary Bone the following, viz...Henry Bone, Elizabeth Bone, Killis Bone, Aggy who married Jacob Holby, Phoebe who married Edward Bone and William Bone; Rachel and Wirrey Bone left this part of the country many years ago and whether they are now alive deponent does not know.....Deponent has seen the wound on the thigh of Lewis Bone which it is said he received in the Battle of Bettis Bridge.
Aaron Knight

Sworn to before me in the Court of Ordinary at
Chesterfield Courthouse in the District and State
Aforesaid. Given under my hand and seal of office,
This 26th March 1849."

5. Eliza Bone, born 1839 Chesterfield County.

B. Elizabeth Bone.

C. Killis Bone, born 1799 Chesterfield County, laborer. Wife, Mary, born 1805. Issue:

1. George Bone, born 1826 Chesterfield County.
2. Sally Bone, born 1832 Chesterfield County.
3. Emma Bone, born 1832 Chesterfield County.
4. Jackson Bone, born 1834 Chesterfield County.
5. Nancy Bone, born 1836 Chesterfield County.
6. Betsy Bone, born 1838 Chesterfield County.
7. Billy Bone, born 1840 Chesterfield County.
8. Mary Bone, born 1841 Chesterfield County.
9. Celia Bone, born 1843 Chesterfield County.
10. Irvin Bone, born 1845 Chesterfield County.
11. Alice Bone, born 1845 Chesterfield County.
12. Annie Bone, born February 1850 Chesterfield County.

D. Aggie Bone married Jacob Holby.

E. Phoebey Bone married Edward Bone.

F. Gilly Bone, died after 1845, unmarried.

G. William Bone.

H. Rachel Bone.

I. Wirrey Bone.

III. John Bone was born ca 1764 in Chesterfield County, South Carolina, died 1822 in Marlboro County. His wife, Jane, was about the same age. The 1800 census shows they had five male children under 10 and 2 female children under 10.

IV. William Bone, Sr., born between 1770 and 1780 in Chesterfield County, South Carolina, died 1832 Madison County. Wife, Nancy, was born 1830-1840 in Madison County. There was an Agreement between the heirs, dated 1838, Madison County Annual Returns, Book E (1837-1841), page 304; Annual Returns Madison County, Book F (1841-1850), page 25, legatees' receipts. The 1820 Madison County Census establishes children living with him...Bailey, George, Polly, Barney and Elizabeth. Issue:[35]

A. John Bone, son of William Bone, Sr., was born 1794 Chesterfield County, South Carolina, married Sally Adair on 8 May 1814 in Madison County. He was living in

---

[35] Revolutionary War Pensions of George, John and Lewis Bone; Madison County deed dated 1806, John Bone "of Clarke County"; 1820 Clarke County Census; Madison County Estates; 1820-1860 Madison County Census; Madison County Marriages; 1850-1900 Paulding County Census; Personal records of Mrs. Alfred V. Thomson, 2325 Barbe St., Lake Charles LA 70601; Dallas City Cemetery, Paulding County; Paulding County Marriages; 1870 Paulding County Census; 1850 Chesterfield County, South Carolina Census..

Carroll County in 1840, according to the census, but was listed on the 1850 Paulding County Census. See ADAIR. Issue:

1. Elizabeth Bone, born 15 April 1815, died 23 April 1889, married on 23 July 1829, Nathaniel Baxter. SEE Baxter.

2. William Bone, born 1819, married on 12 July 1840, Lucinda Box.

3. John Bone, born 1823.

4. James Bone, born 1825.

5. Matthew Bone, born 1828, died 1892, married on 12 May 1849, Sarah Roberts. Issue:

    a.   James Bone, born 1850.
    b.   Emiline Bone, born 1852.
    c.   John Bone, born 1854.
    d.   Thomas Bone, born 1857.
    e.   Zacariah Bone, born 1859.

6. Permelia Elizabeth Bone, born 1831, married on 6 May 1858, Joseph O. Sanders.

B. Bailey Bone, son of William Bone, Sr., was born 1800 in Madison County, died 1859 Dallas, Paulding County, buried Dallas City Cemetery. He married Nancy Evans (born 1802 Madison County, died 1889 Paulding County, buried Dallas City Cemetery) on 13 April 1826 in Madison County, a daughter of William Evans and his wife Celia (Leverett) Evans. SEE Evans. The Estate of Bailey Bone, Will Book 1850-1877, Book B, page 471, Appraisement dated 12 May 1859, Paulding County. Wife, Nancy, was listed on the 1880 Paulding County Census with her daughter, Mrs. Mary Owen. Issue:

1. William Bone, born 26 May 1828 in Madison County, died 4 July 1908 in Dallas, Paulding County, buried Dallas City Cemetery. He married Catherine Crompton, born 19 January 1833, died 27 February 1901, buried in the Dallas City Cemetery. Issue:
    a. Bailey Bone, Jr., born 18 March 1848, died 27 February 1934, buried in the Dallas City Cemetery. Wife, Emma, born 24 November 1847, died 20 July 1926.

2. Celia A. Bone, born 8 October 1831 in Madison County, died 17 March 1910 in Dallas, Paulding County, buried Dallas City Cemetery. She married Anson A. Ables on 9 October 1853 in Paulding County. Anson Ables served in the War Between the States, and was born on 1 March 1829, died 17 March 1862, buried in the Dallas City Cemetery. In 1870, Mrs. Celia Abels was listed on the Paulding County Census with her small children.

3. John Bone, born 3 June 1836 in Madison County, died 3 March 1904 in Paulding County, buried Dallas City Cemetery. He married Nancy J. Shelton on 20 December 1860 in Paulding County. He was a farmer, listed on the 1870-1900 Paulding County Census. During the War Between the States, he served as 2 Cpl in Co. C, 22nd Regiment, C. S. A. Issue:

a. John Martin Bone, born 27 December 1865, died 10 May 1891, buried in the Dallas City Cemetery.

b. Alex Bone, born 1870, died 1872, buried in the Dallas City Cemetery.

4. Henry Bone, born 15 October 1832 in Madison County, died 19 March 1904 in Paulding County, buried Dallas City Cemetery. He married Ella J. Summer on 19 August 1869 in Paulding County. [36] Ella was born on 12 October 1848 and died 7 November 1910, buried in the Dallas City Cemetery. Henry served as a Private in Co. K, 60th Infantry, C. S. A.

5. Nancy Bone, born 1839 in Dallas, Paulding County. She married Ezekiel Owens on 23 February 1862 in Paulding County.

6. Elizabeth Bone, born 1840 in Madison County, died before 1885 in Paulding County, buried in the Dallas City Cemetery. She married (1) Humphrey Collins on 20 August 1853 in Paulding County and after his death (2) Isaac Pace on 24 January 1896 in Paulding County. SEE Collins.

7. Mary F. Bone, born 1849 in Dallas, Paulding County, married Ereck B. Owen.

8. Adaline Bone, born 1850 in Dallas, Paulding County, married Mr. Drake.

C. George Bone, son of William Bone, Sr., was born between 1800-1810 in Madison County, died between 1830-1840 Madison County. He married Cynthia Gore on 4 November 1823 in Madison County.

D. William Bone, Jr., son of William Bone, Sr., was born ca 1801 in Madison County, died between 1840-1850 Madison County, married Salley Williams on 26 March 1818 in Madison County.

E. James Bone, son of William Bone, Sr., was born ca 1802 in Madison County, Georgia, married Milly Sanders on 29 June 1818 in Madison County.

F. Polly Bone, daughter of William Bone, Sr., was born 1804-1810 in Madison County, married Thomas Beard on 9 November 1826 in Madison County.

G. Matthew Bone, son of William Bone, Sr., was born ca 1805 in Madison County, died between 1820-1830 in Madison County, married Elizabeth Strickland on 30 March 1820 in Madison County.

---

[36] NOTE_____ In Memoirs of Georgia (1895), Henry Bone stated that his grandfather was George Bone, a Revolutionary War Soldier who emigrated from Ireland in 1770; also that his father was born in Madison County, Georgia. Henry is mistaken. George Bone could not have been his grandfather because, in 1856 when George's daughter, Martha Stogner of Chesterfield County applied for his pension, she stated that his only living children were herself, and John W. Bone. Also, George Bone died in Chesterfield District, South Carolina in August of 1845. He never lived in Madison County, Georgia.

H. Barney Bone, son of William Boone, Sr., was born 1805 in Madison County, married Judah Allen (born 1805) on 31 January 1833 in Madison County; listed on the 1850 Madison County Census. Issue:

    1. Mary A. Bone, born 1834 in Madison County.

    2. William Bone, born 1837 in Madison County, farmer. He married Nancy (born 1842), listed on the 1860 Madison County Census. Issue: Loucrity Bone, born 1860 Madison County.

    3. Mathew Bone, born 1842 in Madison County.

    4. Martha Bone, born 1848 in Madison County.

    5. Nancy Bone, born 1852 Madison County.

    6. Dock Bone, born 1855 Madison County.

    7. Horsenatt Bone, born 1856 Madison County.

I. Pleasant W. Bone, son of William Bone, Sr., was born 1822 in Madison County. He married Emily C. Adair (born 1824) on 28 July 1840. Issue:

    1. Pheribe Elizabeth Bone, born 1842.

    2. Sarah C. Bone, born 1844.

    3. Nancy W. Bone, born 1846.

    4. Mary Jane Bone, born 1848.

    5. James M. Bone, born 1850, married on 28 August 1873, Nancy Puckett.

    6. Jacob Bone, born 1856, married on 16 March 1884, Julia Guess.

J. Elizabeth Bone, daughter of William Bone, Sr., was born between 1804-1810.

Bradley of Madison County

James O. Bradley was born 1797 in Georgia, died October of 1878 in Madison County. His LWT dated 13 May 1877, probated 1 October 1878, Book B, Page 281, Madison County, in which he named his wife and children; also a grandson, Marion. He married on 20 September 1826 in Madison County, Ann Williams (born 1798 in Northampton County, North Carolina), a daughter of John Williams, Sr. and his wife, Anne (Wade) Williams. SEE Williams. Issue:[37]

I. William Monroe Bradley, born 1828 in Georgia. He married Martha J. Glenn (born 1826 in Georgia) on 24 August 1849 in Madison County. They were residents of Royal township, being listed on the 1880 White County, Arkansas Census. Issue:

    A.   Nancy A. Bradley, born 1858 in Georgia.

    B.   William C. Bradley, born 1863 in Alabama.

    C.   Martha A. Bradley, born 1865 in Georgia.

    D.   Marion M. Bradley, born 1867 in Arkansas.

II. John Walton Bradley, born 1828 Georgia, married Fanny Williams (born 1828 Georgia) on 23 January 1851 in Madison County. Issue:

    A. Robert Bradley, born 1853 Madison County.

    B. James Bradley, born 1855 Madison County.

    C. David R. Bradley, born 1858 Madison County, married Leanor Bullock on 27 November 1879 in Madison County.

---

[37] 1850-1860 Madison County Census; Madison County Wills.

III. Frances Anne Bradley, born 1832 Georgia.

IV. Sarah E. Bradley, born 1833 Georgia.

V. James W. Bradley, born 1835 Georgia.

VI. Nancy M. Bradley, born 1838 Georgia, married on 9 October 1863 in Madison County, James C. Seagraves.

VII. George W. Bradley, born 1840 Georgia.

Brent of Kentucky & Monroe County

Thomas Young Brent descends from the famous Brent family of Kentucky, who trace their lineage to the Magna Charta. Thomas, or "Ty", as he was called, was born 1841 in Louisville, Jefferson County, Kentucky, and died ca 1910 in the Old Soldier's Home in Louisville. He was married on 1 May 1867 in Forsyth, Monroe County, to Jane Smith, the widow of Wesley Clements, who did not come home from the war. SEE Smith.

Thomas Young Brent took charge of the Smith Plantation, near Forsyth, and the community was soon named as "Brent". The 1870 Monroe County Census lists Thomas Y. Brent, 28, Jennie 34, Taylor 1, William Clements 15, Thomas Clements 13, Elizabeth Clements 10, and Elizabeth Fryer 39. (Elizabeth Fryer was Jennie's widowed sister). The Smith plantation had known 20 slaves before the War Between the States, but after the war, suffered for laborers. Ty was enterprising, farming the old plantation after the war, and established a local store, where the neighbors purchased foodstuffs grown on the farm. They, along with Jane's sisters and their children, resided in the old plantation home, which stood at Brent well after the turn of the century, when it was torn down and the ground was used as pasture.

Ty and Jane had two sons:[38]

I. Taylor Young Brent, born 11 February 1869 at Brent, Monroe County, died 30 March 1934, Brent. He married Annie Tindall Hill on 29 January 1893 in Monroe County.

II. Jackson Innis Brent, born 18 December 1871 in Brent, Monroe County, died 5 June 1908 at Brent. He married Mattie Geary.

Brooks of Paulding County

Herman Wood Brooks was born 12 December 1912 in Paulding County, died on 16 September 1991 at his home in Long Beach California. He was the son of John Thomas and Lucy Caroline (Woodall) Brooks. He married Miss Lillian Ruth Starling, born on 3 April 1914 Dallas, Paulding County, Ga, died 24 June 1934, Dallas, Paulding County, SEE Starling. Issue:

---

[38] Brent Bible in the possession of Harry Brent, Riverdale, Georgia (1966); Memoirs of Georgia, and 1880 Monroe County Census.

(Woodall) Brooks. He married Miss Lillian Ruth Starling, born on 3 April 1914 Dallas, Paulding County, Ga, died 24 June 1934, Dallas, Paulding County, SEE Starling. Issue:

I. Thomas William Brooks, born on 4 September 1935 in Dallas, Paulding County, married on 19 April 1964 in Phoenix, Arizona, Sharan Pierce (born on 2 May 1942 in Jamestown, New Jersey, the daughter of Lawrence Grant and Marjorie (Field) Pierce. Issue:

    A. Jeffrey Larence Brooks, born 19 February 1961 in Phoenix, Arizona.

    B. Laura Ruth Brooks, born 22 September 1964 in Paulding County.

    C. John Thomas Brooks, born 2 September 1966 in Phoenix, Arizona.

II. Mary Lee Brooks, born on 2 July 1937 in Dallas, Paulding County, Ga. married 6/29/1963 in Long Beach, California, Richard George Bernhard (born on 22 May 1934 in Los Angeles, California), son of George and Martha Barbara (Koeing) Bernhard. Issue:

    A. Cheryl Ann Bernhard, born on 1 May 1965 in Long Beach, California.

III. James Herman Brooks, born on 16 January 1940 in Dallas, Paulding County, married on 19 December 1959 in Long Beach, California, Clare Elaine Riley (born 5 June 1938 in Beuna Park, California). Issue:[39]

    A. Stacy Deneen Brooks, born on 15 December 1963 in Long Beach, California.

    B. Kari Lynn Brooks, born on 11 November 1967 in Long Beach, California.

IV. Robert Eugene Brooks, born on 10 April 1942 in Dallas, Paulding County, married on 21 April 1963, Beverly Ann Blake (born on 25 March 1942 in Portsmith Virginia), daughter of James Dorist and Bernice Pauline (Poseyj Blake. Issue:

    A. Stephanie Dawn Brooks, born on 19 September 1968 in Long Beach, California.

    B. Jennifer Marie Brooks, born on 16 April 1971 in Long Beach, California.

Brown of Paulding County

G. W. "Pete" Brown was born 2 May 1886, died 7 September 1967. He married Lona Holland, daughter of Henry Clay Holland (born 2 August 1899, died 21 September 1973). Issue:

I. Myrtle Ruth Brown, born 10 August 1908, died 18 May 1987, married Ervin Cleathan Mercer (died 21 November 1982). Myrtle Ruth organized the National Society of Daughters of American Revolution Chapter located in Dallas, known as Edward Hagin Chapter. They had one son: Ervin Lamar Mercer, born 19 May 1928 of Calhoun, Georgia, owner of the aircraft museum located on 1-75. Ervin Lamar Mercer had one daughter: Bonnie Ruth Anderson of Calhoun. Her issue: Ronald, Eddie, Daniel and Andrew Anderson.

---

[39] Holland 1000-1988 by Jeannette Holland Austin.

II.   Leo Curtis Brown, born 29 December 1916, married Louise Love from Wood, Pennsylvania. He resides in Dallas, Texas as a retired Air Force pilot having experienced intense action in the South Pacific during World War II. Issue:

   A. Donald Curtis Brown, born 19 July 1947.
   B. Betty Ann Brown, born 12 September 1951.
   C. William Henty Brown, born 13 July 1955. All reside in Dallas, Texas, except Henry who is a commercial airlines pilot flying the rich from New Yark to the Caribbean.

III.   Murray Lowell Brown, born 2 April 1920, married Frances Osborne of Hartwell, Ga.. They have one son: James Murray Brown born 9 November 1945. Lowell and his wife are retired from Singer Sewing Machine Company and reside in Anderson, South Carolina.

IV.   Edith Lawanna Brown, born 2 March 1925, married Marvin F. Jones, Yorkville. They reside in Dallas, Georgia. Issue: Malinda Dell Jones married (1) John Wilson, Forsyth, Georgia. (div), (2), Nete Hunt, a millionaire from Highlands, North Carolina (no issue). Adopted daughter: Jean Jones Cates, married Wiley Cates in 1973, div. March 1987. Has one dau: Wendy Cates.

V.   Bette Grace Brown, born 1 February 1930, married (2) 13 January 1952, Frank Neils Bacon. (div. 30 November 1970), and, (2) Jerry James Dunn on 29 January 1983. Bette is an Air Force Reservist at Dobbins AFB, Ga. And expects to retire from the Reserves February 1990 as a Senior Master Sergeant. Children of Bette Grace and Frank Neils Bacon:

   A. Ronda Kathryn Bacon, daughter of Frank Neils Bacon, was born 14 November 1952, married (1) 30 July 1970, Richard Winn (div), and, (2) on 13 January 1980, Curtis Davis. Son: William Richard Winn born 12 July 1977. StepIssue: Cuttis Davis, Jr., Timothy Davis, Stephanie Davis.

   B. Renna Joy Bacon, daughter of Frank Neils Bacon, was born 30 July 1957 married (1) Fred Trammell (div.), and (2) Philip Flaig, Forest Grove, Oregon. One son: Kenneth Philip Bacon Flaig, died an infant 27 September 1985, buried in the National Cemetery, Portland, Oregon.

   C. Tamara Jill Bacon, daughter of Frank Neils Bacon, was born 28 August 1958 married 1 September 1979, Thomas Keith Jelks. One daughter: Tori Jill Jelks born 26 March 1983. (Expecting another child in January 1988). She was a school teacher at Hiram, Ga. for several years.

Another family, Glen Smith Brown was born 24 June 1890 in Paulding County, died 11 February 1978 in Paulding County, buried in Marietta, Cobb. County. He married Lottie Lorene Holland, daughter of William Newton Holland, Born 20 May 1893 in Rockmatt, Paulding County, died on 22 November 1971 in Paulding County, buried Kennesaw Memorial Cemetery , Marietta, Cobb County, married on 28 March 1909 in Paulding County. SEE Holland.

Issue of Lottie Lorene Holland and Glen Smith Brown:[40]

---

[40] Holland 1000-1988 by Jeannette Holland Austin.

I.   Paul Brown, born on 8 May 1912 in Dallas, Georgia, died on 8 May 1912, buried High Shoals Church Cemetery, Dallas, Paulding County.

II.   Hardy Gene Brown, born on 14 July 1913 in Dallas, Paulding County, died on 5 July 1914, buried High Shoals Church Cemetery, Dallas, Paulding County.

III.   George Owen Brown, Sr. , born on 22 August 1916 in Dallas, Paulding County, died on 7 April 1969, buried Kennesaw Memorial Cemetery, Marietta, Cobb County, married on 25 December 1938 in Dallas, Louise Imogene Cole (born on 11 September 1919 in Paulding County), daughter of John Alford Cole and Georgia Davis.

IV.   Marvin Lane Brown, Sr. , born on 26 December 1944 in Marietta, Cobb County, married on 20 June 1970, Lavinia Faye Lindley (born on 20 March 1945 in Powder Springs), daughter of Frank Pickens Lindley and Lavinia McCart.

V.   Ellen Elizabeth Brown, born on 15 April 1930 in Powder Springs, married (1) on 29 September 1948, Drewy Russell Andrews (born on 6 October 1924 in Marietta), son of Verd Vestus Andrews and Eva C. Pinion; married (2), Clarence H. Shirley.

Bullock of Virginia, North Carolina;
Madison, Oglethorpe & Paulding Counties

Richard Bullock descends from the family in King & Queen County, Virginia. He was born ca 1695 in Hanover County, Virginia, died 1766 in Granville County, North Carolina. He was married 1706 in New Kent County, Virginia to Anne Henley, a daughter of Leonard Henley, (born 1688 in New Kent County, Virginia, died in Granville County, North Carolina. Issue:

I.   Nathaniel Bullock, son of Richard Bullock, was born 1738 in Granville County, North Carolina, died 1802 in Oglethorpe County, Georgia. He was married on 12 August 1760 in Granville County to Mary Hawkins, a daughter of Philemon Hawkins II and his wife, Delia (Martin) Hawkins, born 1746 in Hanover County, Virginia, died 1833. Issue:

    A.   Nathaniel Bullock.
    B.   Fanny Bullock.
    C.   James Bullock.
    D.   Agatha Bullock.
    E.   Anne Bullock.
    F.   Wyatt Bullock.
    G.   John Bullock.
    H.   Clarissa Bullock.
    I.   Hawkins Bullock, born 19 May 1763 in Warren County, North Carolina, died 1 November 1833 in Hull, Madison County, Georgia. He was married on 12 March 1789 to Frances Roy Gordon, a daughter of Alexander Gordon and his wife, Susannah (Terrell) Gordon, born 8 June 1772 in North Carolina, died 17 January 1835 in Hull, Madison County, Georgia. Issue:

        1.   John Gordon Bullock, son of Hawkins Bullock, was born 3 January 1790 in Georgia, died 4 April 1835.
        2.   Mary Wyatt Bullock, daughter of Hawkins Bullock, was born 16 November 1791 in Georgia.
        3.   Susannah Sherman Bullock, daughter of Hawkins Bullock, was born 16 November 1794 in Georgia.

4.   Alexander Gordon Bullock, son of Hawkins Bullock, was born 13 February 1797 in Georgia, died 9 November 1864. He married Mildred Sorrells on 12 February 1818 in Madison County. She was born 1799 and died 1874. Issue:

> a. Nathaniel Bullock, born ca 1819 in Georgia.
> b. Snead Bullock.
> c. Jackson Bullock.
> d. Alex C. Bullock.
> e. Sarah Bullock.
> f. Elizabeth Bullock.
> g. Frances Bullock.
> h. James Sherman Bullock, born 3 July 1827 in Madison County, died 30 April 1889 in Bremen, Georgia. He was married on 23 June 1868 to Lucia Prudence Redwell in Monroe County. She died in 1879. Issue:
>> i. Robert Gordon Bullock, born 14 March 1874 in Monroe, Walton County.
>> ii. Alva Billups Bullock, born 9 April 1869 in Walton County, died 17 May 1943 in Birmingham, Jefferson County, Alabama, buried in Edwardsville, Cleburne County, Alabama.

5.   Nathaniel Hawkins Bullock, son of Hawkins Bullock, was born 10 December 1798, died 1859 in Dallas, Georgia, buried in the Bullock Family Cemetery, Dallas. He married Salitha Colbert on 3 November 1821 in Oglethorpe County. She died 1851 in Georgia. Issue:

> a.   Alexander G. Bullock, son of Nathaniel Hawkins Bullock, was born 1822 in Georgia. He married Jane Priscilla Matthews, born 1826 in Georgia. Issue:

>> i. Nathaniel Thomas Bullock, born 23 January 1847 in Dallas, Paulding County, died 19 July 1913, buried in the Dallas City Cemetery. He was married to Mary Jane Cooper (born 7 November 1846 in South Carolina, died 1 July 1922, buried in the Dallas City Cemetery) on 27 December 1865 in Paulding County. He was a dealer in dry goods; resident of Dallas, Georgia. Issue:[41]
>>> (1) Alice A. E. Bullock, born 1867 in Dallas, Paulding County.
>>> (2) John H. S. Bullock, Judge. born 1864 in Dallas, Paulding County, died 1946, buried in the Dallas City Cemetery. Wife, Alice M., born 1872, died 1967, buried in the Dallas City Cemetery..
>>> (3) Lou E. Bullock, born 1872 in Dallas, Paulding County, married B. J. Smith on 11 November 1874 in Paulding County.
>>> (4) George N. Bullock, born 1875 in Dallas, Paulding County, married Lula Elliott on 4 September 1892 in Paulding County.

---

[41] 1870-1880 Paulding County Census, Dallas, Georgia.

(5) Alexander Bullock, born 1877 in Dallas, Paulding County.

(6) Albert G. Bullock, born 1879 in Dallas, Paulding County.

ii. Son, born 1850 in Dallas, Paulding County.

iii. James Bullock, born 1852 in Dallas, Paulding County.

iv. Soletras (or Seletram) Bullock (daughter), born ca 1853 in Dallas, Paulding County, married John H. Adair on 3 October 1872 in Paulding County..

v. C. H. Sherman Bullock, born 25 December 1855 in Dallas, Paulding County, died 3 January 1880.

vi. Louisiana or Leanna Bullock, born ca 1857 in Dallas, Paulding County.

vi. Fannie F. Bullock, born ca 1864 in Dallas, Paulding County, married F. M. Matthews on 24 December 1884 in Paulding County.

vii. Richard Bullock, born 1858 in Dallas, Paulding County.

viii. Martha Bullock, born 1862 in Dallas, Paulding County.

ix. Janny Bullock, born 1863 in Dallas, Paulding County

x. Adell B. Bullock, born 29 December 1866 in Dallas, Paulding County, died 3 February 1894.

xi. Delia Bullock, born 1867 in Dallas, Paulding County.

xii. Joseph Bullock, born 1869 in Dallas, Paulding County.

b. Sherman H. Bullock, son of Nathaniel Hawkins Bullock, was born 1828 or 1830 in Georgia, died 1901. He married on 14 May 1857 in Paulding County, Harriett Gann, born 1836. Issue:[42]

i. Antenette Bullock, born 22 October 1857 in Paulding County, died 31 January 1944 Paulding County, buried in High Shoals Cemetery. She married Henry Clay Holland on 22 October 1875 in Paulding County. SEE Holland.

ii Anthony Bullock, born 1858 in Dallas, Paulding County.

c. John F. Bullock, son of Nathaniel Hawkins Bullock, was born 1830 in Georgia.

d. Francis M. Bullock, son of Nathaniel Hawkins Bullock, was born 1832 in Georgia.

e. Albert Bullock, son of Nathaniel Hawkins Bullock, was born 1834 in Georgia.

f. Harriett Bullock, daughter of Nathaniel Hawkins Bullock, was born 28 January 1838, died 16 November 1912, buried in the Dallas City Cemetery, Paulding County.

---

[42] Paulding County Marriages; 1860 Paulding County Census.

6. William Gordon Bullock, son of Hawkins Bullock, was born 27 September 1802 in Georgia.

7. Louisa Nance Bullock, daughter of Hawkins Bullock, was born 3 November 1804 in Georgia, died ca 1881 in Oglethorpe County.

8. Frances Roy Bullock, daughter of Hawkins Bullock, was born 12 November 1806 in Georgia.

9. Richard Henley Bullock, son of Hawkins Bullock, was born 21 October 1810 in Georgia. Wife, Antionett, born 1818 in Georgia; residents of Paulding County in 1880. Issue:

      a. William Bullock, born 1841 in Paulding County.
      b. Albert Bullock, born 1843 in Paulding County.
      c. Henry S. Bullock, born 1845 in Paulding County.
      d. Nathaniel Bullock, born 1848 in Paulding County.
      e. Child, born 1850 in Paulding County.

10. Hawkins Sherman Bullock, son of Hawkins Bullock, was born 1812 in Georgia, died 1850.

Calloway of Bibb & Jones Counties

Josiah Calloway was born ca 1794 in Jones County, Georgia. He married 13 January 1832 in Jones County, Permelia McLane. Issue:[43]

I. William Calloway, born 1828 Jones County.

II. John Calloway, born 1830 Jones County.

III. Henry B. Calloway was born 8 October 1832 in Bibb County, farmer, died 25 October 1901 in Lizella, Monroe County, buried in the Parker Cemetery. He married (1) Georgia Virginia Parker (born 12 February 1843 Bibb County, died 15 October 1865 Bibb County), the daughter of John Brantley Parker and his wife Eliza (Chambliss) Parker, and (2) Sarah A. Chambliss (born 1836). [44]

    Issue by (1) wife:

    A. Lula A. Calloway, born 1862 in Macon, Bibb County, died 11 February 1882 Bibb County.

    Issue by (2) wife:

    B. John W. Calloway, born 1 June 1867 in Macon, Bibb County, died 19 May 1928 in Macon, buried in the Waldron Cemetery, Bibb County.

---

[43] Waldron Cemetery, Bibb County; 1850-1860 Bibb County Census; Jones County Marriages.

[44] 1880 Bibb County Census, District 519. Sarah Chambliss' sister was listed with the family, Ann Chambliss, age 37.

C. Georgia F. Calloway, born 1869 in Macon, Bibb County.

D. Henry Oscar Calloway, born 2 November 1871 in Bibb County, died 3 May 1926 in Bibb County, buried in the Waldron Cemetery, Bibb County.

E. Mary E. Calloway, born 1875 in Macon, Bibb County.

IV. Sarah Calloway, born 1835 Bibb County.

V. Jesse Calloway, born 1837 Bibb County.

VI. Vanhusen Calloway, born 1839 Bibb County.

Camp of England, Virginia, North Carolina; Walton & Paulding Counties

It can be said that the Camp family is one of the most prolific families in America, inasmuch as many of them had more than ten children, and in one case, twenty-six children. There is probably not a member of the Camp family anywhere who does not brag on his ancestor's large family of children. For generations, this family resided in the county of Essex, England. They were deeply religious persons who were dedicated leaders in rural American communities, particularly in Georgia, where strong religious beliefs developed in the backwoods. Many were Baptist and Methodist Ministers whose memories are yet alive by virtue of their uplifting influence. The first known, Thomas Campe, was christened in 1630, his birth registered in the Chignal St. James Parish, in Essex, England. He was married in 1653 at the Holy Cross Parish in Waltham, Essex, England, to Sarah Williamson. Their children were: Thomas Campe (see below), Richard Campe, christened 17 May 1666 in the Nazeing Parish, Essex, England, Ann Campe, christened 17 May 1666 in the Nazeing Parish, Essex, England, Johanes Campe, christened 9 April 1667 in the Chignal St. James Parish, in Mashbury, Essex, England, and Sarah Campe, christened 4 October 1668 in the Nazeing Parish, Essex, England.

Thomas Campe was christened on 20 November 1665 in the Chignal St. James Parish, in Mashbury, Essex, England, and died in 1711 in King and Queen County, Virginia. He was the first Campe to emigrated to America. In 1689 he married Catherine Barron in James City County, Virginia. Catherine was born 1672 in James City County, Virginia, and died 1715 in King & Queen County, Virginia. She was the daughter of Andrew Barron (born 1617) and his wife, Mary (Ewens) Barron. Known Issue:[45]

---

[45] Kemp-Camp Family by R. N. and C. C. Mann, Vol. 1; The Camp Family History by Margaret Fricks Camp; Parish Registers in Chignal St. James Parish, Holy Cross Parish, and Nazeing Parish, Essex County, England; Accomack County, Virginia Marriages; Culpepper County, Virginia Wills; Methodist Church Cemetery, Lebanon, South Carolina; Old Bethlehem Cemetery, Walton County; records of P. L. Stephens, 3919 Beverly Drive, Dallas, Texas 75205; Bible of Mr. E. Russ Williams, Jr., P. O. Box 1074, Bogalusa, LA; 1850-1880 Paulding County Census; Harmony Grove Church Cemetery, Paulding County; High Shoals Baptist Church Cemetery, Dallas, Georgia; 1840-1850 Cobb County Census; personal records of Thomas Camp (1813-1904); William and Mary (1), page 271; personal records of Mrs. Alfred V. Thomson, 2325 Barbe St., Lake Charles, LA 70601; Paulding County Marriages; Rutherford County, North Carolina Deeds; History of Old Tryon and Rutherford Counties by Griffin, pp. 129-130.

I. Mary Camp, born 1708 in King & Queen County, Virginia, died 1758 in Richmond County, Virginia, married on 5 January 1733 James Tarpley.

II. Thomas Camp, born 1691 in King & Queen County, Virginia, died 1751 in Culpepper County, Virginia. This Thomas is the most widely recognized Camp in America, mostly because he was married in 1715 in Westmoreland County, Virginia, to Mary Marshall, the daughter of Thomas Marshall and his wife Martha (Sherwood) Marshall, of the famous Virginia justices. Issue:

    A. John Camp, son of Thomas Camp and Mary, was born 1719 in King & Queen County, Virginia, married on 11 February 1782, Elizabeth Sims.

    B. Marshall Camp, son of Thomas and Mary Camp, was born 1721 in King & Queen County, Virginia, married on 21 November 1805, Lucy Wilkerson.

    C. Ambrose Camp, son of Thomas and Mary Camp, was born 1723 in King & Queen County, Virginia, died 1769 in Culpepper County, Virginia, married Ann Marshall. The LWT of Ambrose Camp, dated 11 March 1769, probated 18 March 1769 in Culpepper County, Virginia. The LWT of Mary Marshall Camp is dated 1757.

    D. Thomas Camp, son of Thomas and Mary Camp, was born 8 February 1717 in King & Queen County, Virginia, died 1798 in Rutherford County, North Carolina. He married (1) in 1738 in Accomack County, Virginia, to Winnifred Starling, and (2) in 1762, Margaret Carney. His LWT was probated in April of 1798 in Rutherford County, North Carolina. His old pre-Revolutionary war house was still standing in the 1960's, and his unmarked grave is located on the site. Winnifred Starling was born 1720 in Accomack County, Virginia, and died 1761 in Culpepper County, Virginia.

Issue of Thomas Camp (1717-1798) and wife, Winnifred Starling:

    1. Edmund Camp, son of Thomas and Winnifred Camp, was born 1739 in Orange County, Virginia, died 1834 in Franklin County, Georgia. He married (1) Mary Ragsdale in 1760, and, (2) Elizabeth Carney.

    2. Mary Camp, daughter of Thomas and Winnifred Camp, was born 5 January 1740 in Orange County, Virginia, died 11 September 1786 in Charlotte County, Virginia, married Thomas Tarpley on 3 April 1759.

    3. Joseph Camp, son of Thomas and Winnifred Camp, was born 1741 in Orange County, Virginia, died before 7 January 1820 in Kentucky. He married Susannah Roundtree.

    4. Lucy Camp, daughter of Thomas and Winnifred Camp, was born 1742 in Orange County, Virginia, married Mr. Hearn.

    5. John Camp, daughter of Thomas and Winnifred Camp, was born 13 October 1743 in Orange County, Virginia, died 1818 in Jackson County,

Georgia, buried in the Methodist Church at Lebanon, near Princeton, South Carolina. He married Mary Tarpley on 1 January 1764.

6. Nathaniel Camp, son of Thomas and Winnifred Camp, was born 1745 in Orange County, Virginia, died after 1832 in Gwinnett County, Georgia, married Winnifred Tarpley, a sister to wives of his brothers (John and Thomas). He was a Revolutionary War Soldier who fought in the Battle of King's Mountain in North Carolina.

7. Thomas Camp, son of Thomas and Winnifred Camp, was born 1747 in Orange County, Virginia, died ca 1811 in Walton County, Georgia, buried in the Old Bethlehem Cemetery in Walton County. He married ca 1763 in Richmond County, Virginia, Nancy Anne Tarpley (born 6 October 1750 in North Farnham Parish, Richmond County, Virginia, died 1814 in Walton County, Georgia, the daughter of James Tarpley and his wife Mary (Camp) Tarpley. Thomas Camp served as a private in 1776, during the Revolutionary War, in the 4th South Carolina Regiment Artillery, commanded by Colonel Barnard Beekman. Issue:
    a. Bradford Camp, son of Thomas and Nancy Anne Camp, was born 5 September 1764 in Laurens County, South Carolina, died 15 April 1838 in Washington Parish, Louisiana, married Mary Drucilla Campbell.
    b. Larkin Camp, daughter of Thomas and Nancy Anne Camp, was born 1767 in Laurens County, South Carolina, died after 1856 in Butler County, Alabama, married Margaret Brewster. Larkin Camp received a 500-acre land grant for his services as a Revolutionary War Soldier on Raburn Creek in Laurens County, South Carolina on 1 October 1798.
    c. Sarah Camp, daughter of Thomas and Nancy Anne Camp, was born 1773 in Laurens County, South Carolina, died after 1849, married on 8 December 1793, John C. Calhoun. Calhoun served in the Revolutionary War from Laurens County, receiving a pension after the war. He was also a Captain in the South Carolina State Militia. He died on 29 September 1838, and his widow, Sarah, was granted a pension (1845) in Laurens County. The LWT of John Calhoun, probated 17 December 1838, Laurens County, South Carolina.
    d. Hosea Camp, son of Thomas and Nancy Anne Camp, was born 1775 in Rutherford County, North Carolina, died in Alabama, married Elizabeth Kennedy on 11 July 1806. He was a farmer and Methodist Minister, listed on the 1850 Paulding County Census, with his wife, Elizabeth.
    e. Sherwood Camp, son of Thomas and Nancy Anne Camp, Baptist preacher, was born 9 March 1777 in Laurens County, South Carolina, died between 1860 and 1870 in Dallas, Paulding County, Georgia, and is buried in the family cemetery near Shady Grove Church. He married Lydia Kennedy on 11 July 1806, the daughter of Edmund Kennedy and his wife Jean. Lydia was born 15 February 1780 in Laurens County, South Carolina, and died between 1870 and 1880 in Paulding County. Issue:

i.   Edmund Kennedy Camp, son of Sherwood
      Camp, was born 25 February 1804 in Jackson,
      Walton County, Georgia, died 22 June 1848,
      married Penelope Willingham on 24 January
      1827.

ii.   Ira Camp, son of Sherwood Camp, was born 1805
      in Jackson, Walton County, Georgia, died 1864 in
      Paulding County. He married Nancy Palmore on
      26 January 1829.

iii. Josiah Washington Camp, son of Sherwood
      Camp, was born 6 August 1808 in Jackson,
      Walton County. He married (1) Louisa Cooper
      (2) Pernecia Holder Fincher.

iv.   Nancy Camp, daughter of Sherwood Camp, was
      born 1812 in Jackson, Walton County, Georgia,
      died between 1880-1890 Paulding County.

v.   Thomas Camp, son of Sherwood Camp, was
      born 21 June 1813 in Jackson, Walton County,
      died 23 March 1904, buried in the High Shoals
      Baptist Church, Dallas, Paulding County. He
      served during the War Between the States in Co.
      K, 60th Georgia Infantry, C. S. A. He married (1)
      Martha Mahon on 11 February 1836, and, (2)
      Mrs. Sarah Elizabeth Smith Hardeman (born 26
      May 1838, died 17 August 1912, buried in High
      Shoals Baptist Church Cemetery)..

vi. Burrell Marion Camp, son of Sherwood Camp, was born 3 October 1822 in Walton County, died 22 May 1912 in Powder Springs, Cobb County, buried in the High Shoals Church Cemetery, Paulding County. During the war he served in Co. E, 9th Georgia Artillery, C. S. A. He married

(1) Mary E. Stegall (born 1826 in Pickens County, South Carolina, died 1869 in Paulding County), buried High Shoals Cemetery, Paulding County, in 1842, the daughter of Bira Stegall and his wife Abigail (Conger) Stegall, and, (2) Sarah Ann Holland (born 22 August 1837, died 12 September 1910, buried in High Shoals Baptist Church Cemetery) on 12 April 1871 in Paulding County. SEE Stegall and Conger. He was an

Elder of the Missionary Baptist Church at High Shoals, near Dallas, Georgia for forty years. Baptisms were performed in the nearby woods, under a waterfall.[46]

Issue of Burrell Marion Camp and Mary E. Stegall.

(1) Abigail Camp, born 1848 at High Shoals, Paulding County, died between 1850-1860.

(2) William Washington Camp, born 1849 High Shoals, Paulding County, died 1930, married Mandy E. Holland on 14 December 1872 in Paulding County.

(3) Lydia Camp, born 26 December 1849 in High Shoals, Paulding County, died 27 August 1883, buried High Shoals Baptist Church Cemetery, Paulding County. She married George Washington Holland. SEE Holland.

(4) Milly C. Camp, born 1852 in High Shoals, Paulding County, died 1948,

---

[46] The waterfall is located to the rear of the old cemetery of High Shoals and is still a popular place for wading and picnicing.

married Tom Pinkard on 26 November 1874 in Paulding County.

    (5)   Nancy Camp, born 1855 in High Shoals, Paulding County, married John Hogue.

    (6)   Pennington James Camp, born 7 December 1857 in High Shoals, Paulding County, died 23 January 1940, married Julia Virginia Leathers on 23 January 1881 in Paulding County.

    (7)   Sarah Camp, born 1859 in High Shoals, Paulding County, died 1930, married John M. Carden on 24 November 1887 in Paulding County.

    (8)   Alex Stephens Camp, born 8 July 1861 in High Shoals, Paulding County, died 17 September 1946 in Paulding County. He married (1) Carrie Matthews (2) Ophelia Rutledge (3) Lilly Rutledge.

    (9)   Joseph Thomas Camp, born 1864 in High Shoals, Paulding County, died 1944, married Lydia Moon.

    (10)   Lavonia Bell Camp, born 13 February 1868 in High Shoals, Paulding County, died 2 March 1951, married Wash Holland.

Issue of Burrell Marion Camp and Sarah Holland:

    (11)   Anna Camp 1871-1951 Paulding County, married Willie F. Lee (died 1947).

    (12)   Rendy Ann Camp, born 1876 in Paulding County, married on 11 August 1892, Taylor Langston.

    vii. Lydia Caroline Camp, born 1824 in Jackson, Walton County, Georgia.

    f.   Burrell Camp, son of Thomas and Nancy Anne Camp, was born 1779 in Laurens County, South Carolina, died 1862 in Carroll County, Georgia, married Elizabeth Moore in March of 1799. In 1856 Burrell Camp was residing in Randolph County, Alabama. He served under General Jackson in the War of 1812.

    g.   Thomas Camp, son of Thomas and Nancy Anne Camp, was born 1781 in Laurens County, South Carolina, married Miss Hamby.

    h.   Nancy Camp, daughter of Thomas and Nancy Anne Camp, was born 1786 in Laurens County, South Carolina, married John Brown.

8.   Starling Camp, son of Thomas and Winnifred Camp, was born 1749 in Culpepper County, Virginia.

9. Hosea Camp, son of Thomas and Winnifred Camp, was born 25 February 1751 in Culpepper County, Virginia.

10. William Camp, son of Thomas and Winnifred Camp, was born 1753 in Culpepper County, Virginia, died ca 1827 in York County, South Carolina. He married ca 1770 Rebecca Wofford. He first settled in Rutherfordton, North Carolina (before 1778), later in Old Camden District on Bowen's Creek. The Camp Bulletin[47] stated that William Camp settled on the Bowen's River in the northwest corner of York County, South Carolina. He received a land grant in South Carolina, 336 acres in 1796. There are two Revolutionary War vouchers paid to William Camp of Morgan District for public claims (on file at the North Carolina State Archives). He was a Baptist preacher, and died in York County.

11. Alfred Camp, son of Thomas and Winnifred Camp, was born 1755 in Culpepper County, Virginia, married Elizabeth Jennings.

12. Benjamin Camp, son of Thomas and Winnifred Camp, was born 1757 in Culpepper County, Virginia, died 1832, married Elizabeth Dukes in 1776.

13. Elizabeth Camp, daughter of Thomas and Winnifred Camp, was born 1759 in Culpepper County, Virginia, died after 1850 in South Carolina, married Reuben Brock. They resided near Honea Path, South Carolina, during the last 45 years of their lives.

14. Joel Camp, son of Thomas and Winnifred Camp, was born 1761 in Culpepper County, Virginia.

Issue of Thomas Camp (1717-1798) and wife, Margaret Carney (born 20 January 1744 Limerick County, Ireland, died 1824 in Rutherford County, North Carolina:

15. Crenshaw Camp, son of Thomas and Mary Camp, was born 5 January 1763 in Rutherford County, North Carolina, died 1808.

16. James Camp, son of Thomas and Mary Camp, was born 1765 in Crenshaw County, Virginia, died April 1817 in Spartanburg County, South Carolina, his LWT dated January 1817, probated April 1817, Spartanburg. He married Sarah Jennings.

17. Daniel Camp, son of Thomas and Mary Camp, was born 1766 in Rutherford County, North Carolina, died 2 April 1798 in Rutherford County, North Carolina. He was married to Sarah McKinney. Daniel lived in Hickory Creek, in Rutherford County. The State of North Carolina granted him 109 acres in Lincoln County which was located on Buffalo Creek, on 20 December 1791.

---

[47] The Camp Bulletin, Georgia State Archives.

In 1795, he was Sheriff of Rutherford County, and in 1797, the county treasurer.[48]

18. Lewis Camp, son of Thomas and Mary Camp, was born 16 January 1768 in Rutherford County, North Carolina, buried in the family cemetery, near the house, in Rutherford County. He married Joanna Neal on 6 November 1800, the daughter of Thomas Neal. After the marriage, they lived near the French River in North Carolina. In 1819, Lewis Camp was deeded 388 acres on both sides of Brush Creek in Rutherford County, by Isaac Vinzant. In 1821, Lewis Camp and John Hord deeded to Benjamin Herndon 260 acres on Bushy Creek and on the First Broad River in Rutherford County.

19. Adam Camp, son of Thomas and Mary Camp, was born 1769 in Rutherford County, North Carolina. [49]

20. Stephen Camp, son of Thomas and Mary Camp, was born 17 September 1771 in Rutherford County, North Carolina, died 1846 in Rutherford County, married Annie Alexander. At the age of ten years (at the close of the Revolutionary War), Stephen Camp accompanied his brother, Benjamin Camp and others, to Cowpens, South Carolina where a battle took place. During the battle, he held the horses and was injured. Stephen Camp's LWT was probated February 1846 in Rutherford County, North Carolina. Annie Alexander was the daughter of Colonel Elias Alexander and his wife, Nancy Agnes (McCall) Alexander. Colonel Alexander was a Revolutionary War Soldier, born 1749, died 1818 in Rutherford County, North Carolina, who migrated from Maryland to North Carolina before the American Revolution; his LWT dated 10 March 1816, Book C, page 101, Rutherford County, North Carolina (named his children).

---

[48] Rutherford County, North Carolina Deeds

Deed Book E-1, page 447. 9 April 1788. Willis Watkins of Spartanburg County, South Carolina deed to Daniel Camp of Rutherford County, 100 acres in said county located on the southside of the Main Broad River.

Deed Book 29-31, page 255. 29 July 1817. The heirs of Daniel Camp, deceased, viz: Archibald Nelson and Elizabeth, his wife; William McKinney, Jr. and Margaret, his wife; Daniel Blackwell and Lydia, his wife; Thomas Camp; Lewis Camp; Deideami Camp. The children and heirs o f Daniel Camp, deceased, deed to Aaron Camp of Rutherford County, land in Rutherford County, located on the southside o f Main Broad River.

[49] Rutherford County Deed Book 45, page 304. 26 April 1845, William and Adam Camp of Spartanburg County, South Carolina and Peter Green and his wife, Eliza, of Rutherford County, North Carolina, deed to John Likes of Rutherford County, for 100 pounds, 334 acres on Mill Creek....being land belonging to the heirs at law of Anna Camp, deceased, William Camp, George Camp, Elias Camp, Julia Fisher, wife of David Fisher, being heirs in part, and Anna Camp, deceased, and Adam and Peter Green and wife, Eliza, for their respective shares in said estate.

44

21. Larkin Camp, son of Thomas and Mary Camp, was born 1773 in Rutherford County, North Carolina.

22. Eunice Camp, son of Thomas and Mary Camp, was born 21 June 1775 in Rutherford County, North Carolina, married Samuel Broadway.

23. Aaron Camp, son of Thomas and Mary Camp, was born June 1778 in Rutherford County, North Carolina, died 6 July 1861. He married (1) Frances Willis Terrell on 2 August 1803, and, (2) Sarah Suttle on 3 April 1817. At the age of 16, Aaron Camp was sent by his father to Halifax County, Virginia, together with his brothers, James and Lewis, to learn house carpeting. Aaron then taught his profession to his son, William Addison Camp. Sarah Suttle was the daughter of George Suttle who died 5 February 1816, and his wife, Nancy, who died 7 July 1837, who came from Virginia to North Carolina with Thomas Camp. George Suttle built the first brick home in Rutherfordton, being wealthy. In 1842, Aaron Camp and his family removed to Walker County, Georgia, along with two brothers o f Sarah (John and Joseph Suttle). John Suttle died at the old in Armuchee Valley, Walker County. Sarah Suttle Camp died 28 November 1869.

24. Ruth Camp, daughter of Thomas and Mary Camp, was born 30 September 1780 in Rutherford County, North Carolina, died 1852, married David Patterson.

25. George Camp, son of Thomas and Mary Camp, was born 24 September 1782 in Rutherford County, North Carolina, died 1835 in Nashville, Tennessee, married Mary Norment. He was a member of the North Carolina State Assembly, serving two terms. He removed from Rutherford County, North Carolina to Spartanburg County, South Carolina; later (in 1830) to Tennessee, near Nashville, where he died.

26. Joshua Camp, son of Thomas and Mary Camp, was born 10 July 1786 in Rutherford County, North Carolina, died 9 January 1849 in Rutherford County, married Nancy Gregory. Joshua was buried alongside his wife in the Thomas Camp Cemetery, near Island Ford, Rutherford County, North Carolina. The LWT of Joshua Camp was probated February 1849.[50]

---

[50] Rutherford Will Book E, page 180.

Henry S. Carlton was born 19 July 1812 in South Carolina, and died 9 July 1795, buried in the Old High Shoals Cemetery, near Dallas, Georgia. He was a farmer, and a resident of Huntsville. He married (1) Elizabeth Rice (born 17 March 1816, died 22 January 1853, buried in the Old High Shoals Cemetery, and (2) on19 March 1857 in Paulding County, Amanda Caldwell Johns (1825-1909), buried in the Old High Shoals Cemetery.

Issue by 1st wife: [51](1860 Paulding)

I.   Susan Carlton, born 1834 in Elbert County.

II.   Malinda Carlton, born 1837 in Elbert County.

III. John Monroe Carlton, born 20 April 1840 in Elbert County. He married Nancy E. Johnson (born 1849 in South Carolina) on 26 December 1868 in Paulding County. They were residents of Buncome, Georgia, in 1880. Issue:[52]

    A. Sarah J. Carlton, born 1869 in Georgia.
    B. William Carlton, born 1871 in Georgia.
    C. Hattie Carlton, born 1873 in Georgia.
    D. Anna Carlton, born 1875 in Georgia.
    E. Ella Carlton, born 1876 in Georgia.
    F. Malcolm Carlton, born 1877 in Polk County.
    G. George Carlton, born 1879 in Polk County.

IV.   Walton Carlton, born 1843 in Elbert County, died 2 July 1863.

V.   William Carlton, born 26 December 1844 in Elbert County, died 28 January 1916. Wife, Ludie E., born 1858 in Georgia. They were residents of Buncombe, Georgia, in 1880. Issue:[53]

    A. Nannie E. Carlton, born 1875 in Georgia.
    B. Mary M. Carlton, born 1877 in Polk County.
    C. William P. Carlton, born 1879 in Polk County.

VI.   Martha Carlton, born 1846 in Paulding County.

VII. Henry Monroe Carlton, born 1847 in Georgia, died 1932. He was known as "Bud". He married Nancy Edie Holland on 2 February 1873 in Paulding County, a daughter of Samuel and Annis Holland. SEE Holland. Issue:
    A. Edna Viola Carlton, born 5 February 1874, died 19 November 1915, married on 8 December 1892, William Edward Williams (born 18 June 1870, died 11 July 1939), the son of Isaac Williams and Amanda (White) Williams.

VIII. James Carlton, born 1849 in Paulding County.

---

[51] 1860 Paulding County Census.

[52] 1880 Polk County Census, Buncombe District.

[53] Ibid.

IX. Mary Jane Carlton, born 28 November 1851 in Paulding County, died 29 January 1936. In 1880, she resided with her brother, William's family in Buncombe, Georgia.

VIII. Robert Carlton, born 1857 in Georgia.

IX. Nancy Carlton, born 1859 in Paulding County.

Carnes of Paulding County

Richard Carnes was born 1810 in North Carolina, farmer, resident of Dallas, Georgia. Wife, Nancy, born 1820 in Georgia. Listed with the family on the 1860 Paulding County Census was Comfort Carnes, born 1753 in Virginia. Issue:[54]

I. Tably Carnes (daughter), daughter of Richard Carnes, was born 1841 in Georgia.

II. James Thomas Carnes, son of Richard Carnes, was born 1 January 1842, died 13 January 1927, married Margaret Catherine Watson, born 21 November 1845, died 5 March 1907, on 12 December 1891. Issue:

   A. Richard Monroe Carnes was born 20 October 1869, died 3 January 1957, married on 12 December 1891, Emma Jane Cochran, born on 23 September 1873, died 15 February 1949, a daughter of William Calvin Cochran (born 15 June 1839, died 19 April 1898) and his wife, Margaret Brown (1843-1881). Issue:

      1. James Calvin Carnes was born 30 September 1895 in Paulding County, died 20 March 1974 in Haralson County, buried in the Whitesburg City Cemetery, Carroll County, married on 13 January 1917/1918, Cassie Grace Holland, born on 19 December 1896 in Rockmart, Polk County, died 9 May 1961 in Carroll County, buried Whitesburg City Cemetery, Whitesburg, Carroll County. SEE Holland. Issue:

         a. Richard Lamar Carnes, son of James Calvin Carnes, was born on 26 December 1918 in Paulding County, married on 8 February 1941 in Carroll County, to Kathleen Annette Richards (born on 10 November 1919 in Carroll County.). Resident of at Whitesburg, Georgia. Issue:[55]

            i. Wyndel Richard Carnes of Whitesburg, born on 2 July 1942 in Coweta County, married on 22 May 1865 in Alabama, Gail Annette Scott (born on 14 August 1946 in Carroll County), the daughter of Brice Virgil Scott (born 10 September 1922), the son of John Calvin Scott (born 29 March 1889, died 6 December 1965 in Carroll County, married on 23 January 1916 to Nora Estelle Morrow (born 5 June 1897, died 2 October 1973 in Carroll County), who was the daughter of John Virgil Morrow (died 10 March 1952) married in 1887 to Sis; married on 8 May 1941 to Mary Nell James (born 15 April

---

[54] Ibid.

[55] Holland 1000-1988 by Jeannette Holland Austin.

47

1926), the daughter of Kie Levis James (born 15 February 1906), who was the son of Sam James and Jerusha Broome; and Mary Burzell Gordon (born 2 February 1909), who was the daughter of John B. Gordon and Susie Sticher. Issue: Mary Kathleen (Kati) Carnes, born on 11 August 1977 in Carroll County, and Holly Nicole Carnes , born on 16 December 1980 in Carroll County.

ii. Lanny Lamar Carnes, born on 2 October 1955 in Coweta County, unmarried.

b.   Ralph Bailey Carnes, son of James Calvin and Cassie Grace Holland Carnes, born on 27 March 1920, married (1) Ethel Davenport (born 29 August 1927). Issue:

i. Priscilla Diane Carnes, born 18 January 1950, married Daniel Denney. Child: Larissa Brent Denney, born on 22 July 1974.

ii. Larinda Carnes, born 1 October 1951, married (2), Jerry Lynn Brown, (2), Vernon Oliver. Child: Wendy Mary Brown , born 7 October 1968.

iii. Candace Carnes, born 20 January 1953, married Larry Davis Brooks. Child: Jamie Carolyn Brooks, born 27 June 1976.

iv. Marlin Keith Carnes, born 21 December 1954, married Carla Brewer (born 6 June 1958). Issue: Tiffany Carnes and Brittany Carnes,

c.   Helen Geneva Carnes, daughter of James Calvin and Cassie Grace Holland Carnes, of Carrollton, born on 15 September 1922, married Wilson Lamar Pate (died 23 December 1954). Issue:

i. Silvia Ronnie Pate, born on 30 March 1941, married Sandra Linderman (born 27 February 1943). Issue: Michelle Pate, born 16 August 1970 (twin) and Michael Pate, born 16 August 1970 (twin).

ii. Melanie Pate, born 16 November 1942, married(1) Mike Delay. No issue.

iii. Myra Pate, born 9 October, 19--, married Walter Jastrzemski. Issue: Kellie Jastrzemski born on 23 March 19----, and Jamie Jastrzemski, born 24 January 19--.

iv. Jane Pate, born 26 September 19-- had one child by (1) husband; married (2), Barry Huff. Issue: Lynn Huff , born 15 August 19-- and John Huff.

v. Beverly Pate, born 7 June 1951, married Ronnie Lewis (born 18 September 1949). Issue: Jeff Lewis, born 11 December 1968 and Tracey Lewis, born 29 November 1974.

d. Madelene Carnes of Whitesburg, daughter of James Calvin and Cassie Grace Holland Carnes, was born 5 February 1923, married John Knight Pate (born 9 May 1923). Child: Wilson Pate, born 9 August 1944 married Brenda Simpson (born 21 August 1948). Child: Jayson Knight Pate , born 8 October 1970.

e. William (Bill) Holland Carnes, of Whitesburg, son of James Calvin and Cassie Grace Holland Carnes, was born on 11 November 1924 in Paulding County, married ob 6 January 1944 to Melissa Louise Gladney (born 23 September 1925 in Carroll County, Ga.) Issue:

i. Sandra Gail Carnes, born 8 September 1944 in Carroll County, married on 27 October 1961 to William Raymond Bryant (born 23 May 1941). Issue: (1) Sandra Dee Bryant, born 26 July 1962 in Coweta County, married on 23 July 1983 in Carroll County, to Jon Melvin Burns. Lives at Whitesburg. Sandra Dee and Jon Melvin Burns had Issue: Nicholas Bryant Burns, born 13 May 1985 in Coweta County, (2) Jenny Leigh Bryant, born 27 January 1973 in Carroll County.

ii. James Richard (Ricky) Carnes of Whitesburg, son of William Holland Carnes, was born 26 December 1946 in Coweta County, married 26 October 1975 to Linda Sue Mashburn (born 30 July 1950 in Carroll County), daughter of Winston G. Mashburn (born 28 June 1920 in Carroll County), who was the son of Arthur M. Mashburn (born 14 September 1881, died 17 October 1951) in Carroll County, and his wife, Ferrell Lee Worley (born 30 April 1893, died 14 February 1928 in Carroll County); married 23 May 1942 in Coweta County. Cora Lee Willfams, born 4 March 1926 in Coweta County, who was the daughter of Joseph Smith Williams and Cora Idella Stallings of Cowe.ta County. Issue: (1) William (Billy) Joseph Carnes) born17 June 1977 in Carroll County, and (2) James Wesley Carnes, born 21 June 1979 in Douglas County.

iii.. Cathy Joan Carnes, daughter of William Holland Carnes, was born 6 August 1948 in Coweta County, married (1) in 1966 to Johnny Van Jackson, Sr., (2) to Joseph Andrew Godwin II (born 10 January 1950. Lives Douglas County. Issue: Johnny Van Jackson, Jr. , born 24 June 1967; Joseph Andrew Godwin III , born 17 June 1977 in Douglas County; and Joshua Lee Godwin, born 15 April 1979 in Douglas County.

f. J. B. Carnes of Whitesburg, son of James Calvin and Cassie Grace Holland Carnes, was born on 16 July 1926, married Doris Carroll (born 25 January 1934). Child: Cars Carnes, born 3 January 1963.

g. Emma Evelyn Carnes, daughter of James Calvin and Cassie Grace Holland Carnes, was born 8 May 1928, married Donald L. Quinn (born 9 February 1928). No issue.

h. Imogene Carnes of Whitesburg, daughter of James Calvin and Cassie Grace Holland Carnes, was born on 6 February 1930, married A. T. Harris (born 29 June 1925). Child: Lisa Renee Harris, born 23 March 1957.

i. Joan Vivian Carnes of Elberton, daughter of James Calvin and Cassie Grace Holland Carnes, was born on 16 February 1932, married Robert (Bob) J. Slocumbe, Sr. (born 28 September 1929). Issue: Lawana Slocumbe born 16 January 1958 and Robert J. Slocumbe, Jr. , born 8 March 1961.

j. Joe Eidson Carnes of Whitesburg, son of James Calvin and Cassie Grace Holland Carnes, was born 8 December 1933 (deceased), married Joyce Annette (Scooter) Sewell (born 14 June 1936). Issue: Sherry Lynn Carnes, born 14 June 1955; Karen Annette Carnes, born 28 March 1963; and Cassie Joyce Carnes, born on 30 March 1973.

k. Lawana Faye Carnes of Mableton, daughter of James Calvin and Cassie Grace Holland Carnes, was born on 14 October 1937 in Carroll County, married on 14 February 1959 in Cobb County, Billy (Buddy) Craven White (born 1 January 1934 in Carroll County), the son of John Murphy White and Lizzie Lou Craven. Issue:

> i. Susan Joy White, born 1 July 1962 in Cobb County.
> ii. John Keith White, born 29 August 1965 in Fulton County,
> iii.Janet Denise White , born 17 April 1970 in Fulton County.

III. Elizabeth Carnes, daughter of Richard Carnes, was born 1846 in Paulding County.

IV. Richard Carnes, son of Richard Carnes, born 1847 in Paulding County.

V. Sarah Carnes, daughter of Richard Carnes, born 1842 in Paulding County.

Carter of Paulding County

Richard J. Carter was born 1837 in Paulding County, died 22 September 1863 in Canton, Mississippi, buried in the Confederate Cemetery. He married on 8 January 1858 Judith Adair, in Paulding County, who was born July 1838 in Carroll County, Georgia, buried in the White Oak Cemetery, Paulding County, Georgia, the daughter of James Lee Adair and his wife Caroline (Evans) Adair. SEE Adair. Issue:[56]

I. James Reuben Carter, born 1859 in Paulding County, married Ellen Moody on 31 July 1878 in Paulding County.

---

[56] 1860 Paulding County Census; Paulding County Marriages.

II. Josephine Carter, born 10 March 1860 in Paulding County, died 20 November 1950 in Atlanta, Fulton County, buried in the White Oak Cemetery, Paulding County.

III. Thomas Carter, born 1862 in Paulding County, married Mary Ellen Pace on 29 May 1881 in Paulding County. He died 20 November 1950 in Paulding County.

Chambless/ Chambliss of Virginia, South Carolina, Bibb & Monroe Counties

This name is spelled variously as Chambliss and Chambless throughout the records; the earliest record denoting "Chamness", John Chambliss was born ca 1630 and was first found in America in 1652, [57]as follows:

> "May 5, 1652, John Chambliss settled in Northumberland County, Virginia.
> July 10, 1621, Ann Chambliss transported by Richard Barrs of York County."

In the Prince George County, Virginia Land Patents, Volume 1, for 1661 to 1771, lands are listed in 1680 which bordered on the land owned by Henry Chamnis. The surnames Chambliss, Chambless and Chamnis are alternately spelled throughout the records. To date, little is known about the John Chambliss (above) before he came to America, and it is only conjecture that he came from France. His issue:

Henry Chambliss was born 1660 in Prince George County, Virginia, died 1719 in Prince George County. He married Mary Moor, the daughter of John Moor. The LWT of Henry Chamnis of Bristol Parish, was probated on 9 January 1719 by Robert Bolling and Mary Chamnis, as executors, in Prince George County. In February of 1720, an inventory was made of the estate of John Chambliss. To his son, John, he bequeathed the plantation "whereon I now live", bounded by the swamp and Miery Branch. The town of Prince George is near the James River. Of course, Petersburg is the capitol of the county. It is presumed that he resided near the James River since most of the plantations (in those days) in this area were along the James River. Apparently, Henry Chambliss owned a plantation of some size, since he directed that his son, John (who inherited the plantation), give to his brothers a hundred plantable apple trees when they come of age. Owing to the various transactions in the county, Henry Chambliss must have resided near his father-in-law, John Moor, who surrendered all his worldly goods to his daughter, Mary Chambliss, widow of John, provided that she maintain him (her father, John Moor). This agreement was recorded on 11 January 1720, and was signed by John Moor and Mary Chamnis.

Issue of Henry Chambliss:[58]

---

[57] Immigrants into Virginia by Nugent.

[58] Bristol Parish Register, Sussex County, Virginia; Sussex County, Virginia deeds; Bible of Littleton Chambliss in possession of Charles Owen Smith of Moultrie, Georgia; Greene County Deeds; Bibb County Marriages & Estates; Georgia's Roster of the Revolution; 1850-1860 Bibb County Census; Columbia County Estates; Warren County Deeds, Administrator's Bonds & Estates; Richmond County Deeds; Bible of Jeptha and Susan Chambliss (see Historical Collectiuons of Georgia, SAR, Vol. 4); Talbot County Cemetery Records; 1850-1860 Panola County, Texas Census; personal records of Mrs. Josephine Huffaker, 5241 Ridgedale, Dallas, Texas 75206; 1850-1860 Monroe County Census; personal records of Elaine Irby, Atlanta, Georgia.

John Chambliss, Sr. was born 1700 in Prince George County, Virginia, died ca 1768 in Sussex County, Virginia. He married (1) Elizabeth Taylor in 1728, and, (2) Sarah Lee. Elizabeth Taylor was the daughter of Thomas Taylor and his wife Elizabeth (Jones) Taylor of Sussex County, Virginia. He inherited his father's lands in Cheraw District, (Marlboro County) South Carolina. A deed in Sussex County, Virginia explains the circumstances:

> "October 16, 1765. Benjamin Simmons of Prince George County, Virginia, et al to James Chambliss of Sussex County, Virginia, John Chambliss, the elder, father of James and John Chambliss, the younger."

Issue: John Chambliss, born ca 1730 in Sussex County, Virginia (below); William Chambliss, born 1738 in Sussex County Virginia, died 1802 in Sussex County; Frank Chambliss, born ca 1740 in Sussex County, Virginia; James Chambliss, born 6 October 1744, christened in the Bristol Parish Register, Sussex County, Virginia; and Thomas Chambliss, died in Richland County, South Carolina.

John Chambliss, born ca 1730 in Sussex County, Virginia, died ca 1777 in Cheraw District, South Carolina. He is believed to have married Mary Littleton ca 1760. As per deeds in Sussex County, some lands of John Chambliss, Sr. were sold to settle the accounts of John Chambliss, Jr. In 1756 and 1757 he was listed as a member of the Welsh Neck Baptist Church on the Great Pee Dee River in South Carolina. The records of the Welsh Neck Baptist Church in Cheraw District, South Carolina note that Mary Chambliss was a member in 1778. In other words, she was still carried on the rolls of the year a year or so after she had removed to Georgia. Also listed were Lucy Chambliss and John Littleton. On 2 April 1773, John Chambliss was granted 250 acres of land in Craven County, South Carolina (Volume 28, page 587, South Carolina Archives). John Chambliss died before 1777, because his widow, Mary Chambliss, is found in Richmond County, Georgia (deed); also in a deed dated 1781 in Warren County, Georgia. The Long Creek Baptist Church in Warren County lists Mary Chambliss, Sr. and Mary Chambliss, Jr. as members (1799-1819 membership rolls), along with Littleton Chambliss and Christopher Chambliss. Mary Chambliss, Sr. would be the widow of John Chambliss. Mary Chambliss, Jr. would be the daughter-in-law of Mary, Sr., the wife of Zachariah Chambliss. The church record provides the death date of Mary Chambliss as 14 October 1817. However, the Bible of Littleton Chambliss lists her death as 15 September 1813. Presumably, the Church recorded "notification of death". Issue:

I.   Christopher Chambliss, born between 1760-1765 in Sussex County, Virginia, died September 1840 in Bibb County, Georgia where he estate was found. He married (1) Mary, and, (2) Rachel Mashburn on 15 August 1821 in Bibb County. He was a Revolutionary War Soldier.[59] Christopher was listed as between the age of 50 and 70 on the 1830 Bibb County

---

[59] Georgia's Roster of the Revolution:

Page 54: "Christopher Chambliss or Chambless, Certificate of Colonel   James McNeill, 2 February 1784, prays for 250 acres. Entitled to same."

Page 68: "Certificate of Colonel James McNeill, petitions for 575 acres bounty land, as per certificate from Hon. John Houston, Esq., 5 April 1784, prays for same in Washington County."

Page 127: "James McNeill, with power of attorney, acknowledges receipt of warrants for Christopher Chambliss and three others."

Census. In 1785 he had land grants in Wilkes County; also, in Washington County, which he never took up. The administration of Christopher's estate was dated September 1840 in Bibb County. It named legatees: Rachel Chambliss, Sr., Thomas G. Jordan, Christopher Taylor (died 19 July 1857 in Harris County, age 53, as per The Christian Index), Ellenor Taylor, William Taylor, Lawson G. Chambliss, Perry Neal, G. W. Davis, Simon Parker, Samuel Chambliss, Jeptha Chambliss, John Danielly, Andrew D. Chambliss, David D. Davis, Elison Taylor (or Ellenor or Eden. Eden Taylor's wife, Mrs. Georgia Taylor, died 22 October 1872 in Monroe County.[60] Issue of Christopher Chambliss and wife, Mary:

A. Mary Chambliss, daughter of Christopher Chambliss, was born ca 1784 in Warren County.

B. Samuel Chambliss, son of Christopher Chambliss, was born 1787 in Warren County, died 1853, his estate probated in Bibb County. He married Jane Danielly (born 1794 in Hancock County, died after 1853 in Bibb County), on 30 May 1814, the daughter of Andrew Danielly and his wife Jane (Harris) Danielly. SEE Danielly. On 22 September 1810 Samuel Chambliss purchased 200 acres on Long Creek from Samuel Camp in Warren County. He sold in 1815, 202-1/2 acres to Robert Carey of Jones County for $400.00. At his father's death in 1840, Samuel purchased 240 acres in Bibb County from his father's estate, as well as three slaves, and numerous other items. On 4 July 1853, Samuel Chambliss and Jackson Chambliss gave bond for $14,000 for the goods and chattels of their father's estate (Samuel). Among those items listed were three spinning wheels, 86 hogs, saddles, a bull, oxen, 30 head o f sheep, gin, and blacksmith tools, and a negro couple (Isaac and Rose), being the same couple which Samuel had purchased from the estate of his father (Christopher Chambliss). Issue:

1. Jane Chambliss, daughter of Samuel Chambliss, was born 1815 in Bibb County, died in Montgomery, Alabama, married William M. Jones on 15 February 1835.

2. Eliza Chambliss, daughter of Samuel Chambliss, was born 5 April 1819 in Bibb County, died 20 September 1893 Lizella, Georgia, buried in the Parker Cemetery. She married John Brantley Parker on 2 February 1841.

3. Andrew Jackson Chambliss, son of Samuel Chambliss, was born 1821 in Bibb County, died December 1866 in Bibb County. He married Mary E. Tapley (born 1820 Baldwin County) on 3 February 1846 in Bibb County. In 1880, Mary was widowed, age 60, and listed with her on the census of Macon, Bibb County (4th Ward) was Joel E. Chambliss, age 29, clerk in the store and Samuel E. Chambliss, age 20, at school. SEE Tapley. Issue:

Page 202: "575 acres in Washington County, bounded East by Ambrose Jones, other sides vacant, Lot 849, Warrant 2439. 5 June 1784."

Greene County, Georgia Deeds

Volume 2, page 46. 22 January 1795. Christopher Chambliss to Richard Foster.

[60] The Christian Index

i.   Jackson Chambliss, son of Andrew Jackson Chambliss, was born 1849 in Bibb County, overseer of the Thomas J. Parker farm, in Bibb County, 1880.

ii.   John H. Chambliss, son of Andrew Jackson Chambliss, was born 1849 in Bibb County.

iii.   Joel Edgar Chambliss, son of Andrew Jackson Chambliss, was born 20 November 1850 in Bolingbroke, Monroe County, Georgia, buried May
1918 in Atlanta and was buried in the Smith Cemetery, Brent, Monroe County. He married Elizabeth Smith Clements on 11 April 1885 in Forsyth, Monroe County (born 14 October 1859 in Muscogee County, died November 1905, buried in the Smith Cemetery. Elizabeth is a daughter of Wesley Clements and his wife Jane (Smith) Clements. SEE Clements. They resided at Bolingbroke, a small community in Monroe County. At the turn of the century, he removed his family to Atlanta, in search of work. But, the summers, they spent on his wife's parents' plantation at Brent, near Forsyth. Joel and his wife are both buried in the old Smith Cemetery at Brent.[61]   Issue:

a.   Mary Brent Chambliss, daughter of Joel Edgar Chambliss, was born 31 March 1886 Macon, Bibb County, died 10 February 1964 in Atlanta, Fulton County, buried at Crestlawn Cemetery in Atlanta. She married Homer James Evans.[62] SEE Evans.

---

[61] The 1910 Census of Fulton County, Atlanta, Ward 3: Homer Evans 24, married 1 year, Mary 22, Joel Chambliss, father-in-law, 58, Estelle, sister-in-law, 18, Eugene, brother-in-law 15, and Prentice, brother-in-law, 9.

[62] "In the evenings, our grandmother, Mary Brent Chambliss, spun tales of her family. We loved to sit around the piano, listening. Proud of her heritage, she told of the piano which her grandfather, Davis Smith, brought from Charleston, South Carolina to their home in Brent. It was said to be the first piano in Monroe County. In 1850, he took his wife, Elizabeth, to Charleston to hear the Swedith soprano, Jinny Lind (brought to America by Barnum & Bailey Circus. Grandmother also told of hos she had a beau that she wished to marry, but that her mother (Elizabeth Smith Clements Chambliss) told her that it was unwise to marry this beau, because he was sickly. He might die at an early age, leaving her uncared for. So, she married my grandfather, Home James Evans, who, after aged 40, fell off a the roof of the house, and died. Thus, leaving my grandmother to survive on a meager pension." -- Jeannette Holland Austin --

b. Edgar Chambliss, son of Joel Edgar Chambliss, was born 1889 in Macon, Bibb County, listed on the 1900 Monroe County Census.

c. Herbert Chambliss, son of Joel Edgar Chambliss, was born July 1890 in Macon, Bibb County, married (1) Irene Violet Bergstrom (2) Anna (3) Civella. Adams Broales on 24 January 1917.[63]

Issue:

Joe Chambliss.

d. Estelle Chambliss, daughter of Joel Edgar Chambliss, was born on 21 June 1892 in Macon, Bibb County. She died in Atlanta, Fulton County. She married (1) Reynard Lewis (2) Calhoun Todd (3) Edward Knight Sparks.[64] Issue: Betty Sparks.

---

[63] "Uncle Herbert came to visit my grandmother (Mary Brent Evans) at 499 North Highland Avenue, in Atlanta, when he was off-duty. He frequently sang to us and cheered us up with his lyrics.... Jeannette Holland Austin"

[64] "Aunt Estelle was a memorable person. She dressed in current fashions, and was opinionated on any subject....Jeannette Holland Austin"

e. Samuel Eugene Chambliss, son of Joel Edgar Chambliss, was born on 7 September 1894 in Macon, Bibb County, died October 1969, near his home in Lithia Sprinigs. He married Ethelyn Murdock (born 4 July 1904, died 29 January 1994) on 3 June 1922. [65] They resided for many years in Lithia Springs, Douglas County. He always spoke well of others, stating that his sister's husband (Homer James Evans), was a "prince of a fellow" Jeannette Holland Austin.

Issue of Samuel Eugene & Ethelyn Chambliss:
    1-Samuel Eugene Chambliss, born 1924.
    2-Mary Eleanor Chambliss, born 1928 married W. K. Whittle, Jr.
    3-Joel B. Chambliss, born 1930.
    4-Martha Jane Chambliss, born 1931, married Mr. Sappingfield.

f. Prentice Norton Chambliss, son of Joel Edgar Chambliss, was born 8 October 1898 at Brent, Monroe County, died 29 July 1995 in Kaneche, Honolulu, Hawaii. He married (1) Bessie Hoffman (2) Mrs. Nancy Anderson McSwain on 6 August 1929, and, (3) Mrs. Jacquetta Marie Urs Calhoun on 22 August 1953.

Issue of Prentice and Bessie:
    1-Patsy Chambliss.

    2-Norton Chambliss.

---

[65] "After many years of marriage, Uncle Eugene and Aunt Ethelyn separated….I was researching my history at the time, and Uncle Eugene and I went on a trip to Bolingbroke, to try and locate a family cemetery. He told me about his namesame (Samuel Eugne Chambliss) who was buried at the Riverside Cemetery, in Macon. It was Uncle Gene who gave me the family photographs, while confiding that his sister (Aunt Estelle) would never release the family portraits. This is how I came to have pictures of the old Smith plantation, and other ancestors. Uncle Gene was an intellectual, a gentleman and a scholar. While thus engaged in various conversations regarding our mutual ancestors. One afternoon in the late 1960s, while Aunt Estelle was waiting to meet Uncle Gene for lunch (as they often did; they were still great friends), she heard an ambulance and saw it take someone away. Later, she learned that person was Uncle Gene….Jeannette Holland Austin"

iv. Eugene Dobb Chambliss, son of Andrew Jackson Chambliss, was born 1854 in Monroe County, died between 1860-1870.

v. Samuel Eugene Chambliss, son of Andrew Jackson Chambliss, was born 29 May 1859 in Monroe County, buried December 1895 in the Riverside Cemetery, in Macon, Georgia.

4. Samuel C. Chambliss, son of Samuel Chambliss, was born 1824 in Bibb County, died 18 December 1889 in Bibb County, buried in the Parker Cemetery, Lizella, Georgia. He married Amanda P. Gilbert on 4 January 1853.

5. Mary (Polly) Chambliss, daughter of Samuel Chambliss, was born 1825 in Bibb County, married Samuel P. Railey on 17 August 1845. Issue:
   a. Fannie Railey, born 1853.
   b. Alida Railey, born 1854.
   c. Evasters Railey, born 1854.
   d. Talbert Railey, born 1861.
   e. Abner Railey, born 1864.
   f. Mollie Railey, born 1869.

6. Rachel Chambliss, daughter of Samuel Chambliss, was born 1828 in Bibb County, married William P. Russell on 5 January 1851.

7. Permelia Chambliss, daughter of Samuel Chambliss, was born 1831 in Bibb County.

8. Frances Chambliss, daughter of Samuel Chambliss, was born 1833 in Bibb County, married William T. Vanzant on 30 July 1853.

9. Sarah A. Chambliss, daughter of Samuel Chambliss, was born 15 May 1835 in Bibb County, died 1 July 1891 in Bibb County. She was the second wife of Henry B. Calloway of Bibb County. SEE Calloway.

10. Lucinda Chambliss, daughter of Samuel Chambliss, was born 1838/1839 in Bibb County, died 12 March 1883, buried in the Parker Cemetery in Lizella, Georgia. She married Malcolm M. Waldren on 27 February 1862, who was born 1832 in Bibb County and died 11 March 1876 in Bibb County, buried in the Parker Cemetery in Lizella. SEE Waldren.

11. Angeline Chambliss, daughter of Samuel Chambliss, was born 2 January 1841 in Bibb County, died 12 May 1904 in Bibb County.

C. Henry Chambliss, son of Christopher Chambliss, was born 1790 in Warren County, died November 1834 in Bibb County. He married Rachel Danielly on 6 October 1809, a daughter of Andrew Danielly and his wife, Jane (Harris) Danielly. SEE Danielly. Issue:
   1. Lawson Green Chambliss, son of Henry Chambliss, was born 24 August 1810 in Warren County, died 23 October 1879 in Jones County, buried in the Juliett Methodist Church Cemetery. He married (1) Martha Elizabeth Russell, born 1818 in Georgia, who died between 1860 and 1870 in Bibb County, and (2) Mrs. Mollie Goggins. [66] Issue:

---

[66] 1850-1860 Monroe County Census, Monroe County Marriages.

a. William Lawson Chambliss, born 6 January 1840 in Forsyth, Monroe County, died 29 May 1911 in Forsyth, buried in the Juliett Methodist Church Cemetery, in Jones County. He married Mollie Harrison. Issue:
  i. Maude Chambliss.
  ii. Sarah Chambliss.
  iv. Henry Chambliss, born 1871
  v. Mattie Lee Chambliss, born 1875.
  vi. Tillie Chambliss, born 1878.
  vii. Pollie Chambliss, born 1878.
  viii. Arthur Chambliss, born January 1880.
b. Elizabeth Chambliss, born 15 December 1841 in Forsyth, Monroe County, died 4 September 1907 in Monroe County, buried in the Willis Cemetery, near Berner. She married (1) Robert Simmons and (2) David E. "Bud" Willis. Issue:
  i. Jennie Bob Simmons, born 21 February 1863, died 26 June 1936.
c. Florence Chambliss, born 1844 in Forsyth, Monroe County, died 1880.
d. Andrew D. Chambliss, born 1846 in Forsyth, Monroe County, married Mary M. Ponder in 1870 in Bibb County. Issue:[67]
  i. Ernest Chambliss, born 1871.
  ii. Oscar Chambliss, born 1873.
  iii. Green Chambliss, born 1873.
  iv. Lula Chambliss, born 1879.
e. Lucy Ann Alice Chambliss, born 22 April 1848 in Forsyth, Monroe County, died 12 November 1924, married Robert M. Williams. Issue:
  i. Robert Williams, born 1861.
  ii. Benjamin Watt Williams, born 1869.
  iii. Andrew Milledge Williams, born 1871.
  iv. Eva Virginia Williams, born 1873.
  v. Edward Mastin Williams, born 1876.
  vi. Charles Thomas Williams, born 1878.
  vii. Vera Maude Williams, born March 1880.
  viii. Myrtle Williams.
f. Sarah A. Chambliss, born 1850 in Forsyth, Monroe County, died 1903, buried in the Parker Cemetery, Lizella.
g. Wiley Chambliss, born 1852 in Forsyth, Monroe County, buried in the Juliett Methodist Church Cemetery, Jones County.
h. Robert S. Chambliss, born 1858 in Forsyth, Monroe County, died 1931 in Jones County, buried in the Juliett Methodist Church Cemetery. He married (1) Fannie Roguemore (born 1858 in Monroe County, died 1902 in Jones County), and (2) Carrie Colvin Grey (born 1869, died 1913 in Jones County, buried in the Juliette Methodist Church Cemetery).
i. Joseph Chambliss, born 1859 in Forsyth, Monroe County.

---

[67] John M. Chambliss Bible, Georgia State Archives.

j.   Virginia Chambliss, died before 1836 in Jones County, married Robert M. Williams.

2. Jane Chambliss, son of Henry Chambliss, was born 22 May 1812 in Warren County, married Perry Neel on 27 August 1841.

3. Mary G. Chambliss, daughter of Henry Chambliss, was born 1 February 1814 in Warren County, died 27 February 1887 in Bibb County, buried in the Parker Cemetery, at Lizella. She married Gardner Lemuel Davis on 17 June 1838. Issue:

a.   Mary Jane Davis was born 2 September 1837 in Bibb County and married William James Dent, the son of John Washington Dent and his wife, Elizabeth (Hoy) Dent. William James Dent was born 16 October 1841 in Bibb County. Mary Jane died 24 February 1887 in Crawford County, and was buried in the Salem Church Cemetery. William James Dent died 28 August 1929 in Roberta, Crawford County and was buried in the Roberta Cemetery, in Crawford County. He married (2) Mrs. Anna E. Dickson Holton and (3) Mrs. Ida Dennis. Issue:
   i.   Walter Braxton Dent, born 23 November 1861.
   ii.   Cynthia Ida Blanch Dent, born 23 November 1863.
   iii.   John Washington Dent, born 24 February 1866, died 28 June 1914.
   iv.   Gardner L. Dent, born 22 March 1868, died 1 January 1939.
   v.   Mary Pauline Dent, born 5 April 1870, died 7 April 1942.
   vi.   Sophronia Elizabeth Dent, born 25 September 1872, died 16 July 1895.
   vii.   Sarah Jane Dent, born 16 February 1875.
   viii.   Varry Pearl Dent, born 23 February 1877, died 10 March 1887.
   ix.   Hoy Dent, born 9 May 1880.
   x.   William Cleveland Dent, born 11 August 1883.

4. Christopher Chambliss, son of Henry Chambliss, was born 2 March 1817 in Warren County, died 22 December 1830 in Monroe County.

5. Lovicy Chambliss, daughter of Henry Chambliss, was born 10 August 1819, died 10 August 1822 in Warren County.

6. Andrew D. Chambliss, son o f Henry Chambliss, was born 4 July 1822 in Warren County, died 10 August 1860 in Talbot County, married Lavinia Pye. Issue:[68]

a.   Mary Chambliss, born 1848 in Talbot County.
b.   Elizabeth S. Chambliss, born 1856 in Talbot County.
c.   Henry Chambliss, born 1847 in Talbot County.
d.   Martha Chambliss, born 1860 in Talbot County.

7. William Henry Chambliss, son of Henry Chambliss, was born 4 October 1824 in Warren County, died 23 January 1885 in Texas. He married Martha

---

[68] 1850-1860 Talbot County Census.

Pye on 7 July 1844. Martha was a daughter of Henry Pye and his wife, Ann (Stockdale) Pye, and was buried in the Dean Cemetery near Tyler, Texas. Issue:

a. Henry Colquitt Chambliss, born 20 December 1845 in Monroe County, died 13 September 1921 in Cleburne, Texas, married on 22 September 1861, Mary Ann Turner, who died 22 January 1917, buried in the old Cleburne Cemetery in Cleburne, Texas. Mary Ann Turner was the daughter of Miles Green Turner and his wife, Martha (McNatt) Turner of Monroe County. She went to Texas with the Chambliss family to teach school. They lived in Smith County, Texas, later in Ellis County, then Cleburne County. Issue:
> i. William M. Chambliss, born 1868, died September 1926.
> ii. Jesse Pye Chambliss, born 17 January 1870, died 11 March 1939.
> iii. Martha Ella Chambliss, born 15 January 1872, died 1907.
> iv. Robert McNatt Chambliss, born 27 September 1875, died 4 October 1904.
> v. Minnie Lenore Chambliss, born 5 September 1877, died 16 June 1950.
> vi. Katherine Antionette Chambliss, born 8 February 1880.
> vii. Henry Mary Chambliss, born 7 June 1882, died 3 December 1935.
> viii. Anna Lee Chambliss, born 13 December 1885, died 1887.

b. Rachel Chambliss, born 1849 in Monroe County.

c. John A. Chambliss, born 1850 in Monroe County, died 1922 in Candler, Texas, buried in the Concord Baptist Church Cemetery, Candler, Texas. He married Mary Fitzgerald who died 1917 and was buried in the Concord Baptist Church Cemetery in Candler, Texas. Issue:
> i. W. Ben Chambliss, 1876-1931.
> ii. James M. Chambliss, 1881-1936.
> iii. Narcissa Chambliss, 1878-1900.

d. Sarah Jane Chambliss, born 12 December 1852 in Monroe County, died 25 August 1867 in Tyler, Smith County, Texas, buried in the Dean Cemetery, near Tyler, Texas.

e. Mary Antionette "Nettie" Chambliss, born 15 November 1854 in Talbot County, died 6 June 1945, buried in the Dean Cemetery, near Tyler, Texas. She was married to the Rev. John Thomas Dean on 21 August 1873. SEE Dean.:

f. William L. Chambliss, born 29 March 1858 in Monroe County, died 14 October 1924 in Swan, Texas, buried I n the Hopewell Baptist Church Cemeteyr, Swan, Texas. He married Fannie Swan, born 5 December 1860 in Swan, Texas, died 24 November 1936, buried same church.. Issue:

> i. William Henry Chambliss, born 28 June 1891 in Swan, Texas, married Miss Dean.

ii. Hasseltine Chambliss, born 24 September 1893 in Monroe County, died Horace Gibson.
iii. Lawson Chambliss, born 17 April 1896, died 3 June 1966 in Swan, Texas.
iv. Mack Chambliss, born 21 May 1900, died 19 October 1945 in Swan, Texas.

8. Joseph Baker Chambliss, son of Henry Chambliss, was born 6 January 1827 in Warren County, died 19 June 1904 in Greenville, Georgia, married on 16 May 1858, Adeline Hobbs. Issue:
    a. Iverson Floyd Chambliss, born 21 April 1861 in Talbot County, died 10 August 1942 in Davis, Oklahoma. He married Lillie Lorena Turnipseed (born 14 October 1866 in Meriwether County) on 21 December 1887. Issue:
        i. Madeline Chambliss, born 14 May 1896.
    b. Jessie Baker Chambliss, born 25 December 1862 in Talbot County.
    c. Joseph Lawson Chambliss, born 28 September 1864 in Talbot County.
    d. William Gardner Chambliss, born 17 March 1866 in Talbot County, died October 1937 at Rocky Mountain, in Meriwether County, and was buried in the Bethel Baptist Church Cemetery. He married on 6 December 1892 in Meriwether County, Josephine Brittain (born 21 September 1873 in Meriwether County, died 29 July 1942 at Rocky Mountain). Issue:
        i. Eunice Bertha Chambliss, born September 1893, died 26 May 1967.
        ii. Marie Frances Chambliss, born April 1896.
        iii. William Urban Chambliss, born 19 July 1899, died 3 March 1941.
        iv. Florrie Chambliss, born 8 October 1901.
        v. Roxie Inez Chambliss, born 31 January 1904.
        vi. Vera Mae Chambliss, born 5 February 1907.
        vii. John Marshall Chambliss, born 25 December 1909.
        viii. Josephine Catherine Chambliss, born 1 April 1913.
        ix. Joseph Alfred Chambliss, born 28 August 1915.
9. John Floyd Chambliss, son of Henry Chambliss, was born 14 March 1829 in Georgia, died in Meriwether County, married on 14 January 1857, Andisa Middlebrooks.

10. Sarah Ann Chambliss, daughter of Henry Chambliss, was born 30 May 1832 in Warren County, died 10 November 1894 in Talbot County, married on 8 December 1853, John Pye. Issue:[69]
    a. Joseph Christopher Pye, born 14 September 1854 in Talbot County, died 20 January 1925 in Woodland, Talbot County. He married on 15 January 1890 in Upson County, Hattie Nohalia Norris (born 30 April 1865 in Thomaston, Upson County, and died 9 July 1945. Issue:
        i. Harvey Norris Pye, born 22 December 1890.
        ii. John William Pye, born 31 August 1892, died 21 July 1965.
        iii. Joseph Christopher Pye, born 26 September 1893, died 14 August 1894.

---

[69] Pye information from the personal files of Mattie Woodall and Jean Marie Jordan.

iv. Annie Rachel Pye, born 11 September 1895.

b. Martha Samantha Pye, born 2 February 1856 in Talbot County, died 10 September 1880 in Talbot County, married John Wesley Woodall.

c. Ida Rachel Pye, born 20 July 1858 in Talbot County, died 15 September 1927 in Talbot County, married on 13 January 1881, Henry Thomas Woodall. Issue:

> i. Sallie Cornelia Woodall, born 7 July 1884, died 29 January 1967.
>
> ii. John Henry Woodall, born 4 April 1886, died 25 August 1965.

d. John Velula Pye, born 1 May 1862 in Talbot County, died 15 March 1933 in Talbot County, married on 9 Decmeber 1884 in Talbot County, Dela Fletcher Woodall. Issue:

> i. Mattie Pye, born 10 June 1885.
>
> ii. Sallie Jessie Pye, born 6 June 1887, died 23 May 1934.
>
> iii. James Fletcher Pye, born 26 September 1891.
>
> iv. William Chambless Pye, born 2 August 1893.
>
> v. Joseph Dela Pye, born 11 March 1898, died 24 August 1924.
>
> vi. John Pye, born 12 April 1904.

e. Narcissus Jane Pye, born 9 October 1867 in Talbot County, died 14 November 1940 in Talbot County, married on 18 December 1891, Benjamin Artemis Smith. Issue:

> i. Willie Joe Smith, born 27 March 1893, died 21 September 1961.
>
> ii. Annie Mae Smith, born 25 October 1894, died 21 February 1944.
>
> iii. Ira Thomas Smith, born 13 September 1896, died 19 August 1966.
>
> iv. Sarah Frances Smith, born 22 January 1899.
>
> v. John Benjamin Smith, born 22 February 1903, died 29 April 1905.
>
> vi. B. C. Smith, born 22 February 1903, died 29 April 1905.
>
> vii. Ludie Pye Smith, born 6 June 1904.
>
> viii. Jennie Lee Smith, born 8 May 1907, died 13 December 1954.
>
> ix. Martha Elizabeth Smith, born 15 March 1910.

f. William Benjamin Pye, born 6 April 1869 in Talbot County, died 28 February 1907, married on 19 December 1894, Estelle Norris (died 15 June 1958). Issue:

> i. Sarah Harriett Pye, born 19 October 1895.
>
> ii. John Cornelius Pye, born 20 January 1898, died 4 March 1965.
>
> iii. Mattie Maude Pye, born 9 September 1902.
>
> iv. Willie Estelle Pye, born 4 February 1907.

D. Mary Lovicy Chambliss, daughter of Christopher. born 15 October 1792 in Warren County, died 28 March 1857 in Barbour County, Alabama. She married Thomas George Jordan on 2 July 1814. SEE Jordan.

E   Jeptha Chambliss, son of Christopher, born 12 March 1798 in Warren County, Georgia, died 14 January 1846 in Talbot County. He married Susan Jones (born 2 April 1805 in Warren County, died 4 August 1862 in Hernando, DeSoto County, Mississippi, buried in the Oak Grove Baptist Church Cemetery) on 1 March 1819, a daughter of Adam Jones, a Revolutionary War Soldier. Issue:[70]

1. Christopher Columbus Chambliss, son of Jeptha Chambliss, was born 11 February 1820 in Warren County, buried in the Chambliss Family Cemetery in Enos, Louisiana. He married Amanda M. Edwards on 16 November 1841. Issue:

a. Albert Chambliss, born 1844 in Muscogee County, married Mary Fleming.

b. John Chambliss, born 1845 in Muscogee County.

c. William Chambliss, born 11 September 1846 in Muscogee County, died 16 May 1913 in West Carroll, Louisiana, buried in the Old Forrest Cemetery. He married (1) Mary Evelyn Neal, and, (2) Dinkyt Huey.

d. Robert Chambliss, born 1849 in Panola County, Texas, married Dorinda Vining.

e. Sarah Chambliss, born 14 March 1851 in Panola County, Texas, died 6 January 1936, married Thomas J. Wright.

f. Susan Chambliss, born 1853 in Panola County, Texas, married Mose Moffett.

g. Nancy Elizabeth Chambliss, born 1855 in Panola County, Texas, married Simeon Wright.

h. Martha Chambliss, born 1858 in Panola County, Texas.

2. Susan Mary Chambliss, daughter of Jeptha Chambliss, was born 7 February 1822 in Warren County, died 6 January 1910 in Gary, Panola County, Texas, married in November of 1837 in Talbot County, William Barclay Young. SEE Young.

3. Jeptha C. Chambliss, son of Jeptha Chambliss, was born 8 July 1823 in Warren County, married Jane Cosby on 9 August 1859. Issue:

a. George N. Chambliss, born 1859 in Stewart County.
b. Neal Chambliss, born 1859 in Stewart County.

---

[70] Bible of Jeptha Chambliss, Historical Collections of Georgia, SAR, Vol. 4; Cemetery Records of Talbot County at the Georgia State Archives; 1850-1860 Panola County, Texas Census; and the personal records of Mrs. Josephine Huffaker, 5241 Ridgedale, Dallas, Texas 75206.

4. Lovicy Chambliss, daughter of Jeptha Chambliss, was born 30 December 1824 in Warren County, died March 1867 in Panola County, Texas, married Hiram Roguemore ca 1843. SEE Roguemore.

5. Harriett Chambliss, daughter of Jeptha Chambliss, was born 22 May 1826 Warren County, died September 1827 in Warren County.

6. Arte Ann Chambliss, daughter of Jeptha Chambliss, was born 24 May 1828 in Warren County, married Ambrose J. Edwards on 19 October 1843. SEE Edwards.

7. Seaborn Chambliss, daughter of Jeptha Chambliss, was born 25 May 1829 in Warren County, married Rebecca. Issue:
       a. Stephen Chambliss, born 1854 in Stewart County.
       b. Benjamin Chambliss, born 1856 in Stewart County.
       c. Edwin Chambliss, born 1857 in Stewart County.
       d. Elias Chambliss, born 1859 in Stewart County

8. Nathan Chambliss, son of Jeptha Chambliss, was born 13 February 1831 in Warren County, died 13 January 1832 in Warren County.

9. Martha Ann Chambliss, daughter of Jeptha Chambliss, was born 7 January 1833 in Warren County, married Thomas J. Baldwin on 10 October 1848.

10. Katherine Chambliss, daughter of Jeptha Chambliss, was born 17 March 1834 in Warren County.

11. Josephus Chambliss, son of Jeptha Chambliss, was born 30 January 1835 in Warren County, died 30 January 1837 in Warren County.

12. Frances M. Chambliss, daughter of Jeptha Chambliss, was born 20 July 1837 in Warren County.

13. Mary Chambliss, daughter of Jeptha Chambliss, was born 13 April 1839 in Warren County, married John H. Mattock on 30 November 1859.

14. George W. Chambliss, son of Jeptha Chambliss, was born 23 February 1842 in Talbot County.

15. Eleanor Chambliss, daughter of Jeptha Chambliss, was born ca 1843 in Talbot County.

16. Frank Chambliss, son of Jeptha Chambliss, was born ca 1844 in Talbot County.

17. Augustus Chambliss, son of Jeptha Chambliss, was born in 1845 Talbot County, died 1859 in Talbot County.

F.   Lawson S. Chambliss, son of Christopher Chambliss, was born between 1790-1800 in Warren County.

II.   Littleton Chambliss, born 9 February 1764 Cheraw District, South Carolina, died 17 January 1822 in Jones County, married ca 1784, Cynthia.[71] Issue:

A.   John D. Chambliss, born 23 January 1785 in Warren County, died 14 March 1857 in Jones County, married Obedience Ledbetter on 20 August 1809. Obedience was born on 27 October 1788 in Warren County, and died on 5 January 1857 in Jones County. Issue:

1.   Sara Jane Chambliss, daughter of John D. Chambliss, was born 21 August 1803 in Warren County.

2.   Mary Chambliss, daughter of John D. Chambliss, was born 31 July 1810, died 15 September 1812 in Warren County.

3.   Zachariah L. Chambliss, son of John D. Chambliss, was born 31 July 1812 in Warren County, died 1879 in Marion County. He married (1) Sarah Jane Howell on 4 December 1835 and (2) Smithy Sherrod on 6 June 1842. The following is an experience which occurred during the War Between the States, written by C. O. Smith, Moultrie, Georgia....

"My grandmother, Smithy Sherrod, was the daughter of Susan Walters Sherrod and Sanders Sherrod. Susan, I believe, was the oldest daughter of Jesse Walters and his wife, Sarah. Smithy Sherrod, born in 1822, married Zachariah L. Chambliss...in 1842, living to the advanced age of 87, dying in November 1909. During the War Between the States, Smithy Sherrod Chambliss and her family suffered severely its tragic consequence. She often told of a terrifying experience of one of her aunts who suffered a severe hip wound by rifle fire in the hands of enemy soldiers....This aunt was seated on her front porch one morning carrying on her domestic duties, and did not have the slightest information that enemy soldiers were anywhere I n the community, or State. She was startled, however, on hearing a noise and looking up saw four yankee soldiers, or officers, on horseback riding toward her homoe, and so into the yard....She naturally was frightened and arose to go into her home when one of the enemy soldiers, taking deliberate aim at her, fired his rifle into her back, causing a severe wound and making her cripple for the remainder of her life. The force of the rifle fire knocked her to the floor where she was found and this lady suffered the remainder of her life, necessitating her use of crutches and cane. This war-time cruelty, according to Smithy Sherrod Chambliss, was the most severe criminal offense civilized man had ever inflicted on a lady up to that time."

4.   William H. Chambliss, son of John D. Chambliss, was born 13 September 1814 in Warren County.

5.   Thomas G. Chambliss, son of John D. Chambliss, was born 10 December 1816 in Warren County, married Martha E. Justice on 1 July 1836.

---

[71] Bible of Littleton Chambliss, in the possession of Charles Owen Smith, Moultire, Georgia. 1850-1860 Madison County Census; Madison County Marriages.

6. Littleton G. Chambliss, son of John D. Chambliss, was born 2 July 1820 in Warren County, married Martha Trerove.

7. Nancy Chambliss, daughter of John D. Chambliss, was born 13 September 1823 in Warren County.

8. John Chambliss, son of John D. Chambliss, was born 21 August 1826 in Warren County.

9. Henry Balden Chambliss, son of John D. Chambliss, was born 20 February 1829 in Marion County, died 22 October 1888 in Buel, Texas, married Augusta Roguemore on 21 April 1868. Augusta was born 1844 and died 21 August 1895 in Panola County, Texas. Henry served during the War Between the States in Co. I, 2nd Regiment, Volunteer Infantry, Beuna Vista Guards, as a private in 1862, 1862; surrendering at Appomattox, Virginia on 9 April 1865. Issue:

    a. Hiram Abiff Chambliss, born 13 February 1870, died 5 November 1895.
    b. Eola Obedience Chambliss, born 3 October 1871, died 22 July 1895. She married James Pogue. Issue:
        i. Leroy Pogue.
        ii. Ida Hatfield Pogue, born 4 August 1891.
    c. Zachariah D. Chambliss, born 17 July 1876, died December 1897. He was married in August 1897 in Morgan Mill, Texas to Ola Harris. Issue:
        i. Zachariah C. Chambliss, born 2 July 1898.
    d. John Thomas Chambliss, born 3 June 1878.
    e. James Henry Chambliss, born 29 January 1883.

B. Littleton Chambliss, son of Littleton Chambliss, was born 1792 in Warren County, died in Covington County, Alabama, wife, Nancy.

C. James Taylor Chambliss, son of Littleton Chambliss, was born ca 1800 in Jones County, married Lilpha Duncan on 24 May 1821.

III. Thomas Chambliss, born ca 1765 in Cheraw District, South Carolina, died 1810 in Columbia County, Georgia. He married Sarah Aldridge, the daughter of James Aldridge, on 6 May 1788. Thomas was a resident of Warren County in 1800. His estate was administered in 1810 in Columbia County by his wife, Sarah. Sarah died 23 July 1821 in Montgomery, Alabama.

IV. John Chambliss, born ca 1766 in Cheraw District, South Carolina.

V. William Chambliss, born ca 1772 in Cheraw District, South Carolina, married Mary Robertson on 19 September 1803. Issue:

A. William Chambliss, born 1802 in Jones County, married Polly Huckaby on 23 December 1823.
B. Levi Chambliss, born 1805 in Jones County, married Caroline Smith on 12 December 1839.

C. Thomas Chambliss, born 1815 in Jones County, married Milly Smith on 10 January 1839.

VI.   Mary Chambliss, born ca 1773 in Cheraw District, South Carolina.

VI.   Zachariah Chambliss, born 1775 in Cheraw District, South Carolina, died August 1874 in Forsyth, Monroe County, Georgia, buried in the Chambliss Family Cemetery, 3 miles from Forsyth, Georgia. Wife, Mary. The LWT of Zachariah Chambliss was probated August of 1874 in Monroe County, Georgia Wills, page 191-192. He was listed on the 1860 Monroe County Census. At the death of Zachariah, B. H. Zellner served as the administrator (1879), and found with the records was this letter.....

"Seventeen years ago, Mr. Thomas E. Chambliss, in a Sunday's evening walk, pointed out to his wife, Mrs. Mary Chambliss, places where he said jars of specia belonging to your father were buried. This was in a piece of woodland just north of the garden and orchard at the McKinney place. Three days before the death of Thomas E. Chambliss, he took up one of the jars which contained nearly $10,000 in gold; she could designate the place where the other jar was buried, but not having been there before in fifteen years, she was not at all certain as to the place. However, after a few hours search, we found it, but it proved to be all silver and only #453.16 as the old coins were counted by the banker at Forsyth."

Issue:

A. John M. Chambliss, son of Zachariah Chambliss, was born 12 April 1797 in Columbia County, died 17 September 1880 in Jones County, buried in the Chambliss Cemetery, Monroe County, on Dames Ferry-Forsyth Hwy, about 5 miles from Forsyth. He was a resident of Baldwin County in 1820, and in Monroe County in 1840, having twelve slaves. He married Elizabeth Jordan (born 1799, died 25 November 1858) on 14 October 1819, the daughter of William Jordan and Anne Medlock. SEE Jordan. In 1880, his wife was E. K. C., born 1825 in Georgia. [72]He was a resident of Baldwin County in 1820, was found in Monroe County in 1840, with twelve slaves. B. H. Zellner served as the administrator of his estate, and wrote this letter:

Issue:

1. William Alexander Chambliss, son of John M. Chambliss, was born 9 November 1820 in Baldwin County. He married (1) on 5 November 1846, Rebecca Johnson, and, (2) on 10 December 1857, Lucy Amelia Pace. Issue:
   a. William Lloyd Chambliss, born 10 December 1848 in Bibb County, died 12 April 1912, married on 13 December 1873 in Covington, Newton County, Sarah Pace. Issue:[73]
      i. Minnie Lee Chambliss, born 22 December 1863.
      ii. Mattie Lou Chambliss, born 21 Sepgember 1865, died 29 September 1866.
      iii. Thomas Eugene Chambliss, born 18 July 1867, died 4 October 1907.

---

[72] 1880 Monroe County Census, District 596.

[73] The Personal records of Edgar F. Chestnut, 8000 Interstate Drive, Little Rock, Arkansas 72206 (1966).

iv. Edgar Stephen Chambliss, born 11 December 1870, died 2 June 1936.

v. Mary Ellen Chambliss, born 30 June 1873, died 2 July 1947.

vi. Lucy Pace CHambliss, born 23 November 1877.

vii. Annie Chambliss, born 3 August 1884.

2. Israel Jordan Chambliss, son of John M. Chambliss, was born 29 August 1822 in Baldwin County. He married on 27 December 1847, Amanda Ellen Stanley. Issue:

a. Charles Stanley Chambliss, born18 September 1850 in Forsyth, Monroe County, died 28 May 1907 in Forsyth, buried in the Forsyth City Cemetery. He married Laura Middlebrooks (born 18 February 1859 in Forsyth, Monroe County, buried in the Forsyth City Cemetery. Issue:

i. Walter Stanley Chambliss, born 4 June 1876, died 18 January 1914.

ii. Israel Chambliss, born 1878.

iii. Ernest Chambliss, born 1880.

iv. Bernice Chambliss, born 6 July 1884, died 28 May 1913.

b. Fannie Chambliss, born 24 December 1852 in Forsyth, Monroe County, married J. R. Hill.

c. Johnnie Lumpkin Chambliss, born 13 June 1855 in Forsyth, Monroe County.

d. Israel E. Chambliss, born 1857 in Forsyth, Monroe County.

3. Mary W. Chambliss, daughter of John M. Chambliss, died 15 February 1907. She married on 20 October 1842 in Monroe County, Gideon T. Johnson. SEE Johnson.

4. Thomas Edmund Chambliss, son of John M. Chambliss, was born 27 February 1824 in Forsyth, Monroe County, died 24 December 1880, buried in the Chambliss Cemetery in Monroe County. He married on 21 October 1852, Mary Cleveland (born 27 July 1833, died 15 February 1907). Listed on the 1860 Monroe County Census as a farmer. Issue:

a. Mary Chambliss, born 27 July 1853 in Forsyth, Monroe County.

b. Elizabeth Jordan Chambliss, born 27 November 1855 in Forsyth, Monroe County, died 19 April 1884, married on 2 September 1880 in Monroe County, J. Frank Roguemore.

c. Edna Armstrong Chambliss, born 3 September 1857 in Forsyth, Monroe County, died 19 April 1884, married on 2 September 1880 in Monroe County, J. Frank Roguemore.

d. Zachariah Cromwell Chambliss, born 24 May 1863 in Forsyth, Monroe County, married on 27 November 1883, Sallie Inman.

e. Mary Ellen Chambliss, born 1 December 1867 in Forsyth, Monroe County, died 1953. She married on 27 August 1885 in Monroe County, Charles Jesse Zellner (born 27 June 1860 in Forsyth, Monroe County, died ca 1946 in Forsyth. Issue:

i. Frances Lucile Zellner, born 26 September 1888.

ii. Charles Jesse Zellner, born 15 August 1890.

iii. Ruth Zellner, born 4 November 1892.

iv. Lois Evangeline Zellner, born 4 October 1894, died 5 August 1895.

v. Louis Edwin Zellner, born 4 October 1894.
vi. Mary Cleveland Zellner, born 3 December 1896.
vii. Winnie Davis Zellner, born 22 July 1898.
viii. Gwendolen Kathleen Zellner, born 31 August 1902.
ix. Thomas Chambliss Zellner, born 21 September 1905.
x. Fannie Cleveland Chambliss, born 13 July 1871 in Forsyth, Monroe County, married on 20 December 1893 in Monroe County, Robert H. Holmes. Issue:
. Elizabeth Holmes.

5. Ann M. Chambliss, daughter of John M. Chambliss, died 24 April 1870 in Forsyth, Monroe County. She married on 9 November 1843, William M. Greene.

6. Nancy Medlock Chambliss, daughter of John M. Chambliss, was born 3 February 1828 in Jones County, died 4 March 1849.

7. Elizabeth Jordan Chambliss, daughter of John M. Chambliss, was born 14 February 1830 in Monroe County, married on 29 November 1847, Gabriel M. Johnson. SEE Johnson.

8. Caroline Frances Chambliss, daughter of John M. Chambliss, was born 23 November 1831 in Monroe County, died 6 May 1864.

9. Emily Angeline Chambliss, daughter of John M. Chambliss, was born 7 July 1838 in Forsyth, Monroe County, died 6 June 1909, buried in the Chambliss Family Cemetery, near Forsyth.. She married (1) Elijah N. Etheridge, and, (2) James Washington Head Ponder.

10. John McPherson Chambliss, son of John M. Chambliss, was born 4 June 1843 in Forsyth, Monroe County, died 20 June 1911. He was buried in the Chambliss Cemetery in Monroe County; farmer.

B. Edmund Chambliss, son of Zachariah Chambliss, was born ca 1802 in Baldwin County, married Amelia Elizabeth Howard.

C. Timothy Chambliss, son of Zachariah Chambliss, was born 1811 in Baldwin County, married Amanda Redding on 13 October 1837.

D. Alexander Chambliss, son of Zachariah Chambliss, died 14 October 1828. He married Martha Sims on 21 April 1825.

E. Joel Chambliss, son of Zachariah Chambliss.

F. Selina Chambliss, daughter of Zachariah Chambliss.

G. Sally Chambliss, daughter of Zachariah Chambliss. She married (1) Lewis Etheridge on 15 January 1815, and, (2) Mr. Durham.

H. Verlinda Chambliss, daughter of Zachariah Chambliss, was born 26 November 1812 in Baldwin County, died 27 September 1836 in Monroe County. She married Gresham McKinney on 24 February 1831.

I. Rebecca Chambliss, daughter of Zachariah Chambliss. She married on 30 August 1836, William Bryant.

J. Nancy Chambliss, daughter of Zachariah Chambliss, was born 30 July 1813 in Baldwin County.

K. Mary Chambliss, daughter of Zachariah Chambliss. She married on 27 December 1825, Joseph W. George.

VII. Ephraim Chambliss, born 1775 in Cheraw District, South Carolina. Wife, Elizabeth.

VIII. Joseph Chambliss, born ca 1776 in Cheraw District, South Carolina, died 1823 in Warren County, Georgia. An Administrator's Bond was issued in Warren County on the estate of Joseph Chambliss, dated 17 November 1823, and on again on April 7th, for the estate of Joseph Chambliss, with Christopher Chambliss as surety. He married Susannah, a daughter of Adam Jones of Warren County. [74] SEE Jones.

Cheatham of Madison County

Isham Cheatham was born 1787 in Chesterfield County, Virginia, and died 1882 in Madison County, Georgia. He was married on 25 February 1813 in Oglethorpe County to Cynthia Jones (born 1795 in Oglethorpe County, died 1850 in Madison County).[75] Issue:

I. Adaline Cheatham.

II. Parmalie Cheatham.

III. Josiah Cheatham was born 1818 in Georgia, farmer. He married on 19 December 1843 in Madison County, Elizabeth P. Williams (born 1824 Danielsville, Madison County), the daughter of Elijah Williams and his wife Nancy (Strickland) Williams. SEE Williams. The family resided at Grove Hill, in Madison County.
Issue:[76]

A Emily. C. Cheatham was born 1844 in Madison County.

B James J. N. Cheatham was born 1846 in Madison County. Wife, Elizabeth, born 1846. Issue:[77]

1. James W. J. Cheatham, born 1868 in Madison County,
2. Jesse R. Cheatham born 1871 in Madison County,

---

[74] The LWT of Adam Jones probated 30 November 1830 in Warren County named his daughter, Susannah Chambliss; 1850-1860 Bibb County Census; Bibb County Estates & Marriages.

[75] 1830-1860 Madison County Census.

[76] 1850-1860 Madison County Census; Madison County Marriages.

[77] 1850-1880 Madison County Census.

C. Birdy E. J. Cheatham was born 1849 in Madison County. Wife, Emily H. They were residents of Grove Hill, Georgia, in 1880.

D. William J. Cheatham was born 1851 in Madison County.

E. Nancy C. Cheatham was born 1854 in Madison County.

F. Caroline D. Cheatham, born 1859 in Madison County.

G. Carlie C. Cheatham (son), born 1865 in Madison County.

IV. Mary Cheatham.

V. Nancy Cheatham.

VI. John J. Cheatham, born 1827 in Georgia, farmer. Wife, Rodah, born 1824 in Georgia.
Issue:
    A. David J. Cheatham, born 1847 in Madison County.
    B. Mary S. P. Cheatham, born 1849 in Madison County.
    C. Rodah E. Cheatham, born 1850 in Madison County.
    D. Georgia Ann Cheatham, born 1852 in Madison County.
    E. Jacob B. J. J. Cheatham, born 1854 in Madison County.
    F. Rispan J. Cheatham (son), born 1854 in Madison County.
    G. Riley C. Cheatham, born 1855 in Madison County.
    H. James J. A. L. Cheatham, born 1857 in Madison County.
    I. Mildred L. G. P. C. Cheatham, born 1860 in Madison County.

VII. Catherine Cheatham, born 16 March 1823 in Madison County, died 20 January 1897, buried in Lystra, Georgia.

VIII. Elizabeth Cheatham, born 1825 in Madison County.

IX. Prudence Cheatham.

Clements of North Carolina, Greene & Putnam Counties

Peyton Clements was born ca 1740, and died 1775 in Granville County, North Carolina. He was first found in Granville County as early as November of 1765 when he sold some land to Frances West, 120 acres, for 50 pounds (Book G, page 291, Granville County). He was married to Elizabeth. His LWT is dated 10 December 1773, probated August of 1782 by William Burford, Executor. He bequeathed to his wife Elizabeth "all land whereon I now live, and a child's part of all of the other estate to be divided among the children." (Granville County Will Book 1, 1772-1787, page 100). His widow, Mary, was found on the 1820 Putnam County, Georgia Census, having five slaves. Mary and her son, Philip Clements, were executors of the Estate of Jesse Clements (another son).[78]

---

[78] NOTE____There is the reasonable argument that Peyton Clements may be a son of Benjamin Clements of Pittsylvania County, Virginia, who died in 1780, leaving a Will. Of course, he did not name a son, Peyton, the latter being already deceased. In 1741, Benjamin Clements of Amelia County, Virginia, patented land on Sycamore Creek on the Stanton River, where he made his home a few years later...The home was known as *Clement Hill* , built about 1748. In August of 1755, Benjamin was a Captain of a company of Rangers in Pittsylvania

I.   David Clements was born ca 1770 in Granville County, North Carolina, died 1851 in Henry County, Georgia. Wife, Nancy. He lived in Putnam County in 1820, with eleven slaves. By the year of 1825, he had sold all of his Putnam County land and removed to Henry County. His LWT dated 1851, page 203, Henry County, Georgia Wills, named his wife and children, leaving the wife a plantation in Chambers County, Alabama, and slaves. For the year of 1834, David Clements was executor of the Estate of John Foster in Henry County Henry County Wills and Bonds, page 334). Issue of David Clements:

A. Turner H. Clements married Mary E. Elliott on 22 February 1842. He was administrator of his father's Estate in 1851, Henry County; was also appointed guardian of his brother's children (Stephen W.), who died in 1857. His bond was $20,000.00 for his father'e estate, with Robert H. Elliott and Stephen W. Clements as securities, dated 3 November 1851 (Henry County Administrator's Bonds, page 134).

B. Stephen W. Clements, died 1857 in Henry County, married Louisa Wyatt on 9 October 1844.

C. Susan Adaline Clements.

D. Elizabeth S. J. Clements.

E. Martha L. Clements.

F. Anna S. Clements, married Mr. Bryan. William L. Crayton was appointed Trustee under the Will of her father, David Clements, for Ann Clements Bryan and her child; he was also appointed Trustee for Rebecca H. Clements.

G. Rebecca H. Clements, married Achison Finley on 10 June 1830.

H. Mary S. Mathew Clements.

I. D. S. Clements.

County, Virginia (History of Pittsylvania County by Clement). Capt. Benjamin Clements later became a prominent resident of Lunenburg County, living in that portion which later became Bedford County (in 1754), and Campbell County (in 1782). Benjamin's father is said to have been William Clements, originally of King William County, who purchased 1225 acres in Amelia County and removed there in 1735 where he became Justice of the Peace and Sheriff. William's LWT was dated 1760 naming his sons, Benjamin, William, John, Francis, and daughters, Elizabeth Ford Ellyson, Anne and Barsheba Major. The LWT of Benjamin Clements was dated 30 March 1780, Pittsylvania County, Vol. B, page 116. Issue: Susannah Clements who married Henry Slaton and settled on Kettle Creek in Wilkes County, Georgia, her LWT dated 29 December 1807 in Wilkes County; Stephen Clements; Isaac Clements; Adam Clements; James Clements; Benjamin Clements, Jr.; John Clements; Rachel Clements and Elizabeth Clements who married Benjamin Wade of Pittsylvania County and their descendants removed to Greene County, Georgia.

[79] Granville County, North Carolina Wills & Deeds; Wake County, North Carolina Deeds; Henry County Wills; Putnam County Deeds & Marriages; Greene County Deeds & Marriages; Putnam County Estates & Annual Returns; Putnam County Tax Digests; Monroe County Wills; Henry County Wills and Estates; Greene County Wills & Estates; 1840-1850 Monroe County Census; Greene County Guardians & Administrator's Returns; Putnam County Guardians & Administrator's Returns; 1820-1840 Putnam County Census; 1850-1860 Harris County Census; Mt. Zion Newspaper dated 5 September 1825; Estate of Mrs. Mary Clements, dated 1825; Putnam County Marriages; Monroe County Marriages; 1860 Muscogee County Census; 1850 Greene County Census; Wake County, North Carolina Marriages; Historical Southern Families, Volume XXIII, by Mrs. John Bennett Boddie.

III.   Jesse Clements was born ca 1775 in Granville County, North Carolina. He married Elizabeth Coleman ca 1788 in Greene County, Georgia. Jesse Clements sold land to Mr. McMarrin in Putnam County on 12 November 1807. The 1813 Putnam County Tax Digests lists Jesse Clements residing in Capt. Jacob Lindray's District. On 4 April 1816, Jesse Clements sold land to H. Dixon, Exec.; Jesse Clements sold to Richard Butt for $400.00, 202-1/2 acres of land, formerly granted to John Morris in 1806 (in Baldwin County, now Putnam County). Issue of Jesse Clements:

A.   Jesse Clements, Jr. born ca 1789 in Greene County, Georgia, died 1833 in Putnam County. He married Betsey Webb on 5 January 1809. Letters ot Administration were issued to Henry Alford and Jeptha Clements on 1 April 1833, for the estate of Jesse Clements, Jr.

B.   Polly Clements, born ca 1791 in Greene County, married Thomas McAdams on 5 January 1809.

C.   Anna Clements, born 1792 in Greene County, married Jesse Bumpass on 3 February 1812.

D.   Elizabeth Clements, born ca 1793 in Greene County, married Ralph Kilgore on 12 October 1810.

E.   Philip Clements, born 1794 in Greene County. The 1840 Monroe County, Georgia Census reflects that Philip Clements owned ten slaves. Philip Clements, as Executor of the estate of Jesse Clements, deceased, sold 161 acres of land in Putnam County to Robert Parham on 22 December 1823.

F.   Gilley Clements, born ca 1797 in Baldwin County, married Jesse Jenkins on 16 February 1823.

G.   Nancy Clements, born ca 1799 in Baldwin County, married Moren Moor on 1 December 1821. She was a minor at the time of her father's death, and Jeptha Clements was appointed as her guardian, the first Return being filed in 1826.

H.   Peyton R. Clements, born 1806 in Baldwin County, married Martha Edmondson on 13 September 1825 in Putnam County. Martha was born 1810 in Putnam County, and was the daughter of Thomas Edmondson and his wife, Patience Spiers. SEE Edmondson and Spiers. Issue:

1. John Clements, son of Peyton R. Clements, was born 1827 in Jones County.
2. Wesley Clements, son of Peyton R. Clements, was born 1830 in Jones County; enlisted as a Confederate soldier in Muscogee County, died during the Civil War. He married ca 1854 Jane Smith, a daughter of Davis Smith of Monroe County. Jane was born 21 March 1836 in Monroe County, died 12 October 1903 in Atlanta, Fulton County, buried in the Smith Cemetery at Brent, Monroe County, Georgia. After the war, when Wesley did not return home, she married (2) on 1 May 1867 in Monoroe County, Thomas Young Brent. He lived on the Smith plantation, operated a store, and was so prosperous there that the community became known as "Brent". SEE Smith. Issue:

i.   William P. Clements, son of Wesley Clements, was born 19 March 1855 in Muscogee County, married Sallie Thweatt on 28 October 1885. He was engaged in merchandising in Dublin, and lived on 400 acres of the Davis Smith plantation in Monroe County.

ii.   Thomas Clements, son of Wesley Clements, was born ca 1857 in Muscogee County.

iii. Elizabeth Smith Clements, daughter of Wesley Clements, was born 14 October 1859 in Muscogee County, died November 1905, Brent, Monroe County, buried in the Smith Cemetery at Brent. She married 11 April 1885 in Monroe County, Joel Edgar Chambliss, the son of Andrew Jackson Chambliss. SEE Chambliss.

3. Asbury Clements, son of Peyton R. Clements, was born 1835 Jones County.
4. Pamela Clements, daughter of Peyton R. Clements, was born 1836 Jones County.
5. Peyton Clements, son of Peyton R. Clements, was born 1840 Putnam County.
6. Whitfield Clements, son of Peyton R. Clements, was born 1843 Putnam County.
7. Martha or Mautna Clements, daughter of Peyton R. Clements, was born 1847 Harris County.

III. Peyton Clements, married Polly Ward on 1 December 1808. Methodist Minister, lived in Harris County in 1850.[80]

IV. Philip Clements married 8 October 1803, Elizabeth. James Daniell deed to Philip Clements of Greene County, appointing Philip Clements as a friend of his attorney to dispose of a child's share of land belonging to Peyton Clements of Granville County, North Carolina, located on the Neece River. Date: 19 October 1790 (Greene County Deed Book I, page 68. In 1793, Philip Clements was First Lieutenant in Company 3, Battalion, Greene County, Georgia.

Issue:

A. Ellis Clements, born 1792 in Greene County. Wife, Polly. Listed on the 1850 Greene County Census.

---

[80] Putnam County Deeds

2 October 1807, Peyton Clements sold land to James Strother; 22 July 1808, Peyton Clements sold land to Fred Race; 5 August 1811, Peyton Clements sold 60 acres in Putnam County to Rowland Brewer; 15 January 1815, Peyton Clements sold 100 acres in Putnam County, Lots 225 and 226 to James Dismarks. (Putnam Deed Book F, 1817-1821, page 209-210); 10 November 1816, Peyton Clements sold to Jerry Watts, 100 acres in Putnam County, Land Lot 225 in 2nd District, formerly Baldwin, now Putnam County, for $475. (Granville County Deed Book H, 1818-23, page119); 24 September 1817, Peyton Clements sold to Peter Tatum for $850, 100 acres, Land Lot No. 225, Dismarks land, formerly in Baldwin County, now Putnam County, and including the waters of Bean Creek (Page 180, Vol. F, 1817-21 Putnam County Deeds); 18 August 1818, Peyton Clements sold to Peter Tatum land in Putnam County; 11 January 1819, Peyton Clements sold land to A. Wallace; 5 December 1820, Peyton Clements sold to William Dennis, 200 acres in Putnam County; 17 March 1824, Peyton Clements sold to S. Breedlove, 201-1/2 acres in Land Lot 58 of Putnam County. (Putnam County Deed Book K, page 486-487); 5 January 1825, Peyton Clements sold 140 acres of Putnam County land to C. G. Hurt.

V. Tyre Clements. Wife, Elizabeth. Tyre Clements took the Oath of Allegiance in 1778, in the Dutch District of Granville County, North Carolina. Tyre and Elizabeth Clements purchased from Lewis Magam on 15 November 1792, 50 acres of land in Greene County, Georgia for $230.00. (Greene County Deed Book B, page 101).

VI. Grisell Clements (female).

VII. William Clements was born ca 1751, died 4 March 1835 in Wake County, North Carolina. He was a Revolutionary War Soldier; Elizabeth applied for a pension as a widow. He married on 15 March 1776 Elizabeth Daniel, in Granville County. Elizabeth died on 13 February 1847 in Orange County, North Carolina. William sold land on Cedar Creek to John Longmire on 30 October 1797 (Granville Deed Book Q, page 353). In 1820, he was a resident of Hatch District, Granville County, but later lived in Wake County. William Clements and Judith Burford sold to Tyre Clements of Greene County, Georgia, on 6 March 1789, land in Washington County, located on Richland Creek, for 25 pounds. (Greene County Deeed Book I, page 233). Issue:

A. Arenia Clements, born 7 March 1808 in Walke County, married Archibald Nichols (born 7 July 1805) in Person County, North Carolina on 14 April 1825.
B. Cary Clements.
C. Mary Clements.
D. Lotty Clements.
E. Woodson Clements, born 22 September 1785, died 24 January 1805 in Walke County, married Kesiah Suskins (born 4 November 1787) on 24 January 1805..
F. Gilly Clements.
G. Anderson Clements, born ca 1791, married (1) Parthena Brasfield on 12 November 1810 in Wake County, North Caorlina, and, (2) Bina Brasfield on 31 May 1819..
H. William Clements, born ca 1793, married 23 September 1811, Jenny Rose.
I. Wiley Clements.
J. Salley Clements.
K. Martha Clements,
L. Elizabeth Clements.
M. Peyton Clements., married (2) Angelina Rencher and removed to Greene County, Alabama.

VIII. Jacob Clements, died September 1823 in Putnam County. On 5 January 1825, Peyton Clements, administrator of the Estate of Jacob Clements of Jasper County, Georgia, sold to Charles Hurt of Putnam County for $600, 140 acres of land located on Little River. (Putnam County Deed Book M, page 7). Issue:

A. Christiana Clements, married Jesse Jenkins on 19 August 1824.
B. Susan Clements, married James Bridges on 6 April 1820.
C. Anna Clements.
D. Thomas L. Clements.
E. William Clements, married Elinor McFarlen on 24 November 1826.

IX. Thomas Clements, died May 1816 in Putnam County. Wife, Anna. The LWT of Anna Clements is dated 4 February 1833, in Putnam County. He was a soldier in the North Carolina Militia of 1771 from Granville County. Taken from the House Journals of 1787, in the House of Commons:

"Henry Burges, being sworn, supports the fact so far as the same relates to a purchase made by Mr. Bonds from Thomas Clements, whom he did not know or had ever seen before or since."

Letters of Administration were issued on 6 May 1816 to his wife, Anna, and his brother, Peyton Clements. Inventory was dated 17 May 1816; Dower dated 4 November 1816. The Annual Returns 1816-1817, Putnam County. On 15 June 1819, Peyton Clements, as administrator of the Estate of Thomas Clements, sold to Jacob Clements of Putnam County for $2000.00, 141-1/2 acres in Putnam County, on Bar Creek. (Putnam Deed Book I, page 209-210). On 25 June 1819, Peyton Clements, as administrator of the Estates of Thomas and Jacob Clements of Putnam County, sold for $2000, 141-1/2 acres of land on Bar Creek in Putnam County. (Putnam County Deed Book I, In 1820, Anna was the owner of six slaves, according to the Putnam County Census.[81] Issue:

    A. Jesse Clements. He was a minor at the death of his father, and his mother, Anna Clements, was appointed as his guardian on 2 September 1816.

    B. Thomas Clements. On 15 November 1822 Thomas Clements received $1602.40 for the sale of Negroes (Archie $700; Peter $225; cash $600; Cash $75).

X.   Jeptha Clements, died November 1847 in Monroe County. Wife, Avey (Elizabeth). He was listed on the 1813 Putnam County Tax Digest, in Capt. Jacob Lindsay's District. On 20 August 1811, Jeptha Clements sold land in Putnam County to James Kendrick. On 27 November 1816, Jeptha Clements sold 98 acres of land in Putnam County to James Dorough. On 14 September 1824, Jeptha Clements sold to J. Lawyers, 252-1/2 acres in Putnam County to Johnson Sawyer for $1512.00, being Lot No. 137 in the 15th District of Baldwin County, and Lot No. 138, 152-1/2 acres (in September 1822). (Putnam County Deed Book L, page 332-333. In September of 1822, Jeptha Clements sold to Thomas T. Napier of Putnam County for $1000, land on Little River, originally in Baldwin County, now in Putnam County, 202-1/2 acres. (Putnam County Deed Book I, page 255-256. The LWT of Jeptha Clements was dated 8 November 1847, probated 13 November 1847, Will Book B, page 4, Monroe County.

Cliatt of Columbia & Richmond Counties

Jonathan and Isaac Cliatt purchased 76 acres of land on Reds Creek from Daniel Richardson, which he sold on 19 December 1789 to Daniel Richardson. On 6 October 1802, in Richmond County, Jonathan Cliatt purchased 88 acres of land from March Chambless, 50 acres of which was originally granted to John Grubbs and 38 acres to Mary Chambliss. On 9 November 1811, Jonathan Cliatt witnessed the sale of 200 acres on Uchee Creek by Sarah Chambless, administratrix of the estate of Thomas Chambless to Elijah Russell, in Columbia County.

The Christian Index dated 1 November 1838, mentioned the death of Jonathan Cliatt in Columbia County, a member of Oak Grove Church. He married on 1 February 1793 in Columbia County, Mary Chambless. On 11 February 1839 in Columbia County, William Cliatt was appointed the administrator of the estate of Jonathan Cliatt, sale of the property on 9

---

[81] On 4 February 1798, Thomas Clements sold to John Tuggle, 150 acres in Granville County, for 50 pounds. (Granville Deed Book), page 567; Thomas Clements sold to David Coley, 252 acres of land and a plantation in Granville County for 100 pds. (Granville Deed Book P., page 224; Thomas Clements sold to Lewis Bledloe, land in Granville County. (Granville Deed Book 2, page 110); Thomas Clements sold to William Williams, land in Putnam County, on 27 September 1806.

January 1840, with the major purchasers as: Mary Cliatt, J. L. Cliatt, Thomas C. Cliatt, William Cliatt, and Minor J. Cliatt. SEE Chambliss. Issue:[82]

I.   Jonathan Cliatt married (1) Ona Zachary, a daughter of William Zachary of Columbia County on 7 January 1813 in Columbia County (2) Milley Moseley in Richmond County on 7 January 1817 (3) Polly Youngblood, widow of Benjamin. Mary's LWT was probated in Columbia County on 20 May 1850, wherein she named her heirs, along with her grandchildren, Eli and Frances Kendrick. In 1822, Jonathan Cliatt, Jr. was appointed the administrator of the estate of Benjamin Youngblood, in "right of my wife", in Columbia County. SEE Youngblood. Issue:

A.   George Hillman Cliatt, born 15 February 1826 in Columbia County. Wife, Laura D., born 1832 in South Carolina. They were residents of Bainbridge in 1880. [83]Issue:
1.   Julien C. Cliatt, born 1866 in Georgia.

B.   William Cliatt, his LWT dated 23 March 1850, probated 5 August 1850, naming his daughter and only child, Mary Caroline Eugenia Cliatt "now a little over five years old." The child is to remain in the care of her grandfather, William Zachary, and if he should die, to go and live with an esteemed relative, George H. Cliett.

II.   Henry Cliatt, born 1801 in Columbia County, died 1839, married Sarah Zachary on 6 April 1815 in Columbia County.

Cobbs of England, Virginia;
Columbia & Wilkes Counties

The family seat was in Chislet, Faversham, County Kent, England, and began with John Cobbs, born ca 1482, a son of Thomas Cobbs. He had one known son, viz: Thomas Cobbs, yeoman, who died 1599 in Eastleigh Court, Lyminge Parish, County Kent, England, and who married (1) Christine Young on 21 January 1544 and (2) Mrs. Agnes Musared in July of 1579 according to the Lyminge Parish Register. The Litigation of the Death of Thomas Cobbs occurred on 6 June 1599 in County Kent, with Robert Hunt, clergyman, being in charge of the documents.

The above Thomas Cobbs (born ca 1525, died 1599) and his wife, Christina Young had two known sons, viz: Edmund Cobbs, born 1560/1563 in Eastleigh Court, married (1) Margaret Musared on 6 July 1584 and (2) Mrs. Ann Elfrith on 14 December 1594; and Ambrose Cobbs, Archdeacon, who died December 1605 in County Kent, England, his LWT being dated 31 December 1605. He married 1584/1585 Angelica Hunt. Angelica died 3 September 1603 in Petham, County Kent.

The marriage of Ambrose Cobbs produced eight children, viz: Susanna Cobbs, chr. 27 November 1586 in Eastleigh Court, Lyminge Parish; Rachel Cobbs, chr. 19 November 1588 (same); Elizabeth Cobbs, chr 1595 (same), married on 4 June 1619 Thomas Smith; Ambrose Cobbs, chr. 25 August 1595, buried 27 August 1595 (same); Jane Cobbs; Edmund Cobbs, died

---

[82] Columbia County Marriages; Richmond County Marriages.

[83] 1880 Decatur County Census, Bainbridge, E. D. 1; The Georgians by Jeannette Holland Austin.

1693 in County Kent; Ambrose Cobbs, Jr., chr. 1603, died before 15 January 1656 in York County, Virginia, married on 18 April 1625, Ann White; and Thomas Cobbs, who died 1702 in County Kent, married on 8 October 1619, Susan White.

Ambrose Cobbs (1603-1656), the emigrant to Virginia, married on 18 April 1625 in Norton, County Kent, Ann White (chr. 19 February 1603 in Bexley, County Kent, a daughter of Robert White and his wife, Susanna (Boulden) White. In 1639, Ambrose Cobbs patented 350 acres of land on the Appomattox River, for himself, and his wife, Ann, daughter, Margaret, and son, Robert. They had four children, viz: Ambrose Cobbs, chr. 12 March 1625 Willesborough, County Kent; Robert Cobbs, Justice, chr. 1 July 1627 Willesborough, County Kent, and died December 1682 in York County, Virginia (wife Elizabeth); Jane Cobbs, born 1629 in Willesborough, County Kent, died 1 December 1634; and Margaret Cobbs.

Robert Cobbs (1627-1682) resided in Marshton Parish, York County, Virginia, and when the parish became known as Bruton Parish in 1674, he was a member of the vestry of the church in Williamsburg, Virginia. His wife, Elizabeth, was born 1634, and died 29 December 1682, her death registered in Bruton Parish. The deposition of Elizabeth Cobbs dated 20 July 1684 in York County, Virginia, gives her age as 50. Their children, viz: Edmund Cobbs, died 21 December 1693 in York County, Virginia,[84] married Mrs. Frances Pierce; Otho Cobbs; Robert Cobbs, died 18 September 1727 in York County, Virginia[85], married (1) Rebecca Pinkethman and (2) Elizabeth Allen; Margaret Cobbs, died 1684, married William Kerle; and Ambrose Cobbs, died 16 June 1718 in York County, Virginia,[86] married Frances Elizabeth Pinkett.

Ambrose Cobbs (ca 1667-1718), his LWT dated 24 April 1718, probated 16 June 1718 in York County, Virginia. He married Frances Elizabeth Pinkett, the daughter of Thomas Pinkett, and

---

[84] The LWT of Edmund Cobbs dated 2 March 1691, probated 7 March 1693 in York County, Virginia. His widow, Frances, later married John Stewart of York County.

[85] The LWT of Robert Cobbs was dated 18 September 1727 in York County, Virginia. "Robert Jones, Jr. and Sarah, his wife, and Dudley Richardson and Martha, his wife, Appellants, vs. James Shields: William Pinketham of York County in the Colony of Virginia, made his will 1 December 1712, by which he gave certain Negroes to his daughter, Rebecca, his only child and heir at law. She married Robert Cobbs, and died in 1715, in the lifetime of her husband, leaving issue, one daughter, Elizabeth, aged 11 years. The said Robert afterwards marries with Elizabeth (the daughter of Daniel Allen) by whom he had two children, the appellants, Sarah and Martha. Robert Cobbs made his will on 10 December 1725, which was proved on 21 February 1725/6, making his wife, Elizabeth, and Daniel Allen, executors." Notes from Barton's Colonial Decisions, page 367.

"After the death of Robert Cobbs, his widow, Elizabeth, married Samuel Weldon and died on 1 August 1747; and the said Elizabeth, daughter of Robert Cobbs by his first wife, married James Sheilds in the lifetime of said Elizabeth Weldon. This case was long drawn out and taken on appeal to the Privy Council in England, where it was still pending in 1753." Virginia Quarterly, Volume VI, page 121.

[86] The LWT of Ambrose Cobbs was dated 24 April 1718 and probated on 16 June 1718 in York County, Virginia.

had seven children, viz: Thomas Cobbs died 1750 in York County, Virginia,[87] married Mary Shields; Frances Cobbs, [88] Robert Cobbs, married Crosia; John Cobb; Edmund Cobb, died 1759 in York County, Virginia; Ambrose Cobbs and Elizabeth Cobbs.

Thomas Cobbs (ca 1689-1750)[89] married Mary Shields of Buckingham County, Virginia, a daughter of James Shields and his wife, Hannah (Marot) Shields. Known issue: Thomas Cobbs, born 1723 in Buckingham County, Virginia, died June 1833 in Columbia County, Georgia; Ambrose Cobbs, died 1783 in Chesterfield County, Virginia;[90] and Matthew Cobbs.

Thomas Cobbs (1723-1833) married Susannah Moon on 7 January 1756, a daughter of Jacob Moon and his wife, Mildred (Cobb) Moon. His LWT was dated 9 April 1831, and probated on 3 June 1833 in Columbia County, Georgia. In this document he stated (about his children) "I outlived them all!". Known issue: Thomas Cobbs, Jr., born 1754 in Virginia, died 13 January 1816 in Columbia County, Georgia,[91] married Catherine Moon; John Cobbs, born 1757 in Virginia, died May 1797 in Columbia County, Georgia,[92] married ca 1782, Elizabeth Beckham; and Sarah Cobbs who married John Benning.

John Cobbs was born 1757 in Virginia, died May 1797 in Columbia County, Georgia, married ca 1782 in Cumberland County, Virginia, Elizabeth Beckham, a daughter of Captain William Beckham and his wife, Catherine.[93] SEE Beckham. Issue of John Cobbs:

I.   Milly Polly Cobbs, born ca 1773 in Cumberland County, Virginia, died after 1830 in Wilkes County, Georgia, married (1) John Lyddall Dixon on 5 November 1793 and (2) Solomon Ellis, Jr. on 5 November 1793; Catherine Elizabeth Cobbs; William Cobbs; Thomas Cobbs who married Polly W. Moore on 14 May 1807; and Lewis Cobbs. SEE Beckham.

II. Lewis Cobbs.

---

[87] LWT of Thomas Cobbs dated 1756, probated 17 September 1750 in York County, Virginia. Thomas Cobbs granted 1,110 acres of land to his sons, Thomas, Ambrose and Matthew in Chesterfield County, Virginia in 1752.

[88] Frances, Robert, John and Edmund Cobbs were named in the LWT of her father, Ambrose Cobbs.

[89] The LWT of Thomas Cobbs dated 1736, probated 17 September 1750 in York County, Virginia. His wife, Mary Shields, was named in the LWT of her father, James Shields, 1727 in York County, Virginia.

[90] The LWT of Ambrose Cobbs, dated 1783 in Chesterfield County, Virginia.

[91] Augusta Chronicle dated 16 February 1816 published the death notice of Thomas Cobbs, Jr. "died 13 January 1816, age 52." Thomas Cobbs, Jr. was named as one of the heirs of Jacob Moon, deceased, in Buckingham County, Virginia.

[92] LWT of John Cobbs dated 26 December 1796, probated 29 May 1797 in Columbia County, Georgia, naming his wife, Elizabeth, and their children.

[93] Elizabeth was named in the LWT of her father, Captain William Beckham, recorded 5 November 1812 in Columbia County, Georgia. He also named his grandchildren. Issue: Thomas, Lewis and Catherine Cobbs.

III.   Thomas Cobbs.

IV.   Catherine Cobbs.

Coles of England and Savannah

Robert Coles was born ca 1655 in London, England. Wife, Elizabeth. Issue:

Joseph Coles was christened on 30 May 1679 in St. Botolph's, Bishopsgate in London, England. Wife, Mary. Issue:

Joseph Coles was christened February 1704 in St. Botolphs without Aldgate in London, England, died 4 March 1734/1735 in Savannah, Chatham County, Georgia. He embarked onboard Oglethorpe's first ship to the Georgia Colony, *the Ann*, on 6 November 1732, arriving in Savannah on 1 February 1733. "Joseph Coles, aged 28, Miller and Baker, Lot 27, Savannah. Reported dead on 4 March 1734 or 1734." Two years' later he was dead.

Joseph Coles was married to Anna Cassells, who was christened on 17 November 1706 in Edinburgh Parish, Midlothian, Scotland, died 1753 in Savannah, married the daughter of John Cassels and his wife, Christian (Wilke) Cassells. After Joseph's death, Anna married Thomas Salter, on 9 September 1736 in Savannah. Thomas Salter arrived in the colony in 1733 and obtained Lot No. 68 in Savannah. On 17 December 1741, Thomas Salter obtained a land grant of 136 acres on Dawbuss' Island, later naming it *Salter's Island*. He was a brickmaker and used the clay on that island to make bricks for the colonists. It was located about three miles south of Savannah. He also owned 500 acres of land on Hutchinson's Island, known as *Deptford Plantation*, which plantation was willed to his grandson, William Thomas Harris, in 1749.

The following deed from Daniel Demetre, Mariner, to Ann Harris, widow, dated 1 April 1752 at Frederica:

> "And whereas, Thomas Salter, late of Savannah, aforesaid, saddler,
> deceased, in and by his Will and Testament in writing duly executed
> bearing date (blank) did give and devise unto the said Anna Salter and
> the said Ann Harris all that his town lott in Savannah with the lands
> thereto appeartaining, they paying off the mortgage which was then
> on the premises (which the said Ann Harris has since discharged); Now
> the said Anna Salter and Ann Harris, for the considerations herein
> before specified, do and each of them doth likewise covenant and grant
> to and with the said James Habersham, Noble Jones and Thomas
> Rasberry and their heirs, and the said town lott and premises, last
> mentioned, and every part and parcel thereof from and immediately after
> the solemnization of the said marriage (between Daniel Demetre and Ann
> Harris, widow) shall be and enure and is hereby intended to be settled and
> assured to the use of the said Anna Salter and her assigns during her
> widowhood, and from and after the death or marriage of said Anna Salter
> (which shall first happen) to the use of the said Daniel Demetre and Ann
> (Harris), his wife, and their assigns during their joint lives and on the life of
> the longer liver of them." [94].

---

[94] Deed Book C-1 of the Colonial Conveyances of Georgia, pages 40-41 from Daniel Demetre, Mariner, to Ann Harris, widow, dated 1 April 1752 at Frederica:

Anna (Cassells) Salter, widow of Thomas Salter, deceased, of Frederica, made her Last Will and Testament dated 19 December 1753. (Colonial Wills). She named her grandson, William Thomas Harris (in care of my daughter, Ann Demetre, until he is age 21), to son-in-law, Daniel Demetre.

Issue:[95]

Anne Coles was born 1723 in England, born 1723 in London, England, and died 1759 in Savannah, Chatham County. She married (1) ca 1737 in the Georgia Colony, William Harris, who died ca 1742 and by him had William Thomas Harris. She married (2) Daniel Demetre of St. Simon's Island, Georgia. Anne Coles Harris Demetre was a very enterprising merchant lady who accumulated wealth during the difficult colonial days. SEE Harris.

Collins of Maryland, South Carolina, Cobb & Paulding Counties

Joseph Collins born in Maryland ca 1730, and removed to Camden District, South Carolina about 1768. A deed for him, recorded in South Carolina Deed Book 4, page 410-411, as follows:

<u>Lease and Release", proved 6 October 1773, recorded 23 March 1774</u>

"Joseph Collins of the Province of Georgia to Thomas Bettey of Camden District, South Carolina, St. Marks Parish, for 10 pounds, 100 acres in Amelia Township which was granted to said Joseph Collins on 1 July 1768." /s/ Joseph Collins /s/ Ann Collins, relinquished dower. Witnesses: Thomas Singleton, William Collins and Jonathan Drake.

His wife, Ann, was born 1740-1750, and is believed to be residing with her grandson, John Collins, Jr., on the 1840 Cobb County Census. Further information on Joseph has not been located. According to his son, John E. Collin's statements when he applied for a pension, John E. left Camden District and settled in Georgia about 1782. Joseph Collins, just prior to the Revolutionary War, appears to have been in Georgia; when, after the war, he was apparently at his home in Camden District, South Carolina. There was a Joseph Collins listed on the 1790 South Carolina Census in Lancaster County, Camden District – 1 male over 16, 1 male under 16, 1 female over 16. There was another Joseph Collins listed in York County, Camden District, 2 males over 16, 5 males under 16, and 4 females.

John E. Collins, is believed to be a son of Joseph and Ann Collins. John E Collins was born 9 December 1760 in Frederick County, Maryland, died 8 March 1851 in Acworth, Cobb County, buried in the Mars Hill Cemetery near Acworth. At the time of his enlistment in the Revolutionary War, he lived in Camden District, South Carolina (with his father). He served as a Captain in the South Carolina Militia during the Revolutionary War. About four years after the war, he removed to Franklin County where he lived for eighteen years (until 1813); then removed to Cobb County.[96]

---

[95] <u>A List of Early Settlers to Georgia</u> by Coulter; Colonial Deeds & Wills.

[96] Comments__ The South Carolina branch of the Collins' family to Cobb County shares a longevity trend. The fact that John Collins removed from Camden District, South Carolina about 1786 and was married in Burke County, Georgia, could explain that some children remained in South Carolina, while others came to Georgia. In this event, probably all of this males listed on the 1840-1850 Cobb County Census were his children. Buried in the same cemetery with John and Phoebe Collins (Mars Hill Cemetery, Acworth) were: Felix, Isabella, and Daniel Collins. The 1820 Cobb County Census shows 3 daughters and 4 sons living at

John Collins was married to Phoebe Sailors on 20 November 1789 in Burke County.[97] SEE Sailors. Some of his children may have been ....John E. Collins, his wife, Charles Singleton and wife, Felix Collins, and the Samuel Collins families resided next door to one another in Cobb County (20th District), 1850 Census.

The Cobb County Estate Records list "John Collins, 1850-1852" and "Francis Collins, 1852". His pension for Revolutionary War Service was dated in Hall County on 27 January 1832. He fought against the Cherokee Indians on the South Carolina frontiers; volunteered as a Private in the Militia under Capt. John McAfee for six months, then Colonel Neal's Regiment, and marched to the Seneca River (Fort Independence), having frequent skirmishes with the Cherokees along the way. In October of 1776, he went to his father's home in Camden District, South Carolina where he remained until October of 1778. Then, he enlisted as a substitute for Moses Kemp, as a Private, in Capt. Thomas Barron's Company and they marched to Brier Creek where General Ashe lay, until 17 March 1779. After that, Daniel McIntire hired him to take his place in the North Carolina Militia for three months under Capt. Benjamin Harden, Colonel Charles McDowell and Lt. Colonel Hugh Tinning; they marched to Charlotte, North Carolina, then to Savannah, Georgia where they joined the forces of General Lincoln and went to Briar Creek, to Bacon's Bridge, on the Ashley River. He served in the North Carolina Volunteers under Capt. John G. Lowman and Colonel Archibald Lytle, when he was appointed Sergeant-Major. On December (2), he was taken prisoner (fall of Charleston, and paroled at Lincoln County, North Carolina.

After being home for about two months, he was taken by a group of tories and carried to where Colonel Ferguson was located (the British) and he was thus charged with violating his parole, found guilty, and sentenced to hang. But he managed to escape, finding the American forces, then engaged himself at the Battle of Guilford, Tarleton's defeat at Cowpens, and Ferguson's defeat at Kings Mountain. Afterwards, he was sent to Henry County, Virginia, but was soon driven away by the British. He enlisted on 12 April 1781 under Colonel Penn, discharged 24 October 1781, and was at the Battle of Jamestown.

He returned to his old home community in South Carolina until March of 1782 when he volunteered to the South Carolina Militia, to serve three months as a Private; was elected Captain; then marched to Orangeburg Court House, then to Four Holes Bridge, and later to Dorchester, then Bacon's Bridge. He continued as a Captain until October of 1782.[98]

---

home. To arrive at the names of the children of Joseph E. Collins, I made a thorough comparison of the family in the Hall and Cobb County Census records, from 1820 to 1860. In each instance, the children matched.

[97] Some references indicate that John Collins married Phoebe Sailors in Burke County, Georgia. It is difficult to assume that this was in Georgia, instead of North Carolina. The reason is that Captain John Collins was still serving in the South Carolina Militia as late as 1789. The first record found of him in Georgia is 1792, when he purchased some land in Elbert County; this seems to be about the date which he first came to Georgia. The Sailors (Saylors) family migrated from Pennsylvania to Burke County, North Carolina, and then to Jackson, Madison and Paulding Counties, in Georgia. The trail of the Collins was from Maryland, to South Carolina, then to Franklin and Paulding Counties. All implications point to Phoebe's relatives being those in Madison and Paulding Counties. Therefore, until otherwise proved, I assume that the marriage took place in Burke County, North Carolina. Unfortunately, Burke County, Georgia and North Carolina county records burned.

[98] Roster of South Carolina Patriots in the American Revolution by Bobby Gilmer Moss

John Collins was found in the Elbert County deed records beginning in 1794, and thereafter was found in Franklin County where he was a Justice of the Peace in that county until about 1811. He removed to Hall County after 1823 when he was on the Franklin County books as being paid for estray horses, and before 1827, when he drew in the Land Lottery, as a Revolutionary War Soldier. [99]

Richard Collins served under Captain John Collins and Colonel Roebuck during 1780 and 1789; William D. Collins served under Captain John Collins and Colonels Thomas and Roebuck 1780-1781; lost a horse at the battle of Fish Dam Ford.

[99] Franklin County Deeds
Book KK, page 135B-136. 27 October 1794. John Collins of Elbert County sold to George Pettigrew of Franklin County for 50 pds., 188 acres adjoining Patton and Beddingfield, which was granted to John White and conveyed by him to said Collins. /s/ John Collins.

Book KK, page 141. 20 February 1794. John White of Elbert County to John Collins of Elbert County, for 50 pds., 188 acres adjoining Patton and Beddingfield, which was granted to John White and conveyed by him to said Collins.

Book L, page 9-10. 23 July 1795. John Collins of Franklin County to James Coiles for 50 pds., 200 acres in Franklin County adj. Beddingfield which was granted to John White on 3 October 1792 and conveyed by White to John Collins on 20 February 1794. (Deed Book L, page 170).

Book NN, page 57-58. 9 July 1800, James Coile (Coil) of Franklin County to John Collins of Franklin County for $40.00, 200 acres on the waters of the Hudson Fork of the Broad River in Franklin County, adj. Mackie, which was granted said Coile on 22 May 1800 by Governor James Jackson.

Book NNN, page 7-8. 18 February 1801. Andrew Burns of Columbia County to John Collins of Franklin County for $100.00, 287-1/2 acres in Franklin County, Eastanolle Creek, surveyed for Allen Brown, adj. John Tolbert, John Kelly and Isham Young which was sold for taxes in 1792.

Book PP, page 83-84. 26 November 18--. John Collins to Green Hill for $245.00, 187-1/2 acres in Franklin County on Eastanolle Creek, surveyed for Allen Brown, adj. John Tolbert, John Kelly and Isham Young which was sold for taxes in 1792.

Book TT, page 82-83. 14 August 1808. Benjamin Cooper of Franklin County to John Collins of Franklin County, $350.00, 100 acres on the Hudson River adj. land laid out for John Sanders, John Ratley, James Brock, being part of 300 acres granted Ralph Banks, 1 March 1786.

Book M, page 64. 9 November 1809. Susannah Collins to Jesse Edwards for $300.00, land on a branch of Falling Creek, 125 acres.

Elbert County Deeds
Book G, page 93. 8 December 1800. Andrew Collins and Campbell Canady and his wife, Margaret, of Abbeville, South Carolina, to Elisha Towns of Elbert County for $700.00, land on the Savannah River, 200 acres granted to the *heirs of Peter Collins, deceased.*

Book H, page 142. 11 July 1801. Elisha Towns and Ankey, his wife, to Thomas Tate, all of Elbert County, for $700.00, land on the Savannah River, 200 acres having been granted the heirs of *Richard? Collins, deceased.*

Issue:

I. James Collins, born 1785 in South Carolina. He was probably the son of a first wife, name unknown. James' wife, Mary, was born 1789 in South Carolina. They were in Georgia by 1813 and are listed on the 1834 Cobb County State Census and the 1840 and 1850 Cobb County Federal Census. Issue:

        A.   Priscilla B. Collins, born 1813 Georgia.
        B.   Temperance C. C. Collins, born 1826 Georgia.
        C.   George W. Collins, born 1844 Cobb County.

II. Charles Collins, born 1780/1790. He married Louisa Pennell on 1 November 1826 in Hall County.

III. John Collins, Jr. born 1780/1790; had an old grandmother (born 1740-1750) residing with him on the 1840 Cobb County Census. Also, he lists very young children, 2 males under 5 years old, male 5-10, male 10-15, female under 5, female 10-15, female 30-40. (Note: This John Collins was not listed on the 1850 Cobb County Census, and had children whose ages match that of Abram, Peggy Ann and Humphrey Collins). He was married to Jincy Saxon on 5 March 1831 in Hall County.

Issue:[100]

        A.   Susanna Collins, born 1824?, married Alexander Veal, and took her little brother, William, to live with her after the death of her mother. Veal was an older man who had a number of children.

        C.   Samuel Collins, born 1830 Hall County, Georgia; lived next door to the Singletons and Felix Collins (which were all dittoed as having been born in Georgia). Wife, Sarah, born 1828 Georgia. Nancy Collins, age 65, (born 1785) was living with them in Cobb County on 1850 Census. In 1860, he was a resident of Cobb County, with Louisa (born 1842), and M. J. (female), born 1860.

        D.   William Collins, born 1848 Cobb County. Listed with the Alexander Veal family (his sister, Susanna), and in 1880 his surname was listed as "Veal".

IV. Felix Collins, born 1801 in Franklin County, Georgia; may have been listed on the 1840 Cobb County Census with John. Listed on the 1850 Cobb County Census with the family of James (Luke) Singleton. Since we know that the Singletons were born in South Carolina, I am assuming that the census taker dittoed the family as having been born in Georgia instead of South Carolina). Felix Collins was born 13 May 1801, died 13 October 1873 in Cobb County,

---

Book A, page 134. 15 February 1792, Zachariah Collins to John Statham of Elbert County for 65 pds., land on the branches of Doves and Falling Creeks, 250 acres. Wife, Sarah, relinquishes her dower.

[100] Comments___-The children of John Collins, Jr. were determined by matching the 1840 list of his children with those persons who were found in Paulding County in 1850. It appears that John, Jr.'s wife died in childbirth (William, born 1848), and was found living with the Alexander Veal family in Paulding County. John, Jr. and his wife both died before 1850.

buried Mars Hill Cemetery, Acworth. In 1860, Felix Collins was listed with the family of Daniel Collins (below).

Presumably, Felix Collins had a number of children. [101]

A. Martha (Peggy Ann) Collins, daughter of Felix Collins, was born 30 October 1828 in South Carolina, died 4 May 1904 in Gwinnett, buried beside her husband in the Methodist Trinity Church Cemetery in Gwnnett County. She married Luke E. (listed as James) Singleton on 24 October 1856 in Paulding County. There is no James Singleton listed on the 1850 Georgia Census. However, the 1850 Cobb County Census, 20th District, lists "Charles Singleton 22, Cally 23, and Felix Collins, age 50, born in Georgia". The 1880 Gwinnett County Census lists him as "Luke", and Peggy Ann was listed as "Martha". The discrepancies reappear, as Martha and Luke are both shown as having been born in South Carolina, not Georgia, and their parents as having been born in South Carolina. I think that South Carolina is correct, because her father did not come to Georgia until after 1840. (There is an S. R. Singleton buried in the Old High Shoals Cemetery, Dallas, Georgia, as having died on 27 October 1878). SEE Singleton.

B. Humphrey Collins, son of Felix Collins, was born 17 September 1835 in South Carolina, and died 17 September 1885 in Dallas, Paulding County, Georgia, buried in the Dallas City Cemetery. He indicated on the 1880 Paulding County Census that both his parents were born in South Carolina.[102] He married Elizabeth

---

[101] Comments__I have been unable to track Felix's movements. He is not found on the 1830 South Carolina Census. I have tracked his father's (John, Sr.), movements through South Carolina and into Georgia. His father came to Georgia before 1800. Felix must have remained in South Carolina until about 1840. I believe that he is the one listed with his old father on the 1850 Gwinnett County Census as being between the age of 30 and 40. A woman of the same age is also listed, and two young children. A son, born 1830-1835), is probably Humphrey Collins. A daughter (born 1820-1825), is probably Martha (Peggy Ann). Martha was the only member of this family to have married in Paulding County, and since Felix Collins was listed with her on the 1850 Cobb County, Census, my conclusion is that his (Felix) wife died before 1850, and that he moved in with his daughter. That leaves a son, Humphrey, to find somewhere on the 1850 Georgia Census. I have thoroughly searched for Humphrey, in every county in Georgia and South Carolina, without any luck. There is an Abram Collins listed on the 1850 Paulding County Census, age 17. I have endeavored to trace this Abram Collins in later census records, and he is just not to be found! Abram Collins was employed as a laborer by Thomas Crayton (Craton) and listed with the family on the 1850 Paulding County Census, 832nd District, living next door to Sherwood Camp. No further records found of him. It is somewhat logical to assume that Humphrey and Abram Collins are one and the same persons. Repeating myself....Martha married in Paulding County, Abram was listed on the 1850 Census, Humphrey married in Paulding County and was first found on the 1860 Paulding County Census. Abram's age is shown as "17". Humphrey was "15" in 1850. However, the exactness of age does not concern me, because of the fact that throughout all the census records where this family resided, the ages vary anywhere from 3 to 5 years difference. When comparing these census ages with the actual tombstone inscriptions, again, a glaring difference emerges.

[102] Comment__ I searched high and low for Humphrey Collins on the 1850 Census of South Carolina and Georgia. However, after 40 years of researching this family, it is my opinion that Abram Collins, age 17, born in South Carolina, working for the family of Thomas Craton

Bone (born 1840 Madison County, died before 1885 Dallas, Georgia), the daughter of Bailey Bone and his wife, Nancy (Evans) Bone. SEE Bone.

Issue of Humphrey Collins:

1. Thomas M. Collins, son of Humphrey Collins, was born 25 July 1856 McPherson, Paulding County, died of cancer on 3 March 1903 in Ben Hill, Fulton County, Georgia, buried in the Dallas City Cemetery. He married on 26 December 1875 Nancy Carrie Lane, the daughter of James C. Lane and his wife, Nancy (Williams) Lane in Paulding County. After his death, Nancy married (2) Isaac Pace, on 24 January 1896, in Paulding County. Nancy was born 4 May 1851 in Paulding County, died 15 October 1940 Paulding County, buried in the Dallas City Cemetery. The obituary of Nancy Carrie (Lane) Collins, as follows:

"Mrs. Carrie Collins of Blanton Road, Ben Hill, died yesterday. She was 88. Surviving are a daughter, Mrs. Ida Wiley, and a sister, Mrs. Judie Butler. Rites will be held at 11:00 this morning at the Chapel of J. Allen Couch Funeral Home with the Rev. George W. Cox and Rev. Marcus D. Drake officiating. Burial will be in Mt. Olivet Cemetery, near Dallas, Georgia." Atlanta Constitution, 16 October 1940. Issue:

a. Ida Genette Collins, born 5 November 1876 McPherson, Paulding County, died 27 August 1961 Dallas, Georgia, buried in the City Cemetery at Dallas, Georgia. She married (1) on 20 August 1899, Radford L. Johns, in Paulding County and (2) Marshall Oscar Wiley. She raised her sister's children (Willie Florence), after her death. SEE Johns.

L-R: Ida Collins Johns;
Nancy Carrie Lane

b. John Thomas Collins, born 17 December 1881 McPherson, Paulding County, died 31 October 1936 in Paulding County, buried in the Mt. Olivet Cemetery, Paulding County. He married Laura Rebecca Jeffries. Issue:

1-Helen Louise Collins, born 9 April 1913 in Dallas, Paulding County, died 20 November 1968 in Atlanta, Fulton County, buried in the Mt. Olivet Cemetery in Dallas. She married William Morgan. Issue: Charles and Dorothy Morgan.
2-Florence Genette Collins, born 29 September 1914 in Atlanta, Fulton County. She married on 23 June 1937, William Carl Foster. They were residents of Atlanta.
3-Margaret Mazeppe Collins, born 25 June 1916 in Dallas, Paulding County, married James Bartow Lowry. Issue: Patricia Lowry, born 15 April 1941 in Atlanta, Fulton County; James

---

(Craton) as a laborer, listed on the 1850 Paulding County Census was Humphrey Collins. Apparently, Abram belongs as a first or second name.

Bartow Lowry, born 30 December 1946 in Atlanta, Fulton County; and Eddie Joe Lowry, born 5 November 1952 in Atlanta, Fulton County.

c. Willie Florence Collins, born 1 September 1884 in McPherson, Paulding County, died 7 October 1914 in McPherson, buried at the High Shoals Church Cemetery in Paulding County. She married on 2 December 1900, James Tom Holland, in Paulding County. The family had just moved into a newly constructed house in McPherson, Georgia, adjacent to the railroad tracks, when Willie climbed into bed one night, and was bitten by a wharf rat. The came down with fever, and died.

2. Louisiana A. Collins, daughter of Humphrey Collins, was born 22 September 1858 McPherson, Paulding County, died 2 February 1898, Paulding County, buried in the Dallas City Cemetery. She married on 14 May 1876, W. H. Johns, in Paulding County.

3. John Collins, son of Humphrey Collins, was born 18 December 1860 McPherson, Paulding County, died 9 September 1862, Dallas, Paulding County, buried in the Dallas City Cemetery.

4. William M. Collins, son of Humphrey Collins, was born 12 September 1863 McPherson, Paulding County, died 17 October 1886 in Paulding County, buried Dallas City Cemetery.

5. Katie E. Collins, daughter of Humphrey Collins, was born 1876 Paulding County, married on 14 August 1895, F. M. Bell, in Paulding County.

6. Mattie Collins, daughter of Humphrey Collins, was born 1882 in Paulding County, married (1) on 28 June 1903, W. M. Wood, in Paulding County (2) on 7 July 1922, J. W. Hindman in Paulding County.

7. Infant son of Humphrey Collins.

V.   Daniel Collins was born 13 June 1813 Hall County, Georgia, died 8 August 1890 Cobb County, buried in the Mars Hill Cemetery. In 1860, the value of his real estate was $7000.00, which is substantial, for that time period. Wife, Isabella, born 1828 Georgia. He married (2) Mary Frances Buchanan (born 1841 in Georgia) in 1859. He is listed on the 1880 Cobb County Census, stating that *his father was born in Maryland*. Issue:[103]

A. George D. Collins, born 1847 Cobb County. He married Laura Gragg on 6 March 1870 in Cobb County. The LWT of John Gragg dated 13 February 1883, probated 8 February 1890 in Cobb County named wife, Livey, and Issue: Mary Ann Avery and

---

[103] 1840-1860 Cobb County Census; Burke County Marriages; Revolutionary War Pension Application #W6735 of John Collins; 1880 Gwinnett County Census; 1880 Paulding County Census; Hall County Marriages; 1820-1830 Hall County Census; Dallas City Cemetery, Paulding County; Bible in possession of Mrs. Florence Foster, Atlanta, Georgia (1960); High Shoals Baptist Church Cemetery, Paulding County; personal bibles and records of Jeannette Holland Austin

Jane Collins; son-in-law, George S. Avery. The LWT of George S. Avery was dated 12 February 1902, and probated May 1904, naming wife, Mary. (Witnesses were: D. H. Collins and J. F. Collins.)

B.   J. F. Collins, born 1852 Cobb County.
C.   J. S. Collins, born 1855 Cobb County.
D.   Hettie B. Collins, born 1865 Cobb County.
E.   Thomas F. Collins, born 1868 Cobb County.
F.   Jessie Collins, born 1871 Cobb County.
G.   Lena Collins, born 1874 Cobb County.

VI.   Richard R. Collins, born 1818 Hall County. Wife, Emeline, born 1826 Ga. Issue:

A.   Sarah B. D. Collins, born 1845.
B.   Elescander Collins (male), born 1847.
C.   Prucilla E. Colliins, born 1848.

VII.   Daughter, born 1804/1810, listed on 1820 Hall County Census.

VIII.   Priscilla Collins, born 1804/1810, listed on 1820 Hall County Census. She married Jarrett Gambling on 4 August 1836 in Hall County.

IX.   Sarah Collins, born 1794-1804, listed on 1820 Hall County Census. She married Granville Thompson on 18 November 1825 in Hall County.

Conger of New Jersey, Gwinnett and Cobb Counties

The name in America was "Belconger", which the family used in England and New Jersey. Benjamin Conger of Woodbridge, Middlesex County, New Jersey changed his name to "Conger" and that is how the name is registered in the Georgia records.

The parish registers in St. Peters Parish, Brooke, Norfolk County, England, list several generations of Belconger, beginning with William Belconger who married in 1575 Ann Ward and had issue: Thomas Belconger, chr 30 May 1578; Katern Belconger, chr 30 August 1579; Elizabeth Belconger, chr. 15 November 1580; Jeffery Belconger, chr 7 March 1584; Judith Belconger, chr. 26 March 1585; William Belconger, chr. 19 June 1586; Ann Belconger, chr. 12 June 1588; John Belconger, chr. 1 September 1589 (married Elizabeth); Antony Belconger, chr. 11 October 1590; and Margery Belconger, chr. 14 January 1592, all in St. Peter's Parish.

John Belconger (above), chr. 1 September 1589 in St. Peter's Parish and his wife, Elizabeth, had issue. Their children are listed in the Great Yarmouth Parish Register in Norfolk, England, as follows: Mary Belconger, chr. 20 November 1616 (married on 26 June 1636 William Curtis); Thomas Belconger, chr. 23 August 1618; Jeffery Belconger, chr. 26 Decer 1619; Judith Belconger, chr. 17 March 1621; Martha Belconger, chr. 17 February 1626; Sarah Belconger, chr. 2 January 1630 (married Valentine Rosse on 19 August 1659); John Belconger, born 8 September 1633, died August 1717 in Woodbridge, Middlesex County, New Jersey.

The emigrant to America was John Belconger (above), born 8 September 1633 in Great Yarmouth, Norfolk, England, died August 1717 in Woodbridge, Middlesex County, New Jersey. He married (1) Mary Kelly on 12 April 1666 (2) Sarah Cawood ca 1689. Sarah Cawood may have been a daughter of Thomas Cawood, Sr. whose inventory of Estate is mentioned

1748 in Middlesex County, New Jersey, his LWT dated 1747. The LWT of John Conger is dated 27 August 1712 Middlesex County, New Jersey.[104]
Issue by (2) wife:

I.   Enos Belconger, born 1687 Middlesex County, New Jersey.

Issue by 2d wife:

II. Joseph Belconger, born 17 May 1692 in Woodbridge, Middlesex County, New Jersey.

III. Lydia Belconger, born 28 April 1698 Woodbridge, Middlesex County, New Jersey.

IV. Benjamin Belconger, born ca 1700 in Woodbridge, Middlesex County, New Jersey, died 10 March 1762 in Morristown, Morris County, New Jersey. He married Experience Ford (born 1702/3 Morristown, New Jersey, died 29 September 1784) ca 1728. Experience was a daughter of John Ford (born 1675) and his wife, Elizabeth Freeman (born 21 March 1681). Benjamin Conger's LWT dated 10 May 1762 Morris County, New Jersey. "Being eighteen years of age, Experience Ford received fifty pounds by her father's will dated 20 October 1721." This establishes her birthdate as 1702/1703, although the Conger Family of America indicates that she was born in 1711.
   Issue:

A.   Daniel Conger, son of Benjamin Conger, was born 1728 Morristown, Morris County, New Jersey, died 1 May 1795 same place, married Mary (ca 1755). Their death dates are recorded in the book, *Presbyterian and Baptist Records of Morristown*, published in 1806. Issue:

   1.   Abigail Conger, daughter of Daniel Conger, married Nathan Guerin on 1 February 1775. She is mentioned in the LWT of her grandfather, Benjamin Conger, dated 1762, Morris County.

   2.   Benjamin Conger, son of Daniel Conger, was born 1757 in Morristown, Morris County, New Jersey, died 21 December 1841 in Cobb County, Georgia. He was mentioned in the LWT of his grandfather, Benjamin Conger, dated 1762, Morris County. Wife, Rachel (married ca 1785). He fought in the American Revolution, his pension application being dated 1 September 1833 in Gwinnett County, Georgia. The widow's application of Mrs. Rachel Conger is dated 1845 in Cobb County. The Conger Cemetery is located on Powder Springs Road, 7 miles from Marietta. No markers. Issue:
         a.   Simeon Conger, born 6 October 1789 in Rockingham County, North Carolina, died after 1851. He married Jane Vowell on 17 September 1812. He made application for the benefits of the Revolutionary War Pension of his father, "for the benefit of his sister, Abigail."

---

[104] Middlesex County, New Jersey Wills; Great Yarmouth Parish Register, Norfolk, England; St. Peter's Parish Register, Norfolk, England; Conger Family of America (1973) by Helen Maxine Crowell Leonard; Morris County, New Jersey Wills; 1800-1820 Pendleton District, South Carolina Census; 1830 Gwinnett County Census; 1850 Cobb County Census; 1860 Cherokee County Census; Gwinnett County Families 1818-1968 by Alice S. McCabe, Paulding County Will Book E (1878-1884), page 17, Inventory of the Estate of Abigail Stegall, deceased.

b. Jonas Conger, born ca 1794 in Rockingham County, North Carolina, died 29 December 1836 in Gwinnett County, Georgia. He married Parthena Pelfrey on 28 December 1816. Georgia, Gwinnett County, Application for land, 28 September 1850, of Mrs. Parthenia Conger, widow of Jonas Conger. Part of this application is the affidavit of Bira Stegall, the husband of Abigail Conger Stegall, stating that he was at the wedding of Jonas Conger. Parthenia was born 1793 in Virginia, and was a widow on the 1850 Cobb County Census. Issue:

    i. Simeon Washington Conger, born ca 1820 Pendleton District, South Carolina, died 8 February 1872, married Eliza Ann McKinney.

    ii. Benjamin Simeon Conger, born 1824 Gwinnett County, Georgia.

    iii. Anna Conger, born 1827 in South Carolina.

    iv. Zachariah Conger, born 12 March 1829 Gwinnett County, died 11 November 1901. He married Pamela Davenport.

c. Abigail Conger, born 1804 Pendleton District, South Carolina, died 9 August 1878 in Paulding County, buried at the High Shoals Baptist Church, in Dallas, Georgia. She married ca 1824 Bira (Birdwell) Stegall and removed to Paulding County.

d. Zachariah Conger, born ca 1805 Pendleton District, South Carolina, died 1849/1850 in Cobb County. Wife, Mary (born 1803 in North Carolina, listed as a widow with children on the 1850 Cobb County Census. Issue:

    i. George B. Conger, born 1833.

    ii. Narcissa Conger, born 1830.

    iii. William B. Conger, born 1836.

    iv. Adaline Conger, born 1838.

    v. Laura A. Conger, born 1844.

    vi. Emeline Conger, born 1847.

e. John Conger, born ca 1806 Pendleton District, South Carolina. Wife, Mary.

3. Jonas Conger, son of Daniel Conger, was born 1758 Morristown, New Jersey. He was mentioned in the LWT of his grandfather, Benjamin Conger, dated 1762, Morris County.

4. Jacob Conger, son of Daniel Conger, was born 1760 Morristown, New Jersey, died 1803 Morristown. He married Phoebe Johnson on 2 March 1787.

5. Zipporah Conger, daughter of Daniel Conger, was born 1764 Morristown, married (1) Jonathan Johnson (2) Samuel Moore. He was mentioned in the LWT of his grandfather, Benjamin Conger, dated 1762, Morris County.

B. Abigail Conger, daughter of Benjamin Conger, was born ca 1732 in Morristown, died 7 December 1810 Morristown, married (1) Simeon Goble on 23 February 1749 (2) Ebenezer Stiles.

C. Benjamin Conger, son of Benjamin Conger, married Elizabeth Goble.

D. Noah Conger, son of Benjamin Conger, was born 5 March 1743 Morristown.

E. Enoch Conger, son of Benjamin Conger, was born 10 August 1744 Morristown, died 12 October 1801, married Susanna Whitehead on 14 November 1762.

F. David Conger, son of Benjamin Conger, was chr. 12 August 1744, First Presbyterian Church, Morristown, New Jersey.

G. Lydia Conger, daughter of Benjamin Conger, was born ca 17 August 1746, died 11 December 1765, married Henry Goble.

H. Elizabeth Conger, daughter of Benjamin Conger, was born 3 March 1751 Morristown, married Benjamin Goble on 3 March 1757.

Cook of Wilkinson County

James Cook was born ca 1750 and died in 1833.. He was married to Margaret Lucile Hawthorne, a daughter of Nathaniel Hawthorne. She divorced him in 1816. Issue:

I. Judith Cook.

II. Lucia Ann Cook.

III. Tabby Cook.

IV. Benjamin Cook.

V. Henry Cook.

VI. Mary Cook, born 1769 in Effingham County, died 1847 in Appling County.

VII. James Cook, died before 1824 in Wilkinson County. Wife, Rebecca. Issue:

    A. Polly Cook, daughter of James Cook, was born 1804 in Georgia.

    B. William Marion Cook, son of James Cook, was born 1809, died before 15 April 1875, possible in Berrien County. He married (1) Nancy Vann (born 1821, died 21 July 1896) , daughter of William Vann, on 20 May 1841 in Wilkinson County. They were buried at the Cook Family Cemetery in Wilkinson County. Issue:

        1. Thomas E. Cook, son of William MarionCook, was born 1842 married Amanda Brooks, killed during the War Between the States, served in Co. D of the 57th Georgia Regiment Volunteer Army of Tennessee, Wilkinson County, Smith Guards. Killed at Vicksburg in 1863.

        2. Martha Ann Cook, daughter of William Marion Cook, was born 1845, married William H. Cauley (born 1840). Issue:

           a. Ella J. Cauley, born 1868, married W. E. Ussery.

           b. Emma E. Cauley, born 1869.

           c. William H. Cauley, born 1871.

           d. Benjamin R. Cauley, born 1877.

           e. Sara F. Cauley, born 1879.

           f. Henry J. Cauley, born 1880, married Gertrude Pharis.

        3. William Jackson Cook, son of William Marion Cook, was born 1846, died 1903, Elizabeth Gilbert, buried in the Cook Cemetery in Wilkinson County.

        4. Amos Rieley Cook, son of William Marion Cook, was born 1849, died 13 October 1881, married Emma Payne. Buried in the Cook Cemetery in Wilkinson County.

5. Benjamin Cook, son of William Marion Cook, was born 24 October 1851 in Wilkinson County, died 15 March 1896, buried in the Cook Cemetery. He married Sarah Cook (1877-1943), a cousin, the daughter of Amos and Mary (Watson) Cook. Buried in the Cook Cemetery in Wilkinson County.
6. Wade Hampton Cook, son of William Marion Cook, was born 10 July 1854, died 5 January 1942, married Fannie Smith (1853-1881), buried in the Cook Cemetery in Wilkinson County.
7. Joel Arnold Cook, son of William Marion Cook, was born 27 June 1856, died 28 January 1938, married Dollie Sarah Constance Patrick (born 30 August 1862, died 20 February 1940), buried in the Cook Cemetery in Wilkinson County. Issue:
    a. Infant sons of Joel Arnold Cook were buried in the Cook Cemetery.
    b. Ruby Lee Cook, daughter of Joel Arnold Cook, married Paul E. Yancey. Issue: Breman Yancey, Max Yancey, David Yancey, Nellie Yancey and Polly Yancey.
    c. Elliott Cook, twin son of Joel Arnold Cook, was born 22 March 1903, married Hardy B. Cannon and had issue: James, Billy, Joe, Pat Cook and Mae Cannon (1903-4 September 2004).
    d. Elberta (Mama Bert) Cook, twin daughter of Joel Arnold Cook, was born 22 March 1903, died 15 April 1897, married Floral Payne, a son of Joel Thomas Payne and his wife, Salina Ann (Butler) Payne. Issue:
        i. Glenn Payne.
        ii. Floral Payne.
        iii. Addie Mae Payne.
        iv. Willie Payne.
        ix. Carliss Payne, married Joe Taylor. Issue:
            1-Donnie Taylor married Patsy Walker and had son, Ricky Taylor (deceased).
            2-William K. Taylor, married Marion and had issue: Timothy and Sabrina Taylor.
            3-Bobby Taylor, died 1993.
            4-Freddie Taylor. No issue.
            5-Gregory Taylor. No issue.
            6-Carol Ruelene Taylor, married (1) Coleman Allen and had issue, Chris Allen, and married (2) Tim Brown and had issue: Todd Brown (issue: Michael and Jessica Brown) and Regina Brown.
        vi. Dollie Clarice Payne, married Paul Eugene Bennett. Issue:
            1-Douglas Eugene Bennett, married (1) Jeannie Stanley and had daughter, Gloria Lynn Bennett, and married (2) Janet Norris and had daughter, Kelli Paige Bennett.
            2-Joseph Ronald Bennett, married Cynthia Fennel and had issue: Chadwick Ronald Bennett and Camille Bennett.
            3-Dollie Elaine Bennett, married Dan Skedsvold, a son of Obert and Dolores Skedsvold. SEE Skedsvold.
        vii. Lindell Iona Payne married Mr. Chamblee.

e. Mattie Ruth Cook, daughter of Joel Arnold Cook, was buried in the Walnut Creek Baptist Church Cemetery, married Richard R. Spires. Issue: Gene Spires.

8. Arthur B. Cook, son of William Marion Cook, was born 1859, died 18 July 1895. Never married. Buried in the Cook Cemetery in Wilkinson County.

9. Doc Barkelou Cook, son of William Marion Cook, was born 4 July 1861, died 3 June 1935, married (1) Becky Register in June of 1882 and (2) Winnie Davison in 1898. Buried in the Cook Cemetery in Wilkinson County.

C. Tabitha Cook, daughter of James Cook, was born 1810 in Wilkinson County, Georgia, died 1890 in Hamilton County, Florida, buried in the Good Hope Baptist Church Cemetery.

D. Amos Cook, son of James Cook, was born 1814 in Georgia, farmer. He married Mary Watson, born 1816. Issue:[105]

      i. Joseph M. Cook, born 1841 in Wilkinson County.
      ii. Henry H. Cook, born 1842 in Wilkinson County.
      iii. Silas F. Cook, born 1844 in Wilkinson County.
      iv. Mary L. Cook, born 1846 in Wilkinson County.
      v. Nancy E. Cook, born 1848 in Wilkinson County, married M. M. Payne.
      vi. Missouri Cook, born 1850 in Wilkinson County, married W. H. Berry.
      vii. Sara Cook, born 1852, married Benjamin Cook.
      viii. Alex A. Cook, born 10 July 1853 in Wilkinson County, died 30 September 1929, buried in the Walnut Creek Cemetery in Wilkinson County. He married Jane Justice.
      ix. Marshall B. Cook, born 1856 in Wilkinson County.
      vi. Bessie Cook, born 1858, married William Henry Patrick Anderson.
      vii. Elizer C. Cook (daughter), born 1861 in Wilkinson County.

E. Elijah Coleman Cook, son of James Cook, was born 22 November 1816, died 15 November 1889 in Berrien County, buried in Milltown.

F. Piety Cook, daughter of James Cook, was born 22 May 1819 in Wilkinson County, died 4 February in Lanier Georgia, buried in the Empire Church Cemetery.

VIII. Nancy Cook, born 1785, died 1850 in Emanuel County.

---

[105] 1880 Wilkinson County Census, District 332.

Craton/Crayton of North Carolina and Paulding County

Samuel.Craton was born ca 1750 in North Carolina. Wife, Mary. Issue:[106]

I. Balis F. Craton, born ca 1776 in Cabarrus County, North Carolina.

II. Mary Jane Craton, born ca 1778 in Cabarrus County, North Carolina.

III. Easter Craton, born ca 1782 in Cabarrus County, North Carolina.

IV. William Craton, born ca 1784 in Cabarrus County, North Carolina.

V. Thomas Howell Craton was born 1784 in Cabarrus County, North Carolina, died 1870 in Paulding County, buried Mt. Olivet Baptist Church Cemetery, Paulding County. He married Sarah Renshaw, born 1784 in North Carolina. They were residents of Dallas, Georgia in 1860. Issue:

> A. John Weaver Craton was born 1808 in Cabarrus County, North Carolina, farmer, resident of Dallas, Georgia in 1860. He served as a soldier in the Confederate Army and died in 1864, buried in the Mt. Olivet Baptist Church Cemetery. The Craton family resided at McPherson, Georgia. Issue:
> > 1. Martha Craton, born 1839 Georgia.
> > 2. Sarah Craton, born 1843 Georgia.
> > 3. James Craton, born 1844 Georgia.
> > 4. Joseph Craton, born 1846 Georgia.
> > 5. William Craton, born 1853 Paulding County.

> B. Joshua Erwin Craton was born 14 May 1819 in Georgia, farmer, lived at Dallas. He died 25 June 1892, buried Mt. Olivet Cemetery, Paulding County. Wife, Amy, was born 11 October 1827 in Georgia, died 24 June 1880, buried Mt. Olivet Baptist Church. Issue:
> > 1. Nancy J. Craton, born 2 June 1847 Georgia, died 29 February 1927, married W. H. Adair on 12 February 1867 in Paulding County. SEE Adair.

> > 2. Sarah Craton, born 1849 Georgia.

> > 3. William I. Craton, born 19 January 1851 Georgia, died 25 July 1886, buried in the Mt. Olivet Baptist Church Cemetery. He was married on 30 November 1869 in Paulding County to Pheriby Emmaline Adair, born 23 September 1852 Dallas, Paulding County, a daughter of John Bluett Adair and his wife, Pheriby C. (Anderson) Adair. SEE Adair. Issue:

> > > a. Mary Ella Craton, born 1871 in Paulding County, married on 20 May 1894, J. V. Braswell.

> > > b. Emma C. Craton, born 1874 in Paulding County, died 1951, married 16 July 1896, Charles C. Gurley.

---

[106] 1860-1880 Paulding County Census; Paulding County. Marriages; 1880 Floyd County..

c. Cora J. Craton, born 1877 Paulding County.

d. Doctor T. Craton, born 15 September 1879 in Paulding County, died 28 October 1918. Wife, Lilly Ophelia, born 9 February 1887, died 2 January 1920, buried Mt. Olivet Baptist Church Cemetery.

e. John Henry Craton, born 29 October 1881 in Paulding County, died 30 October 1961, married Emma Ford, born 29 January 1892, died 19 December 1861, buried Mt. Olivet Baptist Church Cemetery.

Top left: Pleas Craton
Top right: James Tom Holland
Left: Henry Craton - Right: Robert Hicks

f. Joseph R. Craton, born 1884 in Paulding County, married on 22 May 1904, Ethel Atkins.
g. William Isaac Craton, born 1886 in Paulding County, died 1942, married Adaline Gann.

4. Thomas Craton, born 1853 Paulding County, Georgia.

5. Johannah Craton, born 1856 Paulding County

6. Louisa Craton, born 1860 Paulding County.

C. William Isaac Craton, born ca 1821, buried Mt. Olivet Cemetery, Paulding County.

D. Dock Craton, born 1822 in North Carolina, listed on the 1880 Floyd County, Georgia Census. Wife, Rebecca, was born 1818 in Georgia. Issue:

i. Emma Craton, born 1851 in Paulding County.
ii. Joseph A. Craton, born 1857 Paulding County.
iii. John Craton, born 1863 Paulding County.

E. Joseph P. Craton, born 22 February 1824/1825, died 23 June 1890 in Marquez, Leon County, Texas, buried in the Taylor Cemetery. He married Adaline Walston on 27 May 1849 in Paulding County. They were residents of Milam County, Texas, in 1880. Issue:
1. Lucy W. Craton, born 1871 in Milam County, Texas.
2. Ada Craton, born 1874 Milam County, Texas.

F. Sarah Reyan Craton, born 1829.

G. Jack Craton, born ca 1826.

H. Barry Craton, born ca 1828.

I. W. J. Craton, born ca 1830.

J. Martha Ann Craton, born ca 1831.

95

K. Polly Craton, born ca 1833.

Danielly of Maryland
& Hancock & Warren Counties

John Dannely was christened in the year of 1743 in the Saint Lukes Protestant Episcopal Parish, Church Hill, Queen Anne's County, Maryland, as a son of Catherine Dannely. Presumbly, he was same person as John Danielly who resided in Columbia County and died there intestate, in 1806.

In 1774, John Danelly was granted 100 acres in St. Paul's Parish (Richmond County). A Columbia County deed dated 5 August 1786 from John Danelly, John Curry, John Stapler and William Shields, sell 200 acres on Cane Creek in Columbia to Thomas Stapler for 50 pounds, being bounded by lands of Stapler and Telfair. On 19 May 1798, Thomas Stapler and his wife, Ruth, of Hancock County, sold this land to John Sanders for 250 pounds, being 364-1/2 acres on Cane Creek, "it being part of a 300-acre tract granted to said Stapler and part of John Danielly."

A Columbia County deed dated 8 May 1792 suggests (in my opinion) a legatee's deed, conveying 250 acres of a 500-acre tract located on the Great Kiokee Creek, bounded by lands of Claiborne, Castleberry and McDowell. "Thomas Ayres and his wife, Sarah, William Wright and his wife Mary, of Greene County, Francis Danelly and his wife, Elizabeth of Wilkes County, James Danielly and his wife, Bridget, William Ayres and his wife, Frances, and John Ayres and his wife, Mary, all of Columbia County, sell to John Lazenby for 200 pounds sterling...." (John Ayres married Mary Wiley on 10 March 1793 in Columbia County).

Other deed records in Columbia County during this time period (1790's) suggest that John Danielly had sons: Daniel, James, Patrick, Arthur, and possibly daughters, Sarah Ayres, Mary Wright. Since Daniel, James, Patrick, Arthur and Andrew are of the appropriate ages to be sons of John, and that they all owned lands on the Great Kiokee Creek which adjoined lands of Mr. Claiborne and William Castleberry, Sr. in Columbia County, coupled with the fact that these were the only persons with that surname in the State of Georgia during the late 1700's, I am going to rank them as children of the above John Danielly.

Issue:[107]

I.   Francis Danielly of Wilkes County. Wife, Elizabeth. A Columbia County deed dated 10 January 1795, between Samuel Brady and his wife, Mary, Thomas Brady, Margery Brady, Francis Danelly and his wife, Elizabeth, all of Warren County, sell to Robert Allen for 50 pounds, 150 acres on Whiteoak Creek, granted to the heirs of Robert Wilson, deceased, by patent dated 20 September 1796. Another deed, on 27 November 1790, of Francis Danelly and his wife, Elizabeth, of Hancock County; Samuel Brady and his wife, Margaret, to John Darsey

---

[107] Warren County Marriages; Richmond County Marriages; Bibb County Marriages; 1850 Bibb County Census; John Danielly Bible in the possession of K. W. Browning, Rt. 3, Box 300, Ashland, Alabama 36251; Columbia County Deeds & Wills; Richmond County Marriages; 1880 Clay County, Alabama Census; 1880 Crawford County, Georgia Census; 1880 Randolph County, Alabama Census; Bibb County Marriages; Richmond County Deeds; Baldwin County Marriages.

for 25 pounds, 50 acres, being part of a tract granted to William Castleberry, Sr. and by him sold to William Mangham, located on the waters of the Great Kiokee Creek, near Claiborne's.

II.   Daniel Danielly of Columbia County. He married in Richmond County, Elizabeth Prather on 10 April 1788. Elizabeth's LWT was dated 18 November 1821, probated 1 April 1822 in Columbia County. She named Mary, a daughter of her brother, Edward Prather (Edward Prather married Bathena Carroll on 26 February 1798 in Columbia County). Also, sister, Nancy Carroll (Ann Prather married John Carroll on 4 June 1792 in Columbia County). Also, sister, Nancy Prather; sister, Margaret Shaw (Margaret Prather married Charles Shaw on 15 March 1802 in Columbia County). She also named Mary McNeare and Jincy Fudge. On 11 June 1787, John Massey deeded to Daniel Dannelly of Augusta, Georgia, slaves (Bill of Sale), Richmond County Deed Book A-2, Page 24. On 31 May 1787, Henry Allison sold to Daniel Dannelly, 200 acres on Big Kiokee Creek "on which I now live", Richmond County Deed Book IG, page 115.

On 25 July 1794, Joel Dees deeded to Daniel Danelly for 100 pounds, part of a tract granted to Major Richard Call, deceased, located at the head of the Great Kiokee Creek. Another deed, dated 26 December 1798, Daniel Danelly and his wife, Elizabeth, deed to James Hamilton for $470, 200 acres of land located on the Big Kiokee Creek, originally granted to Samuel Morton and by him sold to Ebenezer Smith, and by him sold to Martha Allison, the wife of Henry Allison, and by him sold to Danielly on 30 May 1787. Another deed dated 13 June 1800, Daniel Danelly deeds to John Magrude 200 acres on Kiokee Creek for $40.00. This same tract of land is mentioned by Edward Prather, when he deeds on 8 February 1800, to William Carroll, 40 acres on the Great Kiokee Creek, which was part of a tract granted to Major Richard Call, adjoining Danielly Danielly. And finally, on 5 June 1800, Daniel Danelly and his wife, Elizabeth, deed to Edward Prather for $122, 245 acres on the Big Kiokee Creek, being part of a tract originally granted to Major Richard Call, adjoining Carroll, Danelly and Walker.

Issue:

A. Jincy Danielly, daughter of Daniel Danielly, married David Fudge on 11 January 1819 in Columbia County.

III.   James Danielly who had 135 acres on Cane Creek and on the Great Kiokee Creek. He had a 1787 land grant on Trading Road, and a land grant on Brier Creek (originally in Columbia County, later in Warren and Jefferson Counties). Columbia County deed dated 11 April 1789, James Danelly to Frederick Cobbs for 150 pounds, sold 150 acres on the Great Kiokee Creek, bounded northeast by Danelly, southwest by Warden and Hoge. Another deed, 14 December 1793, James Danelly to John Olive for 100 pounds, 150 acres on the waters of the Great Kiokee Creek, granted to Meshack Matthews on 7 August 1774, bounded northeast by Ninian Offutt Magruder, northwest by James Stewart, all sides vacant at the time of the survey. Land which was granted to James Danelly, recorded in Columbia County Deed Book MMMM, page 927 to 940, was sold to Robert Flournoy, and by him sold to Walter Stewart, all mentioned in a deed dated 25 March 1796 from George Howell of Philadelphia for Walter Stewart who owned 186,688 acres in several counties. This holding was clarified in a deed dated 30 March 1799, James Danelly to Claiborne Newsome for $600, 250 acres of land (being part of two tracts); 150 acres granted to Danelly on 5 July 1787, and 200 acres contiguous, on Trading Road, which was granted him on 6 February 1799. A deed, dated 19 May 1799, of Thomas Stapler and his wife, Ruth, of Hancock County, to Hayden Prior, for 71 pounds, 135 ½ acres of land on Cane Creek, originally granted to James Danelly and Thomas Stapler. This land was referred to again, but this time as being part of land owned by John Danielly (he owned land on Cane Creek, which must have passed to James), in a deed dated 19 May 1798

97

of Thomas Stapler and his wife, Ruth of Hancock County to John Sanders for 250 pounds, 364-1/2 acres on Cane Creek, it being part of a 300-acre tract granted to Stapler "and part of John Danelly." James Danielly also owned land in Brier Creek (later was in Warren, then Jefferson County) was mentioned in a deed dated 29 November 1796 by the tax collector made to William F. Booker in Columbia County. James was one of the executors of the estate of Fuller Spivey dated 3 December 1790 in Columbia County.

IV.   Patrick Danielly, Indian Trader, who had an illegitimate son, James, who was a minor in 1794.

V.   Arthur Danielly was born 1766 in Delaware, died in Baldwin County in 1821. Wife, Sarah, administratrix. On 28 December 1821, cash was paid to Elizabeth Danielly, $4.00. Sarah, the widow of Arthur, was listed on the 1821 Baldwin County Land Lottery. Sarah was listed on the 1850 Bibb County Census, aged 70, born in Delaware.

A.   John Danielly, son of Arthur Danielly, was born ca 1789, married Ellen Luckey on 13 June 1809 in Richmond County. "Died at Milledgeville March 31, 1818, John Danielly, a young merchant who had commanded a company in the Indian War." (Georgia newspaper records). He had a son, William J. Danielly, who married Eliza Slade on 24 January 1828 in Bibb County.

B.   Nancy Danielly, daughter of Arthur Danielly, was born ca 1800, married 31 January 1819 in Baldwin County to George W. Thompson. Listed on the 1850 Murray County Georgia Census, page 184.

C.   Arthur Danielly, Jr., son of Arthur Danielly, was born ca 1800, married Lucinda M. Brown on 16 January 1820 in Baldwin County.

D.   Eliza Danielly, daughter of Arthur Danielly, was married Alexander McGregory on 21 June 1820 in Baldwin County.

E.   James Danielly, son of Arthur Danielly, was named as an orphan in the 1821 Baldwin County Land Lottery.

F.   Mariah B. Danielly, son of Arthur Danielly, married W. E. Boren on 24 September 1829 in Bibb County.

G.   Luesa B. Danielly, daughter of Arthur Danielly, married George P. Wagnon on 11 August 1831 in Bibb County.

H.   Thomas Danielly, son of Arthur Danielly. A deed of Thomas Danielly dated 19 January 1802 in Columbia County, from James Ross, where he paid $140 for 72 acres on Greenbriar Creek, bounded by Ross, James Shields and Fuller.

VI.   Andrew Danielly was born ca 1765, probably in Maryland, died December 1822 in Warren County. He first resided in Hancock County, later removing to Warren County. He married on 29 February 1790 in Richmond County, Jane Harris, a daughter of William Thomas Harris. SEE Harris. Issue:

A   Rachel Danielly, daughter of Andrew Danielly, was born ca 1791 in Hancock County, married Henry Chambliss on 6 October 1809 in Warren County. SEE Chambliss.

B. Jane Danielly, daughter of Andrew Danielly, was born 1794 in Hancock County, died after 1853 in Bibb County. She married Samuel Chambliss on 30 May 1814 in Bibb County.

C. Arthur Danielly, son of Andrew Danielly, was born 1794 in Hancock County.

D. McDade Danielly, son of Andrew Danielly, was born 1801 in Warren County, died November 1882 in Crawford County.

E. John Danielly, son of Andrew Danielly, was born 1 April 1803 in Warren County, died 8 April 1870 in Clay County, Alabama. He married (1) Martha Castleberry on 11 March 1828 (born 6 November 1805 in Georgia, died 6 July 1845 in Monroe County) in Warren County, Georgia , and, (2) Malinda Wood (born 5 January 1828 in Georgia, died 8 February 1912 in Little River, Bell County, Texas) on 23 September 1845. In 1880, the family was listed on the Randolph County, Alabama Census.

Issue of John Danielly and Martha Castleberry:

1. Catharine Baker Danielly, daughter of John and Martha Danielly, was born 21 March 1829 in Warren County, died 6 June 1829 in Warren County.

2. Francis McDade Danielly, son of John and Martha Danielly, was born 10 July 1830 in Warren County, died on 3 May 1863 in Monroe County. He married Elizabeth Pearson on 2 November 1854.

3. Mary Jane Danielly, daughter of John and Martha Danielly, born 31 August 1833 in Warren County, died November 1869 in Monroe County.

4. Anna Danielly, daughter of John and Martha Danielly, was born 26 January 1836 in Warren County, married ca 1856, James M. Pearson.

5. Sarah Ann Danielly, daughter of John and Martha Danielly, was born 17 May 1838 in Warren County, died 9 September 1890 in Pike County. She married Steven A. Kirk.

6. Rhoda Simmons Danielly, daughter of John and Martha Danielly, was born 25 July 1840 in Warren County, died 1 March 1918, married Jasper Alexander Pruet.

7. Martha Caroline Danielly, daughter of John and Martha Danielly, was born 6 December 1842 in Warren County, died 16 September 1908. She married William A. Roberts.

8. John Andrew Danielly, son of John and Martha Danielly, was born 6 July 1845 in Monroe County, died 15 July 1916. He married Susan E. Radney (born 1850 Georgia), listed on the Clay County, Alabama Census in 1880. Issue:
   a. Frances Danielly, born 1868 in Alabama.
   b. Sarah Danielly, born 1871 in Alabama.
   c. John Danielly, born 1873 in Alabama.
   d. Rebecca Danielly, born 1876 in Alabama.

9. Susannah Frances Danielly, daughter of John and Martha Danielly, was born 6 July 1845 in Monroe County, died 2 May 1882 in Monroe County. She married Wilburn Rountree Pruet on 12 September 1867.

Issue of John Danielly and Malinda Wood:

10. Penelope Elizabeth Danielly, daughter of John and Malinda Danielly, was born 25 October 1846 in Monroe County, died 7 June 1889. She married William Young Norman on 16 November 1869.

11. Eliza Ann Danielly, daughter of John and Malinda Danielly, was born 16 October 1849 in Randolph County, Alabama, died 28 July 1872 in Randolph County. She married Henry Mackay Hearn on 19 December 1865.

12. Allen Cleaveland Danielly, son of John and Malinda Danielly, was born 29 August 1851 in Randolph County, Alabama, died 22 November 1900 in Randolph County. He married (1) Virginia Radney, and, (2) Mrs. Lula Still.

13. Josephine America Danielly, daughter of John and Malinda Danielly, was born 12 June 1853 Randolph County, Alabama, died 30 June 1924 in Randolph County. She married Henry Mackay Hearn on 15 January 1874.

14. Mahala Bethany Danielly, daughter of John and Malinda Danielly, was born 25 May 1855 in Randolph County, Alabama, died 30 May 1925 in Randolph County, Alabama.

15. Charity Malinda Danielly, daughter of John and Malinda Danielly, was born 13 April 1857 in Randolph County, Alabama, died 30 September 1862 in Randolph County.

16. Nancy Aldora Danielly, daughter of John and Malinda Danielly, was born 3 December 1859 in Randolph County, Alabama, died 12 July 1935 in Randolph County. She married Francis Glover McCain on 8 December 1875.

17. Jackson Danielly, son of John and Malinda Danielly, was born 3 October 1862 in Randolph County, Alabama, died 13 November 1881 in Randolph County.

18. Levisa Wilson Danielly, daughter of John and Malinda Danielly, was born 18 November 1865 in Randolph County, Alabama, died 6 December 1937 in Randolph County. She married (1) George Washington Barto Huggins on 30 December 1886, and, (2) John Henry Huckabee on 5 December 1895.

F. Ann Danielly, daughter of Andrew Danielly, was born ca 1804 in Warren County.

G. Arthur Danielly, son of Andrew Danielly, was born 1805 in Warren County, married 2 January 1828 in Warren County, Jane Kinsey (born 1806 in Georgia). Issue:

1. Daughter, born 1829.
2. Andrew Danielly, born 1830.
3. John Danielly, born 1836.
4. Missouri Danielly, born 1840.

5. Eliza Danielly, born 1844.
6. Louisa Danielly, born 1847.
7. Sophronia Danielly, born 1850.

H. Francis F. Danielly, son of Andrew Danielly, was born 1808 in Warren County, died ca 1861. He married Mary Sullivan in Monroe County. SEE Sullivan. Issue:
1. William F. Danielly, born 1835 Georgia.
2. John M. Danielly, merchant, born 1828 Georgia, a resident of Monroe County. Wife, Mary Josephine. (born 19 January 1834, died 8 October 1866, buried in the Battle Cemetery in Monroe County). In 1850, he resided in the household of Dr. A. J. Simmons in Monroe County. Issue:
    a. Needham Danielly, born 1843 Monroe County.
    b. Martha E. Danielly, born 1845 Monroe County.
    c. John A. Danielly, born 1849 Monroe County..
    d. William Asbury Danielly, born and died 1 January 1857 in Monroe County, buried in the Battle Family Cemetery.

I. Mary B. Danielly, daughter of Andrew Danielly.

J. Nancy A. Danielly, daughter of Andrew Danielly.

K. Andrew J. Danielly, son of Andrew Danielly, was the Clerk of the Court in Crawford County (1880 Census).

L. Zachariah B. Danielly, son of Andrew Danielly.

M. Francis M. Danielly, son of Andrew Danielly.

Davis of Monroe & Bibb Counties

Gardner Lemuel Davis was born on 5 February 1817 in Germany[108] and died 2 May 1891 in Monroe County, buried in the Parker Cemetery at Lizella, Georgia. He married on 17 June 1838 in Bibb County, Mary G. Chambliss (born 1 February 1814 Warren County, died 27 February 1887 Bibb County), a daughter of Henry Chambliss and his wife, Rachel (Danielly) Chambliss. SEE Chambliss. Issue:[109]

I. Mary Jane Davis, born 2 September 1837 in Monroe County, died 24 February 1887 in Crawford County, buried in the Salem Church Cemetery. She married William James Dent. SEE Dent.

II. Rachel Sophronia Davis, born 1841 in Monroe County, married A. J. Williams.

---

[108] The 1880 Census of Bibb County, District 1085, indicates that Abe Davis' parents were born in Germany.

[109] Parker Cemetery, Monroe County; Bibb County Marriages; Salem Church Cemetery, Crawford County; personal records of Mrs. Jodie Huffaker, 5424 Ridgedale, Dallas, Texas; 1850-1860 Monroe County Census.

III. Abram Josephus Davis, born 25 February 1843 in Monroe County, died 18 February 1911, buried in the Parker Cemetery at Lizella, Georgia. He married Mary Jane Elizabeth Parker, born 29 March 1849 in Bibb County, died 16 October 1910 in Bibb County, a daughter of John Brantley Parker and his wife, Eliza (Chambliss) Parker. SEE Parker and Chambliss. Abe Davis was a grocer, and resided in Bibb County. Issue:[110]

    A. Gardner Davis, born 1869 in Bibb County.
    B. Johnny Davis, born 1871 in Bibb County.
    C. Willie Davis, born 1874 in Bibb County.
    D. Jodie Davis, born 1866 in Bibb County.
    E. Jane Davis, born February 1877 in Bibb County, died same date, buried in the Parker Cemetery, Lizella, Georgia.
    F. Tommie Davis, born 1878 in Bibb County.
    G. Infant, unnamed, born and died on 27 August 1880 in Bibb County, buried in the Parker Cemetery, Lizella, Georgia.

IV. Henry Gardner Davis, born 18 May 1845 in Monroe County, died 8 October 1885. He married Eliza Brown.

V. Sarah (or Annie Davis), born 1850 in Monroe County.

VI. Mary Emma Davis, born 28 September 1868 in Monroe County, died 22 November 1883.

VII. Sally Davis, born September 1869 in Bibb County, married James Robert Hicks.

Dean of Talbot County

Reverend John Thomas Dean was married on 21 August 1873 to Mary Antionette "Nettie" Chambliss, born 15 November 1854 in Talbot County, died 6 June 1945, buried in the Dean Cemetery, near Tyler, Texas. Issue:

I. Martha Frances Dean, born 14 December 1874, died 3 August 1876.

II. Anne Lou Dean, born 10 September 1876, died 28 September 1947.

III. William Walters Dean, born 14 November 1877, died 10 May 1947.

IV. Thomas Dean, born 17 March 1880, died 20 April 1880.

V. Francis Claude Dean, born 28 August 1881, died 8 March 1954.

VI. Nettie Dean, born 26 September 1883.

VII. Clara Dean, born 19 November 1885.

VIII. Bettie Eunice Dean, born 16 March 1888, died 27 November 1965.

IX. Lucy Dean, born 5 June 1890, died 18 November 1893.

X. Ruth Dean, born 22 January 1893.

---

[110] 1880 Census, Bibb County, District 1085.

XI.   Cecil Henry Dean, born 1 June 1895.

XII.   Jessie Martin Dean, born 13 September 1897, died 7 February 1900.

Delk of South Carolina;
Laurens & Wilkinson Counties

Elisha Delk, the son of Kindred Delk of Barnwell County, South Carolina) and his wife, Mary, was born 1792 in Barnwell County, and died 1837 in Wilkinson County, Georgia. He was listed on the 1820-1830 Wilkinson County Census. At the time of his death, guardians were appointed by the court over the orphan children, viz: Seaborn, Elafair, Daniel and Winna (Wineford) Delk. Issue:[111]

I.   Thomas Delk, born 1808 in South Carolina, resided in Laurens County, Georgia as early as 1840. Wife, Dorcas (born 1803 in South Carolina), widowed in 1870. Issue:

  A. Burrell Delk, born 1840 in Georgia.
  B. Martha Delk, born 1843 in Georgia.
  C. Mary Delk, born 1845 in Wilkinson County.
  D. James Delk, born 1845 in Wilkinson County.
  E. Robert Delk, born 1852 in Wilkinson County, farm laborer, residing with his mother at Burgamies, Georgia, in 1880..

II.   David Delk married Frances McLendon on 11 August 1825 in Wilkinson County. [112]

III.   Benjamin Delk.

IV.   Lucretia Delk married Almarire Marshall on 19 July 1838 in Wilkinson County.

V.   Daniel Delk, born 1826, listed on the 1850 Laurens County Census.

---

[111] 1850-1860 Wilkinson County Census; Wilkinson County Marriages; Wilkinson County Court of Ordinary, Minute Book A (1835-1858):

January Term, 1838 – Elisha Delk Estate. Letters of Administration issued to Warren Shiver and A. E. Payne; November Term, 1840 – Benjamin Delk, ward. William R. Smith appoinited his guardian; May Term, 1841 – Elisha Delk Estate. Robert Rozar, administrator, leave to sell Negroes, viz...Hannah, Abram, Jane, Anny and John; March Term, 1842 – Elisha Delk Estate. David C. Butler appointed guardian for Elafair Delk; Martin V. Allen appointed guardian for Daniel Delk; May Term, 1842 – Winna Delk, orphan. William L. Smith appointed guardian; September Term, 1847 – William B. Smith appointed guardian of Seaborn Delk; January Term, 1848 James Waters appointed guardian for Elafair Delk; July Term, 1850 – Elisha Delk Estate. Robert Rozar has fully administred the estate and settled with the distributes; dismissed.

[112] The LWT of Mason McLendon dated 25 September 1826 (Wilkinson County Will Book 1817-1860), names his Mother: Mary Brooks, one negro boy named Isaac, etc. After her death to be divided between John Barnett, Solom B. Murphy and David Delk. Bro-in-law: John Barnett, one negro girl named Nina and one negro boy named Hall. Bro-in-law: David Delk, one negro woman named Dilcey and her children, Elizabeth and Daniel. Nephew: Morton N. Murphy. Niece: Frances Louisa Murphy, one negro man, York and one named Martin. Exrs: Mason McLendon, Samuel Beall.

VI.   Lucy Delk married Niel Pittman on 25 August 1832 in Wilkinson County.

VII.   Wineford Delk, born 10 March 1829, died 18 February 1911 in Laurens County. She was orphaned when about 7 years of age, and her occupation was that of a wever. In 1850 Laurens County, she had one child, Martha Delk, born 1846 in Laurens County. In 1870 Laurens County, two children were listed, viz: Martha, and James Delk (born 1854 in Laurens County). About 1861, she married B. Austin Kilpatrick and had other children. SEE Kilpatrick. In 1920, she was residing in the home of her unmarried daughter in Laurens County, Wineford Patrick "Gennie" and was listed as aged 88 years old.[113]

VIII.   James Delk, born 1826, listed on the 1850 Laurens County Census. Wife, Catherine, borb 1830. Issue:
  A.   Margaret Delk, born 1847 in Laurens County.
  B.   Nancy Delk, born 1849 in Laurens County.

IX.   Elafair Delk, born 1837 in Wilkinson County,

X.   Seaborn Delk married Teresa Catherine Coats, the daughter of Robert Coates in Lauren County, on 14 July 1831.

Dent of Bibb & Crawford Counties

John Washington Dent was born ca 1820 in Georgia. Wife, Elizabeth Hoy. Listed on the 1850 Crawford County Census. Issue:

William James Dent was born 16 October 1841 in Bibb County, died 28 August 1929 in Roberta, Crawford County, buried in the Roberta Cemetery. He married (1) Mary Jane Davis (2) Mrs. Anna E. Dickson Holton on 15 December 1887, and (3) Mrs. Ida Dennis on 29 November 1910. Mary Jane Davis was born 2 September 1837 in Bibb County, died 24 February 1887 in Crawford County, buried in the Salem Church Cemetery, Crawford County, a daughter of Gardner Lemuel Davis and his wife Mary G. (Chambliss) Davis. SEE Davis and Chambliss. Issue:

I.   Walter Braxton Dent, born 23 November 1861 in Crawford County, Georgia, died in Miami, Florida.

II.   Cynthia Ida Blanche Dent, born 23 November 1863 in Crawford County, Georgia, married J. W. McGee on 14 January 1883.

III.   John Washington Dent, born 24 February 1866 in Crawford County, Georgia, died 28 June 1914 in Crawford County, buried in the Salem Churchyard.

IV.   Gardner L. Dent, born 22 March 1868 in Crawford County, died 1 January 1939 in Roberta, Crawford County.

V.   Mary Pauline Dent, born 5 April 1870 in Crawford County, died 7 April 1942 in Roberta, Crawford County. She married Julius Sawyer McGee on 18 May 1892.

---

[113] Laurens County Superior Court, 1833-1857 March 1850 – "State of Georgia vs. Delk. Assault and Battery. Witness: Mathew Mills. 9-1-1851; State of Georgia vs. Delk, Assault and Battery noll prossed by Solicitor General, George W. Jordan."

VI. Sophronia Elizabeth Dent, born 25 September 1872 in Crawford County, died 16 July 1895 in Crawford County.

VII. Sarah Jane Dent was born 16 February 1875 in Crawford County, married Porter Moore.

VIII. Varry Pearl Dent, born 23 February 1877 in Crawford County, died 10 March 1887 in Crawford County.

IX. Hoy Dent, born 9 May 1880 in Crawford County, married Alice Dennis on 17 April 1912.

X. William Cleveland Dent, born 11 August 1883 in Crawford County.

Dixon of North Carolina, Laurens, Richmond, Monroe & Washington Counties

The Dixon family descends from Henry Dixon, Sr., born ca 1700, died Caswell County, North Carolina, his LWT dated 4 August 1795, probated October 1795. Wife, Elizabeth Abernathy, born 20 September 1730 in Prince George County, Virginia, the daughter of Robert Abernathy, Jr. and his wife, Mary. Known children are three sons: Charles Dixon, Tillman Dixon, and Henry Dixon, Jr.

Henry Dixon, Jr. was born ca 1746, and his LWT was dated 1 September 1782 in Caswell County, North Carolina. He predeceased his father. He married on 15 September 1763, Martha Wynne, daughter of William Wynne and his wife, Frances. Issue:[114]

I. Wynne Dixon, born 1764 in Halifax County, Virginia, died 1832 in Caswell County, North Carolina, married (1) Keturiah Payne on 8 January 1786 (2) Rebecca Hart.

II. Robert Dixon, born ca 1744, his LWT dated 26 October 1792, probated January 1793 in Richmond County, Georgia. He married Anne Bacon (born 11 October 1748 Lunenburg County, Virginia, died January 1818 Richmond County, Georgia) on 30 October 1764 in Lunenburg County. The Will of Lyddall Bacon dated 21 1775, probated 12 October 1775 in Lunenburg County, Virginia, Cumberland Parish Register, named his daughter, Anne Dixon, and son-in-law, Robert Dixon. Issue:

A. Tillman Dixon, son of Robert Dixon, was born ca 1765 in Caswell County, North Carolina, married Mary Carlos on 16 November 1789.

B. John Lyddall Dixon, son of Robert Dixon, was born ca 1770 in Caswell County, North Carolina, died 1811 in Laurens County, Georgia. He married Milly Polly Cobbs on 5 November 1793 in Columbia County, Georgia, a daughter of John Cobbs and his wife, Elizabeth (Beckham) Cobbs. Milly married (2) Solomon Ellis, Jr. Issue:
1. John J. Dixon, born ca 1794, died 1838 in Laurens County, Georgia.

---

[114] Caswell County, North Carolina Wills; Lunenburg County, North Carolina Wills; Richmond County, Georgia Wills; Cumberland Parish Register, Lunenburg County, Virginia; Concord Church Cemetery, Meriwether County, Georgia; Administrators and Guardians Bond, Estate of John Lyddall Dixon, dated 5 May 1811, Laurens County: Notes and Accounts of Estate, September Term 1813; Columbia County, Georgia Marriages; Smith Cemetery, Forsyth County, Georgia; Washington Estates.

2. Robert Y. Dixon, died 1830 in Washington County, Georgia. Estate of Robert Y. Dixon (1829-1871), Washington County, distribution to heirs made on 30 December 1830, with Shadrack Dixon as administrator. Issue:
    a. S. Dixon.
    b. Mary Dixon.
    c. Catharine Dixon.
    d. Robert Dixon.
    e. Thomas Dixon.
    f. Henry Casson Dixon.
    g. Shadrack Dixon.
    h. Hezekiah Brown Dixon.
3. Thomas Dixon of Washington County, Georgia.
4. Priskell Dixon of Washington County, Georgia.
5. Elizabeth Dixon, born 1793, in Richmond County, Georgia, died 26 March 1867, Forsyth, Monroe County, Georgia, buried in the Davis Smith Cemetery, Brent, Georgia. She married Davis Smith on 6 January 1820 in Laurens County, Georgia. Her first husband was Mr. Jordan. See SMITH.

C.   Henry Dixon, son of Robert Dixon, was born 8 May 1771 Lunenburg County, Virginia, died April 1867 in Woodbury, Meriwether County, Georgia, buried in the Concord Church Cemetery. Issue:
1. Sarah Parks Dixon married William Spruce on 30 March 1797.
2. Ann Dixon married Mr. Estes.
3. Caroline McDonald Dixon, married Mr. Holt.
4. Maria Felishia Dixon.
5. Mary Bacon Dixon, died before 1792 in Richmond County, Georgia, married Henry Moore McDonald.

III. Roger Dixon, died 1795 Caswell County, North Carolina. He married Mary Jouett in 1794.

IV. Frances Dixon, born 1775 in Caswell County, North Carolina, died after 1860 in Smith County, Tennessee.

V. Henry Dixon, born 1777 in Caswell County, North Carolina, died October 1795 in Caswell County, North Carolina. He married Elizabeth Ramey 10 June 1799.

VI. Elizabeth Dixon, married Nathaniel Williams.

VII. Susannah Dixon, died before 1840 in Bedford County, Tennessee.

Drew of Sumter County

J. J. Drew was born 1813 in Georgia. Wife, Mollie, born 1858 in Alabama, listed with the family resided in Sumter County in 1880. Issue:[115]

I. Robert Drew, born 1853 in Georgia.

II. George Drew, born 1858 in Georgia.

III. Cassie Drew, born 1861 in Georgia.

---

[115] 1880 Sumter County Census.

IV. Thomas Champion Drew, born 1863 in Georgia. He married Sallie Davis, a daughter of Henry Gardner Davis and his wife, Eliza (Brown) Davis. SEE Davis. Issue:

    A. Annie Kate Drew, born ca 1890 Sumter County.
    B. Mary Emma Drew, born ca 1892 Sumter County, married Mr. Clay.
    C. Thomas Floyd Drew, born ca 1894 Sumter County.
    D. Thomas Champion Drew, Jr., born ca 1896 Sumter County.

V. Ed Drew, born 1865 in Georgia.

Durham of Paulding County

Young Marcus Alexander Hadaway Durham was born 1823 in South Carolina, died 02 November 1900 in Dallas, Paulding County, buried High Shoals Church Cemetery. Farmer. He married Mariah Elsberry, born 1828, died 2 November 1900 Paulding County, buried Old High Shoals Cemetery. His sister-in-law, Sarah Holland (born 1823) , was living with them in 1880, at Burnt Hickory. Issue:[116]

I. Mary Durham, born 1847 Georgia.

II. Emily Durham, born 1848 Georgia.

III. Lindsey Elsberry Durham, born 15 September 1852 in Paulding County, died 27 August 1922, buried in the Mt. Olivet Cemetery, Dallas, Paulding County. He married Lisbia Kate Noland (born 12 November 1856, died 20 December 1931, buried at Mt. Olivet Cemetery) on 21 December 1873 in Paulding County. SEE Noland. Issue:

    A. Charles Durham, born 1874 in Paulding County.
    B. William Young Durham, born 22 December 1874 in Paulding County, died 22 February 1842, buried in the Forrest Cemetery in Gadsden, Alabama.
    C. Thomas Walton Durham, born 27 April 1876 in Paulding County, died 24 May 1946 in Dallas, Georgia, buried High Shoals Baptist Church Cemetery. He married Mary Elizabeth Holland (born 26 December 1871 in Paulding County, died 20 May 1928 in Gadsden, Etowah County, Alabama), a daughter of George Washington Holland, and his wife, Lydia (Camp) Holland. SEE Holland. Issue:[117]
        1. Lillie Mae Durham, born 2 August 1901, Dallas, Georgia, married Frank Cochran.
        2. Ben Young Durham, born 16 February 1904 in Dallas, Georgia, married Lola Ledbetter.
        3. Tommie Irene Durham, born 28 March 1907 in Dallas, Georgia, died 14 October 1962. She married Jave Mitchell.
        4. Vera Durham, born 6 March 1909 in Dallas, Georgia, died 6 June

---

[116] 1860 Paulding County Census; Old High Shoals Cemetery; 1880 Paulding County Census.; Paulding County Marriages

[117] 1860 Paulding County Census; Holland 1000-1988 by Jeannette Holland Austin; Thomas Walton Durham Bible, page 207, Georgia Bible Records by Jeannette Holland Austin..

1966, unmarried.

    5.   Willie Ora Durham, born 20 January 1913 in Dallas, Georgia, married Frank Carruth.

D.   Ida Lou Durham, born 29 March 1878 in Paulding County, died 17 December 1960, buried in the Mt. Olivet Cemetery, Dallas, Georgia..

E.   Charles Richard Durham, born 4 December 1880 in Paulding County, died 11 October 1940, buried in the Crestwood Cemetery in Gadsden, Alabama.

F.   Clara Ozella Durham, born 6 April 1886 in Paulding County, died on 3 March 1957, buried in the Mt. Olivet Cemetery, Dallas, Georgia.

G.   Jennie Gertrude Durham, born 13 November 1891 in Paulding County, died 20 June 1976 in Ft. Worth, Texas.

H.   Nancy Florence Durham, born 25 December 1895 in Paulding County, died 27 December 1936, buried in the Mt. Olivet Cemetery in Dallas, Georgia. She was married to Charles Snote Gamel, born 23 November 1893, died 15 July 1919 in Paulding County, buried in the Mt. Olivet Cemetery. SEE Gammell.

I.   George Washington Durham, born 2 June 1898 in Paulding County, died 1 November 1960 in Gadsden, Alabama, buried in the High Schoals Baptist Church Cemetery in Dallas, Georgia.

IV.   Mansas Durham, born 1854 Paulding County.

V.   Thomas J. Durham, born 25 March 1856 Paulding County, died 8 June 1929, buried High Shoals Cemetery, married Sallie (26 January 1865-3 March 1927).

VI.   Sarah Durham, born 1859 Paulding County, married 24 October 1879 in Paulding County, M. S. Turner.

VII.   Mary Durham, born 1860 Paulding County.

VIII.   George Durham, born 1857 Paulding County.

IX.   Rhoda Durham, born 1870 Paulding County.

Edmondson of Virginia, North Carolina, Columbia & Putnam Counties

Thomas Edmondson was born ca 1655, died 1715 in Essex County, Virginia. He married (1) Mary (2) Anne. He lived in old Rappahannock County, Virginia, which county became Essex County in 1692. His LWT was probated in the Essex Court on 20 December 1715. Issue:[118]

I.   James Edmondson, died August 1741 in Essex County, Virginia, his LWT probated 4 August 1743. He married Judith Alleman.

II.   Joseph Edmondson, died 1743 in Craven County, North Carolina, his LWT dated 4 August 1743. Wife, Priselow. Issue:

---

[118] Virginia Magazine of History and Biography; Craven County, North Carolina Wills; Essex County, Virginia Wills; Columbia County, Georgia Marriages; Putnam County Marriages; Columbia County Deeds.

A. John Edmondson, born ca 1704 in Craven County, North Carolina.

B. Thomas Edmondson, born ca 1706 in Craven County, North Carolina, died 1792 in Halifax County, North Carolina, the date of his LWT. Wife, Elizabeth. Issue:

1. William Edmondson, born Halifax County, North Carolina.
2. Judah Edmondson, born Halifax County, North Carolina.
3. Ambrose Edmondson, born Halifax County, North Carolina.
4. Humphrey Edmondson, born Halifax County, North Carolina.
5. Sallie Edmondson of Columbia County, Georgia.
6. Thomas Edmondson of Columbia County, Georgia, married Patience Spiers on 28 February 1791 in Columbia County, Georgia. On 29 January 1799, Thomas Edmondson deeded to Waters Dunn, 33 acres on the Great Kiokee Creek, adjoining said Dunn, in Columbia County. On 25 January 1796, Reuben Dyer deeded to Thomas Edmondson for 80 pounds, 200 acres on the north side of Greenbriar Creek, which had been originally granted to Peter Lawrence (which he conveyed to Dyer on 13 January 1776). Another deed helps to establish the location of his land, viz…1 March 1803, Nathan Harris to Thomas Edmondson for $200, 200 acres on the north side of Greenbriar Creek, originally granted to Peter Lawrence, sold by him to Reuben Dyer on 13 January 1776, and by Dyer to said Harris on 7 July 1771, whereon the said Edmondson lives. Issue:

> a. John Edmondson, born 1794 in Columbia County, Georgia, died 16 April 1852 in Putnam County. He married Lucretia George on 17 September 1818 in Putnam County.
> b. Zachariah Edmondson, born ca 1796 in Columbia County, Georgia, married Mary Godley on 29 March 1823 in Putnam County.
> c. Mary Edmondson, born ca 1798 in Putnam County, died ca 1826. She married Michael Stinson on 14 May 1822 in Putnam County.
> d. Martha Edmondson, born 1810 in Putnam County, Georgia, married Peyton R. Clements on 13 September 1825 in Putnam County. SEE Clements.
> e. Daniel Edmondson of Columbia County, Georgia.
> f. Willie Edmondson of Columbia County, Georgia.

C. Priselow Edmondson, born ca 1708 in Craven County, North Carolina.

III. Benjamin Edmondson, died November 1727 in Essex County, Virginia, his LWT dated 21 November 1727. Wife, Margaret Underwood.

IV. William Edmondson, died 1717 in Essex County, Virginia, his LWT probated 21 November 1727.

V. Bryan Edmondson. Wife, Mary.

VI. Thomas Edmondson. Wife, Constance.

VII. John Edmondson, married Mary Johnson.

VIII. Samuel Edmondson, died 1733 in Essex County, Virginia.

IX.   Sarah Edmondson, married James Bougham.

X.   Anne Edmondson married Miss Hayman.

Edwards of Talbot County

Ambrose J. Edwards was born 1826 in Georgia, farmer. He married on 19 October 1843 in Talbot County, Arte Ann Chambliss, born 24 May 1828 in Warren County, a daughter of Jeptha Chambliss and his wife, Susan (Jones) Chambliss. They were residents of Coldwater, Chattooga County, Georgia, in 1880. SEE Chambliss. Issue:[119]

I.   Narcissa Edwards, born 1844 in Talbot County.

II.   Jeptha Edwards, born 1846 in Talbot County.

III.   Newton Edwards, born 1847 in Talbot County.

IV.   Seaborn Chambliss Edwards, born 1848 in Talbot County.

V.   William A. Edwards, born 1861 in Talbot County.

VI.   Susan F. Edwards, born 1865 in Georgia.

VII.   Anna L. Edwards, born 1866 in Georgia.

VIII.   Julia Q. Edwards, born 1868 in Georgia.

IX.   Henry L. Edwards, born 1870 in Georgia.

Elsberry of Paulding County

Lindsey Elsberry, farmer was born 1788 in either Wilkes or Oglethorpe County, Georgia. He died 19 February 1868 Paulding County, buried in the old Shady Grove Cemetery. He served in the War of 1812. He married Elizabeth Caldwell Hutcherson (born 1793 in North Carolina) on 28 October 1820 in Gwinnett County, died at the age of 98 years, Dallas New Era dated 21 October 1892. He was a farmer, and resided at Dallas, Georgia. Issue:[120]

I.   James R. Elsberry, born 6 April 1825 in Georgia, died 10 August 1891 Georgia. He married Louisa Matthews (born 14 March 1829, died 30 May 1902, buried in the old Shady Grove Cemetery in Paulding County) on 5 August 1852 in Paulding County. Issue:[121]

    A. Elizabeth Elsberry, born 1859 in Paulding County.
    B. Bartone Elsberry, born 31 January 1862, died 8 August 1919 in Paulding County,

---

[119] Talbot County Marriages; 1850 Talbot County Census; 1880 Chattooga County Census, Coldwater District.

[120] 1850 Cobb County Census; 1860 Paulding County Census; Paulding County Marriages, Old High Shoals Cemetery.

[121] 1880 Paulding County Census, Acorn Tree District.

buried in the old Shady Grove Cemetery.

 C. Sarah Elsberry, born 28 February 1866, died 18 December 1928, buried in the old Shady Grove Cemetery.

 D. J. Lindsey Elsberry, born 16 November 1869, died 9 May 1919, buried in the old Shady Grove Cemetery.

II. Sibbie Lavinnie Elsberry, born October 1829 Georgia, married William Edward Holland in 1847 Paulding County.

III. Joseph C. Elsberry, born 1832 Georgia, farmer. He married Catherine Parker (born 1845 in Georgia), on 31 December 1868 in Paulding County. Issue:[122]

  A. Emma Elsberry, born 1870 in Paulding County.
  B. Barbary Elsberry, born 1871 in Paulding County.
  C. Clarinda Elsberry, born 1873 in Paulding County.

IV. Mathew M. Elsberry, born 1834 Georgia, died 11 August 1863 in Mobile, Alabama.

V. Lindsey W. Elsberry, Jr., born 1837 in Georgia, died 1862, buried Old High Shoals Cemetery. He died during the war while serving as a private in o. A, Georgia Volunteers under Capt. Mathews, and died in a hospital on 13 September 1862 in Tennessee. He married (2) Sarah Ann Holland on 30 August 1857 in Paulding County, a daughter of Archibald Holland and his wife, Elizabeth (Hagin) Holland. SEE Holland. He was a Confederate soldier in Company A, 40th Georgia Infantry.

Issue by 1st wife:

 A. Sarah Elsberry, born 1847 in Paulding County.
 Issue by 2nd wife:
 B. Nancy (Nannie) Elsberry, born 1858 in Paulding County. She married John Spinks, born 1845 in Georgia. Issue:[123]
  1. Walton Spinks, born 1872 in Paulding County.
 C. George Elsberry, born 1860 in Paulding County.
 D. Alonzo Elsberry, born 1861 in Paulding County. He was residing with his brother-in-law, John Spinks, in 1880, at Burnt Hickory. He was married to Mary Blanchard on 18 January 1882 in Paulding County.
 E. Mary Elizabeth Elsberry, born April 1862 in Paulding County, died November 1927 in Montgomery, Alabama. She married James Penfield Tatum on 8 March 1878.

VI. J. Richard R. Elsberry, born 7 October 1839 in Paulding County, died 25 August 1923, buried in the New Hope Cemetery, Dallas, Georgia. He served in the Confederate Army in Co. A, 40th Georgia Infantry. Wife, G. R., born 6 April 1845, died 14 January 1912, buried in the New Hope Cemetery. Issue:

  A. George Elsberry, born 7 October 1876, died 10 January 1892, buried in the New Hope Cemetery.
  B. Infant, 1889-1889, buried in the New Hope Cemetery.
  C. Jennie Elsberry, born 8 January 1867, died 28 November 1868, buried in the New

---

[122] Ibid.

[123] 1880 Paulding County Census, Burnt Hickory District.

Hope Cemetery.

D. Nancy E. Elsberry, born 19 January 1873, died 18 February 1966, buried in the New Hope Cemetery.

E. Robert L. Elsberry, born 17 January 1879, died 3 December 1905, buried in the New Hope Cemetery.

Another family, William Monroe Elsberry, was born 6 December 1855 in Paulding County, died 17 May 1918, son of Kirkland Elsberry and Miriam McGregor. He married Permelia (Amelia Ann Holland, born 23 June 1856 in Paulding County, died 10 July 1929), a daughter of Samuel and Annis Holland, on 23 November 1876 in Paulding County.

I. James Lewis Elsberry born September 1877, married Claudia Parker. Issue: Irene, Lucille, Ann, Bernard, Bobby and James Elsberry. (Had 6 girls, 3 boys.)

II. George Elsberry, born 10 July 1879, married Rushie Denton. Issue: Bennett, Harvey, Hayward, Harold and Helen Elsberry.

III. Miriam Frances Elsberry born 1881 married Mendel Buckner. Issue: Ray, Elma and Amelia Buckner.

IV. Samuel J. Elsberry born 14 February 1884, married Jimmie Hulsey. Issue: Lester, Lawrence, Paul and Guy Elsberry.

V. William S. Elsberry, born 8 September 1886, married Fannie Hulsey. Issue: Roy, Bertha, Gertrude and Ruby Elsberry.

VI. Minnie D. Elsberry, born 19 November 1888, married Hayne Bryson. Issue: Harry, Boyd, Jimmie and Margaret Bryson.

VII. Raleigh Elsberry, born 10 May 1891, married Bessie Tittle.

VIII. Carrie Beatrice Elsberry ("Kit"), born 23 August 1893 in Braswell, Paulding County, married Thomas Clifton Holcombe (born 10 February 1886 in Resaca). Issue:

    A. Mary Ann Holcombe Coogan, born 16 November 1921.
    B. Thomas Clifton Holcombe, born 24 July 1924, died November 1925.
    C. .Ray Elsberry Holcombe, born 8 February 1927
    D. Merle Elizabeth Holcombe, born on 14 December 1919 in Rockmart, resident of Brandon, Florida.

IX. Ernest Elsberry was born 8 February 1896, married Tate Townsend. Issue: Ernest Elsberry, Jr. and Willard Elsberry.

Elijah Ethridge was born 1773 in North Carolina, married Gladys Robertson (born 1800) on 28 June 1826 in Monroe County. Issue:[124]

I.   Robert H. Ethridge, born 1820 in Monroe County, married Mary Jane Vaughn (born 1828) in Monroe County. He was a physician. Issue:

    A. Frances Ethridge, born 1844 in Monroe County.
    B. Georgia Ethridge, born 1847 in Monroe County.
    C. John Ethridge, born 1849 in Monroe County.

II.   Elijah N. Ethridge, born 1829 in Monroe County, married Emily Angeline Chambliss (born 7 Jul 1837 in Forsyth, Monroe County, died 6 June 1909), daughter of John M. Chambliss and his wife, Elizabeth (Jordan) Chambliss. After his death, Emily married (2) James Washington Head Ponder. Issue:

    A. Mary Frances Ethridge, born 1 June 1855 in Monroe County, died 1928, married Theo Rumble. Issue:
        1. Theo Rumble, Jr.
        2. Urban Rumble.
        3. Marie Rumble.
        4. Bert Ethridge Rumble.

    B. Elijah Nathaniel Ethridge, born 23 December 1857 in Monroe County, died 1929 in Monroe County.

    C. Willie Ethridge, born ca 1858 in Monroe County.

III. Benjamin Ethridge, born 1830 in Monroe County.

IV.   John H. Ethridge, born 1833 in Monroe County.

IV.   Frances Ethridge, born 1838 in Monroe County.

Evans of Maryland, Wilkes & Madison Counties

The roots of the Evans families in Madison County, Georgia go to the emigrant, David Evans, born ca 1690, the son of James Evans. A deposition dated 1718 in Charles City County, Virginia of David Jones establishes his age as being 28 years old. Again, his age was established in the Charles City County, Virginia Court Orders (1655-1648), page 104, Petition of David Jones, aged 63 (dated 3 August 1657). David migrated to Prince George County, Maryland where he married in the Queene Anne Parish in 1715, Ann (born 1699). They had issue: Eleanor Evans, born 5 October 1716 Queen Anne Parish, Prince George County, Maryland; John Evans, born 21 August 1717 Queen Anne Parish, Prince George County, Maryland; and Arden Evans, born 5 March 1720 Queen Anne Parish, Prince George County, Maryland. Family tradition says that David Evans was married to Anne Arden. There is an obscure reference about 1690 of one, James Arden of the *Potomac Freshes*, mentioned in the

---

[124] 1850 Monroe County Census.

Virginia Land Patents. The estate of David Jones is dated April 1719 in Prince George County, Maryland.

Arden Evans, son of David Evans, married in 1746 Susan Ball, a daughter of Thomas Ball. Arden Evans was a resident of Frederick County, Maryland in 1749, where, along with his wife, Susannah, he was remembered in the LWT of Thomas Ball, being made sole executor. "I give to my daughter, Susanna Evans – one gold mourning ring." Also, "To Lawrence O'Neal and William O'Neal, Jr. a tract of land called *Token of Love*. It appears that Thomas Ball's daughter, Eleanor, was married to an O'Neal of Prince George County, Maryland. See Will Book 26, page 35, Frederick County, Maryland, 1749. Arden Evans lived in the vicinity of Thomas Ball as evidenced by a deed ated 18 December 1750, when Arden Evans sold to Thomas Dowden, stock and household effects. (Frederick County, Maryland Deed Book B, page 318). A witness was William O'Neal. Arden Evans was in the process of disposing of his property in Frederick County, Maryland, when he removed to Bedford County, Virginia when he witnessed a deed (with Joshua and Jesse Abston dated 20 June 1760 made by Ann Childs of Halifax County, Virginia to John Chiles of Albemarle County, Virginia for 100 acres of land located on the north side of the Staunton River. On 26 March 1756, Arden Evans was appointed the overseer of a road to be cleared from Irvin's Ford to Clement's Ford on the Staunton River. (Oldest Order Book, May 1754, August 1761 Bedford County, Virginia). Other Bedford County records reflect that Arden Evans purchased land from Jonathan Jennings of Pittsylvania County, land on Briery Creek, which was a northern branch of the Staunton River, dated 6 May 1769. Also, a map of Arden Evans' land, dated 14 November 1770 in Bedford County Deed Book A, page 126, "Surveyed for Arden Evans 240 acres which, with nine acres, a whole patent, and twenty-two acres, purchased of Charles Lynch (343 acres) in Bedford County on the west side of Otter River." On 29 August 1779, Arden Evans sold the l and on Briery Creek to Thomas Hardy. 25 September 1771, Susannah, the wife of Arden Evans, relinquished her right of dower. (Bedford County Deed Book D, page 163). Apparently, Arden Evans was granted 384 acres of land on 28 February 1779 in Bedford County. He sold this land to Richard Bloxham of Louisa County, being land in Campbell County on the waters of Hills and Cheese Creeks, 384 acres (Bedford County Deed Book 2, page 411).

Issue of Arden Evans and his wife Susan (Ball) Evans:

I.   William Evans, Sr., born ca 1747 in Prince George County, Maryland, died 1807 in Wilkes County, Georgia. He married Susannah Clements. He first purchased land in Bedford County, Virginia on 28 May 1771 from William Callaway, a tract which was located on the north side of Ivy Creek. (Bedford County Deed Book D). He sold this same land on 24 August 1772 to John Fourgerau, and on 28 September 1772, Susannah Evans, his wife, relinquished her right of dower to 100 acres conveyed by her husband to Fougerau (Minutes Court Proceeds, page 3, Bedford County, Virginia). They resided near the Old Kettle Creek battleground, in Wilkes County. He is known to have served in the Revolutionary War, along with his brothers, and to have fought in the Battle of Kettle Creek. On 26 December 1773, William Evans received a land grant in Pittsylvania County, Virginia for 349 acres, located on the northside of Chestnut Mountain, on the Muddy fork of Chestnut Creek (Virginia Land Grants, Vol. E, page 609). Also, another land grant on 27 February 1775 for 315 acres (Book E, page 487, Land Grants, Richmond, Virginia), however, in this instance, William Evans acted as the assignee of Benjamin Clement, who was assignee of Thomas Dillard and Isaac Clements. Again, on 2 August 1777 William Evans acquired land in Pittsylvania County from Benjamin Clement, Jr. and his wife, Mary, of Pittsylvania County, 129 acres, bounded by Benjamin Clements, the Elder. (Pittsylvania County Deed Book 6, page 75). On October 1797 a legacy for Williams Evans was paid by the Benjamin Clement's estate to Charles Lynch, Jr. in

Pittsylvania County. It seems that Charles Lynch, Jr. purchased Evans' share of the estate on 26 November 1790. (Campbell County Deed Book 3, page 80). The LWT of Benjamin Clements reads "One part to Susannah Evans, her heirs or assigns." (Will Book B, page 116, Pittsylvania County.) After the death of William Evans, Sr., Susannah married Henry Slaton whose plantation was located on the site of the Kettle Creek battleground in Wilkes County. Her LWT, Susannah Evans Slaton, dated 29 December 1807 in Wilkes County. Issue:[125]

A. John C. Evans, born 1772, married Bessie Morton on 30 December 1801 in Oglethorpe County.
B. Stephen Evans married Elizabeth Bennett.
C. James Evans married Sallie Bennett.
D. Arden Evans married Elizabeth Carmichael.
E. William Evans, born 23 December 1776, died 14 October 1822, married Elizabeth Combs Hammock on 14 October 1822.

II. Thomas Evans, born ca 1748 in Prince George County, Maryland, died 1838 in Madison County, Georgia. He married Martha Brooks ca 1786. The Estate of Thomas Evans, deceased, Administrator's Bond, 1840, Madison County, Georgia. There was a deed in Elbert County, from Thomas Evans to Philip King, dated 1803. Issue:

A. William Evans, born 1787 Wilkes County. He married ca 1801, probably in Madison County, Celia Leverett (born ca 1780 Wilkes County, died Elbert County), a daughter of John Leverett (born ca 1761) and his wife, Mary. SEE Leverett. A deed of William Evans to Blackshear Dixon in 1837, for 100 acres on Coodey's Creek, Elbert County Deed Book A. Greene County Minutes dated 26 June 1800: Jesse, David, Capt. Evans and William Evans are ordered to work the road, dividing the ridge between Oconee and Appalachee, Phillips Ferry, etc." Issue:

1. Nancy Evans, born 1802 in Madison County, died 1887 in Paulding County, buried in the Dallas City Cemetery, Dallas, Georgia. She married Bailey Bone on 13 April 1826 in Madison County.
2. Elam Evans (son), born 1810-1820 Madison County.
3. Ann Evans, born 1833 Madison County.
4. M. Evans (daughter), born 1836 Madison County.
5. E. Evans (daughter), born 1838 Madison County.
6. W. Evans (son), born 1840 Madison County.

B. David Evans, born 1789 Wilkes County, died March 1866 in Madison County, Georgia. He married Betsy Allen on 29 April 1814. LWT of David Evans dated 16

---

[125] Queen Anne Parish Register, Prince George County, Maryland; Frederick County, Maryland Wills & Deeds, Bedford County, Virginia deeds; Wilkes County, Georgia Marriages, Deeds & Estates; History of Roane County, Tennessee, Vol. 1, by E. M. Wells; Bedford County, Virginia Court Records and Deeds; Pittsylvania County Deeds & Wills; Campbell County, Virginia Deeds; Madison County Estates; Elbert County Deeds; Putnam County Deeds; Oglethorpe County Marriages; 1820-1850 Madison County Census; 1850-1860 Elbert County Census; LWT of John Leverett dated 16 Feburary 1811 Wilkes County named his son-in-law, William Evans.

December 1863, probated March 1866, Madison County Will Book B (1842-96), page 212-213. Issue:

1. William S. Evans, born 1826 Madison County. Wife, Elizabeth.
2. David Evans, born 1829 Madison County.
3. George Evans, born 1833 Madison County.
4. Henry T. Evans, born 1835 Madison County, died May 1874 Madison County. Wife, Elizabeth A. LWT of Henry T. Evans, page 461, Madison County Will Book 1842-96, dated 28 March 1874, probated 7 May 1874, named wife, Elizabeth A., and sons James D. and Henry S. Evans.
5. Pinckney Evans, born 1837 Madison County.

C. Robert Evans, born ca 1791 in Wilkes County, married Mahaley Granger on 12 February 1807.

D. Thomas Evans, Jr., born ca 1793 in Wilkes County, died 10 April 1861 in Athens, Clarke County. He married Clarissa Allen on 9 January 1819. [126]

E. Caroline Evans, born ca 1795 in Wilkes County, married George Rodgers in 1815.

F. Henry Evans, born ca 1797 in Wilkes County married Martha Whitney on 16 December 1811.

G. Elizabeth Evans, born ca 1799 Wilkes County, married John Griffin on 9 January 1817.

III. David Evans, born ca 1751 in Prince George County, Maryland, died 1808 in Wilkes County, Georgia. Wife, Mary. He fought in the American Revolution, while a resident of Wilkes County, Georgia. For his services he was granted on 24 August 1784 a certificate by Colonel Elijah Clarke for his service. He was appointed Lieutenant on 20 June 1812 in a volunteer company of riglemen attacked to the 77th Battalion. The Estate of Davis Evans, dated 1808, Wilkes County; inventory dated 28 March 1808. "Samuel and John Johns and Weaver Cotton, appraisers. David Evans, deceased, Sale 1 November 1808, Wilkes County, Georgia." On 7 August 1809, Hannah Evans, orphan of David, chose her mother, Mary, as guardian; and William and Mary Evans were appointed guardians of Rhody, Sophia and Susannah Evans, minors of David Evans, deceased. [127]

The Petititon of Arden Evans, the administrator of David Evans, deceased, to sell the real estate on Kettle Creek. Petition of Mary Evans, joint Administratrix, that the distributes are willing to sell the Negroes for a division. Signed. "Arden Evans, William Evans, Mary Evans, Jesse Evans, Elizabeth Evans and James Bates". [128] "We, Mary Evans, executor, and Arden Evans, adm., of estate of David Evans, late of Wilkes County, to William Evans, 202-1/2 acres in Baldwin County, now Putnam County, which was drawn by David Evans, the above, deceased." 6 September 1811.[129] Mary Evans, the widow of David Evans, died in 1818, because on 24 September Arden Evans, Anderson Bates and Dempsey gave bond for her estate.[130] Susannah Evans Account with Peter Lunceford. "Your wife, Susannah, was entitled out of estate of David Evans." [131]

---

[126] The death of Thomas Evans, Jr. Death recorded at the Georgia State Archives, Card Catalog File, submitted by grandson, Henry W. Beusse, Athens, Georgia, in 1930.

[127] Page 152, Early Georgia Records, Vol. 1, Wilkes County.

[128] Wilkes County Minutes of the Inferior Court, 1798-1811).

[129] Putnam County Deed Book C, page 100.

[130] Wilkes County Bond Book 1800-1811), page 215.

IV. Arden Evans, born 1755, possibly in Bedford County, Virginia, died in Roane County, Tennessee. Wife, Mary. He served in the Revolutionary War for which he drew a pension, as a Virginia soldier. He was placed on the pension roll on 15 February 1833, Virginia Line. Commencement of pension: 4 March 1831, age 78. (Statement of Roane County, Tennessee, page 514, Pension Roll, Vol. 3, Report of Secretary of War, 1835). Arden Evans received a land grant in Roane County on 10 February 1826, for 80 acres located on Poplar Creek, at the foot of Walling's Ridge.[132]

V. Elijah Evans, died Wilkes County, Georgia. He married Mary Bird on 30 March 1813 in Wilkes County. On 3 May 1811 Elijah Evans sold his land on Kettle Creek (Wilkes County Deed Book B. In 1821, he was the appraiser of the Estate of Jarret Dossy (dated January 1821), Wilkes County. He had two draws in the 1803 land lottery, lots in Baldwin County, 202-1/2 acres. In November of 1828, Elijah Evans of Putnam County sold his land in Baldwin County (now Putnam County), with his wife, Mary Evans, signing the deed. [133]

Evans of South Carolina;
Franklin & Fulton Counties

John Evans was born 1770 in South Carolina, and died between 1860 and 1870 in Franklin County, Georgia. A deed in Jackson County Deed Book J, page 495, dated 25 March 1811, of Francis and Mary Nunn of Jackson County, Georgia, to John Evans of Pendleton District, land on Hurricane Creek. He was living with hisa son, Willis Evans, in Anderson County in 1850. Wife, Ealey. Issue:[134]

I. Zachariah Evans, son of John Evans, was born 1799 in Anderson County, South Carolina. Wife, Lucy.

II. James Oliver Evans, son of John Evans, was born 1805 in Anderson County, South Carolina, died 24 December 1880 in Atlanta, Fulton County, Georgia, buried in St. Paul's Churchyard, Atlanta, according to the Atlanta Consitution dated 24 December 1880. Wife, Frances.[135] Issue:

   A. William Raphael Evans, son of James Oliver Evans, was born 26 October 1843 in Anderson County, South Carolina, died 11 March 1919 in Carnesville, Franklin County, buried in the Trinity United Methodist Church Cemetery. He married Martha C. Nicholson on 7 January 1866.

---

[131] Page 580, Wilkes County Estates. Book H, page 826, Land Grants of East Tennessee.

[132] Book H, page 826, Land Grants of East Tennessee.

[133] Putnam Deed Book M, page 388.

[134] 1850 Anderson County, South Carolina Census; Confederate Pension Records; 1880 Hart County, Georgia Census; DeKalb County Marriages; 1900 Gwinnett County Census; Atlanta City Directory; DeKalb County Estates & Marriages; personal records of Pearl Evans Howard as given to Jeannette Holland Austin.

[135] "My aunt, Mrs. Pearl Howard, the daughter of Charles Crawford Evans, told me that her grandfather's name was Oliver Evans...... Jeannette Holland Austin."

B. John F. Evans, son of James Oliver Evans, was born 1845 in Anderson County, South Carolina, died before 1870 in Franklin County, married Amanda Stephens on 8 December 1865.

C. Lewis H. Evans, son of James Oliver Evans, was born November 1846 in Anderson County, South Carolina. Wife, Martha.

D. Nancy A. Evans, daughter of James Oliver Evans, was born 1848 in Anderson County, South Carolina.

E. Thomas T. Evans, son of James Oliver Evans, was born 1850 in Anderson County, South Carolina, died before 1860.

F. Martha J. Evans, daughter of James Oliver Evans, was born 1851 in Anderson County, South Carolina.

G. Mary E. Evans, daughter of James Oliver Evans, was born 1852 in Anderson County, South Carolina.

H. James H. Evans, son of James Oliver Evans, was born 1855 in Franklin County, Georgia.

I. Sarah F. Evans, daughter of James Oliver Evans, was born December 1857 in Franklin County, Georgia. She was listed on the 1900 Gwinnett County Census as the sister of Frank Juhan; also listed was her mother, Frances Evans.

J. Charles Crawford Evans, son of James Oliver Evans, was born 21 December 1858 in Franklin County, Georgia, died 29 March 1943 in Atlanta, Fulton County, Georgia. He married Martha Josephine Perkins on 20 July 187?? in DeKalb County. She was born 6 January 1863 in DeKalb County, died 19 January 1944 in Atlanta, Fulton County, a daughter of Berry C. Perkins and his wife, Mary Ann Elizabeth (Jordan) Perkins. 9. According to the Atlanta City Directory, Crawford Evans worked on the SIC Line, 1900, a resident of 40 Fairview Street, 3 blocks east of Capitol Avenue. In 1901 he was an engineer for the Atlanta Excelsior & Manufacturing County; in 1902 he was a resident of 691 Capitol Avenue; also in 1903. In 1904, he lived at 121 Estoria Avenue (north from Memorial Drive); in 1806 he lived at 17 Haygood Street (off Capitol Avenue). SEE Perkins. Issue:

> 1. Laura Anne Evans, daughter of Charles Crawford Evans, was born 25 September 1883 in Atlanta, Fulton County, died 26 October 1974 in Atlanta. She married in 1899, William Edward Sealock.

> 2. Homer James Evans, son of Charles Crawford Evans, was born 17 August 1885 in DeKalb County, died 16 July 1943 in Atlanta, Fulton County. He married Mary Brent Chambliss on 25 September 1909 in Atlanta, Fulton County. She was born 31 March 1886 in Macon, Bibb County, died 10 February 1964 in Atlanta, Fulton County, buried Crestlawn Cemetery, Atlanta. She was a daughter of Joel Edgar Chambliss and his wife, Elizabeth Smith (Clements) Chambliss. SEE Chambliss and Clements. Issue:

a. Marguerite Elizabeth Evans, daughter of Homer James Evans, was born 26 May 1910 Atlanta, Fulton County, died February 1984 Atlanta, Fulton County, buried Crestlawn Cemetery, Atlanta. She married Laurel Benjamin Holland on 18 October 1930 in Atlanta, Georgia. SEE Holland.

b. Ruth Evans, daughter of Homer James Evans, was born 23 November 1912 Atlanta, Fulton County, died 23 April 1917, buried in the Crestlawn Cemetery. The story here is that Ruth was sent out to play in the front yard. In those days, there were very few automobiles on the streets. Ruth was playing near the street, dangling her feet over the curb when she was run over by an automobile. The driver of the car was so upset that he offered to send one of his children for Mary Brent Evans to raise.

c. Dorothy Frances Evans, daughter of Homer James Evans, was born 20 October 1918 Atlanta, Fulton County, died 12 January 1997 Decatur, DeKalb County. She married (1) on 6 December 1942 in Atlanta, Harold Claud Smith and (2) Sterling Bryan, Jr.

2. Pearl Evans, daughter of Charles Crawford Evans, was born 4 January 1895 in Rockmart, Paulding County, died ca 1970 in Atlanta, Fulton County. She married (1) on 4 July 1909, Jesse Roy Jackson, (2) on 13 July 1936, Roy Howard, and (3) on 25 December 1947, Roy Howard. For many years, she resided on Ponce de Leon Avenue in Atlanta.

K. Annie Evans, daughter of James Oliver Evans, was born June 1864 in Franklin County, Georgia, died 1918 in DeKalb County, married Frank Juhan in 1888, DeKalb County. The Return of the Estate of Mrs. Annie Juhan was dated 1918 in DeKalb County. She was listed on the 1900 Gwinnett County Census.

III. Elijah Evans, son of John Evans, was born 1823 in Anderson County, South Carolina. Wife, Jane.

IV. Willis Evans, son of John Evans, was born 1824 in Anderson County, South Carolina, died 20 February 1904 in Hartwell, Hart County, Georgia. Wife, Nancy Ann Evans, married 17 September 1846. He served in the Confederate Army, County D., Orr's Rifles (South Carolina). His widow, Mrs. Nancy A. Evans of Hart County, Georgia, drew in his pension. In her application she stated that she was married on 17 September 1846 in Anderson County, South Carolina, and that Willis Evans died on 20 February 1904 in Hart County. They had eight children. The 1860 Census of Anderson County lists Willis Evans as a shoemaker.

V. Garrison Evans, son of John Evans, was born 1 January 1827 in Anderson County, South Carolina, died 14 January 1909 in Hartwell, Hart County, Georgia. Wife, Sarah E. He served in the Confederate Army, County I, (2) South Carolina, Hart County, where he enlisted for three years. Widow, Elizabeth Dutton, whom he married on September of 1897 in Anderson County, South Carolina, collected his pension. Garrison had collected a pension since 1895. He died on 14 January 1909.

Thomas Fambrough, son of Thomas Fambrough, was born ca 1727 in Virginia, where he died in 1791. He married Mary Anderson. Issue:[136]

I. Thomas Fambrough was born ca 1747 Albemarle County, Virginia, died 28 July 1827. Issue:
>   A. Anderson Fambrough.[137]

II. Sarah Fambrough was born 23 October 1760.

III. John Fambrough was born 3 April 1759.

IV. William Fambrough was born ca 1762, died March 1837 in Monroe County, Georgia, his LWT dated 5 November 1836, probated 6 March 1837. Wife: Phoebe. Ch: Robinson, William L.; Katherine Pringle (wife of Coleman S.) Exrs: Robinson, William L. and Allen G. Fambrough.[138] Issue:

>   A. Robinson (or Roberson) Fambrough was born 1788 in Virginia. He married Mary, born 1790. They lived in Monroe County, listed on 1850 Census. Issue:
>
>   >   1. William Fambrough, born 1813 Georgia.
>
>   B. William L. Fambrough was born 1796 in Virginia. He married Sarah M. Akin (born 1797) on 20 July 1837 in Monroe County. They lived in Monroe County, listed on 1850-1860 Census. His LWT dated 9 November 1867, probated September 1868, Monroe County named wife, Sarah, and children. Sarah's LWT was dated March 1869, probated June 1869 in Monroe County, and named her sisters, viz...Mary, the wife of Stephen H. Tucker; Jane, the wife of Robert C. Tucker; Elizabeth Young, widow; Caroline, the wife of William Scarbrough. Her brother, Warren Akin, was the executor. Issue:
>
>   >   1. Thomas M. Fambrough, born 1833 in Monroe County.
>   >   2. Urban C. Fambrough, born 1835/1836 in Monroe County. He married Sarah Jane Pye, a daughter of Benier Pye. They were residents of Monroe

---

[136] Greene County Wills & Estates; 1850 Greene County Census; Clarke County Wills; 1850-1860 Monroe County Census; Monroe County Marriages; Monroe County Wills; Clarke County Marriages; Greene County Marriages; Roster of Revolutionary War Soldiers in Georgia by McCall, Vol. III; Clarke County Guardian Bonds; Clarke County Deeds; Oglethorpe County Deeds.

[137] Oglethorpe County Deeds - Deed Book I, page 240. 31 January 1817, Thomas Fambrough to Anderson Fambrough, both of said county, for affectionate love I do owe my son, Anderson Fambrough, land on the Oconee River, adj. Thomas Fambrough's line and John Greenwood's line. Thomas Fambrough relinquished the right and title to Anderson Fambrough, and Anderson Fambrough binds himself to his son, Thomas Fambrough, when 21 years of age, 100 acres on the Oconee River, including the Spring.

[138] Georgia's Roster of Revolution, Clarke County Deeds.

County in 1860. Issue: Fannie Fambrough, born 1858 in Monroe County and W. B. Fambrough (male), born 1860 in Monroe County. SEE Pye.

3. William N. Fambrough.

4. Nancy H. Arnold married Mr. Arnold.

5. Mary I. Fambrough, married Mr. Fleming.

C. Katherine Fambrough, married Coleman S. Pringle.

D. Allen G. Fambrough, born 1800 in Virginia. He married (1) 11 June 1837 in Monroe County, Mary S. Banks (2) 4 February 1841 in Monroe County, Mary A. P. Pringle. Lived in Monroe County in 1850. Issue:

1. L. C. Fambrough (male), born 1825 Georgia, physician.

2. E. M. Fambrough (male), born 1829 Georgia.

Finch of Paulding County

John Terrell Finch, born 23 February 1832, died 2 February 1909, buried in the High Shoals Baptist Church Cemetery. He served in Co. C, 31 Georgia Cavalry, C. S. A., during the War Between the States. He married Hepsey Farmer, born 19 November 1835, died 23 October 1929, buried in the High Shoals Baptist Church Cemetery. Issue:[139]

I.   Oliver O. Finch was born 3 January 1862 in Paulding County, died 30 September 1945, married Mollie Durham (born 11 April 1865, died 10 January 1941, buried in the High Shoals Baptist Church Cemetery) on 5 January 1885 in Paulding County. Issue:[140]

A. Paul Finch, born 22 May 1898, died 8 October 1900, buried in the High Shoals Baptist Church Cemetery.

II.   Henry Finch, born 1865 in Paulding County.

III. Savannah Finch, born 1867 in Paulding County.

IV.   Terrell Young Finch, born 14 December 1887 in Paulding County, died 20 January 1969, buried in High Shoals Baptist Church Cemetery. He married on 24 June 1906 in Paulding County, Dellie Mae Holland, born 11 March 1889 in Rockmart, died 20 June 1957 in Powder Springs, buried New High Shoals Baptist Church Cemetery, Dallas. SEE Holland.

Issue of Dellie Mae and Terrell Young Finch:

A. Audie Mae Finch, born 15 April 1907 in Paulding County, married on 15 April 1926, Owen Jewel Croker (born 28 February 1905, died 17 June 1973), son of William Edward Croker and Alice Kate Moon. Issue:

1. Ruby Alice Croker, born 29 August 1928 in Pauldfng County, married on 20 September 1824 in Dallas, Georgia, James Russell Clay, Sr. (born 17

---

[139] 1889 Paulding County Census, Burnt Hickory District.

[140] Holland (1000-1988) by Jeannette Holland Austin.

121

October 1916 in Cobb County, Ga.), son of James Willis Clay and Martha Elizabeth Elliott.

2. Ann Grace Croker, born on 15 October 1930 in Paulding County, married on 23 June 1954 in Jacksonville, North Carolina, Russell John Netzinger, Sr. (born 6 December 1929 in Racine, Wise.), son of John Thomas Netzinger and Anna Evelyn Howe.

3. Franklin Roosevelt Croker, born on 29 June 1934 in Paulding County, married on 9 June 1967 in Forsyth, Georgia. Jean Carolyn Roguemore (born 21 December 1934 in Forsyth, Georgia), daughter of William Charles Roguemore and Edna Elizabeth Snow.

4. Marilyn Estelle Croker, born 17 October 1936 in Paulding County, married 30 April 1955 in Paulding County, Loran Crowe (born 4 March 1934 in Paulding County), son of Edgar M. Crowe and Delia Walraven.

5. Audrey Jewelene Croker, born 29 December 1939 in Paulding County, married 10 May 1959 in Paulding County, Eduardo Antonio Aguilar (born 20 February 1937, Santa Ana, El Salvado, C. A.), son of Carlos L. Aguilar and Clementine.

6. William Neil Croker, born 13 October 1942 in Paulding County, married 24 June 1967 in Cobb County, Ga. Henrietta McElroy (born 12 November 1944 in Greensville, Washington County, Mississippi), daughter of Henry McElroy and Margaret Sache.

7. Joy Susan Croker, born 15 August 1948 in Cobb County, married (3) Lee Smith (born 15 May 1932 in Arkansas), son of Vester Smith and Leathy.

B. Norman Eugene Finch, born 14 September 1909 in Paulding County, died on 25 April 1980, married on 11 January 1931 to Azma Grace Porter (born 15 February 1909) in Paulding County, the daughter of Ambrose C. Porter and Anna Bruce.

C. Raymond Woodrow Finch of Breman, born 9 March 1913 in Paulding County, married 7 August 1932 Altha Camp (born 7 January 1913), daughter of John Camp and Coren Abney.

D. John Terrell Finch, born on 21 February 1915 in Paulding County, died 6 September 1972, buried Midway Presbyterian Church Cemetery, Lost Mountain, Powder Springs, married on 16 June 1934 to Dorothy Louise Warren (born 17 November 1917 in Cobb County, Ga.), daughter of John Troy Warren and Bertha Turner.

E. Mary Evelyn Finch of Powder Springs, born on 28 January 1918 in Paulding County, married 22 February to Paul Eugene Pearson (born 16 July 1915 in Paulding County), son of Warner E. Pearson and Lelia Pearce.

F. Elsie Louise Finch, born 23 May 1921 in Paulding County, married on 11 February 1939 to Thomas Harold Hardy (born 11 February 1918) in Paulding County, Ga., son of Leonard Hardy and Dora Goggins.

G. Betty S. Finch of Mableton, born 1 April 1927 in Paulding County, died November of 1987, married on 23 August 1947 Marcus Felton Atcheson (born 7 September 1934 in Pauldfng County), son of Willis Joseph Atcheson and Myrtice Matthews (born 2 March 1909, daughter of John A. Mathews and Eliza Jane Holland, twin with Lucy, who was named by Burrel Marion Camp.)

Foote of Carroll and Cobb Counties

John D. Sandford Foote was born 1822 in South Carolina, married on 22 September 1852 in Paulding County, Emily C. Adair, born 1829 in Madison County, the daughter of William Andrew Adair and his wife, Mary (Meroney) Adair. SEE Adair. Issue:[141]

I.   Frances Foote, born 1860 in Georgia, married Hance Williams.

II.   Sarah Foote, born 1862 in Georgia, died 1894, married John Lee Perrin.

III.   Emma Foote, born 1865 in Georgia, died ca 1956, married William Fletcher Turner.

IV.   Millie Ann Josephine Foote, born 23 November 1872 in Georgia, died 23 November 1959, married Warner Ola.

Forsyth of Paulding County

Martin Forsyth was born 1811 in Georgia, farmer, resident of Huntsville, Paulding County. He married Mary Owen of Paulding County (born 1817 in Tennessee). Known issue:[142]

I. Jonathan J. Forsyth was born on 11 August 1834 in Paulding County, and died 16 April 1889 in Paulding County. He married on 28 October 1858 in Paulding County, Louisa Elizabeth Hagin, born 4 February 1842, died 1932 in Rome, a daughter of Edward Hagin and his wife, Parthenia (Scoggins) Hagin. SEE Hagin. They were residents of Burnt Hickory, in 1880.[143] Jonathan was a farmer and Baptist minister, as well as a school teacher in Paulding County. In 1861, he enlisted as a private/2nd Sgt. In Co. C of the 22nd Regiment of the Georgia Infantry, and was wounded at Sparpsburg, Maryland on 17 September 1862; transferred to the Confederate Navy on 15 April 1864 as a private. On 26 April 1865, he surrendered at Greensboro, North Carolina on the steamer, *Hampton*. After his death, his wife (Lou) resided with her daughter, Willie Forsyth Stewart, in Rome, where she died in 1932. Issue:[144]

    A.   Oziah McCurry Forsyth, son, born October 1859 in Paulding County, died 1900/1910 in Calhoun County, Alabama. After 1900, he lived with his brother, Ves, and worked on the railroad in Anniston, Alabama. In 1883, he was married to Mary A. (born 1856 in Alabama).

    B.   McCurry Forsyth, born 1860 in Paulding County.

---

[141] 1880 Carroll County Census, Villa Rica.

[142] 1860 Paulding County Census; The Hagan-Bryant Genealogies by Tom Hagan.

[143] 1880 Paulding County Census, Burnt Hickory.

[144] Personal records of Mrs. Julian Hardage Morgan, Dallas, Georgia; 1860-1880 Paulding County Census.

C.   Nora Forsyth, born 1862 in Paulding County.

D.   Jonathan Ves Forsyth, born March 1866 in Paulding County, married Mattie Witcher on 30 May 1874 in Polk County. He was a resident of Tallapoosa County and Holt Counties, Alabama..

E.   Martin Edward Forsyth, born 17 November 1868 in Paulding County, died 3 May 1949 in Ragland, Alabama. He was married to Louisa Hattie Baswell on 22 Spril 1891 in Coal City, Alabama.

F.   Cornelius Forsyth, born June 1869 in Paulding County. He was a resident of Rome in 1900.

G.   Mary Elizabeth Forsyth, born 17 August 1871 in Paulding County, died 18 February 1959 in Washington, D. C., buried in the Greenwood Cemetery in Cedartown. She married Wesley H. Henley (died 1921 in Cedartown)..

H.   Fannie Forsyth, born 1874 in Paulding County.

I.   Henrietta Forsyth, born 1877 in Paulding County, married James H. Kilgo in 1895. They were residents of Rome in 1900, but later removed to Tulsa, Oklahoma..

J.   Willie Forsyth, born 4 November 1883 in Paulding County, died 18 February 1957 in Rome, buried in the Myrtle Hill Cemetery. She married Henry J. Stewart (born 6 September 1869, died 27 August 1957 in Rome, buried in the Myrtle Hill Cemetery) in Rome.

K.   Henry Frank Forsyth, born 24 May 1887 in Paulding County, died 6 August 1940 in Birmingham, Alabama. He was married to Annie Guthrie..

II.   Martin Forsyth, born 1838 in Georgia.

Franklin of Warren County

Reverend William Franklin, Revolutionary War Soldier, was born ca 1720 in Virginia, and died 1797 in Warren County, Georgia. A marker was placed at the graves of William and George Franklin by the DAR, in Tennille, Georgia. The old Franklin homesite is located on Feun's Bridge Road near Davisboro, on the l and now owned by Mrs. W. D. Frances. From 1777 to 1790, he was the original pastor of the Little Brier Creek Church in Warren County, first named "Franklin's Meeting House" and was built of logs at a place called Happy Valley in 1777. Iron names in the first building were forged by Vincent A. Tharp from Philadelphia. Later, the church was removed to about one-mile on Little Briar Creek. William Franklin, Sr. and Jr. were listed on the certified list of Georgia Troops in the Revolutionary War, in Georgia. Upon a certificate signed by Colonel Lee dated 7 April 1784, Rev. Franklin was granted 187-1/2 acres of land in Washington County, which he received on 16 August 1784. This land was located on the South Oconee River in Washington County. Pvt. Franklin also appeared on Colonel John Stewart's Regiment's Muster Roll. [145]

---

[145] Deed Book I, page 247, Clarke County. 1 June 1808. William Fambrough of said county to Thomas Fambrough of Oglethorpe County for $600.00, 200 acres in Oglethorpe County on the Oconee River, being part of 575 acres granted to John Burnet.

It appears that William Franklin married twice, one source says first in Virginia, 1743, to Sarah Rebecca Boone (1722-1755), and second to Mary Eason (born 1737). [146]

Issue by 1st wife (Sarah Rebecca):

I. George Thomas Franklin, Sr., born 1744 in Virginia, died 16 February 1816 in Burke County, Georgia. He married in Currituck County, North Carolina, Vashti Mercer (born 1759 in Currituck Bay, North Carolina, died September 1836 in Washington County, Georgia). Issue:

    A. Boyd Franklin.
    B. Sarah Franklin, born 1782, died 1860.
    C. James T. Franklin, born 1795, died 1838, married Harriett Harris. Issue:
        1. George Nicholas Franklin, born 1829, died 1899, married Nancy McAlister.
        2. Mary Franklin.
        3. Owen Franklin.
        4. Thomas Franklin.
        5. Mariah Franklin.
    D. Vashi Mercer Franklin, born 1795, died 11 June 1839 in Georgia, married Daniel Harris.
    E. George Thomas Franklin, Jr., born 1804, died 1879, married (1) Elizabeth Brookins and (2) Nancy McAllister.
        Issue by 1st wife:

        1. Sarah A. V. Franklin, born 1831, married William F. Webster.
        2. Thomas George Franklin, born 1837, died 1909, married Elizabeth Frances Trice.
        3. Louisa M. Franklin, born 1839, married Barnes Moran.
        4. Owen B. Franklin, born 1842.

        Issue by 2nd wife:

        5. Martha A. Franklin, born 1834.
        6. Augustus D. Franklin, born 1836, died 1860.
        7. Catherine A. Franklin, born 1838, married J. Howard Smith.
        8. James Dorsey Franklin, born 1840, died 1915, married Ella E. Boatright.
    F. Martha Franklin.

---

[146] All evidence points to William and Mary Franklin as having a daughter, Martha H. Franklin, who married Alexander Smith. Alexander Smith's son, Davis Smith, gave his first two children the middle name of "Franklin". William Franklin and his wife, Mary, deeded land to Alexander Smith, all of Warren County, on 2 March 1795, for 20 pounds, located on Brier Creek, being 100 acres and part of a 200-acre tract which had been granted to William Franklin, adjoining William White and David Robison. Witnesses: Benjamin Smith and Robert Isaacs. On 5 April 1796, a lawsuit of David Neal, Sr. deeded James White and David Roberson, Sr. of Columbia County, for $12,000 versus William Franklin as Executor of the Last Will and Testament of Ebenezer Starnes of Wilkes County (Starnes' LWT dated 5 April 1796, probated 13 May 1793, Wilkes County).

G. Samuel Owen Franklin, Sr., born 1805 in Washington County, Georgia, died 1867, married Mary Elizabeth Floyd.

Issue by 2nd wife (Mary):[147]

II. Zephaniah Franklin, born 1755, married Mary Walker. Residents of Warren County in 1820. He was a Revolutionary War Soldier who drew land in the 1832 Georgia Land Lottery in Cherokee County (granted 1837). He had at least 5 daughters and one son.

III. William Franklin, Jr., Revolutionary War Soldier, born ca 1756, married Miss Smith.

IV. Martha H. Franklin, born between 1765-1770, died between 1825 and 1829 in Warren County, Georgia, married Alexander Smith. SEE Smith.

Gamel/Gammell of Paulding County

William Gammell was born 1812 in Georgia, farmer. Wife, Mary Ann, born 1814 in South Carolina. Issue:[148]

I. Henry H. Gammell, born 1837 in Georgia.

II. Sarah Ann Gammell, born 1838 in Georgia. She married Joseph B. Thompson on 26 August 1855 in Paulding County.

III. Barbara Ann Gammell, born 1841 in Georgia.

IV. John B. Gammell, born 1844 in Paulding County, married Emiline Hix on 27 December 1874 in Paulding County.

V. William Anthony Gammell, born 1846 in Paulding County, died 1904, marrid Charlotte Mellisa Rapert. Issue:

    A. Semeon Leonadus Christopher Gamel, born 1875, died 1951, married Letta Agnes Donoho. Issue:
        1. Eugene Ulmont Gamel, born 1913. Wife, Marie.
        2. Glenda Gamel, born 1915.
        3. Emily Gamel, born 1918.
        4. Bracy Eldon Gamel, born 1921.
        5. Bryan Gamel, born 1925.
        6. Shirley Gamel, born 1929, married Mr. McMurrey.
    B. Joseph Mont Gamel, born 1878, died 1938, married Amanda Ramsey. Issue: Carl Gamel.
    C. Charles Demar Gamel, born 1880, married (1) Mrs. Amy Inez Martin Dean and (2) Franny Yates. Issue:
        1. Marvin Gamel, 1904-1984.
        2. Edith Gamel, born 1909.
        3. Edna Gamel, born 1911, married Mr. Goddard.

---

[147] Roster of Revolutionary War Soldiers in Georgia by McCall; Warren County Marriages.

[148] 1850 & 1880 Paulding County Census, Paulding County Marriages.

4. Willard Gamel, 1912-1944.
5. Retha Gamel, born 1918, married Mr. Anderson.
6. Charles Shelby Gamel, 1923-1934.
D. Myrtle Luthada Gamel, born 1886, died 1890.
E. Ella Jane Gamel, born 1884, died 1904.
F. Clara Bartelia Gamel, born 1889, married Julius Glenwood Owens.
G. Guy Eaton Gamel, born 1890, married Margie Downey.
H. Ethel Gertrude Gamel, born 1893, married (1) Reuben Grover Chamberlain and (2) John Franklin Anderson.
I. Nova V. Gamel, born 1895, died 1915.
J. Millus Bryne Gamel, born 1897, married (1) Lichford Brooks and (2) Helen Davison.
K. William Dewey Gamel, born 1900, died 1860, married Altheda Mae Hicks.

VI. Charles B. Gammell, born 1847 in Paulding County, farmer. He married Mary F. Adair, born 22 March 1847 in Dallas, Paulding County, a daughter of John Bluett Adair and his wife, Pheriby C. (Anderson) Adair. SEE Adair. Issue:

A. Robert H. Gamel, born 1871 in Paulding County.
B. William W. Gamel, born 1873 in Paulding County.
C. Lucious H. Gamel, born 1875 in Paulding County.
D. Rhodelia Gamel, born 1877 in Paulding County.
E. Charles B. Gamel, born 1879 in Paulding County.

VI. Benjamin Franklin Gammell, born 28 May 1849 in Dallas, Paulding County, died 1 February 1870 in Gustine, Comanche County, Texas, buried in the Siloam Cemetery. He was married on 21 December 1870 in Milam County, Texas, to Alice Elizabeth Lester (born 6 August 1856 Cameron, Texas, died 7 March 1925, buried in the Siloam Cemetery, in Gustine, Texas, a daughter of William Henry Lester and his wife, Martha Anne (McKinney) Lester. Issue:[149]

A. Ewell Bertrum Gamel, born 1 January 1874 in Gustine, Comanche County, Texas, died 1924, buried in the Siloam Cemetery.
B. Wilkes Boothe Gamel, born 9 October 1876 in Gustine, Comanche County, Texas, died 1963.
C. Lozade Gamel, born 10 February 1877 in Gustine, Comanche County, Texas, died 25 December 1964 in Pawhuaka, Oklahoma, buried in the Alfafa Cemetery.
D. Bertie Gamel, born 1880 in Gustine, Comanche County, Texas, died 1921 in Checota, Texas, buried in the Methodist Church Cemetery.
E. Claude Franklin Gamel, born 8 October 1884 in Gustine, Comanche County, Texas, died 18 September 1806 in Dover, Oklahoma, buried in the Siloam Cemetery, in Gustine, Texas.
F. Donnie Gamel, born 1887 in Gustine, Comanche County, Texas, died 1890, buried in the Siloam Cemetery, in Gustine, Texas.

---

[149] 1880 Comanche County, Texas Census, E. D. 30.

Gann of Virginia;
Clarke & Paulding County

Samuel Gann was born 1703 in Virginia, and died 1758 in Winchester, Frederick County, Virginia. Wife, Elizabeth. Issue:

I.   Nathan Gann, born 1729 in Winchester, Frederick County, Virginia, died ca 1832 in Georgia.

II.   Adam Gann, born 1732/1735 in Winchester, Frederick County, Virginia, died 6 August 1812 in Dandridge, Jefferson County, Tennessee.

III. Clement Gann, born 1733 in Winchester, Frederick County, Virginia.

IV.   Nathan Gann, born 1734, died 1843 in Georgia. Issue:

    A. Samuel Gann.
    B. James Gann.
    C. John Gann.
    D. Micajah Gann.
    E. William Gann.
    F. Nathan Gann, born ca 1786, died ca 1854 in Paulding County. Wife, Mary, was born 1796 in Georgia. He married (1) Nancy Summers on 9 January 1809 in Clarke County, and (2) Mary Summers Wilkins on 10 November 1833. Known issue:

        1. John Gann, born 8 January 1812 in Clarke County, died 15 August 1881 in Cobb County.
        2. Robert (Robin) Gann, born March 1815 in Clarke County, died 11 May 1900 in Paulding County.
        3. Elizabeth Gann, born ca 1817 in Georgia.
        4. Seaborn Gann, born 29 July 1818 in Georgia, died 10 November 1809 in Haralson County.
        5. Nathan Gann, Jr., born 1822 in Georgia. Wife, Anna, born 1828 in Georgia. Known issue:[150]

            a. Prudence A. Gann, born 1840 in Georgia.
            b. Nancy Gann, born 1840 in Paulding County.
            c. Mary Ann Gann, born 1844 in Paulding County.
            d. Elizabeth Gann, born 1846 in Paulding County.
            e. Robert Gann, born 1849 in Paulding County.

        6. Francis Gann.
        7. Martha Gann.
        8. Salina Gann, born 1838 in Georgia, married Bozeman Adair, born 1833 Paulding County, on 19 June 1863 in Paulding County. SEE Adair.
        9. William D. Gann, died ca 1863, during the War Between the States.

V.   John Gann, died 1817.

VI.   Samuel Gann, born 1748 in Winchester, Frederick County, Virginia, died 1843 in Madison, Rockingham County, North Carolina.

---

[150] 1850 Paulding County Census.

Gideon of Jackson County

Reverend James Gideon was born in South Carolina, and died 1817 in Jackson County, his LWT dated 6 June 1803, probated 4 August 1817, Jackson County Will Book A, page 68. He married Elizabeth Camp (died before 1850 in Jackson County), the daughter of Nathaniel Camp and his wife, Winnifred (Tarpley) Camp. SEE Camp. After Rev. Gideon's death, Elizabeth married (2) Samuel Stewart and (3) Hardy Howard.[151] Elizabeth is said to have had 22 children in all. Issue:

I. Hosea Camp Gideon, born 1800 in Georgia, farmer. In 1880, he was residing with his grandchildren, William W. Worsham, age 19, and granddaughter, Sallie E. Worsham, age 18, in Maysville, Banks County. He married Easter Morgan on 7 March 1823 in Jackson County.

II. Berry Wilson Gideon, born 1806 in Georgia. Wife, Sally. Issue:

   A. M. P. Gideon (daughter), born 1829 in Georgia.
   B. Flora Gideon, born 1831 in Georgia.
   C. Galean Gideon, born 1834 in Georgia.
   D. Gilead Gideon, born 1836 in Georgia.
   E. Botheliina Gideon, born 1838 in Georgia.
   F. Zenobia Gideon, born 1840 in Georgia.
   G. Sholima Gideon, born 1842 in Georgia.
   H. Thalia Gideon, born 1844 in Georgia.
   I. Tyheginia Gideon, born 1846 in Georgia.
   J. Addinia Gideon, born 1848 in Georgia.

Greene of Monroe County

William M. Greene was born ca 1825, died ca 1847 in Monroe County. He married Ann M. Chambliss who died 24 April 1870 in Forsyth, Monroe County, Georgia, a daughter of John M. Chambliss and his wife, Elizabeth (Jordan) Chambliss. SEE Chambliss. Issue:

I. Ann M. Greene, born 8 January 1845 in Forsyth, Monroe County, Georgia.

II. John Miles Greene, born 23 June 1846 in Forsyth, Monroe County, Georgia.

III. Ellen Frances Greene, born September 1848 in Forsyth, Monroe County, Georgia.

Gruber of Austria &
Effingham County

Peter Gruber, husbandman, was born 1700 in Taxenbuch, Saltzburg, Berchtesgaden or vicinity, Austria. Arrived 12 March 1733/4, Saltzburger. Died 2 December 1740 Ebenezer, buried 4 December 1740, Savannah married on 23 February 1736 at Ebenezer, Marcia Kraher (Mosshammer), the widow of Hans Mosshammer (died 2 September 1735) 23 February 1736 at Ebenezer. After the death of Peter Gruber, Marcie married for the third time, Charles Floerl. Marcie died 1767 Ebenezer. She was the daughter of Peter Kraher, born ca 1694 Saalfelden,

---

[151] The LWT of Hardy Howard, dated 13 August 1859, probated 12 September 1859, Jackson County Will Book A, page 431. Hardy Howard is listed on the 1850 Jackson County Census.

Germany and his wife, Barbara Rohrmoser, born 1696 Augsburg, Schwaben, Bavaria, died 16 Nov 1735. Issue:[152]

I. Peter Gruber, born 17 September 1738 Ebenezer, died 23 September 1738

II. John Gruber, born 1739 Ebenezer, died 23 September, Effingham County married 4 June 1765 Effingham County Miss Mary M. Kalcher from Lindau, Austria. In 1772 he received a Land Grant in Bulloch County. This land grant begins the long lineage of the Groover family in that area. He was deceased by 1802, as his widow, Mary Groover of Bulloch County on 2 January 1802 deeded 50 acres of land, being part of an original land grant to John Gruber, Sr. by King George III of Great Britain for $225.00. Several of their children are listed in the Ebenezer Church data - William, minister, Joshua, Solomon and John. Issue:

A. John Gruber, son of John Gruber, was born 4 March 1766, died 4 April 1836 Brooks County married in 1790 Bulloch County Hannah Lastinger.

B. Solomon Gruber, son of John Gruber, was born 25 January 1769 married 29 Nov 1798 Elizabeth Wise.

C. Joshua Gruber, son of John Gruber, was born August 1772.

D. Charles Gruber, son of John Gruber, was born 1775, died 1829 Bulloch County, married 1813 Sarah Reiser.

E. David Gruber, son of John Gruber, was born 1777, died 1845 Bulloch County married 17 May 1799 Bulloch County, Martha D. Shuffield (Her Will dated 29 January 1849, probated June 1853 Bulloch County).

F. William Gruber, son of John Gruber, minister, was born 30 December 1778, died 1854 Bulloch County, married Mrs. Salome (Gugle) Cooper. Issue:
1. John Gruber, son of William Gruber, was born in 1811 married 4 December 1832 Sarah Bowen and had issue:
a. James Bulloch Groover, miller, was born 1837 in Bulloch County, and married 7 September 1864 Bulloch County, Sarah Januarye Wilson (born 1844 in Bulloch County). Issue:[153]
   i. John J. Groover, born 1867 in Bulloch County.
   ii. James R. Groover, born 1869 in Bulloch County.
   iii. Mary Jane Groover, born 1870 in Bulloch County.
   iv. Emmeline Groover, born 1872 in Bulloch County.
   v. Virginia A. Groover, born 1873 in Bulloch County.
   vi. Ann C. Groover, born 1874 in Bulloch County.
   vii. Eva O. Groover, born 1878 in Bulloch County.
b. Elisha Groover.
c. William Groover.
d. John Groover.

2. Edward Groover, son of William Gruber, was born 1815 married Sarah.

---

[152] Colonial Records of Georgia by Candler; Early Settlers of Georgia by Coulter; Bulloch County Wills, Deeds & Marriages.

[153] 1880 Bulloch County Census, Sink Hole.

3. Harriett Groover, daughter of William Gruber, was born 1818.

4. William Groover, son of William Gruber, was born 1820 in Bulloch County, married Elizabeth M. Lee on 7 December 1848 in Bulloch County. In 1880, his wife was Mary E. (born 1833 in Georgia). SEE Lee. Issue:[154]

        a. Ann A. Groover, born 1856 in Bulloch County.
        b. James A. Groover, born 1859 in Bulloch County.
        c. John J. Groover, born 1860 in Bulloch County.
        d. Lola M. Groover, born 1863 in Bulloch County.
        e. William Groover, born 1866 in Bulloch County.
        f. Malekiah Groover, born 1869 in Bulloch County.
        g. Arthur Groover, born 1872 in Bulloch County.
        h. Lawrence Groover, born 1874 in Bulloch County.
        i. Mary C. Groover, born 1877 in Bulloch County.

5. Easter M. Groover, son of William Gruber, was born 1823 in Bulloch County, married 5 December 1844 in Bulloch County, John D. McElvin (or McElveen) (born 1815), farmer in Brier Patch, Georgia. Issue:[155]

        a. Laura E. McElveen, born 1858 in Bulloch County.
        b. James H. McElveen, born 1859 in Bulloch County.
        c. John D. McElveen, born 1861 in Bulloch County.

6. Sarah A. Groover, daughter of William Gruber, was born 1825, married on 18 May 1854 in Bulloch County, Robert W. Roberts.

7. Charles A. Groover, son of William Gruber, was born 182,9 married on 9 Nov 1854 in Bulloch County, Mary Ann Rushing.

8. Eliza Groover, daughter of William Gruber, was born 1840, married on 22 February 1874 in Bulloch County, Thomas Cone.

9. David Groover, son of William Gruber, was born 1843.

G. Elizabeth Gruber, daughter of John Gruber, was born 1780, married on 20 May 1801 in Bulloch County, Henry Wise.

---

[154] 1880 Bulloch County, Census, Brier Patch.

[155] Ibid.

Hagan/Hagin of Wilkes, Clarke,
Richmond (McDuffie County), Wilkes & Paulding Counties

This name is spelled variously in the records as Hagin, Hagan, and Hagans. To be consistent, I used "Hagin" throughout, however, it must be noted that the Paulding County family frequently used Hagan, and Hagans after the death of Edward Hagin, Jr.[156]

Edward Hagin was born in South Carolina in 1755, probably a resident of Edgefield County, before removing to Georgia with other Quakers, to settle in Wrightsborough. On 30 August 1774, he was among those residents who signed a petition:

"Town of Wrightsborough

We, the Inhabitants of the Town of Wrightsborough and places adjacent, understanding that fourteen persons have drawn up several resolutions respecting the dispute between Great Britain and the Town of Boston, concerning the destroying of a quantity of tea, the Property of the East India Company, and have published them each the Act of the Province, And which we look upon as a great imposition, having no knowledge of them Till they passed; Therefore, we do, in this public manner, deny passing any Concerning them, and disapprove of them altogether, such proceeding as a few Acting for the while without the knowledge, we apprehend being contrary to the rights and privileges of every British subject."

"Notice of the Executive Council Thursday 30 September 1784: This day His Honour, the Governor, signed the following grants in Council, viz: Washington County - Edward Hagin, 287 ½ acres (two)"

Edward and his family removed to Wilkes County in 1786, which is another county where Quakers resided, however they deeded their 200 acres of land on Little River at the mouth of Kettle Creek to Charles Carroll. In 1787 Edward was a Captain of the 9th Company for the Washington County Militia; Coroner in 1790 and 1792. He removed to Clarke County by 1802, because of a deed from Roger Cagle for $400.00, 124 acres located on Barber's Creek, land which was originally granted to Marbury. He fought in the Revolutionary War, being certified as one of the Georgia Troops. Elijah Clarke Certified him as a "refugee soldier" on 7 April 1784 for which he was granted 287 ½ acres of land in Washington County. His Last Will and Testament in Clarke County dated 1805 named "all my children", however, various returns made on the estate, named among the legatees: Edward, Jr. and James.[157]

He was a resident of Wilkes County, where he served as a Captain of the 9th Company in the Georgia Militia in 1795; he was a Coroner in Washington County from 1790 to 1792. As a refugee soldier he was certified by Elijah Clarke on 7 April 1784, for which he received 287 ½ acres of land in Washington County. He later removed to Clarke County where he purchased

---

[156] Much of the recent information comes from the book, *Hagan-Bryant Genealogies* by Tom Hagan; however, all the various census records in Georgia and Alabama were also used as strict guidelines. The above book, however, contains numerous errors, as I think that Tom was speculating in some instances. For one, Wrightsville was located in Columbia (now McDuffie) County, Georgia, and not in South Carolina. Also, he deals with some of the earlier Hagins, which do not match to my findings.

[157] Clarke County Tax Digests & Marriages; 1821 Georgia Land Lottery.

a tract of land in 1802 from Roger Cagle. His LWT was probated in 1805 in Clarke County. He married (1) Elizabeth, who died after 1785 and (2) Hannah.

Known issue:[158]

I. Daniel Hagin, son of Edward Hagin, was born ca 1780 in Wilkes County, died between 1850 and 1860 in Coosa County, Alabama. He married on 1 June 1813, Mrs. Elizabeth Newsome, nee Hinnard, a daughter of John Hinnard.[159] Daniel was listed in the Clarke County Tax Digests from 1811 to 1818; from 1825 to 1830 he was listed in the Georgia Militia Records as a Lieutenant in Appling County; and drew in the 1827 Land Lottery, while a resident of Walton County, designated as a soldier. He was listed on the 1830 Coweta County Census. Issue:

A. Archa Hagin, son of Daniel Hagin, was born 3 April 1813 in Newton County, died 26 December 1885 in Carroll County, buried in the Stripling Cemetery, near Carrollton. He married on 1 October 1835, Malinda George, in Coweta County.[160] Issue:

1. Mary Elizabeth Hagin, born 24 April 1837, married David Holman.
2. John Clark Hagin, born 18 May 1838, died during the War Between the States, in battle. He married Sara Carmichael (she later married Joe Gable). Issue: Abie Hagin and Johnnie Hagin (died as an infant).
3. James Travis Hagin, born 22 October 1839, died 30 August 1861 during the War Between the States, buried in Charlottesville, Virginia.
4. Sara Ann Hagin, born 9 June 1841, married Bennett Evans on 10 December 1867.
5. Minerva Francis Hagin, born 5 December 1842, died 17 November 1915, married G. W. Moore on 17 May 1860 in Coweta County.
6. Martha George Hagin, born 6 August 1844, married Joshua F. Gilbert (died 6 September 1928).
7. Penniah Camp Hagin, born 7 November 1846, married T. Jeff Moore. No issue.
8. Emily Absilla Hagin, born 20 October 1849, married William Fennin Brown on 30 December 1873.
9. Malinda Catherine Hagin, born 17 November 1851, married Joe D. Walker.
10. Louisa Josephine Hagin, born 12 March 1854, married H. W. Culepper.
11. Hiram George Hagin, born 1857, farmer. Wife, Ida O., born 1859 in Georgia. Issue:[161]
    a. Ocrau E. Hagin (son), born 1879 in Carroll County.

---

[158] Georgia's Roster of the Revolution by Lucian Lamar Knight; 1830-1850 Coosa County, Alabama Census; Clarke County Estates, Bonds & Marriages; Paulding County Wills & Estates; 1880 Paulding County Census.

[159] The LWT of John Hinnard probated 4 May 1835 in Fayette County, named his second wife, and sons and daughters (Elizabeth, William, John C., Peninah and Nancy).

[160] Coweta County Chronicles for One Hundred Years.

[161] 1880 Carroll County Census, District 682.

II.   Edward Hagin, Jr., son of Edward Hagin, was born 1782 in Wilkes County, died in Coosa County, Alabama. He married (1) on 9 January 1807, Sally Youngblood, and (2) Heardy Porch on 29 October 1812. SEE Youngblood.

Issue by (2) wife:

D.   Edward Hagin, son of Edward Hagin, Jr., was born 26 August 1807 in Clarke County, died 4 July 1890 in Paulding County, buried in the old High Shoals Baptist Church Cemetery. He served during the War Between the States in Co. A, 9 BN Cav., C. S. A. He married Parthenia Scoggins on 13 January 1828 (born 20 March 1813 in Oglethorpe County, died 24 September 1881 in Paulding County, buried in old High Shoals Baptist Church Cemetery. They were listed on the 1860-1880 Paulding County Census, residents of Huntsville; his LWT was dated 1890 in Paulding County. He owned 240 acres of land and ran a general store which was located on the southwest side of Old Reumus Road, and also served as the Ordinary of Paulding County between 1872 and 1877. Edward and Parthenia were buried in High Shoals Baptist Church Cemetery.

Issue:

1.   Henry Newton Hagin, born 19 September 1830 in DeKalb County, died 4 June 1914 in Paulding County, farmer, resident of Huntsville. He married Elizabeth Stewart (born 1827 in South Carolina) on 31 October 1849 in Paulding County. During the War Between the States, he served as a 2nd Lieutenant in Co. K of the 60th Georgia Regiment Volunteers, and, in 1862, was wounded in the leg at Petersburg, Virginia. He was elected to the State House of Representatives, serving in 1880 and 1881; post master of the Braswell Post Office 1883-1885; and was Justice of the Peace in Braswell, from 1887 to 1909.[162] Issue:

a.   James Edward Hagin, born 19 August 1850 in Paulding County, died 20 April 1905 in Atlanta, buried in the Friendship Baptist Church Cemetery in Braswell. He was married to Emily Crow (born 13 February 1872) on 13 February 1872 in Paulding County. No issue.

b.   William Franklin Hagin, born 22 December 1851 in Paulding County, died 24 September 1890 in Paulding County. He married M. Ellen Davis (born 1856, died 28 June 1891 in Braswell, Georgia[163]) on 19 December 1872 in Polk County. Issue:

i.   Ida Hagin, born 1874 in Georgia, married Mr. Wilson.
ii.   Simeon Hagin, born 1876 in Georgia.
iii.   Walter Hagin, born 1879 in Georgia.
iv.   Claud Hagin.
v.   Clifford Hagin.

---

[162] 1880 Paulding County Census, Burnt Hickory.

[163] The death of Mrs. Ella Hagin (wife of William Franklin Hagin) was recorded in The Paulding New Era on 31 July 1891.

   vi. Fannie Hagin, died 19 October 1889 in Polk County.

   vii. Son, infant, died 28 July 1891 in Paulding County.

c. Samuel Jackson Hagin, born 27 October 1853 in Paulding County, died 18 October 1931. He married Naomi E. Thompson (born November 1856, died 3 December 1920) on 5 November 1874 in Paulding County. They are both buried in the Myrtle Hill Cemetery, Rome. Issue:

   i. Thomas Charles Hagin, born 1875, died 1937, buried in the Myrtle Hill Cemetery, Rome. He married Mable Klein on 27 July 1898 in Floyd County. Issue: Ellen Hagin, born 10 November 1903, died 12 April 1926, buried in the Myrtle Hill Cemetery; and Mae Beth Hagin, married Rufus H. Daniel of Florida.

   ii. Etta Mae Hagin, born 4 December 1881 in Georgia, died 18 September 1977, married in Floyd County on 27 December 1905 to John Alex Wilkins (Born 1871, died 29 October 1938). Both are buried in the Myrtle Hill Cemetery. Issue: Elizabeth Wilkins, born 23 November 1907, died August 1978, married Mr. Wingard;Isabelle Wilkins, born 1 December 1909 in Rome, married William Joseph Pilson (born 20 July 1895, died 2 July 1960); and Jane A Wilkins, born 21 July 1911, died 5 August 1970, married Mr. Coleman.

d. George Thomas Hagin, born 15 August 1856, died 9 June 1887, farmer in Hays, Georgia, married Nancy Jennette Hays (born 1860) on 29 December 1878. Issue:[164]

   i. Willie Floyd Hagin, born 1864 in Newton County.

   ii. Eldorado Hagin.

   iii. Newton Hagin.

   iv. Irwin Hagin.

e. Savage Hagin, born 1857 in Paulding County.

f. Mary Catherine Hagin, born 29 October 1858 in Paulding County, died 11 July 1938, married Samuel D. Denton (born 30 April 1854, died 10 February 1934) on 10 December 1876, a farmer in Round Mountain, Alabama.

g. Sarah Jane Hagin, born 15 January 1861 in Paulding County, married J. Robert Moon on 24 September 1882, a deputy Sheriff in Paulding County (1886-1888); Sheriff in 1889; postmaster 1893-1897. SEE Moon.

h. Parthena E. Hagin, born 18 September 1863 in Paulding County, died December 1914, married Milton Wallis on 10 September 1881 in Paulding County.

i. Amanda E. Hagin, born 16 March 1867 in Paulding County, died 7 March 1960. She married Milton Silas Norton on 15 December 1886.

j. John H. Hagin, born 8 April 1870 in Paulding County, married Elizabeth Bishop (born 29 September 1863) on 10 January 1892. They

---

[164] 1880 Newton County Census, Hays, Georgia.

were residents of Atlanta. Issue: Jessie Hagin, married Hartwell Davis, residents of Selma, Alabama.

    k. Edward H. Hagin, born January 1872 in Paulding County, married Levena in 1900. He was a grocery store merchant in Braswell.

2. Mary Jane Hagin, born 1833 in Georgia, married on 9 May 1852 in Paulding County, to Robert Lewis Spinks.

3. James Jasper Hagin, born 2 May 1836 in Paulding County, died 19 January 1911 in Paulding County. He was a blacksmith and owned a farm at Burnt Hickory in Paulding County. Also, during the War Between the States, served as a 2nd Sgt. In Co. K, 60th Georgia Regiment; elected Jr. Lt. in 1862 and 2nd Lt. in December of 1862. He was wounded during the war, captured at Fredericksburg, Virginia on 13 December 1862, and exchanged at City Point, Virginia in 1863. He was again wounded on 23 July 1863 and admitted to the Confederate Hospital in Charlottesville, Virginia where he was released on 24 August 1863. to be afterwards captured on 19 September 1864 at Winchester, Virginia, send to City Point, Virginia in 1865. Wife, Nancy, born 28 September 1833 in Georgia, was buried in the Flint Hill Cemetery in Paulding County. Issue:[165]

    a. Parthena Hagin, born 1853 in Alabama.
    b. Elizabeth Hagin, born 29 December 1857 in Paulding County, died 28 July 1932, married W. R. Elsberry on 10 August 1881 in Paulding County.
    c. William Hagin, born 1856 in Paulding County.
    d. Parthenia Hagin, born 1858 in Paulding County.
    e. Mary Hagin, born 1860 in Paulding County.
    f. Beulah Hagin, born 1865 in Paulding County.
    g. Frances Hagin, born 1868 in Paulding County.
    h. Russell Hagin, born 1870 in Paulding County.
    i. Louana Hagin, born October 1871 in Paulding County.
    j. Sarah Hagin, born 1872 in Paulding County, married W. R. Rakestraw on 20 April 1890 in Paulding County.
    k. Snowden E. Hagin, born 3 July 1876 in Paulding County, died 1 May 1957 in Atlanta, buried in the Rose Hill Cemetery, Rockmart. She never married, and owned a millinery shop in Rockmart, later removing to Atlanta.
    l. Ella Hagin, born 1877 in Paulding County.

4. Dicy Catherine Hagin, born 25 January 1839 in Georgia, died 11 March 1912, buried in the Rose Hill Cemetery. She married Robert Hays on 6 November 1856 in Paulding County (died 12 December 1885) and they removed to Rockmart.

5. Louisa Elizabeth Hagin, born 4 February 1842 in High Shoals, Paulding County, died 31 December 1932 in Rome, buried in the Myrtle Hill Cemetery in Rome. She married Jonathan J. Forsyth on 28 October 1858 in Paulding County. SEE Forsyth.

---

[165] 1880 Paulding County Census, Burnt Hickory.

6.   Benjamin Franklin Hagin, born 10 December 1845 in High Shoals, Paulding County, died 8 July 1920 in Douglasville, buried in the Holly Springs Baptist Church Cemetery in Paulding County. He established the post office inside the Hagan General Store and named it "Remus, Georgia Post Office", where he was the postmaster from 1885 to 1894. He was also a teacher, deputy sheriff, justice of peace, and was assistant postmaster in Douglasville. During the War Between the States, he served in Co. K, Lee's Battalion Infantry, 4th Georgia Cavalry. He was married to Clarenda Ann Camp (born 8 April 1848 in Paulding County, died 19 July 1903). Both are buried in the Holly Springs Cemetery. Issue:

    i. Cosouth Hagin, born 1870 in Paulding County.

    ii. Bertha Hagin, born November 1872 in Paulding County, died 1939. She married J. Ivy Moody (died 10 January 1902, buried in the Holly Springs Cemetery) in Paulding County on 24 June 1898.

    iii. Ludeala Hagin, born 4 February 1874 in Paulding County, died 13 March 1962 in Douglasville; never married.

    iv. Edward McConnell Hagin, born 27 October 1876 in Paulding County, died 12 January 1974 in Glasville. He married Selena Partain on 25 September 1898. Issue: Virginia Lois Hagin, born 30 April 1900 in Boaz, Alabama, died 11 September 1965 in Douglasville, married George Patrick Gilbert on 3 June 1925; Mira Hagin, born 26 April 1904 in Paulding County, died 27 April 1904; Buena Elnora Hagin, born 22 June 1905 near Yorkville, in Paulding County, married Samuel Thomas Barnes on 28 December 1958; and James Edward Hagin, born and died on 4 July 1911 in Douglasville.

    v. Raleigh Emmett Hagin, born 30 April 1879 in Paulding County, died 27 October 1943 in Atlanta, married Nora Gertrude Lee on 12 August 1900.

8.   Edward F. Hagin, born 1846 in High Shoals, Paulding County, died before 1881.

9.   Thomas Calvert Hagin, born December 1849 in Paulding County, died 13 March 1929 in Polk County, buried in the Rose Hill Cemetery, Rockmart. He married Sarah Jane Lee (born 11 Ocrober 1853, died 20 October 1929) on 14 May 1871. Issue:[166]

    i. Edward Hartwell Hagin, born 6 June 1874 in Georgia, died 8 March 1909. He married Nora Haynes (born 21 January 1882, died February 1901) in 1900. They are buried in the Rose Hill Cemetery.

    ii. Thaddeus Augustus Hagin, born 30 September 1875 in Rockmart, died 18 May 1962 in Rockmart. He married Lula Estelle Waits (born 30 November 1876 in Rockmart), and they were buried in the Rose Hill Cemetery.

    iii. Adna Hagin, born 2 December 1878, died 20 February 1972 in Cedartown, buried in the Rose Hill Cemetery in Rockmart. She married in December of 1905, Julian McDuffie Hardage.

---

[166] 1880 Polk County Census, Buncombe.

iv. Ella Eugenia Hagin, born 3 April 1881, died 5 August 1889, buried in the Old High Shoals Baptist Church Cemetery, near Dallas, Georgia.

v. Wyatt Franklin Hagin, born 26 October 1883 in Georgia, died 21 October 1927 in Polk, County, buried in the Rose Hill Cemetery, Rockmart. Never married.

vi. Thomas Reese Hagin, born 1 March 1886, died 7 September 1886, buried in the old High Shoals Baptist Church Cemetery.

vii. Homer Lee Hagin, born 19 August 1887, died January 1973, buried in the Concord Baptist Church Cemeter in Clanton, Alabama. He was married in 1914 to Essie Mimms (died 30 April 1979).

viii. William Jackson Hagin, born 4 December 1889 in Georgia, died 10 February 1909, buried in the Rose Hill Cemetery in Rockmart, never married.

ix. Robert Luther Hagin, born 7 November 1892, died April 1912.

x. Bertrude Hagin, born 11 October 1895 in Georgia, died 7 July 1983, buried in the Rose Hill Cemetery in Rockmart.

B. Elizabeth Hagin, daughter of Edward Hagin, Jr., was born 1809 in Clarke County, died 22 December 1840, buried in the Holland Cemetery in Paulding County. She married Archibald Holland on 30 December 1823 in Clarke County. SEE Holland. Archibald Holland drew in the 1821 Georgia Land Lottery while a resident of Greene County, Lot No. 82, District 14, in Henry County. This is the same land which was in DeKalb County in 1830 (now Fulton County), now in Atlanta, being 221-1/2 acres encompassing Northside Drive, Luckie Street and downtown Atlanta where the terminal train station is located.

Issue of Edward Hagin and Heardy Porch:[167]

C. Martha Hagin, daughter of Edward Hagin, Jr., was born 1828 in Campbell County.

D. Charles Hagin, daughter of Edward Hagin, Jr., was born 1830 in Campbell County.

E. David Hagin, son of Edward Hagin, Jr., was born 1833 in Campbell County.

F. James Hagin, son of Edward Hagin, Jr., was born 1836 in Campbell County, married Betty Oliver. Issue:

1. James Hagin.
2. Oliver Hagin.

G. Sarah Hagin, daughter of Edward Hagin, Jr., was born 1837 in Campbell County.

H. Amanda Hagin, daughter of Edward Hagin, Jr., was born 1840 in Campbell County.

---

[167] 1850 Coosa County, Alabama Census.

IV.   James Hagin, son of Edward Hagin, was born ca 1784 in Wilkes County, died 1814 in Clarke County. An administrator's bond was issued to Jesse Roberts and Thomas Moore dated 2 May 1814 in Clarke County Bonds (1811-1839), page 35, on the Estate of James Hagin. He was listed on the 1813 Clarke County Tax Digest. He was married to Rachel Annis, born 8 December 1774, the daughter of Thomas and Alice Gayle of Virginia.

Hargett/Hugett of Germany, Maryland, North Carolina
& Cobb County

The Hargett/Hugett family were part of the Palatines (or Germans) who began arriving in Philadelphia in 1727. Johann Henrich Hargett, the progenitor of the family in Mecklenburg and Union Counties, North Carolina, came from Germany, arriving in Philadelphia on 2 October 1749, onboard the ship *Jacob*. He first removed to Anson County, North Carolina. According to various land grants, it appears that he, known as John Henry Hargett in America, removed from Anson County after 1764, to Mecklenburg County to reside on a farm of 200 acres located on both sides of Stewart's fork, near the town of Monroe. John Henry Hargett and his wife, Anna, had about ten children. The LWT of Henry Hargett, Sr. was dated 28 March 1803, probated July 1803, Mecklenburg County, North Carolina. All of his property, his plantation, as well as 100 acres on Stump Lick (on Richardson's Creek), etc. was left to his wife, Nanna Hargett. After her death, the whole estate was to be divided equally among his children, viz: Henry, Peter, Daniel, Joseph, Elizabeth Chaney, Rachel Pellum, Rebekah Broom, Mary Craig, Sarah Holmes and Agnes Laney. Anna died about 1810.

Sons:

I.   Henry Hargett, son of John Henry Hargett), was born ca 1752 in Anson County, North Carolina, died 1827. During the Revolutionary War, he served as a private under Captain Jacob Barnett in Colonel Hampton's Regiment of Light Dragoons (General Sumter's Brigade of South Carolina). He married (1) a daughter of James Finley of Mecklenburg County, who died before 1782. After that he married (2) Anna Broom. His LWT was dated 25 December 1825, probated in 1827, Mecklenburg County. His left his entire plantation to his wife, Anna, then at her death to go to his son, Daniel. He had eleven children. Issue:[168]

    C.   Anny Hargett, daughter of Henry Hargett, was born 12 January 1780, married Eli Presley.

    B.   Henry Hargett, son of Henry Hargett, was born 23 October 1784, married (1) Isabel Presley (born 29 January 1787 in Anson County, North Carolina). They removed to Alabama in 1832, and he died in Franklin County after 1870.

    C.   James Hargett, son of Henry Hargett, was born 1770-1780, married Diana Johnston on 23 December 1800 in Mecklenburg County..

    D.   Casper Hargett, son of Henry Hargett, was born 1789 in North Carolina, farmer; listed on the 1850 Mecklenburg County Census. Wife, Prudence, was born 1802. [169] Issue:

---

[168]   1850-1860 Union County, North Carolina Census; 1850-1860 Mecklenburg County, Census.

[169]   There is a marriage of Casper Hargett to Sarah Finny on 18 December 1856 in Mecklenburg County.

1. Harris Hargett, son of Casper Hargett, was born 1826 in North Carolina, farmer. He married Martha Hall (born 1819) on 21 December 1846 in Mecklenburg County Issue:

    a. Mary Hargett, born 1847 in Mecklenburg County.

    b. Jane Hargett, born 1849 in Mecklenburg County.

2. P. A. Hargett, son of Casper Hargett, was born 1829 North Carolina. Wife, Mary, born 1834. Issue:

    a. Kolman Hargett (daughter), born 1856 in Charlotte, North Carolina.

3. H. Morrison Hargett, son of Casper Hargett, was born 1831 North Carolina. He married Elizabeth Harkey (born 1833 in North Carolina) on 11 September 1851 in Mecklenburg County. Issue:

    a. Prudence Hargett, born 1853 in Charlotte, North Carolina.

    b. William Brown Hargett, born December 1854 in Charlotte, North Carolina. He married Mary Nicholson (born 1853). [170] Residents of Sharon, North Carolina. Issue:

        i. Rosa W. Hargett, born 1874 in Sharon, Mecklenburg County, Noth Carolina.

        ii. Louisa E. Hargett, born 1876 in Sharon, Mecklenburg County, North Carolina.

        iii. Blandina Hargett, born 17 October 1877 in Charlotte, North Carolina, died 23 September 1934 in Smyrna, Cobb County, Georgia. She was married to Sanford C. Austin. SEE Austin.

        iv. Henry Fred Hargett, born December 1879 in Charlotte, North Carolina.[171]

        iii. Willie B. Hargett, born April 1882 in Charlotte, North Carolina,

        iv. Agnes Hargett, born April 1884 in Charlotte, North Carolina.

        v. Lizzie Hargett, born June 1885 in Charlotte, North Carolina.

        vi. Addie T. Hargett, born 24 May 1887 in Charlotte, North Carolina, buried 11 November 1971 in Roseland Park Cemetery, Royal Oak, Michigan.

        vii. Eva Hargett, born June 1888 in Charlotte, North Carolina.

        viii. Oscar Hargett, born November 1890 in Charlotte, North Carolina.

        ix. Grier Hargett, born November 1890 in Charlotte, North Carolina.

        x. Frank Hargett, born September 1893 in Charlotte, North Carolina.

    c. James Hargett, born 1867 in Charlotte, North Carolina.

4. James Hargett, son of Casper Hargett, was born 1837 in North Carolina.

5. Emaline Hargett, daughter of Casper Hargett, was born 1839 in North Carolina.

6. Francis Hargett, son of Casper Hargett, was born 1841 in North Carolina.

7. John Hargett, son of Casper Hargett, was born 1844 in North Carolina.

---

[170] Death Certificate of Blandina Hargett; 1900 Mecklenburg County, North Carolina Census.

[171] The 1880 Mecklenburg County, North Carolina, Sharon, Census indicates that Henry F. Harget was 6 years of age.

E. William Hargett, son of Henry Hargett, was born 22 January 1789 , his descendants removed to Georgia.

F. John Hargett, son of Henry Hargett, was born before 1791.

G. Daniel Hargett, son of Henry Hargett, was born 1790/1800.

H. Nelly Hargett, daughter of Henry Hargett, married Mr. Matthews.

I. Phoebe Hargett, daughter of Henry Hargett, married Mr. Helms.

J. Sarah Helms, daughter of Henry Hargett.

K. Charity Keziah, daughter of Henry Hargett, was born 1803 in South Carolina.

II. Peter Hargett, son of John Henry Hargett, was born 25 July 1754 in Anson County, North Carolina served in the Revolutionary Warin the Charlotte Troops of the Continental Line, under Colonel Thomas Polk. He applied for a pension in 1833, and stated that when he was about 8 or 9 years old that his parents removed to Mecklenburg County.

III. Daniel Hargett, son of John Henry Hargett.

IV. Joseph Hargett, son of John Henry Hargett.

Harris of Paulding County

Green B. Harris was born 1828 in Georgia, and married on 2 March 1848 in Paulding County, Permelia Ann Adair, a daughter of Whitmill H. Adair and his wife, Sarah (Sorrells) Adair. SEE Adair. They resided near Pumpkinvine Creek. Issue:

I. James Cannon Harris, born 1850 in Paulding County.
II. William Harris, born 1852 in Paulding County.
III. Whitmill C. Harris, born 1854 in Paulding County.
IV. Richard A. Harris, born 1857 in Paulding County.
V. Lebanon J. Harris, born 1859 in Paulding County.

Harris of England and Glynn County

William Harris was born 1720 England, clerk of Savannah, died 1737. He came to Georgia in one of General Oglethorpe's early voyages to Savannah. April of 1737 he was granted Lot No. 126 in Savannah by Oglethorpe, it first being possessed by Lawrence Mellichamp who deserted 3 June 1736. The youth of about sixteen years, married Anne Coles, when she was about seventeen years old as she was born 1723 England, (died 1759 Savannah), the daughter of Joseph Coles, Miller and Baker and his wife, Anna Cassells. SEE Coles and Cassells.

He and his wife, Anne resided in the struggling town of Savannah, where he was a Clerk in Thomas Jones' store. However, he died a year later (1737), and Anne was left a young widow with a small infant, William Thomas Harris. Two years earlier (4 March 1735) her father, Joseph Coles, died, leaving her mother, Anna Coles a widow. The two women took up the Frederica lot.

Anne Harris, widow of William Harris. She and her son, William, remained in Savannah, listed as residents of the northern part of the colony in December of 1742. By July of 1743 they were residents of Frederica, along with her mother and a servant. William Harris had been granted 50 acres outside the Town of Frederica by General Oglethorpe, whose policy of General Oglethorpe to grant each "fighting man" 50 acres for life. Here, Anne could raise a garden and her son. So, Anne and infant child, along with her mother, moved into a cottage on Broad Street in Frederica (Lot No. 68). She was listed as a mantuamaker, that is, she was a seamstress who made dresses, and cloaks.

Each charity colonist was allowed 50 acres of land, five acres for a house and a garden in the town in which he lived, and 45 acres for farming outside of the town. Such was the case of William Harris. He was granted the 45 acres outside of Savannah, as we learn from the Last Will and Testament of his son, William Thomas Harris, passed down to his son (William Thomas Harris) an unimproved lot in Savannah as well as a 45-acre lot adjacant to Savannah.

A description of the land granted William Harris at Frederica is that it was "on the Road to the North End, crossing Military Road from the Fort. The former road also led straightway out of the fork easterly from the Town into the farm area." In other words, one of the first streets to cross the main street, practically adjacent to the fort, and a splendid view of the river.

The garden land that went with the Frederica Town Lot, was located two or three miles from the fort in an area described as "the Garden Area", and adjoined that of Lachlin McIntosh, who had 500 acres, James Arkin, who had 400 acres, and James McKay.

From the book, A List of Early Settlers of Georgia by Coulter (From Europe, on their own account): "Will Harris, Lot 126, Savannah, granted April 1737. Anne, wife on her husband's death, she and her son became inmate to Lot 68 with her mother, Ann Cassell Cole Salter. Lawrence Mellichamp possessed it before, who deserted June 3, 1736. Dead 1737. Will, son, born in the Colony."

Women were not allowed land grants, however, since Ann Harris had a son, she and her son became "inmates to Lot 68" in Savannah. This means that her husband had improved his lot, which entitled her, as widow, to receive it. This same type of situation no doubt gave her title to a subsequent lot at Frederica.

From the above accounting, then, it is confirmed that William Harris paid his own passage from England to Savannah, and was not an indentured servant nor convict. This means that he was one of the persons which Oglethorpe recruited in England to come to Georgia as a citizen-soldier to protect the frontiers from the Spanish.

Anna Coles married again on 9 September 1736, Thomas Salter, a Savannah brickmaker, but did not reside with him until later, as Salter was just getting started in the brick business and did not yet have a home for her.

In December of 1741 Salter received a land grant of 136 acres on Dawbuss' Island, which he later named Salter's Island. Formerly, he was listed among the 120 settlers who signed a petition in 1738 complaining about land titles and restrictions on slavery. He preferred this island because its clay was highly adaptable to brick making. The colony needed brick masons, and Salter's industry thrived. In August of 1742, the Common Council recommended that he be given 500 acres near St. Augustine Creek, adjoining Salter's Island. Salter was known to be a diligent worker, however illiterate. In 1746 he discovered that the clay on Hutchinson's Island was superior, and, abandoning the 500 acres on Salter's Island, established himself with a seven-year lease on Hutchinson's Island. Apparently Salter's industry caused him prosperity, as the colony was in need of brick masons, and he later willed Salter's Island to his grandson, William Thomas Harris, who became the owner in 1749. When the garrison at Ft. Frederica was disbanded by General Oglethorpe in 1749, most of the soldiers returned to England. Soon thereafter, the town had a fire. For a while the town remained in tact, continuing to prosper. The widow of William Harris, being in the timber and shipping business, also remained. However, without the soldiers, the town fell into ruins, with the settlers moving off into Glynn and Liberty Counties to begin the ultimately expansive rice and cotton plantations. As William Thomas Harris inherited lands in Liberty County, this is where he moved to plant rice, a valuable commodity in early Colonial Georgia.

 On 12 May 1752, Francis Harris applied before the Board for 500 acres for *his brother*[172] Thomas Harris continguous to lands formerly laid out for him on the north branch of Little Ogeechee River, 200 acres bounding on the west by his lands, south by lands granted to Henry Parker Esq., east by lands granted to William Spencer, and North vacant, and 300 acres bounding on the south by his lands, west by lands granted Capt. Noble Jones, north by lands granted Noble Wimberly Jones, and east by vacant lands; 500 acres granted Thomas Harris. Francis Harris successfully practiced law in Savannah, and obtained a number of land grants for himself. In 1756, Francis Harris built his home, known as "Wild Heron". The Negroes on his plantation pronounced it "hern", and when I visited the area during the 1960's, the locals still referred to the house as "Wild Hern". This story-and-a-half Colonial farm house is located 2 miles from Savannah, on the Grove River. The original land grant specified 1,000 acres, bounded by the Little Ogeechee River. The story goes that this document was removed from the home by one of General Sherman's soldiers in 1864 and taken North. However, in 1909 it was returned to the postmaster at Savannah. The brick used to build the house was brought over from England. Francis Harris returned to England to marry a rich widow, Elizabeth, and she was the one who named the plantation after an ancestral English estate. In 1780, Elizabeth had a palm tree planted at the southeast corner of the house. It was also planted with cassina hedges and scuppernong arbors.[173]

Anne Coles Harris, widow, was an interprising woman, merchandising in shipping timber up and down the coast, having her own vessels. Eventually, she married again, Daniel Demetre, and the activities surrounding that Marchriage are explained in the following deeds and contracts.

The following deeds from Colonial Deed Book C-1: Page 40-41, (Quadriparte Agreement Prior to a Marriage) -Daniel Demetre, Mariner of the Town of Frederica in the Province of Georgia, Ann Harris, widow, of Frederica and Anna Salter, widow, mother of Ann Harris, to Noble Jones and Thomas Raspberry, Gentlemen, and James Habersham, all of Savannah, whereas the said Daniel Demetre is seized and possessed... of a plantation on the Newport River called "Bethany" containing 500 acres bounded south by lands heretofore granted John Rutledge, North by River Newport, and East on marshes of said river....Whereas a marriage is intended shortly to be hand...between the said Daniel Demetre and the said Ann Harris...Daniel Demetre grants to James Habersham, Noble Jones and Thomas Raspberry....the aforesaid premises. And from after the determination of that Estate to such uses as the said Ann in and by her last Will and Testament...And whereas the said Ann Harris is seized and possessed...in a tract of land containing 50 acres on River Newport lately purchased by her of John Rutledge;

---

[172] "his brother's son, Thomas Harris."

[173] White Columns in Georgia by Medora Field Perkerson, page 115.

Now the said Ann Harris doth covenant and grant to and with the said James Habersham, Noble Jones and Thomas Raspberry...the aforesaid 50 acres...after the solemnization of the intended marriage shall be ane enure and are hereby intended to be settled and assured to the use of them. Date: April 2, 1752.

Page 199-203, The Last Will and Testament of Ann Demetre, wife of Daniel Demetre, formerly Ann Harris, widow, dated February 20, 1755, to heir, Daniel Demetre, Mariner. "Ann Demetre does publish and ordain these presents to be her last will and testament. Reference is made to a Marriage settlement written on April 2, 1752 in consideration of a marriage between Ann Harris, widow, and Daniel Demetre. Parties to the marriage settlement were Daniel Demetre, Ann Harris, now Ann Demetre, Anna Salter, mother of Ann Harris Demetre, and James Habersham, Noble Jones, and Thomas Raspberry. A 500 acre plantation called "Bethany" on the Newport River and a 50-acre tract on the same river, the latter purchased by Ann Harris from John Rutledge, were to become the joint property of Ann and Daniel Demetre, then go to the longest liver of us, and later to the heirs of Ann. The same provisions were to apply to a lot of land in the town of Frederica with improvements, also a lot in Town of Savannah with improvements, late Salter's, which would become the property of Ann Demetre after her mother's death. Now that her mother, Anna Salter, is Deceased, Ann Demetre makes a will to bequeath her own property and that which she has inherited from her motherr. Anna Salter's will, dated December 19, 1753, gave to her all her property in Great Britain or any other place. It further stipulated that in case William Thomas Harris, Anna Salter's grandson, should die without heirs, then whatever was given to him by his grandmother's will would go to Ann Demetre. In her own will, Ann Demetre stipulates that her property will go to the heirs of Ann and Daniel Demetre. Ann Demetre also stipulates that if her son, William Thomas Harris, dies without issue and she inherits his property, then it will pass to Daniel Demetre or the children of Ann and Daniel Demetre. Date: 2 August 1758 at Savannah.

Bethany went to William Harris and adjoined Jonathan Bryan's plantation, Walnut Hill, on Salter's Creek. On 7 February 1758, William Harris of St. Andrew's Parish, applied for and received a grant to Salter's Island. He sold this grant in March of 1773 to Miles Brewton of Charles Town, South Carolina for 408 pds. Also, the 500 acres which Salter abandoned, was later acquired by Brewton.

William Harris (died 1737) had a brother, Francis Harris, who came to the colony sometime after James Habersham, because they later joined together as merchants in the colony, establishing one of the earliest commercial houses in Georgia.

Anne Coles Harris Demetre's mother was Anna Coles who married after the death of her husband, (Joseph Coles) Thomas Salter, a brick mason who resided in Savannah. In December of 1741 Salter received a land grant of 136 acres on Dawbuss'Island, which he later named Salter's Island. Formerly, he was listed among the 120 settlers who signed a petition in 1738 complaining about land titles and restrictions on slavery. He preferred this island because its clay was highly adaptable to brick making. The colony needed brick masons, and Salter's industry thrived. In August of 1742, the Common Council recommended that he be given 500 acres near St. Augustine Creek, adjoining Salter's Island. Salter was known to be a diligent worker, however illiterate. In 1746 he discovered that the clay on Hutchinson's Island was superior, and, abandoning the 500 acres on Salter's Island, established himself with a seven-year lease on Hutchinson's Island. Salter's Island was willed to his grandson, William Thomas Harris, who became the owner in 1749.

Page 313-322, James Habersham and Francis Harris, executors of the will of Daniel Demetre, late of Savannah aforesaid, mariner, deceased, who intermarried with Ann Harris, widow, since deceased, who was the widow of William Harris and daughter of (Joseph) Cassell and Anna Cassell, afterwards Anna Salter also deceased, agree to convey specified property to William Thomas Harris in satisfaction of the latter's demands against Demetre's estate. In his will, dated 12 July 1758, Demetre bequeathed to William Thomas Harris a 750 acre plantation called "Bethany" on Dickinson's Neck in the district of Sapelo and Newport, with all livestock, plantation tools and following slaves: Nicholas, Hagar, Tony, Prince, Belinda, Dinah, James and Silvia and their issue. By virtue of the will, dated December 19, 1753, of his now deceased grandmother, Anna Salter, William Thomas Harris lays claim to the aforesaid mentioned slaves....To prevent suits against Demetre's estates, Habersham and Francis Harris pay William Thomas Harris 20 pounds....and sell to Harris ten negroe slaves, namely, Judy and her children, Will and Titus, Jenny, Harry and Priscilla and their children, Harry, Abraham, and London, and Brutus; also a lot at Frederica formerly occupied by the said Anna Salter and Ann Demetre adjoining a lot of John Latter.... Harris agrees to deliver up to Habersham and Francis Harris the following slaves belonging to the estate of Demetre: Ben, old Joe, Minerva and her child Joe, Penny and her child Adam, Jemmy, Jack and long Joe. Date: 27 August 1759, Savannah.

Ann Harris had accumulated a wealthy business at Frederica, and, joining forces with Daniel Demetre, the coxswain at Frederica, built a study business. Together, they transported lumber to Savannah, owning their own sloops, as well as maintained a mercantile store in Frederica. When the garrison was disbanded in 1749, they apparently stayed in the town, probably to about 1753, because in November, some Creek Indians lately from Augustine reported that the Spaniards were preparing to settle the Island of Amelia. Daniel Demetre was the Commander of the Prince George Scout Boat on Frederica, and a letter of instructions was sent him from the Secretary of the Colony that he was to cruise to the Island of Amelia, and farther south into the Florida shores to discover whether the Spaniards were making any settlements within the limits of this province.

They must have been some of the last remaining residents of Frederica. Quite an estate for Ann Harris Demetre was enumerated on the books, and through her husband, as well as her mother's second marriage, her son's inheritance was substantial.

Son of William Harris and his wife, Anne Coles:[174]

I.   William Thomas Harris was born 1738 in Savannah, died June 1786, Liberty County, Ga., date of his LWT. Wife, Mary. William inherited the Liberty County plantation from his mother. His LWT was dated 15 August 1785, probated 20 January 1786 in Liberty County, wherein he bequeathed to his son, John Harris, an unimproved lot in Savannah as well as a 45-acre adjacent lot, to be his after he reached the age of 21 years. This property was part of the land which fell into the hands of his mother. The remainder of his estate, he divided between his three sons, William T. Harris, Jr., John Harris, and James Harris, subject to an encumbrance of testator's wife (Mary), she to have the right of residence on any part of the land. He gave to his daughters, Ann, Mary, Jane and Sabra, as well as to his sons, John, James and William T., and wife, Mary, all of his personal property. Executors were his son, William T. Harris, Jr. and friend, James Gignilliat. He inherited *Dickenson's Neck*, a plantation located near Sapelo and Newport, which was in McIntosh County near the Liberty County border. This was a prosperous plantation of 750 acres, and helps to explain what his son, James

---

[174] Colonial Records of Georgia by Candler; Early Settlers of Georgia by Coulter; Liberty County Wills; Colonial Deeds; Glynn County Wills; Chatham County Wills.

Harris, was doing in McIntosh County. The latter must have taken over the plantation at the death of his father. The above plantation was inherited from the stepfather of William Thomas Harris---Daniel Demetre.

Issue of William Thomas Harris, Sr.:

A. William Thomas Harris, born ca 1758, died 1794 Glynn County Wife, Margaret. He mentioned William Harris, Sr. in his LWT (Glynn County Will Book 1793-1809).
B. James Harris, born ca 1760 Glynn County, died 7 January 1804 in McIntosh County, according to a McIntosh County newspaper article.
C. Ann Harris, born ca 1760 Glynn County She was named in the LWT of her step-grandfather, Daniel Demetre, dated 12 July 1758, probated 10 August 1758 in Chatham County; also named in the LWT of her father.
D. Mary Harris, born ca 1761 Glynn County married Jacob Johns.
E. Sabra Harris, born Glynn County
F. Jane Harris, born Glynn County, died ca 1822 in Warren County, married Andrew Danielly on 29 February 1790. SEE Danielly.
G. John Harris, born ca 1770 Glynn County, died Aug. 1827.

Hamilton of Chatham County

Henry Hamilton was granted a Lot in Hardwicke, July 1760. He left his wife, Frances, all of his lands, houses and tenements in Savannah and Hardwick. Issue:[175]

I.   Thomas Hamilton.
II. Charles Hamilton.
III. Elizabeth Hamilton.
IV. Francis Hamilton.

Hill of North Carolina & Walton County

John Hill, the son of John Hill of North Carolina, was born 1760-1770 in North Carolina, and died ca 1831 in Walton County, buried in the Hill Cemetery at Winder, Georgia. He married in Rutherford County, North Carolina, Annie Naomi Camp (born 1762 Orange County, North Carolina), a daughter of John Camp and his wife, Mary (Tarpley) Camp. SEE Camp. Issue:[176]

I.   Sarah Hill, born 1783 in North Carolina, died January 1858, married Edmund Ragsdale.

II. Margaret Hill, married Sam Clayton.

III. William Hill, born 1791 in North Carolina, died 8 May 1840 in Benton County, Alabama, married Elizabeth Awtry.

IV. Nancy Hill, born 1 January 1793 in North Carolina, died 25 July 1852 in Villa Rica, Carroll County. She married Jacob Awtry.

---

[175] Colonial Records of Georgia by Candler; Early Settlers of Georgia by Coulter.

[176] Hill Family Cemetery, Winder, Georgia.

V. John Hill, born 1797 in North Carolina, died 1881, married (1) Josie Selman (2) Betty Selman.

VI. Winnie Hill, born 1800 in North Carolina, died 1872.

VII. Eliza Hill, born ca 1802 in North Carolina, married Francis Marion Smith.

VII. Carter Hill, born 18 March 1805, buried in the Hill Cemetery at Winder, Georgia. He married (1) Dorcas Tabitha Hosch (2) Nancy T. Mays (1817-1884). Listed on the 1850-1880 Walton County Census, residents of Cut Off, Georgia. Issue:

    A. Frances B. Hill, born 1842 in Walton County.
    D. Susan M. C. Hill, born 1843 in Walton County.
    E. Sarah Elizabeth Hill, born 1846 in Walton County.
    F. Nancy Josephine Hill, born 1848 in Walton County.
    G. Amanda Almedia Ann Hill, born 1850 in Walton County.
    H. John W. Hill, 1850-1853 in Walton County.
    I. Lucy Ella Hill, born 1852 in Walton County.
    J. Martha N. Hill, born 1854 in Walton County.
    K. Cammie Hill, born 1857 in Walton County.
    L. Ida Hill, born 1860 in Walton County.
    M. Z. C. Hill, born 1872 in Walton County.

VIII. Lucy Hill, born ca 1807, married John Franklin.

IX. Richard Hill, born ca 1808 in Georgia, died 1860, married Sarah Elliott.

X. Susan Hill married John Camp. SEE Camp.

XI. Elizabeth Hill, married John Awtry.

Hitchcock of Jasper, Morgan, Oglethorpe, Polk & Paulding Counties

Jesse Hitchcock, Sr., the son of William Hitchcock, Jr., was born 1775 in North Carolina and died January 1827 in Jasper County, Georgia. He was married on 20 June 1803 in Oglethorpe County to Lucy Harris, born 1781 in Hancock County, the daughter of John Harris and his wife, Tiery (Fielder) Harris. Issue:[177]

I. John M. Hitchcock, born 1805 in Georgia, farmer in 222nd District of Paulding County. He married Mary Roberts (born 1827 in South Carolina) on 4 September 1845 in Paulding County. Mary was born 1817 in South Carolina, and died 14 July 1875 in Polk County, buried in the White Oak Cemetery in Paulding County. Issue:

    A. Lucy Ann Hitchcock, born 20 January 1846 in Paulding County, died 6 June 1917 in Caddo County, Oklahoma.

---

[177] Paulding County Marriages; 1860-1870 Paulding County Census; Mrs. Charles B. McGarity, 418 Confederate Avenue, Dallas, Georgia 30132 (1971); personal records of Mrs. Charles McGarity, 418 Confederate Avenue, Dallas, Georgia (1971).

B. John Matthew Hitchcock, born 31 August 1847 in Paulding County, died 14 May 1923 in Paulding County, buried in the White Oak Cemetery.

C. Overton Alberton Hitchcock, born 10 December 1849 in Paulding County, died 19 May 1928. He married Frances Elizabeth Pace on 19 December 1875.

D. Joseph H. Hitchcock, born 1857 in Paulding County.

II. William Lewis Hitchcock, born 1806 in Georgia, died in Morgan County.

III. Mary Hitchcock, born 1807 in Georgia.

IV. James Fielder Franklin Hitchcock, born 1815 Georgia, died in Alabama. He married on 17 October 1839, Mary Casey, in Paulding County.

V. Martha A. Hitchcock, born 1817 in Georgia.

VI. J. Overton Hitchcock, born 1819 in Georgia.

VII. Matthew Hitchcock, born 1820 in Georgia, buried in the White Oak Cemetery, in Dallas, Paulding County. Lived at Dallas, Georgia. Wife, Lucinda, born 1833 in Georgia. Issue:

A. Rouan W. Hitchcock (son), born 1850 Paulding County.

B. Louisa Hitchcock, born 1852 Paulding Couny.

C. Matthew Hitchcock, born 1854 in Paulding County, married Martha New on 23 October 1887, in Paulding County.

D. James Hitchcock, born 1856 in Paulding County.

E. Eliza Hitchcock, born 1859 in Paulding County.

VIII. Jesse Hitchcock, Jr., born 10 July 1822 in Georgia, died 1 May 1910. He married on 17 February 1847 in Paulding County, Sara Ann Adair (19 May 1825-26 December 1886), the daughter of Whitmell H. Adair and his wife, Sarah (Sorrells) Adair. See ADAIR. Residents of Dallas, Georgia, in 1880. Issue:

A. Mary E. Hitchcock, born 1848 in Paulding County.

B. Sarah E. Hitchcock, born 1851 in Paulding County.

C. James Overton Hitchcock, born 1859 in Paulding County. He married Frances Pace on 19 December 1875 in Paulding County.

D. William U. Hitchcock, born 1866 in Paulding County.

IX. Georgia Elizabeth Hitchcock, born 1825 in Georgia, died 10 May 1910 Georgia.

X. Joseph C. Hitchcock, born 7 April 1827 in Georgia. He married Martha Jenkins on 18 January 1851, in Paulding County. Issue:[178]

    A. Joseph B. Hitchcock, born 1861 in Georgia, farmer.

    B. R. Benjamin Hitchcock, born 1863 in Georgia.

    C. Lucetta Hitchcock, born 1866 in Georgia.

    D. Docia Hitchcock, born 1868 in Georgia.

    E. Jennie Hitchcock, born 1871 in Georgia.

Hogan of Virginia, South Carolina & Monroe County

William Hogan "of Edgefield County, South Carolina" was born 1750 in Henry County, Virginia and made his LWT dated 17 February 1805, which was probated on 16 June 1805, recorded in Edgefield County and in Monroe County. He was born ca 1750, from Henry County, Virginia, where he married on 17 January 1780, Nancy Dillard (born 9 September 1753 near Stapleton, Buckingham County, Virgina, died 10 August 1838 in Jones County, Georgia). Issue:[179]

I. Elizabeth Hogan.

II. Winifred Hogan.

III. Nancy Hogan.

IV. Thomas Hogan.

V. Original Hogan, died before 1837.

VI. James Hogan, born 13 December 1780 in Edgefield County, South Carolina. He married Elizabeth Smith, the daughter of Davis Smith. SEE Smith. Davis Smith and Mrs. Elizabeth Hogan were both executors of the LWT of James Hogan, dated 10 March 1847, probated 6 September 1847 in Monroe County. Issue:

    A. Eveline Hogan married Mr. Scarborough.
    B. Emeline Hogan married Mr. Granberry.

VII. William Hogan, born 11 June 1792 in Edgefield County, South Carolina, died 8 March 1853.

---

[178] 1880 Polk County, Census, Rockmart.

[179] Monroe County Wills; Edgefield County, South Carolina Wills.

Holland of England, Virginia, Georgia

Henry Holland was , born ca 1480/1490 at Westminster, London, England, and d. 1561 at Westminster, St. Margarets. The record of his burial is contained in the parish records at St. Margarets. Also, his Last Will and Testament dated 1561 in London, directs that he be buried at St. Margarets and names his children - Thomas, George, Mary and Henry. He also named a grandson, Edward Holland.

Henry was mentioned in trace documents in London with Richard and Thomas Holland. From my studies of Richard and Thomas Holland, both appear to have been , born ca 1480/1490. Thomas was buried at St. Margarets on 29 July 1540. Henry made his Last Will and Testament dated 1561 at Wesminster, London. Two other Hollands, John, buried on 13 August 1547 at St. Margarets, and Robert, made his Last Will and Testament dated 1557 in London (naming wife, Elizabeth, and son, George). These Hollands, Richard, Thomas, John and possibly Robert, appear to be of the age to be either brothers or close-kin to Henry. I have researched with great effort to try and ascertain if either of these show any connection to Henry, or to determine their parents (a son of illegitimate, Thomas or William).

Issue of Henry Holland as follows: **John Holland,** born ca 1519 Westminster, London, England married on 16 June 1529, Agnes Greenway at St. Lawrence, Jewry and St. Mary Magdalene, Milk St., London, England. (Issue: Courtney Holland chr. 16 March 1548 Westminster, St. Margarets); **Thomas Holland, born ca** 1520 Westminster, London, England, died August 1566 Westminster, married on 30 January 1541, Agnes Hyde at Westminster, St. Margarets, London. The Last Will and Testament of Thomas Holland dated August 1566 Westminster, St. Margarets, named his son, Ambrose, and brother, George; **George Holland,** born ca 1521 Westminster, London, England married on 6 September 1541 Elisabeth Wells at Westminster, St. Margarets, London. (Named in LWT of his brother, Thomas, above). He may be the George Holland who was buried in 1554 at St. Margarets Parish; **Agnes Holland,** born ca 1524 Westminster, London married on 3 August 1544 ,William Hall at Westminster, St. Margarets; **Elizabeth Holland,** born ca 1525 Westminster, London married on 4 May 1545, John Patenson, at St. Margarets; **Henry Holland,** born. ca 1527 Westminster, St. Margarets, London married on 30 January 1547, Hyllary Barwarde, Westminster, St. Margarets, London. He was named in the LWT of his father, Henry Holland dated 1561. (Issue: Judith Holland, chr. 11 October 1551 Westminster, St. Margarets, London; Jane Holland, chr. December 1552 Westminster, St. Margarets, London; James or Jacob Holland, chr. 23 July 1553 Westminster, St. Margarets, London; Robert Holland, chr. 3 January 1554 Westminster, St. Margarets; Alice Holland, chr. 10 October 1555, Westminster, St. Martin-in-the-Fields, London; Heugh Holland, chr. 10 October 1555, Westminster, St. Margarets, London, buried 21 November 1555, Westminster, St. Margarets, London; Anna Holland, chr. 30 November 1556, Westminster, St. Margarets, London; Edmonde Holland, chr. August 1557 Westminster, St. Margarets, London); and, **John Holland,** chr. 20 January 1556, Westminster, St. Margarets, died October of 1628 in London, burined on 26 October 1628 in St. Martin-in-the-Fields (parish records) married on 5 March 1583/1584 Mary Mollenax, St. Clement Danes, London. Mary was born ca 1565 at Wigan, Lancashire, the daughter of John Mollenax, as stated in her marriage document dated 5 March 1583/1584 at St. Clement Danes. Her father was deceased at the date of her marriage.

John Holland (1556-1628) had issue---.... two of whom came to Virginia (Gabriel and Richard): Peter Holland, chr. On 25 April 1585, Westminster, St. Martin-in-the-Fields, London, buried 19 August 1593 same parish; Hester Holland, chr. 10 October 1586, Westminster, St. Martin-in-the-Fields, London, buried 1 September 1593, same parish; Constance Holland, chr. 6 April 1587, Westminster, St. Martin-in-the-Fields; Richard Holland, chr. 11 August 1588

Westminster, St. Martin-in-the-Fields, London, buried 16 August 1593, same parish; Elizabeth Holland, chr. 6 June 1591, Westminster, St. Martin-in-the-Fields; Leonard Holland chr. 17 August 1593, Westminster, St. Martin-in-the-Fields; Michaell Holland, chr. 15 March 1595, Westminster, St. Martin-in-the-Fields; Frances Holland, chr. 21 December 1595, Westminster, St. Martin-in-the-Fields; Philemon Holland, chr. 12 October 1597, Westminster, St. Martin-in-the-Fields; Ann Holland, chr. 12 October 1600 Westminster, St. Martin-in-the-Fields and, Gabriel Holland, the son of John Holland (1556-1628) of London, England and his wife, Mary Mollenax of Wigan, Lancashire, England, was chr. 15 February 1596 at Westminster, St.-Martin-in-the-Fields, London. He migrated to Jamestown, Virginia; In 1620, Gabriel and his brother, Richard, he sailed to Jamestowne on the ship *Supply*, arriving at Berkeley on 8 February 1621, at the site of the famous Berkeley's Hundred. [180]

"Thomas Parker, Mayor of Bristol, certificate for sailing on ship "Supply" 18 September 1620. "To the Treasurer Counsell & Company of Adventurers and Planters of the City of London for the first Colony in Virginia. This is to certify that in the good ship called the "Supply" this present XVIII day of Sept. 1620, were shipped from our port of Bristol for plantation in Virginia at the charge of Richard Berkeley, George Thorpe, William Tracy and John Smythe under the conduct of the said William Tracy appointed Captayne and Governor over them this 56 persons whose names ensue who forthwith proceeded in their voyage accordingly: Gabriel Holland, Richard Holland & c., etc.[181]

Gabriel Holland (1556-1628) , son of John. One account relates that he was married to Rebecca, daughter of John George, who was a Lt. Colonel in the Isle of Wight County, Virginia. However, the LWT of Colonel John George dated 1678 in Isle of Wight County names a daughter, Rebecca, who was the relict of Phill. Pardoe, decd. This Colonel John George would have been the age to be a "brother" (of Rebecca), not a father. The above Colonel John George was from Bristol. In Bristol are the following LWT's: Julian George dated 1616, Robert George dated 1628, Edward George dated 1633, Richard George dated 1645, and Eleanor George dated 1665. I have not located these documents, as yet, to determine if a Rebecca Holland is named. It is claimed that George Holland who was found later in Accomack County, Virginia, was Gabriel's son by Rebecca George.

Secondly, Gabriel was married to Mary Pinke, the former wife of William Pinke, alias William Jonas. Gabriel's wife "Mary" was confirmed in the Virginia land records. Mary appears to be the mother of all the children listed here.

Gabriel was a gentleman yeoman and burgess who travelled back and forth to England between 1620 and 1635. Elected a burgess, an honor bestowed only upon prominent land owners, his travels were doubtless on Virginia business. Gabriel, Richard, William and Robert, of the same age group, all apparently kin.[182]

---

[180] NOTE__Richard Holland (chr. 11 August 1588, Westminster, St. Martin-in-the-Fields, London)* came to Virginia in 1620 with Gabriel Holland. He was massacred by Indians at Berkeley's Hundred in 1622.

[181] Records of the London Company, page 405, CXLIL

[182] William Holland was chr. 5 March 1598 Westminster, St. Martin-in-the-Fields, London.

The winter of 1621-1622 brought much illness and hardship to the colonists, whereupon, hundreds died. And worse, the Indians started their massacre of the eastern Virginia seaboard. Sergeant Gabriel Holland was residing at Jamestown at the date of massacre, on 22 June 1622, Boddie states that Gabriel and Richard Holland were killed by the Indians in the massacre at Berkeley Hundred in 1621.[183]

Virginia Genealogical Register - Gabriel Holland was a resident of Virginia 1623-1634.

Journal of the House of Burgess - Gabriel Holland, Burgess, 1623-1624. In 1624 he was seated at Shirley Hundred.

Virginians planted tobacco, using it as money to trade for English goods. In this respect, the London Company acted as Gabriel Holland's agent...paying accunts, etc. In 1629 he acted as a yeoman of James City in administering the estate of Ann Behoute. A yeoman was one who belonged to a class of English freeholders below the gentry. An active member of his community, in 1625 Gabriel Holland signed a petition (along with 30 men) to send a man to England to petition King Charles I that every male who was 16 years or over and who had

"It was testified At this Court by William Holland that he thinketh that there was cast overboard of the tobaccoe was shipped by Mr. Humfrey Rastdell aboard the Anne Fortune for Newfoundland and 200 and he verily thinketh that the rest that wants to ballance the Account was Lost in the weight." Minutes of the Council and General Court, James City, Oct. 1628.

"A Court held the XXVth of October 1624, present Sir Francis Wyatt, Knight and George Sandys, Treasurer, Capt. Roger Smith...Capt. John Martin complayneth yet whereas there were Articles and Covenants drawne betweene him and Mr. Humphrey Rastell for the Transportinge of said Marten, his servante and other goodes unto Virginia. Said Mr. Rastell carried him into New Englande and thare detained him 9 weekes to his great hurte Coste and hinderance.

To which Mr. Rastell replyeth yet his Ship beine leake and the synde Contrary he was enforced to goe for New England and detayned Capt. Martin there no longer, than of necessitie he was Constrayned to doe, And before his owne shipp was redy he hired another shipp to Cary him to Virginia. William Holland, gent. sworne, Examined sayeth there was a leake spring in said shipp, whereby they were in great danger and were forced to heave over board some 40 basketts of bed, which was spoyled by ye leakinge." Minutes of the Council and General Court, 1622-1624

Robert Holland. came to Virginia in 1635 with Gabriel Holland (during one of his return trips from England) on the ship Assurance.

[183] Citing Records of the Virginia Company, Vol. III, p. 396, however, subsequent records on 16 February 1623 prove that Gabriel was a resident in Virginia at College Land (University of Henrico) on the northside of the James River from the falls down to Henrico, about 14 miles from Richmond. Thomas Holland, however, was reported as having been massacred by savages at Capt. Berkeley's plantation, which attack commenced at Falling Creek, some 66 miles from James City. The Virginia Assembly, which first convened in August of 1619, after the massacre, passed one judicious regulation: that no plantation should be seperated from all other plantations by a distance wider than ten miles!

been in Virginia one year, should be required to pay 4 lbs. of merchantable tobacco by or before Oct. 31st. It was decided that Burgess Gabriel Holland (his expenses to be paid for by the King) would go and present the petition to King Charles I. However, the King's quarrel with Parliament grew more bitter as he refused to convene. It was not until 1629 that King Charles I convened Parliament, agreeing to observe (hear) the Petition of Right, an important document in England's Constitution. Therefore, it was not possible for the King to hear the petition of Virginia's House of Burgesses. World Book Encyclopedia #5, p. 2349.

So Gabriel Holland returned to America, embarking on 16 February 1623 to Virginia in the ship "John and Frances". Original List of Persons of Quality Who Went from Great Britain to the American Plantations (1600-1700) by Hotten.

It was not until 1629 that the King agreed to hear the petition. Thus, Gabriel Holland again returned to England to present the document. In 1635, he was still handling colony business, when he returned to Virginia on the ship "Assurance", along with Robert Holland and William Holland. In 1635, Gabriel was recorded as being 35 years old.

While Gabriel was away in England, his wife, Mary Holland, purchased land adjoining 100 acres which she had received from her deceased husband, William Jonas.

> "Mary Holland, 12 acres, Aug. 14, 1624, page 11. Wife of Gabriel
> Holland of the Island of James City, yeoman, lately in the occupation
> of William Pink, alias William Jonas (deceased), her former husband,
> who, at his death gave her his devident of 100 acres of which said 12
> acres is a part adjoining Nathaniel Hutt and Thomas Passmore. Fee
> Rent: 3 pence. Measured by William Claybourne."

> "John Southerne, Gent. of James City, 24 acres in the Island of James
> City, 1 Nov. 1627, p. 55. 12 acres thereof being a neck bounded on the E.
> with a marsh parting this from land of John Johnson, W. on a marsh called
> *Tuckers Hole*, N. on the back river and S. on the highway leading to black
> point; 12 acres lying neare adj. to the former, S. on land of Mary Holland,
> the wife of Gabriel Holland, N. on land of John Johnson, E. on a marsh and
> W. comeing neare unto land of Thomas Passmore; to be accounted parte of
> his first devdt. of 50 acres due for trans. of William Soane who came in the
> *George* in 1621." Cavaliers and Pioneers, p. 3, Part I, by Nugent:

Same book, p. 56-57:

> "John Radish and Bradwell, 16 acres James City Island, 20 May 1637, p. 423.
> 12 acres abutting E. upon land formerly in possession of Mary Holland, W.
> upon the bounds and limits there determined, S. unto the highway running
> close to Goose hill marsh...."

After 1637, there is no further information in the records concerning Gabriel and Mary Holland. The scant James City land records do not mention Gabriel. However, from the above records, we know that he and his wife owned land near the highway in the vicinity of Goose hill marsh. Gabriel may have died about 1660, for, in 1663, his son, John Holland, removed to Nansemond County, Virginia to establish the Holland Family Seat for generations to come.

153

Issue of Gabriel Holland, The Emigrant to Virginia:

George Holland, son of Gabriel Holland, was born in 1633 James City, Virginia, son of Gabriel Holland (and reported as) and Rebecca George. He later lived in Accomack County, Virginia.[184]

Richard Holland, son of Gabriel Holland, was born 1630 in James City, Virginia.[185]

Job Holland, son of Gabriel Holland, was born ca 1630.

Daniel Holland, son of Gabriel Holland, of Northumberland County, Virginia, was born ca 1633 in James City County, Virginia. His LWT dated 17 April 1772 in Northumberland County. Adminstratrix was his widow, Mrs. Joyce Holland. His LWT names his wife, Joyce, and daughter, Elizabeth. The document was half destroyed. On 17 April 1672, Joyce Holland, her servant, Cornelius Mohohory, 17 years old. 17 April 1672, servant of Mrs. Joyce Holland, Mich. Waterland, has runaway. 16 June 1672, Mrs. Joyce Holland registered her mark of cattle. April 21, 1662 Daniel Holland was acquitted of murdering Thomas Hughes. [186]

John Holland, son of Gabriel Holland, was born 1628 James City, Virginia, married Mary. He was the ancestor of the Hollands of Nansemond County, Virginia, North Carolina, South Carolina and Georgia. (SEE John Holland Settles in Nansemond). John is the ancestors of all of those Hollands from Nansemond County, Virginia and Georgia, and in parts of North

---

[184] "William Wroughton, 400 acres on N. side of Lancaster Co. 18 Sept. 1665, p. 406, Beg. at a mark pine standing by an Eagle West, running W.S.W. bounding upon the Court House land and land of William hite, then N.N.W. upon John Merriman, N.W. Nly. upon land of Mr. Nusum, Michael Arms, Danll. Harris and Richard Merryman, N.E. upon land of Doctor Edwards and Thomas Marshall, E. Ely. on land of John Nicholls, William Abby, William Lynhall, Mr. Balls and a former devdt. of said Wroughton. Trans. of 8 pers: George Holland, etc." Cavaliers and Pioneers, Patent Book No. 5, p. 526:

[185] "List of Soldiers 31 December 1680 belonging to apt. Giles Hall: Richard Holland. Richard probably removed to Accomack County, Virginia where he witnessed the LWT of George Crump dated 12 September 1667. Omitted Chapters from Hottens:

[186] The followiing is a remote description of the first land which Daniel Holland owned in Northumberland, 1662. Cavaliers and Pioneers, Patent Book No. 4, p. 359:

> "Richard Gible, 800 acres, Northumberland County, Dec. 1656, p. 66.
> Ely by S. upon a creek dividing this and lands of John Hull, Hugh
> South and James Magregor, N. by E. upon land of Robert Newman
> and W. by N. upon a creek dividing this and land of Mr. Presley...."[186]

Northumberland County, Virginia, 9 December 1662, patent of 800 acres in Newman's Neck to Daniel Holland and William Cornish. Northumberland County, Virginia. 20 February 1671, A Daniel Holland sold John Warner and his wife, Prue Warner, 200 acres formerly owned by Richard Gible.

Carolina. He patented many acres in Nansemond County, located on Kingsale Road and adjoining the North Carolina border, in the present town of Holland, Virginia.[187]

The 1704 Quit Rent Rolls for Nansemond County, Virginia, provided the ages of Hollands, i.e.: John Holland, 700 acres, age 76; Henry Holland, 400 acres, age 47; and Joseph Holland, 100 acres, age 20

The issue of John Holland as follows: James Holland, born 1659; Henry Holland, born 1660; Joseph Holland, born 1661; John Holland, born 1664; and Michael Holland, born 1666

The Issue of John Holland of Nansemond County (James, Henry, Joseph, John, Michael)

James Holland was born 1659. In 1717 James Holland bought 23 acres from Henry Holland, and then in 1733 James Holland owned 295 acres adjoining Henry Holland. No further information.

Henry Holland of Somerton Creek was born 1660 in Nansemond County, VIrginia, d. 1747. He had five sons: Henry, Jr., Joseph, John, William, Sr. and James. James was alive in 1752, mentioned in the processioning of land in Upper Parish.[188]

---

[187] On 20 February 1664, John Holland patented 2500 acres in Nansemond County, Virginia, in the area known today as Holland, Virginia, which is about 13 miles due south of Suffolk. The land grant was granted because he transported 60 persons from England to the colony.

> "Lt. Col. John Blake and Edward Ison, 2500 acres in Nansemond County,
> 20 Feb 1664, p. 154. Trans. of 50 persons: John Holland, etc."
> Cavaliers and Pioneers, Patent Book No. 5, p. 444.

On 20 April 1682, John Holland patented 760 acres in Nansemond County, Upper Parish, beginning and c. at the miles end of Walter Bageley.

On 16 April 1683, John Holland patented 200 acres in Upper Parish, Nansemond, at a place called *Kingsale*. The "Kingsale Swamp" land is located on Kingsale Road in Holland, Virginia.....where two pre-revolutionary houses still stand, as well as other ante-bellum homes. On 20 April 1694, John Holland patented 500 acres on the East side of the Cape.

[188] 29 October 1696, Henry Holland, 472 acres on Back Swamp out of Somerton Creek. Virginia Counties Zero Index by Ura Link Eckhardt. 1704 Nansemond Co. Quit Rents lists Henry Holland, 400 acres. 24 January 1717, Henry Holland deeded 23 acres adjuacent his and James Holland's (above) lands. Evidently part of his patent dated 24 January 1717 for 205 acres in Nansemond. I believe that this additional 205 acres was located adjacent to March's Swamp, just south of South Quay Road and bordering on the east, Holy Neck Road. This 205 acres of Henry Holland eventually fell into the hands of his great-grandson, Frederick H. Holland (son of Capt. Henry J. Holland, ca 1760-1810) who claimed it on the 1867 Nansemond Co. Tax Digest, "205 acres adjoining W. O. Pocason and South Quay Road, 23 miles southwest of the courthouse." Also, "65 acres adjoining M. March." In 1733 Henry Holland of Nansemond Co. sold land to Thomas Vaughan on the east side of the Chowan River in North Carolina (Witnessed by Joseph Holland). 4 August 1733, John Vaughn of Nansemond Co. sold 150 acres on South side of Chowan River (witnesses: Henry, James and Jo. Holland). August 1736, Henry Holland deeded 146 acres between Henry Hedgepath and James Holland on Coronah Swamp. This land, no doubt, was located on Corinth Chapel Road (Hwy 667), between present-day March's Swamp and Holy Neck Road.

Issue of Henry Holland of Somerton Creek (1660 -) :

Henry Holland, Jr. was born ca 1680, died Nansemond County, Virginia, was mentioned in the Vestry Book of the Upper Parish of Nansemond County, Virginia, in the land processioning of 1752, including Henry, Jr., William and Joseph's lands. Also, page 76 mentions processioning lands between Henry, Sr. and Henry, Jr. on 4 March 1752, Henry Holland was a Church Warden in Upper Parish, 1756-1758. Vestry Book of the Upper Parish, Nansemond County, Virginia, page 145: (processioning lands) "All the land belonging to the heirs of Henry Holland, deceased...., 17 September 1759.[189]

Issue of Henry Holland, Jr. : (Henry "the Elder", Job, Robert, John and Solomon), as follows:

Henry Holland, "the Elder", son of Henry Holland, was born ca 1725/35 and was listed on the Nansemond County Tax Records as follows: 1791, Henry Holland vs. Elias Holland; 1794, 125 acres; 1795, James Holland, admr of Henry Holland. Copy of LWT to John Coles dated 1792, Nansemond County.[190]

---

[189] June of 1733 Henry Holland (Jr.) deeded land adjacent to John Holland, Sr., John Winborn, Jr., Ann Ballard and his own land. It appears that James and Henry Holland were re-patenting the 500 acres of their father granted to him inn 1694. (James on same date patented 295 acres in Nansemond County, adajacent to Henry's land). The Upper Parish where Henry Holland, Jr. was Church warden in 1748 was the Old Brick, built about 1642, located adjacent to the Nansemond River, between Suffolk and Reid's Ferry on property known as the George Bunting Farm (Crittenden Road, Hwy 628). It was to this church that Queen Anne made the donation of a red velvet altar cloth, the ancient communion service, the Holy Bible, and the Prayer Books. Every male Inhabitant over the age of sixteen was a tithable must pay his part towards the support of the Church. This, he was usually paad lo tobacco, already a rlch, lucrative crop which the settlers shipped to their agent in London, where their accounts were paid and The number of tithables in the Upper Parish in 1744 was 1,139. Vestry meetings were always held in a member's home in the Town of Suffolk. In 1748 the meeting of the vestry wss held at Mr. Rawlin's house. 1755, 1756 and 1757 meetings were held at the court house in Suffolk. In 1755 Rev. William Webb was the minister at the Old Brick Church, with Henry Holland, vestryman.

[190] "31 August 1747, a committee was appointed to process lands of Henry Holland, the Elder. Also, the lands of Joseph Holland, Sr., John Holland, Joseph Holland, Jr. and James Holland." Vestry Book of Upper Parish, Nansemond County, Virginia, page 29.

"Ordered that James Holland, Jr. and Joseph Holland, Jr....procession all the bounds of land, beginning at Henry Holland's plantation, so down the north side of King Sale Swamp to the county line*, from thence to the head of the Meadow Branch, so to Robert Yeats' Bridge, from thence on the North side South Quay Road to Henry Holland's Plantation." Vestry Book of the Upper Parish of Nansemond County, Virginia, page 62:

In 1747, a description of his property "from Wickam Swamp to county line* to Kingsale Swamp, up said swamp to the county line* ....line between Henry Holland, Jr. and Stephen Darden...line between Holland and John Hedgepeth...line between Holland and William Holland, Sr. and William Sanders."

156

Issue of Henry "the Elder", viz Captain Henry J. Holland.

Captain Henry J. Holland, first son of Henry "the Elder" , was born ca 1760, died ca 1810 Nansemond County, Virginia, according to the 1782 (205 acres) and 1797 (272 acres) tax records. Tax Records show in 1811, Henry Holland's Estate. This is Capt. Henry Holland, Revolutlonary War soldier of Nansemond County, Virginia. He was listed on the 1790 Nansemond County Census with 7 whites, 14 blacks. In 1770, Captain Henry J. Holland belonged to the Nansemond Militia, which numbered 644. On December 11, 1775 the Nansemond Militia contributed to the defeat of Lord Dunmore's forces at Norfolk, Virginia, known locally as the Battle of The Great Bridge. [191]

In 1748 Henry Holland "the Elder" and Henry Holland adjoined lands of Isaac Fleming, James Sumners, Captain William Butler, Henry Hedgepeth, William Butler, William Johnson and Joseph Holland, John Holland and Joseph Holland, Henry Johnson.

In other words, the property commenced at Kingsale Road (Hwy 612) within a few hundred yards of Isle of Wight county line, bordered northwesterly by Kingsale Swamp and Wickam Swamp, thence easterly to the head of Meadow Branch. ** Thence proceeding southerly for a distance of approximately two miles down Kingsale Road to the intersection of Glen Haven Drive (Hwy 653), and including the intersection of Hwy 58 (Holland Road) where there was a bridge, the Robert Yeat's Bridge. Near this intersection (at the Hwy 58 by-pass) was the first Holland, Virginia, known as "Holland's Corner", begun in the 1880's. The old Holland Baptist Church, dating to this period, is all that remains of the old Holland's Corner. Henry Holland "the Elder" apparently owned the original 200 acres at Kingsale (Henry's homeplace at the Isle of Wight Co. line) patented by his great-grandfather, John Holland, in 1683. Later, Capt. Joseph Holland (1741-1804), son of Joseph Holland "of Spivey", owned over 900 acres on Kingsale Road, beginning at the railroad at Holland's Corner.

Henry "the Elder", as well as his son, Capt. Henry J. Holland (also, his children, Lewis Connor, Lawson S., WIlliam, Margaret, Henry J. and Frederick Holland) once lived in this old pre-Revolutionary War house. Family cemetery is to the left of the rear field, in the woods. Near the Isle of Wight county line and over this line, continuing up Kingsale Road, lived WIlliam Holland, Sr. (son of Henry Holland, Jr.) who died 1755 in Nansemond Co. To the right of the house, near the back field, in the woods, lies the old abandoned cemetery. This poorly neglected ground is strewn with auto parts and an old bus, overgrown with weeds, briars, and scrub trees. Even the bus is scarcely visible. Only one tombstone remains, that of Mills Henry Holland (son of Frederick Henry Holland). "Mills H. Holland, Sr.. Born Oct. 23, 1835 Died March 20, 1897". Frederick resided in the old Henry Holland house his father's death (1810) and his brothers (Henry J., Lawson S. , Lewis Connor and William Holland) left for Georgia. This cemetery is an example of the old family burial plots in this 300-year old county....sunken graves, crumbling stones buried under matted leaves, no markers nor identification, no evidence of cemeteries ever having existed. All the old people in this county are buried in family graveyards, yet, where, oh where, are they? Today, no one knows these yards. The relatives who stood over these plots, their tears once sprinkled over the graves, somehow forgot and did not return.

[191] NOTE--... Nine Hundred Virginians and North Carolinians were included in the fight. This news, no doubt, spread quickly across the countryside, reaching the ears of all patriots, causing them to fire their muskets on Christmas Day, as was the custom. In January of 1776 the British got their revenge, when their fleet, lying off Norfolk, commenced a cannonade. Regulars landed setting fire to the town. In the minds of local inhabitants was intense hatred for the British. Again, on 13 May 1779, Sir Henry Clinton, British General, burned the town of

Suffolk. His fleet, which anchored in Hampton Roads, landed a heavy force under General Matthews, who took possession of Norfolk and Portsmouth, committing extensive devastations. No sooner had the word passed of the arrival of the British to the area, than the militia of Nansemond County were called to arms. Suffolk was the place of general rendezvous. About 200 men assembled there with such weapons as they could procure from their own homes. Few of them had muskets, and still fewer, ammunition. The whole of the little army, commanded by Colonel Willis Riddick, proceeded about eight miles along the Norfolk Road, and, on the evening of the 11th of May, encamped in a large uncultivated field, in front of Capt. James Murdaugh's house. To a tavern about a mile below the encampment of the militia, Captain's King and Davis had retired for the night. In front of this tavern (Hargrove's) was a lane with draw bars at its extremity. These were soon heard to rattle; alarmed at this noise, King and Davis seized their muskets and flew to the door. King leapt out and fired to give the alarm.

The British platoon discharged and shot Davis through the heart. King, well acquainted with the countryside, soon reached the VIrginia camp and informed his comrades of approaching British. They had not heard the British musketry discharging so near them, due to the wind, blowing in an unfavorable direction. And Colonel Willis Riddick, not suspecting that the enemy was approaching, had retired to his own home.

The Command, therefore, devolved upon Colonel Edward Riddick.* The militia retraced their steps to Suffolk, which they reached before dawn. Two officers were dispatched to ascertain the situation and force of the enemy. Four miles below Suffolk they halted, and immediately after sunrise, in the entrace of a lane about one-quarter of a mile long, had a full view of the advancing foe and distinctly counted 600 infantry. They rode back in full speed, and, upon calling the militia to arms, only about 100 obeyed the call. The others had dispersed.

A retreat was unavoidable - every man was admonished to take care of himself! Most of the inhabitants had already left their homes. Those who attempted to secure their property or personal efforts were taken prisoners. The British ruthlessly destroyed everything in sight, setting fire to the town. Several hundred hundred barrels of tar, pitch, turpentine and rum had been deposited on lots continguous to the wharves. The heads of the barrels being knocked out, and their contents, which flowed in a commingled mass, caught fire, blazing down the river like torrents of burning laVirginia As the windows blew from the wharves the great violence, these substances, with difficulty soluble in water, rapidly floated to the opposite shore in a splendid state of conflagration, then to the thick and decaying herbage of the marsh.

"This immense sheet of fire, added to the vast columns of undulating flames which ascended from the burning houses of the town - the explosions at intervals of the gunpowder in the magazines - the consequent protection through the air of large pieces of ignlted timber, which flew, like meteors, to antonishing distance - all contributed to form a collective scene of horror and sublimity such as could not be viewed without emotions not to be described." History of Virginia, Vol. 4, Jones & Girardin.

The last skirmish with the British in Nansemond County, took place at South Quay, a thriving town for tobacco planters, who used this port for shipping as well as for receiving foreign goods. It had large tobacco warehouses, and also shipped flour and ships' riggins, having its own Customs House. By 1778 an army's quartermaster's depot was established and wagon trains carried supplies to Suffolk. But it was not until six months before the surrender at

Henry J. Holland died about 1810. Since the records were burned in Nansemond County, we shall never know the exact details- The tax records ls the only guide other than the fact that a mention of funds coming from the Estate of H. J. Holland, deceased, of Nansemond County, Virginia., appear in the Estate of his young son, Henry J. Holland in 1823 Jasper County, Ga. First, there is the mention of postage being paid by the

There is a mention of postage being paid for a letter from Virginia by the estate of Henry H. Holland of Jasper County, Georgia. Then, on February 6, 1824, cash was received by the hands of G. W. Lawrence (probably George Lawrence, son of Charlotte Holland and Jonas Lawrence of Jasper County, Ga., Charlotte being a daughter of Capt. Joseph Holland, from Hardy Cross, the administrator of H. J. Holland, deceased, in Virginia, the balsnce due him as administrator, $270.10. July 12th that same year, cash was received from Major O. Holleman by a draft from Esquire N. Jones of Nansemond County, Virginia, which draft was purchased of E. Jones by Colonel Hardy Cross of Nansemond County, Virginia., the administrator of H. J. Holland, deceased, for $625.00. All this, apparently being the young Henry J. Holland's portion of his father's estate in Virginia. Lewis Connor Holland was administrator of Henry J. Holland's Estate in Jasper County,. in 1823. Lawson S. Holland rented Henry's plantation for 1825, and Lewis Connor Holland purchased one tract of the estate, 101-1/4 acres in 1825 for $304.00.[192]

Sallie's 2 acres later appeared on her youngest son, Frederick H. Holland's tax records in 1821 from Sallie Holland's estate. - 1818-1819 Frederick claimed only 50 acres from Joseph J. Holland, adjoining John and James Holland. In 1820 he claimed 188 acres and 50 acres from James H. Holland of Henry (his uncle). Later, 1825-1826, Frederick acquired the 300 acres belonging to Joseph J. Holland on the Isle of Wight County line (Randolph Scott Holland's land, son of Capt. Joseph Holland), which apparently restored much of the old Henry plantation. Frederick also inherited part of the old Henry Holland s (, born 1660) land patent on Somerton Creek, which he claimed on the 1867 Nansemond Tax Digest as being 203 and 65 acres.

Henry Holland, Jr. had deeded 200 acres of his homestead in 1787 to Stephen Darden, so, in 1794 he claimed only 125 acres on the Tax Digest. However, by 1800 he had acquired 347 acres; then, in 1811, his estate reported only 286 acres. At one point, this dropped by 2 acres, from 288 to 286, apparently the 2 given his widow, Sallie. His son, Frederick, in 1820 was claiming the 286 acres.

Capt. Henry Holland's sons served in the Militia, viz: William, Lawson S., Lewis Connor and Henry J., all in Virginia. The 1812-1814 Nansemond County, Virginia. Militia lists Lawson S. Holland as Com.Sgt. in Capt. Jeremiah Rawls; 5th Regt.; Henry Holland in Capt. Hardy Cross' (admr of Henry J. Holland's estate) and William Holland in Capt. John Cohoon's County[193]

Yorktown that the British reached this port. In July of 1781, the British sent 700 men against South Quay and on July 16th burned it!

[192] Except for these notations, we would never know the father of William, Lawson S., Lewis Connor, Margaret or Henry J. Holland of Georgia.

[193] NOTE--...."During the War of 1812 great uneasiness was felt by the inhabitants of Suffolk lest the British should send small boats up the river from their ships and burn the Town again. In the midst of their fears and suspense, an old itinerant preacher named Theophilus Gates was holding a revival meeting in the old church near the wharf . One night the alarm came

Children of Capt. Henry J. Holland as follows:

Henry J. Holland, son of Capt. Henry J. Holland, was born 1790 Nansemond County, Virginia., died 1823 in Jasper County, married Margaret, born 1792 in Virginia. There is a 1821 lawsuit in Jasper County, Georgia involving John, Lewis C., Henry J. and George W. Holland vs. the Hester Estate. 9 January 1827, Legacy in full to Cornelius Terhuse, guardian for Letitia and Susan Holland, minors. 9 July 1827, Received of L C. Holland, admr, of H. J. Holland, decd, in full of all demands against him as admr received by me, the widow, and one of the legatees. /s/ Margaret Holland. Purchasers on the Estate of Henry J. Holland (of Jasper County, Georgia) 29 January 1824: L. S. Holland, L. C. Holland, Margaret Holland,

---

that the enemy's barges were coming up the s tream. A panic seized the whole community, and Brother Gates' meeting was brought to an abrupt conclusion. The people fied in all directions, and general consternation prevailed- In a few hours, however, it was ascertained to be a false alarm, based upon the fact that a few oyster boats were bringing up a supply of bivalves to the popular establish of Jack Walker, a colored restaurateur, the fame of whose excellent oysters and ginger cakes had secured for him a lucrative business throughout the surrounding area. Sketch Book of Suffolk, by Edward Pollock.

In 1813 the following petition was filed : "The petition of sundry citizens of Nansemond County setting forth the defenceless situation of Suffolk and the county generally: asking for the return of the militia of Nansemond (all of which was at Norfolk) for the protection of the citizens against the public enemy, as well as against insurrection is filed. Calendar of State Papers, Vol. 10, Part 1, p. 235

Apparently, the Holland boys were in Nansemond in 1812. By 1813, however, they had all removed to Georgia. Perhaps the constant tbreat of the British, coupled with the fact of their deceased father's worn out tobacco fields, now only 286 acres left them little alternative. Capt. Henry Holland had already sold some of his lands, and by 1850 many Holland slaves were freedmen. (Frederick lived next door to the Jeremiah Small family in 1850). Many Virginians were driven iinto the Carolina's and Georgia, to find fertile farms.

The names "Lewis Connor" and Lawson S." which appear in this branch of the Hollands was not accidental. One would presume a marriage to Mary Connor the only known daughter of Lewis Connor (his LWT dated 25 October 1752, probated June 1753, Norfolk County, Virginia) and his wife, Margaret. Capt. Henry J. may have been marrled twice. I think that Sallie was a second wife because Frederick was b. in 1800, which was than twenty years after Henry's first son! All speculation.

The above Lewis Connor was the son of Kedar Connor (his LWT pvd 1/20/1698 Norfolk County, Virginia) and his wife, Elizabeth who married second, Thomas Lawson. Mrs. Elizabeth Lawson's LWT dated 1740 Norfolk County, Virginia names children (Kedar and Lewis) and her grandchildren. Her first husband, Lewis Connor (d. 1698) mentioned in his LWT that he had seven children (four sons), however, since this LWT was greatly torn, the other children remain a mystery. Presumably the other two sons did not reach majori ty, since Mrs. Elizabeth Lawson did not name any grandchildren attrlbutable to them. Lewis Connor (d. 1698) mentioned having estates in England and Virginia Mrs. Elizabeth Connor Lawson's second husband, Thomas Lawson, was the son of Lt. Col. Anthony Lawson (b. ca 1620, his LWT dated 1683 Norfolk County, Virginia). Kedar Connor (b. ca 1690) had six Issue: Joseph, Lewis Connor, Charles, Samuel, Lawson and Mary. Mary, his only daughter, apparently married Henry J. Holland.

Joseph Hill, Thomas Mabry, Larey Wekle, Joseph Binford, William Tucker, Parham Mabry, H. T. Wan, James Davis, John Spear, Phillip Crutchfield, and A. Holland. 9 January 1832, Bond of Reuben C. Shorter and William V. Burney, guardian of Susan Holland, minor of Henry J. Holland. The Estate of Margaret Holland, widow of Henry J., 1859, Jasper County, Susan R. Fulton, admx, granted leave to Sell lot in Cherokee County Estate appraised on 21 March 1851. Administratrix' Bond posted on 7 March 1859. See Loose Papers, Jasper County, Georgia.

Children of Henry J. Holland of Jasper County and his wife, Margaret, viz. Susan and Lawson S. Holland.

1--Susan Holland, daughter of Capt. Henry J. Holland, was born 1814 in Virginia and married Mr. Fulton (decd in 1850).; and Letitia Holland.

2--Lawson S. Holland, son of Capt. Henry J. Holland, first a Sgt. in the Nansemond Militia, later Major in the Georgia Militia, was born 1785 in Nansemond County, Virginia., died in Jasper County, Georgia on 2 July 1850.[194]. He married on 5 April 1805, probably in Gates County, North Carolina, Elizabeth Troup.[195] Known issue of Lawson S. Holland:

> i. Calvin Lawson Holland, M. D., son of Lawson S. Holland, was born on 26 September 1815 in Jasper County, died on 17 March 1851 in Coweta County, age 36.[196]. He married on 10 December 1845, Mary Perkins Cook (born 1821, died 3 August 1799- Bible record). She was the daughter of Caleb and Sarah Cook. He left one son. Issue:[197]

---

[194] Southern Recorder dated 18 July 1850

[195] Nansemond County, Virginia. Tax Digest: 1809 - 553 acres; 1811-1816 - 924 acres. Isle of Wight County, Virginia Tax Digest: 1817 - 496 acres to John Copeland. (Note 553 + 496-924 acres). 1821 -"Lawson S. Holland of Georgia", 496 acres; 1824 -"Lawson S. Holland of Georgia", 496, 318.

In 1811, he had 371 more acres. In 1812 Lawson S. Holland was a Com. Sgt. in Nansemond County, Virginia Militia, 5th Regt., and, in 1813 was a Major on the Georgia frontier, stationed at Randolph County, Ga.

1829 Gwinnett County - Fi.Fa. of Lawson S. Holland, 70 acres were sold by John Underwood to William Terry to satisfy the said Fi.Fa.

2 July 1850, the Petition of Elizabeth A. Holland, widow, that her husband had died on 2 July 1850. Letters of Administration were issued to William Kirkpatrick; that the sald Lawson S. Holland had 750 acres in Jasper County adjolning David Meriwether, John Bayon, Isaac L. Walton and Lewis Pou, etc. Nov. 1850, Letters of Admn. were issued to Elizabeth A. Holland. See Loose Papers, Jasper County.[195]

[196] He was buried in a family cemetery, visible from the road, as follows: From Newnan, Ga. go East on Hwy 34 to Stoke Road. Turn South for .4 miles. The (abandoned) cemetery is on the left.

[197] From the Bible of Mrs. T. L. Cook, Newnan, Georgia., dated 1942.

a. Calvin Fitzpatrick Holland, born 18 September 1847, died 12 September 1920, married (1) on 21 January 1897. Margaret R. Tolbert (died 8 August 1899). Their infant son, Alva L. Holland (born 10 July 1899, died 12 October 1899). Calvin married (2) on 21 November 1906, Annie L. Moreland and had: John Clayton Holland, born on 10 March 1908; Calvin F. Holland, born 15 August 1914. In an old letter dated 1863 written by Eudocia Herrington (born 1843) and her mother, Clotilda Holland (born before 1820) by Lavinia Washington (married Colonel Burwell Jordan), Lavinia Jordan says: "I saw the photograph of cousin Dr. Calvin Holland and he is a fine looking man." *

ii. Elizabeth S. Holland, daughter of Lawson S. Holland, was born 12 February 1819, married 30 June 1840 in Jasper County, Charles C. Bussey. She died, age 29, on 5 October 1848 in Morgan County, both in notices from Southern Recorder and Christian Index newspapers. Vining A. Wilson Bible.

iii. Emily Frances Holland, daughter of Lawson S. Holland, was born on 1 December 1821 in Jasper County, married Dr. Franklin George on 14 November 1848 in Jasper County. They were residents of Madison, Morgan County.

iv. Troup Holland, son of Lawson S. Holland, was born 1826 in Jasper County.

v. Mary Holland, daughter of Lawson S. Holland, was born 1830 Jasper County, married George Wilson, born 1826 in Georgia. Issue: Viney Wilson, born 1845 Georgia; Troup Wilson, born 1847 in Georgia.

Lewis Connor Holland, son of Henry J. Holland, , born ca 1780 Nansemond County, Virginia, Virginia, married three daughters of Capt- Joseph Holland (1) Millie Arenthia Holland on 19 December 1803, in Gates County, North Carolina (Bondsman, John Odom), (2) in 1809, Elizabeth Mary Holland Washington (died 1821), and, (3) on 11 December 1827, Lavinia Holland Cargile (she died in 1835), Jasper County, married 4th, Charlotte.[198]

---

[198] 1807-1810 Nansemond Co. Tax Digest - 200 and 315 acres from the Estate of Joseph Holland. Note- He married daughters of Capt. Joseph Holland. This is how he got the land! In 1812 Lewis Connor Holland was a Captain in Randolph County (later Jasper County) ; in 1813, 2d Lt. in Capt. Thomas's Co. on the Georgia frontier. 13 September 1813, Jasper County, deed of Lewis C. Holland to Henry Slappey, .Jasper County verified that he was in Georgia before 1813. Lewis C. Holland drew in the 1820 Georgia Land Lottery while resident of Jasper County, Phillips District, Land Lot 279, 5th Section, Irwin County. Jasper County, Ga. deed dated 18 July 1823, Lewis C. Holland to G. W. Holland on 18 July 1823. Lewis C. Holland was listed on 1830 Jasper County, Ga. Census, died before 1840 in said county. May of 1835 Lewis C. Holland was Exr of LWT of Lavinia Holland, decd; he produced her LWT into Court; appraisers were appointed. See Loose Papers, Jasper County. Also, in 1835 Lewis Connor Holland visited Virginia per the diary of Colonel John R. Copeland (born 11 January 1811) who was from South Quay. 25 April 1844, Jasper County, the Petition of Charlotte Holland, wife of Lewis Connor Holland that she has separate property, negroes, which are secured to her in trust by the appointment of Joseph L. Holland, trustee, who has endeavored to deprive her of said negroes by subjecting them to the payment of debts of Lewis Connor Holland contracted with the said Joseph L. Holland. WHEREAS, Joshua Hill was appointed trustee for Charlotte Holland to replace Joseph L. Holland. See Loose Papers, Jasper County. Nansemond County, Virginia, Deed dated 5 June 1868, Connor Holland to Calvin Holland, both of Nansemond County, 7 acres in Upper Parish, North by Dempsey Boon, East and South by

Issue of Lewis Connor Holland:[199]

    i. Agatha Frances Holland, born 1808 in Nansemond County, Virginia, married Lemuel Q. Lawrence on 25 March 1824 Jasper County.

    ii. Joseph Lawson Holland, born 1811 in Nansemond County, married on 21 March 1836 in Jasper County, Jane M. Morgan.

    iii. Ellen Amanda Holland, born 1813 in Nansemond County, married Blackshear Bryant on 4 September 1853 in Pulaski County.

    iv. Lavinia Washington Holland, born 4 May 1815, died 1 June 1864. [200] Lavinia Holland married on 5 September 1837, Colonel Burwell Jordan. He died on 1 March 1870. Listed on 1850 Pulaski County Census. SEE Jordan.

    v. William Perrian Holland, born 1821 Nansemond County, Virginia.

William Holland, son of Capt. Henry J. Holland, lived in Clarke and Gwinnett County's, Ga. See further on his lineage. SEE William Goes to Georgia.

Margaret Holland, daughter of Capt. Henry J. Holland, , born 1790 Nansemond County, Virginia, unmarried, listed on 1850 Paulding County, Ga. Census near the home of Archibald Holland, her nephew (son of William Holland).

Frederick Henry Holland, son of Capt. Henry J. Holland (by probably his second wife), was , born 1800 Nansemond County, Virginia. He inherited the homeplace on Kingsale Road. In 1850 he was listed on Nansemond Census (wife decd) with only two children. He also boarded a school teacher, Robert Duke. So there must have been a country school house nearby. [201]

Lemuel Holland, West by Newby Newby, Northwest by Louisa Draper's heirs, being land which Connor bought of Lemuel Holland and wife about 1851. Witness: William L. Holland.

[199] I feel that Lewis Connor Holland also had a son, Connor Holland, born 1800 in Nansemond County, Virginia, although his first marriage is not recorded until 1803. Particularly, because of the restricted usuage of the name "Connor" to this branch of the family. Also, Connor (born 1800) named sons, Calvin, William, etc. Connor, born 1800, farmer, married Barbara, born 1800 Virginia (1850 Nansemond Census). Issue: Sophia A., born 1832, John, born 1834, Calvin, born 1836, William, born 1838, Solomon, born 1843.

[200] Bible of Colonel Burwell Jordan and Lavinia W. R. M Holland Jordan.
[201] 1818-1819, 50 acres from Joseph J. Holland, adj. John and Joseph Holland. Land Holdings from the Nansemond County Tax Digest: 1820, 188 acres; 50 acres from James H. Holland "of Henry" (Frederick's uncle); 50 acres from Joseph J. Holland. 1821-1824, 188, 50, 50, 5; 2 acres added from Sallie Holland's estate (Frederick's mother). 1825-1826, 188, 50, 50, 5 and 300 from Joseph J. Holland on Isle of Wight line. (Randolph Holland, Sr.'s land). 1833, 188, 50, 5, 300, 100 (45 and 55), 60 and 100 from Patrick Henry Holland. Frederick Holland was listed on 1820-1830 Nansemond Co. Census. In 1867 he claimed 203 acres adj. W. O. Pocason and South Quay Road 23 miles Southwest of the courthouse (Henry Holland's old land on Somerton Creek); 65 acres adj. M. March and William Davidson, 23 miles SW of courthouse (also Henry's old land); 507 acres adj. Mills H. Holland (his son), 13 miles W of the courthouse. (Henry Holland's Kingsale land).

Issue of Frederick Henry Holland:

i. Mills Henry Holland, Sr., son of Frederick Henry Holland, was born 23 October 1835 and died on 20 March 1897. His house was built on Indian Trail Road in Holland Virginia, located several hundred yards from his father, Frederick Holland, near the intersection of Kingsale Road. He is buried in the old Henry Holland graveyard. He married (2), Martha Adelia. His LWT 1/1/1890:4/1897 names first two children as children by his first wife. Children as follows:
a. Mills Henry Holland, Jr.
b. Fannie A. Holland married____Ballard.
c. Joseph Edwin Holland.

ii. Mary E. Holland, daughter of Frederick Holland, was , born 1838 Nansemond County, Virginia.

iii. Frederick Henry Holland, Jr., son of Frederick Henry Holland, was born 1828 Nansemond County, Virginia.

Job Holland, son of Henry Holland, Jr., was born ca 1730 married Mary Daughtry, the daughter of John Daughtry, Sr. (as per LWT of John Daughtry, Sr. dated 1783 Isle of Wight County), and named as the sister of Joseph Daughtry, his LWT dated 23 September 1740, probated 27 October 1740 in Isle of Wight County, Virginia. Job Holland's LWT was dated 30 August 1789, probated 3 February 1790 in the Wight County, Virginia. Wits: Thomas Daughtry, Uriah Vaughan, Aaron Holland. The estate of Job Holland, p. 309, cash was paid to Simon Boykin, Francis Young, Miles Daughtry. 1800 the LWT of Job Holland mentioned (copy of Jacob Holland, executor, Nansemond County, Virginia., Isle of Wight Order Book 1795/7, "infants under 21, by Thomas Daugherty, their guardian: Elijah and Polly Holland." [202]

Issue of Job Holland, Sr.:

I.   Job Holland, Jr., son of Job, Sr., was , born ca 1765, died 8 January 1829 in Nansemond County, Virginia., was listed on 1820 Nansemond County Census- Job Holland of Nansemond County, Virginia. married (1) Edey Holland on 22 December 1784 in Gates County, North Carolina. Bondsman: Titus Holland, Witness: Christopher Norfleet of Nansemond County, Virginia. He married (2) Patsey Baker.[203] The LWT of Job Holland, Jr. was dated 11 November

---

[202] 3 March 1795 Order Book (1795-1797) Isle of Wight County, Virginia, Meredith, Elijah and Polly Holland, infants under the age of 21 years, by Thomas Daughtry, their guardian, Richard Carson and Betsy, his wife, and Michael Watson and Bathsheba, his wife, vs. Job Holland, defendant in chancery. The persons appointed to make equal division of the slaves in the Bill mentioned, made their report /s/Elisha L. Ballard, Elijah Johnson, Mills Lawrence. Nansemond Deed, Bk R, p. 168. 26 January 1838, Elisha Rawls to Augustus, his son, and along the old Holland line of Jeno Bird to Old South Quay Road, adjoining the old site of a mill, formerly belonging to the heirs of Job Holland.

[203] Job Holland, Jr. owned a mill on present-day Brentwood Road, where he lived. In 1794 Nansemond County, Job Holland, Jr. was granted admn. of Estate of Titus Holland, decd. 1797 lawsuit, Job Holland, admr. vs. Randolph. Titus Holland married (1), 178- Theresa Frasier, Gates County, North Carolina (2) 4 November 1782, Elizabeth Duke, Gates County,

1828 and probated on 12 January 1829, naming his children as, viz: Elizabeth Barnes, Mary Lee and his grandchildren, children of son, of Zachary Holland. Wife of Job, Elizabeth , born 1780 Virginia, lived with Matilda and Stephen Rawls in 1850.

Children of Job Holland, Jr.:

A. Hannah S. Holland, daughter of Job Holland, Jr., was born 1784/94 married (2), Riddick Darden and (2), Solomon Bradshaw.

B. Zachary Holland, son of Job Holland, Jr., was born 1797, died 6 August 1826, married in 1817 Matilda Ann Howell who was born 1800. As a young man, Zachary served as Sgt. in Capt. Jeremiah Rawl's County, 50th Regt., Virginia Militia, during War of 1812. He died young and his widow married Uriah Rawls. The 1850 Nansemond County Census lists: Stephen Rawls, 48, Matilda, 50, Sarah E., 13, Edwin 12, James 10, John Y. 8, and Elizabeth Holland, age 70. Zachary had Issue:

1. Rev. Robert Howell Holland, son of Zachary Holland, was born 16 October 1819 Nansemond County, married Margarette (Margaret) O'Berry. Robert attended Willis H. Holland's school at South Quay. Issue from 1850 Nansemond Census: Eugenia Marion Holland, born 27 July 1850 in Nansemond County.

2. Zachary Everett Holland, son of Zachary Holland, 1821-1889 married in Gates County, North Carolina, Ann Pretlow (born 1820) on 27 September 1843. His estate was appraised in June of 1894 by William T. Holland, Abram T. Holland and Joseph P. Holland. Administrators: Edward E. Holland and Charles E. Holland. Paid heirs: Lizzie A. Holland, widow; Z. E. Holland, Jr. and Annie E. Holland. Edward E. was appointed guardian of Z. E., Jr. 1850 Nansemond County Census: Zachary E., born 1821 Nansemond County, wife, Ann, , born 1820 Southampton County, Virginia Nansemond County Deed Book R, p. 319, 7 April 1843, Albert Rawls and Eliza Ann, his wife, to Zachariah E. Holland of the Upper Parish for $400...land on the road leading from South Quay to Jones & Everitt's Ship...beginning at said road at a common post with Robert Holland's line.

3. Elizabeth Ann Holland, daughter of Zachary Holland, was born 1823 in Nansemond County, married Albert Rawls , born 1813, listed on 1850 Nansemond County Census. Issue: Mary S. Rawls, born 1837, Angelina Rawls, born 1842 and Hugh K. Rawls, born 1848.

North Carolina. Bondsman: Christopher Norfleet. Witness: Law Baker. 10 June 1789, Titus Holland and Trease, his wife, of Newport Parish, Isle of Wight County, Virginia to Epaphroditus Butler, 200 acres on Carr pocasin. In 1796 Job Holland, Jr. and Dempsey Jones appointed admr to settle the estate of Solomon Holland. Job Holland, executor of Alice Holland, deceased, 1795 Nansemond County, Virginia. 1782 Nansemond County, Virginia. Census lists Job Holland, 2 whites. Job was a very large slaveowner, verified by the 1820-1830 Nansemond Co. Census listing 21 slaves. The 1813 Tax Digest, Nansemond County, Virginia.: Job Holland, 667 acres. 1817-1819, Hilliard Holland from Job's Estate, 6 acres on South Quay Road. Hilliard Holland was the husband of Job's granddaughter, Martha Lee Holland.

4. Dixon Howell Holland, son of Zachary Holland, was married on 10 February 1846 in Gates County, North Carolina, to Mary Eliza Sumner. According to the deeds, in 1843 he was a resident of Nash County, North Caroliina. Issue: Mary Dixon Holland married Julius T. Rawles. Had: Mary Edith Rawls who married James Thomas Jones and had: James Robert (Bob) Jones who married Jane Hardy Shaw of Holland, Virginia.

C.   Elizabeth Holland, daughter of Job Holland, Jr. , was born ca 1794, married (2) _____Holland, (2), James Barnes. Issue: William Barnes, Thomas H. Barnes, John P. Barnes (d. young).

D.   Nancy Holland, daughter of Job Holland, Jr., was born 1800 (1850 Nansemond County, Virginia. Census) married James Byrd. Issue: James Byrd , born 1824, Mary E. Byrd, born 1832, Sally M. Byrd , born 1835 and Uriah Byrd, born 1837.

E.   Polly Holland, daughter of Job Holland, Jr., was born 1810/1820, married Isaac Lee, J. P. Issue: Margaret Lee married John Norfleet; Martha Lee married (2), Hilliard Holland, (2), Richard Lee.

F.   Augustus H. Holland, son of Job Holland, Jr., was born on 6 February 1801, and died 30 March 1888, married Anne Winborne on 2 August 1825. Issue:[204]

> 1. Augustus H. Holland, Jr. was born on 4 January 1832, married Mamie E. His LWT dated 12 February 1862, probated November 1864 in Nansemond County, Virginia, naming Margaret. He owned a store at Holland's Corner and after his death his brother, William T., ran it. Served in Confederate service and was killed on 1 July 1862 during the Battle of Malvern Hill. The LWT of Margaret Holland, Sr. His LWT dated 13 February 1862, probated June of 1866, witnessed by William T. Holland and A. H. Holland, Jr. named Eliza A. Byrd, wife of Hillery; Sarah A. Byrd, wife of James; grandson, Jesse J. McClenny.

>> i. William T. Holland , born 11 April 1828, died 12 June 1897 in Nansemond County, Virginia, married Sarah Catharine Abra Cross, the daughter of Abram and Eliza Cross.
>> ii. Catran Hanah Holland, born on 24 June 1834, married James M. C. Duke, son of Isaac V. Duke.
>> iii. Zachary Holland, born on 27 January 1836, died 6 February 1908, unmarried.

II. Meredith Holland, son of Job Holland, Sr., age under 21 in 1800. He was born ca 1784. Listed on 1810 Isle of Wight County, Virginia Census, having two sons born 1800/1810, two daughters 1800/1810. 1787-89 Isle of Wight County Tax Digests: Job Holland, 300 acres in Isle of Wight County. In 1790 he willed to Job and Meredith Holland 150 acres each. In 1823 Meredith Holland about 50 acres, then deeded it to Abram Holland in 1824 (77- 1/2 acres). 1826 Isle of WIght County Tax Records, Meredith Holland's Estate, 60 acres conveyed Abraham Holland by commissioners. 1832 LWT of Abraham Holland to Martha. Probable Issue:

---

[204] Bible of Augustus H. Holland, owned by Miss Novella V. Holland (1938).

A. Abraham Holland, son of Meredith Holland, died 1832.

B. Jordan Holland, son of Meredith Holland, was born 1805 Nansemond County, Virginia. married Margaret, born 1807, listed on 1850 Nansemond County, Virginia. Census. Issue:

    1. Meredith Holland, born 1834 Nansemond County

    2. Ann Holland, born 1836 Nansemond County

    3. Allen Holland, born 1839 Nansemond County

    4. Lucinda Holland , born 1841 Nansemond County

    5. Sarah Holland , born 1842 Nansemond County

    6. Jason Holland , born 1844 Nansemond County

    7. Margaret Holland , born 1847 Nansemond County.

III. Elijah Holland, son of Job Holland, Sr., was born 1794, Isle of Wight County Tax Digest, 100 acres, in said county. 1811, 135 acres Nansemond County. He was under 21 in 1800, guardian appointed. The 1820 Nansemond County Census lists one son , born 1800/1810; four daughters, born 1810/1820. The 1825-1829 Isle of Wight County Tax Books, 150 acres on Blackwater Creek. His LWT was probated on 7 December 1857 in the Isle of Wight County, Virginia naming a grandson (John Robertson) and Issue:.

A. George W. Holland , born 1822 Nansemond County married Susan, born 1815 Nansemond County, listed 1850 Nansemond County Census. Issue: Georgianna Holland, born 1840 and Elijah Holland, born 1847.

B. Elizabeth Holland.

C. Elijah Holland, Jr., listed 1830 Nansemond County, Virginia. Census.

IV. Bathsheba Holland, daughter of Job Holland, Sr., sister of Elijah Holland, married 1795 Isle of Wight County, Virginia, Michael Watson.

V. Elizabeth (Betsy) Holland, daughter of Job Holland, Sr., married on 5 January 1792, Richard Carson, Isle of Wight County, Virginia.

VI. Polly Holland, daughter of Job Holland, Sr., under 21 in 1800.

James, son of Henry Holland, Jr. In 1756 James Holland sold 426 acres in Isle of Wight County, Virginia adj. John Holland, Sr., John Winburn and William Holland. James and Henry, Jr. appear to be deeding Henry's patent of 1696. In 1763, James Holland sold 230 acres, being part of Henry's patent. No further information.

John, son of Henry Holland, Jr. John d. 1786 in Isle of Wight County, Virginia His LWT dated 21 November 1785, probated on 3 October 1786 by Elizabeth Holliday, executrix. Executors named: Wife and Dempsey Hunt. Wife to have use of "my land". Only child named: Joseph Holland.

Solomon, son of Henry Holland, Jr., was born by 1730, appeared in the processioning of lands in 1755 by Upper Parish, Nansemond County Solomon d. 1795 Nansemond County, Virginia. The 1782 and 1790 Nansemond County Census lists 10 whites, 12 blacks, 3/4/1784, Mason and Susannah Johnson of Nansemond County to Solomon Holland of same, 86 acres in Isle of Wight County adj. Aaron Johnson. 1790 Solomon Holland was made guardian of children of Mrs. Anne Holland (wife of Elias). 1791 deed of Solomon Holland to Anne Jones.

1792 Nansemond County, Virginia. deed to Solomon Holland. In 1795 Job Holland, Dempsey Jones were appointed admrs of the Estate of Solomon Holland. 1795 settlement, Estate of Solomon Holland, Nansemond County Heirs: Carr Holland, Brittain Holland, Nathaniel Holland, Dempsey Jones.

Issue of Solomon Holland:

I. John D. Holland, son of Solomon, d. 1791 Nansemond County, Virginia. Estate of John Holland, son of Solomon, ref. est. and settlement of James Holland's estate in accord with John Holland, son of Solomon. In 1790, John, the son of Solomon, was exr of Est. of Henry Winburn, deceased. Nansemond County Tax Digests: John Holland, son of Solomon, 1782, 100 acres; 1787, 91 acres, 275 acres; 1792, "his estate", 100 acres, James Holland, admr of John Holland vs. Holland. James Holland ordered to settle estate of Lemuel Council, admr of John Holland, 1792. Son (listed in tax records):

A. Henry Holland "of John", 1782, 200 acres, Nansemond County, Virginia., 1790 Nansemond County, Virginia Census, 9 whites, 7 blacks.

II. Anne Holland, daughter of Solomon, married Dempsey Jones. The 1850 Nansemond County Census lists Joseph Jones of "D", , born 1815 married Nancy , born 1805. Their Issue: William T. Jones , born 1839; Elizabeth Jones , born 1841; and James R. ones , born 1844. James H. Holland , born 1827 is also listed with the family.

III. Brittain Holland, son of Solomon. The 1802 Nansemond County Tax Digest lists 50 acres for him.

IV. Nathaniel Holland, son of Solomon.

V. Dr. Lemuel Carr Holland, son of Solomon, born 1813, died 21 October 1878, married on 25 May 1836, Catharine B. Woodley (born 1814, died 26 March 1873).[205] Deed in Nansemond County dated 22 March 1866, Lemuel C. Holland of Suffolk to John R. Killy, chosen as trustee, land on the East side of Main Street, North by Henry B. Councill, East by a small branch, South by Jacob H. Duck's estate, West by Main Street. The 1869 Nansemond County Tax Digests lists the Estate of Carr Holland, 128 acres adjoining John Copeland, 6 miles west of the courthouse.

Issue of Dr. Lemuel Carr Holland:

(A) Elfrida Charlotte Holland, daughter of Dr. Lemuel Carr Holland, was born 24 March 1837, died 13 October 1925, married (1) on 21 November 1855, Jesse Bruce Brewer, and (2) on 10 March 1865, Colonel George W. Lewis, died on 5 January 1896, aged 69, Quincy, Illinois.
    1. Mary Augusta Brewer, born 16 October 1856, died 16 December 1936.
    2. Elfrida Alice Bruce Brewer, born 16 October 1856, died 16 December 1936.
    3. Sarah Brewer, born 15 October 1857, died 15 October 1857.
    4. Annie Woodley Brewer, born 5 December 1859, died 13 May 1930, married on 13 December 1888, Fred B. White, born on 25 November 1893. Issue: Jesse

---

[205] Bible owned by Dr. Linwood Car Holland (1947).

B. White, born 6 August 1890, died 27 April 1892 (daughter); W. Harrison White , born on 22 April 1899.

5. George Holland Lewis, born 17 April 1866, died 11 April 1883.

6. Catharine Seymour Lewis, born 19 October 1870, died 2 October 1945, married Mr. Crowder.

7. Clifford Lemuel Lewis, born 6 November 1874, died 25 January 1940.

(B) Granville S. P. Holland, son of Dr. Lemuel Carr Holland, was born 8 December 1838 married (1) Monimia Pinner, and (2) in September of 1879, Nettie Hall. Issue: Annie B. Holland, born 28 October 1867; Lemuel Holland, died 23 August; Linwood Carr Holland , born 24 September 1881; and Granville S. P. Holland, Jr. , born 13 April 1884.

(C) Harrison Woodley Holland, son of Dr. Lemuel Carr Holland, was born on 30 December 1841.

(D) Twin of Dr. Lemuel Carr Holland, born on 5 March 1843.

(E) Twin of Dr. Lemuel Carr Holland, born on 5 March 1843.

(F) Robert Doyle Woodley Holland, son of Dr. Lemuel Carr Holland, born 8 August 1846, died 25 October 1857.

William, Sr., second son of Henry, died 1755 in Nansemond County, Virginia. William's orphans were mentioned in the 1756 Vestry Records of Upper Parish. On 31 March 1747 at a vestry held for the Upper Parish of Nansemond County, lines to be processioned between Henry Holland, Jr. and Stephen Darden; also between William Holland, Sr., etc. 4 March 1752, lines between Henry Holland, Sr. and Henry Holland, Jr., Robert Holland, William Holland, James Holland. In 1755, Henry Holland, William Holland and Daniel Holland. In 1760, James Holland, to heirs of Henry Holland, decd, William Holland. In 1768, Will. Holland, Daniel Holland, Absalom Holland, Henry Holland, Jacob Holland, Joseph Holland. In 1775, Joseph Holland, William Holland, Thomas Holland. Children of William Holland:

I. William Holland, probably a son of William, died 1786 in Isle of Wight County, Virginia. LWT dated 5 February 1785, probated 5 October 1786 by John Darden, Benjamin Holland, Barbary (probably Barnaby) Holland. (Isle of Wight WB 10, p. 53). Page 56, Upon the Motion of William Holland, exr, with Miles Holland (his security), Bond 500 pds. He was bequeathed all his father's land, 100 acres. Issue of William, Jr.:

A. Benjamin Holland, son of William, born ca 1730. His LWT was dated 16 December 1799, probated 7 July 1800, Isle of Wight County, Virginiaa. Witnessess: Mills Butler, Miles Holland, Aaron Holland. Marriage: Gates County, North Carolina. Benjamin Holland to Mary Council on 9 January 1783. Bondsman: John Darden. Benjamin Holland, Barnaby Holland and John Darden were secs. on LWT of Henry Johnson, Sr., Isle of Wight. Isle of Wight County, Virginia Deed, 3 March 1785, Benjamin Holland and wife, Mary to Jacob Wheeler of Southampton County, Virginia for 49 pds., land on northside of Main Black Water Swamp, 200 acres. Children of Benjamin Holland:

1. Ann Holland, daughter of Benjamin, was , born on 1760, married on 17 February 1785 Southampton County, Virginia, Dempsey Carr. (Note that Solomon Holland named one of his children - Carr Holland).

169

2. Elizabeth Holland, daughter of Benjamin Holland, married on 9 April 1788 in the Isle of Wight County, Virginia, John Darden, Jr., the son of John Darden. (Consent of Benjamin Holland). John Darden, Jr. listed on the 1790 Isle of Wight County, Virginia. His LWT dated 23 January 1800, probated 7 April 1800, naming wife, Elizabeth and Issue: Mills Darden, Ziza Darden married on 2 October 1815, Mary Powell, Chasey Darden, Sally Darden. John Darden, Sr. migrated to North Carolina, then Wilkes County, Georgia. In 1788, living from a time in Emanuel County, but died in Wilkes County, Georgia.

3. Patience Holland, daughter Benjamin, married 17 November 1796 in Isle of Wight County, Virginia, Jacob Johnson. (Surety: Eley Johnson).

4. Jacob Holland, son of Benjamin, died 1809 Nansemond County, Virginia. Wife, Tempy? 1798-1867 Nansemond County Tax Digest, 533 acres. 1809 lists 32 acres of his Estate. 1813 Isle of Wight County, Virginia. Tempy Holland, by LWT of Jacob Holland, received 45 acres. The 1782 Tax Records of Nansemond County, Virginia. verifies that Barnaby Holland was the son of William, 100 acres (1796, 7 acres were added). Known Issue:

B. Barnaby Holland, son of William, died 1799 Nansemond County, Virginia., Mills Butler, executor. 1782-1795 Tax Digest, 100 acres; 1796, 7 acres added: 1802-1811, 25 acres, listed for Estate of Barnaby Holland. Son: Aaron Holland, proved by his deed dated 1800 Nansemond County. Issue:

1. Aaron Holland, proved to be the father (of Harrison) from Nansemond County Death Records, viz: Harrison Holland , born 1803, LWT dated 3 December 1866 probated on 11 December 1867 Nansemond County married Sarah C. , born 1803, listed 1850 Nansemond County Census. Issue: Joseph H., Frank and Miles Holland.

II. Miles Holland, son of William.

III. Elisha F. Holland, son of William, married Henrietta, Isle of Wight County Tax Records show an Elisha Holland "to Martha, 84 acres". 1794 Isle of Wight Tax Digest: 200 acres, Nansemond County 1800 Deed of Emancipation from Elisha F. Holland to Grace in Nansemond County, Virginia. 1803 Tax Digest Nansemond County: 322 acres, Nansemond County, 1805 Isle of Wight Tax Records lists: Elisha "of William", 100 acres. Note: He inherited his father, William's, 100 acres in Isle of Wight County, Virginia 1811 - Nansemond County Tax Digest: 422 acres, Nansemond County 1817-1819 Nansemond County Tax Digest lists James, son of Henry Holland, land adj. Elisha and John Holland. In 1829 a division was made of Elisha F. Holland's land. "Omitted in 1829, Lawson F. Holland, 54 acres, from Estate of Elisha F. Holland."[206] Sons:

---

[206] 10 November 1832, Nansemond County Deed: Elarkin Holland and Patience, his wife; Lawson F> Holland and Polly, his wife; James Wright and Media, his wife; Patrick Henry Holland; Braddock Holland and Maria, his wife; William Hoyt and Elmira, his wife, all of Nansemond County, Virginia. To William Odom, Jr. 70 acres which they inherited from Monroe Holland, who devised title from his father, Elisha Holland (William Odom married Keaten Holland, one of the heirs).

A. Lawson F. Holland, son of Elisha F. Holland, his LWT dated 1854 Isle of Wight County, Virginia, naming Margaret Holland, his daughter.

B. Monroe Holland, son of Elisha F. Holland, was born ca 1780. Issue: Elarkin Holland married Patience; Lawson F. Holland married Polly on 7 November 1865 in Nansemond County, Virginia. deed of Polly, the widow of Lawson F. Holland, decd, Dempsey Butler and his wife, Malvina, John Rhodes and his wife, Sally Ann, and John Holland, deed land to Mills H. Holland.

C. Media Holland, daughter of Elisha F. Holland, married James Wright.

D. Patrick Henry Holland, son of Elisha F. Holland, was born 1807 married Ann, , born 1823, listed 1850 Nansemond County Census. Issue: Richard G. Holland , born 1839; Martha S. Holland , born 1841; and Lucy J. Holland , born 1846.

E. Braddock Holland, son of Elisha F. Holland, was born 1809 Nansemond County, married on 16 May 1831 in Gates County, North Carolina, Maria Babb (, born 1817), listed 1850 Nansemond County Census. Children, all , born Nansemond County: John A. Holland , born 1835; Thomas J. Holland , born 1839; Ann M. Holland , born 1841; Clarissa N. Holland, born 1843; Sarah E. Holland , born 1846; Permelia A. Holland , born 1849.

F. Elvina Holland, daughter of Elisha F. Holland, married William Hoyt.

F. Keaten Holland, daughter of Elisha F. Holland, married William Odom. Dau: Mary Louise Odom married WIlliam L. Holland (born 27 September 1835, died 19 November 1893), son of Lemuel Holland.

IV. Absalom Holland, son of William, born ca 1740/1750. Mention of his LWT 1797 Nansemond County, Virginia. LWT received by Andrew Holland, exrecutor, 1796. The 1782 and 1790 Nansemond County Census, 8 whites. He lived in Trumpet Drive area of Holland, Virginia Issue:

A. Andrew Holland, son of Absalom Holland, , born before 1775, d. before 1850. His wife (from tax records), Esther, was born 1778, listed 1850 Nansemond County Census. The 1820-1830 Nansemond County Census shows two sons born 1800/1810, two sons born 1794/1804, son , born ca 1794, and daughter , born ca 1794. Children of Andrew:
> 1. Andrew Holland , born 1820
> 2. Nancy Holland , born 1822
> 3. Betsy Holland , born 1841
> 4. Lemuel H. Holland 1809-5/2/1889 Nansemond County, Virginia. married 1834 Nancy Jones (died 24 April 1907). They lived Southwestern Blvd. and Trumpet Drive, near Holy Neck Christian Church (Holland Corners, now Suffolk, Virginia).[207] Issue:
>> i. William L. Holland, son of Lemuel H. Holland, was born 27 September 1835, died 19 November 1893 in Nansemond County, Virginia. married (1) on 11 November 1858, Mary Louisa Odom, daughter of William Odom and Keaten Holland, married (2) on 17 December 1879 Margaret Susan Holland. Son:

---

[207] Patricia J. Holland, 1525 Lummis Road, Suffolk, Virginia 23437

(a) Hugh S. Holland, born 23 August 1891, died 8 October 1961 in Nansemond County, Virginia. He was married on 29 December 1910, Ada Virginia Carter, born 1 June 1893 Gates County, North Carolina, died 3 December 1918 in Nansemond County, Virginia. Their son: William Horace Holland, born 4 November 1914 in Nansemond County, Virginia. married 31 December 1939, Sarah VIrginia Beall, born 23 February 1918, Nansemond County, Virginia. Their son: William Jerry Holland, born 15 September 1946 in Suffolk, Virginia, married on 2 May 1971 in Jackson, Michigan, Patricia Joanne Finch, born on 11 May 1945 in Jackson, Michigan.

ii. Daughter of Lemuel H. Holland was born 1835/1840 Nansemond County, Virginia.

iii. Lavinia Holland, daughter of Lemuel H. Holland, was born 1837, died 18 March 1884 in Nansemond County, Virginia. married James E. Holland.

iv. Martha Ellen Holland, daughter of Lemuel H. Holland, was born 27 March 1838, died 24 January 1913 in Nansemond County, Virginia, unmarried.

v. George Washington Holland, son of Lemuel H. Holland, was born 27 November 1841, died 10 June 1902 in Nansemond County, Virginia, married on 16 April 1869 in Isle of Wight County, Virginia, Mary Elizabeth Duke.

vi. Matilda Ann Holland, daughter of Lemuel H. Holland, was born 6 October 1845, died 15 December 1933 in Nansemond County, Virginia, buried in the Copeland Family Cemetery, married on 23 April 1867, Elisha Rawls Copeland.

vii. Frances Susan Holland, daughter of Lemuel H. Holland, was born 1846 Nansemond County, Virginia. married on 17 January 1877, Jacob Edward Holland.

viii. John Andrew Holland, son of Lemuel H. Holland, was born 1848 Nansemond County, Virginia, married on 14 May 1874, Annie V. Harrell.

ix. Robert L. Holland, son of Lemuel H. Holland, was born 1851 Nansemond County, Virginia. married (1) on 18 January 1880, Sarah Wright, (2) on 1 March 1894, Mary Ida Badger.

ix. Sarah Holland, daughter of Lemuel H. Holland, was born 1853, died 28 April 1855 in Nansemond County, Virginia., buried in the family cemetery, Lemuel Holland land.

James, third son of Henry Holland, was also mentioned in Vestry Book, as son of Henry, for processioning lands, 4 March 1752. From tax records, "by LWT of James Holland", 250 acres to Alice Holland and Mills Holland, 50 acres. Tax Digests, Nansemond County: 1787-1797, 300 acres; 1798-1801, James Holland, his estate, 200 acres in Isle of Wight County. In 1756 he sold 426 acres in Isle of Wight County, Virginia adjoining lands of John Holland, Sr., John Winburn and William Holland. James and Henry Holland, Jr. appear to be deeding Henry Holland's patent of 1696. In 1763, James Holland sold 230 acres, belng part of Henry Holland's patent. The 1782 Nansemond County, Virginia. Tax Digest speclfies his children, James and Henry. However, James, Sr. and some of his children apparently migrated to Bertle County, North Carolina. The Bertie County deeds make it clear that Hollands in that county came from Nansemond County, Virginia. James Holland, Sr. witnessed a deed of Richard Holland, yeoman, to Davis Jernigan of Nansemond County, Virginia, dated 20 November 1728 for 57S acres on the Chowan River known as "Indian Town" on the southside of Indlan Creek. Patent dated April 1, 1723. The children and grandchildren of James occupied Bertie County in those days, Dempsey, William, Joseph, and Richard. Children of James Holland:

I. James Holland, son of James Holland. His estate in Isle of Wight County, Virginia, was appraised on 18 February 1801. James and Alec (Alice) Holland, adminstrators. Accounts of Eleys and Dardens mentioned. Inventory by Mills and Robert Eley and James Holland. James Holland married Alice Darden, daughter of Hardy Darden and wife, Alice Ely, daughter of Robert Eley IV (LWT dated 29 March 1750, died 1 November 1750, Isle of Wight County, Virginia). Alice Holland's LWT was dated 14 October 1811, probated 4 March 1816, named granddaughter, Patsy Washington Holland and issue: Hardy Dardey Holland, Alice Holland. Alice Holland, in her LWT dated 14 October 1811, probated 4 March 1816 in the Isle of Wight County, Virginia, leaving her entire estate to Hardy Darden Holland, except that he was to take care of her daughter, Alice Holland. She also mentioned a granddaughter, Patsy Washington Holland: Children of James and Alice Holland:[208]

A. Mills Holland, son of James and Alice, was , born 1784/1794. 1810 Isle of Wight County, Virginia Census lists three sons , born 1800/1810. 1814 Nansemond County Tax Digest: Mills Holland "of James", 50 acres..

B. Hardy Darden Holland, son of James and Alice, married Jane. He died intestateintestate before 2 April 1824: John Marshall and Thomas Stephens, admrs, returned acct of Estate. Josiah Holleman appointed guardian of Hardy's children. By LWT of his mother, Alice, left all her estate. Alice "of James", tax digest, conveyed to Hardy Holland, 250 acres.. 1806-1817, Isle of Wight, 250 acres declared near Chapel Swamp; 1818-1821, Isle of Wight County, 247 acres. Hardy Holland married Jincy Clements, 1822 recd 144 acres in tr. because of marriage. 11/23/1809, Hardy D. Holland, his wife, Jane, and his mother, Alice, deeded 3-1/2 acres to Joshua Daniel. Issue of Hardy Darden Holland

    1. Martha Holland.
    2. George W. Holland.
    3. Susan Holland .
    4. James Holland. James Holland appointed guardian.
    5. Caroline Holland. Jincy (Jane) Holland, widow of Hardy D. Holland, deceased, was named as heir of her deceased daughter, Caroline, to represent rights of heirs.
    6. Sally Holland married William Gray Gwaltney of Isle of Wight County, Virginia. Issue:
        i. William Oliver Perry Gwaltney
        ii. Frank Gwaltney
        iii. Sally Gwaltney
        iv. Oceana Winfrey Gwaltney married Samuel Edwin West (born 1838), Confederate Soldier. Issue: Elliott Edwin West married Mary

---

[208] A deed dated 20 April 1794, of James Holland and Alice, his wife, of Isle of Wight County to Elisha Darden of Hertford County, North Carolina, 90 acres on NS of Carrsola Field. 1 February 1802, Mills Eley, Capt. Robert Eley and James Holland, Order of Court, sell to Hardy Holland, Isle of Wight County, 300 acres belng "all land of James Holland, Sr., deceased."

Hunnicutt; Sarah Caroline West married (1) Edwin Warren, and (2) George W. Brown; Mollie West, married Nathaniel Berryman; James Thomas West married Elizabeth Jones; Eugene Gordon West, married Oneta Hardin; Grace West, born on 7 September 1874 in Surry County, married on 27 February 1901, James Robins McClamroch.

C. James Holland, son of James and Alice.

D. Henry Holland, son of James and Alice married Mourning (died after 1820 Nansemond County, Virginia, died 1827 in Nansemond County, Virginia, his estate distributed to David and Eley Holland, and two mulatto girls, Axey and Betsy Holland. Issue:

    1. Amy Holland, daughter of Henry Holland, was born 1798 Nansemond County, Virginia., mulatto daughter of Henry. Listed on 1850 Nansemond County Census. Her family: John , born 1820, Patsey, born 1800. Her LWT was dated 29 May 1874, probated 10 April 1876 in Nansemond County, Virginia., names John as the sole heir.

    2. Betsy Holland, mulatto daughter of Henry Holland.

    3. David Holland, son of Henry Holland, listed 1830 Nansemond County, Virginia. Census.

    4. Eley Holland, son of Henry Holland, born ca 1805 Nansemond County, died on 5 September 1876 in Nansemond County Listed 1830 Nansemond County Census. married (1) Amy who died 1845-1850 in Nansemond County, and (2) Elmira Holland, born 1825/1830 Nansemond County They lived on O'Kelly Drive, near Holy Neck Christian Church (Holland, now Suffolk, Virginia.). Children by Amy:

        i. Henry Holland, son of Eley and Amy Holland, married on 21 February 1861, Nancy Howell.

        ii. Sarah E. Holland, daughter of Eley and Amy Holland, married on 10 January 1867, William E. Hines.

        iii. Hardy Holland, son of Eley and Amy Holland, born 5 June 1836, died 9 August 1909 in Nansemond County, Virginia, buried in the Holland Cemetery, [209]married on 24 March 1870, Louisa Jones.

        iv. Nancy Ann Holland, daughter of Eley and Amy Holland, was born May 1838 in Nansemond County, Virginia, married on 22 December 1865, Henry Jernigan.

        v. David Holland, son of Eley and Amy Holland, was born 1842, died 10 August 1862 in Nansemond County, Virginia, died off disease during the Civil War. Unmarried.

        vi. Mourning Ann Holland, daughter of Eley and Amy Holland, married on 17 February 1872, James Hedgepeth.

    Children by wife, Elmira:

---

[209] Cemetery located on the corner of Rt. #189 and O'Kelly Drive (Holland, now Suffolk, Virginia.)

vii. Margaret Susan Holland, daughter of Eley and Elmira Holland, was born on 28 February 1908 in Nansemond County, Virginia, married on 17 December 1879, William L. Holland.

viii. Jacob Edward Holland, son of Eley and Elmira Holland, married (1) on 17 January 1877, Frances Susan Holland, and (2), Ella C. Holland.

ix. James Holland, son of Eley and Elmira Holland, was born 2 June 1856, died 10 September 1933 in Nansemond County, Virginia, married on 2 January 1887, Elizabeth Fowler.

x. Cherry Marie Holland, daughter of Eley and Elmira Holland, was born 7 January 1864, died 22 February 1933 in Nansemond County, Virginia. He married on 29 January 1885, Joseph Frank Holland.

II. Henry Holland, son of James, Sr., was born ca 1720/1730. Probably removed to Chowan, then Bertie County, North Carolina. Minutes of Chowan County, North Carolina (1735-1748), April, 1748: Deed of Sale, Henry Holland and wife, Ann, to John Watson. Proved by the oath of Michael Watson.

III. Dempsey Holland, son of James, Sr., was born ca 1710/1720 Nansemond County, Virginia. He witnessed the LWT of Epaphroditus Moore of Bertie County, North Carolina dated 11 June 1757, probated in October of 1757. In 1762 he made gift deeds to his sons, Samuel and Abraham. Issue:

A. Abraham Holland, son of Dempsey Holland, was born ca 1740.

B. Samuel Holland, son of Dempsey Holland, was born ca 1742.

C. Mary Holland, daughter of Dempsey Holland, was born ca 1744, married on 26 September 1764 in Bertie County, North Carolina, Edward Toole.

D. Henry Holland, son of Dempsey Holland, was born 1757 Bertie County, North Carolina. Aged 96, he lived with his son, John, 1850 Tattnall County, Georgia Census. Henry married Sarah Clay on 2 September 1783 in Duplin County, North Carolina. His Revolutionary War Pension states he entered service in Duplin County, North Carolina, 1782 militiaman, fought in battle of Eutaw Springs, died on 26 June 1853 in Tattnall County. He removed to Washington County in 1780/1784, thence to Warren County where he lived 4 years, thence to Washingtron County, 1799, in Tattnall County Addendum to pension dated 2 June 1854,, children to receive annual $50 pension of father. Issue:
    1. David Holland, son of Henry Holland, was born 1780 Bertie County, North Carolina, married Priscilla, born 1788 in Burke County. Issue: Polly , born 1826, Dempsey, born 1828, Sarah , born 1830, John , born1832, and Priscilla , born 1840, all in Tattnall County.
    2. Susannah Holland, daughter of Henry Holland, married Francis Benton on 16 January 1810 in Warren County.
    3. John Holland, son of Henry Holland, was born 1785 Washington County, married Rachel , born 1805 Tattnall County. Issue: Martha Cowart , born 1834, Margaret Michael , born 1836 Tattnall County.
    4. Henry Holland, son of Henry Holland.

5. Theophilus Holland, son of Henry Holland.
6. William Holland, son of Henry Holland, was born 1795 in Washington County, Georgia and married Mary (born 1810 Emanuel County). Issue: Thomas , born 1836, Sarah , born 1840, Eliza , born 1842 and James, born 1844, all Tattnall County
7. Frederick Holland, son of Henry Holland, was born 1798 Washington County, married Matilda , born 1800 Bulloch County. Issue: Martha , born 1832, Nancy , born 1834, David H. , born 1836, Polly, born 1838, Matilda , born 1840, all Tattnall County.
8. Dempsey Holland.

E. John Holland, son of Dempsey Holland, was born ca 1764 married Sarah Higgs on 10 February 1784 in Bertie County, North Carolina.

IV. William Holland, son of James, Sr., born ca 1710, listed on 1757 Bertie County, North Carolina Taxables: 1769 Petit Juror in Bertie County There is a marriage of William Holland on 19 May 1769 in Bertie County, North Carolina to Ann Moore. Gift Deed to son, Theophilus Holland dated 12 November 1753 in Bertie County, North Carolina, 125 acres on northside of Cashy Swamp near Wattom Pocoson, "land which I bought in 1734". Gift Deed to son, Snell Holland, May 1754 Bertie County, North Carolina, 125 acres on northside of Cashy Swamp near Watton Meadow, "it being the plantation whereon I now live." Issue:

A. Theophilus Holland, son of William Holland, was born ca 1733, listed on 1757 Bertie County, North CarolinaTaxables.

B. Snell Holland, son o f William Holland, inherited the homeplace.

V. Joseph Holland, son of James, Sr., witnessed the 1755 LWT of Martin Gardner in Bertie County, North Carolina. 1767 Bertie County, North Carolina, Isaac Wimberly to Joseph Holland. Joseph's LWT dated 17 November 1790, probated February 1791 in Bertie County, North Carolina, named his Issue: Joel, Mary, Magdalene, Sarah Thomas; and granddaughter, Rachel Holland.

VI. Richard Holland, son of James, Sr., was found in Bertie County, North Carolina deeds in 1730. John Cotton to Richard Holland on 8 August 1723, land on SS of Roanoke River and Broad Meadow. 9 May 1730, Richard Holland, cooper, to James Brogden, 250 a. on SS of Morratuck River (Broad Meadow)

Joseph, fourth son of Henry Holland, married Phoebe, probably Winburn. Joseph Holland of Kingsale Swamp, which lay in both Nansemond and Isle of Wight County's.- Note that the following deed dated 1 May 1751 proves that Joseph was son of Henry. John Winburn of Nansemond sold to Joseph Holland, son of Henry, deceased, with consent of his wife, Phoebe, 75 acres on the southside of Kingsale Swamp, being part of a patent to Jonathan Robinson, etc., dated 23 April 1681, and by conveyance came to John Winburn's wife from her grandmother, Phoebe Kirl in 1706. Witnesses: Henry, Robert and Job Holland.

Issue of Joseph and Phoebe Holland:

I. Joseph Holland, Jr., son of Joseph and Phoebe Holland, 1715-1799 , known as Joseph "of Spivey". He may have lived west of Henry's original land patent in Nansemond County near Spivey

Swamp and this is why he is referred to thusly. Or, he could have married a daughter of Capt. Mathew Spivie (his LWT dated 1720, Norfolk County, Virginia, leaving small children....Elizabeth, Tamar, Sarah and Judith) In 1777, there was a Joseph Spivey who was paid as reader at Sumerton Church, Cyprus Chappell by the Upper Parish of Nansemond County This located the Spivey's in southern Nansemond County, near Spivey Swamp.

Joseph Holland witnessed the LWT of Isabel Johnson dated 15 August 1773. Also, on 26 February 1782, he was mentioned in the LWT of Henry Johnson, Sr. who names sons-Aaron, William, Henry and bequeathed them lands adjoining Magon Johnson and Joseph Holland. Wits: John Darden, Barnaby Holland, Benjamin Holland, the last two, securities. Joseph is said to have died without a Will in Isle of Wight County in 1799. A copy of the LWT of Joseph Holland was given to Jacob Holland, exr, in 1800, Nansemond County Again, in 1800, Thomas Holland, exr, was given a copy of the LWT of Joseph Holland. A copy of Joseph's LWT was also given to Joseph Holland and his wife in 1800. In 1790, Joseph Holland was assignee of Esther Holland v. Hutchins. Capt. Joseph Holland (his son), for Hodgins vs. Henderson, 1797-1798.[210]

Children of Joseph Holland "of Spivey":

I. David Holland, son "of Joseph", according to tax records, was born 1775/1794. Issue:

> A. David Holland, Jr. listed on 1830 Nansemond County, Virginia. Census. He had three daughters born between 1810/1820.

II. Capt. Joseph Holland, son of Joseph of "Spivey" was born 1747 Nansemond County, Virginia., died 1804 in Nansemond County married Elizabeth Ann Odom about 1762. Capt. Joseph Holland of "Kingsale Swamp" (land in both Nansemond and Isle of WIght County's) His name appears on the tax records of Nansemond and Isle of WIght County's from about 1790.[211]

---

[210] Joseph Holland, Sr.'s lawsuit vs. E. Norfleet (wife of Joseph?), Darden, Hedgepath, Whitfield, Cowper, Allen et ux, Cooper Jenkins, 1793-1796. Mrs. Nancy Holland, admx of Joseph Norfleet, received a settlement on the Estate of Joseph Norfleet in 1791 Nansemond County, Virginia. It appears that Joseph Holland, Sr.'s lawsuits have to do with the LWT of Samuel Holland (inventory dated 18 April 1777 in the Isle of Wight County, where cash was received from: Willoughby Hedgepeth, Moses Darden and Ivy Whitfield. They must still owe on Samuel's estate in 1793-1796. Boddie said that Joseph's children were: Jacob, Job, Solomon, Capt. Joseph and John D. However, Solomon and Job are definitely not his. This leaves: Jacob, James and Capt. Joseph, Jesse and John D. The sons of Joseph Holland, Jr. (1715-1799) of "Spivey", appear to be: David, Capt. Joseph, Jacob, John D., Thomas, Jesse and James. Jacob and Thomas were executors of his LWT in Nansemond County

[211] Capt. Joseph's widow, ELizabeth Holland, of "Jasper County, Ga.", widow of evolutionary War Soldier, received lands in Coweta County, Ga. land lottery. Boddie says he was a Capt. Of Nansemond Militia after the Revolution and that his LWT was destroyed, yet was referred to in the tax records, as leaving lands to his sons, Washington and Randolph, having given lands earlier to Joseph J. His LWT dated 1804 is privately owned by Col. Gordon C. Jones, One Winding Way, Mt. Holly, New Jersey. His widow, Elizabeth Ann, removed to Jasper County, Georgia, where she died after 1835. In 1783 Joseph Holland of Nansemond had conveyed to Capt. Joseph Holland, by John Barnes of Southampton County, 200 acres in Isle of WIght County on the Nansemond County line. About the time of his death (1805), Joseph

Issue of Capt. Joseph Holland:

A. Joseph John Holland, son of Capt. Joseph Holland, 1768-1826, married 1798 Nancy Parker. He was a soldier in the War of 1812 in Capt. Jeremiah Rawl's County The LWT of Joseph John Holland dated 12 October 1826, probated in the Isle of Wight County, Virginia on 1 January 1827. Issue:

1. Willis H. Holland, son of Joseph John Holland, was born 1802. Listed on 1820-1830 Nansemond County, Virginia. Census. In 1820, had one daughter under 10. In all, he had 12 children. He Taught school at South Quay sbout 1835. Nansemond County Tax Digest, 1821-1828, 183 acres, acres; 1829, 229 acres, 66 acres from Mary Ann Saunders adj. James G. Holland, 1830, 234 acres 5 acres friom Amey Holland; 1833 Willis H. Holland to John Holland, 23 acres. According to census records, he had a son , born 1794/1804, 80n , born 1802/1804, daughter , born 1810/1820, daughter , born 1804/1810.
2. Ann Matilda Holland, daughter of Joseph John, married Alexander Norfleet.
3. Joseph John Holland, son of Joseph John Holland, married (1) on 9 December 1824, Sally Council, and (2) Louise Lenox.
4. Nancy Holland, daughter of Joseph John Holland, unmarried.
5. Julia Holland, daughter of Joseph John Holland, unmarried.
6 . Lucy Levinah Holland, daughter of Joseph John Holland, married Mr. Wells.
7. Emelina Virginia Holland, daughter of Joseph John Holland, married on 20 December 1838, Hugh K. Williams.
8. Georgianna Holland, daughter of Joseph John Holland, married on 1 November 1852, Nelson Parker. Marriage License stated that Nelson Parker was from Alabama.
9. John Monroe Holland, son of Joseph John Holland, married Miss Lenow.
10. Samuel Hawkins Holland, son of Joseph John.
11. James Washington Holland, son of Joseph John Holland, born 1 August 1823, died 29 March 1888, buried in the Holland cemetery near Monticello, in Jasper County, married Cordelia Holland, (born 1838), daughter of Jonas H. Holland.

B. Isaac Odom Holland, son of Capt. Joseph Holland, was born 13 April 1770 in Gaston County, North Carolina, married on 1 September 1790, Amelia Brewington (born 10 September 1772). The Nansemond County, Virginia. Tax Digest for 1813, 249 acres. He owned land in Greene County, Ga. in 1803. He was a charter member of the Rising Star Masonic Lodge, Putnam County, Ga.; Tyler of RIsing Star Lodge #33, Eatonton, 8 January 1818; served as Tyler through May of 1818. His Bible record provides the dates of his Issue:

1. Samuel Holland, born on 21 June 1791 in Gaston County, North Carolina, married on 12 December 1812 in Putnam County, Tabitha Kendrick.
2. John Holland, born 12 May 1792 Gaston County, North Carolina, married on 25 December 1818, in Monroe County, Eliza Greer.

Holland conveyed this 200 acres to his son, Joseph J. Holland who lived there and was called Joseph J. Holland of Isle of Wight. His land adjoined that of Thomas Carr, near the present-day Carr Road.

3. Hettie Cale Holland, born 28 May 1793 in Gaston County, North Carolina.

4. Hannah Holland, born 16 August 1794 in Gaston County, North Carolina.

5. Nancy Holland, born 20 March 1799 in Gaston County, North Carolina.

6. Amelia Holland, born 7 November 1800 in Gaston County, North Carolina, married on 23 April 1828 in Monroe County, William Astin.

7. William Holland, born 3 August 1802 in Gaston County, North Carolina.

8. James Cayle Holland was born on 27 December 1804 in Greene County.

9 . Orlando Holland, born on 30 September 1806 in Greene County, died after 1880 in Monroe County. He was married on 8 June 1842 in Monroe County, Miranda Smith, daughter of Davis Smith. SEE Smith. Issue:[212]

    a. William Holland, born 1843 in Monroe County.

    b. John Holland, born 1845 in Monroe County.

    c. Mary Holland, born 1847 in Monroe County.

    d. Orlando Holland, born 1849 in Monroe County.

    e. James J. Holland, born 1855 in Monroe County.

    f. Thomas B. Holland, born 1857 in Monroe County.

    g. Tyrus L. Holland, born 1860 in Monroe County.

    h. Miranda Holland, born 1862 in Monroe County.

    i. Elmira Holland, born 1865 in Monroe County.

10. Elmina Holland, born on 9 January 1809, married on 22 April 1830 in Muscogee County, William Hayes.

11. Julia Ann Holland, born 22 March 1811 in Greene County.

12. Arestus Holland, born on 9 April 1813 in Greene County.

13 Cynthia Holland, born 6 May 1816, Greene County, never married; residing with Orlando Holland's family in 1880, Monroe County..

C. Randolph Scott Holland, son of Capt. Joseph Holland, was born 1788, d. ca 1816, his estate in Isle of Wight County, Virginia Tax Records, 1817-1820, 175 acres in Nansemond County adj. Frederick Holland, 1814 Nansemond County, Virginia. Tax Digest, Randolph Holland, 175 acres from his father, Capt. Joseph Holland. 1815, 66 acres, Isle of Wight County on Nasemond County, Virginia line, by LWT of Joseph Holland of Nansemond County 1817-1820, Estate of Randolph S. Holland, 175 acres in Nansemond County, adj. Frederick Holland, and Isle of Wight County, Virginia line. Had daughter:

    1. Abigail K. Holland, married Thomas Sketchley on 3 February 1816, in Southampton County, Virginia, by the consent of Randolph S. Holland.

D. Charlotte Elizabeth Holland, daughter of Capt. Joseph Holland, married Jonas Lawrence (born On 9 January 1776 in Nansemond County, Virginia.), lived at South Quay at his home, "Elmwood Glen". Jonas Lawrence was the son of Lemuel and Mary Lawrence. Issue: ELizabeth Mary Lawrence, Joseph John Lawrence, Lemuel Lawrence, George Lawrence, and Willis Washington Lawrence.

E. George Washington Holland, son of Capt. Joseph Holland, was born 1772 in Nansemond County, Virginia, son of Capt. Joseph Holland. He married Mary Jane abt 1795.Mary Jane Holland died ca 1798, and their son, George Washington Holland, Jr. , born 1795 was raised by his brother, Jonas H. Holland. The 1814 Tax Digest of Nansemond County, Virginia - George Washington Holland, 200 acres from Capt.

---

[212] 1860-1880 Monroe County Census.

Joseph Holland's Estate (and Randolph Holland, 175 acres from their father). In 1818, Hilliard B. Holland claimed 200 acres on South Quay Road (G. Washington Holland's lands to Uriah Rawls). In 1818, Hilliard B. Holland sold George Washington Holland's 200 acres received from his father, Capt. Joseph Holland in 1814 to Uriah Rawls. After that, George Washington Holland's name disappeared from the tax digest. George Washington Holland's Arithmetic in 1790's mentions William Holland. He served through the War of 1812 from Nansemond County Letters addressed to "Major George Washington Holland" around 1840, were sent from Virginia to Monticello, before stamps were used. In 1817, he sold the land left him by his father and removed to Georgia.

Issue of George Washington Holland (born 1772):

A. Hilliard B. Holland, son of George Washington Holland, (died 1823/4 Nansemond County, Virginia.) is believed to be a son because in 1814 he sold George Washington Holland's land, 200 acres received from said George Washington Holland's father, Capt. Joseph Holland. 1817-1823 Nansemond County, Virginia. Tax Digests, he claimed 200 acres on South Quay Road. 1830-1832; Patsy B. Holland claimed the same 200 acres on South Quay Road received from the Estate of Hilliard B. Holland. In 1833 she deeded it to Eli Joyner. Wife, Patsy, , born 1784 Nansemond County, Virginia., listed on 1850 Census with Elizabeth Duke, age 54, Isaac V. Duke, age 63, Elizabeth Duke 27, William H. Duke 26, James Duke 21, and Mary Duke, 16.

B. George Washington Holland, Jr., son of George Washington Holland, born 1795 in Nansemond County, Virginia, died 6 September 1844, married on 25 January 1816 in Nansemond County, Virginia., Mary Ann Griffin (born 4 May 1799, died 7 May 1840).

Issue of George Washington Holland (born 1795), from Boddie:

1- Richard Odom Holland, born 18 January 1818, died infancy.

2- Dr. Joseph Alfred Holland, born 29 August 1822.

3- Charlotte Elizabeth Holland was born on 31 Septembeer 1822, married Hugh Parks Fitzpatrick. Southern Reporter dated 14 November 1837: "Charlotte E., only daughter of G. W. Holland, married on 7 November 1837, Hugh P. Kirkpatrick, all of Jasper County, Georgia."

4- George Washington Holland, Jr., son of George Washington Holland, was born 30 August 1824, married Elizabeth Sarah Reese, the daughter of Cuthbert Reese and wife, Tabitha Clark. He graduated from University of Georgia and was Professor of English at the Tuskegee Institute. They removed to Texas in 1869. He was a merchang, and bought and sold land in Newnan, Coweta County. Issue: George Cuthbert Holland, Confederate Soldier (right arm broken three times by gun shot wounds, which wounds contributed to his death on 30 August 1869) was born on 8 April 1846 in Jasper County, married on 22 October 1857, Mary Ann Davis (born on 7 December 1850), the daughter of L. G. Davis and wife, Margaret

Aldredge; Joseph Alfred Holland, born 27 March 1848 in Jasper County; Hugh Parks Kirkpatrick Holland, born 10 April 1852 in Coweta County. (Children -- Kirk Davis Holland, born 18 November 1874; William Washington Holland, born 26 September 1876). Hugh Parks Kirkpatrick Holland married (2), on 6 May 1880, Mary Ada Curlee and had: Charlotte Augusta Holland, born on 10 May 1881, Novella Clark Holland, born 21 March 1883, died 5 August 1927; Lois Holland, born 17 January 1892; and Willy Washington Holland, born 30 July 1854 in Jasper County.

5- Virginia L. Holland, born 24 September 1828, died 15 January 1830.

6- Lucius Henry Holland, born 11 October 1830, died 23 June 1834.

7- Mary Ann Holland, born 6 May 1840, married Dr. Hardy Smith. In 1849 Jasper County, Mary Ann Holland, minor; H. P. Fitzpatrick appointed guardian. In 1854, tuition was paid for her to attend college.

F. Jonas Herman Holland, son of Capt. Joseph Holland, was born 1800 in Virginia, died 3 November 1862, buried Holland Cemetery, 2 miles south of Monticello on road to Hillsboro, married (1) 1816, Ann Hines, (2), Mary Ida Scott (died 4 June 1822), (3) in Jasper County, on 8 March 1826, Eunice Adeline White (born 9 July 1809, died 3 October 1832), buried Holland Cemetery, daughter of Colonel Thomas White and Elizabeth Clark, his cousin. Jonas H. and Eunice, in Jonas H. Holland's graveyard on the old Hillsboro Road, Jasper County,. Jonas H. Holland of Morgan County, Ga., Letters of Administration de bonis non on 1 January 1883 in Jasper County. Admrs Bond in amount of $4,000, Estate of Jonas H. Holland, Sr. The petition of Eunice A. Holland, widow, and William W. Holland, her son that Jonas Holland died intestate. Estate valued at $150,000, about 150 negroes, 1 and, money, notes, stock, inventory dated 19 December 1862. 11 June 1866, Return states that cotton belonging to Estate, 15 bales, was burned by the Federal Army on 19 November 1864. [213] Jonas H. Holland came to Georgia on horseback in 1816 from Virginia and built a home in Jasper County He was only sixteen when he married and his bride only thirteen. The parents of both opposed the match, but an uncle (George Washington Holland) gave bond for the bride. Placing the child-bride on horse back, he started upon the long journey through the wilderness, but after arriving in Georgia his youthful bride survived only two years." Georgia's Landmarks, Memorials and Legends, by L. L. Knight, Book I, page 297. His plantation was "Farmingdale" on the old Hillsboro Road, between Monticello and Hillsboro, Georgia. Children of Jonas H. and Eunice Holland:

1. Georgianna A. Holland, daughter of Jonas H. Holland, was born 1830 Jasper County, married Mr. Whitfield on 10 January 1872 in Jasper County. A petition was found in the estate records, of Mrs. Georgianna A. Whitfield stated that she was the former ward of Eunice A. Holland and is married; that Eunice Holland refused to settle. Boring Whitfield, attorney.

---

[213] See Loose Papers, Jasper County.

2. Thomas Randolph Holland, son of Jonas H. Holland, was born 1834 Jasper County, married on 11 November 1847, Catherine Hines. Issue: Jonas Hines Holland, born 18 June 1859, Cordelia Eugenia Holland , born 11/12/1861; William Walter Holland, born 24 September 1866, married on 2 October 1890, Lilly Ora Gibson, lived Overton, Texas in 1935 and had Issue: Mosella Katherine and Evelyn Lois; Thomas (Littleberry) Holland , born on 16 October 1871.

3. George Washington Holland, son of Jonas H. Holland, was born 1836 Jasper County, married Ellen Kirkpatrick, daughter of Hugh Parks Kirkpatrick and wife, Charlotte Holland.

4. Cordelia Holland, daughter of Jonas H. Holland, was born 1838 Jasper County, married James Washington Holland (1863-1888), son of Joseph J. Holland and wife, Nancy. Had daughter: Thetis Holland married Mr. Brown.

5. William W. Holland, son of Jonas H. Holland, was born 1840, Jasper County. His Estate: Executor's Bond for temporary Letters of Admn in 1872 of James W. Holland, Benjamin T. Digby and Boring Whitfield, all exrs. The Estate of James W. Holland was dated 19 September 1889 in Jasper County, with a Return of W. F. Jordan, administrator.

6. Joseph Holland, son of Jonas H. Holland, was born 1842.

7. Jonas H. Holland, son of Jonas H. Holland, was born 1843 Jasper County, married on 9 January 1869, Kate Susan Harris. Issue: Thomas Harris Holland, born on 12 December 1872; Martha Eunice Holland.

8. Eugenia Keturie Holland, daughter of Jonas H. Holland, was born 1847 married Mr. Aven.

9. Adolphus Holland, son of Jonas H. Holland, was born 1850 in Jasper County, married Alice Kirkpatrlck, a cousin, the daughter of Hugh Parks Kirkpatrick and Charlotte Holland. Son: Kirk Holland.

G. Elizabeth Mary Holland, daughter of Capt. Joseph Holland, was born 1784 married Lewis Connor Holland. She died in 1821.

H. Lavinia Holland, daugbter of Capt. Joseph Holland, was born 1786 married (1) ca 1803, Willis Washington (killed during War of 1812), son of Joseph Washington and wife, Zilla Branch of Southampton County, Virginia, having son: Joseph John Washlngton , born 1813. Levinia married (2) in 1817, to John Cargile (died 1819) Jasper County Lavinia's LWT dtd l835 named her Issue: Joseph John Washington Cargile and Reneau , B. M. Cargile.

I. Millie Arenthia Holland, daughter of Capt. Joseph Holland, was born 1792 married Lewis Connor Holland of Nansemond County, Virginia. 19 December 1803 in Gates County, North Carolina. Bondsman: John Odom.

III. Jacob Holland, son of Joseph "of Spivey" and Phebe Holland, was born ca 1750, died 17 October 1815 in Pendleton District, South Carolina, married Dolly Harrison. In 1794 Nansemond County, Jacob Holland and Henry Harrison receive the authority to build a mill.

Jacob Holland was executor of LWT of Joseph Holland "of Spivey" in 1800, as well as surety on the Estate of Capt. Joseph Holland (his brother, who d. 1804 Nansemond County, Virginia). Jacob Holland served in the House of Representatives from Franklin County. In 1789 (now Pendleton District, South Carolina). There are some early deeds of Hollands in Franklin County records; however, most of the records are in Pendleton District deeds . The names of hls chlldren come from a published account. The names of some of Jacob Holland's children, are contained in Deeds of Gift, Pendleton District, South Carolina. From the deed records in Pendleton, there are other Holland's in 1790s: James, Andrew, Daniel, John, Moses, William, and Thomas. I think that James, John and Thomas are Jacob s brothers (from: Boddie, who states that Joseph of Spivey had: Jacob and James, etc.) Pendleton District, South Carolina. Book M, p. 72-73: 'Legatees of Jacob Holland to legatees of Richard Childress, decd, tract of land on Tugaloo River adj. John Holland's land on Big Beaverdam Creek, 200 acres, 3 November 1817. Heirs signed, viz: Jacob, Mary, Robert, Archibald and John Holland, Allen Guest. Children of Jacob and Dolly Holland:

> 1. Benjamin Holland, son of Jacob and Dolly Holland, born 16 October 1816, LWT, Anderson, South Carolina. Wife, Peggy. Issue: Polly, Rutha, Thomas, Sally, John Shannan and Jacob Holland.

> 2. Hugh Holland, son of Jacob and Dolly Holland, was born 1772 Pendleton District, South Carolina Book M, Page 451-2, "Soldier by death of Jacob, late of Pendleton District, Hugh Holland, entered as heirs, appointed my brother, Robert Holland, to receive from my share and keep upon the the expiration of my time from service of USA, 17 January 1815. Hugh apparently removed to South Carolina. No further information.

> 3. Jacob Holland, Jr., son of Jacob and Dolly Holland, was born 1774 married Betsy. Listed on the 1810 Isle of Wight County, Virginia Census, with daughter , born 1800/1810.

> 4. Elijah Holland, son of Jacob and Dolly Holland, was born 1776.

> 5. Archibald Holland, son of Jacob and Dolly Holland, was born 1778, d. 1848 Cherokee County. He was listed on the 1820 Jasper County Census. His estate appraised on 8 September 1848 in Cherokee County. The Return of Jacob Holland, executor, dated 15 September 1848. Cash paid to Elisha Holland and William Holland. Elijah Holland's Note mentioned. Children of Archibald Holland:
> > (a) William Holland, son of Archibald Holland, was listed 1840 Cherokee County, Georgia Census.
> > (b) Elisha Holland, son of Archibald Holland, was born 1800 South Carolina, listed 1820 Jasper County Census, age 16 to 26; 1822-1825 Clarke County Tax Digests; 1840-1850 Clarke County Census. The LWT of Peggy, his wife, dated Anderson County, South Carolina, but of Clarke County mentions her husband, Elisha Holland of Clarke County, Ga. Elisha mentioned on 1821 Clarke County Tax Digest, in Capt. Foster's Distrist; 1824, in Capt. Hugh's District.
> > (c) Jacob Holland, son of Archibald Holland, was listed on 1840 Cherokee County Census.
> > (d) John Holland, son of Archibald Holland, was listed 1840 Cherokee County Census.
> > (e) Harris Holland, son of Archibald Holland.

(f) Isaiah Holland, son of Archibald Holland, was listed 1840 Cherokee County Census.

(g) Nancy Holland, daughter o f Archibald Holland.

(h) Franky Holland, daughter of Archibald Holland, married on 27 March 1834 in Hall County, Thomas C. Martin.

(i) Cassey Holland, daughter of Archibald Holland.

6. John Holland, son of Jacob and Dolly Holland, was born 1780 married Patsy.

7. Margaret Holland, daughter of Jacob and Dolly Holland, was born 1782 married Col. Benjamin Cleveland, son of Absalom. His LWT dated 1830 Pickens County, South Carolina. Executors: Robert, Peggy and Jacob Holland.

8. Mary Holland, daughter of Jacob and Sally Holland, was born 1784 married Allen Guest.

9. Rebecca Holland, daughter of Jacob and Sally Holland, was born 1786 married Caleb Field.

10. Robert Holland, son of Jacob and Sally Holland, was born 20 September 1788, married Sarah Jones (born 7 December 1789 in Virginia, died 12 November 1853), the daughter of Lewis and Charity Jones. Robert's LWT dated 6 February 1856, proved 1869 in Anderson District, South Carolina.

Issue of Robert Holland (from his Bible):

(a) Jincey Holland, daughter of Robert Holland, was born 1 December 1808, died after 6 February 1856, married Thomas Harrison, born 1800. In 1966, Dessie Holland of Hartwell, Ga. wrote me and provided further data on Jefferson Holland, her great-grandfather who married (2) Mary Barton and after her death, (2), Matilda Barton. His children were: John J.; Benjamin T.; Henry M. married Louvenia Parker (had son, Parker Wayne Holland whose daughter is Dessie Holland of Hartwel); James C.; Thomas; William R.; Mary (Polly); Fannie; Sallie; and Susan Holland.

(b) Benjamin Holland, son of Robert Holland, was born on 3 January 1810 in South Carolina, died on 22 July 1905 in Maysville, buried in his brother's cemetery, James Harrison Holland, in Ridgeway Community, Banks County, Ga. married (1), Lucinda Harris, (2), on 19 March 1846, Elizabeth Cauthan of Madison County, Georgia, who didn't live long; (3), married his frist wife's sister, another Miss Harris, (4) married 7 August 1850,, Mahuldah Scott (born 26 September 1813, died 20 July 1871), the daughter of Jane Millican (born 1778) and John Scott (born 1781). At one time Benjamin was very wealthy, but lost his fortune during the Reconstruction days in the South when taxes were raised to high to pay. All of his sons were inn the army (one was killed, one wounded).

(c) Thomas Holland, son of Robert Holland, born 7 February 1811, married Julia Asbury.

(d) Jefferson Holland, son of Robert Holland, was born 28 May 1822, married (1), Mary Barton.

(e) Jackson Holland, son of Robert Holland, was born 19 May 1814, died young.

(f) Margaret Ann Holland, daughter of Robert Holland, was born 14 February 1816, married Ezekiel Stanley.

(g) Mary Ann Holland,daughter of Robert Holland, was born 27 September 1817, died young.

(h) William Wilson Holland, son of Robert Holland, as born 11 January 1819, married (1), Julia Wright (Julia, who had been the wife of William. Her Issue: Robert, Catharine and Nancy, minors, named in LWT of William Cleveland, Pickens County, South Carolina, in 1820).

(i) James Madison Holland, son of Robert and Sarah Holland, was born 27 March 1820, died young.

(j) Robert Holland, Jr. , son of Robert and Sarah Holland, was born 18 January 1822, married Nancy Wright.

(k) Jacob Foster Holland, son of Robert and Sarah Holland, was born 5 February 1824, married Nancy Higley.

(l) James Harrison Holland, son of Robert and Sarah Holland, was born 17 January 1826, married Susan E. Griffith.

(m) Elizabeth Ann Holland, daughter of Robert and Sarah Holland, was born 7 January 1828, married James Latner.

(n) Sarah Ann Holland, daughter of Robert and Sarah Holland, was born 11 June 1830, married Joseph Maret.

(o) Nevels Hayne Holland, son of Robert and Sarah Holland, was born 11 March 1832, married Fannie Harris.

IV. Thomas Holland, Sr., son of Joseph of Spivey, was listed on the Nansemond County, Virginia. Tax Digest 1795-1798, owning 150 acres; 1797-1798, owned 107 acres, and in 1802, 81 acres. He was listed on Nansemond County, Virginia. Tax Records 1795-1798, 150 acres. Thomas Holland married (1) Elizabeth, 3rd, Phoebe Rickman 1779 in Nansemond County, Virginia. (she d. after 1805 in Greene County, Ga.) The Estate of Thomas Holland, Greene County, Ga., Benjamin Holland, administrator, 8 January 1827. Thomas Holland was a Pvt. in Virginia Regiment (3rd and 4th), 4th Co. under Capt. David Arrell. From Jackson Genealogy: Thomas Holland, Rev. War Soldier (born ca 1750) in Nansemond County, Virginia., d. after 1830 married Phoebe Rickman. His first children were born in Virginia Later, he removed to Wilkes County, Ga. (I didn't find him there), drawing land in Troup and Muscogee County's.

In 1820 he lived Greene County, Ga., owner of 20 slaves. Thomas Holland obviously migrated from Nansemond County, Virginia. where he was listed on the tax records; also, his son, Thomas, Jr. (1802-1804, 1811). His son, Harrison P., listed as bound out 1815 in Nansemond County, Virginia.[214]

Issue of Thomas Holland:

A. John Rickman Holland, son of Thomas, was born 8 May 1786, died 10 November 1863 in Dublin, Texas, married 1812 in Putnam County, Elizabeth Walker. Proved by Gift Deed, dated 7 September 1822 in Monroe County, between John R. Walker of Putnam County to Richard Kikpatrick, 202-1/2 acres, Lot 781, 7th Dist. Removed to Texas in 1841. Son:

1. Samuel Eli Holland, born 6 December 1826 in Meriwether County. He came to Texas in 1846, his parents preceding him. In April of 1847 he entered the U. S. Army as Capt. in Austin, Texas, in Samuel Highsmith's County, 6th Texas Cavalry; joined Gen. Taylor's Army in Mexico; was engaged in guerella warfare; discharged 5/1848. He owned land on Hamilton Creek, 3 miles below the town of Burnet. Capt. Holland was married 3 times. (1) 1852 to Mary Scott (had one son, George of Mason County) After her death in March of 1855, he married (2) 6 December 1855 to Clara Thomas and by her had 9 Issue: David B., John H., Sam W., Porter D., Mary R. who married George Lester of Llano County, Martha M. who married Henry Hester, Louisa, Catherine and Elizabeth. Clara Holland died on 8 January 1887. He married (3) on 22 September 1887, Mrs. Susan A. McCarty and had three Issue: Charles Hamilton, Thomas A. and William A. Holland. Capt. Holland was a

---

[214] Pendleton District, South Carolina Deeds:

4 December 1795, Jacob Holland, Jr. of Abbeville County, South Carolina to Daniel Delaney, 200 acres on small creek of Conoross of Savannah River. Witness: Jacob and Thomas Holland. (Could be Thomas, Jr.)

12 April 1799, Frederick Lanier to William Harrison, 200 acres in 96th District on Beaverdam Creek of the Tugaloo River. Witness: Thomas Holland.

18 May 1801, Thomas Harrison, Sr. to William Cleveland, 575 acres on Beaverdame Creek of Tugaloo River. Witness: Thomas Holland.

12 May 1802, Lewis Cobb to Thomas Holland, 256 acres on the ES of 23-Mile River. Note: Jacob Holland, Sr. owned thousands of acres on Beaverdam Creek, Tugaloo River.

After 1801, Thomas Holland removed to Greene County, Ga. Greene County, Ga. Deed Book GG, p. 396-397: "Know all men by these presents that I, Thomas Holland, of Greene County, Ga., do give and deliver unto my son, Harrison Holland of the State of Tennessee a certain negro boy named Isaac".....1 December 1820.

1 December 1820, same deed gift to son, John Holland, Benjamin Holland, and William Hammond, in right of his wife "my daughter, Elizabeth Hammond. "

member of the Texas Mining and Improvement County, which built the Northwestern RR from Burnet to Marble Falls.

B. Harrison P. Holland of Tennessee, son of Thomas Holland, was born 24 October 1779 in Nansemond County, Virginia, deeded Job Holland in 1796, Nansemond County, Virginia. Land. Also, he was bound out in 1796. He was listed on 1815 Nansemond County Tax DIgest as owning 250 acres. He married in Greene County on 2 December 1802 , Elizabeth Rowland, and is listed on 1850 White County, Tennessee Census. Proved by Gift Deed. Issue:

> 1. Rebecca Holland, born 1819.
> 2. Jane Holland, born 1831.
> 3. Nelson Holland, born 1835.
> 4. Amanda Holland, born 1837.
> 5. William Holland, born 1841.

C. Elizabeth Holland, daughter of Thomas Holland, married William Hammond. There is a marriage in Greene County, Betsy Holland to William Smith on 5 February 1802. She must have married William Hammond second.

D. Thomas Holland, Jr., son of Thomas Holland, was born 1780 married Elizabeth Hammond. Nansemond County, Virginia. Tax Records, 1802-1804, Nansemond County, 100 acres; and, in 1811, 108 acres.

E. James Holland, son of Thomas Holland, was born 1785 married Rebecca Hammond, lived in Tennessee.

G. William Holland, son of Thomas Holland, of Washington County, Indiana in 1820; Lawrence County, Indiana 1830-1850 Census. He was born on 11 November 1791 in Virginia, married Phetna McBee. Listed on 1850 Lawrence County, Indiana Census as Merchant. Wife, Letina M., born 1803 in Georgia.

Issue of William Holland:

> 1. Harrison Holland, born 1823 Tennessee married Louisa , born 1826 North Carolina. Issue: Sylvester Holland, born 1847 Indiana; Elizabeth Holland , born 1848 Indiana. Listed 1850 Lawrence County, Indiana Census.
>
> 2. William Holland, born 1830 Indiana.
>
> 3. Melinda Holland, born 1832 Indiana.
>
> 4. Nancy J. Holland, born 1836 Indiana.

G. Nancy B. Holland, daughter of Thomas Holland, married James Goodwin.

H. Sarah Rickman Holland, daughter of Thomas Holland, was born 19 August 1797, married (1) on 19 December 1815 in Greene County, Samuel Nelma, (2) William Hammond.

187

I. Robert Holland, son of Thomas Holland, was born 1800, married Barbara Ann Lunsford.

J. Benjamin Holland, son of Thomas Holland, was born 1805 married Delila. Proved by Gift Deed.

V. Jesse Holland, probably a son of Joseph Holland "of Spivey". In 1791 Nansemond County, Virginia, Joseph Holland, Jr. was made guardian of Jesse's orphans. Joseph, assignee of Esther Holland vs. Cutchins, 1790 Nansemond County Joseph Holland was Exr of LWT of Jesse Holland in 1796, Nansemond County 1793 deed of Joseph Holland, Jr. The 1795 Nansemond County, Virginia. Tax Digest mentions Joseph Holland, Jr., executor's deed.

VI. John D. Holland, son of Joseph Holland "of Spivey" was born 1750 married Elizabeth Daughtrey, daughter of Thomas Daughtrey. This may be him: Pendleton District, South Carolina deed dated 22 August 1793, of Bennet Combs to Thomas Garvin. Witness: John Holland. 4 July 1788, John Holland of Greenville, South Carolina to Levi Murphee, 200 acres on both sides of Buck Creek, 12-Mile River in Abbeville, South Carolina, 9th District. Names of children provided by Kirk Holland. In 1814-1816 John D. Holland was listed on Tax Digest, 96 and 36 acres from William Glover's Estate. In 1817-1827, 96 acres, 36 acres; also 36 1/2 acres from Martha Glover. His widow, Elizabeth Holland, was , born 1700. In 1830 she was a widow residing next door to Robert Daughtry; James R. Holland and his wife, Matilda. In 1828, John D. Holland's land went to Elizabeth. In 1828, 50 acres went to Jason Holland. Children of John D. Holland:

A. Capt. Jason Holland, son of John D. Holland, was born 1805 Nansemond County, Virginia. married Ora, listed on 1850 Census. Issue:

1. John James Holland "Whispering Jim", son of Capt. Jason Holland, was born 5 June 1823, and died 18 March 1890 in Nansemond County, Virginia. He married Margaret Ann Milteer (born 1825, died 22 March 1886). The 1869 Nansemond County Tax Digest lists Margaret H. C. Holland, 232 acres adj. John M. Pierce and James Milteer, 10 miles SW of the courthouse. Issue:
   i. Sarah Aletha Holland, married John Thomas Saunders.
   ii. Judith Ann Holland, married W. C. Peel.
   iii. Benjamin Virginius Holland, born 21 July 1854, died 21 March 1888, married Sallie Alethea Walton. Had: James Truman Holland, born 1886 in Georgia.
   iv. Mary Elizabeth Holland.
   v. Marie Antionette Holland.
   vi. Viola Holland married Frank Wright.
   vii. Lee Ann Holland married Jethro Holland.
   viii. Callie Barnes Holland married William Haslett.
   ix. Maggie Holland married Hudson Bounds.
   x. C. Jason Holland married Emma Sophronia Vining.
   xi. Charles Holland married Deborah Prestlow Sumner of Nansemond County.
   xii. George Thomas Holland married Elizabeth Angeline Sumner.

2. Oliver H. P. Holland, son of Capt. Jason Holland, was born 1838, killed in Civil War.

3. Elizabeth Holland, daughter of Capt. Jason Holland, married Mr. Benton.

4. Hilliard Holland, son of Capt. Jason Holland, married Miss Lee.

5. Elisa Holland, daughter of Capt. Jason Holland.

6. Orrie Holland, daughter of Capt. Jason, married James Murphy. Listed on 21850 Nansemond County Census. Issue: Irene Murphy, born 1832; Martha E. Murphy , born 1836, and Marcilla Murphy, born 1844.

B. John D. Holland, son of John D. Holland.

C. Priscilla Holland, daughter of John D. Holland, married Joshua Daughtrey..

D. Treacy Holland, daughter of John D. Holland, married Jack Anthony Cutchens.

E. Margaret Holland, daughter of John D. Holland, married Joseph Cutchens.

F. Keaten Holland, daughter of John D. Holland, married Mr. West.

G. Honour Holland, daughter of John D. Holland, married Eldred Holland.

H. Matilda Holland, daughter of John D. Holland, born 1806 Nansemond County, Virginia., married James R. Holland, , born 1805 Nansemond County, listed on 1850 Nansemond County Census. 23 August 1869, Nansemond County deed, James R. Holland to his son, Joseph R. Holland, 199 acres adjoining Jason Holland. WHEREAS, about 1851, James R. Holland deeded to William Odom 33-1/3 acres of land adjoining F. H. Holland and Mills Holland. Keziah Holland, nearest of kin, heir of said James R. Holland who died intestate, sold land to William Odom. Issue:

1. John T. Holland, born 1835 Nansemond County
2. Joseph R. Holland, born 1839 Nansemond County
3. Jason Holland, born 1841 Nansemond County 1869 Tax Digest shows 115 acres adj. Joseph R. Holland, 18 miles SW of the courthouse.
4. Etheldred Holland, born 1838 Nansemond County

VII. James Holland, son of Joseph Holland "of Spivey" (1715-1799) was born ca 1740/1750, died before 1799 in Wayne County, North Carolina. There was a land dispute between the Virginia and North Carolina boundary liine, later surveyed and established by William Byrd. James may have lived in that portion of southern Nansemond County, Virginia. which later became Gates County, North Carolina. He married Jerutha White and removed to Dobbs County, North Carolina. He fought in the Battle of Widow Moore's Creek Bridge during American Revolution. In 1799 Wayne County was taken from Dobbs County and in 1791 Dobbs County was abolished. The 1769 Dobbs County Tax Digest lists James Holland and Elisha Holland (his son). The estate of his son, Absalom, was administered in 1799, but James and Jerutha Holland were not mentioned, so it was assumed that they were deceased at this point. James Holland is believed to be buried back of James old plantation which adjoined Howell's old place near the dam and his wlfe with him. In 1948 they were located on the old West Holland place, but grown over for many years. Issue:

A. Elisha Holland, son of James Holland, was born 3 November 1764, died 15 September 1833, buried in the Elisha Holland Cemetery, Pinkney, North Carolina. His headstone is of wood, shield-shaped. Elisha Holland, Sr. is listed on the 1794-1811 Nansemond County, Virginia Tax Digests, 208 acres/ He married (1), Patience Watkins and (2), Patia Peacock, 1806. Elisha and Patience were the parents of eight Issue: Enos, Eli, Woodard, Betsey, Bryant, Curtis, Absalom, and .Elisha. Elisha and Patia were parents of nine children Warren, Ave Nancy), Exum, Jinnett, Ginsey, West, Green, Candace, and Needham. Issue:

1. Enos Holland, son of Elisha Holland, was born 1792 Pinkney, North Carollna, died age 87, blacksmith, married Edith (born 1797 North Carolina). Listed on 1830 Census of Johnson County, North Carolina, later moved to Georgia. Listed on 1860 Colquitt County Census. Issue:

    i.   Mary Ann Holland, born 1 August 1819 in North Carolina, died 19 October 1894, buried with her husband at Union Primitive Baptist Church Cemetery, Lanier County. She was married on 20 September 1837 in Smithfield, North Carolina to Merritt H. Johnson (born 14 February 1815 in Johnston County, North Carolina), son of Wiley and Winnie Johnson. Merritt died on 25 July 1877. Issue: Sarah A. Johnson, born 1844 married Thomas S. Murphy, Wiley Eli Johnson , born 1846, accidently thrown from horse and killed, age 16; Martha Johnson , born 1849; RIchard Seward Johnson , born 1856 married 28 April 1878, Idabelle Shaw, daughter of W. J. Shaw; James Rigdon Johnson , born 1858 married Mary Elizabeth Truett, daughter of Elijah Truett.

    ii. Eson Holland , born 1820 North Carolina.

    iii. Elizabeth Holland , born 1821 North Carolina.

2. Eli Holland, son of Elisha Holland, was born 1792 Pinkney, North Carolina. Listed 1860 Colquitt County, Ga. Census. Issue:

    i.   Marie Holland , born 1847 North Carolina.

    ii. Joseph P. Holland , born 1851 Colquitt County, Ga.

    iii. Woodward D. Holland, born 6 November 1794, died 1853, married Celia (born 15 March 1800). Issue:

        a. Miley Holland

        b. James Holland

        c. Bing Holland

        d. Maniley Holland

        e. Mack Campbell Holland

        f. Paul Anderson Holland

        g. Exum Longwood Holland

        h. Woodward D. Holland

        i. Kathrine Holland

        j. Betsy Holland

3. Betsy Holland, daughter of Elisha Holland, married Jesse Holland, moved to Alabama.

4. Bryant Holland, son of Elisha Holland was born in 1797, married Katie Sasser. Children by first marriage: Martha and Salser Holland.

5. Curtis Holland, son of Elisha Holland, married 1 May 1823, Nancy Holland. Had four children.

6. Absalom Holland, son of Elisha Holland, died age 96 married Nancy Hales. Issue:
  i.   Rufus Holland
  ii   Bardon Holland
  iii. Simon Holland
  iv. Henry Holland
  v.   Richard W. Holland, twin
  vi. William W. Holland, twin
  vii. Elizabeth Holland
  viii. Absalom B. Holland
  ix. Zilpha Holland
  x.   Nancy Holland

7. Elisha Holland, son of Elisha Holland, was born 1805, died 22 November 1901, married Betsy Holland on 26 March 1822. Issue:
  i.   John Holland
  ii. Curtis (or Charles) Holland
  iii. Nancy Holland

8. Warren Holland, son of Elisha Holland, 1807-1864, married Winifred Skipper (, born 1810). Issue:
  i.   Uriah Holland
  ii. Joseph Holland
  iii. Millie Holland
  iv. Patsy Holland
  v.   Needham Holland
  vi. Rachel Holland

9. Ave (Nancy) Holland, daughter of Elisha Holland, was born 24 May 1809, died 14 November 1895, married Major Copeland (born 1803, died 28 September 1885).

10. Exum Holland, son of Elisha Holland, married (1) on 18 September 1831, Penniah Boswell (born 18 April 1811) married (2) Martha Parks. Issue:
  i.   Gaston Holland
  ii. Jincy Holland
  iii. Jinet Holland married Castwell
  iv. Elisha Holland
  v.   West Pratt Holland
  vi. Jane Holland
  vii. Addison Pearson Holland
  viii. Calvin Holland.

Issue by (2) marriage:

  ix. Patrick Holland
  x.   Sarah J. Holland
  xi. Annie B. Holland
  xii. Katherine Holland
  xiii. Martha Holland

11. Jinnett (Ginnett) Holland, son of Elisha Holland, , born 1813/1814 married (1), Betsy Oldham, (2), Susan Barnes.

12. Ginsey (Ginny) Holland , daughter of Elisha Holland, was born 1816 married Arthur Copeland (born 1804)

13. West Holland, son of Elisha Holland, was born 7 June 1820, died 19 September 1903, married Sally Grice (born 5 January 1823, died 26 September 1886). Issue:
      i. Cullen Green Holland
      ii. Ritta Ann Catherine Holland
      iii. Needham Gray Holland
      iv. Arthur Copeland Holland
      v. Martha Holland
      vi. Christopher Columbus Holland
      vii. Lougenia Holland
      viii.Alexander Wayne Holland
      ix. William Gaston Holland
      x. Ransom Beauregard Holland
      xi. Jence Cornelia Holland
      xii. Edith Wise Holland
      xiii. West Bob Holland

14. Green Holland, son of Elisha Holland, was born 13 October 1822, married Elizabeth Barnes (born 12 October 1833). Issue:
      i. George W. Holland
      ii. Joseph Brown Holland
      iii. Kenneth Raynor Holland
      iv. Patience Holland
      v. Celia Holland
      vi. Diana Holland
      vii. Frank Holland
      viii. Sally Holland

15. Candace Holland, daughter of Elisha Holland, was born 12 April 1825, died 19 January 1907, married 19 March 1844, William W. Peacock (born 19 March 1822), moved to Coffee County, Alabama. Issue:
      i. Jincy Holland
      ii. David Holland
      iii. William A. Holland
      iv. Joseph B. Holland
      v. John C. Holland
      vi Alabama Holland
      vii.Patian Holland

16. Needham Holland, son of Elisha Holland, born 6 November 1828, died 29 January 1902, married (1), Smithy Bryant, (2), Pherba Radford (born 10 February 1859, died 2 February 1948). No issue.

B. Absalom Holland, son of James Holland, died 1799 in Wayne County, North Carolina, his inventory dated 19 December 1799. Bond by Elisha Holland dated 13 January 1800.

Joseph, son of John Holland, was born 1661 in Nansemond County, Virginia. Nothing is known about him. The Joseph Holland, Jr. mentioned in the Upper Parish of Nansemond County Vestry Book is believed to be Joseph "of Spivey". Apparently, this Joseph Holland did not reside in Nansemond County, but his descendants may have removed to Northampton County, Virginia.

Michael, son of John Holland, of Goochland and Louisa County's, Virginia He was born 1666 in Nansemond County, Virginia. On 9 July 1724, Michael Holland was granted 400 acres in Henrico County, Virginia adjoining his own land, on southside of Chickahominy. Again, on 16 June 1727, he was granted land on the southside of Chickahominy Swamp and down Meredith's Branch. On 16 June 1726, Michael Holland was granted land on the southside of Chickahominy Swamp, down Meredith's Branch. In 1730, on 12 February, the deposition was taken of Capt. Michael Holland, aged 65, states that he knew Mr. John Bolithoo, late of Princess Anne County, and that said Bolithoo's heirs should inherit his (intestate) estate and that the said Bolithoo was his eldest brother's eldest son. [215]

---

[215] 17 September 1731. Michael Holland received a land grant of 6,350 acres in Louis County, Virginia next to Thomas Machum, probably on the South Ann River. However, at one time, he did reside in Hanover County, Virginia; 2 June 1740. Michael Holland was granted 400 acres on Owens Creek, Louisa County, Virginia.

6 August 1745, William Owen of Goochland County deeded Michael Holland, Sr. for 25 pds. 200 acres on the northside of the James River, Deep Creek; also on Licking Hole Creek. In his LWT dated 10 October 1746, probated 17 March 1746 in Goochland County, Virginia, Michael Holland named his wife, Judith and children. To Judith (wife) he left 800 acres in Louisas County (where Timothy Odenals lives); 800 acres on Lickinghole creek with two plantataions, etc. After her decease, the 800 acres on Lickinghole Creek were bequeathed to son, John. To son, Michael, he bequeathed 400 acres in Louisa County (bought from Caddock). To son-in-law, Pouncey Anderson, 400 acres on Lickinghole Creek, now in his possession; also 500 acres adjacent thereto (200 acres bought from William Owen). To son, Richard, a plantation in Louisa County called "Meredith's Branch" in Henro County (whereon he now lives) containing 500 acres and 450 acres adjoining. To son, George, 700 acres in Louise County (bought from Capt. Davis), 150 acres (bought from Douglas), 500 acres on Lickinghole Creek. "I give to my son, George, in consideration of a promise given from under my hand to Mr. William Ford which obliges me to give my said son, 600 pds., it being on account of his marrying William Ford's daughter, wherein the said William Ford obliges himself to give his daughter, Sarah Ford, 200 pds. To son-in-law, Henry Martin, 522 acres on Lickinghole Creek, 50 acres in Hanover County, about 1/2 mile below the plantation whereon I lived."

Twelve Virginia Counties, page 329: "Richard Burch, whose people purchased from Francis Jardone 400 acres on Ivy Creek, a part of the Michael Holland tract on which Farmington (Virginia) now stands, was a tavern-keeper, first at Stony Point, then at Michie's Old Tavern and then at the noted Swan Tavern in Charlottesville." Page 359: "The Farmington estate was once the property of Michael Holland. It was bought by George Divers in 1788 and the stately house was designed for Mr. Divers by Thomas Jefferson. The place passed by inheritance to Mrs. Isaac White, who sold it to John C. Carter. In 1853 it was sold to General Bernard Peyton, it is now one of the most attractive country clubs in the State"; List of Ships Entering Inwards Upper District James River from 24th July to 29th September 1703 - "DOVE Sloop, built Maryland 1700, 7 tons, Robert Dale, Master, Michael Holland, owner."

A. John, first son of Michael Holland, of Goochland, son of Michael, was born 1696 married 1735 Martha Weeks (dates from Kirk Holland). Bequeathed 800 acres on Lickinghole Creek after the death of his mother. The Douglas Register in Goochland County provides dates of birth of his children, as follows:

1. Judith Holland, daughter of John Holland, born 4 November 1739 in Goochland County, Virginia, married on 4 January 1758, David Parish.

2. Hezekiah Holland, son of John Holland, was born on 14 June 1742 and married on 20 February 1765, Mary Walker. Removed to Fluvanna County, Virginia (His LWT, Will Book II, dated 1816). Issue:
  i. Sally Holland, daughter of Hezekiah Holland, was born 8 September 1765 Goochland County, Virginia
  ii Rachel Holland, daughter of Hezekiah, born 3 August 1767 Goochland County, Virginia.
  iii.John Holland, son of Hezekiah Holland, was born 11 December 1769 Goochland County married 21 December 1795 in Fluvanna County, Virginia, Jane Tandy Rice.
  iv. Shandy Walker Holland, son of Hezekiah Holland, was born 18 December 1785, died 8 November 1821, veteran of War of 1812 married in Fluvanna County, Virginia on 5 November 1811, Lucy Stone, daughter of Caleb Stone and wife, Sallie Ashland (daughter of John Ashland and wife, Frances Shepherd). Issue:
    (a) Sophie Jane Holland, born 1812 married James Pleasant White.
    (b) Sallie Anne Holland married Thomas Shepherd.
    (c) John Clay Holland, born 1819, married Sarah Eliza Kent.
    (d) Emily Susan Holland married Joseph Perkins.
    (e) Hezekiah Russell Holland, born 20 April 1822 in Fluvanna County, Virginia, married Martha Jane Wills.
    (f) Luther Holland married Sallie Frances Nicholson.
    (g) Phillip Archer Holland died in Texas (his remains were returned to the Old Holland Cemetery in Fluvanna County, Virginia)
    (h) Shandy Holland married Martha Sanders.
  v. Hezekiah Holland, son of Hezekiah Holland.

In 1720, 1731 and 1743 Michael Holland was processioning lands in St. Paul's Parish, Hanover County, Virginia Judith Holland (widow of Michael) deeded on 28 May 1751 in Goochland County to William Royadon 400 acres in Fredericksville Parish adj. Silvanius Morris' orphans, John Moore, William Harlow (part of a patent granted to Michael Holland, Gent., deceased 12 September 1738 and by his LWT bequeathed to said Judith Holland).

28 May 1751, Judith Holland of Goochland County deeded to William Harlow, Sr., 400 acres on Sycamore Creek, Morris's corner which was Dansies, including the plantation whereon Timothy Odinaile lives, part of 800 acres granted by patent to *Michael Holland, deceased*.

vi. Michael Holland, son of Hezekiah Holland, was born 30 March 1768 in Goochland County, Virginia, married 20 April 1789 in Louisa County, Virginia, Isabel.

vii. Catherine Holland, daughterof Hezekiah Holland, married Horace Timberlake on 17 January 1799 in Fluvanna County.

viii.Margaret Holland, daughter of Hezekiah Holland.

ix. Dolly Holland, daughter of Hezekiah Holland, married on 1 October 1799 in Louisa County, Virginia, Gentry Morris.

x. Major Holland, son of Hezekiah Holland.

xi. Richard Holland, son of Hezekiah Holland, married on 22 December 1806 in Louisa County, Virginia, Lucy Diggs.

III. Richard Holland, son of John Holland, was born 3 February 1743 in Goochland County, Virginia

IV. Martha Holland, daughter of John Holland, was born 8 April 1745, married on 4 November 1765, Abraham Parish.

V. Nathaniel Holland, son of John Holland, was born on 1 April 1748 in Goochland County, Virginia, married on 23 May 1776 in Louisa County, Virginia, Jeanie Hutson.

VI. John Holland, son of John Holland, of Hanover County, Virginia, was born on 16 June 1735, married (1), Anne, (2), Elizabeth. Listed on 1763 Tithables of Hanover County, Virginia Issue: (From Douglas Register):

A. Anne Holland, daughter of John Holland, was born 12 May 1752 in Goochland County, Virginia, married on 11 July 1770, Absalom Howell, Goochland County, Virginia.

B. George Holland, son of John Holland, was born on 17 February 1757 in Goochland County, Virginia

C. Elizabeth Holland, daughter of John Holland, was born 6 May 1759 in Goochland County, Virginia, married on 24 August 1780, John Hudson.

VII. Michael Holland, son of John Holland, was born 27 December 1737 in Goochland County Michael Holland was processioning lands in Hanover County, Virginia, St. Paul's Parish. 1755, 1759, 1763, land which was Michael Holland's. He was deceased in 1771.

VIII. Alice Holland, daughter of John Holland, was born 12 December 1752 in Goochland County, Virginia, married on 23 May 1773, Henry Nash.

IX. Mary Holland, daughter of John Holland, was born 27 July 1756 Goochland County, Virginia

IX. Lucy Holland, daughter of John Holland, was born 31 March 1758 in Goochland County, Virginia married on 11 February 1778 in Goochland County, Virginia, Solomon Williams.

Michael, Jr., second son of Michael Holland, of Hanover County, St. Paul's Parish, Virginia, son of Michael Holland, was born ca 1695, died 1763 in Amelia County, Virginia He was listed in St. Paul's Parish Records of 1743. Louisa County, Virginia 27 August 1750, Michael Holland of the St. James Northam Parish, Goochland County, Virginia deeded to Stephen Hughes of Fredericksville, Louisa County, Virginia, Planter, 400 acres in Fredericksville Parish on west side of the first mountain (land which William Craddock purchased of Ambrose Joshua Smith 1 June 1738, recorded in Hanover County). Obviously, this is a tract of land which his father, Michael, Sr., bought of William Craddock. Wife, Phebe, relinquished her right of dower. The LWT of William Irby, Amelia County, Virginia dated 10 April 1763, probated 24 October 1765, witnessed by Joseph, Mary and Phebe Holland. Wife, Phebe. Michael Holland fought in the French and Indian Wars of 1754 and was granted 200 acres in 1779. His brother and heir: John Holland. Wife, Phoebe Holland, listed on 1782 Amelia County, Virginia Tax Records. Their son, George Holland, also listed.

Richard, third son of Michael Holland, of Henrico County, Virginia, son of Michael. In 1710 Richard Holland witnessed the LWT of George Froggott, Henrico County, Virginia.[216]

George, fourth son of Michael Holland of Goochland County, married (1) on 27 August 1746 in Goochland County, Sarah Ford,[217] daughter of William Ford. (Surety: Michael Holland), and, (2) on 21 March 1757 in Orange County, Virginia, Mary Coleman (See Douglas Register). Mary was named in the LWT of her father, James Coleman, dated 10/1764 Orange County, Virginia. In 1775 George Holland is listed among the Freeholders of Louisa County, Representatives to the Convention, on 17 March 1775, who made certain Resolves. He was a Patriot, furnishing supplies to Revolutionary forces in Louisa County, Virginia.[218]

---

[216] Louisa County, Virginia deed dated 2 April 1747, between Richard Holland of Henrico County deeded to John Dixon of Hanover County, Virginia, 500 acres on Beaver Creek bounded by lands of Capt. Richard Clough, James Watson, John Michie, John Forsie, Robert Estes, John Rice, on both sides of Beaver Creek; conveyed to A. J. Smith by James Watson; by said Smith conveyed to Michael Holland; by said Holland by his LWT given to his son, Richard Holland. Sarah, wife of Richard, relinquished her dower. Caroline County, Virginia Order Book: June 1717, Suit, John Ravenscroft vs. Richard Holland. Suit, Richard Holland vs. Richard Kennon, admr of Joseph Harwood, deceased.

[217] The Douglas Register.

[218] 27 June 1749, George Holland of Fredericksville Parish, Louise County deeded to Dabney Pettus of St. Martin's Parish, Louisa County, 200 acres on both sides of the South Anna River in Fredericksville Parish, Gilbert Gibson's line near the road. Sarah, his wife, relinquished her right of dower.

Virginia Land Grant: George Holland, 7 July 1763, 370 acres on the southside of the Stanton River in Bedford County, Virginia

Louisa County, Virginia, George Holland was Executor with Thomas Darracott of the LWT of James Beckley of Louisa County, probated on 13 May 1776.

Louisa County, Virginia Deed Book G, page 130-131, 11 June 1791, George Holland and his wife, Mary, of Louisa County to Walker Brume of Caroline County land on Hammond's Creek bounded by Thomas Mitchell, Valentine Meriwether, Joseph Thomson, George Rutherford, Rev. John Todd, Booker Parish.

<u>History of Louisa County, Virginia</u>, page 232: "On Owen's Creek in lower Louisa, among the settlement of the Presbyterian Dissenters, himself, one of them, lived Dr. George Holland. Concerning him little is known except the few chance pieces of information gleaned from several sources. His "Confessions of Faith", printed in 1756, is still in existence, and hence, it is believed that he subscribed to that faith. He was an active practitioner during the Revolution, for he treated a soldier in the COntinental Army, and it was so stated in a petition to recover costs made to the General Assembly. Further, he was living as late as 1794, for Patrick Henry, who knew the old man well, was persuaded to journey to Botetourt County to defend his son, who had killed a man in that country. Mr. Henry pleaded the case so well, picturer this old country doctor and his aged wife, distraught in mind over their son's plight, that the jury lost sight of the evidence and acquitted the young man." See below, Michael Holland.

At one time, George Holland appeared to have owned many acres of land in Goochland County, Virginia and was very well off financially. No doubt it was during his earlier years that he could afford to pay a handsome sum to Patrick Henry. Later, however, it is generally known that he ultimately found himself an old man in a poor financial condition, living well up to about 1800. Note: This George Holland may be the one who died in 1795 Nansemond County, Virginia. with William Holland, Administrator of his Estate.

Indicted for murder, Patrick Henry wins freedom for Michael Holland, son of Dr. George Holland.

"A letter of Mr. Marmaduke Beckwith Morton (1794-1886), written from his home in Russellville, Ky. not long before his death when he was upwards of 90 years...gives some idea of the Revolution when so many sturdy inhabitants pulled up stakes in the Old Dominion...He tells us he was born in Louisa County about four miles from the homes of his uncles, Capt. Samuel Pryor and William Pryor, who lived near each other in Goochland County...Mr. Morton's father was born in RIchmond County in 1753 and was a son of an Englishman named Joseph Morton who married a daughter of Sir Marmaduke Beckwith. The writer goes on to relate that when he was a youngster he was a pupil in an 'old field school' in Goochland where he was taught 'the multiplication table and Arithmetic up to the Rule of Three...The teacher, a man named Michael Holland, used to get drunk Friday evening and remain so until about ten o'clock Monday morning. He was a brother of James Holland who was iindicted for murder and defended by Patrick Henry; also a brother of George Holland

---

Louisa County, Will Book 2, page 238, George Holland and Thomas Darricott, Exrs, of James Beckley, deceased; inventory dated 26 August 1776. WIll Book 2, page 261, named heirs: "Joseph, Elizabeth, Mary and Sarah Beckley, children of my deceased brother, William Beckley, all my estate."

Louisa County, Will Book 2, page 334, Apprraisal of the Estate of William Johnson, 21 November 1777. /s/Thomas Darracott, Joseph Shelton, George Holland, Sr.

Louisa County Will Book 2, page 471, Bond of Ann Parish, Executrix of the estate of Jolley Parish. Secs: George Holland, Bn. Timberland. /s/Ann Parish.

In 1784, Dr. George Holland was named in the settlement of the Estate of Rev. Robert Yancey, Louisa County Louisa County deed dated 24 October 1788, George Holland of Louisa County to Thomas Mitchell, negroes.

who hung two Tories during the Revolutionary War on the Ground Squirrel Road leading from the mountains to Richmond. I have seen the tree on which they were hung."

"About the year 1792, one Holland killed a young man in Botetourt...Holland had gone up from Louisa as a schoolmaster, but had turned out badly, and was very unpopular. The killing was in the night, and was generally believed to be murder...At the instance of the father and for a resonable fee, Mr. Henry undertook to go to Greenbrier court to defend Holland. Mr. Winston and myself were the judges. Such were the prejudices there, as I was afterwards informed by Thomas Madison, that the people declared that even Patrick Henry need not come to defend Holland, unless he brought a jury with him."

"On the day of the trial the court-house was crowded, and I did not move from my seal for fourteen hours, and had no wish to do so. The examination took up a great part of the time, and the lawyers were probably exhausted. Breckenridge was eloquent, but Henry left no dry eye in the court-house. The case, I believe, was murder, though, possibly, manslaughter only; and Henry laid hold of this possibility with such effect as to make all forget that Holland had killed the storekeeper, and presented the deplorable case of the jury's killing Holland, an innocent man. He also presented, as it were, at the clerk's table, old Holland and his wife, who were then in Louisa, and asked what must be the feeling of this venerable pair at this awful moment, and what the consequences to them of a mistaken verdict affecting the life of their son."

"He caused the jury to lose sight of the murder, they were then trying, and weep with old Holland and his wife, whom he painted, and perhaps proved to be, very respectable. All of this was done in a manner so solemn and touching, and a tone so irresistable, that it was impossible for the stoutest heart not to take sides with the criminal...The result of the trial was, that, after a retirement of a half or quarter of an hour, the jury brought in a verdict of not guilty! But on being reminded by the court that they might find an inferior degree of homicide, they brought in a verdict of manslaughter." Patrick Henry, page 376-377.

Patrick Henry worked only for the highest legal fees, as he was always in need of money. Prior to 1768 he had resided in Louisa County, but then purchased a famous old mansion known as "Scotchtown" in Hanover. Henry's eloquence in support of the colonial cause was observed by George Mason. "He is," said Mason," by far the most powerful speaker I ever heard. Every word he utters, not only engages, but commands, the attention; and your passions are no longer your own when he addressed them...." After the Virginia Convention in August of 1774, Roger Atkinson said of him: "He was a very devil in politics, and a son of thunder...."

Issue of Dr. George Holland:

I. Betty Holland, daughter of Dr. George Holland, born ca 1752, married Stephen Robinson.

II. Richard Anderson Holland, son of Dr. George Holland, born 15 February 1762 Goochland County Louisa County, Virginia deed ated 18 October 1788, Richard Anderson Holland of Halifax County, Virginia deeded to Salley Holland, a negro girl, Lucy, etc., which I purchased of "Dr. George Holland".

III. Salley Holland, daughter of Dr. George Holland, was born 26 April 1764 in Goochland County, Virginia, married Nathaniel Carley.

IV. Frankie Holland, daughter of Dr. George Holland, born 8 April 1766 Goochland County, Virginia, married Elijah Lucy.

V. Michael Holland, son of Dr. George Holland, schoolteacher, born 30 March 1768. This is the son defended by Patrick Henry.

VI. Judith Holland, daughter of Dr. George Holland, married George Goodloe.

VII. Mary Holland, daughter of Dr. George Holland, married Charles Burton.

VIII. George Holland, son of Dr. George Holland, of Louisa County, Virginia married 7 November 1779 in Goochland County, Virginia (See Douglas Register) Susannah George, the daughter of James George, who is the surety. (Witness: James Holland). Louisa County, Virginia Deed, page 42, Received of George Holland, Jr., full satisfaction of all debts, costs of suits, etc., Robert Chewning, oath of William Smith. 27 October 1790, the Virginia Gazette published the death of George Holland, Jr. of Goochland County The court appointed Thomas F. Bates as his admr. Child: Keturah Holland, born 1 July 1783.

IX. James Holland, son of Dr. George Holland.

X. William Holland, probably a son of Dr. George Holland, owned 1000 acres on the South Ann River, was born ca 1750, lived in Goochland County married Jane Beckley, probably the daughter of Sir William Beckley (with whom Dr. George Holland had various transactions) whose inventory of estate was filed on 13 July 1772. He owned 1,000 acres on the South Anna River, which flows through Louisa County, Virginia. [219]

William's daughter may be: Katherine Holland who married on 17 January 1799 in Fluvanna County, Virginia, Horace Timberlake.

---

[219] Louisa County, Virginia deed dated 13 June 1785, William Holland and his wife, Jane, convey 95 acres to Thomas Overstreet in Louisa County Louisa County Deed Book H, page 252-253, dated 13 March 1781, William White and Caty, his wife of Louisa to William Holland of the same for 400 pds. Virginial money, 1000 acres in Louisa County on the South Anna River (part of the Watson tract), north-south of the South River.

In the settlement of the estate of Robert Yancey was: Dr. George Holland, William Holland, Capt. Robert Anderson, dated 18 September 1784. He was also named in the settlement of Est. of WIlliam White on 12 February 1798.

Louisa County, Virginia deed dated 7/12/1786, James Pulliam and Agnes, his wife, to Simeon Hall, land adj. William Holland's line.

William Holland witnessed, along with John Bickley, William Timberlake, Peter Crawford, Daniel Powers,Thomas Barnett and John Price, the deed dated 28 June 1786, Louisa County, Robert Duncan and Sarah, his wife, to Edward Smith.

7 January 1793, Louisa County, Virginia Marriage: William Hollins to Elizabeth Cole. Surety: Benjamin Hollins.

Elizabeth, fifth child of Michael Holland, was married to Pouncey Anderson. Her LWT dated 7 July 1791, was probated in Louisa County, Virginia on 8 December 1794. "of the Parish of St. Martins". Names her children and grandchildren. Exrs: Son, Michael Anderson, James Dabney and grandson, Thomas W. Anderson. Will Book 2, page 473, Estate of Pouncey Anderson 12 May 1783. Richard Anderson, Executor.

Children of Elizabeth and Pouncey Anderson:

I.   Michael Anderson. His Issue: Richard, Thomas M., Pouncey, Reuben, Edmund, David, Ann married Edmund Thomson and Elizabeth Anderson.

II. Judith Anderson married James Dabney. Issue: Cisley Dabney married Thomas Shelton, Ann Dabney married Thomas Hardin, Polly, Charity and William Dabney.

III. Richard Anderson. His Issue: Richard, Matthew married Elizabeth, Frances married Christopher Holland, Mary married John Woodson, Kitty married Robert Perkins, Judith, Jane, Susannah, Ann, Shandy and Joseph Anderson.

Judith, sixth child of Michael Holland, of Goochland County, Virginia, was married to Henry Martin. No further information.

Ann, seventh child of Michael Holland, of Goochland County, Virginia. No further information.

Susannah, eighth child of Michael Holland, married (1) on 14 September 1747 in Goochland County, Virginia, Thomas Massie and after his decease married (2) in 1757 William Perkins, Goochland County, Virginia, the son of John Perkins (Named in his LWT, Will Book 4, page 97, Louisa County, Virginia, dated 23 September 1799, probated 9 December 1799) and wife, Mary. Children (from Douglas Register).[220]

Mercy, ninth child of Michael Holland, married William Culbard on 2 January 1759 in Goochland County, Virginia No further information.

William Holland Comes to Georgia

William, son of Captain Henry J. Holland, was born ca 1780 in Nansemond County, Virginia, and removed to Georgia in 1812 according to his grandson, Samuel, in the book Memoirs of Georgia. The Georgia Military Records reflect that in 1813 William was a Private, soldier at Ft. Defiance in Morgan County, Georgia, under Capt. James Barton, in service of the State of Georgia on the frontier line of Morgan County and in the edge of Jasper County at Ft. New Hope from 13 February 1813 when last mustered on 11 February 1814. He seems to have come to Georgia with his brothers, Lewis Connor Holland and Lawson S. Holland. They were all members of the Nansemond County, Virginia. Militia, joining the Georgia Militia when they arrived.

---

[220] Issue: Christian Perkins, born 7 August 1757; William Perkins, William Perkins, born 22 August 1759; Sally Perkins, born 9 August 1763; and Mary Perkins, born 5 May 1763, all in Goochland County, Virginia.

The old homeplace on Kingsale Road in Holland, Virginia had stood since the mid 1700's (still standiing), but now, with its tobacco fields worn out, and father dead (Capt. Henry J. Holland died ca 1810), the probability of a good life in Virginia must have looked bleak. The saying in Virginia was "a farm in Georgia". No doubt, William, who was married, and with two children (Archibald and William), was anxious to find better farmland.

William Holland drew in the 1820 Georgia Land Lottery from Jasper County, Ga. He was listed in the Clarke County, Ga. Tax Digest from 1821 to 1825. The 1820 Clarke County Tax Digest lists William in Capt. Mitchell's District; 1821 in Capt. Berdell's District, 490 acres in Appling County; 1832 in Capt. Foster's District, the same 490 acres; 1823 in Capt. McCree's District, same 490 acres (Archey Holland was now listed with 202-1/2 acres). William is found in the 1830 and 1840 Gwinnett County Census. It is assumed he died there after 1847, since we have never been able to locate any further information. William and Archibald were listed as traders in Lawrenceville, Gwinnett County in 1832. William is listed in the 1830-1840 Gwinnett County Census records, having eight children, five boys and three daughters. Thomas Grady Holland, grandson of Henry Holland, told me that Archibald's mother had ten children and that Archibald had a half-brother, "Bill", who was born in 1786 and died age 84 years. This half brother supposingly came from Mecklenburg County, North Carolina. This tale confirms another tale published in The History of Gwinnett County which relates that one, Samuel Holland, came from North Carolina, settling first in Hall County, later Gwinnett County.

January 28, 1837 estray, Gwinnett County, Ga.: Tolled before William Holland. Letters addressed to William Holland were left at the Post Office in Lawrenceville, dates of: 4-1-1835, 10-1-1839 and 7-1-1840. The Southern Whig mentions 141 acres belonging to William Holland, Dec. 4, 1842. Also, an action (Fi.Fa.) was brought by Lawson S. Holland dated 1829, 70 acres sold by John Underwood to William Terry. There is no record of William ever having lived in North Carolina, but I repeated the above tales since they have some elements of truth. There were seven children of William listed on the 1830 Gwinnett County Census. Archibald makes eight. Since all Hollands have not been identified, it is conceivable that William did have two other children.

A marker erected in the town of Lawrenceville, Ga. states that Robert T. and James Holland were slain on 9 June 1836 in Stewart County during the battle with the Creek Indians. [221]

A study of the census records of Gwinnett County confirm the following children of William Holland:

I. Archibald Holland, son of William Holland, was born 1800 in Nansemond County, Virginia, and died 1868 in Paulding County, married (1) Elizabeth Hagin, (2) Sarah Elsberry. He lived south of Huntsville, today known as Burnt Hickory. SEE Archibald Holland.

II. William Holland, son of William Holland, was born 1805 in Nansemond County, Virginia, died 1896 in Paulding County, buried in Archibald Holland cemetery. William was listed on the 1850 Paulding County Census. Little is known of William except that he never married and travelled around the countryside. He probably lived with his brother, Archibald, from 1850 until his death.

---

[221] Battle of Shepard's Plantation in Stewart County, Georgia. from Historical Collections of Georgia, by White.

III. Robert T. Holland, son of William Holland, was born 1815/20 in Jasper County, Ga., slain on 9 June 1836 in Stewart County, during the Battle of Shepard's Plantation, in a battle with the Creek Indians. He and his brother, James, were given a heroes burial in Lawrenceville, as the detailed accounting in White's Historical Records of Georgia. Their bodies were buried beneath a monument erected near the court house in Lawrenceville to their honor.
He married Martha and had a son, Matthew Crawford Holland who was born 1860 Gwinnett County, according to History of Gwinnett County by McCabe.

IV. James H. Holland, son of William Holland, was born 1815/20 Jasper County, Ga., and was slain on 9 June 1836 in Stewart County, in battle with Creek Indians. Monument in Lawrenceville, Ga. He married Katie Mae Maddox. The Henry Holland family always identified themselves by giving several of their children "Henry" middle names. For tha t reason, I feel certain that James' middle name as "Henry".

V. Daughter of William Holland, was born 1820/25 in either Jasper or Clarke County, Ga.

VI. Samuel Holland, son of William Holland, was born 1825/30 in Clarke County, Ga., wheelwright, farmer, contractor who erected wheat and corn mills around Hall and Forsyth Counties. Samuel married Malissa Bennett in Hall County. Samuel weighed about 250 pounds, while Malissa weighed only about 100 pounds. [222] While attending a meeting held for enlistment in the war, Samuel was so stirred up that he enlisted neat Flowery Branch, Ga. His mother, upon learning of it, mounted a horse and rode after him to bring him back, but was unable to catch up with him. The volunteers spent their first night at the Lawrenceville Camp Ground which went into Atlanta, then to Richmond. At the age of 16 Samuel enlisted in County 1, 24 th Ga. Regt., Wofford's Brigade, Longstreets' Corps, Lee's Army, 1860, fighting in all the battles around Richmond, Virginia He was wounded in The calf of his leg in the second day of fighting on the second day of fighting during the Battle of Gettysburg. While lying wounded on the battlefield, a doctor from Pennsylvania came by, aidiing the wounded and became attracted to the boy, asking him to go with him, but because of Samuel's promise to the boys back home to bring back a pet yankee, he refused. Thus, he was captured, and taken to David's Island, New York, where he recovered and was exchanged, then granted leave of absence to return home. He did not re-enter the service on account of his feeble condition.

Issue of Samuel Holland:

A. Archibald Harrison Holland, son of Samuel Holland, was born 2 August 1844 in Hall County, died 21 February 1931 in Lawrenceville, buried Shadowlawn Cemetery. He married (1) Luvinna Pugh, (2) Jeannette Maulding, 3rd, Mollie Howington, all in Hall County. Archibald was a Missionary Baptist Preacher, democrat, and belonged to The Fraternal Order of The Masons. Issue:
    1. Louvenia Arvaline Holland married Alf Patterson.
    2. Ezekiel Holland married Neppie Warren.
    3. Truman Monroe Holland married Ida Wall.
    4. Cora Lee Holland married Joshua Coffee, then Mr. Wheeler.
    5. Anna Belle Holland married Manassa Sammon.
    6. Willis A. Holland married Cora Webb.
    7. Alice Ophelia Holland, married Bob Sammon.

---

[222] From Jack Holland, Attorney, Lawrenceville, Georgia.

VII. Daughter of William Holland was born 1825/1830 Clarke County.

ARCHIBALD HOLLAND

Archibald Holland, son of William Holland, was born in Nansemond County, Virginia, in 1800, probably on Kingsale Road, where Holland lived for many years. He died September 1869 at Huntsville, Paulding County, Ga., near McPherson, buried in his family graveyard near his homeplace on High Shoals Road (on Alfred Finch farm). Directions: From Dallas, Georgia, take Cartersville Hwy, Confederate Avenue, Rt. 661. Go 3.5 miles and turn left on High Shoals Road. It is about two miles to High Shoals Baptist Church. When the pavement ends, the old Archibald Holland farm is on the right side of the road. A gate leads to the site of the old home site (near road frontage) and the Hagin-Holland tree, Holland cemetery.

In 1823 Archibald was married in Clarke County to Elizabeth Hagin, (born 1809, died 22 November 1840), the daughter of Edward Hagin and Sarah Youngblood. Archibald married (2) Sally Elsberry (born 20 July 1822, died 28 May 1902). Sally was buried Shady Grove Baptist Church Cemetery, Paulding County.

The story of Archibald Holland is given by one of his sons, Samuel Donsel Holland, who, in 1895 had his accounting published in Memoirs of Georgia. Samuel stated that Archibald was the son of William Holland and that he came to Georgia when he was twelve years old. The first records found of him were in Clarke County, his marriage, and listing on the tax digests for 1824 and 1825. Around 1832 be was noted as trading in Gwinnett County, along with his father, William. This must have been during the time he was searching for a home. Archibald apparently left Clarke County with his wife and wife's brother, Edward Hagin, and removed to Atlanta. In 1830 he was listed on the DeKalb County Census, and prior to that time he drew land in the 1827 Land Lottery, 202-1/2 acres now located between Luckie and Spring Streets, where Rich's and the site of the railroad termina. In those days this land was what we call today "Underground A tlanta" (for bridges and roads have been constructed over most of this area). The family story is that Archibald's cows kept bogging down in the mud, and he found the place unsuitable for farming. Thus, in 1840 he was listed on the Cobb County Census.

Archibald's Atlanta farm, which he drew in the lottery, was located in Land Lot 82, 14th District, DeKalb (now Fulton) County, Georgia – 202-1/2 acres. This land is bordered on the West by Northside Drive, North to 9th Street North to South, Williams Street to Alexander Street, the southern border being Simpson Street. West border is Luckie Street. In other words, Archibald owned all the present-day downtown Atlanta prime area which includes Terminal Station, Rich's area, Underground Atlanta, Georgia Tech, the bus station, etc. This is the land which Archibald Holland drew in the 1821 Georgia Land Lottery He moved there between 1825 and 1830 (then DeKalb County) He cows kept getting bogged down in the mud, so searched for more desirable farm lands. About 1833 he lived in Cobb County In 1836 he removed to Paulding County on the old homestead (Huntsville Post Office), later "McPherson", near High Shoals Missory Baptist Church, on Raccoon Creek.

In 1966, I published a book, The Hollands of Paulding County, detailing many Holland ascendants and descendants. During our research, we visited old Samuel Holland's house near Dallas, Ga. and were shown a letter, copied exactly as written, as follows:

"Mr. Archabel Holland State of Georgia
Cob County

From Cuthbert, Georgia December 26
Mr. Archabel Holland Deer 24, 1836

Dear Sir

After my best compliments to you I done agreable to promise about your land. I found about 75 or 100 acres of upland truly as good as that you saw and a hammack with about 10 or 15 acres of first rate of hammack with the rode running threw it and in a rod or two of Mr. Lees. He stated that he was not able to harches his number was 75 lot. I continued to 74 which found it a defrent lot that you stated. It is a real rake and hickry land neals creack running on the north and south line between 74 and 73. It is pine lot 74. Is worth too of it first rate. I think your friend out to send a five dollar bill by letter for my treble and finding out him such a good lot. I would advise him not to sell untill he comes and sees it. If you wish to rite direct it to Cuthbert. Nothing more but remains your friend.

James Martin"

The land mentioned in the above letter ultimately be came Archibald ~ Holland's farm in then Huntsville, Paulding County, which adjoined Hartwell Lee's land. Before 1850, Archibald removed his family to this Paulding County farm. Edward Hagin, his brother-in-law, followed. From Marietta, the family would have travelled the Burnt Hickory Road to the site of Aunt Addie Ross' house, turned left on Sally Hughes Road (now Ga. Hwy 61), turned right onto Braswell Mountain Road, turned left about 300 yards west of Raccoon Creek onto a dirt road, passing through what was later the Thomas E. Ratteree Farm, and settled on 27 acres in Land Lots 792 and 793, Third District, Third Section.

Archibald found a family of nine Cherokee Indians living in this area in a hut made of wooden poles and canes, the exterior plastered with mud, leaves and straw. The Holland's made friends the indian family. Archibald's children often watching the Indian children play ball on a site near the present home of Mrs. Virgil Tibbitts, Sr. When the family left in 1837 for Oklahoma, the Holland's regretted seeing them leave. For many years thereafter, Archibald and his sons tilled these indian fields on Raccoon Creek. Cousin Hubert Holland of Marietta, Georgia says that the Indians had bird names, and that their land was and is known as the "23-acre bottom". Indian artifacts have been found at the foot of this hill; also, a pot of miniballs were dug up at the foot of the bridge over Raccoon Creek.[223]

After Archibald's death, his sons built a house for their step-mother, Sallie, and called it the

---

[223] Thomas Grady Holland, son of Tone Holland, grandson of Henry Holland, told me that Archibald's house was located between the creek (Raccoon) and the church. Specifically, the house was located abou t 800 feet east of the The Archibald Holland Ceme tery, now located on the Alfred Finch Farm, Route 3, Old Marietta-Van Wert Road, Dallas, Georgia. Today (1988), one can find its location neat the Hagin-Holland White Oak Tree, situated upon the ground where houses of bee-hives sit. This location is being mined for rocks. The original Archibald Holland house was built with logs. Everytime they rolled a log, they put a nitch in it, and some of the logs in the house had three nitches. Dorothy and I viewed the land where he lived and determined the location of his house was probably near the road and the now-famous white oak tree, which Elizabeth planted. Typically, this location would have been convenient to the road and convenience for travelling to church and school. Archibald also had a carriage house.

"Aunt Sallie House". In 1860 Archibald is on record as owning five slaves, and the burial ground where he and Elizabeth have laid to rest, according to tradition, have six unmarked slave graves. Archibald told his friends and neighbors that in order to avoid a costly war and ultimate hardship, he would be the first one to free his slaves!

The HOLLAND CEMETERY is located in Land Lot 1043, 18th District, Third Section, Paulding County, on the northside of an unpaved road known as High Shoals Road, having 12 graves 9 of which were marked with unengraved stones. 6 slaves of Archibald Holland were buried here.[224]

Archibald's wife, Elizabeth Hagin, died 22 December 1840, and he married (2) Sally Elsberry (born 26 July 1822, died 29 May 1902), descended from Lindsey Elsberry. Sally was known as "Aunt Sallie" by the children of Archibald and Samuel's old house was called the "Aunt Sally house." Archibald Holland died of cancer.

Archibald's second wife, Sallie Elsberry Holland, beloved teacher, wrote a letter in 1889 to Miss Edna Viola Carlton, one of her pupils at High Shoals School, as follows:

"Dear Edna.

What shall I wish thee. Treasures of earth. Songs in springtime. Pleasures and mirth. Flowers on thy pathway. Skys ever clear. Would this insure thee a happy new year.

Love, Sallie Holland, Remus, Georgia."

Archibald and his first wife, Elizabeth Hagin, had the following Issue:

I. William Edward Holland, son of Archibald Holland, was born 1826 Atlanta, DeKalb County, Georgia, died 12 May 1892 in Paulding County, married 1847 in DeKalb County, Sebbie Lavinnie Elsberry, a daughter of Lindsey Elsberry. Edward was a Confederate Soldier. Lindsey Elsberry owned a mountain near Dallas, Georgia. In 1863 William Edward Holland enlisted in County L, 4th Cavalry, probably to avoid being conscripted into the Infantry. He does not appear on the service rolls for either the 4th Cavalry nor the 4th Cavalry, State Troops, which Cavalry was under over-all command of General Joseph Wheeler. He was captured at the Battle of New Hope Church in 1864 and taken to Rock Island Prison in Illinois. He was released on May 22, 1865 and furnished transportation to Dallas, Ga.

---

[224] Thanks to the efforts of Hubert Holland, Marietta At torney, the bridge over Raccoon Creek was named "The Archibald Holland Bridge." Act of the House, H. R. No. 564-1512, General Assembly of State of Georgia, Adopted In House February 20, 1980; Adopted In Senate Match 5, 1980.

PIONEERS WHO FOUNDED HIGH SHOALS PRIMITIVE BAPTIST CHURCH AND HIGH SHOALS SCHOOL IN 1841 : Edwin and Thena Anderson, Permelia Dodd, Edward and Parthenia Scroggins Hagin, III, Archibald Holland, Hartwell and Sarah Elizabeth Anderson Lee, etc. This famous old school was active from 1841 to 1944 at which time it was discontinued. The old church became dormant in about 1911 and was succeeded by the High Shoals Missionary Baptist Church in 1913. Miss Sallie Elsberry, sister of Mrs. Sibbie L. Elsberry Holland, was one of the first teachers at the High Shoals School. Archibald Holland and his children loved Sallie Elsberry and she married Archibald in about 1842 and helped him raise his children into adulthood.

He took the same two oaths which Humphrey Collins took. His widow, Sebbie, applied for a pension due to his service. The pension stated that he had Auburn hair, blue eyes, was 5 feet, eleven inches tall, and was 39 years of age in 1865. W. H. Crews, a witness on the pension application of William Edward Holland, stated that he knew W. E. Holland had served (as Holland stated) because ~e Crews) had served with him. The command surrendered and was paroled at Kingston, Georgia on 12 May 1865. Crews was with W. E. Holland until he got captured June 1864 at New Hope Church. Crews was present at the surrender in 1865.

Children of Edward and Sebbie Holland:

A. Sarah Holland, daughter of Edward and Sebbie Holland, was born 1848.

B. Archibald Holland, son of Edward and Sebbie Holland, was born 1850 Paulding County, married April 1872, Lucy Baxter, Paulding County.

C. Lindsey Holland, son of Edward and Sebbie Holland, was born 1852 in Paulding County, married on 12 September 1872 in Paulding County, Retency Moody (born1856). They were residents of Phillips, Alabama, in 1880.[225] Issue:
    1. Monroe Holland, born 1875 in Alabama.
    2. Della Holland, born 1875 in Paulding County.
    3. Eric Holland, born 1877 in Paulding County.
    4. Eldora Holland, born 1878 in Paulding County.

D. Starnan Holland, son of Edward and Sebbie Holland, was born 1853 Paulding County.

E. Samuel Holland, son of Edward and Sebbie Holland, was born 1855 Paulding County.

F. Millard Filmore Holland, son of Edward and Sebbie Holland, was born 13 September 1856 and died on 25 December 1928, buried Shady Grove Baptist Church Cemetery, Paulding County, married 26 October 1879, Caroline Hogan (born 13 September 1860). When Millard Holland and his wife, Caroline, could no longer stay on the Holland farm in Paulding County, they removed to A tlan ta and lived with their son and his wife until they died.They loved each other dearly, were a devoted couple, never having a disagreement. Caroline Hogan's mother and father died when she and her brother (George Hogan) were young. Son of Millard Filmore and Caroline Holland:

    1.   William Manon Holland, son of Millard Filmore Holland, was born 24 July 1892 in Paulding County, died 15 November 1952, buried Westview Cemetery, Atlanta, married in Paulding County, 25 October 1914 Evie Barrett. Evie lives in Decatur. "Bill" joined the Atlanta Police Department in 1921, becoming a detective in 1928, serving 14 years as a homocide detective. He retired in 1952 at the age of 60. Bill married Evie in 1914, Paulding County, and they moved in with his parents. They started farming together but when Bill and his father could not agree on how the farm should be run, they moved in with Uncle Henry, who at that time was not married. Evie's first child, Clyde, was born 1916 in Paulding County. In 1918 they removed to Atlanta sad Bill first worked for the Post Office as an automobile mechanic.

---

[225] 1880 Etowah County, Alabama Census, Phillips District.

Bill Holland was very talented. He played the harmonica beautifully, sang in a very deep bass voice with church choirs for years. He led singings in Paulding County and mastered the musical instrumen t "Comet" by playing in the Police Band for many years. Issue of William Manon Holland, all born in Atlanta:

       i. William Clyde Holland, born 22 April 1919.
      ii. Gladys Evelyn Holland, born 22 March 1919.
     iii. Mary Elizabeth Holland, born 25 December 1924.
     iv. Jack Dempsey Holland, born 15 August 1928.
      v. Betty Ann Holland, born 8 November 1930.

G. Mary Holland, daughter of Edward and Sebbie Holland, was born 1858 Paulding County.

H. Benjamin Holland, son of Edward and Sebbie Holland, was born 1859 Paulding County.

I. George Holland, son of Edward and Sebbie Holland, was born 1864 Paulding County, married Mary Elsberry on 20 December 1883 in Paulding County

J. Elvira Holland, daughter of Edward and Sebbie Holland, was born 1864 Paulding County.

K. William Holland, son of Edward and Sebbie Holland, was born 1866 Paulding County.

L. John Holland, son of Edward and Sebbie Holland, was born 1868 Paulding County.

M. Lucy Holland, twin daughter of Edward and Sebbie Holland, was born 20 December 1869, married on 29 December 1889, H. E. Gravett, Paulding County.

N. Eliza Jane Holland, twin daughter of Edward and Sebbie Holland, born 20 December 1869, died 9 January 1941, married 8 January 1890, in Paulding County, John A. Matthews, son of Capt. John Matthews.

II.   Samuel Donsel Holland, son of Archibald, was born in Atlanta, on 15 October 1829, and died in Paulding County on 11 November 1907. He married Annis Lee (born 8 April 1833, died October 1899) , daughter of Hartwell Lee (1810-1868) and his wife, Elizabeth Anderson. Samuel was a Confederate Soldier, enlisting May 10, 1862, County A, 14th Regt, Ga. Vol. Infantry. Discharged after two weeks at Seven Pines, Virginia for enlargement of veins in his leg. After the war, Samuel sought to collect from the Federal Government for damages done to his farm during the war, however, after 25 years, the claim was refused. I saw Samuel's portrait hanging on the wall of his old house...he was six feet tall, black-haired, with a full beard, and dark piercing eyes. Samuel's farm had its cotton gin where long lines of farmers waited at sunrise to have their cotton ginned. Food was prepared from early morning at the house to feed those who were still there at dinner. In the family there is a plate, yellowed from being placed into the oven to keep steaks warm. When Dorothy and I visited this area in 1966, many of the old outbuildings still stood. In 1871, Samuel purchased 110 acres from the Estate of Hartwell Lee, his father-in-law, in Land Lot 831, 18th District, Third Section, Paulding County, as well as Land Lot 794 and south part of Land Lots 790 and 791 in

Third District, Third Section, on Raccoon Creek. In 1873, Samuel claimed 40.3 acres, Paulding County tax digest.

Samuel's Last Will and Testament dated 21 November 1904, probated 14 January 1907, mentioned his homeplace on Raccoon Creek and "more particularly described in a deed made by myself as administrator of my father, Arch Holland, deed, to myself as an individual in a deed dated 27 September 1869, my said homplace comprising the whole of the lands described in said three deeds, except that portion hereto deeded by me to Sarah A. Camp." [226] Upon the death of Annis, Samuel married Miss Emma Fricks, a teacher, and moved to Dallas, where they lived until his death on 11 November 1907.

Issue of Samuel and Annis Holland:

A. Nancy Edie Holland, daughter of Samuel and Annis Holland, (1854 -1879) Paulding County, married on 2 February 1873, Henry Monroe ("Bud") Carlton (1850-1932) in Paulding County, the son of Henry S. Carlton and Elizabeth Rice Carlton. SEE Carlton.

B. James Holland, son of Samuel and Annis Holland, was born 1852 in Paulding County, married Sophronia Hubbard (1851-1925). Issue:

1. Mary Holland, born 1800, married Dansby and had: Dan Dansby (had Donnie Mae and Charles Dansby); Tivola Dansby; Heslip Dansby of Rockmart, Georgia.; Una Mae Dansby married S. J. Noland of Rockmart. (son, Robert Jackson Noland, lawyer in Douglasville.); Robert Paul Dansby (son, Robert Durham Dansby); Clarice Dansby born 1916 of New Jersey (son Edmund); and Wilma Dansby born 1916, twin to Clarice.

2. Charles L. Holland, born 1877, died ca 1963. Issue: James Henry Holland married Lois Locklear (daughter, Ann Holland); Lucille Holland married Rolander (Betty Faye and Geneva Rolander); Laura Holland married Bunyan Bishop; Walter Holland married Myra Locklar, Marietta City Councilman; Ernestine Holland married Sam Wheeler, Atlanta.; Charlene Holland married W. S. Shanks.

3. Chesley Holland married Edith Suit. Issue: Heslip, Kennon, Dennis, Sally, Joanne and Betty Jean Holland.

 4. Homer H. Holland, born April 1888, died 24 February 1929, married Helen Moore (born 21 April 1894, died 10 November 1957. Issue: Woodson Holland, born 2 January 1912, died 2 February 1862, married Inez Johnson (had a daughter, Gall Holland, who married Mr. Waddell); and Maggie Ruth Holland, born 5 November 1914, married Roy Pulliam (Issue: Frank, Roy, Johnny and Zane Pulliam).

C. Thomas Wyatt Holland ("Buddy"), son of Samuel and Annis Holland, was born 3 February 1874, died 19 November 1957, buried High Shoals Cemetery, in Dallas, Paulding County. He married on 5 December 1894, Roma Belle Jones (born 19 August 1878 in Paulding County, died 1945 in Paulding County) daughter of Don

---

[226] Paulding County Deed datee 27 September 1869, Paulding County Deed Bk O, pp. 197, 265.

Jones. He was the" dandy" of all the Holland men - never wearing coarse or heavy shoes. Even in the fields, Buddy wore his dress shoes.

"An interesting anniversary will be celebrated Saturday, December 9, by Mr. and Mrs. Buddy Holland, natives and lifelong citizens of Paulding County, at their home in Marietta where they have been residing for seven months. Mrs. Holland is the daughter of the late Don Jones. Mr. Mr. Holland will be 71 years of age in February. For 65 years, he has lived on the old Holland farm - a farm that has a very unusual history in that it has been in the Holland family for 120 years. Thus, when Queen Victoria was a young girl and the War of 1812 was fresh memory to America, a Holland was tilling the acres, which, for so long have furnished sustenance to an outstanding Paulding family. Mr. and Mrs. Holland received congratulations of many friends of this significant event." <u>Dallas New Era</u>, dated 12 August 1942.

Issue of Thomas Wyatt (Buddy) and Belle Holland:

1. William Odus Holland, son of Thomas Wyatt Holland, was born on 20 April 1896 and died 29 January 1959, buried High Shoals Cemetery married (1) Nettie Brown (born 3 November 1897, died 8 April 1922) and (2) Estelle Sheppard (born 4 December 1907) and had issue: Lois Holland married Hoyt Locklear and Thelma Holland married Woodrow Tibbitts.

2. Nettie Josephine Holland, daughter of Thomas Wyatt Holland, was born born 1 June 1897.

3. Addie Mozelle Holland, daughter of Thomas Wyatt Holland, was born on 21 May 1901, married Julius H. Hollingshed (born 6 January 1897, died 15 August 1972, buried High Shoals Cemetery. Issue: Estelle Hollingshed married Cleo Clupp of Rockmart; Thomas Levi Hollingshed married Louise Hunton; J. T. Hollingshed married Ann Roper from Cummings; Edgar Ray Hollingshed; Wendell Hollingshed married Beverly Milholland; Cecil Hollingshed married Emma Jean Hamby; and Alta Fay Hollingshed married Sammy Aikens.

4. Dessie M. Holland, daughter of Thomas Wyatt Holland, was born born 17 Nover 1902.

5. Donnie Viola Holland, daughter of Thomas Wyatt Holland, was born 5 May 1904, died 2 April 1980, married on 7 November 1920, Ernest Coleman Bell, born in Braswell on 5 February 1897, died 2 August 1892, Paulding County, both buried New Hope Cemetery. SEE Bell.

6. Annie Lou Holland, daughter of Thomas Wyatt Holland, was born on 4 February 1906, died 3 March 1909, buried High Shoals Cemetery.

7. Thomas Ira Holland, son of Thomas Wyatt Holland, was born 4 February 1907.

8. Samuel Donsel Holland, son of Thomas Wyatt Holland, was born 1912.

9. Mamie Ophelia Holland, daughter of Thomas Wyatt Holland, was born 6 October 1913.

10. Calvin Lewis Holland, son of Thomas Wyatt Holland, was born 30 May 1916, died 4 April 1918.

11. Infant son of Thomas Wyatt Holland, was born October 1922.

    i. Irma Holland, daughter of Thomas Wyatt Holland, born 12 August 1924 in Paulding County, married W. M. Weaver of Smyrna.

D. Permelia (Amelia Ann) Holland, daughter of Samuel and Annis Holland, was born 23 June 1856 in Paulding County, and died on 10 July 1929, daughter of Samuel and Annis Holland. She was married on 23 November 1876 in Paulding County, to William Monroe Elsberry, born 6 December 1855 in Paulding County, died 17 May 1918, son of Kirkland Elsberry and Miriam McGregor. SEE Elsberry.

III. Elizabeth Holland, daughter of Archibald, was born 1833 in Atlanta, died 1915, buried High Shoals Cemetery, Paulding County, married Gilbert Peter Matthews (born 13 June 1831, died 15 August 1898), buried High Shoals Cemetery, served in Confederate Army, Pvt., County C., (2) GA State Line. SEE Matthews.

III. Harrison Ramsey Holland, son of Archibald Holland and Elizabeth Hagin, was born in Cobb County, 29 June 1831, died of typhoid fever in Rome, Georgia on 3 August 1863. He married on 30 May 1851 in Paulding County, Sarah Elizabeth Anderson (born 1833), leaving his wife to raise four small children. His body was buried in the Holland Cemetery in a grave marked with a slate rock. (Replaced 1975 with a marble monument).

Quoting from Hubert Holland: "She (Sarah Elizabeth) was aware of the universal principle that 'the home is the most important source of education for children and they should be taught by excellent parental example and counsel.' Thus, by excellent example and intelligent counsel, she taught her children the value of education, work, recreation and morality and helped and encouraged them to formulate and pursue intelligent goals. She and her four children worked very hard on her small farm in Paulding County, attended religious services regularly at the High Shoals Primitive Baptist Church, enjoyed fishing and swimming in Raccoon Creek and each child graduated from the High Shoals School. "Unfortunately, most of the land in the High Shoals Community was hilly and when cleared for cultivation became infertile very rapidly due to erosion. Her sons later married and mese of them purchased fertile farms in Polk County, Georgia, and farmed and raised their families there. It is interesting to note that from 1852 to 1898 there wee no public high school in Paulding County, and during this period many parents moved to Polk County and o ther counties in order the t their beloved children could be afforded the opportunity to earn a high school diploma in the county of their residence."

Issue of Harrison Ramsey and Sarah Elizabeth Anderson Holland:

A. Edwin A. Holland, son of Harrison Ramsey Holland, was born 1854 Paulding County, died 1917 in Polk County, married on 17 January 1875, Frances Taylor. They had ten Issue:

1. John W. Holland 1889-1948 unmarried,

2. Josie Holland married L. O. Benefield. Issue: Charlie and Lottie Benefield.

3. Bill Holland, son of Edward A. Holland, 1877-1949 married Maude Collins.

4. Noble C. Holland, son of Edward A. Holland, 1887-1961 married Grace Witcher. They owned and operated a deity farm in Polk County for many years and had three children, viz:

> i. Ralph T. Holland, Retired U. S. Air Force General, married on 14 March 1944, Kathleen L. Lummus (born 1900 Bloomburg, Texas, the daughter of Sam Lummus (1897-1959). As told to Cousin Hubert Holland, "while returning home from the hay fields at sunset and walking to the dairy barn to milk the cows at dawn during the 1920s, little Ralph T. Holland often watched Canadian geese fly gracefully across the sky, going North in the spring and South in the fall. At about age 9, this lad decided that he would learn to fly and become a pilot. His parents were devout Christians. General Holland married Kathleen Lummas in Texas. They had two children, 'Barbara and Jane, who died of natural causes at very early ages.[227]

---

[227] SECRETARY OF THE AIR FORCE   AV 29-74291
OFFICE OF: INFORMATION AREA CODE 202/76-74291
COMMAND SERVICES UNIT BOLLING AFB, D.C. 20332

"Major General Ralph T. Holland is Commander, Warner Robins Air Logistics Center, Robins Air Force Base, Georgia. The Warner-Robins ALC is logistics manager for the F-15 air superiority fighter and for most of the U.S. Air Force transport aircraft, helicopters, air-to-air missiles, airborne electronic equipment, surface motor vehicles, and ground support equipment. General Holland was born on Nov. 16, 1920, in Cedartown, Ga., where he graduated from high school in 1937. he attended West Georgia College, Carrollton, Ga., for two years prior to enlisting in the U.S. Army Air Corps as an aviation cadet in August 1941. He graduated from advanced flying school in March 1942 with a commission as second lieutenant and his pilot wings. He then served as an instructor pilot until November 1943, when he joined the 462d Bombardment Group, Hays, Kans. In April 944 the group was transferred to India and for the next year he flew as a B-29 aircraft conrmander In the China-Burma-India (CBI) Theater. The 462d Group moved to Tinian Island in the Western Pacific in March 1945, and three months later he returned to the United States, after having flown 35 combat missions and 500 combat hours in the B-29 aircraft. General Holland reverted to inactive duty in June 1945 and resumed his college education. He was graduated from Emory University, Emory, Ga., in 1947, with a bachelor of arts degree in business administration, became personnel manager for Scripto Manufacturing County, and later joined the sales department of theWestinghouse Electric Supply County. During the Korean War, he was recalled to active military duty in March 1951 and was assigned to the 2d Bombardment Wing, Hunter Air Force Base, Ga., as a deputy squadron commander, and later served at Barksdnle Air Force Base, La., and on Okinawa. In October 1954 he began a four-year assignment with the Director of Procurement and Production, Deputy Procurement and Chief of Staff, Materiel, Headquarters U.S. Air Force, 89 Chief of the Bombardment Branch, From August 1958 until July].9T9, he was a student at the Air War College, Maxwell Air Force Base, Alabama. After graduation, he returned td Strategic Air Command (SAC) os Vice Commender and later became Commander of the 341et Bombardment Wing at Dyess Air

211

ii. Louise Holland, daughter of Noble C. Holland, was born 10/1922 married Jim Wilkerson.

iii. N. A. Holland, daughter of Noble C. Holland, was born 1/1913 married John Rutledge. John and N. A. Holland Rutledge still own a part of the Noble C. Holland Dairy Farm and keep the beautiful old home which was formerly owned by her beloved parents in an excellent state of repair.

5. Ella Holland, daughter of Edwin A. Holland (1875-1901), married Charlie McBrayer.

6. Martha Holland, daughter of Edwin A. Holland (1873-1957), married J. H. Benefield.

7. Henry Tate Holland, son of Edwin A. Holland, died 1919 married Fannie Curr. Child: Cecil Holland married Lucille Whitehead and had son, Van Holland, born Polk County. Van Holland and his wife, Mar tha, have toured in various nations throughout the world. While in Great Britain several years ago, Van researched his Holland lineage from John Holland 1664 (migrated to Virginia in about 1664) back to 1250 A. D. Notation from Dallas New Era 8 January - "Mr. Otis Cooper and Van Holland opened a store."

Force Base, Tex. In June 1961 he became Vice Commander of the 96th Bombardment Wing at Dyetis. In June 1962 he was assigned to the office of the Inspector Ceneral, SAC, Offutt Air Force Base, Nebr. He became Deputy Commander of SAC's 3d Air Division at Andersen Air Force Base, Guam, in June 1965. During that assignment, he flew c~mbat missions in addition to participating in command and control of U-52 and KC-135 Air Force operations support of Southeast Asia operations. In July 1966 General Holland reeurned to the United States as Commander of the 7th Bombardment Wing, Carswell Air Force Base, Tex., and in July 1967 became Commander of the 42d Air Division, Blytheville Air Force Base, Ark. In July 1968 he was assigned as Commander of the 810th Strategic Aerospace Division, Minot Air Force Base, N. Dak., and in August 1969 became Vice Commander of the Warner Kobins Air M~~eriel Area se Kobins Air Force Base, Georgia. General Holland was transferred to the Republic of Vietnam in November 1971 and assumed duties as Deputy Chief of Staff, Logistics, Headquarters Seventh Air Force., at Tan Son Nhut Airfield, and in September 1972 became Deputy Commander of the Seventh Air Force. He became Deputy Chief of Staff for Logistics, Headquarters Pacific Air Forces, at Hickam Air Force Base, Hawaii, in February. In August 1974 General Holland was reassigned se Commander of Warner Robins Air Logistics Center, AFLC, at Robins Air Force Base, Georgia. His military decorations and awards include the Distinguished Service Medal, Legion of Merit with three oak leaf clusters; Distinguished Flying Cross with two oak leaf clusters, Air Medal with five oak leaf clusters; Abr Force Commendacion Medal; Distinguished Unit Citation Emblem with three oak leaf clusters; Air Force Outstanding Unit Award Ribbon with one oak leaf cluster, and from the Republic of Vietnam the Air Force Distinguished Service Order, First Class, and Air Service. Medal, General Holland is married to the former Miss Kathleen Lummus, a native of Palestine, Texas. His hometown is Cedartown, Georgia. He was promoted to the grade cf major general effective April 2, 1973 with date of rank August 1, 1969."

8. Lena Holland, daughter of Edwin A. Holland, born 1891 married S. L. Carlton. Issue: Mrs. H. N. Shepard born 1922 of Aragon, Ga.; Mrs. Harold Miller born 1926 of Rockmart; and John Ed Carlton born 1915 of Rome, Ga.

9. Starling Holland, son of Edwin A. Holland, 1895-1902.

10. Seward Holland born 1898 married Mollie Wilkerson.

B. Henry Clay "Doc" Holland, son of Harrison Ramsey Holland, was born 2 January 1856 in Paulding County, died 20 August 1927, son of Harrison Ramsey Holland, married on 22 October 1857, Antenette Bullock, born 22 October 1857, died 31 January 1944, the daughter of Sherman Bullock and Harriett Gann. He was called "Dec" Holland because he performed medical services on humans as well as animals. "Mom said a man had fallen and cut his face open. He came to Doc's house and my grandfather sewed his face up without any deadening assistance except a big swig of whiskey (homemade moonshine). He was a coarse and crude type person, apparently as a result of years of piecing together everything and everybody."[228]
Children of Doc Holland:

1. Lucy Mae Holland, daughter of Henry Clay Holland, born 30 December 1876, died 28 October 1955, married on 5 August 1892, Tom Jones, died 23 August 1966, buried at High Shoals Church, near Dallas. Issue:

    i.   Hettie Jones of Hardy Street, Dallas, Ga. 30132, over 90 years old.
    ii. Deltha Jones, died age 2.
    iii. Dorothy Jones, deceased.
    iv. D. L. Jones, deceased.
    v. Quinton Jones.
    vi. Herschal Jones, decd. A Jr. High School is named for him in Dallas, Georgia.
    vii. Ray Jones, d. age 2.
    viii.Clara Mae Jones, decd.
    ix. Bernice Jones, decd.
    x. Felton Jones.
    xi. Paschal Jones.

2. Martha Ann (Mattie) Holland, daughter of Henry Clay Holland, born 20 October 1878, married (1) on 15 November 1892, Tom Elsberry (1869-1909, buried in the High Shoals Baptist Church Cemetery, (2) Bill Camp. Mattie's children by Tom Elsberry:
    i.   Virgil (Dick) Elsberry.
    ii. Ben Elsberry.
    iii. Docia Elsberry.
    iv. Rayford Elsberry.
    v. Clifford Elsberry.
    vi. Millie Elsberry.
    vii. Tommy Elsberry.
    Mattie's children by Bill Camp:
    viii. Julian Camp.

---

[228] From Bette Brown Dunn, granddaughter.

ix. Myrtle Camp Bullard of Hiram, Ga.

x. Lucy Belle Camp Brown.

3. Robert Edward Holland, son of Henry Clay Holland (born 22 December 1880, died 1 June 1956), married Mattie Austin. Issue:

    i. Bertie Holland, decd.

    ii. Lucille Holland.

    iii. Sharon (Chad) Holland.

    iv. H. C. Holland of Dallas, Georgia.

    v. Mildred Holland, deceased.

    vi. Hazel Holland.

    vii. Woodson Holland, deceased.

    viii. Lilly Holland, decd.

4. Lilly Ola Holland, daughter of Henry Clay Holland, was born 5 September 1884, married 7 May 1901, B. M. "Roe" Bowman. Issue:

    i. Otis Bowman, decd.

    ii. Henry Bowman, decd.

    iii. Butler Bowman, decd.

    iv. Gladys Bowman, decd.

    v. Gertrude Bowmen.

    vi. Clarice Bowman Barren of Dallas, Georgia.

    vii. Audine Bowman.

    viii. Lillian Bowman.

    ix. Willard Bowman.

    x. Hazel Bowman, died when a small child.

5. Infant son of Henry Clay Holland.

6. Albert Jackson Holland, son of Henry Clay Holland, was born 20 January 1887, married (1) Minnie Dunaway (died 27 January 1922) and (2), Mrs. Winnie Howell German. Issue:

    i. Sheryl J. Holland, born 1 October 1912, married Nora Lee Carter.

    ii. Joe Bailey Holland, born 27 January 1915, married Christine Cochran of Dallas, Georgia.

    iii. Evelyn Sophronia Holland, born 6 November 1919, married Parker Womack of Paulding County. (Daughter, Eloise Womack married Winford Harding.).

7. Lona Holland, daughter of Henry Clay Holland, born 2 August 1899, died 21 September 1973, married H. W. "Pete" Brown (born 2 May 1886, died 7 September 1967). SEE Brown.

8. Edde Holland, daughter of Henry Clay Holland, daughter of Henry Clay Holland, born 29 December 1891, died 7 March 1914, married Charlie Thomason. Issue: infant son and daughter; Willie T. Thomason married Bill

214

O'Conner; Louise Thomason married (1) Wallace Allsup, (2) George Deason (children, Edwin Allsup married Emma Jones and Joellen Allsup married Billy Naugher).

9. Jodie Holland, daughter of Henry Clay Holland, born 3 May 1894, married Walter C. Hunt. Issue: Jewell Hunt married Gene Tibbett of Marietta; R. J. Hunt married Evelyn Atcheson; Gid Clay Hunt married Vera Wills; Ella Hunt married John Moore; and Joeddta Hunt married J. T. Wood.

10. Jesse ("Tige") Holland, son of Henry Clay Holland, born 8 October 1897, died ca 1964, married Fannie Carnes. Issue: Gueston, Wilfred (Woody), Emery, Betty Faye and Guy Holland.

11. Harrison Holland, son of Henry Clay Holland, was born 2 May 1900, married Madge Cantrell of Birmingham, Alabama. Issue: Lydia Fay Holland married Humby and Annie Holland.

C. Samuel D. Holland, son of Harrison Ramsey Holland, was born 20 August 1858 and died 19 January 1924, buried High Shoals Cemetery, Paulding County, married on 6 September 1883 in Paulding County, Miss Georgia Johns (born 8 October 1868, died 7 June 1906). SEE Johns. Issue:

1. Walter Holland, son of Samuel D. Holland, was born 18 August 1884, died 18 July 1886 , buried High Shoals Cemetery.

2. Oscar Holland, son of Samuel D. Holland, 1896-1962, married Birtie Holland. Issue: Frances Holland, married J B. Irwin of Atlanta; Evelyn Holland married Warner Hill; Hewell Holland married Walter Hughes; Georgia Holland married Dewey Samples; and Edna Elizabeth Holland married William Earl Armistead. (children, William Earl, Jr., Edwin and Gary Armistead).

3. Snowdie Holland, daughter of Samuel D. Holland, was born 1889 unmarried.

4. Dora Holland, daughter of Samuel D. Holland, born 1891 married Charles W. Statham. Issue: William Robert Statham; Mildred Evelyn Statham married Donald Crawley; Mary Frances Statham married Charles Denham; Eva Lois Statham; and Dorothy Helen Statham, deceased.

5. Effie Holland, daughter of Samuel D. Holland, was born 9 October 1898, died 15 September 1965, buried High Shoals Cemetery, Paulding County, married William Robert Parlier.

6. Addie Holland, daughter of Samuel D. Holland, was born 1895, died February 1974, married Alvin Hulsey of Atlanta. Issue: Maudie Hulsey born 1924 married Harold Lee (daughter, Janice Gall Lee born 1956); Charles Everett Hulsey; and Ezra Ralph Hulsey.

7. Samuel Chester Holland, son of Samuel D. Holland, born 1897, died 1968, unmarried, buried High Shoals Baptist Church Cemetery, Paulding County.

8. Charles Lee Holland, son of Samuel D. Holland, was born 1898 of Powder Springs, married (1) Elizabeth Nolan, (2), Era Thompson. Son, Charles Lee Holland, Jr. married Miss Trouter.

9. Emmett Holland, son of Samuel D. Holland (1900-1954), married Lora Lyle, had daughter: Marguerite Holland, unmarried.

10. Augustus Owen Holland, son of Samuel D. Holland, 19021961 married Rosie Aiken. Child: Martha Jane Holland married Hugh Martin.

11.. George Holland, son of Samuel D. Holland, unmarried.

D. Joe Holland, son of Harrison Ramsey Holland, was born 1860 Paulding County, married Emma Dunaway. Child: Corinthy Holland of Rockmart, unmarried.

E. Amanday Holland, daughter of Harrison Ramsey Holland married Burrell Camp, buried at Runcombe Primitive Baptist Church, Polk County. They owned a farm near Rockmart and had three girls: Stella Camp who was killed in a car wreck when Ford automobiles first began on the road; Millie Camp married Mr. Sprowls, lived Rockmart; and Edna Camp.

V. Henry Holland, son of Archibald Holland, was born in Cobb County on 11 August 1835, and died 15 December 1870 in Paulding County. He was married on 15 December 1870 to Sarah Carlton (born 15 August 1833, died 28 May 1901). The family story is that upon returning home one day, Henry's horse became frightened as he turned into the road to his home. He lost his seat, but his foot was caught in the saddle and he was dragged down the ravine to the doorstep of his house where his wife disengaged his foot. While recovering from these severe injuries, he contracted pneumonfa and died.

Issue of Henry and Sarah Carlton Holland:

A. Amanda Holland, daughter of Henry and Sarah (Carlton) Holland, was born 1855 married 30 October 1881 in Paulding County, Seabie Z. Noland of Rockmart.

B. James Monroe Holland, son of Henry and Sarah (Carlton) Holland, was born 28 January 1857, died 16 May 1931, Merchant, married on 10 August 1879, Marinda Ann Durham, born 29 March 1854, died 16 December 1930, the daughter of William H. Durham (1822-1900) and Mariah Elsberry (1827-1898). Both buried Dallas City Cemetery.

Issue of James Monroe Holland:

1. Sally Dosher Holland, daughter of James Monroe Holland, was born 26 July 1880, died 26 September 1907, married on 28 December 1898, R. M. Matthews. Issue: Annie Florence, Lillian and Linnie.

2. Henry Young Holland, son of James Monroe Holland, was born 27 September 1881, died 17 July 1938, married (2) on 15 October 1905, Beatrice E. Griffin, (2), Grace Marie Owens (Mrs. Holland later remarried R. Johns.) Issue: Lois Holland, born on 13 May 1907, married Leon Wills (children, James Holland Wills (born 18 January 1935) and Franklin Leon Wills (born 15 December 1947); Ned Eugene Holland (born 23 November 1911, married on 8

216

April 1939, Katharine Leigh Rhodes, daughter of Edgar Rhodes (children, Sandra Holland (born 19 May 1940, married Ray Parkins), Ned Eugene Holland, Jr. (born 9 December 1942) and William Holland (born March 1946); Van Buren Holland (born 10 August 1913, married on 10 November 1934, Ethel Wright (children, Curtis Wright Holland (born 29 August 1935), Henry Young Holland (born 11 December 1938), Ann Louise Holland (born 14 April 1943), Ethel Marie Holland (born 14 April 1943) and Linda Holland (born 19 January 1949); Ralph Griffin Holland; Zuma Louise Holland (born 23 December 1917, married 21 December 1941, E. C. Bullock, Jr. (children, Robert Bullock (born 4 October 1945) and Allen Bullock (born 5 May 1953); Max Holland (born 19 July 1906, died 8 November 1907); and infant son (born 28 December 1909, died 30 December 1909).

3. Ivey R. Holland, son of James Monroe Holland, was born 1 November 1883, died 4 February 1954, married (1) on 27 August 1905, Roma Brown of Dallas, and (2) on 9 August 1920, Sabra Bertram. Issue:

   i. Inez Holland, born 21 March 1908 in Dallas, Georgia, married Don Trammell (Son: Don, Jr. (born Rome, 11 July 1931, married Cecilia Cooper).

   ii. Gladys Holland (died April 1987) married James R. Davis, resides in Alabama. Child: Virginia Davis married Densen Franklin.

   iii. Rev. James B. Holland, born 9 July 1921, died 8 June 1946. His daughter, Donna Louise Holland married Larry Reed (Their son, Cullen).

   iv. William Dean Holland, born 25 December 1927. His daughter: Karen Holland married Philip Arcadapane. Their son: Adam Arcadapane.

   v. Betty Holland, born 27 March 1929 in Rome, married Emory Lanier.

   vi. Sabra Louise Holland, born and died 1 February 1930.

   vii. Eleanor Holland, born 20 December 1932, married Orville R. Davis. Issue: Orville R. Davis III, born on 29 November 1949 (Orville's Issue: Jason D. Davis, Meredith Davis, and Kalla Davis); Elaine Davis born 23 July 1953, married Kelby Dee Watt. (Their daughter, Cynthia Nanette Watt).

4. William S. Holland, son of James Monroe Holland, was born 2 May 1886, married on 15 September 1902 at Mt. Olivet, Georgia, Anne Julia Trice. Issue: Willie S., Jr., Murphy, Paul and Pauline Holland.

C. James Archibald Holland, son of Henry and Sarah (Carlton) Holland, was born 22 April 1859, died 1 July 1920 in Paulding County, buried High Shoals Cemetery, Paulding County, married on 14 May 1879, Ruby Ann Crew (born 13 November 1862, died 24 November 1915), buried High Shoals Church Cemetery, Dallas. Children of James Archibald Holland and Ruby Ann:

1. Lena Holland born 1880 Paulding County, married (1) Charles Eugene Davis (1878-1906) who owned a farm 3 miles from Rockmatt. By him she had three boys and one girl. Only one survived, i.e.: Joseph King Davis (called Joe K.) (1902-1983). Lena married (2), Henry Finch, Sr. of Dallas, Ga. She was Henry's third wife. They had: Henry (Bubba) Finch, Caroline Finch, Zelma F inch. Henry Finch, Sr. married (1), Ida House, 2d,----, 3rd, Lena Holland Davis. Charles Richard Davis born 1926 is the son of Joe K. Davis and married Rita (born 1931). They reside in Birmingham, Alabama.

2. Ben Holland.

3. William Walter Holland, born 4 July 1883, died 19 February , buried High Shoals Cemetery, married Ada Finch (born 12 October 1885, died 25 October 1967, buried High Shoals Cemetery. Issue: Oliver A. Holland, born 29 August 1910, died 10 September 1910; infant son, born 15 August 1913, died 10 September 1913.

4. Deborah Haskins Holland, born 2 September 1887 Dallas, died on 15 February 1907, married (1) on 15 September 1902, Jesse Coleman born 31 July 1873 in Roswell, Georgia, died 2 December 1967. He married (2) in 1908 Ludy Ann Monk (born 29 September 1887, died 7 March 1971).

5. Dura Holland.

6. Mattie Lee Holland was born on 27 January 1905, married O. Virgil McCard. Issue: J. Harold McCard, born 21 September 1921, and Jean McCard, born 13 March 1927, married Jack Manning, son of Vernon E. Manning.

7. Tennie Holland was born on 22 February 1890 and died on 8 June 1901, buried High Shoals.

8. Timmy Holland, died young.

9. Mattilee Holland.

D. John H. Holland, son of Henry and Sarah (Carlton) Holland, was born 1861 Paulding County, married on 18 January 1885 in Paulding County, Lula Finch. Issue:

1. Hattie Mae Holland married on 5 December 1917, William Edward Williams (born 18 June 1870, died 11 July 1939), his (2) wife. (children--Carl Leon Williams, born 15 December 1918 and Billy Jack Williams, born 2 July 1929.
2. Ida Sarah Holland, daughter of John H. Holland married Wells.
3. Loyd T. Holland, son of John H. Holland.
4. Myrtle Holland, daughter of John H. Holland, married Williams.
5. Amanda Holland, daughter of John H. Holland, married Jordan.
6. Oma Holland, daughter of John H. Holland, married Pearce.
7. Clarence Holland, son of John H. Holland.
8. Henry Holland, son of John H. Holland.
9. Arthur Holland, son of John H. Holland.

E. Martha Amanda (Mendy) Holland, daughter of Henry and Sarah (Carlton) Holland, was born 28 May 1864 in Paulding County, died 3 May 1942 in Polk County, buried in the.Hills Creek Baptist Church Cemetery, Rockmart, Polk County, married (1) on 20 November 1892 Paulding County, S. P. Elsberry, and (2) on 18 September 1881, Seaborn ("Seab") Jackson Noland (born 4 September 1860, died 16 February 1921), the son of William Aubrey Noland (born 17 January 1828 in Walton County, died 29 August 1884 in Paulding County) and his wife, Sarah Elizabeth (Cheeves) Noland (born 17 January 1839, died 1 June 1904), buried Old High Shoals Baptist Church Cemetery, whom he married on 19 January 1856 in Carroll County). SEE Noland.

F. Harrison Ramsey "Tone" Holland, son of Henry and Sarah (Carlton) Holland, born 4 May 1870, died 24 January 1954, married 13 January 1893, Dorothy Jones (born 23 December 1873, died 30 April). Hubert Holland remembers Tone Holland as being a very sweet man and hard-working. He had a long mustache and wore a big hat. Tone raised sweet potatoes and had a sweet potato house - a building where a fire was built under the floor to dry out the sweet potatoes.

Seated (left-to-right): James Tom Holland,
Tone Holland, Samuel Marion Holland.
Standing (left-to-right): Silas Casey Holland,
?, Hart Holland. Photo date: 4 August 1893

Issue of Harrison Ramsey "Tone" Holland and Dorothy:

1. Allie Lee Holland born 1893 in Paulding County, died 1979 in Long Beach, California, married Thomas James Starling, Sr. (born 13 March 1889 in Stoke Newington, London England, died 12 May 1935 in Carrollton, Carroll County) the son of Thomas James and Rose Hannah (Brown) Starling. Allie Lee Holland Starling is buried Forest Lawn Cemetery, Cypress, California. Thomas James Starling is buried at New Hope Cemetery, Paulding County, Ga. SEE Starling.

2. Ludie Ann Holland, daughter of Tone Holland, was born 1895 Paulding County a. William Silas Monk of High Shoals, Georgia and had: Frances Monk, John Monk of Atlanta, -Charles Monk of Greenville, South Carolina and Wayne Monk of Maryland.

3. Thomas Grady Holland, son of Tone Holland, was born 28 November 1897 in Paulding County, died 7 October 1967. He married Georgia Wills of Bartow County, born 25 December 1896. Thomas Grady Holland told me that he is six feet tall and has weighed as such as 293 pounds. and had:

   i. Henry Grady Holland, son of Thomas Grady Holland, was born 20 September 1921,, died 14 May 1949, married Jean Deboard, born 11 June 1931, of Smyrna. Son: Michael Henry Holland, born 2 August 1954, married Dianne Garrett of Cumming.

219

ii. Ella Mae Holland, daughter of Thomas Grady Holland, was born 9 January 1924, married John Harrington of Little Beck, Arkansas. Son: Stephen Harrington, born 1 November 1952.

iii. Dorothy Virginia Holland, daughter of Thomas Grady Holland, was born 15 February 1826, married Robert Myron Zimmerman of Kansas City, Missouri. Issue: Bobby Zimmerman, born 21 November 1952; Susan Zimmerman, born 29 June 1962.

iv. Mary Louise Holland, daughter of Thomas Grady Holland, was born 28 April 1929, married William Lester of Marietta. Issue: Earl Lester, born 23 January 1955,, married Cheryl Mitchell, born 5 December 1956. Cheryl married (2) Dr. Dennis Fielder; Ellen Lester, born 20 September 1964, unmarried.

v. Johnny Andrew Holland, son of Thomas Grady Holland, was born 5 January 1933, married Selba Jean Fouts. Issue: Linda Holland born 29 October 1960, married Treg Brown.

4. Willie Archibald Holland, son of Tone Holland (1901-1953) married Ruby Waite, died in Birmingham, Alabama. Issue:

    i. Willie Archibald Holland, Jr.
    ii. Gene Holland.
    iii. Dorothy Holland married Jack Robins.
    iv. Ann Holland.

5. Forrest R. Holland, son of Tone Holland, born 2 May 1904, died 14 January 1965, married Vera Pearson, born 28 January 1911, died 27 November 1957. Issue:

    i. Forrest Robert Holland, born 1952.
    ii.Infant, died 23 February 1932.

6. Harrison Ramsey Holland, son of Tone Holland, was born 1912 married Mildred Jerdon.

7. 1910-1910, baby, 3 mos. old.

8. Lessie May Holland, daughter of Tone Holland, born 1 June 1900, died July 1900, twin.

9. Millie Fay Holland, daughter of Tone Holland, born 1 June 1900, died July 1900, twin.

G. William Newton Holland, son of Henry and Sarah (Carlton) Holland, was born on 16 April 1867, died on 20 December 1938 in Paulding County, was buried New Hope Baptist Church Cemetery, Dallas, Paulding County. He married on 8 January 1888 in Paulding County, Fannie Evely Noland (born 8 January 1868 in Dallas, Georgia, died 4

1918 photo of William Newton Holland Family

October 1939 in Polk County)., also a daughter of William Aubrey Noland and his wife, Sarah Elizabeth Cheeves, buried in the Old New Hope Baptist Church Cemetery, in Dallas, Georgia.

Issue of William Newton Holland:

1. Dellie Mae Holland, daughter of William Newton Holland, was born 11 March 1889 in Rockmart, died 20 June 1957 in Powder Springs, buried New High Shoals Baptist Church Cemetery, Dallas, Georgia, married on 24 June 1906, Terrell Young Finch (born 14 December 1887) in Paulding County, died 20 January 1969 in Dallas, Georgia, buried High Shoals Baptist Church Cemetery, son of E. Oliver Finch (born 28 February 1805, died 17 June 1973), the son of William Edward Croker and Alice Kate Moon. SEE Finch. Issue:

2. William Aubrey Holland, son of William Newton Holland, was born Rockmart, Polk County, on 13 July 1891, died in Paulding County on 26 April 1966, buried Narroway Baptist Church, Dallas, Paulding County, married on 24 December 1911, Otela Igasccia Nix (born 29 August 1896 in Forsyth County, died 2 May 1971), buried in the Narroway Baptist Church Cemetery, Paulding County, the daughter of Dr. Charles Newton Nix (born 29 October 1864, died 24 March 1935) and Harriet Wilbanks (born 31 March 1872, died 12 December 1937), both buried New Canaen Paulding County. [229]

---

[229]   Aubrey Holland's obituary best describes him, published in the Dallas New Era:
"MR. AUBREY HOLLAND, RESPECTED AND BELOVED DALLAS MAN, PASSES Mr. William Aubrey Holland, well known and respected Dallas man passed away early Tuesday morning, April 26, 1966 at PauldLng Memorial Hospital. He was 74 years old. He had been in ill health for the past several months and a patient at the hospital for a week. Mr. Holland was born in Polk County on July 13, 1891, the son f the late William N. and Fannie Noland Holland. He had been married for 55 years to the former Otelia Nix, who survives. He had 1Lved in Paulding County for 65 years. Mr. Holland was wail known throughout the county. He had been associated with Wilbanks Gin County for many years prior to his retirement. He was a man of integrity and one who numbered his friends by his acquaintances...Funeral services were held Wednesday, April 27, at 2 o'clock P. M. at Narroway Baptist Church where he had been a member for 50 years...Besides his wife, he is survived by one daughter, Mrs. J. T. Morris of Dallas; one grandson, Mr. Jack Morris; one granddaughter, Miss Linda Morris; two brothers, J. M. Holland of Acworth and H, P. Holland of Atlanta; two sisters, Mrs. Glen Brown of Acworth, and Mrs. J. D. Carnes of Marietta; three brother-in-laws, Mr. Wade Goode of Bronswood, Mt. T. Y. Finch of Dallas and Mr. James Carnes of Whitesburg; and two sister-in-laws, Mrs. Clarice Holland of Atlanta sad Mrs. Dewey Holland of Savannah."

Issue of William Aubrey Holland:

 i. Infant Holland, born 9 March 1918, died 9 March 1918 in Paulding County, buried High Shoals Baptist Church Cemetery, Paulding County.

 ii. Mamie Lou Holland of Dallas, born 13 June 1919 in Paulding County, married on 22 October 1938 in Paulding County to J. T. Morris (born 11 October 1913 in Paulding County, died 30 April 1976, buried Dallas Memory Gardens, Paulding County, Ga.), son of Parks Henderson Morris (born 28 February 1878, died May 1951) and Ida Anderson (born 1888, died 21 December 1934), both buried Mt. Zion Baptist Church Cemetery, Paulding County. Issue:

  a. Jackie Dean Morris, born on 27 August 1939 in Fulton County, unmarried.

  b. Linda Lee Morris, born 30 September 1946 in Vero Beach, Indian River, Florida, married (1) Joe Lamar Postell (born 15 August 1946). Issue: Janet Leigh Postell (born 1 September 1969 in San Diego, California), and James Wesley Postell (born 8 October 1971 in Fulton County).

3. Lottie Lorene Holland, daughter of William Newton Holland, was born 20 May 1893 in Rockmart, Paulding County, died 22 November 1971 in Paulding County, buried Kennesaw Memorial Cemetery , Marietta, Cobb County, married on 28 March 1909 in Paulding County, Glen Smith Brown (born on 24 June 1890 in Paulding County, died 11 February 1978 in Paulding County, buried Marietta Cobb County.) SEE Brown.

4. James Monroe Holland, son of William Newton Holland , was born in Rockmart, Polk County, on 6 March 1895, died 8 November 1968 in Paulding Ca., Ga., buried Narroway Baptist Church Cemetery, Dallas, Paulding County, married on 10 January 1918, Clara Isabel Carnes, born in Paulding County on 31 October 1900, died 23 January 1983 in Paulding County, daughter of Richard Monroe Carnes (born 20 October 1869, died 3 January 1957), who was the son of James Thomas Carnes (born 1 January 1842, died 13 January 1927) and Margaret Catherine Watson (born 21 November 1845, died 5 March 1907) and Emma Jane Cochran (born 23 September 1873, died 15 February 1949), whom he married on 12 December 1891, the daughter of William Calvin Cochran (born 15 June 1839, died 19 April 1898) and Margaret Brown (1843-1881). James Monroe Holland was a school teacher at Harmony Grove School, and this is where he met his wife. After she graduated from his 7th grade, they were married. Later, he became a preacher at Narroway Baptist Church.

Children of James Monroe and Clara Holland:

 i. Lewell Gerome Holland, son of James Monroe Holland, born 14 October 1918 in Acworth, married at Dallas, Georgia on 28 December 1943, Vera Mae Lee, on 28 November 1943, Vera Mae Lee was born 28

November 1923 in Dallas, Georgia, the daughter of Ivey J. Lee and Hattie Camp. Children of Lewell Gerome Holland:

    a. Patricia Jane Holland, born 14 April 1945, unmarried.

    b. James Lewell Holland, born 1 September 1950 in Cartersville, unmarried.

    c. Carol Lawanna Holland, born 8 July 1954 in Dallas, Georgia, married in married 1979 Frank Pepper (died 1980. No issue.

    ii. Hubert Glenn Holland, son of James Monroe Holland, was born 15 November 1930 in Acworth, attorney in Marietta, married on 27 June 1959, Naomi Corley, born 9 March 1939 in Dallas, Georgia, tax accountant, the daughter of Amos Corley and Florence Malinda Tibbitts. No children.

5. Cassie Grace Holland, daughter of William Newton Holland, was born on 19 December 1896 in Rockmart, Polk County, and died on 9 May 1961 in Carroll County, buried in the Whitesburg City Cemetery, Whitesburg, Carroll County. (See group photo) married on 13 January 1917 or 1918 James Calvin Carnes (born 30 September 1895 in Paulding County, died on 20 March 1974 in Haralson County, buried in the Whitesburg City Cemetery, Carroll County). SEE Carnes.

6. Mattie Evelyn Holland, daughter of William Newton Holland, was born 3 July 1899 in Rockmart, Polk County, and died on 26 December 1965 in Americus, buried in Bronwood, Terrell County, Ga., (See group photo) married 16 December 1917 in Paulding County, Wade Herman Goode of Bronswood (born 28 September 1897 in Pickens County, died on 5 March 1969 in Albany, buried Bronwood), the son of James Wootsen Goode and Mary Sophranie.

7. Theodore Roosevelt Holland, son of William Newton Holland, was born 10 July 1901 in Rockmart, died 7 July 1943 in Atlanta, buried New Hope Baptist Church Cemetery, Dallas, married on 28 October 1923 in Paulding County, Clarice Wills (born 11 February 1904 in Paulding County, died 13 August 1978 in East Point, Fulton County, buried New Hope Baptist Church Cemetery, Paulding County), daughter of Dennis Franklin Wills and Lou Caroline Matthews. Issue:

    i. Joyce Evangeline Holland of Doraville, born on 9 August 1924 in Atlanta, married (1) on 9 July 1946 in John Lee Goodroe, Jr. (born 28 October 1918 in Waycross, Ware County), son of John Lee Goodroe, Sr. and Dora Bolton.

    ii. Janice Holland, daughter of Theodore Holland, was born 8 September 1927 in Atlanta, Fulton County, married (1) Thomas Hill Mebane, (2) John Wallace. Has two children.

    iii. Clyde Theodore Holland, son of Theodore Holland, was born 28 October 1938 in Atlanta, unmarried.

8. Dewey Lee Holland, son of William Newton Holland, was born 25 July 1904 in Dallas, Paulding County, died ca 1952, buried in Savannah, Ga., married abt. 1942 Susan Miller. No children.

9. Henry Pearman Holland, Sr. of Atlanta, Ga., son of William Newton Holland, was born on 1 August 1906 in Dallas, Georgia, died on 17 February 1977, buried in the Kennesaw Memorial Cemetery, Marietta, Cobb County, married on 2 November 1924, Linnis Crowe. Issue:

        a. James Douglas (Duggan) Holland.
        b. Henry Pearman Holland, Jr.
        c. Helen Holland married Mr. Tidwell.

10. Melba Zurlene Holland, daughter of William Newton Holland, of Marietta, was born on 27 February 1911 in Paulding County, married on 27 December 1930, J. D. Carnes (born 19 March 1908, son of Zack Carnes). Melba is 76 years of age (1987), confined to a wheelchair. Child: James Donald Carnes, born 25 November 1933, teacher at Georgia State College, Atlanta, Ga., lives Tallahassee, Florida. Don is a professor of History at the Florida State University, having travelled extensively throughout Europe in search of the history of the Hollands and Carnes.

VI. Sarah Ann Holland, daughter of Archibald Holland and Elizabeth Hagin, was born 22 August 1837 in Paulding County, and died 12 September 1910 in Paulding County, married (1) on 30 August 1857, Lindsey W. Elsberry in Paulding County, and (2) Burrell Marion Camp on 7 August 1870 Paulding County. Lindsey Elsberry served in the Civil War as a Pvt. in County A., Ga. Volunteers under Capt. Mathews, and died in a hospital on 13 September 1862 in Tennessee. He was the son of Lindsey Elsberry and Elizabeth Caldwell. Sarah had three children by Lindsey Elsberry, viz: Nannie, Alonzo, and Mary Elizabeth Elsberry, and two children by Burrell Marion Camp, viz: Anna and Rendy Ann Camp. SEE Elsberry and Camp.

VII. George Washington Holland, the son of Archibald Holland and Elizabeth Hagin was born 15 July 1839 at High Shoals, Paulding County, died 10 June 1896. Wash Holland was approximately 5 feet 9 inches tall, weighing over 250 pounds, blue-eyed, black-haired man who lived at High Shoals on a farm. Jesse Lee Holland, grandson of Henry Holland, told me that Wash Holland weighted about 270 pounds. He served in the Confederate Army in Virginia under General Lee, and was at the second Battle of Manassas (29 August through 30 August 1862) where he was wounded on the last day. Surgeons probed for the ball imbeded in his hip, but were unable to remove it. He was captured at the Battle of South Mountain and Antietam, later paroled 29 September 1862 at Warrenton, Virginia.[230]

---

[230] George Washington Holland in the Confederate Service, By Dorothy Holland Herring

"It is not known when he joined the company, since organization entailed a month or so and even then, the Confederate Service could not handle all the companies offered them and many had to wait until they could be accommodated. The Company was mustered in at Camp McDonald August 31, 1861 (A camp of instruction located north of Marietta, near Kennesaw, now called the Four-Lane). Prior of enlistment was *for the duration*. George Washington Holland was elected Third Sgt. (and was to so remain for the war) and Wyatt Lee, Corporal. Benjamin McCurry was elected Capt. of the Company and Robert Jones elected Colonel of the regiment. The regiment left for Virginia September 30 - Nov. 1, 1861. Nov. and Dec. 1861. Roll for Company "C" shows George Washington Hollan;i-present. The regiment was ssigned to General Blanchard's Brigade. It is not known if they were in Richmond or at Norfolk. Jan. and Feb. 1862. Roll for Company "C" shows George Washington Holland present. Blanchard's Brigade was by this time at Norfolk assigned to Major. Gen. Huger's (pronounced "U-Gee") Division, a semi-independent command, under the command of Gen. Joseph E. Johnston. Mar. and April 1862. Roll for Company "C" shows George Washington Holland present. Still at Norfolk. May 10, 1862. Samuel D. Holland arrived in Company "C", 22nd Regt. May 24, 1862. Norfolk evacuated. Division moved to Petersburg. Samuel D. Holland discharged.

Battle of Malvern Hill. Huger's Division, a large division about 9,000 or 10,000 strong (General J. E. Johnston said it was only about 8,000 but his figures have been successfully disputed) had been on garrison duty at Norfolk, Virginia. When Federal General George B. McClelland began his Penisula Campaign it was obvious that Norfolk would have to be given up. Its situation and lack of an adequate Confederate Navy made this imperative. Afterwards, president Davis accused Confederate General Johnston of evacuating Norfolk precipitously and abandoning equipment, etc. Major General Huger moved on Petersburg to await Johnston's orders to meet the threat posed by McClelland. Huger's Division, at this time, consisted of three brigades: Mahones, Armisteads and Blanchards. Yorktown and Williamsburg were given up after fighting a rear guard action and the Confederate Army withdrew north of the Chickahominy River and offered battle to the Federal forces pursuing. This was the position General Johnston had wanted to be from the start. May 29th, Huger's Division joined the main army and encamped east of Richmond on Gillis Creek north of the Williamsburg Road. Huger had bad luck; due to his Battle of the Axes he missed the Battle of Seven Pines fought on May 30th and 31st He subsequently missed all the Seven Days' Battles until the last one, Malvern Hill. Meantime, on June 1, 1862, Ambrose Ransom Wright, formerly Colonel of the 3rd Georgia Regt., took command of Blanchard's Brigade. On this same date, Robert E. Lee took command of the army after General Joe E. Johnston had been severely wounded at Seven Pines. Lee had no be tter luck than J ohn s ton commanding this unwieldly army. Confederate law forbade any military unit larger than a division and it was like operating twelve puppets with only ten fingers. Lee planned to attack with his whole army and drive the enemy from Richmond and perchance, from Virginia. The various divisions could not get into position at the right times and/or were impeded from carrying out their instructions however and the attacks were made by two or more divisions. Each day he tried again with the same results, while the Federals occupied the best positions. The enemy began withdrawing but couldn't be caught then either, as their withdrawals were made in better order than the Confederate advances. On June 29th, Huger was ordered to take the Charles City Road and strike the retreating Federals below White Oak Swamp. General Holmes was to take possession of Malvern Hill. Huger made no attack and when General D. H. Hill sent to ask why, Huger replied the toad was obstructed by fallen timber. The next day Mahone's Brigade skirmished with Federal General Slocum , but o therwise the division did no thing . Biovouacked at Brightwell's Farm just south east of White Oak Swamp, General Wright was ordered to start at daybreak the next morning, move down New Road, locate the enemy, and cover the enemy's left flank (which was commanded by Federal General Franklin). Accordingly, Wright having passed down New Road behind the Confederate artillery positions, and found no Federals except sttagglets: be reported to General Stonewall Jackson that he had completed his assignment. Apathically, Jackson told Wright he had no orders for him and suggested he retrace his steps and rejoin his division. Obediently and without debate, Wright marched back up the road and without assistance or a guide found Brackett's Ford at a distance of one mile. Enemy skirmishes, heavily obstructed and well covered by artillery, were discovered on the south bank. Then Wright marched three miles further upstream and crossed at Fisher's Ford. Jackson had not detailed an officer to see how Wright fared nor had he directed a report be made to him. The Division marched down Quaker Road to Longbridge Road about two miles and took position on the Confederate right, with brigades from General McGruder's Division. In the center was D. H. Hill and to the left, Whiting, Longstreet t and A. P. Hill remained at Longbridge Road in reserve, having fought alone the day before at Frayser's Farm. Generals Wright and Armistead made a reconnaissance of their own front. Armistead, not realizing he was the seniour officer on that flank (Huger remained behind on Longbridge Road), made no effort to extend his observations westward or to inform Lee. Armistead found ground where his own and Wright's men could be protected. The signal to advance was to have been a yell from Armistead when he observed Confederate artillery had broken the enemy's line. This condition wasn't met so the order to advance was given at about 4:45. Wright and Mahone 2500 strong emerged from the woods yelling and cheering. Wright was exhuberant; bareheaded, he waved his hat on the tip of his sword. There was a delay, however, and D. H. Hill, in the center, met the enemy alone and after a struggle of one and half hours was compelled to fall back. At sunset, the brigades on the right advanced, but they did not move together and were beaten in detail. They crossed a meadow half a mile though a ravine towards the Crew House on the hill. From 50 to 100 guns opened on them as soon as they appeared in the wheatfields, tearing great gaps in them, but the heroes reeled on and were shot down by reserves at the Federal guns, which a few reached. Heavy fire from Federal gun-boats in the James River raked them. General D. H. Hill said it was not war -it was murder!

May 31, 1862. Battle of Seven Pines, Hugers Division failed to take part due to General Longstreet's error for which Huger was blamed. George Washington Holland admitted to Chimbarago Hospital #4 at Richmond, Virginia for diarthea. This was a hospital complex located on a ridge east of Richmond. June 1, 1862. Ambrose Ransom (ranse) Wright was appointed Brig. Gen. in place of Blanchard. He was a 31-yr. old Georgia lawyer who had enlisted as private and was elected Colonel of the 3rd Ga. Infantty Regt. July 1, 1862. George Washington Holland returned to duty.

July 1, 1862. Battle of Malvetn Hill. July 8, 1862. Gen. Richard H. Anderson given command of Huger's Division. Gen. Huger transferred to the Trans-Miss. Dept. Hence: Gen. Lee II Corp. Longstreet, Anderson's Division, Wright's Brigade.

Battle of Second Manassas. When General McClelland retreated to his newly established base at Hartison's Landing, he settled down to recruit his men and await reinforcements from Lincoln. Only when he had his force up to 150,000 men would he resume operations against the Confederates, who now numbered 200,000 he claimed. Convinced McClelland was never going to achieve anything, Lincoln, instead of reinforcing McClelland began to draw off troops for duty in Northern Virginia. Then he ordered McClelland to bring his remaining forces to Alexandtia, Virginia where they, too were withdrawn from him, and added to General John Pope's army. So McClelland was a general without an army. He asked permission to accompany his troops and share their lot, even though he had no command. Permission was denied him. When Lee noted these withdtawals, he detached Jackson on July 13th to Gordonsville to deal with General Pope. In the meantime, Lee had formed the army with two "wings", commanded by Jackson and Longstreet. General Huger, who's performance had satisfied neither Johnston nor Lee, was transferred to TransMississippi along with General McGruder. Huger's division wasgiven to General Richard Heron Andetson to command on July 8, 1862. Anderson's Division was placed under the command of Longstreet.

By <u>August 15 th</u>, Longstreet's "wing" was di s pa tched to Gordonsville to join Jackson. leaving behind only the division of D. H. Hill to oppose McClelland. Jackson rapidly matched north, struck at Manassas Junction and captured supplies there and was gone before Pope could get wind of him. He finally found him at the old battlefield at Manassas. Elated, he attacked with his whole army! Jackson had chosen this position in advance. It was an old, unfinished railroad cut and was perfect for defense. The attack was fierce and sustained, but Jackson held out, for Longstreet was coming. Unknown to the Federals, Longstreet had left Gordonsville, encountered a small number of Federals at Thoroughfare Gap, which he brushed away, and was nearing the battlefield! Anderson's Division had been left behind at Gordonsville as a rear guard sad then they, too, headed for Thoroughfare Gap. On August 29th, Longstreet's lead divisions arrived at Manassas and formed at Wartenton-Gainesville-Centerville Pike just west of Pageland Lone. The next day, when most of his force had arrived, Lee anxiously asked if he was ready to attack Jackson was taking a beating. "Not yet!" Longstreet replied. The next day Lee again asked and again Longstreet said "Not yet ! " Federal Gene ral Pope did not know Longstreet was there; indeed was convinced that Longstreet was still at Gordonsville. That night, <u>August 30th</u>, Anderson's Division arrived. They marched forward almost into Federal lines but were alerted by General Hood just in time, Anderson withdrew to the rest and waited. The next day, <u>August 31st</u>, Longstreet finally advanced about 3:00 in the afternoon. It was not altogether a surprise, for Federal General John FitzPorter had discovered his presence and turned his division to face Longstreet, disobeying an order to attack Jackson. Pope refused to believe Longstreet was there and did so, long afterward. (FitzPorter was court-martialled for this and kicked out of the service. He probably had saved the army). Anderson's Division went in last, about 4:30, following General Flood, who was attacking the guns at the Henry House. Anderson's Division took the extreme right flank, the tip end of the scissors and by nightfull the Federals were in full retreat. George Washington Holland was wounded in this action. From Wright's Brigade 32 were killed, 150 wounded, and 8 missing. Anderson's Division: 72 killed, 364 wounded and 8 missing. Longstreet reported his losses as 663 killed, 4016 wounded and 46 missing. <u>Aug, 20, 1862. Battle of Second Manassas</u>. Brigade losses: 32 killed; 150 wounded, 8 missing. George Washington Holland was wounded (after 4:00 p.m., probably assaulting Henry House Hill). He "was snot in left hip and ball sagging down to near the knee, cutting one of the leaders in two, causing me to use crutches at times and a stick always. The wound has caused stiffness in hip joint and where the ball now is it has caused at various times the thigh to rise and cause a great deal of pain. (Aunt Lula Holland Reaten said that the surgeons probed but could not remove the ball. This wound caused his death in 1896, probably blood poisoning). Wounded left shoulder by a piece of shell, breaking left shoulder blade and can partly open and shut hand but cannot hold anything in the hand, giving me severe pain at times (Aunt Lula said he shoulder drooped)." This first wound was from a minnie ball, fired from a rifle, the second probably from artillery fire." Quotes from his pension application in 1893. <u>Sept. 29, 1862</u>. The next card says "Captured and paroled at Warren ton, Virginia, Sept. 29, 1862." He may have been in a hospital in Warrenton that was subjected to a raid on this date and   paroled the same day. It seems unlikely he was captured August 30 when the Confederates drove the Federals from Henry Hill. <u>Oct. 11, 1862</u>. George Washington Holland began convalescent leave of 60 days. While home, he received an additional 72 days upon certificate of a surgeon in Atlanta. During this time, General Lee invaded Maryland and the Battle of Sharpsburg was fought. Wright's Brigade served under Stonewall Jackson who had first captured Harper's Ferry. They arrived just in time for Sharpsburg. A. R. Wright and Col. Jones wounded in battle <u>Sept. 15th</u>. <u>Jan. 19, 1862</u>. George Washington Holland paid commutation rations for 60 days at Atlanta and examined by a surgeon who extended his leave for another 72 days. <u>Feb. 22, 1863</u>. George Washington Holland returned to duty at Fredeticksburg and applied for commutation rations for 72 days. Signed by Lt. Col. Joseph Wasden, a Lt. Commanding Co. R. of 22nd Regt. Wyatt Lee was now a Lt. in Company "C".

Chancellorsville. February 22, 1863 George Washington Holland returned from his convalescent leave. He could not walk except with the aide of a stick, nor could he hold anything in his left hand. These injuries would prevent him from matching and handling a rifle, but as a non-commissioned officer he probably was already mounted and armed with a pistol. He found Wright's Brigade camped south of Chancellorsville on the east side of Telegraph Road which runs southwesterly from Fredericksburg They were located just south of Massaponax Church, which was made famous a yeat later when General Grant had the pews taken out sad set under the trees and a series of photographs were made from a second-stoıy window.   George Washington Holland filed a claim for commutation of rations he furnished traveling home and back. This claim was notarized by a Justice of the Peace and was signed by Lt. Col. Wasden of the 22nd Regt. This was a trivial bit of red tape, but not usually found in Confederate soldiers muster cards. This brigade commander, A. R. Wright, was a lawyer in civilian life and it is possible that he advised George Washington Holland to file this claim. This may appear mote pertinent in events to follow. The Brigade was the only force in the immediate vicinity and they remained there until April 29th. That night, at 9:00 p.m., in a drenching rain, they marched north on Telegraph Road to just north of Massaponax Church and turned right. They took a position by a cemetery in the tear of General Early, as a reserve for him. Not needed for this purpose, they returned to Telegraph Road, turned right or north. A military road had been cut to the left, or west, linking Telegraph Road with Plant Road. They took this toad to Plank Road, taking position near Tabernacle Church. Plank Road was just what the name implies - wooden planks were laid across the road to provide passage in rainy weather. This Plank Road, called Orange Plank Road, tan parallel to Orange Turnpike to the north and ended at Orange Turnpike near Tabernacle Church. Zoar Church was also near here.Wright's Brigade took a position at Tabernacle Church, facing the road, towards the north. They had marched 27 miles that day! The reason for their movements was that the Federals, under General Joe Hooker, had crossed the Rappahannock River and were advancing towards a crossroads where they Chancellor family lived in a large two-story house.   April 30, 1863. The next day. Wright's Brigade turned, astrude Plank Road, facing towards Chancellorsville to meet the enemy should they advance down Plank Road. The Corps Commander, General Longstreet, was absent with two of his divisions having left behind Anderson's and McLaws' Divisions now under the personal command of General Lee. Lee, aware of Anderson's lethargic nature, directed him to go personally to U. S. Ford where two of his brigades were stationed and escort them back to Wright's position. (Usually Lee gave instructions to a general and left it up to him how he would carry out the instructions). These two brigades were commanded by Generals Mahone and Posey. Anderson brought Mahone sad Posey to the line already formed by Wright and extended it across to Orange Turnpike. At 2:00 p.m. that same day (April 30) Lee sent Anderson detailed instructions to dig trenches and prepare positions for additional troops he planned to send. This was the first time in history field fortifications were preplanned. They were also to cook rations for two days. The men worked on the trenches all night and then at 4:30 a. m., May Ist, they were ordered to advance. Wright and Posey took Plank Road and Mahone took Orange Turnpike. Just south of Aldritch, they took positions facing the road, Wright on the south side. The enemy was just ahead and it was now 12:30 p.m. When the soldiers saw Lee and Jackson riding down the road, a cheer went up. The men had complete faith in General Lee and probably had no idea how serious the situation was. Not only was Longs tree t absent with two of his solely needed divisions, bu t Lee had been forced to leave a division under General Jubal Early in Fredericksburg to hold in check Federal General Sedgewick, as well as a brigade to guard a bridge. Federal General Joe Hooker, however, had perfected plans that couldn't fail. His advance was strictly according to plan and everything was perfect. All that was needed was to follow through and administer the killing stroke. Hooker had a high opinion of himself and never moreso than now. Overcome with elation, he had made such remarks "God have mercy on Lee for I will have none" and "The Army of Northern Virginia is the legitimate property of the Army of The Potomac." He was right, too! His plans would work beautifully. His excitement grew until the night of April 29th, when he was beside himself with anticipation. By morning his mood had plunged to the bottom; he was haunted with all the "what if's" and became paralyzed, unable to act. The army continued to advance on its previous orders, but when the new orders and the go-aheads were sought, he withdrew into himself. His lead units had reached Chancellorsville, turned right and encamped near Wilderness Church in the absence of orders. It was these troops General Stuart's Cavalry had discovered, without protection to their right flank! Delighted, he took this news back to Lee. Meantime, Federal troops, under General Slocum, had begun advancing down Plank Road where Anderson's three brigades awaited them. There was some skirmishing, then unexpectedly, Slocum withdrew. (Hooker had become frightened). Ramseur's Brigade of Rodes Division was brought up to assist Wright and Posey, while the remainder of Rodes Division took a position on the right flank of Plank Road. A. P. Hill's Division came up behind Rodes in support. On hearing the news Stuatt brought, Jackson immediately proposed to flank them. He explained the route he would take and then Lee asked "Who would you take?" "My whole corps," Jackson answered. His corps included the division of Hill and Rodes, now in position on Plank Road. Jackson's plan would leave Lee with two divisions to face the whole Federal Army! Lee swallowed hard and said: "Okay." Jackson sent along a member of his staff with a local guide to check out the route so there could be no mistakes. At mid-day all the troops on Plank Road moved up north of the previous Federal advance, to above Decker. Wright was still in the front line. They slept here. The next morning, May 2nd, 8:00 a. m. Wright drew back south of Decker. Jackson pulled out his troops and begins his march. At 5:00 p.m. General Anderson, on his own, has Wright march south to the junction of Furnace Road and follow that to Catherine's Furnace to feel out the Federals. They drew up on the right of the toad, facing northwest. This move was to divert the Federals from learning of Jackson's advance. The 23rd Georgia Regt. just west of the furnace was sacrificed so that Jack son' s tail could be freed. In some sections the men were six feet apart, even after Kershaw's Brigade came to fill the gap between McLaw's left and Anderson's tight. Jackson's wagon train was attacked and Posey sent to their aide. Wright was sent in support. Posey found himself hotly engaged. Jackson arrived on the Federal's flank about this time, finding them not only with an unprotected flank, but no picketts posted. The Federals had stacked arms and were cooking their supper. They noticed a sudden rush of rabbits and other small animals from the woods running wildly through their campside, but only wondered. The Confederates suddenly burst from the woods, Yelling and firing. in panic, the Federals fled, bumping into other units who also fled, only a few having the presence of mind to a ttemp t a defense. The charge took them nearly to Chancellorsvflle before they met any real defense. By nightfall this had been silenced. Exhausted, the men tested. Jackson planned for A. P. Hill, bringing up the rest and still fresh, to launch an attack at 9:00 when all his troops would be up. North Carolina Troops were in the front line and they camped beside a narrow road off old Orange Turnpike, just west of Chancellorsville. Stonewall decided to recover the Federal position, and with his staff rode up this small road and took the first lane to the right. They could hear the Federals in their camp and satisfied, Stonewall retraced his steps. He hadn't gone very far down this road -- coming from the direction of the enemy -- when the N. 6. Troops, still edgy, opened fire on them. "Stop firing, we're friends," the group called out. The troops had heard that before, however, and continued their fire. Repeated calls were to no avail and Stonewall Jackson was hit in the arm, but kept his seat. We was struggling to control his horse and his aides suggested he dismount and they would carry him out. A litter was rigged up and four men picked it up, but the fire was so heavy, one was shot and another took his place. The litter was dropped several times before Stonewall Jackson could be gotten out. A. P. Mill had arrived on the scene and was shot in the foot. Finally, the North Carolina troops were prevailed upon to cease fire and the party made their way out. A. P. Hill was second in command, but as he was wounded, the next in command was deemed too inexperienced to take over, so General Stuart was given temporary command.

A. P. Hill's attack, therefore, was not made, and the next day Stuart resumed the general attack. Back at Catharine's Furnace, the morning of flay 3, 1563, Wright and Posey were a mile beyond the other forces - inviting destruction. At 7:30 Mahone joined them and turning the brigades facing north they began moving in that direction over difficult ground; the forge was too small to cover their front. Su ppor ted by three guns on their left, Wright, with 1600 men, swept the tangle of woodland on a front of one mile. Re contracted his line them, and threw out skirmishers. Led by General Lee, they forced the Federals back until the Rained the heights at Fairview and commanded the enemy guns. Stuart had pushed his attack hard but made no headway until he had almost reached the conclusion his attack had failed. Just then, he heard guns from Fairview and the enemy in front ran. It was Lee! Just in time! The two forces were re-united, forming a solid line with Wright's Brigade in the center. Wright con tinued to mee t resistance, They were the first to reach Chancellorsville, where the Chancellor house was on fire. Seeing Lee ride up to the Chancellor house, Anderson's men were wildly jubilant. It was about 10:00 a.m. Federal General Joe Hooker had been unable to give orders when Jackson's attack took place. He was suffering from dislocation of the brain. He had made the Chancellor house his headquarters, and in the afternoon was standing on the porch when a shell struck a column nearby. He fell off the porch - on his head. Though he was able to mount his horse, he gradually became paralyzed the rest of his life. Lee had given orders to pursue the enemy when he got news tha t Federal General Sedgefield at Fredericksbutg had a ttacked Early and had broken out. Lee's tear was threatened. He detached two brigades, Wilcox and ---- to Salem Church to attack the Federals in front of that place and Early could attack the rear. Wilcox could not bring himself to attack and repeated orders from Lee did no good. Lee finally had to give up hope of pursuit and personally lead Wright's Brigade and launched the attack himself. The threat was finally removed, but the day was gone. Another lost opportunity! April 16, 1863. George Washington Holland paid $23.76 commutation rations for 72 days upon notarized receipt signed by Joseph Wasden who had been elected Lt. Col. 6/2/1862. George Washington Holland gave receipt to J. L. Keith, Asst. Quartermaster. July 2, 1863. Second Day at Gettysburg. Wtigh t' s Bri gade assaulted Federal Center on Cemetery Ridge at either 5:30 or 6:30 p.m. The Brigades on either side failed and Wright found himself surrounded, 1 mile in front of all other Confederate forces. They cut their way out, losing most of the brigade. Col. Wasden was killed (Wright erroneously called him Col. Hall). Adj. J. D. Daniel was captured. July 3, 1863. Third Day at Gettysburg, Picketts Charge, Wright's Brigade standing by to support the charge but Gen. Lee decided not to support it. Various members of Company "C" were captured this day, including Wyatt Lee, so it is possible the regiment itself went into the charge, though I have found no mention of this. Brigade Loss: 40 killed, 295 wounded, 333 missing. June 14, 1863. Anderson's Division started for Culpepper. George Washington Holland followed the next day. They (with Fender Division) proceeded to Culpepper, Front Royal, Bertyville, Charlestown, Shepardsown, Boonsborough to Hagerstown. Thence, the line of advance was Cbambersburg and Faye tteville. The troops matched 15-20 miles a day, with no stragglers. Pendet and Heth proceeded to Cashtown. 5:00 a.m. Heth's Division marched to Gettysburg where it was believed only Federal Cavalry met Feds in force. July 1, 1863. Anderson's Division, still at Fayetteville, moved to Cashtown. Heth's Division attacked an unknown Federal Force at Gettysburg. They

Because of wounds received, Wash Holland was sent home where he remained from October 11, 1862 to March 1863 when he returned to General Lee's Army in Virginia and fought in the Battle of Chancellorsville May 1, 1863 where he was wounded again. He also fought at Gettysburg. He later received the meager pension of $50.00 per month, having achieved the tank of Sergeant and receiving shell wounds in his tight arm and a ball in his leg. Because of war wounds Wash Holland could only plow for short intervals, and sent his sons to plow while he heed. He spent much time reading the Bible, local newspaper and a Republican newspaper, The Cincinnati News. Hollands were Republicans. The farm of his father-in-law, one mile southeast of McPherson, was heavily wooded, and Burrell Camp, having no sons to clear the land, swapped farms with Wash Holland. The children attended High Shoals and Mt. Olivet .schools, a walk of about three miles. Wash Wash solved this problem by donating land at Candy Ridge for a school, helping build it, and boarding the teachers.

George Washington Holland was married on 18 January 1866, in Paulding County, Lydia A. Camp (born 26 December 1849, died 27 August 1883), the daughter of Rev. Burrell Marion Camp and his wife, Mary E. Stegall. When already a grown man, Wash declared that he would wait for the lovely Lydia Camp to grow up and marry her. It was said that she had auburn hair and "was a pretty little thing". When Lydia was dying in 1853, two years after the birth of their last child, she selected her husband's second wife. SEE Camp. [231]

Wash Holland married (2) on 20 December 1883 in Paulding County, Mary Jane Henderson Elsberry (buried Friendship Cemetery, Paulding County), the daughter of Robert Mitchell Henderson and Louise Goode. Her brothers and sisters were: W. C. Henderson of Villa Rica, James Thomas Henderson of Villa Rica, Noah Jeff Henderson of Villa Rica, and J. H. Henderson of Dallas, Louise Mitchell Henderson, born 14 April 1852, died 9 November 1943, married Floyd Madison McClung, lived at Dallas, buried at Mt. Zion. Mary Jane Henderson Elsberry (later Holland) married (1) on 11 September 1859 in Paulding County, M. M.

---

were successful, but sustained heavy casualties. Federals increased their forces. July 2, 1863. 4:00 p. m. Anderson's Division were to attack by Brigade: Wflcox first, Perrys, Wrights, then Posey, with Mahone in Reserve. 6:20 p.m. the attack begins.

April 10, 1865. George Washington Holland was captured and received at Harts Island, in the New York Harbor, from New Bern, North Carolina. Received by Capt. Perkins and assigned to Co. 25. Member of Company "A", 22nd Regt. June 15, 1865. George Washington Holland released on oath of allegiance. Remarks: Born Jones County, and place of residence, Jones County, Ga. Complexion: Light. Hair: Light. Eyes: Grey. Height 5 ft. 9 in. (Note: There was no such person in Co. "A", but Co. "C". There was no such person in Jones County, Ga. There were no Jones Co. companies in 22nd Regt. and no such person served in a Jones Co. Co. So this is an error).
Casual ties:

[231] Wash's daughter, Lula Holland Keaten who lived in Atlanta. I me t her for the first time When I went to visit her in Atlanta before Uncle Alton died. Aunt Lula told me what she knew about the family, but did not know her great-grandfather's (William) name. Her grandfather, Archibald, was the first Holland to Paulding County, and since his father, William, died before 1840, his children could not have remembered much about him. Aunt Lula did say that she had an Uncle William who travelled a great deal and sometimes visited them on the farm.

Elsberry, and she was the mother of two children by her first husband, M. M. Elsberry, viz: Walton L. Elsberry, born 21 November 1862, died 29 May 1950, buried Cullman, Alabama, married 15 November 1887 in Paulding County, Fannie Hagan; and Lou Elizabeth Elsberry, born 20 July 1860, died 29 September 1938, married on 21 December 1881, Patrick Henry Winn (born 1 February 1859, died 17 June 1901), both buried at Friendship Cemetery, Paulding County.

Issue of Wash and Lydia Holland:[232]

A. Johnny Holland, son of Wash and Lydia Holland, born and died 1866.

B. Silas Casey Holland, son of Wash and Lydia Holland, was born 13 January 1868, died 15 July 1933. He married (1) Vicki Moon, and, (2) Susie Elizabeth Keaten. SEE Keaten.

1. Lydia Holland, daughter of Silas Casey Holland, married John Lang. Issue:

i. Barbara Lang who married Bill McCollum.
ii. Ruth Lang who married Jack Sanders.

2. Hettie Holland, born 1882, married Jim Estes. Issue: Herbert Estes married Louise Brown of New Mexico; Ima Estes a. Ist Cecil Otwell, (2), Vernon Brooks; Inez Estes, married (1) J. T. Norton, (2) Julius Cangelosi of New Jersey (children, Everett Norton, Janet Cangslosi, Laarie Cangelosi); and Reba Holland Estes married Ben Hill (children, Ramona, Susan and Vicki Hill).

3. Mary Holland, deceased, married Shirley Adams. Issue: Floy, Leslie, Dewey and I. J. Adams.

4. Emery Holland, born 1900 married Hattie Waite. Son, Jack Holland.

5. Louella Holland, born 1904, married Ed Hill. Son, Jerry Hill, born 1930, married Mary Morcock.

C. Mary Elizabeth Holland, daughter of Wash and Lydia Holland, was born 26 December 1871, died in Gadsden, Alabama. On 20 May 1928, she married Thomas Walton Durham, born 27 April 1876, died 24 May 1946. SEE Durham.

D. Charles Hartwell Holland, son of Wash and Lydia Holland, born 22 May 1874, died 1 July 1934, married on 17 October 1900, Alice V. Howell (born 27 March 1881, died 6 November 1925).

Issue of Hart and Alice Holland:

---

[232] 1880 Paulding County Census, Burnt Hickory.

1. Thelmer Holland, born 1 June 1907, died 28 February 1948, married Elsie Lee Johnson who was born on 29 September 1913. Thelmer worked for the railroad. When he was fired from his job, he came home and shot himself. Buried Mt. Olivet Baptist Church Cemetery, Dallas, Georgia.

2. Clarence D. Holland (1901-1965), married Irene Bullock. Had a store in Dallas. During the 1920's. Issue of Clarence and Irene Holland:

    i. Clarence D. Holland, Jr., born 1921, married Gloria Burnet (Issue: Jack, Steve, Mike and Gloria Jean Holland).

    ii. Josephine Holland, born 22 October 1927, married William Daniel Crawford in 1948. Her Issue: William Daniel Crawford, Jr., born 1953; Jeffry Crawford, born 1955.

3. Virginia Holland, born 1916, married Lake Sisson. Issue: Alice Louise Sisson, born 1942; Virginia Elizabeth Sisson, born 1944, married William Harrison, Jr.; Cindy Lake Sisson; and Dorotheanna Sisson, born 1951.

4. Louise Holland born 1913 Paulding County, married Roger Nixon Reynolds, Jr., (born 1918 Atlanta, Georgia), resides near Winston Salem, North Carolina. Issue of Louise Holland Reynolds:

    i. Linda Reynolds born 1941 Miami, Florida married Dr. Robert D. Fox.
    ii. Dr. Roger Nixon Reynolds III, born February 1947 in Winston Salem, North Carolina.
    iii. Susan Nixon, born 1955 in Winston-Salem, North Carolina, (div.)

E. James Tom Holland, son of Wash and Lydia Holland, was born in Paulding County on 11 October 1876, and died in Paulding County on 26 February 1939. He was buried Mt. Olivet Baptist Church Cemetery. He owned a store at McPherson, Georgia, where railroad section-hands lived in huts. He was married to Willie Florence Collins (born 1 September 1844, died 7 October 1914) on 2 December on 1900 at Dallas, Georgia, the daughter of Thomas M. Collins and Nancy Carrie Lane, all buried at Mt. Olivet Baptist Church Cemetery, neat Dallas, Ga. "Sister" died at the age of 30. Tom had just built a new house at McPherson and they moved into it before it was completely finished. One night, she crawled into bed and was bitten by a rat. Shortly afterwards, she was sick with fever. The doctor was called, but she soon died. The house was never finished, and Tom Holland lived it until his death. After her death, her sister, Ida Collins Johns helped raise the Holland children. Of necessity, the Holland boys became independent and self-sufficient, all of them learning to cook from an early age. SEE Collins.

Tom, as he was known, had influenza in February of 1939, and was at home sick, when some neighbors came to his home, because they needed groceries. Tom was too sick to walk, so the neighbors put him inside of a wheelbarrow, and pushed him to the store. Tom worked as a section hand for the Southern Railroad, and for two years was foreman at a mill at Vinings, Ga. He also farmed, but 10-15 years before his death he ran Dallas Grocery Company at Dallas, Ga., cotton buyers and dealers in staples and grains and feeds. Also, Tom was a Trustee for Willow Springs School.

233

Unlike his father and his stout uncles, he was a tall, slender man with dancing eyes and long eyelashes, eviden try taking af ter his mother, Lydia Camp Holland reportedly a "pretty little thing." Tom Holland ran the store at McPherson many people lived on credit, while others never paid. In 1939, while too sick to work, a local resident insisted be open up the store. It was a cold February and Tom, too sick to walk, was put inside a wheelbarrow and wheeled to the store. Not long afterward, he died. Later, relatives felt that the experience in inclement weather had "done him in." After his death, the store was run for several years by Pleas Craton. The old account book is at Pleas' house, inside a bureau drawer, with page after page of unpaid hills by citizens of McPherson. Tom Holland owned a house "across the creek" at McPherson which he later rented to a sharecropper who raised cotton in the 180-acre bottom land. Later, he built a house identical to Hart Holland's, however, Tom never really finished his.[233]

Issue:

1. Eugene Holland was born 22 September 1901, and died 27 December 1965, He married Mable Smith, the daughter of William J. and Mattie Smith. After their divorce, Mable married (2) Robert A. Blackwell. By her second husband she had Issue: Robert J. Blackwell and Mary Alice Blackwell who married Arthur Woodrum, Professor at Georgia Southern, Statesboro. In his younger years, Eugene was a Master Mechanic, which meant good pay and status over other mechanics. In 1923, Eugene was a member of the Capitol City Lodge #642, F. & A. M., holding a highly respected office in the Masons. After his wife divorced him, he became a roamer, grieving over his loss. When he refused to pay child support, his wife had him jailed several times. Once she had him released upon the advice of Uncle Alton who said "He can't make money in jail." Yet, he swore never to pay child support. Little is known of his career after that. As a child we seldom saw him. Once, he lived with us on Whitefoard Avenue, occupying the back room. In 1955 he attended daddy's funeral in Charlotte, North Carolina. He was timid, tall, slender, handsome, having silver hairs around the temples. He was found dead with bruises on his face. The family thought he was probably beaten and robbed.
Issue:

i. William Thomas Holland, born 28 February 1926, Retired Lt. Colored in U. S, A. F. married Lillian Jones (divorced). Bill resides in at Sharpsburg, Georgia. (Peachtree City).

2. Laurel Benjamin Holland, son of James Tom Holland and Willie Florence Collins, was born 13 February 1902 in McPherson, Paulding County, Georgia, near Dallas. He died July 28, 1959 in Charlotte, North Carolina. Daddy was a short, blackheaded mao with gray eyes, stocky build, immensely handsome in

[233] MCPHERSON, GA. (ghost-town). Directions: Hwy 275 thru Dallas. 1.8 miles from City Limits turn tight, High Shoals Road (unpaved). Sign on right: Mt. Olivet Church. Pass under railroad tressle. Turn left on Bob Howell Road. Pass McPherson Baptist Church test. about 1913) on right. Enter unpaved road to above site. McPherson was a village of abt 40 houses, where railroad sectionbands lived. Although this site is not flat and has a deep ravine, houses were tightly situated. Crossing the tracks, the depot was between two buildings.

his youth. As children we used tosay that he resembled the movie star, George Raft. Daddy's appearance typified that of modern-day Hollands, with round innocent eyes, but a set, determined expression. Daddy had brothers, Eugene and Alton. Daddy and Alton loved to return to McPherson and visit their relatives, even after both were married and had families of their own. Daddy frequently stuffed his five children into the Ford for weekend visits. During the early years of their marriage, daddy travelled, selling insurance. Consequently, our family lived briefly at Cowpens, South Carolina as well as Abbeville, where Dorothy was born. He married 1st, Helen Smith of Villa Rica, by whom he had 3 children. Helen and the children died young. He married 2nd, Marguerite Elizabeth Evans on 18 October 1930 in Atlanta.

Issue of Laurel Benjamin and Marguerite Elizabeth Evans Holland:

> i. Marianne Holland, daughter of Laurel Benjamin Holland, was born on 4 November 1931 in Atlanta, married (1) 29 April 1950, Haig Daniel Keishian, son of Haig Keishian and Iona Mitchell of Atlanta and had three Issue: Karen Joy, Julia Gay and Stephen Daniel Keishian. Marianne married (2) Robert DeCotte Tobin and had one son, Robert DeCotte Tobin, Jr. Issue by 1st husband:

>> a. Karen Joy Keishian, daughter of Marianne Holland Keishian and Haig Daniel Keishian, was born 7 January 1956 in Atlanta.

>> b. Julie Gay Keishian, daughter of Marianne Holland Keishian and Haig Daniel Keishian, was born 5 March 1960 in Atlanta. She resides in Boone, North Carolina.

>> c. Stephen Daniel Keishian, son of Marianne Holland Keishian and Haig Daniel Keishian, was born 10 June 1964 in Atlanta.
> Issue by 2nd husband:
>> d. Robert DeCotte Tobin, Jr., son of Marianne Holland and Robert DeCotte Tobin, was born 13 March 1975 in Atlanta.

> ii. Laurel Benjamin Holland, son of Laurel Benjamin Holland and Marguerite Elizabeth Evans was born on 8 April 1934 in Georgetown, South Carolina, died 1999 in Cary, North Carolina. He was married on 16 June 1954 Barbara Cowan in Charlotte, North Carolina. Barbara was born on 19 December 1935, the daughter of Kenneth Cowan. The family resided in Cary, North Carolina, where Ben was postmaster for many years. Issue of Ben and Barbara Holland:

>> a. Linda Sue Holland, born 4 July 1955 in Charlotte, North Carolina married on 15 September 1973, Mare Paine, born on 25 January 1953. Issue: Leslie Anne Paine, born 9 September 1976, Abigail Leigh Paine,

235

born 11 June 1978, and Megan Alisa Paine, born 8 July 1981.

b. Anna Lisa Holland, born 28 July 1961 in Charlotte, North Carolina, married on 19 February 1984 Michael Fosdick, born 6 July 1953. Issue: Rebecca June Fosdick, born 7 August 1984, Christina Michelle Fosdick, born 20 October 1986.

c. Kenneth Edward Holland, born 22 February 1964 in Charlotte, North Carolina.

iii. Jeannette Holland, daughter of Marguerite Elizabeth Evans and Laurel Benjamin Holland, was born on 28 July 1936 in Atlanta. She married (1) on 25 April 1853 in Rockmart, Georgia, Edwin Gerald Stucki (divorced), son of Edwin Gottfried Stucki and his wife, Sarah Elizabeth Lee of Atlanta, and had one daughter, Suzanne Teri Stucki, born 27 March 1960 in Atlanta, Georgia. Jeannette married (2), 1975 Kenneth Milton McCall (divorced), and (3), on 13 May 1977 at Jekyll Island, Georgia, Jerry Franklin Austin.
Issue of Jeannette Holland:

a. Suzanne Teri Stucki, daughter of Jeannette Holland and Edwin Gerald Stucki was born on 27 March 1960, Crawford Long Hospital, Atlanta, Georgia. Teri married Kevin Skedsvold. Teri was baptised a member of The Church of Jesus Christ of Latter-Day Saints. Teri graduated from Aiken High School, Aiken, South Carolina, and attended Charleston College, Charleston, South Carolina, and Georgia State College, where she graduated in 1987 .She is employed as a real estate agent. SEE Skesvold.

b. Christopher Lewis Austin, son Jeannette Holland Austin and Jerry Lewis Austin, was born on 19 March 1978, Clayton General Hospital, Riverdale, Georgia. School. Baptized 20 March 1988, The Church of Jesus Christ of Latter-Day Saints. Christopher died in Roswell, Georgia on 28 December 2002. SEE Austin.

iv. Dorothy Elizabeth Holland, born 24 July 1937 in Abbeville, South Carolina, married William Frank Herring in Charlotte, North Carolina. Issue:

a. Frankie Herring.

v. Marie Eleanor Holland, born 1942, married (1) Bing Robinson (2) Derwood Johnson (3) Donald Carroll Roach, (4) Robert Bennett.

a. Deborah Ann Robinson, daughter of Marie Holland and Bing Robinson, was born 17 March 1959 in Charlotte, North Carolina married December 1987 Harold Walley, Rock Hill, South Carolina. (6 children). Issue:

> i. Linda Marie Walley, born September 1983.
> ii. Susan Walley, born 1 April 1987.
> iii. George Walley.

b. Gary James Robinson, son of Marie Holland and Bing Robinson, was born 15 June 1960 in Charlotte, North Carolina, married on 6 December 1886 to Leta Dover, Salt Lake CIty, Utah Temple, both members of The Church of Jesus Christ of Latter-Day Saints. Son: Michael Scott Robinson, born 16 October 1987, Charlotte, North Carolina, and John Robinson..

c. Julie Renee Robinson, born 5 July 1961, married on 17 October 1978, Robert Wallace (divorced). Daughter: Taniese Eleanor Wallace, born May 1979, Tucker, Georgia.

d. Anthony Ray Johnson, son of Marie Holland Robinson Johnson and Derwood Johnson, was born on 4 April 1968 in Statesville, North Carolina. Anthony is a very talented comedian, and has entertained in The Comedy Inn in Charlotte. Has three children.

3. Thomas Alton Holland was born on 25 January 1906 in Paulding County, and died in Atlanta on 11 November 1869, He as married on 13 March 1929 to Nona Belle Thomas (born 13 August 1905 in Paulding County, died 17 June 1985 in Douglasville, Georgia, buried in the Willow Springs Baptist Church Cemetery, Dallas, Georgia.. Uncle Alton lived in the West End Section of a Atlanta for many years and died about 1965 of lung cancer. All three of the Holland brothers were fun-loving boys, loving to drink and gamble. Uncle Alton had a wonderfully sweet wife, Nona Belle, whom he married in Dallas, Georgia. At first, daddy courted Aunt Nona, then met Mama. Aunt Nona later recounted to me that she had her mind set on "catching one of them Holland boys!" Aunt Nona was easy-going, kind and kind and gentle, bearing troubles with smiles. Son:

a. Thomas Alton Holland, born on 8 February 1931 in Atlanta, married Jean Stinchcomb (divorced) and had one child, Nona Lee Holland, who was born on 28 April 1955 in Atlanta, married on 7 November 1986, Gary Wilshire (residents of Roswell, Georgia). They have one child: Stephen Holland Wilshire, born on 28 September 1987.

VII. William Holland, son of George Washington Holland, 1879-1886.

VIII. Lula Ann Holland, daughter of George Washington Holland, was on 31 March 1881, married on 8 May 1898, William Robert Keaten (born 31 October 1876, died 1962) of Carroll County. She died in 1967 or 1968, Atlanta, Ga. Before her father's death (George Washington Holland), he told her to go with her grandpa Burrell Marion Camp who swapped farms with her father. She was fifteen years old at the time and recalled her father's tales about the Civil War. Two years later, she married and moved to Douglasville, where all her children were born. SEE Keaten.

Howard of Jackson County

Hardy Howard was born 1777 in South Carolina and died 1859 in Jackson County, Georgia. He married Elizabeth Camp, a daughter of Nathaniel Camp and his wife, Winnifred (Tarpley) Camp. SEE Camp. Hardy Howard's LWT dated 13 August 1859, probaed 12 September 1859 in Jackson County Will Book A, page 431. Hardy Howard is listed on the 1830-1840 Jackson County Census. After his death, Elizabeth married (2) Samuel Stewart, and (3) Rev. James Gideon. Elizabeth Camp had 22 children in all. The LWT of her second husband, James Gideon, dated 6 June 1803, probated 4 August 1817 in Jackson County Will Book A, page 68.

Issue:[234]

I.   Samuel Howard.

II.   Emily Almeda Howard, born 12 March 1824, married Hugh M. Niblack on 25 September 1839 in Jackson County.

III.   Amanda Howard, married Green M. Duke.

IV.   Harper H. Howard married Malinda C. Borders on 4 January 1838 in Jackson County. Issue:
    A.   John Howard, born 1842 Jackson County.
    B.   Harper Howard, born 1844 Jackson County.

V.   Elizabeth Howard, married Mr. Webb.

VI.   Hartsford Howard married Louisa C. Niblack, on 4 August 1845 in Jackson County..

VII.   Malissa Howard, married G. V. Braselton on 29 November 1845 in Jackson County.

VIII.   Homer R. Howard, born 10 December 1829 Jackson County, died 28 March 1903, buried in the Howard Family Cemetery on Hwy 124 East, Jefferson, Georgia. Wife, Martha E., born 25 January 1837, died 4 March 1910. They were residents of Jackson County, in 1880. Issue:[235]
    A.   Zachira T. Howard (son), born 1855 in Jackson County.
    B.   Harry R. Howard, born 1860 in Jackson County.
    C.   Robert L. Howard, born 1865 in Jackson County.

---

[234] Jackson County Wills; 1830-1850 Jackson County Census; Jackson County Tombstones by Jeannette Holland Austin.

[235] 1860-1880 Paulding County Census; Paulding County Marriages.

D. Julius O. Howard, born 1867 in Jackson County.

E. James W. Howard, born 1870 in Jackson County.

F. Frank Howard, born 1875 in Jackson County.

G. Lillie A. Howard, born 1878 in Jackson County.

Howell of Paulding County

Thomas C. Howell was born 1834 in North Carolina. He married Adaline Robinson on 16 December 1854 in Paulding County, however, Sarah, born 1836, was listed as his wife on the 1860 -1880 Census. The family was listed on the 1880 Paulding County Census, Dallas, Georgia. Issue:[236]

I.   Henry Howell, born 1855 in Paulding County, married Laura Baxter on 1 October 1872 in Paulding County.

II.   Joseph B. Howell, born 27 October 1857 in Paulding County, died 30 October 1891 in Dallas, Paulding County, buried in the Mt. Olivet Cemetery. He married Judy Emma Lane (born 26 March 1859, died 3 January 1942 Dallas, Georgia, buried Mt. Oliver Cemetery), the daughter of James C. Lane and his wife, Nancy (Williams) Lane. SEE Lane and Williams. Issue:
    A.   Alice Howell.
    B.   Winnie Howell.
    C.   Lee E. Howell, born August 1874 in Paulding County.
    D.   Joe Howell.

III. Green Howell, born 1860 in Paulding County, farmer.

IV.   Mary J. Howell, born 1869 in Paulding County.

V.   Thomas C. Howell, born 1871 in Paulding County. He married Lucinda Bradbury on 22 June 1892 in Paulding County.

VI.   Benjamin F. Howell, born 1873 in Paulding County. He married Mattie Mintz on 14 September 1890 in Paulding County.

Huckaby of Lee & Jones Counties

James Huckaby was born ca 1772 and died 1840-1850 in Lee County, Georgia. Issue:[237]

I.   Felix Huckaby was born ca 1799, married Nancy Brown on 30 December 1816 in Jones County.

II.   William Huckaby was born ca 1801 in Monroe County, died ca 1859, married Nancy Reaves on 20 December 1821 in Jones County.

III. Mariah Huckaby was born 1803 in Monroe County.

---

[236] 1880 Jackson County Census, District. 245.

[237] Jones County Marriages; 1850 Lee County Census.

IV. Polly Huckaby was born 1805 in Monroe County, died 16 September 1881, married William Chambliss on 23 December 1823 in Jones County. SEE Chambliss.

V. Jane Huckaby was born 18 February 1807 in Monroe County, married Jessie Slocumb on 23 December 1828 in Jones County.

VI. Seaborn J. Huckaby was born 1808 in Jones County, died 13 October 1855.

VII. Simon Huckaby was born 1810 in Jones County. Wife, Elizabeth, born 1812 in Georgia. Listed on 1850 Lee County Census. Issue:

    A. James Huckaby, born 1835 Lee County.
    B. Elizabeth Huckaby, born 1836 Lee County.
    C. Felix A. T. Huckaby, born 1838 Lee County.
    D. Samuel W. Huckaby, born 1840 Lee County.
    E. Nancy Huckaby, born 1843 Lee County.
    F. John Huckaby, born 1844 Lee County.
    G. Charles T. Huckaby, born 1845 Lee County.
    H. Mariah Huckaby, born 1846 Lee County.
    I. Narcissa R. Huckaby, born 1849 Lee County.
    J. Unnamed daughter, born 1850 Lee County.

VIII. George Washington Huckaby was born 4 December 1811 in Jones County, died 12 May 1881, married Elizabeth Tinsley. Listed on 1850 Sumter County Census.

IX. Charles Pinckney Huckaby was born 29 November 1813 in Jones County, died 20 December 1865. Wife, Narcissa, born 1820 in Georgia. Listed on 1850 Lee County Census. Issue:

    A. Louisa Huckaby, born 1837 Lee County.
    B. Mary M. Huckaby, born 1839 Lee County.
    C. James G. Huckaby, born 1844 Lee County.
    D. William F. Huckaby, born 1846 Lee County.
    E. Martha Huckaby, born 1847 Lee County.

X. James Andrew Huckaby was born 1815 in Jones County, died 1864, married Nancy L. Forehand.

Johns of Paulding County

John Johns was born ca 1780 and was listed on the 1820 Madison County, Georgia Census. He had 4 sons and 4 daughters. Apparently he died after that. The 1860 Paulding County Census lists Pheba Johns, born 1780 in Virginia with two daughters matching the ages of John John's children, viz, Harriett and Ann. Living nearby was her son, W. Johns. Known Issue:[238]

I. Harriett Johns, born 1816 in South Carolina, never married.

II. Ann Johns, born 1818 in South Carolina, never married.

---

[238] 1830 Madison County Census; 1860-1870 Paulding County Census; Paulding County Marriages; Mt. Olivet Cemetery, Dallas, Georgia.

III. W. Johns, born 1820, died before 1880, farmer at Dallas. Wife, Elizabeth, born 1824, who is listed on the 1880 Paulding County Census, Dallas, Georgia, with her children. Issue:

A. James J. Johns, blacksmith, born 1842. He married Elender Moore (born 1839 Georgia) on 18 December 1860 in Paulding County. Issue:
    1. Georgia Johns, born 8 October 1868, died 7 June 1906 in Paulding County. She married Samuel D. Holland.
    2. Sarah Johns, born 1867 Paulding County.
    3. John Johns, born 1868 Paulding County.
    4. William Johns, born 1869 Paulding County.

B. Margaret Johns, born 1846.

C. John Johns, born 1852.

D. Bartlett Johns, born 1854.

E. Mary Johns, born 1854.

F. William H. Johns, born 10 February 1855 Paulding County, died 25 August 1941 Dallas, Paulding County, buried Mt. Olivet Cemetery. He married on 14 May 1876, Louisiana Collins, the daughter of Humphrey Collins and his wife, Elizabeth (Bone) Collins. SEE Collins. Issue:[239]
    1. Radford L. Johns, born 3 August 1878 in Paulding County, died 23 November 1914, buried Dallas City Cemetery. He married on 20 August 1899, Ida Genette Collins. SEE Collins.
    2. Robert L. Johns, born 1876 Paulding County, died 1962. Wife, Margaret E. (1882-1940), buried Dallas City Cemetery.
    3. W. L. Johns married Mattie Brown.
    4. Son, born 12 January 1881 Dallas, Paulding County, buried 1884 in Mt. Olivet Cemetery.
    5. W. H. Johns, born 6 November 1882, died 15 April 1950, buried in Dallas City Cemetery.
    6. Son, born 28 May 1886 Paulding County, died 28 May 1888, buried in Mt. Olivet Cemetery.
    7. Son, born 26 November 1894 Paulding County, buried in Mt. Olivet Cemetery.

G. Pearce Johns, born 1855 Paulding County, married (1) Mahaley Parris on 20 February 1881 in Paulding County and (2) on 4 May 1883 in Paulding County, Susan Clelan.

H. Missouri Johns, born 1856 Paulding County.

I. Lydia Johns, born 1859 Paulding County.

J. James Johns, born 1860 Paulding County.

---

[239] 1880 Paulding County Census, Dallas District.

K. Martha Johns, born 1861 Paulding County.

L. Mary Johns, born 1863 Paulding County.

M. Elizabeth (Letitice) Johns, born 1863 Paulding County.

N. Lou Johns, born 1865 Paulding County.

N. Georgia Johns, born 1867 in Paulding County.

Johnson of Virginia;
Bibb & Monroe Counties

William Johnson was born 1753 in Amelia County, Virginia and died 26 October 1838 in Bibb County, Georgia. He died 26 October 1838, his LWT dated 2 March 1837 and probated November 1838 in Bibb County, naming wife, Million S., and all of his children. Executors were: Million S. Johnson, Peter Stubbs, and son, Gideon Johnson. His deceased son, Joel Mac Johnson, was mentioned. Issue:

I. Gideon T. Johnson was born 18 April 1786, died 2 February 1839 in Monroe County, his LWT probated on 3 April 1839 in Monroe County, naming wife, Mary. Issue:[240]

> A. Rebecca Johnson, born 23 September 1826, died 7 January 1849, married 5 November 1846 in Monroe County, William Alexander Chambliss. She is buried in the Salem Methodist Church Cemetery.
>
> B   William Johnson.
>
> C. Thomas Johnson.
>
> D. Gabriel M. Johnson, born ca 1830, married Elizabeth Jordan Chambliss on 29 November 1847 in Monroe County. SEE Chambliss.
>
> E.   Louisa Johnson married Archibald Lany.
>
> F.   Martha Johnson, born 1800 in Georgia, married Turner Brown (born 1783 in Virginia). Issue:[241]
> > 1. Amanda Brown, born 1836 in Bibb County.
> > 2. Lucy Brown, born 1837 in Bibb County.
> > 3. Mary Brown, born 1842 in Bibb County.
>
> G. Mary Johnson.
>
> H. Sarah Johnson.

II. Caleb Johnson.

---

[240] Salem Methodist Church Cemetery, Hwy 87, Monroe County; Monroe County Marriages.

[241] 1850 Bibb County Census.

III. A. M. Johnson.

IV. Lord Johnson.

V. Albert Johnson.

VI. William B. Johnson, married Caroline B. Bailey on 10 October 1833 in Bibb County.

VII. Morgan P. Johnson, born 1826 in Bibb County. Wife, Sarah, born 1831 in Georgia. Issue:[242]
- E. William Johnson, born 1846 in Bibb County.
- F. Eliza Johnson, born 1847 in Bibb County.
- G. Martha Johnson, born 1849 in Bibb County.

VIII. Mary Ann Johnson married Mr. Turk.

IX. Rebecca Johnson married Mr. Turk.

X. Susan D. Johnson married William F. Clark on 10 December 1839 in Bibb County.

XI. Elizabeth Johnson married William Harrington on 25 September 1834 in Bibb County.

XII. Vastile Johnson.

XIII. Millison H. Johnson.

XIV. Ann Miriam Johnson.

XV. Joel Mac Johnson, died before 1837.

XVI. Luther R. Johnson (not 18 in 1837), was born 1823 in Bibb County, married Elizabeth S. Hollingsworth on 18 June 1844 in Bibb County. Elizabeth was born 1825 in Georgia. Issue:

- A. Robert Johnson, born 1845 in Bibb County.
- B. Maretta Johnson, born 1847 in Bibb County.

Jones of Virginia & Warren County

Adam A. Jones was born 1759 in Virginia and died 1 October 1830 in Warren County, Georgia, buried in the Jones cemetery at E. Jewell's Mill, in Warren County. Wife, Susan. Issue:

I. Seaborn S. Jones married Polly Taylor on 20 December 1817 in Warren County.

II. Nathan Jones.

III. Thomas Jones married Kiddy Bazemore on 4 July 1805 in Warren County.

IV. Patsy Jones.

---

[242] Ibid.

243

V.   Aaron Jones married Disey Willaby on 12 February 1800 in Warren County.

VI.   Simon Jones.

VII.   Adam Jones, Jr., Rev., married Nancy Baxley on 18 September 1821 in Warren County.

VIII. Elijah Jones married Margaret Beall on 9 April 1808 in Warren County.

IX.   Stephen Jones married Mary Beall on 14 April 1824 in Warren County.

X.   Susannah Jones, married Jeptha Chambliss on 1 March 1819. SEE Chambliss.

XI.   Elizabeth Jones, born 1785/1790, baptized on 25 April 1811 in the Long Creek Baptist Church, in Warren County, died ca December 1843 in DeSoto County, Mississippi.

Jordan of North Carolina, Alabama, Warren & Jones Counties

William Jordan, a Lieutenant in the Revolutionary War, was born 31 March 1744 in Richmond County, North Carolina, died 23 September 1826 in Warren County, Georgia. In 1786, he married in Virginia, Anne Medlock, born 17 March 1759 in Virginia, died 29 November 1817 in Warren County, Georgia, a daughter of Charles and Agatha Medlock. They are buried near Warrenton, Georgia, near the home which they built in 1794. This home was remembered by his great-granddaughter, Theo M. Jordan (Mrs. J. P. Wood), as being a two-story building of logs, having an immense fireplace. Lieutenant Jordan was wounded in the thigh with a musket ball by the Tories, captured, but released from prison at Wilmington, North Carolina when Lord Cornwallis surrendered at Yorktown, Virginia on 19 October 1791. He served under General Nathaniel Greene. [243]

Issue:

I.   Henry William Jordan, born 17 April 1787 in Richmond County, North Carolina, died 25 October 1872 in Bulloch County, Georgia. He married on 21 July 1814 in Warren County, Mary Lovicy Chambliss, the daughter of Christopher Chambliss. She was born 15 October 1792 in Warren County, died 28 March 1857 in Barbour County, Alabama. SEE Chambliss.

II.   Thomas George Jordan, born 22 July 1788 in Richmond County, North Carolina, died 25 October 1872 in Bulloch County, Alabama. He married on 21 July 1814 in Warren County, Mary Lovicy Chambliss, daughter of Christopher Chambliss. Mary Lovicy Chambliss was born 15 October 1792 in Warren County, died 28 March 1857 in Barbour County, Alabama. SEE Chambliss. Issue:

   A. Abry Henry Jordan, son of Thomas George Jordan, was born 27 April 1815 in Warren County, Georgia, died 25 August 1815 in Warren County.

---

[243] NOTE_____ See the Manuscript Section, Georgia State Archives. The William Jordan File states that William Jordan was a son of James Jordan and is the great-grandfather of Mrs. T. R. Prideaux, Box 1463, Lubbock, Texas.

B. Eleanor Myllie Jordan, daughter of Thomas George Jordan, was born 6 January 1816 in Warren County, Georgia, died 26 July 1879 in Dade County, Alabama, married Rev. Pitt M. Calloway, Baptist Preacher.

C. Henry William Jordan, son of Thomas George Jordan, was born 27 June 1817 in Warren County, Georgia, died 24 December 1858 in Barbour County, Alabama.

 D. Ira Thomas Jordan, son of Thomas George Jordan, was born 9 January 1819 in Jones County, died 8 November 1888 in Midway, Alabama. He married (1) in 1845, Mary Temperance Feagin, daughter of Thomas Feagin and his wife Temperance (Wilson) Feagin. Mary was born 22 February 1824, died 22 September 1868. They are buried in the cemetery adjacent to the Baptist Church in Midway, Alabama. He married (2) Missouri E. Feagin, sister to his first wife. (No issue by the second wife). Issue:

1. Nora Jordan, daughter of Ira Thomas Jordan, married Lafayette Thornton.

2. Alry Gunn Jordan, son of Ira Thomas Jordan, died April 1921, married his cousin, Almira "Dumpy" Feagin, died March 1931, buried in Midway, Alabama.

 3. Walter Joshuaway Jordan, son of Ira Thomas Jordan, was born 29 November 1851 in Society Hill, Macon County, Alabama, died 2 June 1918 in Midway, Alabama. He married (1) Marie Antoinette Katharine Parmalee Carlisle on 2 November 1875. Marie was born 31 October 1853 in Milltown, Chambers County, Alabama, died 14 September 1976 in Brundidge, Alabama. Their only child: Walter Carlisle Jordan, was born 3 September 1876 in Brundidge, Alabama, died soon after his birth. Walter married (2) Lilla Green Carlisle, the daughter of Green Whatley Carlisle and his wife Mary Elizabeth (Leverett) Carlisle. Lilla was born 26 May 1858 in Brundidge, Alabama, died 13 August 1936 in Montgomery, Alabama. They were both buried in Brundidge, Alabama. Issue:

   a. Rev. Ira Lafayette Jordan, son of Walter Joshuaway Jordan, was born 7 December 1880 in Midway, Alabama, died 3 May 1929 in Tuscaloosa, Alabama, married Lollie Eddins on 12 June 1918 in Tuscaloosa.

   b. Carlisle Alry Jordan, son of Walter Joshuaway Jordan, was born 11 December 1881 in Midway, Alabama, died 6 December 1946 in Dothan, Alabama, married 22 November 1909, Isabelle Maude Henderson, the daughter of Daniel Pleasant Henderson and his wife, Abigail Jane (Legg) Henderson. Isabelle was born 29 September 1882 in Chattanooga, Tennessee, died 31 July 1959 in Atlanta, Fulton County, Georgia, buried in Forrest Hill Cemetery, Chattanooga, Tennessee. Issue:
   i. Jean Marie Jordan
   ii. Carlisle Alvin Jordan.

c. Walter Roy Jordan, son of Walter Joshuaway Jordan, was born 14 April 1885 in Midway, Alabama, died 30 March 1853 in Dothan, Alabama, buried in Ozark, Alabama, married (1) 26 November 1912, in Charlotte, North Carolina, Annie Mae Hunter (born 2 January 1893 in Charlotte, North Carolina, died 7 March 1913 in Montgomery, Alabama. He married (2) on 24 June 1916 in Ozark, Alabama, Ethel Eva Pippin, born 9 September 1893 in Ozark, Alabama, died 15 April 1953 in Dothan, Alabama.

d. Lucille Grace Jordan, daughter of Walter Joshua Jordan, was born 7 November 1888 in Midway, Alabama, married 3 January 1912 in Midway, Alabama, Eugene Clifton Cooner (born 23 November 1880, died 23 February 1947 in Montgomery, Alabama, buried Greenwood Cemetery.

4. Mary Alice Jordan, daughter of Ira Thomas Jordan, was born 1857, died 21 August 1919, married Isaac Cheney Thompson (born 1855) in 1877.

5. Ida Lee Jordan, daughter of Ira Thomas Jordan, married Rev. Turner Goodrum, buried in Cedartown, Georgia.

6. William Jordan, son of Ira Thomas Jordan, was born 8 February 1861, died 16 February 1862, buried in Midway, Alabama.

7. Lillie Jordan, daughter of Ira Thomas Jordan, married Barney Ivey.

E. Louise B. Jordan, daughter of Thomas George Jordan, was born 18 October 1820 in Jones County, Georgia, died 29 September 1822 in Jones County.

F. Narcissa Eliza Jordan, daughter of Thomas George Jordan, was born 2 February 1822 in Jones County, died 2 November 1843 in Montgomery County, Alabama.

G. Thomas William Jordan, son of Thomas George Jordan, was born 2 May 1823 in Jones County, Georgia, died 10 September 1823 in Jones County.

H. Albert Crawford Jordan, son of Thomas George Jordan, was born 21 August 1824 in Jones County, Georgia, died 1 August 1899 in Caplen, Texas, had eleven children.

I. Samuel Varn Jordan, son of Thomas George Jordan, was born 5 February 1826 in Jones County, Georgia, died 14 August 1855 in Macon County, Alabama.

J. Mary Ann Lovicy Jordan, daughter of Thomas George Jordan, married (1) John Martin White who died 9 July 1859 leaving her with eight minor children, and, (2) William Long and had by him three children.

K. Melissa Ann Jordan, daughter of Thomas George Jordan, was born 27 July 1829 in Jones County, Georgia, died 14 December 1916 in Marillo, Texas, married J. Sanford Calaway.

L. Warren Jordan, son of Thomas George Jordan, was born 16 February 1831 in Talbot County, Georgia, died 4 January 1861 in Barbour County, Alabama, married 21 December 1852, Elizabeth Temperance Myrick (born 30 March 1833, died 2 May 1912).

M. Walter Golightly Jordan, son of Thomas George Jordan, was born 3 September 1832 in Talbot County, Georgia, died 28 January 1906 in Tuscaloosa, Alabama.

N. William Christopher Jordan, son of Thomas George Jordan, was born 10 July 1834 in Talbotton, Talbot County, Georgia, died 22 September 1923 in Woodland, Talbot County, Georgia, buried in Midway, Alabama. His wife, Frances A. Thornton, was born 1 May 1838, died 30 December 1917 in Midway, Alabama. They married on 14 February 1858 in Barbour County, Alabama. He was a member of County B, 15th Alabama Regt., C. S. A., and wrote a book entitled *Some Events and Incidents During the Civil War*, published in 1909 by Paragon Press, Montgomery, Alabama. Issue:[244]

1. Ira Thomas Jordan, married Susie Smith.
2. Theodosia Jordan, born 1856, married in 1878, James Pinckard Wood.
3. Lovina Jordan.
4. Carry T. Jordan (twin) married Margaret Mabson.
5. Curry T. Jordan (twin).
6. Early Jordan.
7. Pitt Jordan, unmarried.
8. Annie Jordan.
9. Mildred Jordan.

III. Charles Jordan, born 29 July 1790 in Richmond County, North Carolina, died 18 July 1829 in Bibb County, Georgia.

IV. Joshua Medlock Jordan, born 10 July 1792 in Richmond County, North Carolina, died March 1860 in Butts County, Georgia.

V. Israel Sneed Jordan, born 11 October 1793 in Richmond County, North Carolina, died 18 July 1829 in Bibb County, Georgia.

VI. Mary Walton Jordan, born 28 August 1794 in Warren County, Georgia, died 5 October 1871 in Hancock County, married Mr. Howell.

VII. William Warren Jordan, born 31 March 1797 in Warren County, Georgia, died 18 April 1854 in Crawford County, Georgia, married Miss Wilson.

VIII. Elizabeth Jordan, born 22 August 1798 in Warren County, Georgia, died 25 November 1858, aged 60 years, in Forsyth, Monroe County. She married on 14 October 1819, John M. Chambliss. SEE Chambliss.

---

[244] Jean Marie Jordan, Atlanta, Ga.; Monroe County Marriages; 1850 Barbour County, Alabama Census; Barbour County, Alabama Marriages; The Austin Collection by Jeannette Holland Austin, Volume I.

Jesse Jordan was born 1785 in Virginia, died September 1863 in DeKalb County, Georgia, buried in the Wesley Chapel cemetery, Decatur, Georgia. He was married in Edgefield County, South Carolina in 1809 to Rachel Bird (born 1790 Edgefield District), the daughter of Solomon Bird who named his daughter in his LWT dated 1810. Jesse was probably a son of William Jordan. Issue:[245]

I.   Elijah B. Jordan, born 1810 in Edgefield County, South Carolina, died before 1860 in DeKalb County, Georgia, married Lucy Stephens on 26 May 1836. Listed on the 1850 Cobb County Census.

II.   William Jordan born 1813 in Edgefield County, South Carolina, died 1895 in DeKalb County. He married ca 1835 Berdellia. Issue:

    A.   Margaret E. Jordan, born 1837 in DeKalb County, Georgia.
    B.   Martha Jordan, born 1839 in DeKalb County, Georgia.
    C.   Mary Ann Elizabeth Jordan, born 1839 in DeKalb County, Georgia. She married Berry C. Perkins on 2 November 1853. SEE Perkins.
    D.   Sarah P. Jordan, born 1842 in DeKalb County, Georgia.
    E.   Emily Jordan, born 1844 in DeKalb County, Georgia.
    F.   Rachel Jordan, born 1849 in DeKalb County, Georgia.

III.   Sarah A. Caroline Jordan, born ca 1814 in Edgefield County, married Robert Hollingsworth.

IV.   Nancy A. Jordan, born 1815 in Edgefield County, married N. A. Hannada.

V.   Solomon E. Jordan, born 21 November 1819 in Edgefield County, died 25 January 1878. He married Mary A. F. Warren on 11 January 1844.

VI.   Mary Eliza Jordan, born 15 June 1825 in Edgefield County, South Carolina, died 3 August 1895, married on January 1843, Silas Pritchard (born 14 October 1814 South Carolina, died 14 June 1896). The family is listed on the 1880 Lost Creek, Cleburne County, Alabama Census. Issue:

    A.   Silas W. Prichard, born 1857 in Georgia.

    B.   Evy Prichard (daughter), born 1865 in Alabama.

    C.   Elijah C. Prichard, born 1868 in Alabama.

VII.   James Jordan, born 1836 in DeKalb County, Georgia.

VIII.   Larden A. Jordan, born 1837 in DeKalb County, Georgia.

---

[245] DeKalb County Wills; Edgefield County, South Carolina Wills; 1850 DeKalb County Census; DeKalb County Marriages; 1880 Cleburne County, Alabama Census; 1880 DeKalb County Census.

IX.   Sarah Ann Jordan, born 1838 in Georgia, married Joel J. Crockett, born 1837 in Georgia. They lived in the Phillips District of DeKalb County. Issue:

   A. James Crockett, born 1860 DeKalb County.
   B. Mary Crockett, born 1862 DeKalb County.
   C. Julia Crockett, born 1870 DeKalb County.
   D. Joe Crockett, born 1872 DeKalb County.
   E. Hegburt Crockett, born 1875 DeKalb County.
   F. Caroline Crockett, born 1878 DeKalb County.

X.   Demares L Jordan, born 1840 in DeKalb County, Georgia.

Jordan of Jasper & Pulaski Counties

Colonel Burwell Jordan died on 1 March 1870. He was married to Lavinia Washington Holland (born 4 May 1815, died 1 June 1864) [246] on 5 September 1837 in Jasper County. Listed on 1850 Pulaski County Census. SEE Jordan.
      Issue of Lavinia W. Holland and Col. Burwell Jordan:

I.   Leonidas James Augustus Jordan, born 15 June 1841, died 10 July 1842 in Jasper County.

II.   Julius Tennille Jordan, born 12 January 1845.

III. Burwell Lawson Jordan, born 5 December 1847, died 6 June 1892, married on 8 May 1872, Caroline R. Mason (she died on 19 April 1921). Issue: Ella Mason Jordan, born 23 February 1873, died 25 May 1933, married Daniel Allen Penick (no issue); Lee Mason Jordan, born 26 March 1876, died 3 May 1927, married Frances Carter (no issue) and Julia R. Jordan, born 18 February 1878.

IV.   Anna Safford Jordan, born 4 March 1850.

V.   Leander Benjamin Jordan, born 3 May 1852.

Kalcher of Ebenezer

Ruprecht Kalcher was born ca 1710, from Lindau, Austria, arrived 28 December 1734, died Ebenezer, Georgia 10 January 1752 m. ca 1734 at Ebenezer, Margaretha Gunter. Managed the orphans home.

Issue:[247]

I.   Ursula Kalcher born 14 November 1735 Ebenezer, Georgia, died 13 March 1769.
II.   Marcia (Mary) Kalcher, born 15 December 1738 Ebenezer, died 15 March 1760.
I.   Mary Magdalene Kalcher, born 1740/1741, married on 4 June 1765 in Effingham County, John Gruber. SEE Gruber.

---

[246] Bible of Colonel Burwell Jordan and Lavinia W. R. M Holland Jordan.
[247] Colonial Records of Georgia by Candler; Early Settlers of Georgia by Coulter; Effingham County Marriages.

Keaten of South Carolina;
Carroll & Douglas Counties

Sarah Keaten was born 1775 in South Carolina and was listed on the 1850 Carroll County Census with issue, Sarah, born 1810 Georgia, Anna, born 1817 Georgia, and John P., born 1812 Georgia. Probable issue, from the 1850 Carroll County Census - [248]

I. Cader (Kader) Keaten, born 1797 in Georgia. Carroll County Deed Book G, page 397, "Campbell County... Keeder Keeton to Seaborn E. Smith of Campbell County for $400, Land Lot 172 in the 2nd District of Carroll County (now Douglas County), 3 February 1851. Witness: Isham Keaten. Issue:

    A. Mary Keaten, born 1830 Georgia.
    B. Elizabeth Keaten, born 1832 Georgia.
    C. Isham Keaten, born 1834 Georgia.
    D. Sarah Keaten, born 1836 Georgia.
    E. Martha Keaten, born 1838 Georgia.
    F. Mary Keaten, born 1840 Georgia.
    G. Susan Keaten, born 1842 Georgia.
    H. William Keaten, born 1844 Georgia.
    I. Wiley Keaten, born 1846 Carroll County.
    J. Jackson Keaten, born 1849 Carroll County.

II. Sarah Keaten, born 1810 Georgia.

III. John P. Keaten, born 1812 Georgia.

IV. William Keaten, born 1814 Georgia. Wife, Susan, born 1816 Georgia. Issue:

    A. John D. Lafayette Keaten, born 1840 Georgia, farmer, listed on the 1870-1880 Carroll County Census. Wife, Sarah, born 1840 Georgia. Issue:
        1. Mary A. C. Keaten, born 1865 Carroll County.
        2. James William H. Keaten, born 1868 Carroll County.
        3. Sarah A. Keaten, born 1875 Carroll County.

    B. Cader Keaten, born 1843 Carroll County. Listed on the 1870 Carroll County Census as a farmer. Wife, Sarah, born 1850 Georgia. Issue:
        1. Susan Keaten, born 1868 Carroll County.
        2. Ella Keaten, born 1870 Carroll County.

    C. Sarah Keaten, born 1845 Carroll County.

    D. Henry H. Keaten, born 1846 Carroll County. Listed on the 1870 Carroll County census as working on a farm. Wife, Margaret, born 1843 Georgia. Issue:
        1. Lula Jane Keaten, born February 1870 in Carroll County.
        2. Tobie Keaten, born 1871 Carroll County.

---

[248] 1850 Carroll County Census; Carroll County Deeds; Bible of William Robert Keaten, owner Lula Keaten (deceased); personal knowledge of Jeannette Holland Austin; 1880 Douglas County Census; Social Security Death Index.

3. Enoch A. Keaten, born 1872 Carroll County.

4. Viola (or Flora) Keaten, born 1874 Carroll County.

5. Minnie Keaten, born 1875 Carroll County.

6. Alice L. Keaten, born 1876 Carroll County.

 7. William Robert Keaten, born 31 October 1876 (or 1878) in Carroll County, died 1962. He married Lula Ann Holland, daughter of George Washington Holland on 8 May 1898. SEE Holland. Issue:

a. Willie Audrey Keaten, born 18 May 1899 Douglasville, died 11 February 1904.

b. Clarice Lorraine Keaten, born 15 June 1901 Douglasville, died 31 January 1904.

c. Clarence Aubrey Keaten, born 5 January 1905 Douglasville, married Nettie Winn on 8 October 1927.

d. John Coburn Keaten, born 17 December 1906 Douglasville, married on 9 February 1929 Elon McCullough.

e. Lottie Kathryn Keaten, born 10 April 1912 Douglasville, married Fred E. Rowden on 17 November 1931.

f. Keader (Kader) Carlton Keaten, born 10 January 1917 Douglasville, married (1) Margaret Hudson (2) Kathryn Griffin on 9 March 1946. He died on 1 April 1990.

g. Wayne Holland Keaten, born 29 April 1909 Douglasville, married (2) Ruby Jenkins (2) Edna Wiley. He died 7 November 1999 in Santa Clara, California.

E. Mary Keaten, born 1848 Carroll County.

F. Hester Keaten, born 1850 Carroll County.

V. Anna Keaten, born 1817 Georgia.

Kilpatrick of Laurens & Wilkinson Counties

B. Austin Kilpatrick was born 1810 in Georgia, died ca 1877. The first record found of him was an Indenture in Wilkinson County, between Andrew W. Ard and Samuel M. Carswell. November 3, 1846. Wilkinson County, Georgia, D.S. Conveys 202 1/2 acres, lot No. 230 in 23rd district of Wilkinson County from Andrew W. Ard to Samuel M. Carswell for $600. Signed by Andrew W. Ard, Matthew T. Carswell, *B. Kilpatrick*. He married Wineford Delk ca 1862, probably in Laurens County. Before they were married, she had a daughter, Martha Delk, born 1846 in Laurens County and a son, James Delk, born 1855 in Laurens County, who were residing with their mother on the 1850-1870 Laurens County Census . SEE Delk. It appears that this generation changed their name from Kilpatrick to "Patrick." Issue:

I. Martha E. Kilpatrick, daughter of B. Austin Kilpatrick, was born 1844 in Laurens County, married George S. Watkins (born 1845) on 1 June 1864 in Laurens County. Issue:

A. G. B. Watkins, born 1869 in Laurens County.

B. Infant child, born 1870 in Laurens County.

II.   Sarah Constance (Dollie) Kilpatrick, daughter of A. Austin Kilpatrick, was born 30 August 1862 in Laurens County, married Joel Arnold Cook (born 27 June 1856, died 28 January 1938). SEE Cook.

III.   Esther L. Kilpatrick, daughter of B. Austin Kilpatrick, was born 1866 in Laurens County.

IV.   Wineford Kilpatrick ("Gennie"), daughter of B. Austin Kilpatrick, was born 2 June 1869 in Laurens County, died 1 March 1951, buried in Northview Cemetery, Section 1, Row 3, Laurens County.. She later called herself Gennie Patrick.

Lane of North Carolina, Madison & Paulding Counties

Fred Lane died 1798 in Craven County, North Carolina, the date of his LWT. Issue:

I.   William Lane, Revolutionary War Soldier, son of Fred Lane, was born 20 September 1752 in Craven County, North Carolina, died 6 January 1835 in Green County, North Carolina. He applied for a pension (R6140) on 12 February 1833, aged 81 years, stating that he'd entered the service under Colonel Samuel Campbell, volunteering for 3 months; went to Craven County, North Carolina in 1776; term expired August 1776. After that he was a substitute for Rutherford Nelson for 3 months under Capt. Silas Stevenson and marched to Wilmington and Brunswick. He again volunteered for 3 months under Capt. Blackard and was in a skirmish under Capt. Battle, went to Georgetown, South Carolina; volunteered again for 18 months, marching to Halifax under Major Blount and Major Coleman; sent to General Washington to dispatch letters, returned, and having been injured by a wagon, was discharged after 4 months. This was in 1779. In 1780, he was in Newbern under Capt. Green, guarding prisoners for 2 months; discharged; lost his papers when his house burned down in 1786. His application stated that he was born on 20 September 1752 in Craven County, about 25 miles from Newbern.

The application of Elizabeth Jackson, aged 59 on 26th December next, dated at Duplin County, North Carolina on 18 October 1847, states that she is the only surviving child of William Lane, deceased, of Green County, North Carolina, and that he died on 6 January 1835 without a living widow or any children.

Another application, this time of William T. Jackson, dated 17 October 1848 in Duplin County, North Carolina, aged 46, stating that he was a grandson of William Lane, deceased, who died on 5 January 1834, his grandmother having died before he could recollect and his grandfather left two children, viz...Lucretia Suggs, a widow who died in about 12 months hereafter, leaving two children, one who is dead and the other, Lydia, who intermarried with William Wilson, residents of Onslow County, North Carolina; Elizabeth Jackson, her mother, now living in Duplin County, North Carolina. That two of the sons of William Lane....James and Laban...emigrated to Kentucky forty odd years ago and it is over 20 years since they were heard from and 8 or 10 years before the death of Jackson's grandfather they had not been heard of.

Issue:[249]

A. James Lane, son of William Lane, was born ca 1776 in Craven County, North Carolina, married Dolly Phipps on 18 May 1793. He may have removed to Kentucky.

B. Laban Lane, son of William Lane, was born 1780-1790 in Craven County, North Carolina, died September 1833 in Madison County, Georgia. He did not emigrated to Kentucky, but to Georgia, as he was listed on the 1817 Madison County, Georgia Tax Digest. A deed from Laban Lane to Brunnell J. Wiley dated 16 October 1823, in Madison County Deed Book E, page 356. He was found on the 1830 Madison County, Georgia Census with 3 sons under 5, one son 15-20, male 50-60, one daughter 15-20, daughter 20-30, female 40-50. His estate was dated 1833 in Madison County, when William M. Lane was appointed guardian of James E. Lane and Harrison G. Lane, minors of Labog Lane, along with James Carrithers.(2 September). Issue:

   1. William M. Lane, son of Laban Lane, was born 1802 in Jackson County, Georgia, married Elsey C. Burroughs on 27 December 1827 in Madison County.

   2. Minerva Lane, daughter of Laban Lane, was born 1813 in Madison County, married William B. Williams on 4 May 1835 in Madison County. SEE Williams.

   3. John D. Lane, son of Laban Lane, was born 16 February 1814 in Madison County, died 1 December 1846, buried in the old Danielsville Cemetery in Madison County. He married Emily Allen (born 10 September 1816, died 5 January 1895, buried in old Danielsville Cemetery) on 15 November 1838 in Madison County. She was listed on the 1850 Madison County Census, with their children. Issue:

      a. Mary Lane, born 8 July 1840 in Madison County, died 11 December 1917, buried in the old Danielsville Cemetery, married Robert J. Sorrells on 7 November 1866 in Madison County. SEE Sorrells.
      b. Martha Lane, born 1842 Madison County.
      c. Archibald Lane, born 1845 Madison County.
      d. John D. Lane, Jr., born 5 May 1847 in Madison County, died 23 November 1899, buried in the old Danielsville Cemetery.

   4. James Clayton Lane, son of Laban Lane, was born 26 April 1818 in Madison County, died 20 June 1896 Dallas, Paulding County, married Nancy Williams (born 19 May 1818 Danielsville, died 27 June 1905 in Dallas) on 27

---

[249] Craven County, North Carolina Wills, Revolutionary War Pension of William Lane; Madison County Tax Digest; 1830-1850 Madison County Census; Madison County Marriages; Madison County Estates; Paulding County Deeds; 1850-1880 Paulding County Census; Paulding County Marriages; Paulding County Cemeteries.

December 1839 in Madison County, the daughter of Elijah Williams and his wife Judith (Adair) Williams. SEE Adair and Williams. He was born and raised in Madison County and came to live in Paulding County during the 1840's, with his wife. They were both buried in the Mt. Olivet Cemetery at Dallas. A Paulding County Deed dated 10 December 1859, headed Henry County, between John C. Gillman and James Lane of Paulding County, for land in the 2nd District, 3rd section of originally Cherokee, now Paulding County, being Lot 437 and containing 40 acres. Another deed dated 17 November 1881, between J. C. Lane and Fredric Thompson, for land in the 2nd District of the 3rd Section of Paulding County, being five acres, in the northwest corner of lot of land, No. 136.[250] Issue:[251]

> a. Permelia Elizabeth Lane, daughter of James Clayton Lane, was born 1 October 1840 in Dallas, Paulding County, died 16 February 1920 in Atlanta, Fulton County, buried in the Hollywood Cemetery (Hudson Lot), on Hightower Road and Northwest Atlanta. During her later years, she moved to Bolton, Georgia. Never married.

> b. Berry Tilman Lane, son of James Clayton Lane, was born 6 July 1843 in Athens, Georgia, died 13 August 1928 in Clarendon, Donley County, Texas, married Katherine (Eva) Hudson (born 18 May 1844 in Putnam County, died 22 April 1925 Wichita Falls, Texas, buried in the Rosemont Cemetery) on 29 November 1866 in Paulding County. He served in County A, 40th Georgia Regiment, Volunteer Infantry, Army of Tennessee during the Civil War. He was a blacksmith and a

---

[250] "James and Nancy moved to Paulding County, Pumpkinvine District on about 1845. Records indicate they settled on Land Lot No. 500. This is located West of Dallas on Georgia State Highway 120 near where Lane Creek now crosses the highway. Settlers helped them build a log house. Son after they moved into the house, James had to return to Madison for more of their belongings. He traveled with a wagon drawn by oxen and was gone three months. Nancy stayed alone during this time, keeping up with the farm chores. They farmed and operated a waterwheel powered grist mill on Lane Creek. He also had a blacksmith shop at the mill. The grist mill was expanded into a cotton mill, and the machinery was driven by a #6 horsepower steam engine....The equipment had a power cotton press which was modern for that day...All accounts indicate that the business prospered. Their son, George, was a partner in the business. The family seat was located on 6 acres of land, in Land Lot No. 438, adjacent to Lane Creek. The later family home is still standing and has been renovated by present owners. It is located just West of Lane Creek on right side of 120 Highway. The story has been handed down that the foundation of that house was constructed with wooden pegs driven into the holes. All of the original lumber was hand planed by James and sons. They reared a large family in that two storied home...James and Nancy lived a healthy life. He became sick one day and died the next, this was June 20, 1896. The funeral was conducted under a large oak tree in the front yard of their home....Nancy lived 9 years after her husband died. Her daughter, Elizabeth, stayed with her and they continued living in the same house. Nancy died May 27, 1905. She is buried beside James in the Lane Cemetery." Ref: Horace A. Lane, 1044 Six Flags Drive, Austell, Georgia 30001. (1981).

[251] Family Bible of James C. and Nancy Lane in possession of Tom Lane, 2092 Ben Hill Road, East Point, Georgia (1965).

resident of Paulding County in 1870. About 1875, he went West, later settling in Clarendon County, Texas. [252]

Issue of Berry Tilmon Lane:

i. John Thomas Lane, born 18 September 1867 in Atlanta, DeKalb County, died 18 June 1951 same place. He married Nora Colbert on 9 August 1892. Issue:
    a. Thomas W. Lane, born July 1893 Paulding County.
    b. Emma L. Lane, born October 1894 Paulding County.

---

[252] "B. T. Lane. A son of J. C. Lane, a prominent farmer of Georgia, and educated in that State, the subject of this sketch began life for himself in the year 1867, and starting in business with only a very limited amount of capital, ranks at this date among the most influential and popular citizens of Nevada County. He is engaged in farming and mercantile pursuits, and in 1885 founded the postoffice of Lanesburg. He is a member of the Masonic lodge, and is a faithful Democrat in politics...In 1879 they (he and wife) moved to Arkansas, and entered the mercantile business in 1884, but the stock was burned out in February, 1885, and again in 1889. Yet true genius surmounts all obstacles, and thus Mr. Lane succeeded in spite of misfortune. He enlisted in the Civil War in 1861, under Maj. Kemp and figured in many of the celebrated battles, experiencing the usual hardships of war, but serving until May, 1865." Biographical and Historical Memoirs of Soutern Arkansas, page 572. According to various estate records, he was emassed a considerable estate. When he died, a representative visited relatives in Atlanta, searching for heirs. A Gin Sale occurred in Paulding County on 18 November 1896, between the following heirs-at-law of James C. Lane, deceased, to-wit: Berry Tilman Lane of the State of Texas, by his lawful attorney-in-fact J. E. Butler; Sarah Frances Landers of Cobb County in the said State of Georgia; Permelia Elizabeth Lane; Eliza Davis; Nancy Carrie Collins and Judith (J. E.) Butler of Paulding County of the first part, to George W. Lane of Paulding County, of the second part. They sold the James C. Lane mill and gin, located in the Northeastern part of Land Lot 438 in the 2nd District and 3rd Section of Paulding County, having situated thereon...one steam cotton gin, mill and all of the fixtures, being Northside 150 feet long, East side, 120 feet long, Northside 120 feet, Westside 135 feet long, containing two-fifths of an acre. All of the above heirs signed this sales deed. His estate was died up in court by the heirs (J. T. Lane, Ella Simond, Henry Simond, W. T. Lane, R. K. Lane, C. W. Lane, Orine Lewis, Ira Lewis, Julia Alexander, Otis Alexander, J. T. Lane, Jr., Beulah Lane, Flora Lane, Pauline Lane, Rose Mary Lane and Lloyd Noel Lane, the last three parties being minors, by their next friend, W. T. Lane, and "there appearing by answer and waiver of citation under due authority upon behalf of Roy Abbott, Hazel Kraus, Dollie Neilsen et vir, Alex Neilson, Edna Wright et vir, Don Wright and Mrs. Lula T. Lane, and all parties named...." Waiving having a trail Wichita County, Texas, and a Judgement was issued on 16 August 1926, which disclosed the following facts:
1. Mrs. A. C. Lane, wife of B. T. Lane, died in Wichita Falls, Texas April 23, 1925. That B. T. Lane died in Wichita Falls, Texas, August 15, 1928.
2. J. T. Lane, Ella Simond, wife of Henry Simond, W. T. Land, R. R. Lane, C. W. Lane, J. W. Lane who died during the month of October 1918, Mollie Abbott who died May 23, 1926.
3. That J. T. Lane, Ella Simond, W. I. Lane, R. K. Lane and C. W. Lane are now living and each is over 21 years of age.
4. That the residence was 1009 – 15th Street, Wichita Falls and 1506 Elizabeth Street, and other cash account

255

    c. Effie N. Lane, born October 1896 Paulding County.

    d. Freddie Lane, born December 1898 Paulding County, buried in the High Shoals Church Cemetery.

    e. Eva Lane, born 1900 Dallas, Paulding County.

    f. Grace Lane, born 1901 Dallas, Paulding County.

    g. Hattie Lane, born 1903 Dallas, Paulding County.

    h. Sylva Lane, born 1909 Paulding County.

ii. James Walker Lane, born 4 May 1869 in Dallas, Paulding County, died 16 August 1919, same place. Wife, Lula T.[253] Issue:

    (a) Orine Lane married Ira Lewis.

    (b) Julia Lane married Otis Alexander.

    (c) J. T. Lane, Jr.

    (d) Beulah Lane.

    (e) Flora Lane.

    (f) Pauline Lane.

    (g) Lloyd Lane, died in France.

    (h) N. N. Lane, died December 1927.

iii. Maryelder Lane, born 25 August 1871 in Athens, Clarke County, died 21 May 1926, married Edwin Oscar Abbott in November 1898.

iv. George W. Lane, born and died 11 November 1874, Dallas, Paulding County, buried in Pumpkin Vine Cemetery.

v. Missouri Ella Lane, born 15 November 1875 in Dallas, Paulding County, died 6 June 1957, married Henry Simond.

vi. Wesley Irving Lane, born 15 June 1876 in Dallas, Paulding County, died 17 February 1951.

vii. Robert Kirk Lane, born 19 March 1879 in Dallas, Paulding County, died 21 March 1944.

viii. Carey Foster Lane, born 21 November 1881 in Lansbury, Arkansas, died 2 August 1950.

---

[253] "Laneburg, Arkansas. August 4, 1890. Mr. J. C. Lane, Dallas, Georgia. Dear Grandpa, I will write you a few lines. This leaves all well except Johny's wife. She is sick but is not dangerous. Pa and Mollie got home Saturday morning. They got here all rite and had no accidents. Well, Grandpa you have no idea how proud I was of my pants. I expect I will stand up with my wife with them on. Jonie liked his very much but could not fill them up. He is too little anyhow. Crops are very sorry here. There are some places that they have not had rain in 8 weeks. You bet Pa was sick when he got home (financially).....Yours in Love to all, James W. Lane." Copied from the original letter by Horace A. Lane, November 26, 1980.

c. John W. Lane, son of James Clayton Lane, was born 25 May 1846 in Dallas, Paulding County, died during the Civil War, in Chickamauga, Georgia.

d. Sarah Frances Lane, daughter of James Clayon Lane, was born 27 December 1848 in Dallas, Paulding County where she died on 16 August 1921, buried in the New Harmony Grove Church Cemetery in Mableton. She married Abe J. Landers on 16 November 1873 in Paulding County.

e. Eliza Frances Lane, daughter of James Clayton Lane, was born 25 February 1850 in Dallas, Paulding County, died 13 June 1933 in Dallas, buried in the Dallas City Cemetery. She married Lon Davis on 12 December 1875 in Paulding County.

f. Nancy Carrie Lane, daughter of James Clayton Lane, was born 4 May 1851 in Dallas, Paulding County, died 15 October 1940 in Ben Hill, buried in the Mt. Olivet Cemetery in Dallas. She was a daughter of Thomas M. Collins. SEE Collins. The obituary of Nancy Carrie Lane Collins, Atlanta Constitution, dated 16 October 1940, as follows: "Mrs. Carrie Collins of Blanton Road, Ben Hill, died yesterday. She was 88. Surviving are a daughter, Mrs. Ida Wiley and a sister, Mrs. Judie Butler. Rites will be held at 11:00 this morning at the Chapel of J. Allen Couch Funeral Home with the Rev. George W. Cox and Rev. Marcus D. Drake officiating. Burial will be in the Mt. Olivet Cemetery, near Dallas, Georgia."

g. George Washington Lane, son of James Clayton Lane, was born 14 May 1854 in Dallas, Paulding County, died 31 December 1934 same place, buried in the Lane Cemetery (Pumpkin Vine) in Dallas, Georgia. He married Martha Josephine Hawkins (born 29 January 1863, died 1 November 1945, buried Pumpkinvile Cemetery) on 13 November 1879 in Paulding County. Issue:[254]

> i. Hattie Cora Lane, daughter of George Washington Lane, was born 21 September 1881 in Paulding County, died 6 August 1882, buried in the Lane Cemetery, Dallas, Georgia.
>
> ii. Hannah Alena Lane, daughter of George Washington Lane, was born 6 February 1883 in Paulding County, died 15 November 1884, buried in Pumpkinvine Cemetery, Dallas.
>
> iii .James Tilman Lane, son of George Washington Lane, was born 5 August 1885 in Paulding County, died 18 August 1960, married Devie Motes. Issue: Charles R. Lane, born 20 September 1918 in Paulding County, died 30 March 1981 in Mableton, married Bernese Pace; and Louise Lane, married Mr. Lemasters.

---

[254] Family Bible of George W. Lane and Martha Josephine Lane in the possession of Tom Lane, 2092 Ben Hill Road, East Point, Georgia (1965).

iv. John Williams Lane, son of George Washington Lane, was born 5 March 1888 in Paulding County, died 15 January 1889, buried in the Pumpkinvine Cemetery, Dallas.

v. Mauddy Beatrice Lane, daughter of George Washington Lane, was born 23 June 1889 in Paulding County, died 6 September 1889, buried in the Pumpkinvine Cemetery, Dallas.

vi. Thomas Theodore Lane, son of George Washington Lane, was born 14 July 1891 in Paulding County, died 7 February 1981 in East Point, Fulton County. He married Myrtle Buford. Issue: Lucy Lane married Mr. Rouse; Horace A. Lane; and Marvin Lane.

vii. Jesse Andrew Lane, son of George Washington Lane, was born 29 July 1897 in Paulding County, died 4 June 1964, buried in the Pumpkinvine Cemetery, Dallas.

viii. Lillian Irene Lane, daughter of George Washington Lane, was born 18 August 1902 in Paulding County.

h. Judith (Judy) Emma Lane, daughter of James Clayton Lane, was born 26 March 1859 in Dallas, Paulding County, died 3 January 1942, buried Mt. Olivet Cemetery in Dallas. She married (1) Joseph B. Howell and (born 27 October 1857, died 30 October 1891, buried Mt. Olivet Cemetery), (2) J. E. Butler (born 26 October 1866, died 29 January 1900, buried Mt. Oliver Cemetery) on 29 January 1892 in Paulding County.

i. Thomas J. Lane, son of James Clayton Lane, was born 18 October 1862 in Dallas, Paulding County, died 18 April 1864, buried in the Pumpkinvine Cemetery.

5. Harrison Lane, son of Laban Lane, was born 1825 in Madison County, married Judith Leak Maddox on 15 September 1844 in Madison County.

C. Lucretia Lane, daughter of William Lane, was born ca 1782 in Craven County, North Carolina, married Mr. Suggs.

D. Elizabeth Lane, daughter of William Lane, was born 26 December 1788 in Craven County, North Carolina, died in Duplin County, North Carolina, married Mr. Jackson.

II.   Ann G. Lane, daughter of Fred Lane, was born ca 1759 in Craven County, North Carolina.

III. John S. Lane, son of Fred Lane, was born ca 1760 in Craven County, North Carolina.

IV. Henry B. Lane, son of Fred Lane, was born ca 1762 in Craven County, North Carolina.

V.   Mary B. Lane, daughter of Fred Lane, was born ca 1764 in Craven County, North Carolina,

VI.   Daniel Lane, son of Fred Lane, was born ca 1768 in Craven County, North Carolina.

VI.   Shrine Lane, son of Fred Lane, was born ca 1772 in Craven County, North Carolina.

Lee of North Carolina & Bulloch County

The Lee family in Bulloch County, Georgia came from James Lee whose LWT was dated 1777 in Edgecombe County, North Carolina, naming issue: William, Root, Travis, Winnie and James.

I.   James Lee, born 1755 in North Carolina, died 1806 in Bulloch County. He was married on 3 November 1760 in Edgecombe County, North Carolina to Agnes Cade. The family removed to Bulloch County about 1784. Issue:[255]
  A. Phillip Lee, born ca 1760 in North Carolina.

I.   Obedience Lee, born ca 1764 in North Carolina.

III.   Milbry Lee (daughter), born ca 1766 in North Carolina.

IV.   Sarah Lee, born ca 1768 in North Carolina.

V.   Drury Ludwell Lee, born 1771/1777 in Edgecombe County, North Carolina, died 1797 in Wake County, North Carolina.

VI.   Lydia Lee, born 1771/1777 in Edgecombe County, North Carolina.

VII.   Abel Lee was born 1770 in North Carolina. He lived for awhile in Marlboro, South Carolina where it is said that he was married.[256]

Issue:

  A.   Sarah Lee, born 1806 in South Carolina, unmarried; died October 1880 in Leefield, Bulloch County.
  B.   William Lee, born ca 1809 in Bulloch County.
  B.   Abel Lee, Jr., born 1812 in Georgia, farmer, died 4 May 1892 in Hillsborough County, Florida, buried in the Fellowship Cemetery. Wife, Mary (born 1826). Issue:

---

[255] 1820-1870 Bulloch County Census; Bulloch County Wills, Deeds & Marriages; Edgecombe County, North Carolina Wills.

[256] Bulloch County Deeds

Deed Book FF, page 396. Abel Lee and his wife, Mary, deed to Agnes Calhoun, 300 acres on the Northeast side of the Great Pee Dee River on Hagin's Prong of Three Creek; 100 acres granted to Joseph Hagins on 2 November 1784 by Alexander Craig, Department Surveyor, in another tract containing 100 acres conveyed by Mary Hagins to Jonathan Meekings on the fork of Three Creek.

1. Elizabeth Lee, born 1844 Bulloch County.
2. John Lee, born 1847 Bulloch County.
3. Ann Lee, born 1848 Bulloch County.
C. Martha Lee, born 1815 Bulloch County, unmarried.
D. Jane Lee, born 1820 Bulloch County, unmarried.
E. Isaac Lee, born 1825 Bulloch County.

VII. James Ludwell Lee, born 1775 in Edgecombe County, North Carolina, died September 1840 in Bulloch County, Georgia, the date of his LWT 13 July 1840, probated September 1840. Wife, Patience. [257]

Issue:
A. Thomas Lee.
B. Jesse Lee.
C. Eliza Lee.
D. _____Lee married Joshua Kirkland.
E. James Lee, Jr., born 1806 in Bulloch County. He married Lucy Lanier (born 1815 Georgia) on 1 February 1827 in Bulloch County. The LWT of James Lee, Jr. was probated on November 1864 in Bulloch County. Issue:
    1. William A. Lee, born 1828 Bulloch County.
    2. Loving Lee, born 1834 Bulloch County.
    3. James Lee, born 1838 Bulloch County.
    4. Sarah Lee, born 1841 Bulloch County, married Mr. Williams.
    5. George W. Lee, born 1843 Bulloch County.
    6. Henry C. Lee, born 1847 Bulloch County.
    7. Morgan Lee, born 1849/1850 Bulloch County.
    8. Roxey Ann (or Mazey) Lee, married Wiley Williams on 8 February 1846 in Bulloch County..
    9. Eliza Ann Lee, married James Sumerlin.

F. David Lee.
G. William Lee.
H. John Lee.
I. Sarah Lee married Jesse Bird on 15 September 1831 in Bulloch County..
J. Elizabeth Lee married Augustus Lanier on 11 December 1840 in Bulloch County.

VIII.John Lee, born 1775 in Edgecombe County, North Carolina, died 1795.

---

[257] Bulloch County Deeds

Book 3A, page 142-146. 11 December 1840. Augustus Lanier signed as having received of James Lee and William Lee, executors of the Estate of James Lee, Sr., it being part of the property bequeathed to wife, Eliza, by the deceased. James Lee, Jr. signed a similar receipt as the guardian of Thomas Lee.

Book 3A, page 160-163. March 1843. Annual Return of William Lee, Sr. and James Lee, Jr., the executors of the LWT of James Lee, Sr., deceased. Return for 1842: Paid the following legatees: James Lee, Jr., David Lee, William Lee, William Lee as guardian for Thomas Lee, Augustus Lanier, Jesse Bird, Sharp Roberts, Mitchell Lanier, John Lee. Jackson Bird signed for Jesse Bird.

IX. David Lee, born 1780 Edgecombe County, North Carolina, died 1829 in Bulloch County, Georgia. He had deed transactions in Bulloch County from 1801 to 1803. The 1803 transactions deed some land to General Lee. (Bulloch County Deed Book AAA, page 325. On 29 January 1817, there is a deed of gift from David Lee for the natural love and affection for his son, Pearcy Lee....25 head of cattle.

XI. General Lee was born 1784 in Edgecombe County, North Carolina, died 1862 in Bulloch County, Georgia. He married on 25 December 1809 in Bulloch County, Nancy Cook, who was born 1793 in Georgia. His LWT dated 13 April 1861, probated August 1862 in Bulloch County, named his wife, sons and daughters, and a granddaughter, Eliza Groover. Issue:

    A. General G. W. Lee, born 1817 in Georgia, farmer, listed on the 1850 Bulloch County Census. Wife, Loving (born 1829 Georgia). Issue:
        1. William Lee, born 1850 in Bulloch County.
        2. Joshua O. Lee, born 1870 Bulloch County.
    B. John Lee.
    C. Jane Lee, born ca 1819, married Jackson Wilson on 26 July 1838 in Bulloch County.
    D. Mary Lee, born ca 1822, married Jasper Wilson on 7 December 1843 in Bulloch County. Issue:
        1. E. James Lee.
    G. Nancy Lee married W. H. Macleon.
    .H. Ann Lee married William Lester.

X. William Lee, Sr. was born 1790 in Edgecombe County, North Carolina, died December 1870 in Bulloch County, Georgia. He married (1) ca 1817 (name unknown), and, (2) on 7 January 1844 in Bulloch County, Miss Sarah Lowther, who was born 1797 in Georgia, and died 1870 in Bulloch County. The LWT of William Lee, Sr. is dated 7 July 1870, probated the December Term of 1870 in Bulloch County. He named his *sister*, Sarah Lee; also son, James M. Lee; and grandchildren, viz: James Frank Lee, Newton R. Lee, Ann E. T. Lee, the children of his son, John Lee. The LWT of Sarah Lee (2nd wife) was dated 7 May 1872 and probated 4 October 1880 in Bulloch County. In it, she named her cousin, Martha Foy of Effingham County; her nephew, Newton R. Lee; her niece, Ann E. Rogers. Named as trustees were: James M. Lee and Winfield S. Lee.[258]

Issue by (1) wife: [259]

---

[258] Bulloch County Deeds

Deed Book AAAA, page 425. 24 February 1821. William Lee of Bulloch County deeded to Elizabeth Lowther for $57.00, 73 acres of land located on the East side of Spring Creek on the waters of Belcher's Mill, which adjoins lands belonging to the heirs of John Lowther.

The above deed compares in description to a deed of Stephen Bowen, Planter of Montgomery County to John Everett, dated 7 November 1800, for 117 acres located near Mill Creek, near a place formerly called Belcher's, old cowpens, now a plation of the aforesaid John Everett called *Spring Grove*. (Montgomery County Deed Book A, page 66).

[259] 1820-1880 Bulloch County Census; Bulloch County Deeds, Marriages & Estates; Personal Information of Sarah E. Lee Stucki, Orlando, Florida (deceased); Brooklet-Brannen Cemetery; New Hope Cemetery' Lester Family Cemetery; Edgecombe County, North Carolina Wills.

A. John Lee, son of William Lee, Sr., was born 1818 Georgia. He married Deeree Henly (born 1827) on 21 January 1841 in Bulloch County. Issue:

    1. James Frank Lee, born 3 December 1844 in Bulloch County, died 18 April 1878, buried in the Brooklet-Brannen Cemetery in Bulloch County. Wife, Julia (born 1852).

    2. Newton Lee, born 1849 Bulloch County.

    3. Ann E. T. Lee, born 1851 Bulloch County.

B. William Lee, Jr., son of William Lee, Sr., was born 1820 Bulloch County, married (1) Sarah McCall on 5 April 1842 in Bulloch County, and, (2) on 11 October 1864, Mrs. Ann Perry in Bulloch County. Mrs. Perry was born 1836 in Georgia. The 1880 Bulloch County Census, William, Jr. stated that his parents were born in North Carolina. His LWT dated 5 December 1892, probated 11 October 1892 in Bulloch County, named his daughters, viz: Margaret R. Gesandea, Caroline Eliza Sutton, Sarah Martha Parrish; and sons, Frank P. Lee, James B. Lee and Andrew J. Lee.

    Issue by (1) wife:

      1. Elbert Lee, born 1843 in Bulloch County. He married on 18 August 1864 in Bulloch County, Ann E. Groover, the daughter of Samuel E. Groover. Anna was born 1845 in Bulloch County. There is a deed in Bulloch County Deed Book FM, page 177, of Samuel E. Groover to Ann E. Lee. This deed refers to Ann E. Groover, daughter of Samuel Groover. Issue:

        a. Martha L. Lee, born 1862 Bulloch County.

        b. Elizabeth Lee, born 1863 Bulloch County.

      2. John M. Lee, born 1847 Bulloch County.

      3. William Baker Lee, born 1850 Bulloch County, married on 30 November 1870, in Bulloch County, Sarah J. Lee. Listed on the 1870-1880 Bulloch County Census, 47th District, Briar Patch. Issue:

        a. William Cassels Lee, born 17 October 1873 in Bulloch County, died 11 March 1933 in Brooklet, Georgia. He married Anna Cornelia Groover (born 25 September 1879 in Bulloch County, died 22 February 1954 in Savannah, Chatham County), the daughter of James Bulloch Groover and Sarah Ann (Wilson) Groover of Buloch County.

        b. Florence L. Lee, born 1874 Bulloch County.

        c. Leslie Lee, born 1876 Bulloch County.

        d. Sarah E. Lee, born 1877 Bulloch County.

        e. Mattie I. Lee, born August 1879 Bulloch County.

      4. James B. Lee, born 1851 Bulloch County, married 6 October 1875 Carrie P. Pretorious in Bulloch County.

      5. Franklin P. Lee, born 1853 Bulloch County.

      6. Margaret R. Lee, born 1855 Bulloch County, seamstress, married Mr. Gesandeau.

      7. Andrew J. Lee, born 1856 Bulloch County. Unmarried in 1880.

      8. Carolina Eliza Lee, born 1858 Bulloch County, married Mr. Sutton.

      9. Sarah Martha Lee, born 1860 Bulloch County, married Mr. Parrish.

      10. Sarah W. J. Lee, born 1863 Bulloch County, unmarried in 1880.

D. James M. Lee, son of William Lee, Sr., was born 1824 Bulloch County, married 27 February 1845, Margaret Hagins in Bulloch County. Issue:

    1. Lawrence Lee, born 1846 in Statesboro, Bulloch County.

2. Winfield Lee, born 1848 in Statesboro, Bulloch County.
3. Sarah Lee, born 1849 in Statesboro, Bulloch County.

E. Benjamin Cook Lee, son of William Lee, Sr., was born 1824 in Bulloch County, Georgia. He married Sarah Waters (born 1822 in Statesboro) on 25 February 1841 in Bulloch County. She was a daughter of Thomas Waters, Sr. and his wife, Hannah (Stuart) Waters. Issue:
1. Nicey E. Lee, born 26 December 1842 in Statesboro, Bulloch County.
2. Jasper Lee, born 1844 in Statesboro, Bulloch County.
3. Jane Caroline Lee, born March 1845 in Statesboro, Bulloch County.
4. Ann Lee, born 1846 in Statesboro, Bulloch County.
5. Morgan Watson Lee, born 19 May 1849 in Statesboro, Bulloch County, died 2 September 1928 in Starke, Florida, buried in Middleburg, Florida.
6. Hannah Lee, born 1851 in Bulloch County.
7. Ida Lee, born 1857 in Statesboro, Bulloch County.
8. Alice Lee, born 1859 in Statesboro, Bulloch County.
9. Lilly Lee, born 1861 in Statesboro, Bulloch County.
10. Rosey Lee, born 1863 in Statesboro, Bulloch County.
11. Robert E. Lee, born 1865 in Statesboro, Bulloch County.

Leverett of Wilkes County

William Leverett was born ca 1727 in England, died 1805 in Wilkes County, Georgia. He married Bridget. The Minutes of the Inferior Court, Wilkes County (1811-1817), page 96, Abraham Leverett was appointed administrator of the Estate of William Leverett, deceased, dated 1805. Wilkes County Annual Returns (1811-1819), page 19, Abraham Leverett, administrator of the Estate of William Leverett, deceased, filed Annual Return dated 1811, which included Notes of William Leverett, Jr., Thomas Leverett, Henry Leverett, and Abraham Leverett.[260]

Issue:[261]

I. William Leverett, Jr., born ca 1753 in Wilkes County, died 1812 in Putnam County. The LWT of William Leverett, Jr. dated 7 January 1812 in Putnam County Will Book A, page 14-15.

---

[260] Wilkes County Deeds

25 January 1790. William Leverett and his wife, Bridget, deed to Benjamin Baldwin, 200 acres in Wilkes County, bounded on the South by Little River, West by Richard Johnson, and North by Baldwin, East by Robert Leverett

Greene County Deeds

5 June 1792, Deed Book I, page 603. William Leverett of Wilkes County deeds to William Ashmore of Greene County for 50 pounds sterling, 250 acres of land on the waters of Island Creek.

[261] Wilkes County Marriages, Deeds & Estates; Lincoln County Marriages; Greene County Deeds; Putnam County Wills; Revolutionary War Pension of Thomas Leverett; Georgia Roster of the Revolution, page 192; Lincoln County Wills.

II.   Thomas Leverett, Revolutionary War Soldier, was born 12 May 1755 in Wilkes County, died 8 June 1834 in Troup County. He married (2) Mary G. Griffin on 3 July 1789 (2) Elizabeth Johnston on 8 March 1801. He served on the Continental Line, in Georgia, and received a pension (#W4264), which included a bible record; resided in Putnam County for nineteen years (widow applied for pension).

III.   Henry Leverett, born ca 1757 in Wilkes County, died 1820 in Lincoln County. On 10 January 1820 in Lincoln County, Mathew Leverett was appointed administrator of the Estate of Henry Leverett, deceased.

IV.   Abraham Leverett, born ca 1759 in Wilkes County, died in Lincoln County. He married Martha White on 12 March 1818.

V.   John Leverett, born ca 1761 in Wilkes County, died November 1818 in Wilkes County. Wife, Mary. The LWT of John Leverett was dated 16 February 1811, probated 2 November 1818, Wilkes County, named daughter, Celia, the wife of William Evans (his son-in-law). "To Mary, all the property for life except a horse to go to daughter, Patsy Leverett." Final division made to all of the children, with son, Joel P. Leverrett and son-in-law, William Evans, as executors.Issue:

> A.   Joel P. Leverett, born 29 June 1783 in Anson County, North Carolina, died 30 June 1866 in Washington County, Georgia. He married Mary E. Bishop on 18 November 1827.
>
> B.   Joseph Leverett, of Wilkes County, Georgia.
>
> C .John Leverett, of Wilkes County, Georgia.
>
> D.   Patsy Leverett of Wilkes County, married Travis W. McKinney on 13 December 1808 in Wilkes County.
>
> E.   Celia Leverett, born ca 1780 in Wilkes County, died in Elbert County. She married William Evans ca 1801. SEE Evans.

VI.   Elizabeth Leverett, born ca 1763 in Wilkes County, married George Tucker, a Revolutionary War Soldier. Wilkes County Deed dated 27 January 1790, Sanders Walker and his wife, Sarah, deed to George Tucker, 287-1/2 acres of land located on the waters of Rocky Creek in Greene County.

VII.   Daughter who married Peter Ashmore.

VIII.   Daughter who married Benjamin Reason.

IX.   Robert Leverett, born ca 1769 in Wilkes County, died September 1806 in Lincoln County. Wife, Patsy. LWT of Robert Leverett, dated 18 September 1806, Lincoln County.

X.   Seley Leverett, born ca 1771, lived in Lincoln County.

XI.   Absalom Leverett, born ca 1773, died 1817 in Wilkes County. He married Anne McElroy on 7 January 1799. Minutes of the Inferior Court of Wilkes County (1817-1824), page 30, Estate of Absalom Leverett, deceased. Anne Leverett and Silas Catchings were appointed administrators. On page 118, the petition of John Moreman, security for Anne Leverett, guardian of the minors of Absalom Leverett, deceased, to be released as such. According to a petition of Anne Leverett, widow of Absalom, her husband died in 1817.

Littleton of Warren & Wilkes Counties

Thomas Littleton who died in Jones County, North Carolina, his LWT dated May of 1792, naming wife, Mary and two Issue: William Littleton and Leah Johnson, appears to be the Thomas Littleton of Kent County, Delaware who first migrated to Craven County, North Carolina along with his brother, Edmond. Craven County later became Jones County. By implication, they also appeared to have had Savage Littleton (born 1752 Kent County, Delaware, a Revolutionary War Soldier, who applied for a Pension and Mark Littleton, before before 1740, both of whom appeared on the 1794 Warren County, Georgia Tax Digests. William Littleton appeared on the Wilkes County Georgia Tax Records.[262]

My primarily interest in the Littleton family in Georgia is to prove the parents of Mary, the wife of John Chambliss, born ca 1730/1740 who married him about 1760 in Cheraw District, South Carolina (he died there in 1777) was a Littleton. After his death, she migrated to Warren County, Georgia by 1781. Mary Chambliss, Sr. and Mary Chambliss, Jr. are both listed as members of the Long Creek Baptist Church (1799-1819 Membership Rolls) along with her sons, Littleton Chambliss and Christopher Chambliss. The church record gives her death as 14 October 1817, however, the Bible of Littleton Chambliss gives her death as 15 September 1815.

William Littleton was born in 1762. According to his declaration for a pension made in Wilkes County (Minutes of Inferior Court 1824-1827), page 128, dated 7 May 1827, he stated that he was 65 years of age, and he enlisted on 1 July 1782 for 18 months in the State of North Carolina in a company commanded by Capt. Elijah Moore, Capt., Alex. Brevard, 2nd Capt. and Capt. Rhodes, in the 1st North Carolina Regiment commanded by Lt. Col. Archibald Lyttle, under the command of Major Gen. Nathaniel Greene in the line for the State of North Carolina; that he was discharged on 1 July 1783 in Charleston, South Carolina, having served in no battles. On 18 March 1818, he drew 250 acres of land in Walton County, which he sold to Henry Conner for $250.00 (about 1822). That he was a shoemaker and farmer when he was able to work, and that he has no family. (Pension was granted).

Also, further validating his claim to having served in the Revolutionary War, he gave an affidavit (Wilkes County Minutes of Inferior Court 1817-1824, pp. 81-83) for Joseph Hurley, stating that said Hurley was a soldier in the Continental Line in the First North Carolina Regiment (serving as 1st Sgt., and Orderly Sgt.), "while I was 1st sergeant", and that Hurley served to the close of the war.

William Littleton was listed as *William Littleton, Jr.*, on the 1785 Wilkes County Tax Digest, 1 poll. "Georgia,Warren County} This indenture made and executed this the Fourth day of January in the year of our Lord one Thousand Eight hundred and forty five between James W. Smith of the County and State aforesaid of the one part and *William Littleton* of the same place of the other part witnesseth that I, James W. Smith for and in consideration of the sum of Two hundred Dollars to him in hand paid at or before signing Sealing and delivering these presents the receipt hereof is hereby acknowledged hat this day granted bargained sold and conveyed and do by this presents grant bargain and sell unto the said William Littleton his heirs and assigns for ever all that tract lot or parcel of Land lying and being in the said County of Warren on the waters of Cattail Creek containing Two Hundred acres be the same more or

---

[262] Wilkes County Minutes of the Inferior Court & Tax Digests.

less joining lands of Vinson Johnson and others it being better known as the property of Neal ?Hure and being sold by the sheriff as there property to have and to hold said bargained premises and I the said James W Smith will forever warrant and defend the rights and titles I bind myself my heirs executors administrators jointly & ____ unto the said William Littleton his heirs and assigns forever in fee simple.

In witness whereof I the said James W. Smith hath hereunto set my hand and seal this day and year above written

In presence of us, James W Smith and James B Smith

Recorded the ?20ᵗʰ day of
S R Culpepper J. P. February 1846

James Pilcher Clerk

Matthews of Paulding County

Jeremiah Matthews was born 1757, died September 1842 in Newton County, Georgia. He married Sarah Johnson, born 1766, died 1850 Newton County. Issue:

I.   William Matthews.

II.   Burrell Matthews.

III.   Elbert Matthews.

IV.   Cary J. Matthews, born 1800, died 1878 Paulding County. He married Sarah Smith, born 1802, died 1883 Paulding County. Issue:

> A.   Peter Gilbert Matthews was born 13 June 1831, died 15 August 1898, buried in the High Shoals Cemetery in Paulding County. He married on 4 Febrary 1850 in Paulding County, Elizabeth Holland, daughter of Archibald Holland, born 1833 in old Atlanta, Ga., died 1915, buried High Shoals Cemetery, Paulding County, Ga. He served in Confederate Army, Pvt., County C., 2nd GA State Line. SEE Holland. Issue:[263]
>
> > 1.   George W. Matthews, born 1858 in Paulding County, married (1) on 24 December 1884 in Paulding County, Fannie Bullock, and, (2) Nora Hudson (born 1857), daughter of Doc Hudson.[264] Issue:[265]
> > a.   Nancy M. Matthews, born 1876 in Reynolds, Taylor County.

---

[263]   1860 Paulding County Census; Paulding County Marriages; Holland 1000-1988 by Jeannette Holland Austin; 1880 Paulding County Census

[264]   "Atlanta Constitution, 3/13/1928. Dallas, Georgia. Funeral Tuesday, of Mrs. Ledie Adair, 74. Nephew: J. H. Bullock, Sr. Three sons: A. L. Adair of Dallas; S. L. Adair of Atlanta; and J. A. Adair of Atlanta. Two sisters: Mrs. F. M. Matthews and Mrs. George Matthews, both of Dallas, Georgia.

[265]   1880 Taylor County Census, Reynolds District.

b. John H. Matthews, born 1878 in Reynolds, Taylor County.

2. James Casey Matthews, born 1865 in Paulding County, married on 1 December 1887 in Paulding County, Rody Frances Durham. He died 1924.

3. Arch Matthews, born 1869 in Paulding County, married (1) Nora Orr, (2) Georgia Lyle.

4. Lem Matthews, married on 30 August 1885 in Paulding County, M. T. Sloan.

5. Samuel Matthews, born 31 October 1872 in Paulding County, died 8 April 1892, buried High Shoals Cemetery, married on 9 July 1891 in Paulding County, Oma Crew.

6. Jesse Matthews, married (1) Miss Smith, (2) Mrs. Mollie Elsberry Tatum. Issue: Thomas, Peter, Minnie, Willie, Carney (died age 10), and Walter R. Matthews, married Frances Jones, daughter of Ben C. and Elizabeth Jones of Yorkville.

7. Thomas Matthews, born 31 August 1875 in Paulding County, died 9 November 1934, married (1) Anna Hicks, and (2) Mrs. Julia Aiken, 3rd, Mattie Aiken, cousin of Julia.

B. Benago Matthews.

C. Mary Matthews.

D. Sarah Matthews.

E. William Matthews.

F. Jeremiah Matthews.

G. Jesse Matthews.

H. Amanda Matthews married Mitchell Adair on 25 September 1853 in Paulding County..

I. Nancy Matthews.

V. Lewis M. Matthews.

VI. Elijah W. Matthews.

VII. Polly Matthews.

VIII. Cady Matthews married Mr. Johnson.

IX. Sarah Matthews married Mr. Bacon.

X. Jeremiah Matthews, born 1815 Georgia, farmer. Wife, Mary A. (born 1817 Georgia. They

267

lived in Paulding County. Issue:

    A. Joseph Matthews, born 1840 Georgia.
    B. William B. Matthews, born 1844 Georgia.
    C. Sarah Matthews, born 1847 Georgia.
    D. Richard Matthews, born 1849 Georgia.
    E. Amanda Matthews, born 1851 Georgia.
    F. Jeremiah M. Matthews, born 1854 Georgia. He married Elizabeth Stidham on 19 December 1878 in Paulding County.
    G. Mary Ann Matthews, born 1857 Paulding County.

McGarity of Milton & Paulding Counties

W. C. McGarity was born 1851 in Georgia. He married Sarah E. Jones (born 1853 in Georgia) on 10 November 1872 in Paulding County. They were residents of Double Branch, Georgia, in 1880.[266] Portions of old Milton County fell into Douglas, Fulton and Paulding Counties. Issue:

I.   Green J. McGarity, born 1873 in Milton County.

II.   Charles B. McGarity was born 1874 in Milton County. He married on 29 June 1916 in Paulding County, May Belle Hitchcock, a daughter of James Overton Hitchcock and his wife, Memmine (Bone) Hitchcock. Issue;

    A. Janet Adair McGarity married J. Mac Barber.
    B. Marcia McGarity married Thomas H. Rogers, Jr.
    C. Mable McGarity married John A. Chambers.
    D. Georgia McGarity married Rochford Johnson.

III.   John H. McGarity, born 1876 in Milton County.

IV.   Willis A. McGarity, born 1878 in Milton County.

McGee of Crawford County

The family in Crawford County began with David McGee who married Elvira Hammock and had issue, John McGee, as follows:

John McGee, born 13 November 1831, died 3 October 1903 in Crawford County. He was married to Sara Ann Sawyer, born 10 March 1835, died 11 November 1876 in Crawford County, the daughter of Watson Sawyer and his wife, Susanna (Castleberry) Sawyer. Issue:[267]

I.   Sara Ella McGee, born 23 March 1855 in Crawford County, died 24 December 1927.

II.   John Wilson McGee, born 22 December 1856 in Crawford County, died 5 March 1936.

III.   Emma Jane McGee, born 9 November 1858 in Crawford County.

---

[266] 1880 Milton County Census, Double Branch District.

[267] Personal records of Jeannette Holland Austin.

IV. Julius Sawyer McGee was born 25 January 1864 in Crawford County, died 7 February 1928. He was married on 18 May 1892 in Crawford County to Mary Pauline Dent, born 5 April 1870 in Crawford County, died 7 April 1942 in Roberts, Georgia, a daughter of William James Dent and his wife, Mary Jane (Davis) Dent. SEE Dent. Issue:

    A. Jason R. McGee, born 25 October 1893 in Crawford County, married Bonnie E. Martin on 2 January 1918, a daughter of Allen L. Martin and his wife, Claudia (Sutton) Martin. Issue:

        1. Jason R. McGee, Jr., born 22 December 1918, married Millicent Schrushy.
        2. Allen Martin McGee, born 13 October 1920, married Clara Taylor.
        3. Claudia Virginia McGee, born 26 April 1933, married Joseph A. Scott.

    B. Irma McGee, born 22 October 1896, died 2 December 1897 in Crawford County.

    C. Julius McGee, born 25 October 1897 in Crawford County, married Ludy Mae Corley.

    D. Paul McGee, born 29 January 1900 in Crawford County, died 3 March 1967, married Helen Lynch. Issue:

        1. Helen McGee married Frederick Hackmann.
        2. Ronald McGee married Margie.
        3. Janet McGee married Dennis Pearsall.

    E. Cathryn McGee, born 20 August 1902 in Roberta, Crawford County, married Clyde McClure.

    F. Mary Myrtis McGee, born 21 January 1905 in Roberta, Crawford County, married George William Jacobs, II on 28 August 1927.

    G. Sarah Virginia McGee, born 2 July 1907, died 17 January 1916 in Roberta, Crawford County.

    H. Minnie Pauline McGee, born 2 November 1911 in Roberta, Crawford County, married Edgar Jackson Smith.

    I. William Dalton McGee, born 16 November 1913 in Roberta, Crawford County, Georgia, married Mary Christine Smith on 13 February 1942. Issue:

        1. Carol McGee, born 2 April 1945 in Macon, Bibb County.

V. Minnie Lee McGee, born 4 May 1865 in Crawford County, died 14 May 1868.

VI. Edgar Lee McGee, born 4 April 1866 in Crawford County, died 22 January 1937.

Travis McKinney was born ca 1733 in Virginia, and died before 1800 in Lincoln County, Georgia. He and his wife, Ann, came to Georgia from Amelia County, Virginia. Issue:

I. John McKinney was born 1759 in Virginia, and died 25 August 1837 in Lincoln County, Georgia.

II. William McKinney was born in 1765 in Virginia and died 1813 in Baldwin County, Georgia. He was married to Jane Gresham who died in Monroe County. Issue:

A. George McKinney, son of William McKinney, was born ca 1790 in Lincoln County.

B. William McKinney, son of William McKinney, was born 9 December 1794 in Lincoln County, died 8 March 1854 in Upson County.

C. John McKinney, son of William McKinney, was born 1800 in Lincoln County, died 21 July 1877 in Talbot County. Wife, Julia A. (born 1805 in Georgia). Issue:[268]

   1. Elizabeth J. McKinney, born 1826 in Georgia.
   2. John H. McKinney, born 1828 in Georgia.
   3. Joshua T. McKinney, born 1830 in Georgia.
   4. Sarah A. McKinney, born 1832 in Georgia.
   5. James H. McKinney, born 1834 in Georgia.
   6. Monroe M. McKinney, born 1836 in Georgia.
   7. Margaret J. L. McKinney, born 1838 in Georgia.
   8. Elizabeth McKinney, born 1842 in Georgia.

D. Gresham McKinney, son of William McKinney, was born 22 September 1802 in Lincoln County, died on 10 April 1845 in Monroe County, married (1) on 24 February 1834 in Monroe County, Verlinda Chambliss (born 26 November 1812 in Baldwin County, died 27 September 1836 in Monroe County), a daughter of Zachariah Chambliss and his wife, Mary, and (2) Patience Gresham on 8 January 1839 in Wilkes County. Issue:

   1. William Zacharias McKinney, born 20 November 1831 in Monroe County.

   2. Alexander Gresham McKinney, born 7 October 1832 in Monroe County.

   3. Bianco Elizabeth Verlinda McKinney, born 17 April 1834 in Monroe County.

   4. Joel Jackson McKinney, born 20 November 1835 in Monroe County.

   5. John C. McKinney, born 1840 in Monroe County.

E. Travis McKinney, son of William McKinney, was born 10 April 1805 in Lincoln County, died 6 July 1875 in Monroe County.

---

[268] 1850 Monroe County Census.

III. Mary McKinney, daughter of William McKinney, was born ca 1767 in Virginia.

IV. Anney McKinney, daughter of William McKinney, was born ca 1769 in Virginia.

Mercer of Virginia, North Carolina; Wilkes County

CHRISTOPHER MERCER was christened on 8 July 1612 at St. Albins Abbey, Hertford, England and m. Mary Simson, the daughter of Thomas and Sarah Simson on 3 November 1644 at Stepney Parish, London, England. He migrated to Lower Norfolk, Virginia, where his estate was listed in 1711. His son:

THOMAS MERCER of Lower Norfolk County, Virginia, married 1671 Kathren Bigge (or Biggs), the daughter of John Bigge and wife, Joan Norsworthy. His LWT was dated 1718 Lower Norfolk County, Virginia.
His son:

JOSEPH MERCER was born 1680 Norfolk, VA and died May of 1765 in Norfolk, Virginia. He married Amy Ives.
His son:

JAMES MERCER was born 1713 in Norfolk, Virginia, and removed to Currituck Co., North Carolina about 1767. He was listed on the 1755 Currituck County., North Carolina Tax Digest, Along with Jeremiah and Thomas Mercer. James removed to Wilkes Co., Georgia by 1777 where he was found listed receiving 150 acres on first branch that makes into Harden's Creek (where he is camped)the "ceded lands" in 1777, having a wife, two sons and five daughters, from 13 years old to 3 months old.

James Mercer married (1) Ann Jones (ca1723-ca 1748) of Princess Anne, Virginia, daughter of John Jones and Ann Spann, losing her early, thus left to raise their three children. He m. 2d, Sarah Simmons of Currituck, North Carolina and by her had seven children. He was a devotee to the High Church, and was violent opposed to all other religious denominations, especially Baptists.

> "...but being a man of vigorous and discriminating mind, and thinking for himself, when he came by conversion under the influence of vital, experimental piety, he was naturally led into that course of investigation which gradually carried him beyond the circle of educational prejudice and ecclesiastical tradition, and established him in a faith and practice more in harmony with the simplicity of the gospel. He soon began to question the validity of sprinkling as Scripture baptism, and in accordance with the rubric of the Episcopal Church, which ejoined immersion, except when the health of the child might seem to require a milder mode, he had two of his children dipped.

> The first was Jesse, who was immersed in a barrel of water at the clergyman's house....At last he gained consent to attend a Baptist meeting, and listened to a discourse from one of their
> ministers.

> His prejudices began to yield, and he was inclined to cherish more kind and charitable feelings towards the people he had so long despised.....

> "About this time he removed with his family to Georgia and settled in Wilkes Co. Having at length become thoroughly convinced of the propriety of believers' baptism,

271

he was baptised in the year 1775 by Alexander Scott, and became a member of the Kiokee Church...Very soon he was licensed by his church to preach, and at once commenced a career of ministerial labor and usefulness characterized by much zeal and ability. The name of Silas Mercer will ever occupy an honored place in the records of American Baptists."

Sunday meetings were frequently held in the log-cabin home of James Mercer and his wife, and his grandson, Jesse Mercer, remembered this as a time when he felt the spirit of the Lord.

Issue of James Mercer, and his 1st wife, Jane Jones:

I. Lydia Mercer, daughter of James Mercer.

II. Rhoda Mercer, daughter of James Mercer.

III. Jacob Mercer, son of James Mercer and Sarah, born ca 1739.

IV. Thomas Mercer, son of James Mercer and Sarah, born ca 1741.

V. Sarah Mercer, daughter of James Mercer and Sarah, born ca 1743.

VI. Chloe Mercer, daughter of James Mercer and Sarah, born ca 1745.

VII. Mary Mercer, daughter of James Mercer and Sarah.

Issue of James Mercer and his 2nd wife, Sarah Simmons:

VIII. Silas Mercer, son of James Mercer, born 1745 near Currituck Bay, North Carolina, died 1796 Wilkes County, Georgia where he had moved in 1767. His mother died when he was an infant. He married (1) Dorcas Green, born 18 December 1743 in Stafford Co., Virginia, Overwharton Parish. She died on 7 September 1819 in Wilkes County, and was the daughter of William Green, Sr. and Ann Robinson. Ann Robinson married on 18 December 1743, William Green in Overwharton Parish. Silas Mercer married (2) Ann Thompson, daughter of Samuel Thompson of Wilkes Co., 15 May 1828. His mother died when he was an infant.

During the American Revolution, Silas Mercer was a Chaplain for the North Carolina Troops. Apparently after the war, he left Currituck County, North Carolina, to settle in Wilkes County, Georgia. The first record in Wilkes Co. was in 1777 when Silas Mercer, from North Carolina, having a wife, one son and one daughter, aged from 4 to 2 years old and 3 indentured children, received from the "ceded lands" in Wilkes Co., being 100 acres on a Little Spring branch about a mile below his father's land at a place called "Indian Ladder". [269]

---

[269] A deed of Silas Mercer and his wife, Dorcas of Halifax Co., North Carolina to Dempsey Battle of Edgecombe County, North Carolina, 750 acres on a branch of Shoulderbone Creek, being an original Grant to said Mercer in July of 1784.

Silas Mercer deeded to the heirs of John Mulkey, decd, viz, Nancy, John, Elizabeth, Mary and James, 250 acres on Hardins Creek, 6 December 1785.

William Greene of Wilkes Co., Ga. Deeded to Silas Mercer of Wilkes Co., Ga. For $20.00, 287 ½ acres of land in Washington Co. on Little Beaverdam fork of Richland Creek, boarding the Academy line. 6 December 1785.

Silas Mercer died in 1796, as we find appraisers appointed on 13 September 1796, in Wilkes Co., said appraisers being Thomas Grant, Thompson Bird, James Patterson and Phillip Wilhite. The Southern Centinel and Universal Gazette dated 18 August 1796, published his death...."Rev. Silas Mercer, minister of the Baptist Church on Little River, Wilkes County, died 1 August 1796". He was buried at Ficklen, Georgia, between Sharon and Washington, and it is believed that this is near the spot where he originally settled. It is near Phillips Mill Church and not very far from Bethesda, where both Silas and Jesse's homes were located -- on the north prong of Little River. Jesse Mercer, his son, was appointed administrator. 23 February 1801 a bond for 287 ½ acres of land in Greene County on Richland Creek, originally the land grant to William Green, Sr., Jesse Mercer, admr of Estate of Silas Mercer. Thomas Cartwright asked for good titles.

A petition of Rev. Jesse Mercer, admr of Rev. Silas Mercer, deceased, to sell 320 acres of land "being the whole of the real estate of said deceased". (1802)

Jesse Mercer, administrator of the estate of Silas Mercer, record in his annual return, "Cash arising from the sale of a paper on the estate., viz, solder's bounty, $218.75". Also, paid his mother's dower. 23 May 1812. Heirs of Silas Mercer were named in the estate proceedings.

Issue of Silas Mercer and wife, Dorcas:

December 1787, a Warrant for 200 acres was given to the heirs of John Mulkey, decd, adj. Silas Mercer, etc., in lieu of an old warrant and survey of their deceased father.

Silas Mercer and wife, Dorcas, deed to Samuel Walker, 200 acres on Legets branch of Fishing creek agreeable to a land grant in 1784 to said Mercer. 10 February 1789.

James Burke of Burke Co., Ga. gave Power of Attorney to Silas Mercer of Wilkes Co. "so far as concerns a bounty of 700 acres allowed me for service in Third Company of Troops", 11 February 1790. On the same day he agreed to sell this land to Silas Mercer as soon as clear titles could be made.

Deed of Silas Mercer and his wife, Dorcas, of Wilkes County, Georgia. to Elisha Battle of Edgecombe County, North Carolina, 300 acres on Fishing Creek of the Oconee River near Washingtn Co., being the original Land Grant dated 1785 to said Mercer. 9 April 1791.

Rev. Silas Mercer labored in The Sardis Church (originally called Hutton's Fork), which was constituted by him in 1785. It was then located in Wilkes Co. (now Taliaferro Co.)

In 1785, he also constituted The Bethesda Church , also Powell's Creek Church, in Powellton, Hancock Co., Ga., which was constituted in July of 1786 with twenty-six ministers. By February 1797, his son, Jesse Mercer, assumed the church as its pastor.

Silas Mercer, James Mercer, James Mercer and Jacob Mercer were listed on the 1793 Wilkes County Tax Digest, Turner's District.

 A. Jesse Mercer, son of Silas Mercer, was born 16 December 1769 in Halifax County, North Carolina in 1745, died 6 September 1841 at the house of brother James Carter in Indian Springs, married (1) Sabrina Chivers (born 1769, died 23 September 1826) in January of 1788. The notice of the death of Sabrina appeared in the <u>Georgia Journal</u> dated 10 October 1826. "Mrs. Sabrina Mercer, wife of Jesse Mercer, 55 years, died 9/13/1826 in Andersonville, South Carolina at the house of Mr. J. Harrison of billious fever. Her body was removed during the construction of Hartwell Dam by the Corps of Engineers and reinterred in Penfield Cemetery, Greene Co., Georgia, at the request of the Georgia Baptist Association. Sabrina Chivers was the aunt of Robert Chivers, who was father of the famous Georgia poet, Thomas Holley Chivers.

Jesse married (2) Nancy Simons (died May 1841) on 11 December 1827 in Wilkes County, buried Washington Baptist Church, Wilkes Co. Jesse Mercer came to Georgia at the age of four years, about 4 December 1773, with one sister, two years of age, and five other (indentured) children.

From the records of the Phillips' Mill Church, he was made a candidate for baptism on 7 July 1787, and was subsequently baptised by his father, Rev. Silas Mercer. Before he was twenty years old, he was ordained a minister by Phillips' Church. His first effort to preach was made in the "humble log-house of his grandmother, where the people had asseumbled for a Sunday prayer meeting....In January 1788, being then nineteen years of age, he was united in marriage to Miss Sabrina Chivers, a most devotedly pious young woman, and a member of the Phillips' Mills church...." <u>Baptist Denomination in Georgia</u>, page 384-385.

"Mr. Mercer was not, in the strictest sense, an educated man. At the time of his marriage his education was comparatively limited, but, in his great anxiety to increase his scanty store of knowledge, he sold his little farm and moved with his wife into a little house on Fishing Creek, near a respectable school, under the charge of Rev. Mr. Springer, a Presbyterian minster of considerable learning and talent. Here he contined for two years, in the meantime filling his engagements with the Hutton's Fork (now Sardis) Church in Wilkes Co. After attending the school of Mr. Springer for two years, he returned to his father's, and continued another year in the study of the lanaguages under Mr. Armor. "After all, Mr. Mercer never attained a very profound knowledge of the ancient languages, though his knowledge was sufficient to enable him to examine difficult passages. ...

"The Sardis church (originally called Hutton's Fork), gathered by the labors of Silas Mercer, was the first church over which Jesse Mercer was caled to preside as pastor....Shortly after the death of his father, he was called to take his place in that pulpit, which he accepted and entered on the work some time in 1796. This church he served regularly for thirty-nine years...During his connection with the church he baptized into its fellowship something like two hundred and thirty persons."

Jesse Mercer also preached at the Bethesda Church from 1796 until 1827, where his membership resided from 1807 to 1816.

On 4 February 1797, Jesse Mercer assumed charge of Powell's Creek Church in

Powellton, Hancock County and remained its minister until 1825. About February of 1818, he removed his family from Greene Co. to Powellton, where he resided for seven or eight year. From 1820 to 1826 he was pastor of a church in Eatonton, Putnam County.

After attending the General Convention in 1826, upon passing through the upper part of South Carolina, his wife was brought low by disease, and died on 23 September 1826, at Andersonville, Pendleton District. He then returned to Wilkes County to reside. In December of 1827 he became pastor of a church in Washington, Georgia. In 1833 Jesse Mercer purchased <u>The Christian Index:</u>, published in Philadelphia by Dr. Brantly, and moved it to Washington Co. By 1840, the newspaper was tendered by the Baptist State Convention, and removed to Penfield, Georgia. From 1795 until the session of 1816, Jesse Mercer officiated as the clerk of the Georgia Association; he was moderator of the Georgia Baptist Station Convention, 1839-1841.

> "He gave, also, much of his influence, and contributed liberally of his means, to sustain a Baptist college in the District of Columbia. The Mercer University, from its beginning to the close of his life, he devoted his best energies, giving large sums of money to its endowment while he lived, and making it the principal legatee of his estate.....

> "The personal appearance of Mr. Mercer was well calculated to arrest the attention of the beholder, and fix a lasting impression on his mind. No one that ever saw him would be likely to forget him. In height he rose somewhat above the ordinary standard; in his young days he was spare, but in his advanced years when in health, he was moderately corpulent. Time had gradually removed the greater portion of his hair, leaving at last but a few thin, straight locks on the sides and back of his head, which still retained their original dark brown color. His extreme baldness revealed to all the exact size and confirmation of the citadel of his noble mind. This conformation was very remarkable. The horizontal length of his head, from his eye-brows back, was very great, while his forehead seemed to rise upward with a gently receding slope even to the very crown, exhibiting a most striking development of which phrenologgists term the organs of benevolence, veneration and firmness. His eye, which was of a hazel color, and rather small, and deeply sunk, was clear and sparkling, and beamed with a sweet, mingled expression of affection and intellience. What he appeared to be, he really was."

At the time of his death, on 6 September 1841 at Indian Springs, in the home of brother James Carter, he threw his arms around the neck of his nephew, who was present, and drawing him close to his lips, said, "*I have no fears.*"

Jesse Mercer was buried in the churchyard near where the Mercer Chapel now stands, and remained there until after 1848, when the Georgia Baptist Convention set apart a burial site for the Penfield Community in Greene Co., and reinterred it, locating it on the highest spot in the cemetery. This displeased the Washington Church, as they wanted his remains buried beside his last wife, and it caused some contention for years to come.

On 22 January 1847, David E. Butler, executor of Jesse Mercer, decd, William F. Baker, the other executor, having removed to Mississippi), deeded to Jacob Printup, lot southeast of Crawfordville known as the brick house and lot formerly owned by Hermon Mercer adjoining John Rhodes, 146 acres. Taliaferro Deed Book D, page 185.

On 1 March 1847, David E. Butler, executor of Jesse Mercer, decd, deed to Gilbert Kent, a 3-acre lot in Crawfordville, on east by Town, south by Augusta Road, east by Washington Road, north by Bartholomew Lot, now John Janes lot, and west by Thompson's lot, which said lot was deeded by Hermon Mercer to Jesse Mercer 1 December 1838. Taliaferro Deed Book D, page 209.

Issue of Jesse Mercer:

    1. Miriam Mercer born ca 1798, died 9 months later, 1799, in Virginia.

    2. Miriam Mercer born ca 1803, died 1814 in Greene County, was buried in the Bethesda Cemetery; later reinterred Penfield Cemetery in Greene County on 5 November 1943.

B. Anna Mercer, daughter of Silas Mercer, born 10 December 1774, married in Georgia, William Robertson (born 16 January 1771) on 28 June 1792. She was christened at Phillips Mill Church in 1789, and died in 1852 in Lincoln, Tennessee. Issue:

    1. Gilbert Robertson, born 15 August 1794, married Matilda Andrews (born 1801) in Georgia, in 1817. Issue:

        a. Silas Mercer Robertson, born 13 December 1833, died 18 October 1910, married in Tennessee in August of 1865, Prudence Ann, born 29 June 1837. Issue:

            i. Vincent Franklin Robertson born 27 May 1867 in Lincoln County, Tennessee, married Addie Lorena Cunningham (born 19 September 1885) on 18 December 1912 in Sevier County, Tennessee.

            ii. Thomas William Robertson, born 6 March 1874.

            iii. Ezekiel Wagner Robertson, born 9 October 1877.

    b. Winnie Ann Thornton Robertson, born 6 December 1835, died 29 July 1896.

C. Mary Mercer, daughter of Silas Mercer, was born ca 1776, Wilkes County, the daughter of Silas Mercer, died infancy.

D. Daniel Mercer, son of Silas Mercer, was born 1780 in Wilkes County, died 26 February 1830 in 1830 Henry County, married Sarah Tuggle of Greene Co., (b. ca 1812) died without issue. [270]

---

[270] Henry Co. Deeds: Book C/D, page 518: "Greene Co., Daniel Mercer of said county deeds to William Tuggle, 12 November 1825 for $550, in consideration for a negro boy named Miles; Book F, page 22, Sarah Mercer to Ransom Tuggle on 1 September 1830 for $300.00, 101-1/4 acres in Lot 31 of 11th District; Book G, page 419, Samuel Wyatt on 10 January 1835 received of John Mercer $500.00,full payment of a certain negro woman named, Nancy, aged ca 30.

E. Mourning Mercer, daughter of Silas Mercer, was born ca 1782 Wilkes Co., Ga., daughter of Silas Mercer, died infancy.

F. Hermon Mercer, son of Silas Mercer, was born 1784 in Wilkes County, died 13 January 1854 in Ochusee, Jackson County, Florida, son of Silas Mercer, his name being given from the Biblical "Mount Hermon", married Elizabeth Andrews 3 September 1802 in Greene County, Hermon, being among the first settlers to Taliaferro County, made the town plan for Crawfordville. His brick mansion was built in the early 1830's, facing the Janes house, and adjoining lot of William Janes (which was on the northeast corner of Broad and Ray, formerly Reynolds Streets). The home was razed in the 1950's

His son, Dr. Leonidas B. Mercer, married Lovicia Janes, daughter of William Janes, Sr. Also, William Janes', son, William, Jr., married Rebecca, a daughter of John Mercer (the half brother of Silas Mercer, Jesse and Hermon's father).

He was among the first five justices in Taliaferro Co., and presided over the first Inferior Court on15 May 1826; also was first city commissioner. His influence was felt throughout the community of Crawfordville, taking an active part in civil affairs.

Hermon and his brother, Joshua, were long-time members of the Baptist Church and among the members of Palmyra Church in Lee Co. during the formative years. He helped found the First Baptist Church in Albany.[271]

---

[271] 4 April 1828, Hermon Mercer gave a promissory note to Jesse Mercer in the amount of $3310.00, for 500 acres on Little River, adj. Robert's land, which included the mills formerly belonging to William and Thomas Janes. (Note Satisfied). Taliaferro Deed Book A, page 96.

8 May 1836, Hermon Mercer deeded Thomas J. Shackelford, Crawfordville Lot No. 27, containing a near one acre in the Plan of the said Town, adjoining Academy on the north and Davant's Lot, which is now Calloways. Taliaferro Deed Book A, page 233.

16 October 1837, Hermon Mercer deeded Thomas Shackelford, Crawfordville Lot No. 29, north of the railroad, north by street and Mrs. Gresham's lot, owned by said Mercer, and west by street and lot belonging to the Estate of William Janes. Taliaferro Deed Book A, page 332.

11 January 1839, Hermon Mercer deeded to Joel E. Mercer, the west half of Lot No. 22 through which the Georgia Railroad runs, adjoining Thomas Wynn, being 4 ½ acres....as well as the eastern half of Lot No. 28 bounded on the east by Washington Street, being 4 ½ tenths of an acres. Taliaferro Deed Book B, page 495.

31 December 1838, Hermon Mercer deeded to Jesse Mercer of Wilkes Co. That parcel of land whereon "my brick house stands" and other outhouses and the land adjoining, lying southeast of Crawfordville, 150 acres, for $5000. Also, a certain lot, 3 acres, in Crawfordville, south by the Augusta Road, East by Washington Road, North by Bartholomew's lot, and west by Thompson's lot. Taliaferro Deed Book C, page 13-14.

10 August 1839, Hermon Mercer deeded to Gutus Lockett, a Crawfordville Lot lying near the Big Spring on the southside of the Georgia Railroad, Mercer's Wood and Iron Shop lot, north by the Georgia Railroad, E by Thompson's land, south by the lot of A. G. Taylor, and west by the street at the east of Crawfordville. Taliaferro Deed Book A, page 299.

G. Mount Moriah Mercer, son of Silas Mercer, was born 1781, died 1822, joined the church at Williams' Creek in 1809, married Nancy Ann Edge (born 1798) of Wilkes Co. in 1815 Oglethorpe County; listed on 1820 Taliaferro County Census, and died in Oglethorpe County, leaving widow and three children. Issue:

    1. Jim Mercer, son of Mount Moriah Mercer.

    2. Ann Moriah Mercer, daughter of Mount Moriah Mercer.

    4. Elizabeth Mercer, daughter of Mount Moriah Mercer, married James H. B. Shackelford.

H. Joshua Mercer, son of Silas Mercer, was born 20 July 1788 in Wilkes County, died 4 February 1869 in Gordon, Henry County, Alabama. He married Mary D. Wells. He was also a preacher, was raised his brother, Mount Moriah Mercer's three orphan children. He was a member of the Baptist Church at Palmyra, Lee County, Georgia. From the Minutes of Palmyra Baptist Church, "after prayer by Rev. Joshua Mercer, the committee, agreeable to instruction, reported the following resolution which was unanimously adopted, to-wit: "Resolved that we will call the church Palmyra, in honor of our ancient and beautiful city in Syria built by King Solomon." (2/26/1837)

Issue of James Mercer and his 2nd wife, Sarah Simmons, continued:

IX. Vashti Mercer, daughter of James Mercer and Sarah, born after 1759, died after 1816 Georgia, married in Currituck County, North Carolina, George Franklin of Currituck County (born 1744, died 1816 Burke County, Georgia), a son of William Franklin. SEE Franklin

XI. James Mercer, son of James Mercer and Sarah, born 1769 in Halifax, North Carolina, married Elizabeth Williamson on 11 April 1807 in Wilkes County.. He died in December 1850 in Coweta County. His older brother, Silas Mercer, also receiving the "ceded lands".

XII. John Mercer, Colonel, born 1778 Wilkes County married Sarah Chivers. Listed 1850 Lee County, Georgia Census. The LWT of John Mercer, Lee Co., page 44-47, names sons and daughter. John Mercer was a trustee of Penfield School in Greene Co., which later became Mercer University. He came from Oglethorpe Co. to Lee Co. with his son, Dr. Leonidas B. Mercer, during the 1830's, to settle Crawfordville, and was instrumental in founding the Palmyra Baptist Church.

Issue:

A. Rebecca C. Mercer married William Janes, Jr. on 14 December 1826 in Taliaferro County.

B. Joel Elreath Mercer.

C. Dr. Leonidas Bennington Mercer, born 1803 in Georgia, married in Taliaferro County on 23 August 1826 Lovicia Janes (born 1811 in Virginia, died 13 Ocotber 1841), a daughter of William Janes and Selah Graham, of Crawfordville, Georgia.[272] They were married by Hermon Mercer. He married (2) Mary Ann Hilsman, (born

---

[272] Notice of this marriage appeared in the Georgia Journal.

1824 Ga.) on 20 September 1842 in Hancock County, daughter of Bennett Hilsman and Lowella Harvie. Listed 1850 Lee County Census.

Leonidas B. Mercer was active in Palmyra Baptist Church (Lee Co.), beng a deacon there, and appointed in 1837, along with William Janes and Joshua Mercer, to a committee to raise subscriptions for building an academy and house of worship. L. B. Mercer, John Mercer and James B. Mercer were appointed to draft plans for the house.[273]

Dr. Mercer, according to a historical marker in Crawfordville, was trustee of Crawfordville Academy (later Alexander Stephens Institute), said to be one of the finest of the early Georgia academies (chartered 1826). Among the first trustees were: Archibald Gresham, Hermon Mercer and Leonidas B. Mercer.

In George White's Historical Collections of Georgia, Dr. Mercer is said to have cleared one of the worst shoals on the Flint River, which helped improve navigation to Albany.

Dr. E. Merton Coulter, in his book, Georgia, A Short History, page 287, he stated that Dr. Mercer was appointed gy Governor Towns in 1849 on a committee to study school plans for the State. And, in the book, College Life in the Old South says that Dr. Mercer was a trustee of the University of Georgia.

Dr. Mercer was a doctor, geologist, naturalist, weather observer, writer, lecturer, farmer, legislator from Lee County and Delegate for Georgia. From the Second District....Also, President of the Atlanta Fair in 1857.
His LWT recorded in Terrell County Book A, page 11-12, dated 16 August 1860, probated 29 January 1859. Executors: Leonidas Mercer, William Janes, John B. Gilbert. Wits: Jeremiah Hilsman, James Pope, Leemon D. McLendon.

Issue of Dr. Leonidas B. Mercer and Lovica Janes:

1. Selah Ann Rosemon Mercer, daughter of Dr. Leonidas B. Mercer and Lovicia Jane, born 24 July 1836, died 1897, married Council B. Wooten on 10 March 1859. They were parents of Mrs. W. T. Tift of Albany, W. E. Wooten, and John Wooten.

2. Joel Edward Mercer, born 1832 Ga.

3. John Thomas Mercer, killed in War Between the States.

---

[273] William Janes deeded L. B. Mercer, his son-in-law, land in Taliaferro Co., 7 April 1827. Taliaferro Deed Book A, page 75.

On 2 February 1830, Archibald Gresham and Leonidas B. Mercer, deacons of Bethal Baptist Church at Crawfordville deed to George Tilley two acres on headwaters of the Ogeechee, formerly owned by Elijah Williams. Taliaferro Deed Book A, page 182.

On 6 August 1836, Leonidas B. Mercer deed land to Mary McCormick. Taliaferro Deed Book A, page 364.

Issue of Dr. Leonidas B. Mercer and Mary Ann Hilsman:

4. Mary Gertrude Mercer.

5. Frances Addison Lamar Mercer, born 10 January 1847, married (1) Dr. James L. D. Perryman of Leary, Georgia and had one child, Lee Perryman. She married (2) David Buckner Jones and had one child, Erin Mercer Jones who m. David Brady Sherman. They had issue: David Mercer Sherman of Albany, born 6 August 1906, married on 16 June 1829 Ernestine Ayers Walker, born 3 August 1909 (had sons, John Mercer Sherman, born 20 August 1945 and David Maurice Sherman, born 6 July 1943), and Dr. Henry Thomas Sherman of Valdosta, born 11 August 1910, married Ruth Morgan (had Issue: Henry Thomas Sherman, Erin Mercer Sherman and Mercer Lancaster Sherman).

6. Moriah Twigg Mercer.

Miles of Marion & Schley Counties

F.C. Miles married Mary Jane Munford (Monford). The family removed from Marion County Schley County in 1895, and they were buried in the Ellaville Cemetery in Schley County. Issue:

I. Essie Ophelia Miles, born 22 March 1896 in Ellaville, Schley County, died 4 March 1976 in Columbus, Georgia. She was a Nurse. She was the second wife of William Eugene Bennett, born 26 January 1822, died 13 February 1940, buried in Bigsby, Oklahoma, and married him ca 1922. Issue:

   A. Frank Lewis Bennett, twin, born 1923 in Wilkinson County.
   B. Louise Bennett, twin, born 1923 in Wilkinson County, died age 4 months.
   C. Paul Eugene Bennett, born 27 July 1924 in Camden, Arkansas, died 23 February 2000.

II. Oscar Miles, born 15 August 1897 in Schley County, died 25 October 1960, buried in Ellaville Cemetery. He was married to Bessie Mae Sorrells on 20 July 1918 who "now resides in Magnolia Manor Retirement Center in Americus, Ga." Issue:[274]

   A. Louis Weldon Miles, born 12 April 1920, resident of Bonifay, Florida.
   B. James Oscar Miles, born 4 May 1922, a resident of Americus.
   C. Raymond Alford Miles, born 19 May 1925, a resident of Bainbridge.
   D. Ruthie Elois Miles, born 5 February 1927 in Schley County, m arried Claude F. Fripp, Jr. on 26 April 1948. Claude died 21 April 1968, buried in Parkhill Cemetery, Columbus, Georgia.
   E. Clinton Miles, born 15 November 1929, a resident of Albany.
   F. Betty Joyce Miles, born 21 November 1932, a resident of Albany.
   G. Patricia Miles, born 13 March 1936., a resident of Columbus.
   H. Glenn Autry Miles, born 29 January 1940, a resident of Albany.

---

[274] History of Schley County, Georgia by the Schley County Preservation Society 1981-1982.

The Moody family of Paulding County come from a long line of Moody's from Charles City County, Virginia, through North Carolina, thence to Georgia.

Thomas Moody died 1656 in Weyanoke Parish, Charles City County, Virginia where his death was recorded on 3 October (Register). He married Ann Lawrence, a daughter of William Lawrence of Charles City County, Virginia. They had two known sons, viz:

I.   Samuel Moody, was born 1652 in Weyanoke Parish, Charles City County, Virginia, died after 1704.

II.   Robert Moody, was born 1654 in Weyanoke Parish, Charles City County, Virginia. He had a son, viz:

A.   Robert Moody, II, who died in Granville County, North Carolina, who married Ann ca 1722 in Prince George County, Virginia. Issue:[275]

1.   Robert Moody, III, son of Robert Moody II.
2.   John Moody, son of Robert Moody II, was christened 1723 in Bristol Parish, Virginia, died after 1790 in Franklin County, North Carolina. He married Miss Jackson and had issue:
     a.   William Moody, son of John Moody, was born ca 1740, died ca 1819, lived in Granville County, North Carolina. Issue:
          i.   John Moody, son of William Moody, of Granville County, North Carolina, died ca 1829.
          ii.   Thomas Moody, son of William Moody, born ca 1764 in Granville County, North Carolina, died 13 February 1851 in Pike County, Georgia. Wife, Sarah. Issue:
                (a) Henry Moody, son of Thomas Moody, was born 1790, of Chatham County, North Carolina.
                (b) Nancy Moody, daughter of Thomas Moody, was born 1795, of Chatham County, North Carolina, died February of 1857.
                (c) John S. Moody, son of Thomas Moody, was born 28 August 1798 of Chatham County, North Carolina, farmer, died 13 January 1886, buried in the Moody Place Cemetery, Yorkville, Georgia. Wife, Elizabeth, born 1813 in South Carolina. Issue:[276]
                     (1) Ezekiel W. Moody, born 1833 Georgia, died 1915. Miller. He married on 25 December 1857 in Paulding County, Emaline (Milly) Adair (born 2 February 1836 in Carroll County, died 26 August 1894 in Cobb County), a daughter of James Lee Adair and

---

[275] 1860-1870 Paulding County Census, Paulding County Marriages.

[276] 1860-1870 Paulding County Census.

his wife, Caroline (Evans) Adair. SEE Adair. Issue:[277]

> (i) Nathaniel Moody, born 1858 in Paulding County.
> (ii) Elizabeth Moody, born 9 September 1858 in Paulding County, died 22 December 1952.
> (iii)William Moody, born 1861 in Paulding County.
> (iv) James Moody, born 1865 in Paulding County.
> (v) Nathaniel G. Moody, born 3 February 1868 in Paulding County, died 4 August 1957.
> (vi) Caroline Jane Moody, born 25 December 1870 in Paulding County.
> (vii)Ezekiel W. Moody, born 1873 in Paulding County.
> (viii)Martha Emiline Moody, born in 1877 Paulding County.

(d) Gilley Moody, daughter of Thomas Moody, was born 1800, died before July 1827 in Georgia.
(e) William Moody, son of Thomas Moody, was born 12 March 1805 in Twiggs County, Georgia, died 10 November 1887 Moseley's Bluff, Union, Louisiana, where buried.
(f) Margaret Moody, daughter of Thomas Mooday, was born ca 1807 in Pike County, Georgia, died 1830/1831.
(g) Risa Moody, daughter of Thomas Moody, was born 1808 in Upson County, Georgia, died 1850-1851.
(h) Thomas Moody, son of Thomas Moody, was born 26 October 1811 in Georgia, died 29 October 1864 in Dallas, Paulding County, buried in the White Oak Cemetery. He was married on 24 May 1835 to Retency Hill Chapman (born 25 April 1820 Georgia, died 8 April 1884 in Paulding County, buried in the White Oak Cemetery), a daughter of Mrs. Deborah Chapman. After Thomas died, Retency and her children moved in with John S. Moody (1870 Paulding County Census. Issue:

> (1) Mary P. Moody, daughter of Thomas Moody, was born 1839 Paulding County.

---

[277] Ibid.

282

Living with John S. Moody on the 1870 Paulding County Census.

(2)   William T. Moody, son of Thomas Moody, was born 1841 Paulding County.

(3)   Celesta (or Calista) Moody, daughter of Thomas Moody, was born 17 August 1842 in Paulding County, died 9 March 1909, buried in Iredel, Bosque County, Texas. She married Joseph M. Cason on 24 December 1875 in Paulding County.

(4)   Leander Drucilla Moody, daughter of Thomas Moody, was born 3 October 1843 in Paulding County, died 28 April 1903, buried in Iredell, Bosque County, Texas.

(5)   Elizabeth Moody, daughter o f Thomas Moody, was born 1844 Paulding County, died 1930 in Henegar, DeKalb County, Alabama, buried in the High Point Cemetery.

(6)   Green B. Moody (or Debring), son of Thomas Moody, was born 1846 Paulding County, married Mary J. Cogburn on 13 January 1867 in Paulding County.

(7)   Ezekiel Moody, son of Thomas Moody, was born 1848 in Paulding County, married Polly Ann Cole on 22 December 1867 in Paulding County.

(8)   Elizabeth Moody, daughter of Thomas Moody, was born 1848 in Paulding County. Living with John S. Moody on the 1870 Paulding County Census.

(9)   Martha Jane Moody, daughter of Thomas Moody, was born 1850 Paulding County.

(10)   Caroline Moody, daughter of Thomas Moody, was born 1852 in Paulding County. Living with John S. Moody on the 1870 Paulding County Census.

(11) Samuel Moody, son of Thomas Moody, was born 1851 Paulding County. Living with John S. Moody on 1870 Paulding County Census.

(12) John M. Moody, son of Thomas Moody, was born 1852 Paulding County. Living with John S. Moody on 1870 Paulding County Census.

(13) Retensa Moody, daughter of Thomas Moody, was born 1853 Paulding County, married Lindsey Holland on 12 September 1872 in Paulding County. SEE Holland. Living with John S. Moody on 1870 Paulding County Census.

(14) Sophronia Moody, daughter of Thomas Moody, was born 5 May 1857 Paulding County, died 10 February 1893, buried in the White Oak Cemetery in Paulding County. Living with John S. Moody on 1870 Paulding County Census.

(15) Ellen Moody (or Emma) , daughter of Thomas Moody, was born 1859 Paulding County married H. R. Coal on 30 December 1877 in Paulding County. Living with John S. Moody on the 1870 Paulding County Census.

(16) Cassandra Moody, daughter of Thomas Moody, was born 1862 in Paulding County. Living with John S. Moody on the 1870 Paulding County Census.

    iii. Frances Moody, daughter of William Moody, of Granville County, North Carolina.
    iv. William Moody, son of William Moody, of Granville County, North Carolina.
    v. Ezekiel Moody, was born 1784 in Granville County, North Carolina, died before 1810.
    vi. Benjamin Moody, son of William Moody, was born 1767 in Granville County, North Carolina.
    vii. Joel Moody, son of William Moody, was born 1771 in Granville County, North Carolina, died 1852.
    viii.Riley Moody, son of William Moody, was born 1773 in Granville County, North Carolina.

  b. John Moody, Jr., son of John Moody.
  c. Jesse Moody, son of John Moody, died February 1788 in Greenville County, South Carolina.
  d. Fanny Moody, daughter of John Moody.
  e. Joel Moody, son of John Moody.

3. Joel Moody, son of Robert Moody, II.
4. Humphrey Moody, son of Robert Moody II.
5. Laurena Moody, daughter of Robert Moody II.

6. Frances Moody, daughter of Robert Moody II.
7. Daniel Moody, son of Robert Moody II.

Monfort/Montford/Munford of New Jersey;
Greene & Marion Counties

The Montfort family seat was in Holland, with the emigrant coming to New York during the early 1600's. The Georgia family begins with Wilhellemus Monfort, christened on 3 August 1744 in Harlingen, Montgomery, Somerset County, New Jersey. He died 19 September 1805. Wife, Ann, died 16 September 1829. Issue:

I. Peter Monford, born 1771/1772, died 8 September 1828 in Greensboro, Greene County.

II. James William Monford, born 1780/1800. He married Matilda Jane Patrick on 3 January 1822 in Greene County. Issue:
  A. Thomas Peter Monfort, born ca 1825 in Greensboro, Greene County. He married Charlotte Everingham (born 1837), listed as a widow with two children on the 1860 Marion County Census. She was also listed in the Marion County Homestead Records 1866-1921. Issue:
    1. Lewis Monfort, born 16 March 1851, died 1 August 1924 in Edison, Clay County. He married Mary Hamilton of Marion County. Issue:
      a. Minnie Monfort, born ca 1871, died ca 1873 in Marion County.
      b. Ella Monfort, born in Marion County.
      c. Thomas Peter Monfort, born 3 August 1872 in Marion County, died 25 July 1907 in Columbus, Muscogee County, Georgia, buried in Doyle, Marion County.
    2. Mary Monfort, born 1854 in Marion County. She married F. C. Miles. SEE Miles.
  H. William Wiley Monfort, born 17 July 1829 in Greene County. He married Emaline Russ on 11 January 1859 in Marion County.

III. Mary Monfort, born 1780/1781, died 23 September 1832.

IV. Rebecca Monfort, born ca 1782, died after 1836 in Greene County.

V. John S. Monfort, born 1790/1799, died between 1836 and 1850 in Greene County.

Moon of Pennsylvania, Virginia
Elbert, Greene & Madison Counties

Simon Moon, was christened on 11 April 1700 in Bucks County, Pennsylvania, and died November 1748 in Frederick County, Virginia, his LWT probated 11 November 1748. He left his "present dwelling" to two sons, James and Jacob Moon. To his son, Richard, and daughter, Mary Moon, he left a young grey mare. The remaining estate to be divided between James and Jacob and young daughters, Mary and Rachel. His son, James Moon and son-in-law, Henry Bowen, were executors. He married Leaurey Humphrey on 27 September 1721. The family were Quakers who left Pennsylvania to remove to the Hopewell Meeting in Frederick County, Virginia, then in 1759 to North Carolina. Hinshaw's Encyclopedia of Quaker Genealogy registered their births.

Issue:[278]

I. James Moon, born ca 1720 in Frederick County, Virginia.

II. Jacob Moon, born ca 1717 in Frederick County, Virginia, died 1793 in Greene County, Georgia. He married Mildred Cobb, a daughter of Bishop Cobb. SEE Cobb.. Albemarle County, Virginia Deed Book 3, page 249-251, Henry Martin deeded to Jacob Moon of Albemarle County, land on 8 May 1760. The Middle Creek Quaker Meeting House in the Village of Arden (Berkley County, now West Virginia), was founded in 1775 by Jacob Moon, a Friend, who named it for her former home village in Virginia. Issue:

A. Susannah Moon, born ca 1740, married Thomas Cobbs on 7 January 1756. SEE Cobbs.

B. Patsy Moon, born ca 1748 in Frederick County, Virginia, married Charles Martin.

C. Jacob Moon, Jr., Captain in the Revolutionary War, was , born ca 1750, died September 1781 in Bedford County, Virginia. He died of wounds that he received at Guilford Court House, North Carolina during the Revolutionary War. His LWT dated 2 March 1781, probated 24 September 1781 in Bedford County, named his brothers, William and Archelaus. He married Nancy Ann Ammons in 1778. After Jacob's death, Nancy married Samuel Hancock on 5 January 1784, per military records. Issue:

1. Christopher Moon was born on 11 August 1781 in Virginia, probably Bedford County.

D. Archalaus Moon, born ca 1754, married Ann Anderson on 29 December 1784. Archalaus was named as a brother of Jacob Moon, Jr. in Jacob's LWT dated 2 March 1781, probated 24 September 1781 in Bedford County, Virginia.

1. Pleasant Moon, born ca 1756.

E. Jesse Moon, born ca 1758, died October 1780 in Bedford County, Virginia.

F. Sally Moon, born ca 1760, married Silas Moorman.

G. William Moon, born 26 November 1770, married Charlotte Digges on 3 November 1793. He died 7 January 1811 in Elbert County. Wife, Sarah.[279] Issue:

---

[278] Frederick County, Virginia Wills; Bucks County, Pennsylvania Wills; Greene County Wills; Hancock County Wills; Hinshaw's Encyclopedia of Quaker Genealogy; Bedford County, Virginia Wills.

[279] The LWT of James Bell, dated 17 September 1807, Codicil 27 April 1808, probated January 1810, Elbert County. Sons : Joseph (eldest), James, William, Thomas, David, Jonathan. Daus: Patsy, Nancy. Married Daus: Polly, Elizabeth and Sarah Moon. Exrs: Wife, Olive and son, Joseph. Wits: Peter Wyche, Andrew Woodley, James Glover. Codicil mentions that Daughter, Nancy, married, has recd most of her legacy. Wits: Robins Andrews, Elizabeth Andrews, William Davis, William D. Davis, Reuben Davis.

1. Pleasant Moon, born 1771 in Elbert County, died March 1818 in Elbert County, his LWT dated 25 January 1818, probated 2 March 1818 in Elbert County; wife, Sarah and her brother, James Bell, were named as executors. Wife: Sarah. Issue:

    a. William H. Moon married Susan Moon on 25 October 1825 in Elbert County.
    b. James B. Moon married Mary Davis on 2 August 1821 in Elbert County.
    c. Pleasant Moon, born 1814, farmer. Wife, Susannah, born 1825 in Georgia. Issue:
        i. Olivea A. Moon (daughter), born 1843 in Madison County.
        ii. Susan (or Louisa) Moon, born 1844 in Madison County.
        iii. Wrenn Emalene Moon, born 1847 in Madison County.
        iv. Jonathan Moon, born 1854 in Madison County.
    d. John P. Moon.
    e. Gabrilla Moon.

2. Archelaus Moon, born 1776, died 1842 in Madison County. Wife, Matilda. Known issue:[280]
    a. Archelaus P. Moon, born 1816 in Danielsville, Madison County. Wife, Gabrilla, born 1817 in Georgia. No known issue.
    b. William T. Moon, born 1823 in Danielsville, Madison County. Wife, Martha C., born 1823 in Georgia. Issue:
        i. Susan G. Moon, born 1848 in Madison County.
        ii. Elizabeth A. Moon, born 1851 in Madison County.
        iii. Archelaus P. Moon, born 1858 in Madison County.

3. Martha Moon, born 1777, married Mr. Blake.

4. Robert Moon, born 1779, died 1824 in Jackson County.

5. Susannah Moon, died before 1828 in Georgia, married David Power on 15 October 1807 in Elbert County.

6. Jacob Moon, born 1792, died before 1810 in Elbert County.

7. Jesse Moon, born 1791, died before 1808 in Georgia.

8. John Moon.

9. Sally Green Moon married Mr. Power.

III. Richard Moon, born 1724, registered at the Hopewell Meeting (Quaker) in Frederick County, Virginia, died February 1795 in Hancock County, Georgia. He married on 4 February 1746, Susannah Beeson. The LWT of Richard Moon was probated 27 February 1795 in Hancock County, Georgia.

---

[280] 1850-1860 Madison County Census.

IV.   Mary Moon, born ca 1726.

V.   Hannah Moon, born 2 February 1729 in Chester County, Pennsylvania, died in Orange County, North Carolina.

VI.   Rachel Moon, born ca 1730.

VII.   Margaret Moon. Frederick County, Virginia. "Thomas Brown of Frederick County, Virginia married Margaret Moon, daughter of Simon Moon of the same place on 10 June 1748. New Garden Meeting, North Carolina."

Moon of Paulding County

John Moon was born 1831 in Georgia, resident of Dallas, Georgia in 1860. Wife, Sophronia, was born 1831 in Georgia. Issue:[281]

I.   Lewis Anthony Moon, born 1857 in Paulding County.

II.   Robert L. Moon, born 21 September 1853 in Paulding County, died 12 January 1899, buried in the Dallas City Cemetery. He married Sarah Jane Hagin (born 15 January 1861, died 9 April 1925, buried in the Dallas City Cemetery) on 24 September 1882 in Paulding County. SEE Hagin. Issue:

>   A.   Roland Moon, born 30 January 1891, died 10 December 1912, buried in the Dallas City Cemetery.

>   B.   Lloyd Moon.

>   C.   Bessie Moon, born 14 January 1885, died 9 December 1944, buried in the Dallas City Cemetery. She married Alex G. Spinks (born 15 June 1877, died 9 February 1935, buried in the Dallas City Cemetery. They were residents of Kentucky.

>   D.   Clara Moon, married Mr. Partee; schoolteacher in Dallas, then in Cuthburt, Georgia.

III.   Mary Moon, born 1860 in Paulding County.

III.   Harriet Moon, born 1862 in Paulding County, married T. B. Bullock on 30 December 1883 in Paulding County.

V.   Frances S. Moon, born 1864 in Paulding County, married Mr. Spinks.

---

[281] 1860-1870 Paulding County Census; The Hagan-Bryant Genealogies by Tom Hagan, Jr.; Paulding County Marriages.

Noland of Walton & Paulding Counties

Peyton Noland was born 1793 Wilkes County, married Sarah Moseley (born 1795 Wilkes County.) Issue:[282]

William Aubrey Noland was born 17 January 1828 in Walton County, died 29 August 1884 in Paulding County, buried in the old High Shoals Baptist Church Cemetery. He married on 19 January 1856 in Carroll County, Sarah Elizabeth Cheeves, born 17 January 1839, died 1 June 1904, buried in the High Shoals Cemetery in Paulding County. He served during the War Between the States as a 1st Lieut., in the 12th Georgia Regt, C. S. A.
Issue:

I.   Lesbia Kate Noland, born 12 November 1846 in Villa Rica, died 20 December 1931 in Paulding County, buried in the Mt. Olivet Baptist Church Cemetery. She married on 21 November 1873, Lindsey Elsberry Durham.

II.   Buddy Aubrey Noland, born on 15 September 1858 in Dallas, died 10 August 1897 in Pittsburg, Texas, buried in the Rose Hill Cemetery. He married on 2 February 1890, Jennie Harlan.

III.   Seaborn (Seab) Jackson Noland was born 4 September 1860, died 29 August 1884 in Paulding County, married on 18 September 1881, Martha Amanda (Mendy) Holland, daughter of Henry Holland. SEE Holland. Issue of Martha Amanda Holland and Seaborn Jackson Noland:

> A.   William Henry Noland was born on 25 August 1882 in Polk County, died on 22 March 1926, buried in the Hills Creek Baptist Church Cemetery, Rockmart, Polk County. He married (2) Jessie Mae.

> B.   Sarah Evelyn (Evie) Noland, born 26 September 1885 in Polk County, on 4 December 1956, buried in the Baptist Cemetery, Yorkville, Paulding County. She married on 28 November 1909, Joseph Elijah (Buddy) Davis (born 16 April 1882 in Yorkville, Paulding County, died 20 February 1962, buried in the Baptist Cemetery, Yorkville), the son of Joe H. Davis and Mary Jones. Issue: Joe Leroy Davis, born 10 November 1910 in Polk County, died 26 September 1965, buried in Bainbridge, married on 2 October 1942 in Lumpkin, Stewart County, Grace Elizabeth Sanders (born 16 April 1921 in Crisp County, died 21 February 1974, buried in Bainbridge): Seaborn Jackson Davis, born 28 January 1816, died 7 August 1936; and Jewell Evelyn Davis of Lumpkin, Georgia, born 26 August 1920 in Rockmart, married on 7 April 1945 in Columbus, Robert Lee Mitchell (born 16 March 1910 in Cave Springs, Floyd County, died on 6 March 1981, buried in Lumpkin, Georgia), the son of Isaiah L. Mitchell and Susan Kitchens.

> C.   Varannie (Rannie) Noland, born on 9 February 1890 in Polk County, died on 30 December 1971, buried in the Rose Hill Cemetery, Rockmart, Georgia. She married on 7 October 1917 in Rockmart, Charlie Robert Godfrey (born 9 January 1895, died 23 March 1963, buried in the Rose Hill Cemetery, Rockmart), son of Sherman Henry Godfrey and Ada Balew.

---

[282] Holland 1000-1988 by Jeannette Holland Austin.

IV.   Georgia A. Noland, born on 9 September 1862 in Dallas, died on 15 February 1834 in Dallas, buried I n the Old High Shoals Baptist Church Cemetery, married on 17 April 1884, John T. Monk.

V.   Mattie D. Noland, born 8 November 1865 in Dallas, died 27 April 1946 in Rockmart, buried in the Hills Creek Baptist Church Cemetery, married on 27 November 1884, Benjamin F. Denton.

VI.   Fannie Evelyn Noland.

VII.   William Allison ("Willie") Noland, born on 10 March 1870 in Dallas, diew on 8 July 1939 in Freestone, Texas, buried in the Dew Cemetery, married on 8 November 1894, Helen Gertrude Johnson.

VIII.   Battavia Jane ("Bat") Noland, born 18 January 1872 in Dallas, died on 6 September 1915 in Rockmart, buried in the Rose Hill Cemetery, married on 22 January 1898, Robert E. Lee.

IX.   Edwin ("Ed") Dayton Noland, born 17 December 1874 in Dallas, died on 14 September 1943 in Rockmart, Georgia, buried in the Rose Hill Cemetery. He married on 24 November 1907, Cora Carlton.

X.   Sallie L. Noland, born 2 April 1877 in Dallas, died 1880 in Dallas, Georgia, buried in the Old High Shoals Baptist Church Cemetery; unmarried.

XI.   Ora Emily Noland, born 28 February 1880 in Dallas, died 5 July 1948 in Dallas, buried in the Dallas City Cemetery. She married on 5 November 1896, O'Connell W. ("Con") Crew.

XII.   Samuel ("Sam") Clemen Noland, born 5 March 1881 in Dallas, died 6 November 1938 in Rockmart, buried in the Hills Creek Baptist Church Cemetery cemetery. He married on 12 February 1905, Mary Magdalene ("Maggie") Gentry.

IX.   Cleveland ("Cleve") D. Noland, born on 8 October 1884 in Dallas, died in Avon Park, Florida, married Addie Moore.

O'Neal of North Carolina & Monroe County

Alford O'Neal was born 1794 in North Carolina. Wife, Margaret, was born 1800. Issue:[283]

I.   Scott O'Neal, born 1827 in Georgia.

II.   Susan O'Neal, born 1830 in Georgia.

III.   Elizabeth O'Neal, born 1832 in Georgia.

IV.   Francis O'Neal, born 1834 in Georgia.

V.   Claton O'Neal, born 1836 in Georgia.

---

[283] 1850-1860 Monroe County Census.

VI.   Griffin O'Neal, born 1838 in Georgia, farmer, a son of Alford and Margaret O'Neal of Monroe County. He married Evaline Sullivan (born 1838 in Georgia), a daughter of Sallie Sullivan (born 1800 in North Carolina. Mrs. Sullivan resided with the family in Monroe County in 1880. SEE Sullivan. Issue:

    A.   Sarah O'Neal, born 1854 in Monroe County.
    B.   Mary O'Neal, born 1857 in Monroe County.

VII.   Martha O'Neal, born 1840 in Monroe County.

VIII.   Nuton S. O'Neal, born 1842 in Monroe County.

Parker of Bibb County

Simon Parker.. Wife Elizabeth. Simon Parker of Talbot County was named in the LWT of Lemuel Crittenden, dated 21 May 1855, probated 24 June 1855 in Talbot County. Issue:[284]

I.   John Brantley Parker was born 11 March 1811 in Bibb County, died 23 September 1833 in Bibb County. He married Eliza Chambliss (born 5 April 1819 Bibb County, died 1893, buried in the Parker Cemetery, Lizella, Georgia) on 2 February 1841 in Bibb County. They were resents of Bibb County, in 1880. SEE Chambliss. He served as a deacon in the Primitive Methodist Church. Issue:

    A.   William Jackson Parker, born 17 December 1841, Bibb County, died 15 January 1920, Bibb County, buried in the Parker Cemetery, Lizella, Georgia. He married Narcissa Jane Neel, the daughter of Perry Neel and his wife, Jane Chambliss (born 22 May 1812). Narcissa Jane was born 27 August 1842 in Bibb County, died 5 October 1887, buried in the Parker Cemetery. Issue:

        1.   Janie Eliza Parker, born 10 February 1876, Bibb County, died 7 December 1885, Bibb County.

        2.   Willie Franklin Parker, born 19 January 1879 Bibb County, died 15 September 1879, buried in the Parker Cemetery.

    B.   Georgia Virginia Parker, born 12 February 1843, Bibb County, died 15 October 1865, buried in the Parker Cemetery. She married Henry B. Callaway. SEE Callaway.

    C.   John Andrew Parker, born 28 March 1845, Bibb County, died 6 July 1864 in Virginia.

    D.   Mary Jane Elizabeth Parker, born 29 March 1849 in Bibb County, died 16 October 1910 in Bibb County. She married in 1876 Abram Josephus Davis.

    E.   Josephus Parker, born 1851, Bibb County.

---

[284] 1850 Bibb County Census; Bibb County Marriages.

F. Franklin Jefferson Parker, born 11 June 1851, Bibb County, died 1 Januiary 1933, buried in the Parker Cemetery.

G. Simon Samuel Alonzo Parker, born 20 June 1859 Bibb County, died 1 January 1933, buried in the Parker Cemetery. He married (1) Anna Brown Callaway (2) Fannie May Brown.

H. Henry Christopher Parker, born 29 November 1861 Bibb County, married Laura Reese.

Parris of Paulding County

George Sylvester Parris was born 1825 in North Carolina, shoe and boot maker. He married on 26 June 1852 in Paulding County, Sarah Ann E. Adair (born 1826 in Madison County), a daughter of William Andrew Adair and his wife Mary (Meroney) Adair. His family was listed on the 1880 Cherokee County, Alabama Census. SEE Adair. Issue:[285]

I.   Mary Ann Parris, born 1853 in Paulding County.

II. John L. Parris, born 1855 in Paulding County.

III. Nathan Parris, born 1857 in Paulding County, married Elizabeth Wisner on 25 October 1885 in Paulding County.

IV. Amanda Parris, born 1859 in Paulding County.

V.   Milla Parris, born 1863 in Paulding County.

VI. Joseph N. Parris, born 1865 in Paulding County.

VII. Thomas Mitchell Parris, born 1869 in Paulding County.

Perkins of Maryland, North Carolina;
DeKalb & Habersham Counties

This large family begins with Richard Perkins of Harford County, Maryland, who died 1705 in Baltimore County. Wife, Mary, died 20 February 1735, listed in St. George Parish Register, Harford County, Maryland. After the death of Richard, she married (2) John Belcher, on 16 March 1706. He settled at the head of Mosquito Creek in Baltimore County according to a survey certificate dated 15 December 1683..." to be laid out 100 acres for Richard Perkins, cooper, called *Perkinson*."

Issue: Richard Perkins, born 9 July 1689 on Mosquito Creek, St. George's Parish, Harford County, Maryland, married Mary Sherrill; Elisha Perkins (below); William Perkins, born 15 March 1692 on Mosquito Creek, St. George's Parish, Harford County, Maryland, died 1760 in Susquehanna, Maryland, married Elizabeth Cottrell and named in the LWT of John Cottrell dated 22 January 1721 in Baltimore, Maryland; Mary Perkins, born 2 April 1695 on Swan Creek, St. George's Parish, Harford County, Maryland; Sarah Perkins, born 15 December 1699

---

[285] Paulding County Marriages; 1860 Paulding County Census; 1880 Cherokee County, Alabama Census, Township 10.

and died 28 December 1699 in Swan Creek, St. George's Parish, Harford County, Maryland and Martha Perkins, born 31 March 1701 n Swan Creek, St. George's Parish, Harford County, Maryland.

Elisha Perkins was born 9 June 1697 in Swan Creek, St. George's Parish, Harford County, Maryland, died May of 1742 in Orange County, Virginia. He married Margaret Sherrill on 1 December 1718. There is a deed for him dated 3 December 1719, where he patented for 50 acres of land on the Susquehanna River (now in York County, Pennsylvania), called Elisha's Lot, which he sold to John Cooper on 29 January 1721. On 8 April 1721, in a Baltimore Court Proceeding, his mother, Mrs. Mary (Perkins) Belcher, made clemency for her son, Elisha Perkins, who was accused of stealing a horse from John Baldwin. Elisha removed to Spotsylvania County, Virginia, where (Deed Book B, page 117) a deed was found for him when he purchased 470 acres of land from Francis Kirtley and wife, Frances, on 6 April 1731; this land was later sold to Thomas Wright Belfield on 7 October 1734 (Spotsylvania Deed Book C, page136). A Baltimore County, Maryland deed, between William and Richard Perkins stated that Elisha Perkins was "now deceased"). (28 November 1741, Deed Book A, page 123-131).

Elisha's wife, Margaret (Sherrill) Perkins, the daughter of William Sherrill, was involved in various legal proceedings (Orange County, Virginia, Book 1, page 243,300,316,329 and Order Book 3, pp.292,477; Order Book 4, pp.104,232,253). The Grand Jury found that Christopher Hoomes lived in adultery with the wife of Elisha Perkins in St. Mark's Parish. [286]

That Elisha Perkins was brought into court and was accused of barbarously using his wife, Margery, who had sworn peace against him, wherein Margaret Perkins asked for separate alimony against her husband (case was dismissed). Another case of Margaret Perkins, alias Sherrill, a bastard child in St. Mark's Parish (case dismissed); other complaints ensued stating that Margaret Perkins disturbed the peace for which (on 26 January 1745) the Grand Jury sentenced her to go to jail for one year, but on 28 March 1745 she was set free by the Sheriff.

Issue of Elisha Perkins and his wife, Margaret (Sherrill) Perkins:

I. Elizabeth Perkins, born 18 November 1719, St. George's Parish, Harford County, Maryland, died January 1835 in Independence County, Arkansas. She married Jacob Sherrill. Elizabeth is traced to her father, Elisha Perkins, when Jacob and Betsy (Elizabeth was known as Betsy) Sherrill sold land which was inherited from her father, Elisha Perkins, on 6 April 1796 in Berkeley County, Virginia (Deed Book 12). After the death of her husband, Jacob Sherrill, Elizabeth was listed on the 1810 Lincoln County, North Carolina Census, daughters 10-16, son 10-15, son under 10, and female 26-45. Her other sons, Eli and Colbert, were of age and were listed separately. Her LWT is recorded in Lincoln County, North Carolina, dated 14 October 1834, probated January 1835 and is headed "Elizabeth Sherrill of the County of Independence and Territory of Arkansas named her nieces, Polly C. Sherrill and Sally A. Sherrill. Also her sons, Eli and Alfred Sherrill, and daughters, Nancy and Polly Sherrill.

II. Phillis Perkins.

---

[286] NOTE____ A case was brought in the Courts against Margaret Perkins, alias Sherrill, who'd had a bastard child in St. Mark's Parish (dismissed). Apparently, she named the child, William Sherrill, because the LWT of Christopher Hoomes dated 28 May 1780, probated 21 February 1785 in Culpepper County, Virginia, bequeathed to William Sherrill, son of Margaret Sherrill, alias Margaret Perkins, the tract of land whereon Christopher Hoomes lived.

III. Ute Perkins. According to the Augusta County, Virginia records, Ute Perkins, alias Anderson, was the leader of the *Perkins Gang*. He was arrested in 1747. Frederick County, Virginia Order Book page 497 (undated)...."Adam Sherrill, being brought before the Court as a harbourer of Ute Perkins, a horse thief, and it appearing to the Court that the said Perkins is guilty of the same, it is ordered that the Sheriff take the said Perkins into his custody until he enters into recognizance in the sum of One Hundred Pounds Sterling with good securities in the sum of fifty pounds sterling each, in case the said Perkins shall not be of good behaviour, for a twelve month and a day...."

IV. Margaret Perkins.

V. Richard Perkins.

VI. Joshua Perkins inherited 1 shilling in his father's Last Will and Testament.

VII. Elisha Perkins, born 31 August 1734 in St. George's Parish, Harford County, Maryland, died August 1759 in Frederick County, Maryland, the date of his LWT.

VIII. John Perkins, born 15 September 1733 in Frederick County, Virginia, died 13 April 1804 in Burke County, North Carolina. He married Catherine Lowrance (born 13 August 1742 at Peapack, Somerset County, New Jersey, died 5 October 1819 in Burke County, North Carolina), a daughter of Alexander Lowrance and his wife Mary (Evelan) Lowrance.. He served in the Revolutionary War and was a State Senator from Lincoln County, North Carolina in 1795) as was his son, Ephraim Perkins, in 1805). His descendants were in Burke, Caldwell and Lincoln Counties of North Carolina. He was famously known as "Gentleman John Perkins", as he lived lavishly, owning vast acreage in North Carolina and had many slaves. John Perkins appeared in the inventory of the goods and chattels of Burill Grigg, deceased, in Anson County, North Carolina, along with Avington Sherrill, Adam Sherrill and Elisha Perkins. He was enumerated on the 1763 Anson County Taxables and there was an Anson County deed dated 10 December 1763 between Thomas Bingham and John Purkins for 100 pounds, for 200 acres on Brown Creek, beside the old Catawba Path. On 28 April 1778, he received a land grant of 300 acres on the John's River, adjoining Samuel Simpson and Andrew Rudolph. The Lincoln County Court of Please Quarter Sessions on the first Monday in April 1796...."Be it remembered that on 6 April 1796, Aquilla Sherrill, James Abernathy and Moses Abernathy, the subscribing witnesses to a deed of John Perkins and Catherine, his wife, to Christopher Thrasher on 4 April 1796. Issue:

A. Elisha Perkins, born 18 October 1760 in Edgefield County, South Carolina, died 1795 in Burke County, North Carolina. Wife, Jean.

B. Mary Perkins, born 6 October 1762 in Edgefield County, South Carolina, married Rev. Robert Johnson Miller on 5 March 1787.

C. Ephraim Perkins, born 6 November 1764 in Edgefield County, South Carolina, married Elizabeth Abernathy on 1 February 1796.

D. John Perkins, born 11 February 1767 in Edgefield County, South Carolina, married Nancy Abernathy on 26 January 1817.

E. Joseph Perkins, born 2 December 1768 in Union, South Carolina, married Melissa Lavender.

F. Burwell Perkins born 21 May 1771 in Edgefield County, South Carolina, died 20 January 1773.

G. Alexander Perkins, born 6 December 1773 in Island Ford, Burke County, North Carolina. Wife, Miss Moore.

H. Sarah Perkins, born 6 January 1776 in Island Ford, Burke County, North Carolina, married Thomas Snoddy.

I. Ann Perkins, born 27 December 1780 in Island Ford, Burke County, North Carolina.

J. Elijah Perkins, born 27 December 1777 in Island Ford, Burke County, North Carolina, died after 1830 in Habersham County, Georgia. He was found in Habersham County in 1820; a deed dated 3 January 1823, from John Middlebrooks to Elijah Perkins of Habersham County, for land in the 75th District (Book B, page 13). He had fourteen children, as found on the early census records. Wife, Melissa Lavender. Issue:[287]

1. Reuben B. Perkins, born 1800 in Island Ford, Burke County, North Carolina, died November 1870 in DeKalb County. Wife, Martha Ann. LWT dated 5 October 1862, probated 11 November 1870, DeKalb County. He drew in the 1827 Land Lottery in Habersham County; listed on 1850-1870 DeKalb County Census. Issue:

   a. Valeria Ann Perkins, born 1832 in Habersham County, married John M. Hawkins on 12 December 1851 in DeKalb County.

   b. Berry C. Perkins, born 1833 in Habersham County. He married Mary Ann Elizabeth Jordan (born 1839 in DeKalb County) on 2 November 1855 in DeKalb County, the daughter of William Jordan and his wife, Berdelia. SEE Jordan. Issue:

      i.   Albert Perkins, born 1855 in DeKalb County.
      ii.   William T. Perkins, born 1859 in DeKalb County.
      iii. Martha Josephine Perkins, born 6 January 1863 in DeKalb County, died 19 January 1944 in Atlanta, Fulton County. She married Charles Crawford Evans on 20 July 1879 in DeKalb County. SEE Evans.
      iv.   Lis Perkins, born ca 1865 in DeKalb County. Never married.
      v.   Frank Perkins, born ca 1867 in DeKalb County, Georgia.

   c. Mary Caroline Perkins, born 1836 in Habersham County, married John Jones on 5 May 1852 in DeKalb County.

---

[287] 1810-1820 Burke County, North Carolina Census; 1820-1830 Habersham County, Georgia Census; Habersham County Deeds; St. George's Parish Register, Harford County, Maryland; Lincoln County, North Carolina Wills; 1850-1870 DeKalb County Census; DeKalb County Marriages; personal records of Mrs. Pearl Howard (1966), Atlanta, Georgia, whose grandmother was Martha Josephine Perkins.

d. Martha Elizabeth Perkins, born 1843 in DeKalb County, married Russell T. Ayers on 27 November 1866 in DeKalb County.

e. William F. Perkins, born ca 1845 in DeKalb County.

f. James A. Perkins, born ca 1847 in DeKalb County.

2. Hiram B. Perkins, born 1805 in Island Ford, Burke County, North Carolina. He married Susan Ray on 14 June 1829. Hiram B. Perkins deeded land in Land Lot 42 of the 11th District of Habersham County, 250 acres, on 1 December 1828 (Deed Book G, page 112). He was listed on the 1850 Murray County, Georgia Census.

3. William A. Perkins, born 1815 in Island Ford, Burke County, North Carolina. Wife, Mary A.

Ponder of Monroe County

Daniel Ponder was born ca 1730 in Buffalo Gap, Augusta County, Virginia, died in Elbert County, Georgia. He married Jemima Bennett, born 1730/1740 Cedar Creek Delaware, died ca 1784, the daughter of Stephen Bennett and his wife, Margaret. Issue: [288]

I. Mary Ponder, born York County, South Carolina, died 1810/20 York County, South Carolina.

II. Daniel Ponder, born before 1755 in Buncombe County, North Carolina, died 1815/1817 in Monroe County, Georgia.

III. James Ponder, died ca 1826 Greenville District, South Carolina.

IV. Abner J. Ponder, born 1755, died Dec 1832 in Bon Aqua Springs, Hick County, Tennessee, buried Ponder-Perkins Cemetery. He married Jane Knox on 23 October 1802, Oglethorpe County.

V. John Ponder born 1757/1758 Buffalo Gap, Augusta County, Virginia, died 25 October 1804 in Oglethorpe County, Georgia. He married Margaret Cummings (born 1759, died 22 May 1842 in Monroe County, Georgia). The LWT of Margaret Ponder in Monroe County, Georgia, dated 13 December 1836, probated 7 July 1842, names children...James, Amos, John Lewis, Daniel, Silas, Malinda Gilleland and Jemima D. Mitchell. Monroe County deed, Book A, page 110, Elias Goff of Hall County to John H. Ponder of Monroe County, for $200.00, 202-1/2 acres of land being Lot 129 in the 13th District of Monroe County, on Rockey Creek, 27 December 1821. [289]

---

[288] 1850 Monroe County, Georgia Census; Ponder Family Bible (Georgia State Archives); 1830 Monroe County Census; Monroe County Marriages; Ponder Family Cemetery, Route 83, Forsyth to Monroe; Monroe County: A History; Monroe County Deeds; 1860 Monroe County Census

[289] Oglethorpe County Deeds

Deed Book A, page 11. "Wilkes County, Georgia". 15 November 1791, Martin Dreadwilder of Elbert County to John Ponder of Wilkes County, for 50 pounds, 230 acres on Clouds Creek in Wilkes County

Issue:

A. Melinda Ponder married Mr. Gilleland.

B. Jemima B. Ponder married Mr. Mitchell.

C. Mary Anne Ponder, died 4 April 1864 Oglethorpe County, Georgia.

D. James Ponder. Listed on 1830 Monroe County Census.

E. Silas Ponder, his LWT dated 26 October 1836, probated 10 November 1836, Monroe County, named wife, Lucille (sp?), and children. Listed 1830 Monroe County Census. He married Leadda Dardin on 31 May 1827 in Monroe County. Issue:
1. Laurancy E. Ponder.

2. Peggy Ann E. Ponder.

3. William A. Ponder.

4. Martha Ponder.

F. Amos Ponder born 6 December 1785 in Oglethorpe County, Georgia, died 6 February 1851 Monroe County, buried Ponder Cemetery, Monroe County. Listed 1830 Monroe County Census. He married Nancy Milligan (born 17 October 1800, died 5 June 1853). They are buried on the old Ponder homeplace, in the Ponder Cemetery. Issue:
1. Oliver W. P. Ponder born 1822 in Monroe County, died May 1864 Monroe County He married Nancy Ann Amanda Rogers (born 1826) in Monroe County on 25 January 1844. His LWT dated 26 March 1864, probated 2 May 1864 in Monroe County. Issue:

        a. Mary E. Ponder, born ca 1846.
        b. Amos J. Ponder, born 1847.

2. James Washington Head Ponder born 3 May 1825 Monroe County, died 26 Jan 1890 Monroe County, married Emily Angeline Chambliss, daughter of John M. Chambliss and his wife, Elizabeth Jordan See CHAMBLISS. Issue:

a. Henry Oliver Ponder born 10 November 1863 Monroe County, died 18 September 1926 Glenmora, Rapides Parish, Louisiana, buried Forest Hill Cemetery, married Annie Lorena Peninger (27 November 1879 Sugartown, Louisiana-11 March 1964 Lake Charles, Louisiana, buried Glenmora, Rapides Parish. Issue: Lydia Emily Ponder, born 25 August 1906 Forest Hill, Rapides Parish, Louisiana, died 10 May 1908, Glenmora, Rapides Parish, Louisiana; and Annie Louise Ponder, born 27 November 1913 Forest Hill, Rapides Parish, Louisiana, married 19 December 1935, Alfred Valerie Thomson.

b. Lulie Milledge Ponder born 28 September 1876 Monroe County, died 22 July 1966 Greenville, Greenville County, South Carolina, buried Forsyth, Monroe County, Georgia, married John Gordon Smith on 7 Nov 1894.

c. William Zachariah Ponder born 1878 Monroe County, Georgia.

3. Lewis (Louis) A. Ponder born 1829 Monroe County.

4. Peggy Ann Ponder born ca 1829 Monroe County, married Uriah M. Gilder.

5. Letha Ann Ponder born ca 1830 Monroe County.

6. Lucinda Ponder born ca 1832 Monroe County, married Jacob Gilder.

7. Mary Jane Ponder born ca 1834 Monroe County.

G. John Lewis Ponder born 13 February 1788 Oglethorpe County, Georgia, died 29 April 1865 in Tallapoosa County, Alabama. He was listed on the 1830 Monroe County Census.

H. Daniel Ponder, born 31 October 1794 Oglethorpe County, Georgia, died 6 November 1867 in Monroe County, Georgia, buried Ponder Cemetery, Monroe County, which was the old Ponder homestead. (On the Silas Thomas place) He married (1) on 29 October 1823 in Monroe County, Jane E. Lewis (born 7 November 1809, died 6 May 1837). He married (2) on 2 July 1838, Elizabeth McMickle (1 April 1811-1 Jan 1880). LWT of Daniel Ponder dated 14 November 1866, probated 6 January 1868, Monroe County, Georgia, names wife, Elizabeth.

Issue by (1) wife (Jane E. Lewis)

1. Catharine Austin Lewis Ponder was born 3 August 1824.

2. Agness M. Lewis Ponder was born 8 April 1826.

3. Jane Emily Lewis Ponder was born 26 January 1828, died 20 October 1862.

4. Peggyan Cuming Ponder was born 24 January 1830.

5. Marey Moore Ponder was born 26 March 1832.

6. Martha Ponder, born 1834 Monroe County.

7. Elizabeth S. Ponder, born 1837 Monroe County.

Issue by (2) wife (Elizabeth McMickle):

8. Nancy M. Ponder was born 14 August 1839, married 14 December 1862.

9. Coosa Ponder, born 1840 Monroe County (daughter).

10. Amos M. Ponder was born 12 August 1841, married 12 October 1869.

11. Daniel J. Ponder was born 4 January 1843, died 6 May 1865.

12. John L. Ponder was born 19 May 1844, married 12 December 1877.

13. James M. Ponder was born 1 January 1846, married 14 December 1869.

14. Emma (Safrona) Ponder was born 5 March 1847, married 19 October 1880.

15. Ella (Levonia) Ponder was born 5 March 1847, married 27 November 1867.

16. William P. Ponder was born 20 December 1848.

17. Georgia A. Ponder was born 14 September 1850, died 7 October 1878, married William F. Hale (5 December 1842-10 October 1907) on 29 December 1868. Issue: Mary E. Hale, born 21 March 1870; Edgar Hale, born 25 July 1871; W. Frank Hale, born 27 September 1873; Georgia E. Hale, born 7 January 1876; and Ada L. Hale, born 21 September 1878.

Francis Power of Elbert County made his LWT there on 20 November 1793, but it was probated in Madison County on 3 August 1818. He named his wife, Elizabeth, and Issue: William Power and Elizabeth Wood, the wife of James Wood. Executors were his wife, son, William, son-in-law, James Wood, and William Stokes of Elbert County. Issue:

I.   Elizabeth Power married James Wood.
II. William Power.

Another family, David Power was born 1780/1790 and was listed on the 1820 and 1830 Madison County Census having 3 sons under 10, son 10-16, and 2 daughters under 10. In his LWT dated 17 June 1840, probated 21 September 1840 in Madison County, he named his wife, Margaret and Issue: Jesse R. Power, Francis E. Power, Sarah Power and Polley Murry. (Clearly, one son is missing, who has to be William Power who predeceased him, because David named William's children as his grandchildren, viz: Susan M. Power and George W. Power. He was apparently married twice, having married (1) Susannah Moon on 15 October 1807 in Elbert County, and (2), Margaret Hopkins on 11 May 1828 in Madison County. Susannah Power was named as a daughter of William Moon in his LWT dated 7 May 1810, probated 7 January 1811 in Elbert County (also named was Sally Green Power, a daughter who married James Power). Issue:

I.   William Power. His LWT dated 31 December 1834, probated 14 January 1835 in Madison County, named his wife, Elizabeth and children, Susan M. and George W. Power, with his father, David Power, as executor. He married Elizabeth Grimes on 3 July 1827 in Madison County.

II. Jesse R. Power, married Julia Ann Hopkins on 14 December 1834 in Madison County.

III. Francis E. Power, Sr., born 1813 in Georgia, married Elizabeth P. Woode (born 1819 in Georgia) on 17 February 1837 in Madison County. Listed on the 1860 Madison County Census. Issue:

   A. Jesse G. Power, born 1843 Madison County, married Minerva Louisa Power on 29 November 1859 in Madison County.
   B. Mary Power, born 1845 Madison County.
   C. Martha A. Power, born 1847 Madison County, married Isaac D. Vaughan ca 1875 in Madison County.
   D. Elizabeth F. Power, born 1849 Madison County, married William W. Carithers on 19 August 1868 in Madison County.

IV. Sarah Power married William G. Power on 28 September 1831 in Madison County.

V.   Polley Power married Isham Murry on 23 November 1834 in Madison County.

Another family, James Power was born 1780/1790. His LWT dated 23 October 1838, probated 12 January 1839 in Madison County naming wife, Elizabeth. Also, sons: William Williamson Power and Francis Power. Daughter, Elizabeth T. David. The 1840 Madison County Census lists Elizabeth as head of household, born 1780/1790 and having one male under 5, one male 15-20, one female under 5, one female 5-10, one female 10-15, and 1 female 20-30. Clearly, James did not name all of his daughters in his Will. Known issue:

I.   William Williamson Power, married Martha Grimes on 4 May 1831 in Madison County.

II.   Francis Power.

III.   Elizabeth T. Power, born ca 1808, married John David on 13 November 1828 in Madison County.

Another family, James M. Power, born 1812 in Georgia, Baptist clergyman. On 6 August 1829 in Madison County, he married Eliza R. Moore, born 1811 in Georgia. Issue:

I.   Elizabeth Power, born 1832 Georgia.

II.   John M. Power, born 1834 Georgia, farmer.

III.   Mary J. Power, born 1837 Georgia.

IV.   Winney A. Power, born 1839 Georgia, married George G. Brown on 15 December 1859 in Madison County.

V.   Frances Power, born 1842 Madison County.

VI.   Eliza J. Power (daughter), born 1845 Madison County.

VII.   Sarah M. Power, born 1847 Madison County.

VIII. Margarett J. Power, born 1849 Madison County.

IX.   William L. Power, born 1851 Madison County.

X.   Ophelia Power, born 1854 Madison County.

XI.   Olivea Power, born 1856 Madison County.

Another family, John M. Power was born 1805 in Georgia, laborer. He was married to Keddy Ann Maxwell on 15 June 1823 in Madison County, who was deceased by 1850. The 1830 Madison County Census shows a son under 5 years of age, as well as a daughter under 5, and a daughter between the age of 5 and 10. Sometime after he married, he removed to Meriwether County, where he found on the 1850 Census. Issue:

I.   Wiley B. Power was born 1825 in Georgia. He married Mary A. Williams, born 1837 in Danielsville, Madison County, Georgia, the daughter of Elijah Williams and his wife, Nancy (Strickland) Williams. SEE Williams.[290] Issue:

       A. Esther A. Power, born 1855 in Madison County.

       B. Elizer F. Power, born 1858 in Madison County, married C. H. Turner on 16 December 1880 in Madison County.

---

[290] NOTE__ Wiley B. Power was established as a son of John M. Power by the 1830 Madison County Census.

C. Mary E. Power, born 1860 in Madison County.

II.   J. Power (son), born 1833 Madison County.

III.   D. Power (son), born 1838 Madison County.

IV.   F. Power (son), born 1843 Georgia.

V.   W. Power (son), born 1845 Georgia.

Pye of Monroe County

Henry Pye was born ca 1799 in Georgia, died 20 March 1826 in Monroe County, Georgia. He married on 19 January 1818 in Putnam County, Ann Stockdale (born ca 1797 near Tarboro, North Carolina, died 27 March 1841 Monroe County, Georgia). The LWT of Mrs. Ann Pye dated 19 May 1837, probated 6 July 1841 in Monroe County, named children, viz: Jesse, John and Martha. Executors were Benjamin Haywood and Spencer Sullivan. Issue: [292]

I.   Jesse Pye was born 7 September 1819 Putnam County, Georgia, died 6 February 1844, married Louvenia M. Sullivan on 15 November 1841 Monroe County. Listed on 1830 Putnam County Census. His LWT dated 11 October 1844, probated 11 February 1844 in Monroe County, named wife, Delilah. Mentioned "My sons". Known issue:

A. Sarah F. Pye.

B. Arabella A. Pye.

II.   John Pye was born 3 August 1823 Monroe County, married (1) on 1 February 1843, Priscilla W. Sullivan (2) 8 December 1853, Sarah Ann Chambliss, in Monroe County. Issue:

A. Jesse Binire Pye (17 January 1844-27 April 1874).

B. John Henry Pye (24 July 1845-8 October 1850 Monroe County).

C. Mary Ann Pye (3 June 1848-2 September 1848 Monroe County).

III.   Martha Pye was born 12 May 1825 in Monroe County, Georgia, died 23 March 1878 Tyler, Texas, buried Dean Cemetery, Tyler, Texas, married William Henry Chambliss on 7 July 1844. SEE Chambliss.

Another family, Benier Pye was born 1807 in Georgia, died 1876 in Forsyth, Monroe County, married Cuzziah (born 1809). His LWT dated 20 November 1876, probated 28 November 1876, Monroe County. Issue:

I.   William A. Pye, born 1834 Monroe County, listed on the 1880 Talbot County Census. Wife, Martha M., born 1841 in Georgia. Issue:

A. Jefferson D. Pye, born 1862 Georgia.

B. Anna E. Pye, born 1867 Georgia.

C. Charles W. Pye, born 1869 Georgia.

---

[292] Monroe County Marriages; Dean Family Cemetery, Tyler, Texas; Monroe County Wills; 1850 Monroe County Census.

D. Nonie Pye (daughter), born 1872 Georgia.

    E. Donie Pye (daughter), born 1872 Georgia.

    F. Robert Pye, born 1874 Georgia.

    G. Mattie Pye, born 1878 Talbot County.

II. Shady Ann Pye, born 1837 Monroe County, married Mr. Freeman.

III. Sarah Jane Pye, born 1838 Monroe County, married Urban C. Fambrough (born 1836).

IV. Martha S. Pye, born 1840 Monroe County, married Mr. Flynt. Issue:

    A. Martha Flynt.

    B. Kerziah Flynt.

V. John E. Pye, born 24 September 1843 in Forsyth, Monroe County. Wife, Julia, born 7 February 1842, died 3 July 1872. Issue:

    A. Benier Gimberly (or Wimberly) Pye, born 28 July 1868, died 8 July 1869 Forsyth, Monroe County.

    B. Eula Pye (daughter), born 12 December 1870, died 16 July 1872 Forsyth, Monroe County.

VI. Mary R. Pye, born 1846 Monroe County, married Mr. Tally.

Ragsdale of Virginia, South Carolina;
Cherokee, Clayton, Cobb, DeKalb, Paulding & Walton Counties

Peter Ragsdale, Revolutionary War Soldier, was born ca 1726 in Prince George County, Virginia, and died in Greenville County, South Carolina on 16 September 1799. He served during the war as a Sergeant under Capt. Samuel Hopkins' Co., 6th Virginia Regiment, Colonel Hendricks, commander.[293] Also, a NSDAR marker was erected in the Lebanon Churchyard. His home was located on Bluestone Creek. His wife, Sarah Charlton, died in Laurens County, South Carolina in 1842. They had seven children. Elijah Ragsdale, along with his brothers, Larkin, Richard and Francis Asberry Ragsdale, settled in Georgia. Issue:[294]

I.   Larkin Ragsdale, Revolutionary War Soldier, born in Lunenburg County, South Carolina, died before 1850 in Newton County. Wife, Nancy. Issue:
    A. Charlton Ragsdale, born 1804 in South Carolina. Wife, Mary.
    B. Mark M. Ragsdale, born 1806 in South Carolina, married Matilda Westley of DeKalb County.
    C. Temperance Ragsdale, born 1808, married William Westley.

III.   Richard Ragsdale, born ca 1765 in Lunenburg County, Virginia, died in Cherokee County, his LWT dated 1847 (Will Book A, pp. 4-5), proven by his nephew, Sanders Walker Ragsdale (son of brother, Elijah). He was married to Susanna Allen on 1 December 1791 in Mechlenburg County, Virginia. Susanna resided with her son, Larkin Ragsdale, in Cherokee County (1850 census) Issue:
    A. Ira Ragsdale.
    B. Larkin Ragsdale, born 1800 in South Carolina, farmer. He married Judy Gibson on 15

---

[293] Henings Statues of Virginia, Vol. 7, pp. 206-209.

[294] Elijah Ragsdale, born Virginia 11/1/1778 to South Carolina, died Georgia 5/1/158 by June Hart Wester.

November 1842 in Cherokee County. She was deceased before 1850. This was probably a second marriage. Issue:[295]

    1.   Spencer Ragsdale, born 1829 in Georgia, married Sarah Ann Gibson on 5 December
    2.   1848 in Cherokee County.
    3.   John S. Ragsdale, born 1832 in Georgia married Melissa A. Smith on 30 July 1851 in
    4.   Cherokee County.
    5.   Susan Ragsdale, born 1852 in Cherokee County.
    6.   Hiram Ragsdale, born 1852 in Cherokee County.
    7.   Olly Ragsdale (daughter), born 1860 in Cherokee County.

  C. Charlton Boyd Ragsdale, born in South Carolina, married Sara Tate.
  D. Mary Ragsdale married Mr. Sessions.
  E. Elizabeth Ragsdale married Mr. Roach.
  F. Martha Ragsdale married Mr. Williams.
  G. Susanna Ragsdale married James O. Phillips.
  H. Melissa Ragsdale married Mr. Dudley.

IV.   Fanny Ragsdale, died in Laurens County, South Carolina, married John Ridgeway, Revolutionary War Soldier. Issue:

  A. Betsy Ridgeway married Thomas Lindley.
  B. John Ridgeway.
  C. Richard Ridgeway married Elizabeth Waldrop.

V.   Edmond Ragsdale, born 1774 in Mechlenburg County, Virginia, served as a Justice of the Peace in Greenville County, South Carolina.

IV.   Elizabeth Ragsdale, born 15 July 1775 in Mechlenburg County, Virginia, died 10 March 1854 in Walton County, Georgia. She was married to Abner Camp, a member of the extensive Camp families in South Carolina and Georgia. Issue:[296]

  A. Edmond Camp married Mary Reynolds.
  B. Arthur Camp married (1) Eliza Martin and (2) Nancy Maxwell.
  C. Russell Camp married Mary Shepherd.
  D. Satira Camp married Harvey Treadwell.
  E. Hiram Camp married Peniah Reynolds.
  F. Martha Camp married John W. B. Allen.
  G. Mary Camp married Reuben Manning.

V.   Elijah Ragsdale, born 1 November 1778 in Virginia, died 1 May 1858 in Paulding County, buried in the old Baptist Cemetery in Powder Springs, Cobb County. Wife, Mary, died 1860-1867, as she was listed on the 1860 Paulding County Census, age 81. They were residents of Greenville County, South Carolina in 1800, but soon thereafter removed to Jackson County, Georgia where Elijah was listed on the 1803 Tax Digest. His LWT wad dated on 10 April 1858, Paulding County Wills, Sales Bills, etc., Book A, pp. 374-376, (probated on 8 June 1858) where he bequeathed everything to his wife, "Mary with whom I have lived in the strictest quiet for fifty-nine years...." Included was a town lot in the town of Dallas, Georgia, being in Block C, Land Lot No. 15. Issue:

  A. Francis Asbury Ragsdale (known as "Berry Ragsdale"), born 27 November 1803, died 30 November 1887, married Frances Morris (born 20 November 1807, died 26 May 1860), a daughter of James Morris of DeKalb County. His LWT was dated 5 December 1887, DeKalb County Will Book B,

---

[295] 1850-1880 Cherokee County Census, Wild Cat, Georgia; Cherokee County Marriages

[296] Camp-Kemp Families, Vol. I & II, by Mrs. Robert Mann; Elijah Ragsdale, born Virginia 11/1/1778 to South Carolina, died Georgia 5/1/1858 by Jane Hart Wester.

pp 235-236. "I direct that all my children, to-wit: Almeda Blankenship, Francis E. Crowley, Arnaveeny Clark; also my granddaughter, Loula Ragsdale, daughter of my son, James L. Ragsdale, deceased, shall each receive an equal share of my estate at my death." Issue:[297]

    1. Almeda Ragsdale, born ca 1828, died after 1898, married John B. Blankenship on 17

    2. December 1843 in DeKalb County.

    3. Frances E. Ragsdale, born 9 September 1831, died 28 September 1928, married Seaborn Crowley on 30 November 1854 in DeKalb County.

    4. Elijah M. Ragsdale, died during the War Between the States, on 21 January 1863 in Howard's Grove, Virginia, General Hospital..

    5. James Lafayette Ragsdale, served during the War Between the States in Co. I, 18th Alabama Infantry, and died during the war. He married Martha Louise Hooker..

    6. William A. Ragsdale, died 3 May 1863 near Fredericksburg, during the War Between the States.

    7. Marshall K. Ragsdale, born 1839, died 14 September 1862 from wounds received during the War Between the States at Crampton's Gap in Maryland.

    8. Nancy Arbazine Ragsdale, born 1843, died after 1889, married Joseph B. Clarke in DeKalb County..

    9. Warner L. Ragsdale, born 1847, died 14 September 1862, at the age of 15 years, during the War Between the States, at Crampton's Gap, in Maryland..

    10. Armenda Ragsdale married Mr. Dulin.

B. Mason M. Ragsdale, born ca 1805 and died February 1872 in Clayton County. Wife, Mary, left her LWT in Will Book A, page 104, Clayton County, recorded 23 May 1889, bequeathing her daughter, Martha A. Ragsdale, 35 acres of land and the homeplace; other property (71 acres) to be sold and divided between the four children, viz: James Ragsdale, Cleveland Ragsdale, Mary Fielder and Martha A. Ragsdale. Issue:

    1. William C. Ragsdale, born 27 October 1828, died in Weatherford, Texas, married on 12 May 1853, Caledonia D. Camp..

    2. Mary Jane Ragsdale.

    3. James Berry Ragsdale.

    4. Jesse Cleveland Ragsdale.

    5. Sarah Frances Ragsdale.

    6. Martha A. Ragsdale.

C. Sanders Walker Ragsdale, born 1809 in Georgia, farmer, resident of Dallas. Wife, Sarah, born 1814 in Georgia. Issue:[298]

    1. Mary Ragsdale, born 1838 in Georgia.

    2. Sanders Ragsdale, born 1845 in Georgia.

    3. Elijah Ragsdale, born 1846 in Georgia.

    4. James Ragsdale, born 1848 in Georgia.

    5. Jane Ragsdale, born 1849 in Georgia.

    6. Thomas Ragsdale, born 1853 in Paulding County.

    7. Isaac Ragsdale, born 1860 in Paulding County.

D. Joseph Ragsdale, born 9 May 1811, died 28 December 1890, married on 25 December 1831, Lucinda Carter (born 13 December 1814, died 15 February 1896). In 1848 they were residents of Cobb County, and in 1860, residents of Dallas, Georgia. His LWT dated 1890 in Paulding County wherein he appointed his son, John Warner Ragsdale, as the executor. Issue:[299]

    1. Mary J. Ragsdale.

---

[297] 1850-1860 DeKalb County Census; DeKalb County Marriages.

[298] 1860 Paulding County Census; Paulding County Marriages.

[299] Ibid.

2. Martha Ann Ragsdale married William Griffin 21 January 1855 in Paulding County. William Asbury B. Ragsdale married (1) Charlotte Denson on 1 January 1857 and (2) Laura Denson on 11 April 1886 in Paulding County.

3. Emily Ragsdale married Levi Cooper on 19 August 1855 in Paulding County.

4. Caroline Ragsdale.

5. George Washington Ragsdale, born 1843 in Georgia, married Elizabeth C. Gray on 2 March 1862 in Paulding County.

6. John Warner Ragsdale, born 1850 in Paulding County, married M. E. Trammel on 22 December 1869 in Paulding County.

E. John Clarence Ragsdale.

F. Elijah Newton Ragsdale.

G. William Mayfield Ragsdale.

H. James Armstrong Ragsdale.

I. George Washington Ragsdale.

VII. Francis Asberry Ragsdale (called "Berry"), was born in Mechlenburg County, Virginia, died 1843 in Anderson County, South Carolina. He married Priscilla Chandler of Laurens County, South Carolina. Issue:

A. Daniel S. Ragsdale, born 1811, died 1850, married Mary Eskew.

B. Mary Ann Ragsdale, born 1814, died 1853 married Henry Middleton Gaines.

C. Fannie Ragsdale married George Davis who was killed during the Battle of Atlanta.

D. Elizabeth Ragsdale, born 1817.

E. Matilda Ragsdale.

F. Francis Asberry Ragsdale, 1824-1868, married Sarah Ellison.

G. John F. Ragsdale, 1827-1876, married (1) Letha Ann Austin and (2) Elizabeth Cox Brock.

H. Emily Ragsdale, 1823-1857, married Richard Sanders Smith.

Roberts of Paulding County

James Roberts was born 1791 in North Carolina, died October 1860 in Paulding County. Wife, Martha, born 1798 Georgia. His LWT dated 3 August 1860, probated 1 October 1860, Paulding County. ".... Issue: $25 to Emily Elizabeth Baxter when she arrives at age or marries, and $25 to John Marion Baxter when he arrives at age or marries. My five Issue: Polly Hitchcock, wife of John Hitchcock, Fanny Cogburn, wife of Zachariah Cogburn, Susannah Starnes, wife of Thomas Starnes, Wesley H. Roberts and Sarah Bone, wife of Matthew Bone. Negro woman, Anner of dark complexion, about 16 years of age, to be sold at Dallas. Executor: Son, Wesley H. Roberts."

I. Wesley H. Roberts, born 1813 in South Carolina, a resident of Huntsville, in Paulding County in 1860. Wife, Elizabeth, born 1815 in North Carolina. "to collect debt for support of wife, Patty, during her life or widowhood, upon said Wesley H. Roberts giving bond and security for $1,000. At wife's death or marriage, to be divided among three Grandchildren: $50 to Wesley H. Roberts when he becomes of age or marries. Issue:[300]

A. William Roberts, born 1838 Georgia.

B. Elizabeth Roberts, born 1844 Georgia.

C. John Roberts, born 1846 Georgia.

D. Mary F. Roberts, born Georgia.

E. James Roberts, born 1854 in Paulding County.

II. Polly Roberts, born 1817 in South Carolina, married John Hitchcock on 4 September 1845 in Paulding County. SEE Hitchcock.

---

[300] 1860 Paulding County Census; Paulding County Wills & Marriages.

III.   Fanny Roberts, born 1818 in South Carolina, married Zachariah Cogburn (born 1815 in South Carolina,
farmer. Residents of Dallas, Georgia in 1860. Issue:

    A. Henry Cogburn, born 1843 in South Carolina.

    B. Mary Cogburn, born 1848 in South Carolina.

    C. Sarah Ann Cogburn, born 1852 in South Carolina.

IV.   Susannah Roberts married Thomas Starnes.

V.   Sarah Roberts married Matthew Bone on 12 May 1849 in Paulding County. SEE Bone.

Roguemore of Monroe County

Hiram Roguemore was born 21 December 1821 in Georgia, died 1866. He married Lovicy
Chambliss, a daughter of Jeptha Chambliss and his wife Susan (Jones) Chambliss of Monroe
County. SEE Chambliss. Issue:[301]

I.   Augusta Roguemore, born 1844 Georgia, died 21 August 1895 in Panola County, Texas,
married on 21 April 1868, Henry Balden Chambliss, in Monroe County. SEE Chambliss.

II.   James Murphy Roguemore, born 7 February 1847 in Georgia, died 16 December 1922 in
Texas, married on 31 October 1871, Laura Victoria Spivey, in Monroe County.

III.   Zachariah T. Roguemore, born 1849 in Georgia.

IV.   Susan Zillah Ann Roguemore, born 17 October 1850 in Panola County, Texas, died 28
October 1932, married Elijah Hanks Woolveston on 15 October 1866.

V.   Thomas Peter Roguemore, born ca 1852 in Panola County, Texas.

VI.   Jeptha Roguemore, born 1853 in Panola County, Texas.

VII.   Seaborn Roguemore, born 1855 in Panola County, Texas.

VIII.   A.Delbert Roguemore, born ca 1855 in Panola County, Texas, died 1892 in Panola
County, married Sarah Elizabeth Parrish on 1 September 1880.

IX.   Elizabeth Roguemore, born 1857 in Panola County, Texas, married Robert Waller on 1
October 1874.

X.   Lovicy Roguemore, born 1859 in Panola County, Texas.

Sailors of Switzerland, Maryland,
South Carolina, North Carolina and Georgia

Abram Sailors was born ca 1710 in Lucerne, Switzerland. Abram is said to have come from
Switzerland in 1737 to settle in Maryland. One source says he and his brothers landed at the
Port of New Orleans. Another quotes Strassburger's Pennsylvania German Pioneers, page 42,
where among the Palatine passengers of the ship "Pennsylvania Merchant," commanded by
John Stedman, is one Abram Saler. That boat landed at Philadelphia 10 Sept 1731 from Dover,

---

[301] Monroe County Marriages; 1860 Panola County, Texas Census.

and before that from Rotterdam. Other sources says our Abram may have settled along the Susquehanna River on the border between Maryland and Pennsylvania. Janel Woodbury says Abraham Saylors or Zoellers was born 1710 in Lucerne, Switzerland. He married Catherine Seyleria about 1731 in Switzerland. Abraham came on the ship Harle to Philedelphia, PA 1 Sep 1736. The descendants claim that John Sailors, born ca. 1756, was 20 years younger than his sister Mary, born ca. 1736 in Germany. She married Michael Hechelman/Hackleman. Abram Sailors had a large family of children.

The family lived in the Shenandoah Mountains, near the Pennsylvania- Maryland borders. They later crossed into North Carolina, South Carolina, and Indiana.
Known issue:[302]

I.   Mary Sailors, born ca 1733, died 8 June 1824 in South Carolina. She married Michael Hechelman/Hackleman.

II.   Philip Sailors.

III.   Abram Sailors, Jr., born 1743 in Maryland.

IV.   Leonard Sailors, born ca 1748 in Maryland. . .In <u>The North Carolina Booklet,</u> Vol. IX, <u>The History of Lincoln County</u> by Alfred Nixon: At July Term, 1770, "Thomas Camel came into court and proved that the lower part of his ear was bit off in a fight with Steven Jones, and was not taken off by sentence of law; certified by whom it may concern." At a later term, "James Kelly comes into open Court of his own free will and in the presence of said court did acknowledge that in a quarrel between him and a certain Leonard Sailor on the evening of the 2nd day of June, 1773, he did bite off the upper part of the left ear of him, the said Leonard Sailor, who prays that the same be recorded in the minutes of the said court." This confession gave James Kelly such standing in the esteem of his Majesty's Justices that at the same term it was ordered by the Court that James Kelly serve as constable in the room of George Trout and that he swear in before Thomas Espy, Esq." From the court entries biting off ears was a popular way of fighting, but whole ears were at least an outward sign of honesty. Known issue:
    A.   Leonard Sailors married Amy Gant.
    B.   Frederick Sailors married Elizabeth Cameron.

V.   Daniel Sailors, born 1753 in Maryland.

VI.   John Sailors, born ca 1756 in Maryland d: April 03, 1833 in Lincoln County, North Carolina. Another source says that he died in Rush County, Indiana. About 1775, John Sailors went to Lincoln County, North Carolina. On 19 October 1779, he signed a petition to have Burke County annexed to Lincoln County, North Carolina. About 1784, he went to Abbeville, South Carolina. Later, in 1786 he owned some land in South Carolina as his name appeared on the 1787 tax digest for 96th District, 60 acres. Three of his children were born in South Carolina, before he removed to Scott County, Kentucky about 1810, then to Franklin County, Indiana, later settling in Rush County, Indiana in 1822. He is buried on the south bank of Little Flat Rock Creek; bur. SE qtr. of section 7, range 11, twp 13, 6 mi. SE of Rushville .

    Others who appear to be some of the children of Abram Sailors, are enumerated as follows:

---

[302] Jackson County Wills, Deeds & Marriages; 1850-1860 Madison County Census.

VII.   Phoebe Sailors, born ca 1760 married on 20 November 1789 in Burke County, John E. Collins. [303] SEE Collins.

VIII.   Michael Sailors was born ca 1756 in Pennsylvania and removed to Burke County (later Lincoln County), North Carolina as a child. He was a Revolutionary War Soldier, enlisting from Burke County. According to his Revolutionary War Pension, he removed to Willaimson County, Tennessee where he died in 1850. He was found on the 1801 Elbert County Tax Digest.

IX.   Christopher Sailors was born 1760 in North Carolina and died after 1850 in Madison County, Georgia. He first lived in Jackson County where he was listed as a petit juror in Jackson County (Jackson County Minutes 1801-1803, page 52-83). He married a daughter of Thomas Little. He was residing with his son, Christopher, Jr. in Madison County (1850 Census).[304]

Issue of Christopher Sailors:

A. William Sailors, born 1788 in Wilkes County, Georgia, died 1869 in Madison County. He married Betsy Beard (license) on 29 January 1811 in Jackson County. Elizabeth (Betsy) was born 1795 in Georgia. Issue:
   1. Minerva Sailors, born 1826 in Georgia.
   2. Rachel Sailors, born 1830 in Georgia.
   3. Crawford Sailors, born 1834 in Georgia.

B. David Sailors, born 1790-1795 in Georgia, died 1855 in Madison or Jackson County.

C. James Sailors, born 1790-1795, died 1840-1850.

D   Daughter, born ca 1794, died after 1820.

---

[303] NOTE__ I could be wrong on this, but I believe that Phoebe is one of the many children of Abram Sailors.
[304] Jackson County Deeds

Deed Book E, page 557. 16 February 1811. George Washington Wilson to Christopher Sailors, both of Jackson County, for $250.00, 100 acres on Sandy Creek, it being part of a tract whereon George Wilson, Sr. now lives on the southeast side thereof and lying on both sides of the creek.

Deed Book E, page 542. 22 July 1811, George Wilson, Sr. to Christopher Sailors, both of Jackson County, for 60 pounds, 30 acres located on the south side of Sandy Creek. Wilson gave 100 acres to his son, George, and which William Sailors bought from George W. Wilson on the northeast side of same.

Deed Book G, page 162. 2 August 1816. Martin Anthony of Franklin County to John Sailors of Jackson County, for $236.00, 119 acres on Sandy Creek. Witness: George Wilson, Sr. and Christopher Sailors.

E. John Sailors, born ca 1796 in Georgia, died 1866 in Jackson County, his LWT dated 25 September 1866, probated 15 October 1866 in Jackson County. He married Nancy Betsy McGennis on 21 December 1815 in Jackson County. Issue:

    1. Mary Ann Virginia Sailors.
    2. Alexander Sailors married Sarah Chandler 7 October 1847 in Jackson County.

F. Abner Sailors, born 1803 in Georgia, died after 1880 in Jackson County. He married Levina Wilson on 1 December 1823 (date of license) in Jackson County. Wife residing with him in Jackson in 1880, was Palina (born 1806 in Georgia).

G. Frances Sailors, born ca 1805, died 1870-1880 in Georgia, married William Williams 1826 in Jackson County.

H. Christopher Sailors, Jr., born 1806 in Jackson County, died after 1880. He married Merra Dunston on 16 January 1845 in Jackson County. Wife, Nancy, born 1817, listed with the family on the 1850 Madison County Census. Wife, Artemisea (born 1815 Georgia), listed with the family on 1860 Madison County Census. Issue:

    1. Milly Elizabeth Sailors, born 1845 Madison County.
    2. Charles W. Sailors, born 1848 Madison County.
    3. Lucinda Florida Sailors, born 1850 Madison County.
    4. Clarisea Sailors, born 1856 Madison County.
    5. Mercy Sailors, born 1859 Madison County.

Salter of Liberty County

Samuel Salter was appointed Commissioner of Roads near Sunbury, Liberty County, in 1773. In April of 1768 he was paid for executing a negro; in 1772 was Inquirer and Tax Assessor for St. Andrew's Parish. Died in Liberty County in 1790, the date of his will. His wife was Martha, who was born in Charles Towne, South Carolina, who died March 18, 1767, aged 24.[305]

He took advantage of the need for bricks in Savannah, and located on Hutchinson Island. He married Anna, the widow of Joseph Coles and mother of Ann Harris Demetre, the widow of William Thomas Harris of Frederica. This was an industrious family, and Salter apparently enjoyed some success in his trade. At his death, he owned Lot No. 9 in Wilmington Tything Derby Ward, a house and Lot No. 8 in Torvers Tything Deckers Ward (occupied by William Spencer), and Salter's Island (which he bequeathed to his grandson, William Harris, son of Ann). Salter's Island was located about three miles from Savannah. Anna Salter, his widow who named her grandson, William Thomas Harris, her daughter, Anne Demetre, and daughter, Pennellope Cassell. Land in Great Britain was mentioned.

Salter was granted 500 acres of land on a piece of Marsh located near Augustine Creek. He arrived in Georgia on 17 December 1733 and was appointed Constable. Godson: John Anderson. In 1739 he was Tythingman. In December of 1741 he was granted 500 acres on

---

[305] Colonial Records of Georgia by Candler; Early Settlers of Georgia by Coulter; Colonial Deeds.

Dawbus Island, south of Savannah, three miles below the town. He married Anne, the widow of Joseph Coles on 9 September 1736. His LWT dated 28 October 1752. Wife, Anne died December 1753 in Frederica, naming her grandson, William Thomas Harris "following in care of my daughter, Ann Demetre", in her Will. (See William Harris). Issue:

I. Anna Salter married Daniel Demetre, according to a Marriage Contract.
II. Pennellope Salter married Mr. Cassell.

Sanders of Paulding County

Jonathan Sanders was born ca 1799, and married Lucy Adair (born 1800) on 31 May 1817. SEE Adair. Issue:

I. William Sanders.

II. Darcus Sanders.

III. Joseph Sanders.

IV. Permelia Sanders.

V. Agnes Sanders.

VI. Needham Sanders.

VII. Lucy Sanders.

VIII. Mary Sanders.

IX. Millie Sanders, born ca 1820, died before 1869, married on 25 May 1837, Kenion Tarpley Hulsey. Issue:

    A. Joseph Pate Hulsey, born 8 June 1839, died 18 November 1887.
    B. James Bartley Hulsey, born 22 April 1841.
    C. Needham Whit Hulsey, born 23 July 1843, died 20 February 1916.
    D. William T. Hulsey, born 23 June 1846, died 1923.
    E. Hillborn Quincy Hulsey, born 15 September 1848, died 2 September 1921.
    F. Thomas Russell Hulsey, born 8 February 1950, died 7 May 1921.
    G. John Sims Hulsey, born 28 April 1853.
    H. Charles L. Hulsey, born 18 September 1855.
    I. Kenion Tarpley Hulsey, born 19 August 1862.
    J. Julius McCain Hulsey, born 23 December 1863, died 23 July 1936.

Singleton of Gwinnett County

Mary Singleton was born ca 1750-1760 in South Carolina and was listed with a male born 1760 to 1770 on the 1840 Gwinnett County Census. This family is to Pinckeyville and represents the progenitor of all Gwinnett County Singletons. Apparently, her sons were Dennis Singleton (born 1813), Jefferson Singleton (born 1814) and Luke E. Singleton (born 1819), all born in South Carolina.[306]

Another connection is *Cynthia Singleton*, born 1802 in South Carolina, listed next door to Dennis and Luke in 1870. Cynthia was widowed on the 1850 DeKalb County Census, when she lists her son, Wilson Singleton (born 1830 in South Carolina) and daughter, Martha A. Singleton (born 1837). Wilson married Pheaby A. (born 1831 in Georgia), and they were listed on the 1880 Jackson County, Alabama Census, with issue: Mary Ann Singleton, born 1850 Georgia; Martha E. Singleton, born 1855 Alabama; and St. Luke Singleton, born 1879 Alabama.

Dennis Singleton was born in South Carolina in 1813 and died in 1884(per family record)in Gwinnett County, GA; he is buried in Singleton Cemetery. Dennis and Thomas Jefferson Singleton served in the Reed Company during the Creek Wars of 1836. Dennis was first listed as head of household in 1840 Gwinnett County (Pinckneyville) census, along with a 15-20 year-old female and two 5-10 males. The property of Dennis was located in the Crooked Creek Road-Spalding Drive area. (1-1/2 acres for Shiloh Baptist Church came from this property in 1883), and the Singleton Cemetery is located near the church on Spalding Drive. Dennis married (1) Elizabeth Waits (born 1817, died after 1860), the daughter of Mark and Hannah Waits, originally of South Carolina. Issue of Dennis Singleton and wife, Elizabeth:

    A. Julius C. Singleton, born 1840, buried in Singleton Cemetery.

    B. Philo V. Singleton, born 1 January 1842, died 14 January 1914, buried Mt. Carmel Methodist Church, Gwinnett County. He was a Confederate veteran. He was listed on the 1880 Gwinnett County Census, resident of Pinckneyville. Wife, Rosa, was born 1858 in Georgia. Issue:
        1. Lizzie Singleton, born 1872 in Gwinnett County.
        2. Cora Singleton, born 1873 in Gwinnett County.
        3. Ina Singleton, born 1876 in Gwinnett County.

    C. John M. Singleton, born 1845, died in Civil War, buried Singleton Cemetery. (no dates) His Civil War files indicate that he died at Camp Douglas, in Illinois).

    D. Alford (Alfred) P. Singleton, born 1847, C.S.A., died 1921; CSA-enlisted 1863 County H. He is buried in the Norcross Town Cemetery. He married Mary (born 1857 Georgia), daughter of Luke Singleton. Listed on the 1880 Gwinnett County Census. Issue:
        1. Sam Singleton.
        2. Lafayette Singleton, born 1873 in Gwinnett County.
        3. Moses Singleton.
        4. Dess Singleton.
        5. Mattie Singleton.
        6. Marietta Singleton, born 1875 in Gwinnett County.

    E. Adaline E. Singleton, born 1849, buried Singleton Cemetery.

    F. Julia Ann Singleton, born 1851, died 1875, buried Singleton Cemetery.

---

[306] Comment_Mary is believed to have come to Georgia from Camden District, South Carolina about 1831, and may be the wife of Thomas Collins.

Dennis married (2) Sarah Snow (born 9 December 1831, died 6 February 1911) in 1854. She is buried in Singleton Cemetery. Issue of Dennis Singleton and wife, Sarah, as follows: [307]

G. Sylvester (S. V.) Singleton, born 1855, died 1917, married Lula Carroll (born 1862 in Alabama; buried Arizona. Issue: P. J. and George. They were listed on the 1880 Gadsden, Etowah County, Alabama Census.

H. Mazaline (Malrene) Elizabeth Singleton, 1857-1921, married Benjamin Franklin Honea; buried Singleton Cemetery: Issue: Charlie, Kate, Alma, Ludie, Paul, Ben, Dock (Sylvester) and George

I. Dennis P. Singleton, born 31 January 1859, died 29 December 1886, not married, buried Singleton Cemetery

J. Austin M. Singleton, 1861-1944 married Emma Cowan, then Mary Chloe Harper; buried Singleton Cemetery; child from first marriage: Emma Darling, who married Sam Singleton; children from second: Hugh, Pearl, Johnny, Frank, Joe, Gertrude, Lou, Lois, and Winnie

K. Sarah Singleton, born 26 April 1864, died 11 September 1894, not married, buried Singleton Cemetery.

L. Lou (Lula) G. Singleton, born 25 May 1867, died 30 January 1935, no children, buried Singleton Cemetery.

M. Toccoa Singleton, born 1868, married John T. Scott in 1894, Milton County, GA; buried at Mt. Pisgah; Issue: Guy, Glenn, J. T., and George.

N. Eva (Evie) Singleton, born 1871, married Charlie (C. J.) Dalton in 1903 in Milton County, GA; moved to Gadsden, AL area (maybe Albertville);children :Charlie, D. C., Bernice, Eula, and Paul George Washington 1876-1952; married Mary Magdalena Hawes 1876-1964 (daughter of Frances Parker 1849-1928 and Peyton L. Hawes 1845-1920, both buried in Norcross Town Cemetery).

O. George Singleton, born 22 September 1875, died 22 January 195o (or 1952), buried in Singleton Cemetery, in Gwinnett County. Wife, Lena, born 26 January 1876, died 20 December 1964, buried Singleton Cemetery. Issue of George and Lena:

1. Edward Earl Singleton, born 19 September 1898, died 8 July 1972 buried Singleton Cemetery; no children.
2. Leila Ruth Singleton, died 1991; married Olan Sparks; no children Bess Evelyn 1906-7, married Jesse Harold Sellars; one child; Jesse buried in Singleton Cemetery.
3. Birdie Lou Singleton (1908-2001), married Robert Pruitt (Allen)

---

[307] Gwinnett County Deaths 1819-1989 by Alice Smythe McCabe; 1840-1880 Gwinnett County Census; Gwinnett County Marriages; Singleton Family Cemetery; Mt. Carmel Methodist Church Cemetery; Norcross Town Cemetery; Methodist Trinity Church Cemetery; 1880 Jackson County, Alabama, Census; 1880 Gadsden County, Alabama Census; 1880 Gwinnett County Census.

4. Mary June Singleton (1912-1998), married 1912-1998 married J. Otwell Kelley; both buried in
Singleton Cemetery; two children.
5. S. V. Singleton (1917-1977), married Joyce Anderson: one child

Thomas Jefferson Singleton was born 1814 in South Carolina. He married Tresham (Tempy Ann) Dickens on 6 September 1838 in Gwinnett County. Issue:

A. John Singleton, born 1840 Gwinnett County.
B. William Singleton, born 1842 Gwinnett County.
C. James Singleton, born 1844 Gwinnett County.
D. Ephraim Singleton, born 1846 Gwinnett County.
E. Mary Ann Singleton, born 1848 Gwinnett County. She married Alford P. Singleton, son of Dennis (see above).
F. Jefferson Singleton, born 1850 Gwinnett County.

Luke E. Singleton was born 2 September 1815 in South Carolina, farmer, died 30 January 1904 in Gwinnett County leaving a wife, three sons, and one daughter. The 1880 Gwinnett County Census lists both his parents as having been born in South Carolina. Luke Singleton (listed as James) married Peggy Ann (Martha) Collins on 24 October 1856 Paulding County. One census records her nickname "Cady", while the 1880 Census lists her as "Martha". She was born 30 October 1828 in South Carolina, and died on 4 May 1904 in Gwinnett County. Martha is believed to be a daughter of Felix Collins of Cobb County. On the 1850 Cobb County Census, Felix Collins (born 1800) is listed as a member of her family. Martha and Luke are buried in the Methodist Trinity Church Cemetery in Gwinnett County. SEE Collins.
Issue:

A. John Robert Singleton, born 11 March 1852 in Gwinnett County, buried in the Mt. Carmel Methodist Church Cemetery.
B. Joseph T. Singleton, born 9 November 1854, died 1 September 1924, Gwinnett County, buried in the Mt. Carmel Methodist Church Cemetery.
C. Georgia Singleton, born 5 August 1845 Gwinnett County, died 13 November 1918 Gwinnett County, married Joseph T. Goza, buried in the Trinity Methodist Church Cemetery.
D. William A. Singleton, born 19 June 1859 in Gwinnett County, died 12 March 1933 in Gwinnett County. Wife, Minnie Anna Goza, born 4 May 1861, died 22 March 1923. Both are buried in the Singleton Cemetery, Gwinnett County.
Issue:
1. Ida B. Singleton, born 24 February 1886, died 11 March 1932, buried Singleton Cemetery.
2. Zerah M. Singleton, born 3 May 1884, died 1 October 1938, buried Singleton Cemetery.

Skedsvold of Norway, North Dakota,
& Richmond County

Ole Gunderson Skjedsvold Haugen lived in Vaga (formerly Vaage), in PeerGynt Country, in the Gudbrandsdalen region of Norway. The old stave church was mentioned in the records as early as 1100, however, the churches were built mostly between 1100 and 1400.

Gudbrandsdalen, Vaago Kirko.

Two of his sons, Anton and Jacob Skedsvold traveled from Norway ca 1895, and settled in McKenzie County, North Dakota. Known issue of Ole Gunderson Skedsvold:

I.   Jacob Skedsvold returned to Norway after the death of his father to live in the family home in Vaga.

4th row, L-R: Ole Lillegren, Ole Tiegen, Jacob Skedsvold, Hans Lunde and Syver Hanson.

3rd row, L-R: Nils Lund, Carl Holte, Ole Eidsness, Gust Gern, M. O. Eidsness

2nd row, L-R: Mike Thompson, Mike Jacobson, Syver Syverson, Bert Olson.

1st row, L-R: Lars Strate, Knut Botten.

314

Lillehof Township

II. Ole O. Skedsvold, born 1870 in Norway. He was married in 1887 in Norway to Raquilda H. (born 1867 in Norway). His land is listed on the adjacent Township Map for Lillehof, North Dakota.

Issue:[308]

A. Oscar Skedsvold, born

B. Clara R. Skedsvold, born 1902 in Ramsey County, North Dakota.

C. Pauline Skedsvold, born 1903 in Ramsey County, North Dakota.

D. Carl Skedsvold, born 1905 in Ramsey County, North Dakota.

III. Hans Olson Skedsvold, born 1874 in Norway, a resident of Brocket, North Dakota.

IV. Anton Skedsvold, born 25 August 1884 in Norway, died 26 February 1978 in Culbertson, Roosevelt County, Montana,[309] buried in the Alexander Cemetery in McKenzie County, North Dakota. He was found on the 1910 Ramsey County Census, age 25, lodger. Wife, Anna, born 25 November 1889, died May 1979 in Culbertson, Roosevelt County, Montana.[310] Issue:

A. Obert Skedsvold, son of Anton Skedsvold. Wife, Delores (born 5 August 1920, died 29 July 1996 in Charbonneau, McKenzie County, North Dakota).[311] Issue:

1. Dan Skedsvold of Augusta, Fulton County, Georgia married Dollie Elaine Bennett, a daughter of Joseph Ronald Bennett and his wife, Cynthia (Fennel) Bennett), in Laurens County. Dan Skedsvold, retired, DSM Chemicals' senior environmental specialist in Augusta. Issue:

---

308 1910 Ramsey County, North Dakota Census.

309 Social Security Death Index, ss#502-32-9872.

310 Social Security Index.

311 Social Security Death Index, ss#502-58-6638

a. Paula Rhee Skedsvold, unmarried.

b. Sandra Delores Skedsvold, resident of Augusta.

c. Daniel Brett Skedsvold.

d. Kevin Obert Skedsvold, married 17 November 1990 in Atlanta, Fulton County, Suzanne Teri Stucki (born 27 March 1960 Atlanta, Fulton County), a daughter of Edwin Gerald Stucki and Jeannette Holland. Kevin is a partner with the Atlanta law firm of Donahue, Hoey & Skedsvold, LLC, specializing in insurance and workmen's compension. Issue:

1-Sarah Elizabeth Skedsvold, born 26 December 1993, Atlanta.
2-Miles Christian Skedsvold, born 14 September 1995, Atlanta.

Sarah and Miles Skedsvold

B. Gunder T. Skedsvold, son of Anton Skedsvold, was born 1921, died 27 September 1998. His obituary appeared in the *McKenzie County Farmer*. In 1940, he was a member of the Montana State National Gudard.

Smith of Carroll County

William J. Smith married Mattie, and resided in Carrollton. Known issue:

I.   Mable Smith married Eugene Holland (born 1901), divorced. She married (2) Robert Blackwell.

II.   Helen Smith, born 9 July 1906 in Villa Rica, Carrollton, Georgia, died 25 February 1929 at McPherson, Paulding County. She married Laurel Benjamin Holland and by him had two or three children who died as infants.

Smith of Laurens & Monroe Counties

Alexander Smith was born about 1765, died 1820 Laurens County, Georgia. Alexander Smith came from North Carolina to Georgia about 1791. His wife was Martha, probably Martha Franklin. SEE Franklin. Evidence points that Alexander came from North Carolina as one of his sons, Matthew Smith, was born 1780 in North Carolina; found on 1850 Dooly County, Georgia Census.[312]

---

[312]   Laurens County Deeds, Book H, Page 169, 12/7/1815. Alexander Smith of Laurens County for $800, 200 acres of land, being part of a tract granted to Thomas Fort and part of a tract granted to Hugh McKollock in James Hogan's corner; John Montford's corner. Signed, his mark.

Laurens County Returns 1811-23, Page 125, Alexander Smith Estate. Davis Smith, administrator. 1/7/1822. "To Davis Smith. note and interest $73.39. J. Hogan's account. $2.90,"

Laurens County Administrator's and Guardian's Bonds, Page 124, Davis Smith, John Thomas, Lewis Sanders of Laurens County make bond for $10,000, as administrators Est. Of Alexander Smith, decd., 7/3/1820.

Martha H. Smith, widow, drew in the 1821 Land Lottery, then a resident of Laurens County, Georgia. She drew Land Lot 222 in the 12th District of Monroe County. Note that this is the identical land which she deeded to her son, Davis Smith. [313] No further records have been found on Martha H. Smith. Her son, Davis Smith, referred to "my Hogan plantation" in his marriage contract, this land appearing to be in Monroe County adjoining his other lands there, and it may be that his mother was a "Hogan" before she married Alexander Smith. It is believed that she died between 1825 and 1829, since she did not appear on the 1830 Census.

Issue:[314]

I.   Matthew Smith, son of Alexander Smith, was born 1780 North Carolina, listed on 1850 Dooly County, Georgia Census, married on 19 February 1809 in Laurens County, Unity Register. Listed on 1830 Laurens County Census. On 1850 Dooly County he is listed as age 70, with wife, Abigail, age 73. Also listed with them were Nancy Spill, age 90, born in South Carolina and Mary Spill, aged 68, born South Carolina. It appears then, that his second wife was Abigail Spill, a daughter of Nancy Spill.

His wife, Abigail, was born 1777 in North Carolina; listed on the 1850 Dooly County Census, along with Nancy Spill, age 90, born in South Carolina and Mary Spill, age 68, born in South Carolina. Dooly County Returns and Vouchers, Vol. 2, July Term 1855, Page 101, 205, Mathew Smith was made guardian of Susan E. Bridges.

His LWT is on Page 150 of Dooly County Wills, 1847-1901, and headed:

> "Mathew Smith of Lee County". He named his wife, Abigail, with whom he
> had lived for 6 years. Will dated 28January 1860. He married on 22 November 1853,
> Abigail Bridges. His daughter, Elizabeth Smith married David D. Culpepper
> On 8 November 1833 in Laurens County. Names in Will wife's son, William Bridges
> and her daughter, Susan Bridges. His son-in-law, Jeremiah Broxton. Two daughters:
> Eliza Culpepper's children, and Zelpha Broxton's children.

David Culpepper was one of the appraisers of the estate of Alexander Smith in Laurens County dated 29 September 1821. He could not write!. David Culpepper is also listed on the 1830 Laurens County Census. There is one other reference to land belonging to Davis Smith in Laurens County, part of which adjoins the estate of Henry Cutpepper, deceased, and also adjoins the land of Alexander Smith, deceased, deed dated 1825 (see reference below). David Culpepper was probably a son of Henry Culpepper of Laurens County.

Laurens County Inventories, Book A, Page 62-4, "Appraisers of Estate of Alexander Smith: Winfield Wright, David Culpepper (his mark) Lewis Sanders and M. G. Oliver. " 9/29/1821

[313] Monroe County Deed Book D, Page 15, April 1, 1824. Martha H. Smith of Dooly County and Davis Smith of Laurens County for $250, land in Monroe County, Georgia, located in the 11th district and being Land Lot 202.

[314] Monroe County Wills; Monroe County Marriages; Monroe County Cemetery (Smith Cemetery); Laurens County Deeds; Monroe County Deeds; personal records of Jeannette Holland Austin.

III. Davis Smith, son of Matthew Smith, was born 1791 Washington County, Georgia, died 1868 Monroe County, Georgia, leaving a Will of that date which was left unprobated. He married (1) Hannah Ferth on 23 July 1816 in Laurens County and had one son by her, then married (2) on 6 January 1820 in 1820 Laurens County Mrs. Elizabeth Dixon.Jordan. They moved to Monroe County about 1821. In 1830, Davis Smith owned 20 slaves, a figure which put him in the "planter class". During 1850 and 1860, some of his married daughters and their husbands lived with the family inside the house. [315]

All of the children of Alexander Smith appear to have ended up on the plantation of Davis Smith, his son. Davis Smith is the ancestor of the author and I have heard many family stores, as well as seen the old plantation house. It was a large two-story white frame, built about 1821, with a hallway down the center ~ the house and rooms on each side. An old photograph taken about the turn of the century shows a slave, called Sarah Low, who refused to leave after the war, as well as family members.

Davis Smith raised cotton primarily, having his own store and warehouse. It was an enterprising community in his day and later called "Brent, Georgia, " out from Forsyth, after his daughter, Jane's second husband, Thomas Young Brent, who kept it going. My grandmother told of how her grandmother, Jane Smith, attended Wesleyan Female College, studied music, and how her father and mother went to Charlestown to see Jenny Lynn sing when she was in America, bringing back the first piano to Monroe County. Elizabeth Dixon Jordan Smith taught her children music and how to play the piano.

During the War Between the States, with Davis Smith's sons off to War, and his son-in-law, Wesley Clements, the first husband of Jane Smith, a planter with 77 slaves, the family tried to

---

[315] Laurens County Deeds

Book G, Page 196, Davis Smith of Laurens County to James Hogan of Laurens County for $200, 100 acres, orig. the Thomas Fort tract. 10/13/1812.

Book H, Page 214, Davis Smith of Monroe County to Henry Montford of Laurens 1/6/1825 for $800 land on Big Creek, 272 1/2 acres, being part of three different surveys. One part granted to Hugh McKullock; Thomas Fort and William Nelson, bounded on the west by Mary Stokes, southeast by the estate of Henry Culpepper, deceased; and north by Alexander Smith, deceased.

Book J, Page 309, Davis Smith of Monroe County to H. Z. Frutrelt of Laurens County for $50, 150 acres on Big Creek adjoining Turner Mason and Thomas Pullin.

Book H, Page 188, Davis Smith of Monroe to John Thomas, 343 acres, 1/7/1823.

Book H, Page , Davis Smith to Mathew Smith, 1/7/1825.

Book I, P. 54, Ira Stantey to Davis Smith of Monroe County, 202-½ acres 1/8/1828.

Book G, Page 194, Alexander Smith to Davis Smith.

Book H, Page 169, 12/7/1815 Alexander Smith of Laurens County for $800 to Davis Smith, 200 acres of land, being part of a tract granted to Thomas Fort and part of a tract granted to Hugh McKollock in James Hogan's corner; John Montford's corner.

hold together. When Sherman came through Atlanta, burning his way southward, some yankee soldiers found the plantation, just out of Forsyth, Georgia. Davis Smith, fearing the consequences of being found, climbed a tree and hid from the yankees. However, as they approached the house on horseback, he feared they would hear the ticking of his pocket watch. The yard was planted with cedar trees which lined the walkway to the street, the walk kept swept clean.

Davis Smith made a Will dated 1868 in Monroe County, but was incomplete, so not probated, instead, his estate administered. After his death, Thomas Young Brent, husband of Jane Smith, ran the plantation, up until around 1900, when Jane's brothers and sisters moved to Atlanta. Jane Smith Clements Brent had a daughter, Elizabeth Smith Clements who married Joel Edgar Chambliss.They moved to Atlanta, however, Elizabeth Smith Clements Chambliss and her mother, Jane Smith Clements Brent contracted typhoid fever about the same time and fell sick. Since Elizabeth was a Christian Science Healer, she received no medical care, and thus died in 1905, two years after her mother, Jane. Both are buried in the Smith Cemetery, at Brent, near Forsyth.

For years after the death of Dais Smith, the family members would return to the old abandoned plantation for summertime visits, but never returned there to live.

"My grandmother, Mary Brent Chambliss Evans, recalled visiting the old plantation during summer vacation. "About the turn of the century," she said, "it was necessary for the family to relocate in Atlanta to find work. After the devastation to the homes during War Between the States, no one could afford to hire laborers, and so, the old communities lay wasted." When I first found the old Smith family cemetery at Brent, it was about 1965. My sister, Marianne, was with me on that cold February day. "Do you want to go?" I asked her. "No," she shuttered. The wind howled fiercely across yellowed pasture grass, and I felt it whip through my clothing, as I climbed the hillside to the cemetery. The site was surrounded by a slate rock wall. As soon as I entered the cemetery and saw the gravestones ensnarled with thorny briars, a chill went through me. A neglected cemetery of long years past, yet, once so tenderly cared for, with descriptive gravestones and planted flowers. I knew to my knees, and traced my fingers over the vague indentions. David Smith and Joel Chambliss was there; also Lizzie's parents, grandparents, great aunts and uncles."
--Jeannette Holland Austin--

Davis Smith's children were:

A. William Frankling Smith was born on 29 June 1817 in Laurens County, died June 30, 1842 Monroe County, Georgia - child by first wife, Hannah Ferth.

B. Martha Franklin Smith was born on 29 December 1820 in Laurens County, died on 5 October 1821 in Laurens County.

C. Miranda Smith was born on 23 March 1822 in Monroe County, died on 19 October 1909 in Monroe County, married Orlando Holland. SEE Holland.

D. Mary Warren Smith was born on 11 April 1823 in Monroe County, married on 13 August 1840, Urbane Billingsley, died 6 June 1841 in Monroe County.

E. Tyrus Thomas Smith was born on 25 July 1824 in Monroe County, married on 19 December 1844, Eliza J. Hill, died about 1905 Monroe Counties

F. Davis Smith, born 20 May 1825 in Monroe County, unmarried.

G. John Dickson Smith, born 10 May 1828 in Monroe County, died 30 August 1839, buried in the Smith Cemetery in Brent, Georgia.

H. James Smith, born 14 February 1830 in Monroe County, married Rebecca Bartlett on 20 July 1851 in Monroe County.

I. Elizabeth Smith, born 14 June 1832 in Monroe County, married James H. Fryer. He must have died after 1850, because she was listed with the Davis Smith family in 1860, aged 28, and again in 1870, aged 38.

J. Judson Smith, born 26 July 1833 in Monroe County, died 6 September 1864, married Isabeth E. Potts on 18 December 1856 in Monroe County.

K. Jane Smith was born on 21 March 1836 in Monroe County, died 1905, buried in the Smith Cemetery in Brent, Georgia. She married (1) ca 1854 Wesley Clements, who died in the Civil War, and (2) on 1 May 1867 in Monroe County, Thomas Young Brent who died 12 October 1903 in Monroe County, and was buried in the Smith Cemetery at Brent. SEE Brent & Clements.

IV. Jeremiah Smith, son of Matthew Smith, was born 1795 Washington County, Georgia, died 1861 in Monroe County, buried at Brent, Georgia in Monroe County in the old Smith Cemetery, along with all above persons. Jeremiah married Milly Bailey on 26 November 1826 in Bibb County, Georgia, and was listed on the 1830 and 1840 Bibb County Census. He was listed on the 1850 and 1860 Monroe County Census alone, living next door to the Davis Smith family. The only son known: Georgia Messenger, published in Macon, Georgia, "David Washington Smith, son of Jeremiah Smith, died 14 June 1828 in Macon, aged 9 months, 10 days."

V. Elizabeth Smith, daughter of Alexander Smith, was born 1800 Georgia, died May 1865 Monroe County. She married James Hogan, although marriage was not located in Laurens or Monroe County records. However, they married about 1820. January 7, 1822, the Estate of Alexander Smith lists J. Hogan's account, in Laurens County. 23 May 1865, Davis Smith was appointed administrator of the Estate of Elizabeth Hogan. He was also administrator of the Estate of James Hogan, probated 6 September 1847 in Monroe County. 60. She is listed on the 1850 Census with 22 slaves, while Davis Smith lists 77. Also, Davis Smith, in his Will, refers to "my Hogan Plantation. " James Hogan died before 1850, as Elizabeth was listed as a widow on the 1850 Monroe County Census, living with her was Zephiah Smith, born 1832; the 1860 Census shows her as aged 60. SEE Hogan.

VI. Mable Smith, daughter of Matthew Smith, was born on 10 January 1812. She is buried in the family cemetery at Brent, Georgia, Monroe County, on Davis Smith's plantation. She must have died after 1830. No death date recorded.

Richard Tully Sorrells was born 26 February 1808 in Georgia, died 7 February 1828 Madison County, Georgia. He was the son of William Alexander Sorrells, and his wife, Dorcas (Sanders) Sorrells. He married Evelina L. Brown (born 14 January 1810, died 20December 1890) on 7 February 1828 in Madison County. Issue:

I.   William Alexander Sorrells, born 2 December 1828 in Madison County, died 8 January 1883.

II.   Benjamin W. Sorrells, born ca 1832 in Madison County, died 21 February 1864.

III. Sarah Ann Sorrells, born ca 1834 in Madison County.

IV.   Desdemona Sorrells, born ca 1838 in Madison County.

V.   Richard Tully Sorrels, born 6 April 1840 in Madison County, died 23 June 1858.

VI.   Robert Jackson Sorrells, born 10 May 1840 in Madison County, died 13 October 1918. He married on 7 November 1855 in Madison County, Mary Lane, born 8 July 1840 in Madison County, died 11 December 1917, buried in the old Danielsville Cemetery, in Madison County, a daughter of John D. Lane, born 1841 in Georgia, residents of Grove Hill, in 1880. SEE Lane. Issue:[316]

> A. Richard Tully Sorrells, born 29 July 1868 in Madison County, died 8 April 1949, buried old Danielsville Cemetery.
> B. Mattie R. Sorrells, born 1870 in Madison County.
> C. George F. Sorrells, born 1872 in Madison County.
> D. Mary Susan Sorrells, born 20 September 1874 in Madison County, died 28 January 1957, buried in the old Danielsville Cemetery.
> E. Willie M. Sorrells, born 1876 in Madison County.
> F. John Carlton Sorrells, born 5 January 1877 in Madison County, died 1860, buried in the old Danielsville Cemetery. Wife, Myrtie Hix, born 1884, died 1950.
> G. Rufus Jackson Sorrells, born 1 November 1880 in Madison County, died 22 January 1971, buried in the old Danielsville Cemetery. He married Emma Sue Coile, born 2 February 1888, died 24 January 1969.

VII. Dorcas A. Sorrells.

VIII. Ann Sorrells, born 17 August 1845 in Madison County, died 25 June 18888.

IX.   Zachariah Taylor Sorrells, died 18 November 1858.

X.   Maurine Sorrells.

XI.   Catherine Brown Sorrells, born 7 April 1853 in Madison County, died 23 January 1934.

---

[316] 1880 Madison County, Census, Grove Hill.

Sparks of Franklin County

Thomas Sparks, the son of Thomas and Margaret Sparks, was born 1760-1770 in Franklin County, Georgia. He was married to Sarah Camp, born ca 1787 in Pendleton District, South Carolina, a daughter of Edmund Camp and his wife Elizabeth (Carney) Camp. After Sarah's death, Thomas Sparks married Ms. Callahan. Issue:[317]

I.   Mary Sparks, born 1815-1820 Georgia.

II. Sarah Sparks, born 1815-1820 Georgia, married Joseph Benton Camp.

III. Elvira Sparks, born 1823 in Georgia, died 1900, married James Hicks Wilbanks.

IV. Louisa Sparks, born 3 March 1825 in Georgia, died 1863, married William R. Perry Wilbanks.

V.   Harriet M. Sparks, born 12 September 1827 in Georgia, died 23 August 1904, married (1) Benjamin Smith (2) William R. Perry Wilbanks on 2 February 1864 in Franklin County.

VI. Jeremiah Sparks, born 1834 in Georgia, married Frances E. Eskew on 5 October 1854 in Franklin County.

VII. Frances Sparks, born 28 May 1835 in Georgia, married William Hayes, in Franklin County (no date provided).

Spiers/Spears of Maryland and Lincoln County

William Spiers (Spears) was born ca 1705 in Baltimore, Maryland. Wife, Mary. Issue:

I.   Phoebe Spears, born 3 April 1726 in Anne Arundel County, Maryland.

II. Patience Spears, born 13 June 1728 in Anne Arundel County, Maryland.

III. Abentha Spears, born 7 June 1730 in Anne Arundel County, Maryland.

IV. Charlotty Spears, born 6 September 1734 in Anne Arundel County, Maryland.

V.   Jeremiah Spears, christened 8 September 1736 in Anne Arundel County, Maryland.

VI. Anletty Spears, born 24 April 1738 in Anne Arundel County, Maryland.

VII. Zachariah Spiers, christened 22 May 1740 in Anne Arundel County, Maryland, died 1806 in Lincoln County, Georgia. Wife, Rhoda. His LWT dated 22 April 1806 in Lincoln County

---

[317] Franklin County Marriages; 1830 Franklin County Census.

322

Will Book 1796-1808, page 62. He first lived in Columbia County, Georgia, as per a number of deeds in Columbia County.[318]

Issue of Zachariah and Rhoda:[319]

A. Hezekiah Spiers, born ca 1768, died in Lincoln County, Georgia.

B. Patience Spiers, born ca 1770, died October 1826 in Putnam County, Georgia, her LWT dated October 1826. She married Thomas Edmondson on 28 February 1791. SEE Edmondson.

VIII. Zephaniah Spears, born 7 June 1742 in Anne Arundel County, Maryland.

IX. John Barney Spears, christened 25 September 1744 in Anne Arundel County, Maryland.

X. William Spears, christened 28 October 1746 in Anne Arundel County, Maryland.

XI. Joshua Spears, born 31 May 1748 in Anne Arundel County, Maryland.

Spinks of Paulding County

B. F. Spinks, farmer, resident of Huntsville, in Paulding County, was born 1824 in Georgia. Wife, Della, was born 1826 in Georgia. Issue:

I. John W. Spinks, born 1848 in Paulding County, farmer. He married (1) Eliza Jane Bullock on 24 December 1868 in Paulding County, and (2) Sally, born 1849 in Georgia. Issue:[320]

A. James W. Spinks, born 1871 in Paulding County.

---

[318] Columbia County Deeds
3 April 1793, Isaiah Wright and his wife, Rebecca, to Zachariah Spiers, for 74 pounds, five shillings, 165 acres on Big Kiokee Creek, willed to Isaiah by Dyonisius Wright.

5 April 1794. Nathaniel Cocke mortgaged a Negro fellow named Joe, and a Negro woman named Agatha "who live with Mr. Wright" to Zachariah Spears, for 80 pounds.

February 1795, Benjamin Finney and his wife, Anne, deed to Zachariah Spires, for five shillings, 100 acres granted to Littleton Yarborough, whereon said Finney now lives, to include the plantation and dwelling place. Anne relinquished her dower.

13 August 1797, William Tindall to Zachariah Spiers for one dollar, 10 acres on the northside of Uchee Creek.

15 November 1797, Zachariah Spiers to Jonathan Ward of Richmond County for $150, 113 acres on the north side of the Uchee Creek, bounded by William Tindall, James Tinsley, William Booker, A. Crawford and Zachariah Chambliss.

[319] Putnam County Wills; Lincoln County Wills; Columbia County Deeds; Anne Arundel County, Maryland Parish Register.

[320] 1880 Paulding County Census, Dallas.

B. John T. Spinks, born 1873 in Paulding County, married Dora Anderson on 1 February 1893 in Paulding County.

C. Cary B. Spinks, born 1875 in Paulding County.

D. Alexander Spinks, born 1877 in Paulding County.

E. Benjamin L. Spinks, born 1879 in Paulding County.

II. Abihesholan (Abre) Spinks (daughter), born 1860 in Paulding County, married W. H. Childers on 11 April 1878 in Paulding County.

Starling of Carroll & Paulding Counties

Thomas James Starling, Sr. was born 13 March 1889 in Stoke Newington, London England, and died 12 May 1935 in Carrollton, Georgia, a son of Thomas James and Rose Hannah (Brown) Starling. He married Miss Allie Lee Holland, born 1893 in Paulding County, died 1979 in Long Beach, California, buried Forest Lawn Cemetery, Cypress, California. Thomas James Starling is buried at New Hope Cemetery, Paulding County. SEE Holland.

A letter dated 1966 from Allie Lee Starling to me described her school days:

"I went to the old McGregor schoolhouse down on Raccoon Creek...a one room affair with a fireplace on one end. Our teachers were poor and we had no books to amount to anything .... It was where the old Holland private cemetery was- it was near Uncle Buddy Holland's passing it one time and my parents said there were graves there.

We had two or three graves on our old farm place that we used to call the nigger graves and we were told they died of smallpox."

Lyn Starling, granddaughter of Allie Lee Holland Starling, wrote me on 14 August 1987: "Allie Lee was naturalized on June 6, 1928 Greensboro, North Carolina, even though we was born in Paulding County The imigration law was that a woman who married a noncitizen, she became a citizen of whatever country the husband came from.

"Thomas James Starling, Sr. came to Paulding County, Georgia to live with his aunt and uncle, Mr. and Mrs. William M. and Mary Anderson. William, born on 4 June 1856 in England, died 15 February 1920 in Paulding County. Mary, born 31 May 1859 in England, died in Paulding County It is thought Mary Anderson and Rose Hannan and Elsie Jenkins were sisters, Mary being the eldest and the daughters of Mrs. Brown of Great Misenden, Buckinghamshire, England.

"William and Mary came to the USA to work in the gold mines in Georgia. The first date we put Thomas into the USA is when he arrived at the port of New York on 21 November 1907, on the vessel 'Majestic' White Star Lines from Southampton, England on 13 November 1907. He taught at Harmony Grove School prior to 1917 with Rev. James Monroe Holland. Petition for Naturalization on 10 February 1922. Declaration of Intention dated 10 July 1925. Certification of Naturalization dated 10 December 1927. On 3 April 1910 in Dallas, Paulding County, he married Allie Lee Holland, born on 13 October 1893 in Paulding County, died on 6 October 1978 in Bellflower, California. Daughter of Mr. and Mrs. Harrison Ramsey "Tone" and Dorothy Frances (Jones) Holland, Sr.

Issue of Thomas Starling, Sr.:[321]

I.   Thomas James Starling, Jr., born on 27 May 1911 in Dallas, Paulding County, married on 10 August 1940 in Washington, D. C., Norma Loraine France, born on 17 March 1922 in Washington, D. C., the daughter of Charles Theodore and Zelda Loraine (Berrett) France, Sr. Issue:

A. Rosemary Starling, born on 12 August 1941 in Washington, D. C., married (1) 22 May 1968 in Carmel Monterey, California Jack Allen Dail (born 13 August 1934, died 1 September 1973 in Washoe County, Nevada, married (2) Robert Howard MaCartney (born 17 December 1933 in California). Issue:

1.   Jennifer Alish Dail, born 22 January 1971 in Carmel, California.
2.   Eric Ray MaCartney, born 11 September 1974 in Carmel, California.
3.   Kevin Starling MaCartney, born 3 February 1978 in New Haven, Connecticut.

B. Thomas James Starling III, born 13 November 1943 in Long Beach, California, married on 2 May 1970 in Parks, Nevada, Holly Lisle Villman (born on 31 December 1948 in Vancouver, B. C., Canada), daughter of Bruce and Dorothy Addaide (Elliott) Villman. Issue:

1.   Janet Lee Starling, born 25 January 1971 in Martinet, California.

C. Lynn Loraine Starling, born 1 December 1944 in Long Beach, California.

II.   Lillian Ruth Starling, born 3 April 1914 in Dallas, Paulding County, died on 24 June 1934 in Dallas, Paulding County, married Herman Woodrow Brooks (born on 12 December 1912 in Paulding County, died on 16 September 1981 at home in Long Beach, California), the son of John Thomas and Lucy Caroline (Woodall) Brooks. SEE Brooks.

III.   Robert Edward Starling, born 9 September 1915 in Dallas, Paulding County, married Birdie Shaw. Issue:

A. Kenneth Edward Starling, Sr. , son of Robert Edward Starling, was b. 10/17th Decatur, married 20 October 1957 in Decatur, Rebecca Jean Stewart, daughter of Vaughn Morton Stewart. Issue:

1.   Kenneth Edvard Starling, Jr., son of Kenneth Edward Starling, Sr., was born on 17 October 1958.

2.   Vaughn Hugh Starling, son of Kenneth Edward Starling, Sr.

3.   Jon Robert Starling,son of Kenneth Edward Starling, Sr.

4.   Catherine Lynn Starling, dan. of Kenneth Edward Starling, St.

5.   Thomas Marshall Starling, son of Kenneth Edward Starling, Sr.

---

[321] Ref: Holland 1000-1988 by Jeannette Holland Austin.

B. Brenda Ann Starling, married Russell Anderson Davis.

III. William Holland Starling, born 6 September 1919 in Newark, New Jersey, married on 5 April 1941, Kathryn Ellen McCorrick. Children.

A. Carol Lee Starling, born on 4 December 1941, married Gordon Wonacott. Children of Carol Lee Starling and Gordon Wonacott:

1. Robert Wonacott.

B. William Curtis Starling, born 2 May 1943.

Stegall of South Carolina, Mississippi; Bartow, Cobb & Paulding Counties

William Steggall (born 1609) sailed on the *Plaine J(o)aane* from London, England on May 16, 1635. His son was Samuel Stegall (Sr.) (born abt. 1645). His wife was named Jane.
After considerable research, I have found that the name "Stegall" is Anglo-Saxon (and therefore Germanic), traditionally from East Anglia, particularly Norfolk with some occurrences in Suffolk. There are many variants in spelling, including Stegol, Steagle, Stiggle, Stiggles, Stagold, Stickle, Stickles, and even Style and Styles. In one dictionary of English surnames, "Stegall" is listed as a variant of "Styles", as in this example: "Styles - Topographic name for someone who lived near a steep ascent. OE Stigol (a derivation of stigan - to climb, or OE Stigel - a man who lived near a stile). Vars. Stile, Stiles, Stiggle, Steggall, Steckle, Steckles." Another source essentially agrees: both "Styles" and "Stegall" evolved from Old English Stigol or Steogol, a derivative of stigan, "to climb", or from Old English Stige meaning "a man who lived near a stile", or "dweller by the stile or steep ascent". The name "Stegall" in its various forms and the word "stile" are historically and linguistically related to the German names Stiegel, Sti(e)gler, Stiegelmeyer, and Stegelman and also to the modern German word Stiege meaning "staircase," and the modern verb steigen meaning "to climb, to ascend." (By the way, a "stile" was not made of wood as it is today, but denoted a place to climb over the large embankments of mud and dirt that marked the boundaries of property: toeholds or footholds were carved into the dirt at an angle, and this passage over the embankment was called a "stile." Thus the stile was always "a steep ascent.") In this country, as in England, the spelling of "Stegall" has had many forms. Apparently the first immmigrant to this country with the name spelled it "Steggall", but today the most common spellings are "Stegall", "Stiegall", "Steagal"; in the United States "Stegall" is the most common. Because of the similarity of this name to some German names, it is quite possible that German immigrants with names like those previously mentioned may now be known as "Stegall."

Several people with variants of the name Stegall have found their way into historical records, including Reginald atte Stighel - 1227, William de Stile - 1229, Richard de Stigele, Robert de la Stiele - 1275, Roger Attestichell - 1305, Edmond Stegyll (or Stekyll), and Richard Stegold - 1524, many of these names showing obvious Norman-French changes.[322]

---

[322] Hanks, Patricia and Flavis Hodges. A Dictionary of Surnames, p. 517.
For those of you who are interested in linguistics, the normal development of the name from the Old English "Stigol" or "Steogol" would be to "Stile" or "Style", but in surnames, "Stigele" became "Stigle" and the continuant "g" became a stopped "g", hence "Stiggle". And often "gl" is

Samuel (Sr.) and Jane had a son named Samuel Stegall, Jr. (born abt. 1698). Samuel Stegall, Jr. was baptized on 26 March 1699. (The Vestry Book of the St. Peters Parish (Episcopal Church) New Kent and Jane City Counties, of Virginia).

The parents of Richard Stegall of Pickens County, South Carolina is believed to be George Stegall, born ca 1726 and his wife, Agnes (Bottomley) Stegall of Brunswick County, Virginia, however, as of yet, this has not been established factually to my satisfaction.. There is a deed in Lunenburg County Deed Book 10, page 294, dated December 1766 between Willian and Jane Turner to George Stegall, all of Lunenburg County, for 40 pounds, 135 acroes on the upper sde of Little Creek, below Stony Creek. Recorded 11 December 1766. In 1769, this 135 acres was listed in the tithes of Cumberland Parish, Lunenburg County.[323]

Richard Stegall was born 4 July 1754 in Brunswick County, Virginia, died 28 July 1836 in Pickens County, South Carolina. In 1793, he sold his land on the Indian River, in Virginia, to Aaron Harbour and removed to Pickens County, South Carolina where he purchased 2,000 acres of land. Richard married (1) Betsy Hensley , (2) Peggy Gillespie and (3) Margaret Davis (born 20 June 1790, died 22 February 1880), in 1813. Mrs. Margaret Stegall, widow of Richard Stegall, deceased, appointed William Holcombe as her attorney to collect from the estate. Witness: R. A. Stegall. (Pickens County Estates). [324] *Richard Stegall's S.C. LWT, dated 16 March 1831, and found in Pack 90, Clerk of Courts Office, Pickens Co., S.C. mentions the following eleven Issue:Bird, Spencer, Blackwell, Linny Yancy (2 ch: Elizabeth and Baylis Yancy), Artemus, Susan, Benjamin, Kelly, Nancy, Patsy Denny and five children of his son Hensly Stegall, deceased.. He* does not mention a wife. When the will was filed, it mentioned widow, Margaret and nine children to wit, Benjamin, Patsy Denny, Nancy, Kelly, Birdwell, Blackwell, Linny Yancy, Richard A. Stegall, Susan Williams and two children deceased, Hensly and Spencer Stegall.

---

interchanged with "cl", hence "Stickle". Middle English "Stegele" is from Old English "Steogol" and similarly developed to "Stiggle" and "Steckle". Dictionaries that specify this meaning are: Reaney, Hanks and Hodges, and others. The "Steddall" who came in 1637 is assumed to be "Steggall" until research proves otherwise. Reaney, P.H., op cit.

[323] Indenture made 5 January 1765, between Thomas Twitty Senr. of Saint Andrews Parish, Brunswick County and Peter Twitty his son of same, for Naturall Love and Affection, and five pounds, sell to Peter Twitty, one certain tract or parcell of land containing Four Hundred acres, it being part of a Larger Tract lying and being in the County of Brunswick on the North Side of Meherrin River & bounded as follows Begining at the mouth of Rattle Snake Branch on Briery Creek runing up the sd. Branch as it Meanders to Russells Path, from thence to the Head of the Bull Branch on Williams's Line thence down the branch to Edmund Ruffins Line, thence along the sd. Ruffins Line to Jno. Greshams Line thence along the said Greshams Line to John Johnsons Line, thence along the said Johnsons Line to Brierey Creek, thence across the sd. Creek to Richard Hagoods Corner White Oak on James Thorntons Line, thence along the sd. Thorntons Line to a Corner Red Oak on *George Stegall's Line* thence down the said Line to the begining. Signed Thomas Twitty. Witnesses: John Russell, John Twitty, Ralph Gresham. Court 25 February 1765, Indenture proved by the oaths of John Russell John Twitty & Ralph Gresham the witnesses thereto ... page 11-12.

[324] Pickens County, South Carolina Estate Records; Bartow County, Georgia Estates; Paulding County cemetery records; 1850 Cobb County Census; Paulding County Wills; Paulding County Marriages; the personal records of Mrs. Midge Byrum Coker, Rt. 2, Marquez, Texas 77865.

Spencer Stegall died leaving a widow Sarah Stegall and seven children to wit: Hensly, William, Robert, Peter, Elizabeth and two other names unknown. Richard Stegall, Senr. was helpless about 11 years before his death and could not walk. Benjamin Stegall appointed Kelly Green Stegall as his lawful attorney in the matters of his father's estate. Kelly Green Stegall assigned those rights to John Bowen. Margaret Stegall appointed William Holcombe as her attorney. Nancy Stegall, Lumpkin Co., GA, appointed her son, George W. Stegall as her lawful agent. George W. Stegall assigned rights to John Bowen. Richard A. Stegall and Abel Williams appointed John Bowen their lawful attorney.

Issue by (1) wife (Betsy Hensley):

I.   Blackwell Stegall, born 1797 in Pickens County, South Carolina, died June 1861 in Bartow County, Georgia, buried in the family lot at Altoona, Georgia. He married Sarah Calagia in 1814. The LWT of Blackwell Stegall, dated 8 August 1859, probated 21 June 1861 in Bartow County, Georgia Will Book A, page 213. Issue:

   A. Emsley Stegall, born 6 January 1812 in Pickens County, South Carolina, died 25 November 1888 in Emerson, Georgia. Wife, Sarah Allen Lockey. Known child:
       1. Robert Blackwell Stegall, born 1842 in Cartersville, Bartow County, Georgia, died 25 November 1888 in Emerson, Georgia. He was educated in the "Old Field Schools", and later attended high school in Cartersville. On his 20th birthday, he enlisted in the 14th Georgia Regiment, C. S. A., on June 15th, and was sent to Virginia where he saw service in the Seven Days' Battle around Richmond. He had organic trouble, and was released from a hospital in Richmond. In the fall of 1863, he was a brakeman on the old Western and Atanta Railroad. When General Sherman came through Atlanta in July of 1864, he went to Columbus, Georgia where he obtained work on the Muscogee Railroad, being the conductor of freight trains until the latter part of May 1865. When the U. S. Government quit operating the W. & A. Railroad, he was one of the first conductors to run a train from Atlanta to Chattanooga. He served 14 years, terminating on 6 November 1878. Then, he worked for the Alabama Great Southern Railroad until 31 December 1925 when he was retired. During this time, he resided on his little farm, which was ne mile south of the Tennessee line, at Roswell, Georgia. He met his first wife, Mrs. Carrie Murphy, while working in Columbus.[325]

   A. John Stegall, born 13 June 1820 in Spartanburg County, South Carolina, died 1 November 1878 in Pickens County, South Carolina, buried in Long Swamp Cemetery. He married Elizabeth Fitzsimmons.

   B. Hensley Stegall, born 1826 in Pickens County, South Carolina, died 24 November 1882, married Conni Witherstein.

   C. Patsy Stegall, married James M. Brooks on 14 August 1840.

   D. Mary Stegall, married Harry Thomas.

   E. Margaret Stegall, married Ross Lawhorn.

   F. Harriet Stegall, married Riley Payne.

---

[325] History of Walker County, Georgia, page 433-434.

G. Salley Stegall, married Fleming Cox.

H. Jane Stegall, born 11 June 1837, died 11 March 1923.

I. Tandy Stegall, born 11 June 1837, died in Atlanta, Fulton Conty, Georgia, married Mr. Carmichael.

II. Hensley Stegall, born 1798 in Pickens County, South Carolina, died July 1826 in Anderson County, South Carolina. He married Fanny Holeman. The LWT of Hensley Stegall dated 10 July 1826 in Anderson County Will Book A, page 329. "Children I have had by Fanny Hoeman: Spencer, Caroline, Mary Elizabeth, William Warren. My father, Richard Stegall, now living."

III. Bira (Birdwell) Stegall, born 1799 in Pickens County, South Carolina, died after 1860 in Dallas, Paulding County, Georgia. He married Abigail Conger ca 1824. On 30 November 1830, Bira Stegall was deeded by his father, Richard Stegall, 400 acres in Pickens County, South Carolina, being a border rock tract on the Saluda River. A deed from Birdwell Stegall to Blackwell Stegall for 23 acres on St. George's Creek in Pickens County. (Pickens County Deed Book C-1, page 240). Bira Stegall served in the South Carolina Militia under Captain A. Hamilton. He was in the War of 1812 for which he received pension #WC5933. He removed to the High Shoals community, near Dallas, in Paulding County, where he attended the High Shoals Primitive Baptist Church. Bira and his wife, Abigail, are buried in the old cemetery. He married Abigail Conger (born 1804 in Pendleton District, South Carolina, died 8 August 1878 in Paulding County, Georgia), a daughter of Benjamin Conger and his wife, Rachel. SEE Conger. Abigail's estate was administered in Paulding County Will Book E (1878-1884), page 17, the inventory. Issue:

   A. Hensley Zachariah Stegall, born 1826 in Pickens County, South Carolina, died 14 February 1909 in Energy, Comanche County, Texas, buried in the Pottsville Cemetery in Hamilton, Texas. He married Mary Ann Palmer (born 21 June 1833 in Cobb County, Georgia, died 14 December 1925 in Upshur County, Texas, in December of 1849, a daughter of John Palmer and his wife Mary (Camp) Palmer. Issue:

      i. Eliza L. Stegall, born 14 February 1851 in Tishomingo County, Mississippi, died 15 April 1940. She married James Burchman.
      ii. John Stegall, born ca 1853, died 10 November 1932 in Upshur County, Texas, buried in the Hopewell Cemetery. He married on 10 November 1890, Ada Hammonds.
      iii. Richard Stegall, born ca 1861, married Amelia Wilson.
      iv. Martha Elizabeth Stegall, born 23 November 1862in Tuka, Tishomingo County, Mississippi, died 11 January 1947 in Marquez, Leon County, Texas, buried in the King Cemetery. She married on 27 July 1878, Harmon White Bynum.
      v. William Stegall, born ca 1863 in Alcorn County, Mississippi, married Belle Kilpatrick.
      vi. Tommy Stegall, born ca 1864.
      vii. Elisha Washington Stegall, born 1865, died 1934, married Martha Shephard.
      viii.Margaret Adeline Stegall, born ca 1866, married Henry Joseph.

ix. Henry Stegall, born ca 1868 in Alcorn County, Mississippi, married Lizzie Harper.

x. Robert Stegall, born 26 December 1872, died 4 April 1948, buried in the Pleasant Hill Cemetery in Pritchett, Texas. He married Nancy Cox Stanley.

B. Mary E. Stegall, born 1826 in Pickens County, South Carolina, died 1869 in Paulding County, Georgia, buried in the High Shoals Baptist Church Cemetery. She married in 1842 in Paulding County, Burrell Marion Camp, a son of Sherwood Camp. SEE Camp.

C. William Stegall, born 1837 Georgia.

D. Nancy Stegall, born 1837 Georgia.

E. Narcissa Stegall, born ca 1839 in Georgia.

F. Lena Anna Stegall, born 15 June 1821 in Pickens County, South Carolina, died in Drew County, Arkansas. She married on 8 August 1839, Joseph Stepp.

IV. Spencer Stegall, born ca 1799 in Pickens County, South Carolina. He married Sallie Conger. SEE Conger.

V. Lindy Stegall, born ca 1800 in Pickens County, South Carolina. She married Miles Yancy.

Issue of Richard Stegall and (2) wife, Peggy Gillespie:

VI. Terrell Stegall, born in Pickens County, South Carolina.

VII. Nancy Stegall, born Pickens County, South Carolina.

VIII. Patsy Tenny Stegall, born Pickens County, South Carolina.

IX. Benjamin Stegall, died 1838 in Lauderdale County, Alabama. Kelly Green Stegall was appointed attorney as representative of his father's estate on 29 September 1838, which mentioned the Estate of Richard Stegall, deceased.

Issue of Richard Stegall and his 3rd wife (Margaret Davis):

X. Richard Artemas Stegall, born 3 June 1814 in Pickens County, South Carolina, died 3 March 1866. He married (1) Susanna Roberts (2) Elizabeth Ann Roberts. Richard A. Stegall and Abel Williams, heirs of Richard Stegall, deceased, appoint John Bowen as their attorney on 14 November 1838. Witness: Richard A. Stegall (Pickens County Estates).

XI. Susanna Roberta Stegall, born 1 August 1816 in Pickens County, South Carolina. She married Abel Williams.

Sullivan of North Carolina & Monroe County

Zachariah Sullivan was born 1770 in North Carolina, and was first found in Georgia on the 1820 Putnam County Census. Thereafter, he removed to Monroe County where the family was found on the 1850 and 1860 Census Records. Wife, Nancy, born 1785. His LWT was dated 25 July 1854 (no probate date) in Monroe County and named his children, Isaac, Spencer, Hilliard H., Nancy W. Miller, and a son-in-law, Francis Danielly. Issue:

I. Spencer Sullivan, born 1795 in North Carolina. Wife, Sarah, born 1799. His LWT dated 3 January 1870, probated October 1878 in Monroe County, named his children and grandchildren, Mary and Zachariah Sullivan, children of his, George W. Sullivan. Sarah resided with her daughter, Evalina O'Neal in Monroe County, during 1880. Issue:

    A. James M. Sullivan, born 1821 in Georgia. Wife, Ally C., born 1821. Issue:
        1. John S. Sullivan, born 1843 in Monroe County.
        2. James M. Sullivan, born 1844 in Monroe County.
        3. Charles W. Sullivan, born 1845 in Monroe County.
        4. Thomas C. Sullivan, born 1848 in Monroe County.
    B. Stephen H. Sullivan, born 1826 in Georgia, farmer. Wife, Mary, born 1830 in Georgia. Issue:
        1. Zachariah Sullivan, born 1859 in Monroe County.
    C. William Sullivan, born 1827 in Georgia.
    D. Zachariah M. Sullivan, born 1828 in Georgia.
    E.. Evalina Sullivan, born 1832 in Georgia, married Griffin O'Neal. SEE O'Neal.
    F. Nancy E. Sullivan, born 1842 in Monroe County.
    G. George W. Sullivan, born 1843 in Monroe County, resided with his sister, Evalina O'Neal and his mother in 1880 Monroe County. Issue:
        1. Mary Sullivan.
        2. Zachariah Sullivan.

II. Isaac Sullivan, born 1797 in North Carolina, died after 1860 in Monroe County.. Issue:

    A. Ann Sullivan, born 1840 in Monroe County.

III. Hilliard H. Sullivan, born 1811 in North Carolina, died before 1880. Wife, Sabina, born 1816, a resident of Monroe County in 1880. Issue:[326]

    A. Mary A. Sullivan, born 1837 in Georgia.
    B. Samuel W. Sullivan, born 1839 in Georgia.
    C. Virginia Sullivan, born 1841 in Monroe County married Mr. Dumas. Her LWT dated 16 February 1891 in Monroe County named her mother, Sabrina Sullivan; brother, O. H. Sullivan; sister, Mit Sullivan; and heirs: E. S., Missouri L. and Emma A. Sullivan. SEE Dumas.
    D. Ellen Sullivan, born 1843 in Monroe County.
    E. Missouri L. Sullivan, born 1847 in Monroe County.
    F. Emma Sullivan, born 1850 in Monroe County.
    G. Josephine Sullivan, born 1854 in Monroe County.
    H. Joseph Sullivan, born 1856 in Monroe County.
    I. Otis H. Sullivan, born 1859 in Monroe County.
    J. Martie Sullivan (daughter), born 1866 in Monroe County.

IV. Mary Sullivan, born 1814 in Georgia, married Francis F. Danielly. SEE Danielly.

V. Nancy Sullivan married Mr. Parker.

---

[326] 1880 Monroe County Census, District 557.

VI. Eliza W. Sullivan, married Mr. Miller.

Tapley of Baldwin, Bibb, Monroe & Warren Counties

The name Tapley is a rare name in the records. The first record I found of the name in Virginia, was Adam Tapley located in Prince George County as early as 1679. (Prince George was taken from Charles City County in 1704). [327]

---

[327] Prince George County Deeds:

12 May 1714. Thomas Harrison of Prince Georgia County authorizes Thomas Simmons of same ot be the attorney to acknowledge a deed to Adam Tapley for 100 acres of land. Indenture between Thomas Harrison of Westopher Parish, Prince George County and *Adam Tapley* of the same, 100 acres, adj. lands of Sanders' Tapley, Richard Hamlin, Capt. Harrison, and an old field of Christopher's.

5 Aug 1714. *Adam Tapley* of Westopher Parish, Prince George County, to Thomas Harrison, 100 acres of land bounded by Sanders Tapley and Richard Hamlin.

9 June 1717. *Adam Tapley* of Westopher Parish, Prince George County, planter, to Randle Platt, merchant, 100 acres, which acreage was purchased by Alexander Davidson from Rice Pritchett in 1681, and by Davison and his wife assigned to *Adam Tapley, father of said Adam Tapley*, land bounded by Symond's Swamp and Richard Hamilin; except 10 or 15 acres that John Owen formerly bought of Adam Tapley; the other part is 26 acres purchased by Adam Tapley, father of said Adam Tapley, from Elizabeth Drayton, widow, by deed of sale dated 3 Jan 1679.

27 Dec 1720. *Adam Tapley* of Prince George County to *Alexander Tapley* of the same, 100 acres of land located on the East side of Powell's Creek, formerly in the possession of *Thomas Tapley, deceased,* and by him given in the *Will of Alexander Tapley*

Virginia Patent Book No. 8:

"Adam Taply and William Harryson, 1,068 acs., Charles City County, in Jordan's Par: on S. side of James River, 21 April 1690, p. 78. Beg. at Maj. Poythres; near Aroocock Path; & near Nich. Whitmore. Trans. of22 pers: Elfrid Snow, Tho. Oxly, Ja. Allin, Geo. Rudder, Antho. Scarlett, Ja. Lewis, Robert White, Edw. Hutchison, Jno. Whiting, Wm. Rosse (or Roffe), Sarah Moore Tho. Osborne, Tho. Randall, Ruth Everett, Rich. Isham, Geo. Nelson, Robt. Wells, Andrew Isham, John Willoughby, Robert Norton, Joshua Royston, Richard Mallard."

Virginia Patent Book No. 12:

"Adam Tapley, 430 acs. (N. L.) Surry County; on N. side of the Three Creeks; adj. William Macklin's land; & Nicholas Hatch; 22 Feb. 1724, p. 225. 45 Shill."
Adam Tapley is listed on the 1704 Virginia Quits as owning 377 acres in Prince Georgia County. Also listed is Sanders Tapley, 300 acres, and Thomas Tapley, 300 acres.

With Adam Tapley's land interests in Surry County, note Moses Tapley, as follows -

Surry County, Virginia Deed Book #8, p. 188, on 5 May 1732 Richard Smith deeded to Moses Tapley 250 acres (being the land granted to said Smith on 22 Feb 124). Ann Smith relinquished her Right of Dower. Witness: James Mathis, Jr., James Loftin and Adam Tapley.

Members of the family must have drifted into Georgia from Virginia and North Carolina, where we find continous repetitive first names, i. e....Adam, Mark and Joel.

Mark Tapley was born ca 1740, died 1788 Warren or Columbia County, Ga. The family appears to have originated in South Carolina. There is so little data on it that I traced all the Tapley's in Georgia and put them together in family groups. The collage is fairly accurate; however, lacks substantiating proofs. Issue: [328]

I. William Tapley, born ca 1790 in South Carolina, died before 1850 Bibb County, married E. (Elizabeth?); listed 1830 Bibb County Census. Issue:

> A. Teresa Ann Tapley, born ca 1816 Baldwin County.
> B. Cezza Tapley, born 1817 Baldwin County, married Matthew Hughes on 29 December 1850 Bibb County.
> C. Clara Tapley, born 1820 Baldwin County.
> D. Mary E. Tapley, born 1820 Baldwin County, married Andrew Jackson Chambliss on 3 Feb 1846 Bibb County. SEE Chambliss.
> E. Winifred Tapley, born 1820 Baldwin County.

Tolbert of Madison County

Allen Tolbert was born ca 1780. He married on 24 July 1824 in Madison County, Permelia Adair (born 1805 in Jackson County), a daughter of Bozeman Adair. SEE Adair. He was listed on the 1830 Madison County Census, having a son under 5, 2 sons 20-30, 2 daughters under 5, and 2 daughters, 20-30. Known issue:[329]

I.   Harmon Tolbert, born 10 November 1806 in North Carolina, died 21 September 1892, buried in the Tolbert Cemetery on Martin Road, in Madison County, farmer. He married Pamela (or Permelia) Williams (born 24 May 1809 in Georgia, died 20 December 1903, buried in the Tolbert Cemetery) on 18 March 1830 in Madison County. SEE Williams. Issue:[330]

> A. Judah (or Judy Ann E.) Tolbert, born 1831 Madison County.
> B. Sarah A. T. Tolbert, born 1833 Madison County.
> C. Lucy E. Tolbert, born 1835 Madison County.
> D. Josiah T. Tolbert, born 1838 Madison County.
> E. William A. Tolbert, born 6 October 1842 in Madison County, died 12 March 1917, buried in Union Baptist Church Cemetery, farmer. He married Sarah A. O'Kelly, Sarah, born 16 February 1845, died 20 February 1936, buried in Union Baptist

---

[328] Cavaliers and Pioneers by Nell Marion Nugent, Vol. II and III; The Quit Rents of Virginia 1704 by Annie Laurie Wright Smith; 1850 Bibb County, Ga. Census; 1820 Baldwin County Census; 1830 Monroe County, Ga. Census; Prince George County, Virginia Deeds; 1840-1850 Bibb County Census; Bibb County Marriages; 1820-1830 Baldwin County Census; Baldwin County Marriages.

[329] 1830 Madison County Census; Madison County Marriages; 1850 Madison County Census; Paulding County Marriages.

[330] 1860 Madison County Census.

Church Cemetery, the daughter of B. F. O'Kelley on 21 February 1865 in Madison County. They were residents of Nowhere, Georgia, in 1880. Issue:[331]

1. Roda A. Tolbert, born 1866 Madison County, married James M. Sailors on 28 February 1889 in Madison County.
2. Mattie F. Tolbert, born 7 July 1867, died 29 February 1936, buried in the Union Baptist Church Cemetery in Madison County.
3. L. E. Tolbert (daughter), born 1875 Madison County.
4. Mary E. Tolbert, born 6 September 1877, died 17 October 1967, buried in the Union Baptist Church Cemetery in Madison County. She married E. C. Edwards on 27 September 1896 in Madison County, and had issue: Charles T. Edwards, 1898-1960, buried in the Union Baptist Church Cemetery in Madison County.
5. M. L. Tolbert (daughter), born 1879 Madison County.

F. Levi J. Tolbert, born 1845 Madison County.
G. Martha J. Tolbert, born 1848 Madison County.
H. Harmon Hezekiah Tolbert, born 3 May 1851, died 26 May 1936, buried in the Harmon Tolbert Cemetery in Madison County. He married Martha Ann Jane Gambrilla (born 4 May 1856, died 20 April 1936, buried in the Harmon Tolbert Cemetery in Madison County), a daughter of Jeptha F. and Clarissa Gobert Smith of Jackson County.

II. Hezekiah Tolbert, born 1829 in Madison County, married ca 1850 Artempie Walston. Issue:

A. Savannah Tolbert, born 1851, died after 1880.
B. Delany Myrtle Tolbert, born 7 December 1853, died 29 July 1907.
C. James B. Tolbert, born ca 1856.
D. Mary Elizabeth Tolbert, born January 1858, died 10 August 1948.
E. Fannie C. Tolbert, born September 1860.
F. William A. Tolbert, born 1868.

III. Mary Ann F. Tolbert, born 1832 in Madison County, married William B. Hight on 29 September 1849 in Madison County.

IV. Delany Tolbert, born 1834 in Madison County, married Lewis Matthews on 12 July 1853.

V. Allen C. Tolbert, born 1836 in Madison County, died 12 June 1862, married Sarah Thomason on 18 January 1855, in Paulding County. Issue:

A. Charles P. Tolbert, born 1856, died 16 July 1937.
B. Walker Tolbert, born 1858, died 24 March 1891, married Martha Evaline Cantrell.
C. William A. Tolbert, born 16 December 1860, died 9 September 1937, married Emma South.

---

[331] 1880 Madison County Census, Nowhere District.

Edward Wade, Sr., Revolutionary War Soldier, was born ca 1727 in Virginia.[332] He died November 1790 in Greene County, Georgia. He took the Oath of Allegience in Pittsylvania County, Virginia in 1770; served as a private in the Virginia Troops under Captain William Witcher.

He married ca 1748 Mary Clements of Pittsylvania County, Virginia, born 1730, died between 1790 and 1792 in Greene County. In 1768, Edward Wade and Mary Wade and James Wade bought for 20 pds., 175 acres on both sides of the Frying Pan Creek in Pittsylvania County, being an original land grant to Timothy Dalton. Also, the same year, Edward Wade sold 226 acres of land to Stephen Bennett, his son-in-law, on both sides of Frying Pan Creek, adj. lands to James Wade. Witness: Benjamin Clements. In 1777, Edward Wade, Sr., Daniel or David Wade, Edward Wade, Jr. and Peyton Wade signed the Oath of Allegiance in Pittsylvania County, Virginia, Edward and Peyton having served in the Pittsylvania County Militia in Capt. Witcher's Company. *His brother, James Wade,* was also in the 6th Virginia Regt., and was killed during the war.

They were also listed on the List of Tithables for that year. The LWT of Edward Wade, recorded in Will Book A (1786-95), Greene County, dated 18 February 1790, probated on 4 November 1790. *The History of Halifax County...*"A reference to Edward Wade by a grandson in after years all allude to him as an English scout and hunter....Another grandson wrote...My grandmother on my mother's side was named Mary Clemens. They were both born and raised in Virginia. (James Daniel Easley).; he also said that David Wade and his wife, Agnes, named a son, Thomas Clements Wade and my grandfather and great-grandfather were named Edward Clements Wade."

Issue:[333]

I.   Peyton Wade, Revolutionary War Soldier, born 25 February 1755 in Pittsylvania County of Halifax County, Virginia, died 15 June 1831 in Morgan County, Georgia. He served under Captain William Witcher during the war, and took the Oath of Allegienace. He married Martha Perkins ca 1790. Issue:

---

[332] Comment_Some people believe that this Edward Wade was a son of Robert Wade of Halifax County, Virginia who named a son, Edward in his will. However, it appears to me that Edward Wade of Halifax County remained in Halifax County (later deeds) and that he did not appear to be the same person as Edward Wade, Sr. who removed to Georgia. There may be some connection between Benjamin Wade who died in Granville County, North Carolina in 1785 and Peyton Clements, who died in Granville County in 1775.

[333] Greene County Wills & Marriages; Pittsylvania County, Virginia Deeds; History of Halifax County, Virginia, page 110; McCall's Roster of the Revolution; Wade Genealogy by Mrs. Francis Banister Rabb, page 249; Nowlin-Stone Genealogy, page 35 (1916).; The Georgians by Jeannette Holland Austin, page 362; Morgan County Marriages; AFN:FSJS-9L, Ancestral File, The Church of Jesus Christ of Latter-Day Saints; Men of Mark in Georgia, by William F. Northen, Vol. V.

A. Jesse Perkins Wade, born 24 May 1794 in Greene County, died 26 November 1872 in Blackshear, Pierce County, Georgia, buried in the West End Cemetery, Quitman (Brooks County), Georgia. He married on 7 October 1813 in Morgan County, Georgia, Bethenia Middlebrooks (born 19 October 1798, died 24 December 1882). Issue:

1. Elizabeth Ann Wade, born 7 May 1815 Greene County, died before 1900 in Texas.
2. Peyton L. Wade, born 12 September 1817 in Morgan County, died before 1900 in Rusk County, Texas. Issue:
    i. Louisa B. Wade.
    ii. Melville S. Wade.
    iii. Elizabeth E. Wade, born in Rusk County, Texas.
3. Isaac Middlebrooks Wade, born 18 February 1820 in Hickman County, Tennessee, died 1873 in Rusk County of Young County, Texas.
4. Martha L. Wade, born 8 June 1823 in Morgan County, died young.
5. James Dawson Wade, born 13 February 1826 in Newton County, died 9 March 1910, near Quitman, Brooks County.
6. Archibald P. Wade, born 21 March 1828 in Newton County, died before 1900.
7. Edward Clemens Wade, born 25 August 1830 Oxford, Newton County, died 5 April 1911 in Los Angeles, California, buried in the Laurel Grove Cemetery in Savannah, Georgia.
8. William Parks Wade, born 16 August 1833 Georgia, died 1897 in Brooks County.
9. Seaborn Howard Wade, born 18 September 1836 in Newton County, died 26 December 1873 Savannah, Georgia.
10. Milton Carter Wade, born 30 May 1840 in Whitfield County, Georgia, died 14 August 1921, buried in the West End Cemetery, Quitman, Georgia.

B. Peyton Lisby Wade, Jr., born 23 October 1795 in White Plains, Greene County, Georgia, died 21 December 1866 in Screven County, Georgia, buried in the Brick Church Cemetery in Screven County. He married twice, and after his first wife died (no children), he married Miss Elizabeth Robert, a daughter of William Henry Robert and his wife, Mary Maner, (born 7 November 1817 in Robertville, South Carolina, died 4 October 1883, buried in the Brick Church Cemetery. Issue:

1. Robert Maner Wade, born 5 March 1840 in Screven County, died 7 December 1904 in Athens, Clarke County. He married 15 March 1864 Frederica Washburn (born 31 August 1844, died 21 June 1916 in Athens, Georgia. The plantation was called *Lebanon Forest* in Screven County. He attended the Military Institute in Marietta, graduating in the class of 1860. Then he studied medicine in Savannah until 1862, later serving in the First Georgia Regiment, as a Lieutenant, War Between the States. Later on, he was promoted to the rank of Captain, and ultimately surrendered with General Joseph E. Johnston in 1865. After the war, he attendede the University of Maryland, where he graduated in 1872, having completed his medical studies. Issue:

   i. Peyton Lisby Wade, born 9 January 1865 in Screven County, died 29 August 1919 in Fulton County. He graduated from the University of Georgia in 1886, ranking 5th in the A. B. degree, having excelled in every way. He studied law under his uncle, U. P. Wade, in Sylvania.
   ii. Eugene Washburn Wade, born 1 November 1867 in

Screven County.

    iii. Edward Ingersoll Wade, born 24 September 1869 in Whitfield County.

    iv. Rosalie Wade, born 23 November 1871 in Whitfield County.

    v. Robert Maner Wade, born 17 November 1876 in Whitfield County.

    vi. Frederick Habersham Wade, born 5 November 1879 in Atlanta, Fulton County.

2. Peyton Lisby Wade, born 1841 in Screven County, died 16 November 1861, during the War Between the States.

3. Edward Clemens Wade, born 1843 in Screven County, died 1865 while being held as a prisoner during the War Between the States.

4. Ulysses Perkins Wade, born 9 March 1845 in Screven County, died 15 November 1897 in Screven County.

5. Rosalie Melvina Wade, born 22 January 1847 in Screven County, died 8 January 1885 in Brooklyn, New York.

6. William Crawford Wade, born 7 February 1849 in Screven County, died 26 February 1925 in Macon, Bibb County.

7. Jesse Turpin Wade, born 24 August 1851 Screven County, died 30 August 1918 in Augusta, Georgia.

8. Archibald P. Wade, born 28 September 1853 in Screven County, died 19 May 1855.

9. Samuel Asbury Wade, born 3 January 1856 in Screven County, died 2 November 1905. Never married.

10. Walter Barnwell Wade, born 12 July 1858 in Screven County, died 20 October 1882. Never married.

11. Arthur Bartow Wade, born 24 May 1861 in Screven County, died 20 June 1890. Never married.

C. Martha Wade, born 22 March 1798 in Greene County, Georgia, died in Red River County, Texas.

D. Elizabeth Wade, born 1799/1807 in Greene County, Georgia, died in Texas

E. Archibald P. Wade, born in Greene County.

F. Edward Wade born in Greene County.

G. Frances India Wade, born 27 December 1807 Greene County, died 2 October 1853. She married Henry Vidette.

II. Edward Wade, Jr., Revolutionary War Soldier, born 1760 Pittsylvania County, Virginia, died between 1830 and 1840 in DeKalb County, Georgia.

III. Lucy Wade, born between 1760 and 1770 in Pittsylvania County, Virginia, married Peyton Nolin.

IV. Thomas Wade, born between 1760 and 1770 in Pittsylvania County, Virginia.

V. Chloe Wade, born between 1760 and 1770 in Pittsylvania County, Virginia, married Thomas Easley.

VI. Anne Wade, born between 1760 and 1770 in Pittsylvania County, Virginia, died after 1830 in Madison County, Georgia. She married John Williams, Sr. on 11 November 1788 in Madison County.

VII. Christian Wade, born between 1760 and 1770 in Pittsylvania County, Virginia, died before 1790, married Mr. Dalton.

VIII. Mary Wade, born 17 March 1761 in Halifax County, Virginia, died 13 August 1829, married Thomas Burford of Greene County.

IX. David Wade, born between 1770 and 1780 in Pittsylvania County, Virginia, died between 1830 and 1840 in Hall County, married Agnes Hardy.

X. Grissel Wade, born between 1775 and 1794 in Pittsylvania County, Virginia, married Stephen Bennett.

Waldren of Bibb County

M. J. Waldren was born 1827 in North Carolina. She was left a widow before 1850, and resided in Bibb County. Issue:[334]

I. Malcolm Waldren, born 1832 in North Carolina, died 11 March 1876, married Lucinda Chambliss on 27 February 1862 in Bibb County. SEE Chambliss. Issue:
    A. Samuel Waldren, born 1869 in Bibb County, died 21 July 1871.

II. John Waldren, born 1835 in Georgia.

III. Henry Waldren, born 1838 in Georgia.

IV. Thomas Waldren, born 1843 in Georgia.

Williams of Virginia, North Carolina;
Madison & Paulding Counties

John Williams was born about 1650 in Virginia, and married 1671 in Isle of Wight Co, Virginia, Anne Whitley, the daughter of John and Ann Whitley. John died Aug 1687 in Isle of Wight County, Virginia. Anne died Apr 1694 in Isle of Wight County, Virginia. LWT of John Williams dated 9 Mar 1690, probated 9 Aug 1692 Isle of Wight County, Va. 20 Aug 1687 Estate of John Williams, appraisal, p. 270. P. 61, Estate of John Williams who died intestate, to son, John.

LWT of Mrs. Anne Williams dated 9 Apr 1694 Isle of Wight County, Va. Gift deed to her children, viz... John, William, Thomas, Mary, Nicholas (age 17), Richard, Jane, Eliza Wright, dated 1694 Isle of Wight County, Va. Isle of Wight County, Va. Deed Book and Wills 2, p. 105, marriage of John Williams to Anne Whitley.

Issue:

I. John Williams, son of John Williams of Isle of Wight County, Virginia, was born ca 1672 in Virginia. He married in 1696, Isle of Wight County, Virginia Elizabeth Taberer Copeland,

---

[334] 1850 Bibb County Census.

the daughter of Thomas Taberer.[335]

II. Mary Williams, daughter of John Williams of Isle of Wight County, Virginia, born ca 1682.

III. Jane Williams, daughter of John Williams of Isle of Wight County, Virginia,born ca 1684.

IV. William Williams, son of John Williams of Isle of Wight County, Virginia, born ca 1686.

V. Nicholas Williams, son of John Williams of Isle of Wight County, Virginia, born 1687.

VI. Richard Williams, son of John Williams of Isle of Wight County, Virginia, born ca 1687.

VII. Eliza Williams, daughter of John Williams of Isle of Wight County, Virginia, was born ca 1687, married Mr. Wright.

VIII. Thomas Williams, son of John Williams of Isle of Wight County, Virginia, captain, born ca 1680, died November of 1759. He was married in 1726 in Isle of Wight County, Virginia to Mrs. Susanna Davis (born ca 1684 in Isle of Wight County), the relict of John Davis. Thomas died in November 1759 in Nottaway Parish, Southampton County, Virginia. His LWT was dated 6 October 1758, and probated on 8 November 1759 in Southampton County, Virginia, naming his son, Nathan, and his grandson (son of Nathan) as heirs.[336] Issue:

> A. Nathan Williams, born ca 1700 in Southampton County, Virginia, died in July of 1758 in Northampton County, North Carolina. He was married in 1721 in the Isle of Wight County, Virginia to Rebecca Eley, the daughter of Robert Eley and his wife, Jane (Braswell) Eley,[337] who was born 1700 in Nansemond County, Virginia. Rebecca died 1784 in Northampton County, North Carolina. The LWT of Nathan

---

[335] Isle of Wight County, Virginia deed of John Williams of the Isle of Wight Co. Deed Book 1, p. 223. Also, Will and Deed Book 2, p. 350.

[336] Bertie County, North Carolina Deed- William Willson to Thomas Williams for #100, 609 acres of land on the northside of Casshy Swamp. May Court of 1734. Book D, Page 54.

Northampton County, North Carolina Deeds

Thomas Williams of Bertie County, North Carolina to William Bryan of Northampton County, 20 December 1742, for #20 Virginia money, 200 acres of land, joining Sandy Run.

Southampton County, Virginia Deeds

Deed Book 7, Page 173, 11-28-1788, John Williams of Halifax County, North Carolina sold to Amos Stephenson of Southampton County, Virginia for #45 all that tract of land given to Jacob Williams by Thomas Williams, deceased, in his Last Will and Testament, and descended to the said John Williams by the death of Jacob Williams, on the southside of the Nottaway River in Southampton County, Virginia, and the northside of Togathunting Swamp, containing 100 acres.

[337] Rebecca Eley Williams was named in LWT of her father, Robert Eley dated 5 Apr 1738, probated 1739 Isle of Wight County, Virginia

Williams was dated 8 April 1751, probated July 1758 in Northampton County, North Carolina. The LWT of Rebecca Ely was dated 1784 in Northampton County, North Carolina. Nathan Williams and his wife removed from Virginia to settle in Northampton County, North Carolina, where he became sheriff. [338] Nathaniel Williams, friend, and Colonel John Dawson, were appointed executors of the LWT of William Arrington, Northampton County, North Carolina, dated 1752. Arrington was originally from Isle of Wight County, Virginia. Issue:

1. Eley Williams, born ca 1722.[339]

2. Nathan Williams was born about 1724 in of Isle of Wight, Virginia, and married 1764 in the Isle of Wight County, Virginia, Selia Eley, at the Pagan Creek Meeting, Isle of Wight County, Virginia. [340]

3. Thomas Williams, born ca 1730 in Southampton County, Virginia, died December 1815 in Northampton County, North Carolina. LWT of Thomas Williams dated 15 Jan 1815, probated Dec 1815 Northampton County, North Carolina; LWT of Thomas Williams, Southampton County, Va. Named his grandson, Thomas Williams, son of his deceased son, Nathan, dated 6 Oct 1758, probated 8 Nov 1759. He was married in 1750, Isle of Wight County, Virginia, to Mrs. Sarah Warren, who was born about 1734. Sarah died 1790/1800 in Northampton County, North Carolina. After her death, Thomas married Jennet. He owned extensive lands in North Carolina.[341]

---

[338] Northampton County, North Carolina Deeds

1735 - Nathan Williams to Joynor, Book D, Page 232.

William Liles of Northampton County to John Jacob Liles and Lucy Liles, his children, 3-2-1755, for love and affection, his whole estate to be divided among the said children "by my two friends, James Washington and Nathan Williams."
8-20-1755, Nathan Williams, Sheriff, to John Person of Southampton County, Virginia, 100 acres of land.

[339] Edgecombe County, North Carolina Deeds

Book C, Page 244, Charles Herrington of Orange County, North Carolina to Eley Williams, 3-1-1765, #35 Virginia currency, 380 acres on the northeast side of Peachtree Creek adjoining lands of William Hill, John Odom and Drury Herrington in Granville County, land lying in both counties.

Book D, Page 363, Eley Williams of Halifax County, North Carolina, to Stephen Pace of Northampton County, 1-5-1771, for #40 Virginia currency, 380 acres in Edgecombe and Bute Counties, on the north bank of Peachtree Creek.

[340] Hinshaw's Encyclopedia of Quaker Genealogy.

[341] Southampton County, Virginia Deeds

Deed Book 1, Page 81 - 4-12-1750, Thomas Williams and his wife, Sarah, of the Province of North Carolina, sell to John Bowen, Jr. and Mary, his wife, Hardy Hart and Jane, his wife, Arthur Hart and Martha, his wife, all of North Carolina , of the second part, and John Holding

Issue:

> i. Jesse Williams, born ca 1750, died December 1782. in Greene
> County, Georgia. He married ca 1770 in Northampton County, North
> Carolina, Martha (born ca 1754).[342] The LWT of Jesse Williams dated
> 22 Nov 1782, probated Dec 1782.Greene County, Georgia, Book 4
> (1817-42), p. 93-95, proceedings also probated in Northampton
> County, North Carolina. Jesse Williams, in his LWT, named his
> father, Thomas Williams of Northampton County, North Carolina.[343]

of the Co. of Southampton in VA of the third part, for #36 a certain tract of land containing 180 acres in Southampton County, on the southside of Lithwood Swamp, being part of a patent granted Bartholomew Andros for 320 acres by date of 6-16-1714 and by said Andros conveyed to Robert Warren, Jr., Thomas Warren and John Warren, 10-26-1719...deceased, by the LWT of Thomas Warren to his wife, Sarah Warren, and after her death to his son, Thomas Warren and his heirs; but the said Thomas Warren, Jr., dying an infant with no heirs, the said land was devolved to his four sisters, Mary, Jane, Martha and Patience Warren, and whereas, the said Sarah Warren, relict of Thomas Warren, hath intermarried with the said Thomas Williams and they being willing to sell their right, being the first part, etc., and whereas, the said Mary, Jane and Martha hath intermarried with the said John Bowen, Hardy Hart and Arthur Hart.

Bertie County, North Carolina Deeds 1753-1757 –

Thomas WIlliams to William Hollowell of Perquimans County, for #28, 200 acres, landing adjoining William Andrews, Thomas Andrews, at Mill Branch.

Page 112. Thomas Williams to Nicholas Skinner, for #28, 200 acres, 11-11-1754. Page 125. Thomas WIlliams to Marmaduke Norfleet of Perquimans County, 2-10-1756, for #120, 385 acres on the northside of Roanoke River, adjoining lands of George Williams, Mary Williams' corner, granddaughter of George Williams deed. Part of a tract granted to George Williams 4-6-1722.

Northampton County, North Carolina Deeds

Page 290. Thomas Williams, Sr. to Samuel Lands, 11-1760, Book 3, Page 73.
Thomas Williams to Benjamin Bishop, 10-10-1771, Book 5, Page 115.
Thomas Williams to Winifred Wooten, 10-25-1772, Book 5, Page 154.
Thomas Williams to Jesse WIlliams 5-3-1773, Book 5, Page 256.
Thomas Williams to James Norton, Book 6, Page 239, 8-6-1778.
Thomas Williams to John Rives, 6-17-1789, Book 8, Page 107.
Thomas Williams to Odom Potress, 6-22-1795, Book 10, Page 51.
Thomas Williams to William E. Williams, 9-10-1799, for $250.00, land on the southside of the Meherin River. Book 10, Page 438.

Granville to Thomas Williams of Northampton County, North Carolina for 3 shillings Proclamation Money, 679 acres of land. 10-30-1753.

[342] Believed to be Martha Hart.

[343] Northampton County, North Carolina deed dated 3 May 1773, Thomas Williams to son, Jesse Williams, Book 5.

Issue:[344]

    a. John Williams Sr., born 1760/1770, died July 1849. SEE John Williams of Greene County, Georgia.

    b. Thomas Williams, born 1770/1780 in Northampton County, North Carolina, and married 12 Dec 1808 in Jackson County, Eliza Kirkley..

    c. Brittain Williams, born ca 1770 in Northampton County, North Carolina, died September 1863 in Harris County, Georgia. He married 27 Nov 1798 in Jackson County, Pamela Bell. The LWT of Brittain Williams dated 21 Dec 1847, Codicils dated 24 Jan 1855 and 7 Aug 1857, probated Sep Term 1863. Harris County Wills (1850-1875). His LWT names six grandnephews, sons of his nephew, Thomas A. Williams, John Thomas Williams, James Finnemore Cooper Williams, Benjamin Henry Williams, Charles Williams, Brittain Williams and Ozices Stoval Williams. In his Codicil, he named daughters of nephew, Thomas A. Williams - Sarah Lucinda and Joel Frances. Also, the widow of his nephew, Thomas W. Williams - Elizabeth B. Williams. He was listed on the 1805 Georgia Land Lottery as a resident of Greene County; listed on the 1830 Harris County Census.

    d. William Hart Williams, born ca 1775 in Northampton County, North Carolina.

    e. Polly Williams, born ca 1782 in Northampton County, North Carolina. She married on 11 April 1807 in Jackson County, Georgia, David Moore.

ii. Jefferson Thomas Williams, born 1774/1784 in Northampton County, North Carolina; married on 26 January 1828 (same county), Nancy E. Daughtry.

iii. Samuel Curl Williams, born 1774/1795 in Northampton County, North Carolina

iv. Anthony Richard Williams, born ca 1775 in Northampton County, North Carolina.

v. Sarah Williams, born ca 1780 in Northampton County, North Carolina, married Richard Long.

vi. Julietta Tucker Williams, born 1790/1800 in Northampton County, North Carolina.

vii. Rebecca Marcum Williams, born 1790/1800 in Northampton County, North Carolina.

viii. Caroline Matilda Williams, born ca 1800 in Northampton County, North Carolina.

ix. Evalina Sally Williams, born ca 1800 in Northampton County, North Carolina. She married Thomas Nicholson.

---

[344] Northampton County, North Carolina Wills & Deeds.

4. Martha Williams, born ca 1732 in Southampton County, Virginia.
5. Jane Williams, born ca 1734 in Southampton County, Virginia.
6. Lucy Williams, born ca 1736 in Southampton County, Virginia.

B. Thomas Williams, born ca 1727, died November of 1766 in Southampton County, Virginia.
C. Chaplin Williams, born ca 1729. "Chaplin Williams, son and heir of Capt. Williams, deceased, of Southampton County, Virginia, summoned to appear in Court to answer a bill....."Virginia Gazette, published 11 April 1771.
D. Benjamin Williams, born a 1731 in Virginia.
E. Joseph Williams, born ca 1733 in Virginia.
F. Elizabeth Williams born ca 1737 in Virginia, married Mr. Jones.
G. Anne Williams, born ca 1739 in Virginia, married Mr. Pitman.
H. Mary Williams, born ca 1741 in Virginia, married Mr. Baisden.
I. Patience Williams, born ca 1743, died before 1758 in Southampton County, Virginia. She married Mr. Gregory.
J. William Williams, born ca 1745, died February 1783 in Southampton County, Virginia, his LWT dated 1 December 1782, probated 13 February 1783. Wife, Sarah.

John Williams of Greene County, Georgia, the son of Jesse Williams, was born 1760/1770 in Northampton County, North Carolina. He married on 11 November 1788 in Greene County, Georgia, Anne Wade, a daughter of Edward Wade and his wife, Mary (Clements) Wade. Anne was born 1760/1770 in Pittsylvania County, Virginia. John died July 1849 in Madison County, Georgia. Anne died after 1830 in Madison County. After Anne's death, he married Frances. The LWT of John Williams, Sr., dated 29 May 1843, probated Jul 1849 in Madison County Will Book B (1842-95), Page 45-6, named wife, Frances, and Issue: to Robert 80 acres and the homeplace; Eliza; Birdy; Nancy; Anna Bradley; Elsey Strickland; Dolly Thompson. Also names the children of his deceased daughter, Sally Bone, i.e.: William Russell, Allen Bone and Jasper Bone. Listed 1830-1850 Madison County Census. Issue:

I. Elijah Williams, born 1787 in Northampton County, North Carolina, and died January 1880 in Madison County, Georgia. He was married on 7 August 1806 in Madison County, to Judith Adair, the daughter of Bozeman Adair, Sr. Judith was born September 1790 in South Carolina. Judith died 7 September 1823 in Madison County. SEE Adair. The: LWT of Elijah Williams dated 5 Feb 1872, probated 7 Jan 1880 Madison Cunty, named his daughters: Permelia Tolberts, Sally Sanders, Nancy Lane, Elizabeth Cheatham, Anna C. Strickland, Martha H. Thomas, Mary A. Power. Sons: William B., John Britton S. and Birdy O. Williams. 1813 Madison County, Ga. Tax Digest, Capt. Daniel Taylor's District, 1 poll, 170 acres. Listed on the 1830-1880 Madison County Census. He married (2) on 30 October 1823 in Madison County, Nancy Strickland (born 1801 in Madison County), and (3), Elisabeth (died after 1880, born 1793 in North Carolina). On 1 December 1879 in Madison County, Permelia Tolbert, Elizabeth P. Cheatham, Anne C. Strickland, Mary A. Powers, Birdey C. Williams and John F. Williams of Madison County and Sallie H. Sanders of Floyd County, Nancy C. Williams Lane (Mrs. James C. Lane), Huldah G. Baxter and Nancy C. Massey of Paulding County, Marltner A. Thomas and Eliza Massey of Banks County, heirs-in-law of Elijah Williams, deceased, requested the will to be probated in solemn form on the first day in December of 1879 in Danielsville. The records of the Union Baptist Church in Madison County, which church Elijah helped to institute and was its first moderator, reflect that Elijah Williams died 3

Issue by (1) wife:

A. John Y. Williams, born 1808 in Madison County, and married 29 Jul 1840 in Madison County, Sarah Ann Strickland (born 1800 in Georgia). Listed 1860-1870 Madison County Census. He died October of 1862 in Madison County; a bond was issued on Estate of John Y. Williams, on 6 October 1862.

    1. Louisa J. Williams, born 1841 in Madison County, married J. R. Crawford on 14 January 1866 in Madison County.
    2. Mary E. Williams, born 1843 in Madison County, married John R. Crawford on 26 October 1873 in Madison County.
    3. A. E. Williams, born 1845 in Madison County.
    4. Nancy C. Williams, born 1847 in Madison County.
    5. Child, born 1850 in Madison County.

B. Brittain S. Williams, born ca 1809 in Madison County. He was married on 25 December 1834 in Madison County to Menta Hampton.

C. Permelia Williams, born 1810 in Madison County. She was married on 18 March 1830 in Madison County to Harmon Tolbert (born 1807 in North Carolina). [346] SEE Tolbert.

D. Sarah L. Williams, born 1813 in Danielsville, Madison County, and married 26 December 1834 in Madison County, Augustus Sanders.

E. William B. Williams, born 1815 in Danielsville, Madison County, and married 4 March 1835 in Madison County, Georgia, Minerva Lane (born 1813 in Georgia). The Bond of John Y. Williams, on the Estate of William B. Williams, Madison Cunty Bonds (1856-65). The Estate of his wife, Minervy Williams, Madison Co. Bonds, Page 249. John Y. Williams and Birdy O. Williams Bond dated 1 September 1856.[347] In 1860,

---

[345] The LWT of Elijah Williams, probated 1 December 1879 in Madison County. "State of Georgia, Madison County. To: Permelia Tolbert, Elizabeth P. Cheatham, Anne C. Strickland, Mary A. Powers, Birdey C. Williams, and John F. Williams of said county, Sallie H. Sanders of Floyd County, Nancy C. Williams Lane (Mrs. James C. Lane), Huldah G. Baxter, and Nancy C. Massey of Paulding County, Marltner A Thomas and Eliza Massey of Banks County, heirs in law of Elijah Williams, deceased....You are hereby notified that we as executors of Elijah Williams, late of Madison County will on Monday the first day in December in the year of 1879 will move in the Court of Ordinary of Madison County to be held in the Court House in Danielsville of the State of Georgia in said county to probate the ten last wills and testaments of the said Elijah Williams, deceased. By the attesting witnesses thereto and on solemn form to with one said will dated the fifth of February in the year of 1872 and attested by J. W. Gunnells, Henry Smith and Gabriel Nash, and the other nine wills dated on February 14, 1879 and attested by John F. Kirk, Gabriel Nash and John F. Williams and to have said wills admitted to record and you are satisfied to be present and file objections you may have to same. This 7th day of October 1879. /s/ Birdey C. Williams and John F. Williams, executors.
[346] 1850 Paulding County Census; 1870 Madison County Census.

[347] Listed 1850 Madison County Census.

children, Permelia A. Williams, age 14, Nancy J. Williams, age 12, and Harmon H. Williams, age 9, were living with the Harmon Tolbert family in Madison County. Issue:

1. Judah A. Williams, born 1837 in Madison County.
2. Eliza A. Williams, born 1838 in Madison County.
3. Huldah G. Williams, born 1841 in Madison County.
4. Emily C. Williams, born 1843 in Madison County.
5. Permelia Williams, born 1845 in Madison County.
6. Nancy C. Williams, born 1847 in Madison County.
7. Harmon H. Williams, born 1851 in Madison County.

F. Nancy Williams, born 19 May 1818 in Danielsville, Madison County, died 27 June 1905 in Paulding County. She was married on 27 December 1839 in Madison County to James C. Lane (born 26 April 1818 in Madison County), the son of Laban Lane. Nancy died 27 Jun 1905 in Dallas, Paulding County. James C. Lane died 20 Jun 1896 in Dallas, Paulding County. SEE Lane.

Issue by (2) wife:

G. Elizabeth P. Williams, born 1824 in Danielsville, Madison County, and married 19 Dec 1843 in Madison County, Josiah Cheatham (born 1818 in Georgia). SEE Cheatham.[348]

H. Birdy O. Williams, born 1828 in Danielsville, Madison County, and married 4 Oct 1865 in Madison County, Nancy Bone. He was a resident of Nowhere, Georgia, in 1880, farmer; in his household was his sister, M. (Mary) A. Power, and his step-mother, Elizabeth Williams (born 1797 in North Carolina. SEE Bone.

I. Anna C. Williams, born 1832 in Danielsville, Madison County.

J. Martha A. Williams, born 1835 in Danielsville, Madison County.

K. Mary A. Williams, born 1837 in Danielsville, Madison County. She married Wiley B. Power (born 1825 in Georgia). SEE Power.

L. Lucinda N. Williams, born 1841 in Danielsville, Madison County.

II. Birdy Williams, born 1790 in Northampton County, North Carolina; married in 1808, Nancy. His LWT, Madison County (1842-96), Page 244-245, dated 17 December 1870, probated the January Term of 1872, leaves "to my wife, Nancy, with whom I have lived for 62 years, 250 acres and homeplace." Named Issue: James M. Williams and Amanda J. Baxter. [349] Issue:

A. James M. Williams.
B. Amanda J. Williams, married Mr. Baxter.

III. Anna Williams, born 1798 in Northampton County, North Carolina. She was married on

---

[348] Listed on 1850-1860 Madison County Census.

[349] Listed 1850-1870 Madison County Census.

20 September 1824 in Madison County, to James Bradley. SEE Bradley.

IV. Elsey Williams, born 1800/1810 in Madison County, married on 18 December 1823 in Madison County, Hardy Strickland, a son of Hardy Strickland, Sr. She and her husband, Hardy Strickland, Jr. were listed on the 1830 Madison County Census.

V. Salley Williams, born 1800/1810 in Madison County, Georgia. She married on 26 March 1818 in Madison County, William Bone, Jr., son of William Bone, Sr. and wife, Nancy. SEE Bone.

VI. Robert Williams, Sr., born 1805, died November 1875 in Madison County. He was married on 31 December 1818 in Madison County, to Nancy Williams. The LWT of Robert Williams, Sr. was dated 2 October 1873, probated November 1875 in Madison County Will Book B, page 263-266.

VII. Mary G. Williams, born 1807, married B. M. Thompson; listed on the 1830 Madison County Census.

Williams of Paulding County

Isaac Williams was born 1835 in Georgia, farmer, resident of Eutah, in Paulding County. He married Amanda White (born 1850 in Georgia) on 3 December 1868 in Paulding County. Issue:[350]

I. William Edward Williams was born 18 June 1870, died 11 July 1939. He married Edna Viola Carlton (born 5 February 1874, died 19 November 1915) on 8 December 1892 in Paulding County. Issue:

A. Lillian Emma Williams, born 30 April 1894, died 13 October 1979, married on 18 February 1916, Henry Grady Hutcheson (born 8 February 1890, died 8 September 1954). Issue:

1. Henry Hamilton Hutcheson.
2. Helen Louise Hutcheson.
3. William David Hutcheson.
4. John Robert Hutcheson.
5. Margaret Susan Hutcheson.
6. Vivian Jeanette Hutcheson.

B. Samuel Edward (Ned) Williams, born 12 April 1896, died 7 May 1956, married Minnie Irene Gamel. Issue:

1. Roland O. Williams.
2. Gladys Williams.

C. Myrtice A. Williams, born 16 May 1898, died 26 December 1980, married Dewey Roberson. Issue:

1. Margaret Roberson.
2. Billy Roberson.

---

[350] 1880 Paulding County Census, Eutah District.

D. Charles Henry Williams, born 5 April 1900, died 22 August 1959, married Willie Mae Moore. Issue:

    1. Richard Williams.

    2. Robert Williams.

E. William Carlton Williams, born 13 September 1902, married 3 February 1929, Carrie Mae Sills (born 21 May 1904).

F. Winnie Bell Williams, born 30 July 1906, died 21 March 1921.

G. Jessie Mae Williams, born 2 June 1911, died May 1944, married Fred Cole. Child:

    1. Freddy Cole.

II. Rebecca Williams, born 1874 in Paulding County.

III. Thomas Williams, born 1879 in Paulding County.

Williamson of Butts, Hart & Jackson Counties

John Williamson, Sr. died 1831 in Butts County, leaving his LWT dated 25 February 1831 and probated on 7 November 1831. He married Nancy Leslie. His will named his son, John, and his grandson, Nathan, as well as his other children. Issue:

I. Sally Williamson married Mr. Moon.

II. Polly Williamson married Mr. McClusky.

IV. William Williamson died 1834 in Jackson County, his LWT dated 17 December 1832, probated 3 November 1834, naming his nephews:James Williamson McCleskey, Eusebius McCleskey, Madison West McCleskey, Milton T. McCleskey; James, Jackson, Hartwell and Robert Moon. Elizabeth and Betsy Moon, land drawn by Boler Moon. Nieces: Margaret, Mary and Elizabeth McCleskey. Sisters: Jinny Doss, Sally Moon, Polly McCleskey. Half-bro: James Mitchell. To the children of his sister, Betsy Powers. Executor, Adam Williamson.

IV. Jenny Williamson married Edward J. Doss on 19 March 1809 in Jackson County.

V. Adam Williamson.

VI. Elizabeth Williamson married Mr. Powers.

VII. Micajah Williamson, attorney at law, his LWT was probated in September of 1803, in Jackson County, naming his wife, Polly, as sole executrix. Also, named his brother, William.

VIII. John Williamson was born 26 March 1780 in Virginia and died 1849 in Jackson County, Georgia. He married Winifred Camp (died 1873 in Jackson County), a daughter of Nathaniel Camp and his wife, Winnifred (Tarpley) Camp. Micajah Williamson was the administrator of the estate of his father, John Williamson, and filed a Return dated 1 January 1851 in Jackson County, Jackson County Estates, Book A, page 117. Issue:

A. Nathan Camp Williamson, born 17 September 1804, married Irena Summerlin on 21 October 1832 in Butts County.

B. John Leslie Williamson, born ca 1806 married Caroline J. Shotwell on 29 March 1832 in Jackson County.

C. Nancy Williamson, born ca 1808 in Jackson County, died in Hart County.

D. Sarah Williamson died in Hart County.

E. Micajah Williamson, born 1810 in Jackson County, died in 1881.

F. Eliza Williamson, born 1811 in Jackson County, died 1889.

G. William Harper Williamson, born 1813, died 1814 in Jackson County.

H. Andrew Jackson Williamson, born 1815 in Jackson County.

I. Louisa Williamson, born 1816 in Jackson County.

J. Jasper Marion Williamson, born 1818 in Jackson County married Mary A. Davis on 10 April 1842 in Jackson County (she died before 1880). The family removed to Texas before 1860. Issue:[351]
  1. Gally Williamson (son), born 1860 in Texas.
  2. Samiea Williamson (daughter), born 1867 in Texas.
  3. Ida Williamson, born 1868 in Texas.
  4. Annie Williamson, born 1874 in Texas.

K. Cranston Berrian Williamson, born 17 September 1817 in Jackson County, died 17 February 1900, buried in the Bethany Methodist Church Cemetery, Brockton, Georgia. He married Eliza Jane Jarret (born 3 January 1827, died 14 March 1889, buried in the Bethany Methodist Church Cemetery) on 30 September 1842 in Jackson County. Issue:[352]
  1. Floret G. Williamson (daughter), born 1864 in Jackson County.
  2. Harris M. Williamson, born 1871 in Jackson County.

L. Mary E. Williamson, born 1821 in Jackson County.

M. Adam A. Williamson, born 1823 in Jackson County married Betsy Horton on 18 January 1810 in Jackson County (she died before 1880). Issue:[353]
  1. William W. Williamson, born 1860 in Jackson County.
  2. Talulah C. Williamson, born 1860 in Jackson County.
  3. Adam C. Williamson, born 1863 in Jackson County.
  4. John J. Williamson, born 1867 in Jackson County.
  5. Leonard L. Williamson, born 1876 in Jackson County.

N. Winifred M. Williamson, born 1825 in Jackson County.

O. Gilbert Lafayette Williamson, born 12 May 1827 in Jackson County, farmer, died 18 May 1906, buried in the Bethany Methodist Church Cemetery, Hwy 335, Brockton, Georgia. Wife, Caroline F. (born 3 March 1837 in Georgia). Issue:[354]
  1. John M. Williamson, born 1862 in Jackson County.
  2. Ada Williamson, born 1868 in Jackson County.
  3. Eva L. Williamson, born 1870 in Jackson County.

---

[351] 1880 Smith County, Texas, Precinct 1.

[352] 1880 Jackson County Census, District 245.

[353] 1880 Jackson County Census, District 253.

[354] 1880 Jackson County Census, District 257.

4. George L. Williamson, born 1871 in Jackson County.

5. Thomas H. Williamson, born 1874 in Jackson County.

6. Nathan C. Williamson, born 1877 in Jackson County, died 1965, buried in the Bethany Methodist Church Cemetery, Brockton, Georgia.

7. Abbott B. Williamson, born 1879 in Jackson County.

P. James Columbus Williamson, born 1829 in Jackson County.

Q. George W. Williamson, born 1830 in Jackson County.

Wilson of Bulloch County

Andrew Wilson was born 1796 in North Carolina and died 1858 in Bulloch County. Wife, Mary (born 1807 in Georgia). His LWT was dated 8 December 1857, probated 9 January 1858 in Bulloch County. Issue:[355]

I. Jasper Wilson, born 1821 in Bulloch County, died March 1897, died intestate in Bulloch County in 1896. James H. Groover was elected administrator of his estate on 1 March 1897. He married on 7 December 1843 in Bulloch County, Mary M. Lee (born 1828 Georgia, died December 1900), the daughter of General Lee and his wife, Nancy (Cook) Lee. Mary's LWT was rather detailed, naming her children and grandchildren. SEE Lee. Issue:

A. Sarah A. Wilson, born 1845 in Bulloch County, married Mr. Groover.

B. James R. Wilson, born 4 September 1848 in Bulloch County, died 26 February 1909.

C. Jackson W. Wilson, born 1851 in Bulloch County.

D. Virginia Wilson, born 1854 in Bulloch County.

E. Lewis J. Wilson, born 1856 in Bulloch County.

F. Ann E. Wilson, born 1867 in Bulloch County, married Mr. Roberson.

II. Mary Wilson married William Lee. See LEE

III. Rebecca Wilson, born 1832 in Georgia, married Thomas Knight.

IV. Amelia Wilson, born 1834 in Georgia, married Solomon Hagin.

V. America Wilson, born 1841 in Georgia.

VI. Leila Wilson, born 1845 Bulloch County.

VII. Sally Wilson.

VIII. Martha Frances Wilson.

IX. Andrew Jackson Wilson, born 1849 in Bulloch County, farmer. Wife listed with him on 1880 Statesboro Census was Rachel A. (born 1850), Wife listed on his LWT was Sarah. His LWT dated 28 June 1883, probated 7 April 1884 in Bulloch County, named his brother, Jasper Wilson; also his children. They were residents of Statesboro, in 1880. Issue:

A. Mary M. Wilson.

B. Julia E. Wilson.

C. Ann P. Wilson married William Alderman.

---

[355] Bulloch County Wills & Estates; 1850-1870 Bulloch County Census; Bulloch County Marriages; 1880 Bulloch County Census, Statesboro District.

D. Moses B. Wilson.

E. William J. Wilson.

F. James L. Wilson.

G. Lola Wilson, born 1868 Georgia.

H. Joseph A. Wilson, born 1870 Georgia.

I. Leanney A. Wilson, born 1876 Georgia.

J. Emaline Wilson, born 1879 Georgia.

Woodall of Talbot County

Robert Woodall was born 1824 in Georgia, and was deceased before 1880. He married Cornelia, born 1830 in Georgia, farmer. Her husband was deceased by 1880, and she lived with her two sons in Talbot County, viz: Henry Woodall, born 1857 and Seaborn, born 1861. Issue:[356]

I. William Woodall, born 1849 in Talbot County.

II. Lucy Woodall, born 1852 in Talbot County.

III. James Woodall, born 1854 in Talbot County.

IV. Fletcher Woodall, born 1855 in Talbot County.

V. Henry Woodall, born 1857 in Talbot County, married 13 January 1881, Ida Rachel Pye (born 20 July 1858 in Talbot County, died 15 September 1927 in Talbot County, a daughter of John Pye and his wife, Sarah Ann (Chambliss) Pye. SEE Chambliss and Pye. Issue:

A. Sallie Cornelia Woodall, born 7 July 1884 Woodland, Talbot County, Georgia, died 29 January 1967.

B. John Henry Woodall, born 4 April 1886 Woodland, Talbot County, Georgia, died 25 August 1965, buried in the Woodland Cemetery in Talbot County, married on 18 May 1910, Berta Mae Matthews. Issue:

1. Dorothy Rachel Woodall, born 10 October 1912 in Talbot County, married Robert Henry Wilson on 12 September 1914.

2. John Henry Woodall, born 22 October 1917 Talbot County, married (1) Catherine Gay on 5 September 1940, and (2) Elizabeth Harmon on 28 December 1948. Issue:

a. Larry Craig Woodall, born 12 March 1943.

b. Charles Alvin Woodall, born 10 October 1945.

---

[356] 1880 Talbot County Census; Talbot County Marriages; personal records of Mattie Woodall, Woodland, Georgia; 1860 Talbot County Census.

William Alonzo York was the son of Sarah York of Rabun County. She was born 1828 and was widowed, residing at Clayton, Georgia, with her children, viz: Walhalla C. York (daughter), born 1858; William A. York, born 1867; and Martha I. York, born 1879 in Rabun County.

William Alonzo York was married to Savana Rowe and had issue:

I.   Ernest Alonzo York, born March 1893 in Meriwether County, married Eunice Bertha Chambliss in 1912, the daughter of William Gardner Chambliss and his wife, Josephine (Brittain) York. SEE Chambliss. Issue:

    A. Bertha Lucrete York, born September 1913 in Meriwether County, married Guy Jackson.
    B. William Ravner York, born 1916 in Meriwether County.
    C. Geraldine York, born 1921 in Meriwether County.
    D. Ernestine York, born 1930 in Meriwether County.

II.   David York, born October 1895 in Meriwether County, married in 1923, Marie Frances Chambliss (born April 1896 in Meriwether County), the daughter of William Gardner Chambliss and his wife, Josephine (Brittain) Chambliss. Issue:

    A. Josephine York, born September 1924 in Orlando, Florida, married in 1953, John Rohan.

    B. Huntley Avery York, born February 1926 in Sarasota, Florida, married in 1952, Shellie Avo Maynard (born 9 June 1921). Issue:
        1. Michael Avery York, born 11 February 1954 in Atlanta, Fulton County.
        2. Brenda Joyce York, born 23 May 1955 in Atlanta, Fulton County.
        3. Jeffrey Lane York, born 3 September 1956 in Atlanta, Fulton County.

    C. Marilyn York, born January 1941 in Meriwether County.

Young of Talbot County

William Barclay Young was born 17 February 1815/1816 in Georgia, died 28 April 1895 in Panola County, Florida, buried in the Clayton Cemetery. He was married 2 November 1837 in Talbot County to Susan Mary Chambliss (born 7 February 1822, died 6 January 1910 in Gary, Panola County, Texas), a daughter of Jeptha Chambliss and his wife, Susan (Jones) Chambliss. SEE Chambliss. They were residents of Panola County, Texas in 1880, Precinct 8. Issue:[357]

I.   John C. Young, born 1839 in Talbot County.
II.   James Young, born 1840 in Talbot County.
III. Harriet Young, born 1842 in Talbot County.
IV. William Young, born 1843 in Talbot County.
V.   Nathan Young, born 1845 in Talbot County.
VI. Susan Young, born 1847 in Talbot County.

---

[357] 1850 Talbot County Census.

VII. Martha Young, born June 1850 in Talbot County.

Youngblood of Germany, South Carolina
and Columbia County, Georgia

Heinrich Jungblut was born ca 1660 in the Rheinland of Germany and was married to Margret Schuckman on 9 December 1681 in Lipss, Muesten, Germany. They had issue:[358]

Peter Jungblut, christened on 4 August 1686 in Katholisch, Vilich, Rheinland, Prussia, and died in Prince George County, Maryland. He married (1) Barbara, ca 1704 and (2), Elizabetha Catharine ca 1712. He was a Palatinate refugee to Lancaster County, Pennsylvania in 1728. On 6 March 1739 a "Patent for Naturalization was issued to Peter Youngblood of Prince George County, Maryland, native of Germany, to William and Peter, his sons, and Sarah and Mary, his daughters." Issue:

I.   Margretha Elisabetha Youngblood, christened on 17 September 1706 at Roemisch, Katholische, Bischofsdron, in the Rheinland.

II.   Peter Youngblood, born between 1705 and 1720 in the Rheinland, died in Pennsylvania. Issue:

    A. William Youngblood.

    B. Sarah Youngblood.

    C. Mary Youngblood.

    D. Peter Youngblood, Captain, died in 1788, Richmond County, Georgia. He was married(1) on 26 November 1750 in Harford County, Maryland to Mary Whealis, and had by her two known sons, viz....Samuel and Abraham, as proved by a publication in the Augusta Chronicle and Gazette, Vol. XI-500, dated 1 July 1767....A case in the Supreme Court of George Youngblood, for himself and the heirs of Abraham Youngblood, vs. the heirs and creditors of P. Youngblood....show that George and Abraham, sons of Peter Youngblood, deceased, had a gift deed from their father dated 27 November 1777 for 200 acres on White Oak Creek, Columbia County. Peter married (2) Susannah and had a number of children. A Richmond County deed recorded in Deed Book IG, page 106-107, entered 8 May 1789 (dated 5 October 1788) from Susannah, Samuel and Joseph Youngblood, William Wilson and J. Rebecca (Youngblood) Wilson, his wife, Lewis and Margaret Youngblood, the widow of Peter Youngblood, deceased, Samuel Youngblood, Joseph Youngblood, William Wilson and Rebecca, his wife, Cain Gentry and Liddy, his wife, Lewis Youngblood, Sarah (Sally) Youngblood, Susanna Youngblood and Margaret Youngblood, all of the State of South Carolina, and Lewis Barnes of Richmond County, Georgia, were all named as heirs of Peter Youngblood. Further evidence of Peter's children is a Columbia County deed dated 27 November 1777, entitled Deed of Gift, from Peter

---

[358] Hogsden Library, Savannah, Georgia; Columbia County Marriages; Richmond County Marriages; Richmond County Deeds; Columbia County Deeds; Edgefield County, South Carolina Deeds & Wills; <u>Southern Indian Youngbloods, Their Ancestors and Descendants</u> by Lawrence L. Lant (1968).

Youngblood, Sr. of Richmond County, Georgia, to his sons, Abraham and George Youngblood, 200 acres on Whiteoak Creek to include the plantation. Martin Mellown, a witness, swore on 6 April 1784 that Peter Youngblood "is now deceased". Signed, George Ray, John Youngblood, Martin Mellown and Lewis Youngblood. George Youngblood appeared and deposed that he and his brother, Abraham Youngblood (now deceased), possessed the above tract, but that the deed was destroyed by fire. Another deed, dated 26 January 1774 in Edgefield County, "Peter Youngblood of Granille County, North Carolina" (was South Carolina) deeded to John Frazier, planter, 100 acres on the southside of Beaver Creek of the Savannah River in Granville County. Signed, Peter and Mary Youngblood.

Issue by (1) wife, Mary Whealis:

1. Samuel Youngblood, born ca 1754 in Edgefield County, South Carolina. Samuel Youngblood and his wife deeded to Nathan Youngblood land in Hancock County in 1794.

2. Abraham Youngblood, born ca 1767, died before 1799 in Columbia County, Georgia. He married Amey McNeill on 1 March 1787 in Columbia County. Letters of Administration were issued to George Youngblood on 8 March 1799 in Columbia County, on the Estate of Abraham Youngblood. Amey, Abraham's wife, was named in the LWT of her father, Daniel McNeill, dated 23 October 1804, probated 18 June 1805 in Columbia County, which named his wife, Sarah and children, viz: Daniel, Jesse, Sarah Reeve, Ann Lastly, Amey Youngblood and Mary Robertson; also grandchildren, John, Daniel, Caby and Ann Youngblood.

Issue by (2) wife, Susannah:

3. George Youngblood, born ca 1768. George Youngblood "of Edgefield County, South Caroliina" sold the land deeded to him by his father, Peter Youngblood, on 16 April 1797 to Jesse Offutt. Edgefield County Deed Book 18-351, dated 3 December 1799, George Youngblood deeded Daniel Mazyeke, the eldest captain in the late seconod Regiment of foot in the State aforesaid on Continental establishment, 150 acres of land surveyed for Robert Larry on 26 January 1773 and 4 April 1775, conveyed on 2 January 1776 in the 96th District, on Mine Creek of the Little Saluda River. The Estate of George Youngblood was dated 30 January 1808, Edgefield County. Nancy Youngblood, the widow, was administratrix. She married 2nd, H. W. Lowe. Ira Youngblood (died 1829) and Eleanor Youngblood, minors, had an interest in the Estate of Emalie Youngblood. Henry W. Lowe was appointed the guardian of Ira, Eleanor, Erasmus J., Emaliine, and Matilda Youngblood. The 1790 Census of Edgefield County lists George Youngblood, one man, no boys, 3 females. Issue:

a. Ira Youngblood.
b. Eleanor Youngblood.
c. Erasmus J. Youngblood, married Eliza Wigfall, the daughter of Levi Durand Wigfall. Eliza died, leaving five children, viz: Erasmus H., Arthur, Lewis, Eliza and Jacob.
d. Emaline Youngblood.

e. Matilda Youngblood.

4. Sally Youngblood, born ca 1786 in Edgefield County, died ca 1812 in Clarke County, Georgia, married Edward Hagin on 9 January 1807 in Clarke County. SEE Hagin.

5. Bartley Youngblood of Richmond County, Georgia.

6. Joseph Youngblood of Edgefield County, South Carolina. Richmond County Deed Book IG-58, 21 October 1788, Joseph and Margaret Youngblood of Augusta, deed to Lewis Barnes. Mentions, Peter Youngblood, deceased; his widow, Susannah Youngblood; Samuel Youngblood; Joseph Youngblood; Rebecca, wife of William Wilson; Liddy, wife of Cain Gentry; Lewis Youngblood; Sarah Youngblood; Margaret Youngblood; and Susannah Youngblood, "Now all of the State o f South Carolina."

7. Rebecca Youngblood, died 1804 in Edgefield County, married William Wilson. The LWT of Mrs. Rebecca Wilson dated 22 April 1804, probated 5 December 1805 in Edgefield County, South Carolina.

8. Liddy Youngblood married Cain Gentry.

9. Lewis Youngblood, born February 1822, married Mary, lived in Edgefield County. The LWT of Lewis Youngblood dated 11 February 1822, probated 23 February 1822 in Edgefield County. A division of the estate in 1846 shows Whitfield Brooks, share of widow, 1/3rd, Basil Youngblood, 1/3rd, widow, 1/3rd or 1/7th of 2/3rds; children, Thomas and Martha; Sarah, the wife of John McNeil; Catherine, the wife of J. S. Hollister; and Martha, the daughter of Gideon Youngblood who married W. J. Bickers. Issue:

    a. Abner Youngblood.
    b. Gideon Youngblood.
    c. Thomas Youngblood.
    d. Basil Youngblood.
    e. William Youngblood.

10. Margaret Youngblood married James Cone on 8 January 1807.

11. Peter Youngblood, Jr. of Edgefield County, married Sarah Jane Still. A Columbia County deed dated 1 April 1797 of Peter Youngblood of Richmond County, Georgia, to James Culbreath, 300 acres of land on Trading Path, originally granted to the said Peter on 6 August 1793.

INDEX

355

Adair, John Gibson 6
Adair, John H. 35
Adair, John Henry 7
Adair, John L. 3
Adair, John Thomas 10
Adair, John W. 4, 7, 10
Adair, Jonathan W. 10
Adair, Jones 2
Adair, Joseph 1, 10, 11, 12
Adair, Joseph A. 10
Adair, Joseph Alexander 1
Adair, Joseph Fisher 2
Adair, Joseph H. 4
Adair, Joseph Henry 8
Adair, Joseph Warren 5
Adair, Joseph, Jr. 1
Adair, Judith 3, 9, 50, 254, 343
Adair, Julia R. 10
Adair, Karl 2
Adair, L. 5
Adair, Lizzie 10
Adair, Louanna Moselle 8
Adair, Louise E. 5
Adair, Louise H. 6
Adair, Lucy 11
Adair, Lucy 310
Sanders, William 310
Adair, Lucy J. 6
Adair, Lula Jane 8
Adair, Malinda 4
Adair, Margaret Elizabeth 5
Adair, Margaret Eugenia 11
Adair, Marjorie 10
Adair, Martha 9
Adair, Martha A. 8
Adair, Martha Ann 3
Adair, Martha B. 8
Adair, Martha Delany 4
Adair, Martha J. 6
Adair, Martha Jane 8
Adair, Mary 2, 4, 9, 11
Adair, Mary A. 4, 6
Adair, Mary Ella 10
Adair, Mary F. 8, 127
Adair, Mary Jane 3
Adair, Mary Josephine 8
Adair, Mary L. 10
Adair, Mary Radcliff 2
Adair, Mary Rebecca 11
Adair, Mattie Elizabeth 6
Adair, Mattie J. 9
Adair, Memie C. 6

Adair, Memory Amanda 8
Adair, Milla E. 3
Adair, Milton R. 9
Adair, Mitchell 267
Adair, Mitchell S. 3, 10
Adair, Nathan M. 3
Adair, Ophelia 11
Adair, Patrick 6
Adair, Permelia 11, 333
Adair, Permelia Ann 141
Adair, Permelia Ann 5
Adair, Pheriby Emmaline 9, 94
Adair, Robert 11
Adair, Robert Emmitt 8
Adair, Robert Lee 7
Adair, Robin 2
Adair, Rufus L. 10
Adair, Salina Laura 9
Adair, Sallie 2
Adair, Sally 11, 13, 27
Adair, Sally Amanda 5
Adair, Sara Ann 5, 148
Adair, Sarah 2, 3, 9
Adair, Sarah A. Malinda 8
Adair, Sarah Ann 11
Adair, Sarah Ann E. 4, 292
Adair, Sarah C. 4, 9
Adair, Sarah E. 8
Adair, Sarah Frances 9
Adair, Sarah R. 10
Adair, Sherman L. 10
Adair, Susan 2
Adair, Sydney A. 5
Adair, Talitha Ann 4
Adair, Thomas 1, 11
Adair, Thomas B. 9
Adair, Thomas F. 9
Adair, Thomas Franklin 8
Adair, Thomas Jackson 7
Adair, Thomas L. 6
Adair, Vina A. 4
Adair, W. H. 94
Adair, Whitmell H., Jr. 6
Adair, Whitmell Harrington 4
Adair, Whitmill H. 5, 141, 148
Adair, William 2, 3, 11, 12
Adair, William Andrew 3, 193, 292
Adair, William Bozeman 9
Adair, William H. 8, 10
Adair, William Harrison S. 8
Adair, William J. 5, 6
Adair, William Levi 9

Baxter, Margaret A. J. 14
Baxter, Martha E. 14
Baxter, Mary A. 14
Baxter, Mary A. F. 13
Baxter, Mary F. 7, 14
Baxter, Mary M. 14
Baxter, Mitchell M. 13
Baxter, Nancy 9
Baxter, Nathaniel 13, 14, 27
Baxter, Richard S. 14
Baxter, Robert E. L. 14
Baxter, Sarah A. 14
Baxter, Stockley S. 14
Baxter, Thomas J. 14
Baxter, Wesley H. 13
Baxter, William 14
Bazemore, Kiddy 243
Beall, Margaret 244
Beall, Mary 244
Beard, Betsy 308
Beard, Thomas 28
Beckham, Catherine 15, 79
Beckham, Elizabeth 16, 79, 105
Beckham, G. 16
Beckham, Henry 16
Beckham, James 15
Beckham, John 16
Beckham, Lydia 15
Beckham, Mary 16
Beckham, Phillis 16
Beckham, Sherwood 16
Beckham, Simon 15, 16
Beckham, Solomon 16
Beckham, Stephen 16
Beckham, Tabitha 15
Beckham, Thomas 16
Beckham, William 15, 16
Beckham, William, Captain 15, 79
Beckley, Elizabeth 197
Beckley, James 196
Beckley, Joseph 197
Beckley, Mary 197
Beckley, Sarah 197
Beckley, William 197
Beckley, William, Sir 199
Beekman, Barnard, Colonel 39
Beeson, Susannah 287
Belcher, John 292
Belcher, Mary 293
Belconger, Ann 88
Belconger, Antony 88
Belconger, Benjamin 89

Belconger, Elizabeth 88
Belconger, Enos 89
Belconger, Jeffery 88
Belconger, John 88
Belconger, Joseph 89
Belconger, Judith 88
Belconger, Katern 88
Belconger, Lydia 89
Belconger, Margery 88
Belconger, Martha 88
Belconger, Mary 88
Belconger, Sarah 88
Belconger, Thomas 88
Belconger, William 88
Belfield, Thomas Wright 293
Bell, David 286
Bell, Donnie Lynn 17
Bell, Doris Jeanette 17
Bell, Ernest Blake 16
Bell, Ernest Coleman 16, 209
Bell, F. M. 87
Bell, James 286, 287
Bell, James Calvin 17
Bell, Jonathan 286
Bell, Joseph 286
Bell, Joshua Ernest 16
Bell, Kenneth Ernest 16
Bell, Kenneth James 16
Bell, Lydia Margaret 17
Bell, Marie Kenneth 16
Bell, Myra Susan 17
Bell, Nancy 286
Bell, Pamela 342
Bell, Patricia June 17
Bell, Patsy 286
Bell, Rachel Wynette 17
Bell, Ronald Coleman 17
Bell, Sarah 287
Bell, Thomas 286
Bell, William 286
Bell, Wilma Ione 16, 21
Bell, Wyatt Coleman 17
Benefield, J. H. 212
Benefield, L. O. 211
Bennett, Camile 92
Bennett, Chadwick Ronald 92
Bennett, Dollie Elaine 92, 315
Bennett, Douglas Eugene 92
Bennett, Elizabeth 115
Bennett, Frank Lewis 280
Bennett, Gloria Lynn 92
Bennett, Jemima 296

Bridges, William 317
Brittain, Josephine 351
Broadway, Samuel 44
Broales, Civella Adams 55
Brock, Elizabeth Cox 305
Brock, James 83
Brock, Nancy E. Moody 14
Brock, Reuben 43
Brockington, Daryl Robertson 17
Brockington, David Oliver 17
Brockington, Sera Elizabeth 17
Brookins, Elizabeth 125
Brooks, Amanda 91
Brooks, Herman Wood 31
Brooks, Herman Woodrow 325
Brooks, James Herman 31
Brooks, James M. 328
Brooks, Jamie Carolyn 48
Brooks, Jeffrey Larence 31
Brooks, Jennifer Marie 31
Brooks, John 5
Brooks, John Thomas 31, 325
Brooks, Kari Lynn 31
Brooks, Larry Davis 48
Brooks, Laura Ruth 31
Brooks, Lichford 127
Brooks, Martha 115
Brooks, Mary Lee 31
Brooks, Robert Eugene 31
Brooks, Stacy Deneen 31
Brooks, Stephanie Dawn 31
Brooks, Thomas William 31
Brooks, Vernon 232
Brooks, Whitfield 354
Broom, Anna 139
Broom, Rebekah 139
Brooms, Jerusha 48
Brown, Allen 83
Brown, Amanda 242
Brown, Bette Grace 32
Brown, Betty Ann 32
Brown, Donald Curtis 32
Brown, Edith Lawanna 32
Brown, Eliza 102
Brown, Eliza 107
Brown, Ellen Elizabeth 33
Brown, Evelina L. 321
Brown, Fannie May 292
Brown, G. W. 31
Brown, George G. 300
Brown, George Owen, Sr. 33
Brown, Glen Smith 32, 222

Brown, H. W. 214
Brown, Hardy Gene 33
Brown, Jerry Lynn 48
Brown, Jessica 92
Brown, John 42
Brown, Leo Curtis 32
Brown, Louise 232
Brown, Lucinda M. 98
Brown, Lucy 242
Brown, Lucy Belle Camp 214
Brown, Margaret 47, 222
Brown, Marvin Lane, Sr. 33
Brown, Mary 242
Brown, Mattie 241
Brown, Michael 92
Brown, Murray Lowell 32
Brown, Myrtle Ruth 31
Brown, Nettie 209
Brown, Paul 33
Brown, Reginia 92
Brown, Roma 217
Brown, Rose Hannah 219, 324
Brown, Sylvia 16
Brown, Thomas 288
Brown, Tilmon Powell 6
Brown, Tim 92
Brown, Todd 92
Brown, Treg 220
Brown, Turner 242
Brown, Wendy Mary 48
Brown, William Fennin 133
Brown, William Henry 32
Broxton, Jeremiah 317
Broxton, Zelpha 317
Bruce, Anna 122
Brume, Walker 196
Bryan, Ann Clements 72
Bryan, Jonathan 143
Bryan, Sterling, Jr. 119
Bryan, Turner 24, 25
Bryant, Jenny Leigh 49
Bryant, Sandra Dee 49
Bryant, Smithy 192
Bryant, William Raymond 49
Bryson, Boyd 112
Bryson, Harry 112
Bryson, Hayne 112
Bryson, Jimmie 112
Bryson, Margaret 112
Buchanan, Mary Frances 87
Buckner, Amelia 112
Buckner, Elma 112

362

Buckner, Mendel 112
Buckner, Ray 112
Buford, Margaret Elizabeth 5
Buford, Myrtle 258
Bullard, Myrtle Camp 214
Bullock, Adell B. 35
Bullock, Agatha 33
Bullock, Albert 35, 36
Bullock, Albert G. 35
Bullock, Alex C. 34
Bullock, Alexander 35
Bullock, Alexander G. 34
Bullock, Alexander Gordon 34
Bullock, Alice A. E. 34
Bullock, Alice M. 34
Bullock, Allen 217
Bullock, Alva Billups 34
Bullock, Anne 33
Bullock, Antenette 35, 213
Bullock, Anthony 35
Bullock, Antionett 36
Bullock, C. H. Sherman 35
Bullock, Clarissa 33
Bullock, Delia 35
Bullock, E. C., Jr. 217
Bullock, Elizabeth 34
Bullock, Fannie 265
Bullock, Fannie F. 35
Bullock, Fanny 33
Bullock, Frances 34
Bullock, Frances Roy 36
Bullock, Francis M. 35
Bullock, George N. 34
Bullock, Harriett 35
Bullock, Hawkins 33
Bullock, Hawkins Sherman 36
Bullock, Henry S. 36
Bullock, Irene 233
Bullock, Jackson 34
Bullock, James 33, 35
Bullock, James Sherman 34
Bullock, Janny 35
Bullock, John F. 35
Bullock, John Gordon 33
Bullock, John H. S. 34
Bullock, John Pickney 9
Bullock, Joseph 35
Bullock, Leanor 30
Bullock, Lou E. 34
Bullock, Louisa Nance 36
Bullock, Louisiana 35
Bullock, Martha 35

Bullock, Mary Wyatt 33
Bullock, Nathaniel 33, 34, 36
Bullock, Nathaniel Hawkins 34
Bullock, Nathaniel Thomas 34
Bullock, Nickalus Hawkins 9
Bullock, Richard 33, 35
Bullock, Richard Henley 36
Bullock, Robert 217
Bullock, Robert Gordon 34
Bullock, Salina M. 10
Bullock, Sarah 34
Bullock, Sherman 213
Bullock, Sherman H. 35
Bullock, Snead 34
Bullock, Soletras 35
Bullock, Susannah Sherman 33
Bullock, T. B. 288
Bullock, William 9, 36
Bullock, William Gordon 36
Bullock, Wyatt 33
Bumpass, Jesse 73
Burch, Richard 193
Burchman, James 329
Burford, William 71
Burnet, Gloria 233
Burns, Andrew 83
Burns, Jon Melvin 49
Burns, Nicholas Bryant 49
Burroughs, Elsey C. 253
Burton, Charles 199
Butler, Alfred Keith 21
Butler, Alice Elizabeth 21
Butler, Bradly Keith 21
Butler, David E. 275, 276
Butler, J. E. 258
Butler, Judie 86
Butler, Patrick Christian 21
Butler, Salina Ann 92
Bynum, Harmon White 329
Cade, Agnes 259
Cagle, Roger 132, 133
Calagia, Sarah 328
Calaway, J. Sanford 246
Caldwell, Elizabeth 224
Calhoun, Jacquetta Marie Urs 56
Calhoun, John C. 39
Call, Richard, Major 97
Callahan, Miss 322
Callaway, Anna Brown 292
Callaway, Henry B. 291
Calloway, George F. 37
Calloway, Henry B. 36, 57

Calloway, Henry Oscar 37
Calloway, Jesse 37
Calloway, John 36
Calloway, John W. 36
Calloway, Josiah 36
Calloway, Lula A. 36
Calloway, Mary E. 37
Calloway, Pitt M., Rev. 245
Calloway, Sarah 37
Calloway, Vanhusen 37
Calloway, William 36
Cameron, Elizabeth 307
Sailors, Daniel 307
Camp, Aaron 44
Camp, Abigail 41
Camp, Abner 303
Camp, Adam 43
Camp, Alex Stephens 42
Camp, Alfred 43
Camp, Altha 122
Camp, Ambrose 38
Camp, Anna 42, 224
Camp, Annie Naomi 146
Camp, Arthur 303
Camp, Benjamin 43
Camp, Bill 213
Camp, Bradford 39
Camp, Burrell 42, 216, 231
Camp, Burrell Marion 41, 42, 224, 231, 230, 330
Camp, Clarenda Ann 137
Camp, Crenshaw 43
Camp, Daniel 43
Camp, Edmund 38, 303, 322
Camp, Edmund Kennedy 40
Camp, Edna 216
Camp, Elizabeth 39, 43, 129, 238
Camp, Eunice 44
Camp, George 43
Camp, Hiram 303
Camp, Hosea 39, 43
Camp, Ira 40
Camp, James 43
Camp, Joel 43
Camp, John 38, 122
Camp, Joseph 38
Camp, Joseph Benton 322
Camp, Joseph Thomas 42
Camp, Joshua 43
Camp, Josiah Washington 40
Camp, Julian 213
Camp, Larkin 39, 44

Camp, Lavonia Bell 42
Camp, Lewis 44
Camp, Lucy 38
Camp, Lydia 41
Camp, Lydia A. 231
Camp, Lydia Caroline 42
Camp, Marshall 38
Camp, Martha 303
Camp, Mary 38, 303, 329
Camp, Mary Marshall 38
Camp, Millie 216
Camp, Milly C. 41
Camp, Nancy 40, 42
Camp, Nathaniel 39, 129, 238
Camp, Pennington James 42
Camp, Rendy Ann 42, 224
Camp, Russell 303
Camp, Ruth 43
Camp, Samuel 53
Camp, Sarah 39, 42, 322
Camp, Sarah Suttle 43
Camp, Satira 303
Camp, Sherwood 39
Camp, Starling 42
Camp, Stella 216
Camp, Stephen 43
Camp, Thomas 38, 40, 42, 43
Camp, William Addison 43
Camp, William Washington 41
Camp, Winifred 347
Campbell, Mary Drucilla 39
Campbell, Samuel, Colonel 252
Campe, Ann 37
Campe, Johanes 37
Campe, Richard 37
Campe, Sarah 37
Campe, Thomas 37
Canady, Campbell 83
Cangelosi, Julius 232
Cannon, Hardy B. 92
Cannon, Mae 92
Cantrell, Madge 215
Cantrell, Martha Evaline 334
Carden, John M. 42
Carey, Robert 53
Cargile, B. M. 182
Cargile, John 182
Cargile, Joseph John Washington 182
Cargile, Reneau 182
Carithers, William W. 299
Carley, Nathaniel 198
Carlisle, Green Whatley 245

Castleberry, Susanna 268
Castleberry, William, Sr. 96
Castwell, Mr. 191
Catchings, Silas 1=264
Cates, Jean Jones 32
Cates, Wendy 32
Cates, Wiley 32
Cauley, Benjamin R. 91
Cauley, Ella J. 91
Cauley, Emma E. 91
Cauley, Henry J. 91
Cauley, Sara F. 91
Cauley, William H. 91
Cawood, Sarah 88
Cawood, Thomas, Sr. 88
Cgambliss, Edwin 64
Chamberlain, Reuben Grover 127
Chambers, John A. 268
Chamblee, Mr. 92
Chambless, March 76
Chambless, Mary 76
Chambliss, Albert 63
Chambliss, Alexander 69
Chambliss, Andrew D. 53, 58, 59
Chambliss, Andrew Jackson 53, 74, 333
Chambliss, Angeline 57
Chambliss, Ann 51
Chambliss, Ann M. 129
Chambliss, Ann M. 69
Chambliss, Anna Lee 60
Chambliss, Annie 68
Chambliss, Arte Ann 110
Chambliss, Arte Ann 64
Chambliss, Arthur 58
Chambliss, Augustus 64
Chambliss, Benjamin 64
Chambliss, Bernice 68
Chambliss, Caroline Frances 69
Chambliss, Charles Stanley 68
Chambliss, Christopher 52, 53, 59, 244
Chambliss, Christopher Columbus 63
Chambliss, Cynthia 65
Chambliss, E. K. C. 67
Chambliss, Edgar 55
Chambliss, Edgar Stephen 68
Chambliss, Edmund 69
Chambliss, Edna Armstrong 68
Chambliss, Eleanor 64
Chambliss, Elias 64
Chambliss, Eliza 36, 53, 102, 291
Chambliss, Elizabeth 21, 58, 70
Chambliss, Elizabeth Jordan 68, 69, 242

Chambliss, Elizabeth S. 59
Chambliss, Ellen Frances 129
Chambliss, Emily Angeline 69, 113, 297
Chambliss, Eola Obedience 66
Chambliss, Ephraim 70
Chambliss, Ernest 58, 68
Chambliss, Estelle 55
Chambliss, Eugene Dodd 56
Chambliss, Eunice Bertha 61, 351
Chambliss, Fannie 68
Chambliss, Florence 58
Chambliss, Florrie 61
Chambliss, Frances 57
Chambliss, Frances M. 64
Chambliss, Frank 52, 64
Chambliss, George N. 63
Chambliss, George W. 64
Chambliss, Green 58
Chambliss, Harriett 64
Chambliss, Hasseltine 61
Chambliss, Henry 101
Chambliss, Henry 51, 57, 58, 59, 98
Chambliss, Henry Balden 66, 306
Chambliss, Henry Colquitt 60
Chambliss, Henry Mary 60
Chambliss, Herbert 55
Chambliss, Hiram Abiff 66
Chambliss, Israel 68
Chambliss, Israel E. 68
Chambliss, Israel Jordan 68
Chambliss, Iverson Floyd 61
Chambliss, Jackson 54
Chambliss, James 52
Chambliss, James Henry 66
Chambliss, James M. 60
Chambliss, James Taylor 66
Chambliss, Jane 291
Chambliss, Jane 53, 59
Chambliss, Jeptha 53, 63, 110, 244, 306, 351
Chambliss, Jeptha C. 63
Chambliss, Jesse Pye 60
Chambliss, Jessie Baker 61
Chambliss, Joe 55, 69
Chambliss, Joel B. 56
Chambliss, Joel E. 53
Chambliss, Joel Edgar 54, 74, 118, 319
Chambliss, John 51, 52, 63, 66
Chambliss, John A.60
CHambliss, John D. 65
Chambliss, John Floyd 61
Chambliss, John M. 67, 113, 129, 247, 297
Chambliss, John Marshall 61

Chambliss, William Lawson 58
Chambliss, William Lloyd 67
Chambliss, William M. 60
Chambliss, William Urban 61
Chambliss, Zachariah 52, 67, 270, 323
Chambliss, Zachariah C. 66
Chambliss, Zachariah Cromwell 68
Chambliss, Zachariah D. 66
Chambliss, Zachariah L. 65
Chamnis, Henry 51
Champion, Gretchen Sloan 21
Champion, James Donald 21
Chandler, Priscilla 305
Chandler, Sarah 309
Chandler, William 15
Chaney, Elizabeth 139
Chapman, Deborah 282
Chapman, Retency Hill 282
Chasey, Levi, Colonel 1
Cheatham, Adaline 70
Cheatham, Birdy E. J. 71
Cheatham, Carlie C. 71
Cheatham, Caroline D. 71
Cheatham, Catherine 71
Cheatham, David J. 71
Cheatham, Elizabeth 70, 71, 343
Cheatham, Emily C. 70
Cheatham, Emily H. 71
Cheatham, Georgia Ann 71
Cheatham, Isham 70
Cheatham, Jacob B. J. J. 71
Cheatham, James J. A. L. 71
Cheatham, James J. N. 70
Cheatham, James W. J. 70
Cheatham, Jesse R. 70
Cheatham, John J. 71
Cheatham, Josiah 70, 345
Cheatham, Mary 71
Cheatham, Mary S. P. 71
Cheatham, Mildred L. G. P. C. 71
Cheatham, Nancy 71
Cheatham, Nancy C. 71
Cheatham, Parmalie 70
Cheatham, Prudence 71
Cheatham, Riley C. 71
Cheatham, Rispan J. 71
Cheatham, Rodah 71
Cheatham, Rodah E. 71
Cheatham, William J. 71
Cheeves, Sarah Elizabeth 219, 289
Chew, Larkin 15
Chewning, Robert 199

Childers, W. H. 324
Chiles, John 114
Chiles, M. L. 22
Chivers, Robert 274
Chivers, Sabrina 274
Chivers, Thomas Holley 274
Claiborne, Jr. 96
Clark, Arnaveeny 303
Clark, Elizabeth 181
Clark, Mary A. 11
Clark, William F. 243
Clarke, Elijah 132
Clarke, Elijah, Colonel 116
Clarke, Joseph B. 304
Clay, James Russell, Sr. 121, 122
Clay, Mr. 107
Clayton, Sam 146
Clelan, Susan 241
Clement, Benjamin 114
Clement, Benjamin, Jr. 114
Clement, Mary 114
Clements, Anderson 75
Clements, Anna 73, 75, 76
Clements, Anna S. 72
Clements, Arenia 75
Clements, Asbury 74
Clements, Benjamin 115
Clements, Cary 75
Clements, Christiana 75
Clements, D. S. 73
Clements, David 72
Clements, Elizabeth 30, 71, 73, 75
Clements, Elizabeth S. J. 72
Clements, Elizabeth Smith 54, 74, 118
Clements, Ellis 74
Clements, Gilley 73
Clements, Grisell 75
Clements, Jacob 75, 76
Clements, Jane Smith 319
Clements, Jeptha 73, 76
Clements, Jesse 71, 73, 76
Clements, Jesse, Jr. 73
Clements, John 73
Clements, Lotty 75
Clements, Martha 74, 75
Clements, Martha L. 72
Clements, Mary 335, 343
Clements, Mary 71, 75
Clements, Mary S. Mathew 72
Clements, Nancy 72, 73
Clements, Pamela 74
Clements, Peyton 71, 74, 75

368

Cook, Missouri 93
Cook, Nancy 93, 261, 349
Cook, Nancy E. 93
Cook, Nora 7
Cook, Pat 92
Cook, Piety 93
Cook, Polly 91
Cook, Rebecca 91
Cook, Ruby Lee 92
Cook, Sara 93
Cook, Sarah 92
Cook, Silas F. 93
Cook, Tabby 91
Cook, Tabitha 93
Cook, Thomas E. 91
Cook, Wade Hampton 92
Cook, William Jackson 91
Cook, William Marion 91
Cooner, Eugene Clifton 246
Cooper, Benjamin 83
Cooper, Cecilia 217
Cooper, Levi 305
Cooper, Louisa 40
Cooper, Mary Jane 34
Cooper, Otis 212
Copeland, Arthur 192
Copeland, Elizabeth Taberer 338
Copeland, Major 191
Corley, Amos 223
Corley, Ludy Mae 269
Corley, Naomi 223
Cornett, Martha J. 4
Cornwallis, Lord 244
Cosby, Jane 63
Cottrell, Elizabeth 292
Cowan, Barbara 235
Cowan, Emma 312
Cox, George W., Rev. 86
Craddock, William 196
Craig, Mary 139
Craton, Ada 95
Craton, Amy 94
Craton, Balis F. 94
Craton, Barry 95
Craton, Cora J. 95
Craton, Dock 95
Craton, Doctor T. 95
Craton, Easter 94
Craton, Emma 95
Craton, Emma C.94
Craton, Jack 95
Craton, James 94

Craton, Johannah 95
Craton, John 95
Craton, John Henry 95
Craton, John Weaver 94
Craton, Joseph 94
Craton, Joseph A. 95
Craton, Joseph R. 95
Craton, Joseph T. 95
Craton, Joshua Erwin 94
Craton, Lilly Ophelia 95
Craton, Louisa 95
Craton, Lucy W. 95
Craton, Martha 94
Craton, Martha Ann 95
Craton, Mary 94
Craton, Mary Ella 94
Craton, Mary Jane 94
Craton, Nancy J. 94
Craton, Nancy Jane 8
Craton, Polly 96
Craton, Rebecca 95
Craton, Samuel 94
Craton, Sarah 94
Craton, Sarah Reyan 95
Craton, Thomas 95
Craton, Thomas Howell 94
Craton, W. J. 95
Craton, William 94
Craton, William I. 9, 94
Craton, William Isaac 95
Craven, Lissie Lou 50
Crawford, A. 323
Crawford, Anderson 15
Crawford, J. R. 344
Crawford, John R. 344
Crawford, Peter 199
Crawford, Thomas, Colonel 23, 24
Crawford, William Daniel 233
Crawford, William Daniel, Jr. 233
Crawley, Donald 215
Crew, Oma 267
Crew, Ruby Ann 217
Crews, W. H. 206
Crocker, John Wendall 17
Crockett, Caroline 249
Crockett, Hegburt 249
Crockett, James 249
Crockett, Joe 249
Crockett, Joel J. 249
Crockett, Julia 249]
Crockett, Mary 249
Croker, Ann Grace 122

371

372

375

Elsberry, Barbary 111, 112
Elsberry, Bartone 111
Elsberry, Ben 213
Elsberry, Bertha 112
Elsberry, Bobby 112
Elsberry, Carrie Beatrice 112
Elsberry, Clarina 111
Elsberry, Clifford 213
Elsberry, Docia 213
Elsberry, Elizabeth 111
Elsberry, Emma 111, 112
Elsberry, Ernest, Jr. 112
Elsberry, G. R. 111
Elsberry, George 111
Elsberry, Gertrude 112
Elsberry, Helen 112
Elsberry, Irene 112
Elsberry, J. Lindsey 111
Elsberry, J. Richard R. 111
Elsberry, James Lewis 112
Elsberry, James R. 110
Elsberry, Johnnie 112
Elsberry, Joseph C. 111
Elsberry, Kirkland 112, 210
Elsberry, Lindsey 110, 205
Elsberry, Lindsey W. 224
Elsberry, Lindsey W., Jr. 111
Elsberry, Lou Elsberry 232
Elsberry, Lucille 112
Elsberry, M. M. 232
Elsberry, Mariah 107, 216
Elsberry, Mary 207
Elsberry, Mary Elizabeth 111, 224
Elsberry, Mary Jane Henderson 231
Elsberry, Mathew M. 111
Elsberry, Millie 213
Elsberry, Minnie D. 112
Elsberry, Miriam Frances 112
Elsberry, Nancy 111
Elsberry, Nancy E. 112
Elsberry, Raleigh 112
Elsberry, Rayford 213
Elsberry, Robert L. 112
Elsberry, Roy 112
Elsberry, Ruby 112
Elsberry, S. P. 219
Elsberry, Sally 203
Elsberry, Samuel J. 112
Elsberry, Sarah 111, 201
Elsberry, Sibbie Lavinnie 111, 205
Elsberry, Tom 213
Elsberry, Tommy 213

Elsberry, Virgil 213
Elsberry, W. R. 136
Elsberry, Walton L. 232
Elsberry, Willard 112
Elsberry, William Monroe 112
Elsberry, William Monroe 210
Eskew, Frances E. 322
Eskew, Mary 305
Espy, Thomas 307
Estes, Herbert 232
Estes, Ima 232
Estes, Inez 232
Estes, Jim 232
Estes, Mr. 106
Estes, Reba Holland 232
Estes, Robert 196
Etheridge, Elijah N. 69
Etheridge, Lewis 69
Etheridge, Robert H. 113
Ethridge, Benjamin 113
Ethridge, Elijah 113
Ethridge, Elijah N. 113
Ethridge, Elijah Nathaniel 113
Ethridge, Frances 113
Ethridge, Georgia 113
Ethridge, John 113
Ethridge, John H. 113
Ethridge, Mary Frances 113
Ethridge, Willie 113
Evans, Ann 113, 115
Evans, Annie 119
Evans, Arden 113, 114, 115, 116, 117
Evans, Bennett 133
Evans, Capt. 115
Evans, Caroline 9, 116
Evans, Celia 264
Evans, Charles Crawford 118, 295
Evans, David 113, 115, 116
Evans, Dorothy Frances 119
Evans, E. 115
Evans, Elam 115
Evans, Eleanor 113
Evans, Elijah 117, 119
Evans, Elizabeth 116
Evans, Elizabeth A. 116
Evans, Frances 118
Evans, Garrison 119
Evans, George 116
Evans, Hannah 116
Evans, Henry 116
Evans, Henry S. 116
Evans, Henry T. 116

Evans, Homer James 54, 56, 118
Evans, James 113, 115
Evans, James D. 116
Evans, James H. 118
Evans, James Oliver 117
Evans, Jesse 115, 116
Evans, John 113, 117
Evans, John C. 115
Evans, John F. 118
Evans, Laura Anne 118
Evans, Lewis H. 118
Evans, M. 115
Evans, Marguerite Elizabeth 119, 235
Evans, Martha 118
Evans, Martha J. 118
Evans, Mary 116, 117
Evans, Mary Brent Chambliss 319
Evans, Mary E. 118
Evans, Nancy 1, 27, 85, 115
Evans, Nancy A. 118
Evans, Nancy Ann 119
Evans, Pearl 119
Evans, Pinckney 116
Evans, Rhody 116
Evans, Robert 116
Evans, Ruth 119
Evans, Sarah E. 119
Evans, Sarah F. 118
Evans, Sophia 116
Evans, Stephen 115
Evans, Susanna 114
Evans, Susannah 116
Evans, Thomas 115
Evans, Thomas T. 118
Evans, Thomas, Jr. 116
Evans, W. 115
Evans, William 27, 115, 264
Evans, William Raphael 117
Evans, William S. 116
Evans, William, Sr. 114, 115
Evans, Willis 117, 119
Evans, Zachariah 117
Everingham, Charlotte 285
Fambrough, Anderson 120
Fambrough, E. M. 121
Fambrough, Fannie 121
Fambrough, John 120
Fambrough, L. C. 121
Fambrough, Mary 120
Fambrough, Mary I. 121
Fambrough, Nancy H. 121
Fambrough, Phoebe 120

Fambrough, Robinson 120
Fambrough, Sarah 120
Fambrough, Thomas 120
Fambrough, Thomas M. 120
Fambrough, Urban C. 120
Fambrough, Urban C. 302
Fambrough, William 120
Fambrough, William L. 120
Fambrough, William N. 121
Fanning, Colonel 23, 24
Farmer, Hepsey 121
Feagin, Almira 245
Feagin, Mary Temperance 245
Feagin, Missouri E. 245
Feagin, Thomas 245
Fennel, Cynthia 92
Ferguson, Colonel 82
Ferth, Hannah 319
Field, Caleb 184
Fielder, Dennis, Dr. 220
Fielder, Mary 304
Fielder, Tiery 147
Finch, Ada 218
Finch, Audie Mae 121
Finch, Betty S. 123
Finch, Caroline 218
Finch, E. Oliver 221
Finch, Elsie Louise 122
Finch, Henry 121, 218
Finch, Henry, Sr. 218
Finch, John Terrell 121, 122
Finch, Lula 218
Finch, Mary Evelyn 122
Finch, Norman Eugene 122
Finch, Oliver O. 121
Finch, Paul 121
Finch, Raymond Woodrow 122
Finch, Savannah 121
Finch, Terrell Young 121, 221
Finch, Zelma 218
Fincher, Pernecia Holder 40
Finley, Achison 72
Finley, James 139
Finney, Anne 323
Finney, Benjamin 323
Fitzgerald, Mary 60
Fitzsimmons, Elizabeth 328
Flaig, Philip 32
Fleming, Mary 63
Fleming, Mr. 121
Fletcher, Henry 20
Floerl, Charles 129

Hale, W. Frank 298
Hale, William F. 298
Hales, Nancy 191
Hall, Jmartha 140
Hall, Simeon 199
Halsey, Robert 15
Hamby, Emma Jean 209
Hamby, Miss 42
Hamilton, Charles 146
Hamilton, Elizabeth 146
Hamilton, Frances 146
Hamilton, Francis 146
Hamilton, Henry 146
Hamilton, Thomas 146
Hammock, Elizabeth Combs 115
Hammock, Elvira 268
Hammonds, Ada 329
Hampton, Jmenta 344
Hancock, Samuel 286
Hannada, N. A. 248
Hardage, Julian McDuffie 137
Hardeman, Sarah Elizabeth Smith 40
Harden, Benjamin, Capt. 82
Hardin, Thomas 200
Harding, Winford 214
Hardy, Agnes 338
Hardy, Leonard 122
Hardy, Thomas 114
Hardy, Thomas Harold 122
Hargett, Addie T. 140
Hargett, Agnes 140
Hargett, Anny 139
Hargett, Blandina 12
Hargett, Blandina 140
Hargett, Casper 139
Hargett, Charity Keziah 141
Hargett, Daniel 139, 141
Hargett, Emaline 140
Hargett, Eva 140
Hargett, Francis 140
Hargett, Frank 140
Hargett, Grier 140
Hargett, H. Morrison 140
Hargett, Harris 140
Hargett, Henry 139
Hargett, Henry Fred 140
Hargett, Henry, Sr. 139
Hargett, James 139, 140
Hargett, Jane 140
Hargett, Johann Henrich 139
Hargett, John 140, 141
Hargett, John Henry 139

Hargett, Joseph 139, 141
Hargett, Kolman 140
Hargett, Lizzie 140
Hargett, Louisa E. 140
Hargett, Mary 140
Hargett, Nanna 139
Hargett, Nelly 141
Hargett, Oscar 140
Hargett, P. A. 140
Hargett, Peter 139, 141
Hargett, Phoebe 141
Hargett, Prudence 139, 140
Hargett, Rosa W. 140
Hargett, Sarah Helms 141
Hargett, W. B. 12
Hargett, William 141
Hargett, Willie B. 140
Harkey, Elizabeth 140
Harlan, Jennie 289
Harmon, Elizabeth 350
Harper, Lizzie 330
Harper, Mary Chloe 312
Harrington, John 220
Harrington, Stephen 220
Harrington, William 243
Harris, A. T. 50
Harris, Ann 143, 144, 145, 146
Harris, Ann 80
Harris, Anne 142, 145
Harris, Daniel 125
Harris, Francis 143
Harris, Green B. 141
Harris, Green B. 5
Harris, Harriett 125
Harris, James 145, 146
Harris, James Cannon 141
Harris, Jane 47, 53, 98, 145, 146
Harris, John 145, 146, 147
Harris, Kate Susan 182
Harris, Lebanon J. 141
Harris, Lucy 147
Harris, Margaret 146
Harris, Mary 145, 146
Harris, Nathan 109
Harris, Ola 66
Harris, Renee 50
Harris, Richard A. 141
Harris, Sabra 145
Harris, Thomas 143
Harris, Whitmill C. 141
Harris, Will 142
Harris, William 81, 98, 141, 142, 143, 144

Holland, Cassie Grace 47
Holland, Catherine 195
Holland, Cecil 212
Holland, Celia 192
Holland, Charlene 208
Holland, Charles Hartwell 232
Holland, Charles L. 208
Holland, Charles Lee 216
Holland, Charles Lee, Jr. 216
Holland, Charlotte 182
Holland, Chesley 208
Holland, Christopher 200
Holland, Christopher Columbus 192
Holland, Clarence 218
Holland, Clarence D. 233
Holland, Clarence D., Jr. 233
Holland, Clyde Theodore 223
Holland, Cora Lee 202
Holland, Cordelia Eugenia 182
Holland, Corinthy 216
Holland, Cullen Green 192
Holland, Curtis 191
Holland, Curtis Wright 217
Holland, D. L. 213
Holland, David 192
Holland, Deborah Haskins 218
Holland, Della 206
Holland, Dellie Mae 121
Holland, Dellie Mae 221
Holland, Dennis 208
Holland, Dessie 184
Holland, Dessie M. 209
Holland, Dewey Lee 224
Holland, Diana 192
Holland, Dolly 195
Holland, Donna Louise 217
Holland, Donnie Viola 16, 209
Holland, Dora 215
Holland, Dorothy 220
Holland, Dorothy Elizabeth 236
Holland, Dorothy Virginia 220
Holland, Dura 218
Holland, Edde 214
Holland, Edith Wise 192
Holland, Edna Elizabeth 215
Holland, Edwin A. 210
Holland, Effie 215
Holland, Eldora 206
Holland, Eleanor 217
Holland, Elisha 183, 189, 191, 192
Holland, Eliza Jane 123, 207
Holland, Elizabeth 191, 195, 200, 210, 265

Holland, Elizabeth May 182
Holland, Ella 212
Holland, Ella Mae 220
Holland, Elvira 207
Holland, Emery 215, 232
Holland, Emily Susan 194
Holland, Emmett 216
Holland, Eric 206
Holland, Ernestine 208
Holland, Ethel Marie 217
Holland, Eugene 234, 316
Holland, Eugenia Keturie 182
Holland, Eunice A. 181
Holland, Evelyn 215
Holland, Evelyn Lois 182
Holland, Evelyn Sophronia 214
Holland, Exum 191
Holland, Ezekiel 202
Holland, Fannie 184
Holland, Forrest R. 220
Holland, Forrest Robert 220
Holland, Frances 215
Holland, Frank 192
Holland, Frankie 199
Holland, Franky 184
Holland, Gall 208
Holland, Gaston 191
Holland, Gene 220
Holland, George 195, 196, 197, 199, 207, 216
Holland, George W. 192
Holland, George Washington 107
Holland, George Washington 41, 224, 225, 226, 227, 228, 229, 230, 231, 238
Holland, George, Dr. 198, 199
Holland, George, Jr. 199
Holland, George, Sr. 197
Holland, Georgia 215
Holland, Georgianna A. 181
Holland, Ginsey 192
Holland, Gladys 217
Holland, Gladys Evelyn 207
Holland, Gloria Jean 233
Holland, Green 192
Holland, Gueston 215
Holland, Guy 215
Holland, H. C. 214
Holland, Harris 183
Holland, Harrison 215
Holland, Harrison Ramsey 210, 213, 219
Holland, Hart 234
Holland, Hattie Mae 218
Holland, Hazel 214

Holland, Helen 224
Holland, Henry 191, 216, 218, 289
Holland, Henry Clay 31, 35, 213, 214
Holland, Henry J., Capt. 201
Holland, Henry M. 184
Holland, Henry Pearman, Jr. 224
Holland, Henry Pearman, Sr. 224
Holland, Henry Tate 212
Holland, Henry Young 216, 217
Holland, Heslip 208
Holland, Hettie 232
Holland, Hewell 215
Holland, Hezekiah 194
Holland, Hezekiah Russell 194
Holland, Homer H. 208
Holland, Hubert 204, 210, 219
Holland, Hubert Glenn 223
Holland, Hugh 183
Holland, Ida Sarah 218
Holland, Inez 217
Holland, Irma 210
Holland, Isabel 195
Holland, Isaiah 184
Holland, Ivey R. 217
Holland, Jack 232, 233
Holland, Jack Dempsey 207
Holland, Jacob, Jr. 183, 186
Holland, James 199, 201, 208
Holland, James Archibald 217
Holland, James B., Rev. 217
Holland, James C. 184
Holland, James Douglas 224
Holland, James H. 202
Holland, James Henry 208
Holland, James Lewell 223
Holland, James Monroe 216, 217, 222
Holland, James Tom 87, 233
Holland, James W. 182
Holland, Jane 191
Holland, Janice 223
Holland, Jeannette 236, 316
Holland, Jefferson 184, 185
Holland, Jence Cornelia 192
Holland, Jesse 215
Holland, Jesse Lee 224
Holland, Jincey 184
Holland, Jincy 191, 192
Holland, Jinet 191
Holland, Jinnett 192
Holland, Joanne 208
Holland, Jodie 215
Holland, Joe Bailey 214

Holland, John 191, 193, 194, 195, 196, 207, 212
Holland, John C. 192
Holland, John Clay 194
Holland, John J. 184
Holland, John M. 218
Holland, John Shannon 183
Holland, John W. 210
Holland, Johnny 232
Holland, Johnny Andrew 220
Holland, Jonas Herman 181
Holland, Jonas Hines 182
Holland, Joseph 191, 193, 196
Holland, Joseph B. 192
Holland, Joseph Brown 192
Holland, Josephine 233
Holland, Josie 211
Holland, Joyce Evangeline 223
Holland, Judith 193, 194, 199, 200
Holland, Karen 217
Holland, Katherine 191, 199
Holland, Kenneth Edward 236
Holland, Kenneth Raynor 192
Holland, Kennon 208
Holland, Keturah 199
Holland, Laura 208
Holland, Laurel Benjamin 245, 246, 316
Holland, Lavina Washington 249
Holland, Lawson S. 200, 201
Holland, Lena 213, 218
Holland, Lessie May 220
Holland, Lewell Gerome 222, 223
Holland, Lewis Connor 200
Holland, Lilly 214
Holland, Lilly Ola 214
Holland, Linda 217
Holland, Linda 220
Holland, Linda Sue 235
Holland, Lindsey 206, 283
Holland, Lois 209, 216
Holland, Lona 31, 214
Holland, Lottie Lorene 32, 222
Holland, Louella 232
Holland, Lougenia 192
Holland, Louise 212, 233
Holland, Louvenia Arvaline 202
Holland, Loyd T. 218
Holland, Lucille 208, 214
Holland, Lucy (Negro) 198
Holland, Lucy 195, 207
Holland, Lucy Mae 213
Holland, Ludie Ann 219
Holland, Lula Ann 237, 251

Holland, Luther 194
Holland, Lydia 232, 233
Holland, Lydia Fay 215
Holland, Maggie Ruth 208
Holland, Major 195
Holland, Mamie Lou 222
Holland, Mamie Ophelia 210
Holland, Mandy E. 41
Holland, Margaret 195, 241
Holland, Marguerite 216
Holland, Marianne 235
Holland, Marie Eleanor 236
Holland, Martha 191, 192, 195, 212
Holland, Martha Amanda 219, 289
Holland, Martha Ann 213
Holland, Martha Eunice 182
Holland, Martha Jane 216
Holland, Mary 195, 196, 199, 207, 208, 232, 341
Holland, Mary Elizabeth 107, 207, 232
Holland, Mary Louise 220
Holland, Matthew Crawford 202
Holland, Mattie Evelyn 223
Holland, Mattie Lee 218
Holland, Mattilee 218
Holland, Max 217
Holland, Melba Zurlene 224
Holland, Mercy 200
Holland, Michael 193, 195, 196, 197, 199
Holland, Michael Henry 219
Holland, Michael, Jr. 196
Holland, Mike 233
Holland, Mildred 214
Holland, Millard Filmore 206
Holland, Millie 191
Holland, Millie Fay 220
Holland, Monroe 206
Holland, Mosella Katherine 182
Holland, Moses 183
Holland, Myrtle 218
Holland, N. A. 212
Holland, Nancy 191
Holland, Nancy Edie 46, 208
Holland, Nathaniel 195
Holland, Ned Eugene 216
Holland, Ned Eugene, Jr. 217
Holland, Needham 191, 192
Holland, Needham Gray 192
Holland, Nettie Josephine 209
Holland, Noble C. 211, 212
Holland, Nona Lee 237
Holland, Oliver A. 218

Holland, Oma 218
Holland, Orlando 319
Holland, Oscar 215
Holland, Parker Wayne 184
Holland, Patian 192
Holland, Patience 192
Holland, Patricia Jane 223
Holland, Patrick 191
Holland, Patsy 191
Holland, Peggy 183, 184
Holland, Permelia (Amelia Ann) 210
Holland, Permelia Ann 112
Holland, Phebe 196
Holland, Philip Archer 194
Holland, Rachel 191
Holland, Rachel 194
Holland, Ralph Griffin 217
Holland, Ralph T. 211
Holland, Ramsey Ramsey 220
Holland, Ransom Beauregard 192
Holland, Rebecca 184, 187
Holland, Richard 195, 196
Holland, Richard Anderson 198
Holland, Richard W. 191
Holland, Ritta Ann Catherine 192
Holland, Robert Edward 214
Holland, Robert T. 201, 202
Holland, Rufus 191
Holland, Rutha 183
Holland, Sabra Louise 217
Holland, Salley 198
Holland, Sallie Anne 194
Holland, Sallie Elsberry 205
Holland, Sally 192, 194, 208
Holland, Sally Dosher 216
Holland, Samuel 46, 200, 202, 208
Holland, Samuel Chester 215
Holland, Samuel D. 215, 241
Holland, Samuel Donsel 203, 207, 209
Holland, Sandra 217
Holland, Sarah 42, 107, 206, 241
Holland, Sarah Ann 41, 111, 224
Holland, Sarah J. 191
Holland, Seward 213
Holland, Shandy 194
Holland, Shandy Walker 194
Holland, Sharon 214
Holland, Sheryl J. 214
Holland, Silas Casey 232
Holland, Simon 191
Holland, Snowdie 215
Holland, Sophie Jane 194

Holland, Starling 213
Holland, Starnan 206
Holland, Steve 233
Holland, Susannah 200
Holland, Tennie 218
Holland, Thelma 209
Holland, Thelmer 233
Holland, Theodore Roosevelt 223
Holland, Thomas Alton 237
Holland, Thomas Grady 204, 219
Holland, Thomas Harris 182
Holland, Thomas Ira 209
Holland, Thomas Littleberry 182
Holland, Thomas Randolph 182
Holland, Thomas Wyatt 208, 209, 210
Holland, Timmy 218
Holland, Tom 233, 234
Holland, Tone 204
Holland, Truman Monroe 202
Holland, Uriah 191
Holland, Van 212
Holland, Van Buren 217
Holland, W. E. 206
Holland, Walter 208, 215
Holland, Warren 191
Holland, Wash 42, 224, 232, 233
Holland, West 192
Holland, West Bob 192
Holland, West Pratt 191
Holland, Wilfred 215
Holland, William 197, 199, 207, 217
Holland, William A. 192
Holland, William Aubrey 221
Holland, William Clyde 207
Holland, William Dean 217
Holland, William Edward 111, 205, 206
Holland, William Gaston 192
Holland, William Manon 206
Holland, William Newton 221
Holland, William Newton 32
Holland, William Odus 209
Holland, William of Georgia 200, 201, 202, 203
Holland, William R. 184
Holland, William S. 217
Holland, William Thomas 234
Holland, William W. 191
Holland, William Walter 182, 218
Holland, Willie Archibald 220
Holland, Willie Archibald, Jr. 220
Holland, Willis A. 202
Holland, Woodson 208, 214

Holland, Zilpha 191
Holland, Zuma Louise 217
Holliingshed, Julius H. 209
Hollingshed, Alta Fay 209
Hollingshed, Cecil 209
Hollingshed, Edgar Ray 209
Hollingshed, Estelle 209
Hollingshed, J. T. 209
Hollingshed, Thomas Levi 209
Hollingshed, Wendell 209
Hollingsworth, Elizabeth S. 243
Hollingsworth, Robert 248
Hollins, Benjamin 199
Hollins, William 199
Hollis, John W. 9, 11
Hollis, Margaret 11
Hollis, P. M. 7
Hollowell, William 341
Holmes, Elizabeth 69
Holmes, Robert H. 69
Holmes, Sarah 139
Holt, Mr. 106
Holton, Anna E. 59
Holton, Anna E. Dickson 104
Hooker, Martha Louise 304
Hopkins, Julia Ann 299
Hopkins, Margaret 299
Hopkins, Samuel, Capt. 302
Hord, John 43
Horton, Betsy 348
Hosch, Dorcas Tabitha 147
House, Ida 218
Howard, Amanda 238
Howard, Amelia Elizabeth 69
Howard, Elizabeth 238
Howard, Emily Almeda 238
Howard, Frank 238
Howard, Hardy 129, 238
Howard, Harper 238
Howard, Harper H. 238
Howard, Harry R. 238
Howard, Hartsford 238
Howard, Homer R. 238
Howard, James W. 238
Howard, John 238
Howard, Julius O. 238
Howard, Lillie A. 239
Howard, Malissa 238
Howard, Martha E. 238
Howard, Robert L. 238
Howard, Roy 119
Howard, Samuel 238

392

McGregory, Alexander 98
McIntire, Daniel 82
McKinney, Alexander Gresham 270
McKinney, Ann 270
McKinney, Anney 271
McKinney, Bianco Elizabeth Verlinda 270
McKinney, Eliza Ann 90
McKinney, Elizabeth 270
McKinney, Elizabeth J. 270
McKinney, Gresham 69, 270
McKinney, James H. 270
McKinney, Joel Jackson 270
McKinney, John 270
McKinney, John C. 270
McKinney, John H. 270
McKinney, Joshua T. 270
McKinney, Julia A. 270
McKinney, Margaret J. L. 270
McKinney, Martha Anne 127
McKinney, Mary 271
McKinney, Monroe M. 270
McKinney, Sarah 43
McKinney, Sarah A. 270
McKinney, Thomas 270
McKinney, Travis 270
McKinney, Travis W. 264
McKinney, William 270
McKinney, William Zacharias 270
McKinnhey, John 270
McKleroy, Rebecca B. 14
McKullock, Hugh 318
McLane, Permelia 36
McLendon, Frances 103
McLendon, Leemon D. 279
McLendon, Mason 103
McMickle, Elizabeth 298
McMillican, Susanna 15
McMurrey, Mr. 126
McNatt, Martha 60
McNeil, John 354
McNeil, Sarah 354
McNeill, Hester, Colonel 2324
McPherson, H. H. 11
McSwain, Nancy Anderson 56
Mebane, Thomas Hill 223
Medlock, Agatha 244
Medlock, Anne 244
Medlock, Anne 67
Medlock, Charles 244
Mellown, Martin 353
Melson, William 20
Mercer, Ann Moriah 278

Mercer, Anna 276
Mercer, Chloe 272
Mercer, Christopher 271
Mercer, Daniel 276
Mercer, Dorcas 273
Mercer, Elizabeth 278
Mercer, Ervin Cleathan 31
Mercer, Ervin Lamar 31. 32
Mercer, Francis Addison Lamar 280
Mercer, Hermon 276
Mercer, Jacob 272
Mercer, James 271, 272, 278
Mercer, James B. 279
Mercer, Jesse 273, 274, 275, 276
Mercer, Jim 278
Mercer, Joel Edgar 279
Mercer, Joel Elreath 278
Mercer, John 279
Mercer, John Thomas 279
Mercer, John, Colonel 278
Mercer, Joseph 271
Mercer, Joshua 276, 278, 279
Mercer, Leonidas B. 279
Mercer, Leonidas B., Dr. 276, 278
Mercer, Leonidas Bennington, Dr.. 278
Mercer, Lydia 272
Mercer, Mary 272, 276
Mercer, Mary Gertrude 280
Mercer, Miriam 276
Mercer, Moriah Twigg 280
Mercer, Morning 277
Mercer, Mount Moriah 278
Mercer, Rebecca C. 278
Mercer, Rhoda 272
Mercer, Sabrina 274
Mercer, Sarah 272
Mercer, Selah Ann Rosemon 279
Mercer, Silas 272, 273, 278
Mercer, Thomas 271, 272
Mercer, Vashti 125
Mercer, Vashti 278
Meriwether, Valentine 196
Meroney, Mary 123
Meroney, Mary 292
Meroney, Mary 3
Michie, John 196
Middlebrooks, Andisa 61
Middlebrooks, Bethenia 336
Middlebrooks, Laura 68
Miles, Betty Jouce 280
Miles, Clinton 280
Miles, Essie Ophelia 280

Miles, F. C. 280
Miles, F. C. 285
Miles, Glenn Autry 280
Miles, James Oscar 280
Miles, Louis Weldon 280
Miles, Oscar 280
Miles, Patricia 280
Miles, Raymond Alford 280
Miles, Ruthie Elois 280
Milholland, Beverly 209
Millar, Anne 19
Miller, Harold, Mrs. 213
Miller, Nancy W. 331
Miller, Robert Johnson, Rev. 294
Miller, Susan 224
Millican, Mary J. 4
Milligan, Nancy 297
Mimms, Essie 138
Mintz, Mattie 239
Mitchell A. 6
Mitchell, Capt. 201
Mitchell, Cheryl 220
Mitchell, Iona 235
Mitchell, Isaiah L. 289
Mitchell, James 347
Mitchell, Jave 107
Mitchell, Jemima D. 296
Mitchell, John 16
Mitchell, Mr. 297
Mitchell, Robert Lee 289
Mitchell, Thomas 196
Mitchell, Thomas 197
Moffett, Mose 63
Molton, Aggy 24
Monford, James William 285
Monford, Mary 295
Monford, Peter 285
Monford, William Wiley 2985
Monfort, Ella 285
Monfort, John S. 285
Monfort, Lewis 285
Monfort, Mary 285
Monfort, Minnie 285
Monfort, Rebecca 285
Monfort, Thomas Peter 285
Monfort, Wilhellemus 285
Monk, Charles 219
Monk, Frances 219
Monk, John 219
Monk, John T. 290
Monk, Ludy Ann 218
Monk, Wayne 219

Monk, William Silas 219
Montford, John 318
Montfort, Peter 285
Montgomery, Rebecca 2
Moo, John 51
Moody, Ann 281
Moody, Benjamin 283
Moody, Caroline 283
Moody, Caroline J. 14
Moody, Caroline Jane 282
Moody, Cassandra 283
Moody, Celesta 283
Moody, Daniel 284
Moody, Donna Lyn 17
Moody, Elizabeth 281, 282, 283
Moody, Ellen 50, 283
Moody, Ezekiel 283
Moody, Ezekiel W. 9, 281, 282
Moody, Fanny 283
Moody, Frances 283
Moody, Frances 284
Moody, Gilley 282
Moody, Green B. 283
Moody, Henry 281
Moody, Humphrey 283
Moody, James 282
Moody, Jesse 283
Moody, Joel 283
Moody, John 281
Moody, John M. 284
Moody, John S. 281, 282, 283
Moody, John, Jr. 283
Moody, Laurena 283
Moody, Leander Drucilla 283
Moody, Margaret 282
Moody, Martha Emiline 282
Moody, Martha Jane 283
Moody, Mary P. 282
Moody, Nancy 281
Moody, Nathaniel 282
Moody, Nathaniel G. 282
Moody, Retency 206
Moody, Retensa 284
Moody, Riley 283
Moody, Risa 282
Moody, Robert 281
Moody, Robert III 281
Moody, Robert, Jr. 281
Moody, Samuel 281, 283
Moody, Sarah 281
Moody, Sophronia 283
Moody, Thomas 281, 282

410

Stegall, Lena Anna 330
Stegall, Lindy 330
Stegall, Margaret 328
Stegall, Margaret Adeline 329
Stegall, Martha Elizabeth 329
Stegall, Mary 328
Stegall, Mary E. 231
Stegall, Mary E. 330
Stegall, Mary E. 41
Stegall, Nancy 327, 328, 339
Stegall, Narcissa 330
Stegall, Patsy 328
Stegall, Patsy Tenny 330
Stegall, Peter 328
Stegall, Richard 327, 328, 329, 330
Stegall, Richard A. 328
Stegall, Richard Artemas 330
Stegall, Robert 328, 330
Stegall, Robert Blackwell 328
Stegall, Salley 329
Stegall, Samuel 327
Stegall, Samuel, Jr. 327
Stegall, Sarah 328
Stegall, Spencer 327, 328, 330
Stegall, Susan 327
Stegall, Susanna Roberta 330
Stegall, Tandy 329
Stegall, Terrell 330
Stegall, Tommy 329
Stegall, William 328, 329
Stegall, William 330
Steggall, William 326
Stephens, Amanda 118
Stephens, Lucy 248
Stephens, Mary 16
Stephens, Tristan, Captain 23
Stepp, Joseph 330
Stewart, Elizabeth 134
Stewart, Henry J. 124
Stewart, James 97
Stewart, John, Colonel 124
Stewart, Samuel 129
Stewart, Samuel 238
Stewart, Vaughn Morton 325
Stewart, Walter 97
Stewart, Willie Forsyth 123
Stgarling, Thomas James 324
Sticher, Susie 48
Stidham, Elizabeth 268
Stiles, Ebenezer 90
Still, Lula 100
Still, Sarah Jane 354

Stinchcomb, Jean 237
Stinson, Michael 109
Stockdale, Ann 301
Stockdale, Ann 60
Stone, Caleb 194
Stone, Lucy 194
Strickland, Anna C. 343
Strickland, Anne C. 343
Strickland, Elizabeth 29
Strickland, Elsey 343
Strickland, Hardy 345
Strickland, Hardy, Jr. 346
Strickland, Nancy 300
Strickland, Nancy 343
Strickland, Nancy 70
Strickland, Sarah Ann 344
Stuart, Hannah 263
Stubbs, Peter 242
Stucki, Edwin Gerald 236
Stucki, Edwin Gerald 316
Stucki, Edwin Gottfried 236
Stucki, Jeannette Holland 13
Stucki, Suzanne Teri 236, 316
Suggs, Lucretia 252
Suggs, Mr. 258
Suit, Edith 208
Sullivan, Ally C. 331
Sullivan, Ann 331
Sullivan, Charles W. 331
Sullivan, E. S. 331
Sullivan, Ella W. 332
Sullivan, Ellen 331
Sullivan, Emma A. 331
Sullivan, Evaline 291, 331
Sullivan, George W. 331
Sullivan, Hilliard H. 331
Sullivan, Isaac 331
Sullivan, James M. 331
Sullivan, John S. 331
Sullivan, Joseph 331
Sullivan, Josephine 331
Sullivan, Louvenia M. 301
Sullivan, Martie 331
Sullivan, Mary 101, 331
Sullivan, Mary A. 331
Sullivan, Missouri L. 331
Sullivan, Mit 331
Sullivan, Nancy 331
Sullivan, Nancy E. 331
Sullivan, O. H. 331
Sullivan, Otis H. 331
Sullivan, Priscilla W. 301

411

414

Wilshire, Gary 237
Wilshire, Stephen Holland 237
Wilson, Amelia 329, 349
Wilson, America 349
Wilson, Andrew 349
Wilson, Andrew Jackson 349
Wilson, Ann E. 349
Wilson, Ann P. 349
Wilson, Emaline 350
Wilson, Jackson 261
Wilson, Jackson W. 349
Wilson, James L. 350
Wilson, James R. 349
Wilson, Jasper 261, 349
Wilson, Joseph A. 350
Wilson, Julia E. 349
Wilson, Leanney A. 350
Wilson, Leila 349
Wilson, Levina 309
Wilson, Lewis J. 349
Wilson, Lola 350
Wilson, Martha Frances 349
Wilson, Mary 349
Wilson, Mary M. 349
Wilson, Miss 247
Wilson, Moses B. 350
Wilson, Mr. 134
Wilson, Rebecca 349, 352
Wilson, Robert Henry 350
Wilson, Sally 349
Wilson, Sarah A. 349
Wilson, Sarah Ann 2362
Wilson, Sarah Januarye 130
Wilson, Temperance 245
Wilson, Virginia 349
Wilson, William 352, 354
Wilson, William J. 350
Wingard, Mr. 135
Winn, Nettie 251
Winn, Patrick Henry 232
Winn, Richard 32
Winn, William Richard 32
Wise, Elizabeth 130
Wise, Henry 131
Wisner, Elizabeth 292
Witcher, Grace 211
Witcher, Mattie 124
Witcher, William, Captain 335
Wofford, Rebecca 43
Womack, Eloise 214
Womack, Parker 214
Wonacott, Gordon 326

Wondacott, Robert 326
Wood, Elizabeth 299
Wood, J. P., Mrs. 244
Wood, J. T. 215
Wood, James 299
Wood, James Pinckard 247
Wood, Malinda 99,100
Wood, W. M. 87
Woodall, Charles Alvin 350
Woodall, Cornelia 350
Woodall, Dela Fletcher 62
Woodall, Dorothy Rachel 350
Woodall, Fletcher 350
Woodall, Henry 350
Woodall, Henry Thomas 62
Woodall, John Henry 62, 350
Woodall, John Wesley 62
Woodall, Larry Craig 350
Woodall, Lucy 350
Woodall, Lucy Caroline 31, 325
Woodall, Robert 350
Woodall, Sallie Cornelia 62, 350
Woodall, William 350
Woodbury, Janel 307
Woode, Elizabeth P. 299
Woods, Miss 2
Woodson, John 200
Woolveston, Elijah Hanks 306
Wooten, Council B. 279
Wooten, John 279
Wooten, W. E. 279
Worley, Ferrell Lee 49
Worsham, Sallie E. 129
Worsham, William W. 129
Wright, Benjamin F. 8
Wright, Eliza 338
Wright, Ethel 217
Wright, Isaiah 323
Wright, Mary 96
Wright, Rebecca 323
Wright, Simeon 63
Wright, Thomas J. 63
Wright, William 96
Wyatt, Louisa 72
Wynne, Frances 105
Wynne, Martha 105
Wynne, William 105
Yancey, Breman 92
Yancey, David 92
Yancey, Max 92
Yancey, Nellie 92
Yancey, Paul E. 92